Starting & Running a Small Business
For Canadians
ALL-IN-ONE

FOR
DUMMIES®

Starting & Running a Small Business For Canadians

ALL-IN-ONE

FOR DUMMIES®

by John Aylen, Margaret Kerr,
JoAnn Kurtz, Henri Charmasson, John Buchaca,
Neil Milton, Diana Byron, Paul Tiffany,
Steven D. Peterson, Nada Wagner, Lita Epstein,
Cécile Laurin, Harold Messmer,
Barbara Schenck, John Arnold, Ian Lurie,
Marty Dickinson, Elizabeth Marsten,
Michael Becker

John Wiley & Sons Canada, Ltd.

Starting & Running a Small Business For Canadians All-in-One For Dummies®

Published by
John Wiley & Sons Canada, Ltd.
6045 Freemont Boulevard
Mississauga, Ontario, L5R 4J3
www.wiley.com

For general information on our other products and services, please contact our Customer Care Department within the U.S. at 877-762-2974, outside the U.S. at 317-572-3993, or fax 317-572-4002.

For technical support, please visit www.wiley.com/techsupport.

Wiley publishes in a variety of print and electronic formats and by print-on-demand. Some material included with standard print versions of this book may not be included in e-books or in print-on-demand. If this book refers to media such as a CD or DVD that is not included in the version you purchased, you may download this material at http://booksupport.wiley.com. For more information about Wiley products, visit www.wiley.com.

Library and Archives Canada Cataloguing in Publication

   Starting & running a small business for Canadians all-in-one for dummies / John Aylen ... [et al.]. Includes index.

Issued also in electronic formats.

ISBN 978-1-118-17282-7

   1. New business enterprises–Canada–Management. 2. Small business–Canada–Management.
3. Self-employed–Canada.

I. Aylen, John II. Title: Starting and running a small business for Canadians all-in-one for dummies.

HD62.5.S835 2012   658.1'1410971   C2012-900468-5

ISBN 978-1-118-17282-7 (pbk); ISBN 978-1-118-22387-1 (ebk); ISBN 978-1-118-22389-5 (ebk); ISBN 978-1-118-22391-8 (ebk)

Manufactured in the United States of America

1 2 3 4 5 RRD 16 15 14 13 12

WILEY

About the Authors

John Aylen has a small business that provides marketing and communications services to businesses, institutional clients and not-for-profit organizations of all sizes. He is a regular guest lecturer at the Dobson Centre for Entrepreneurial Studies at McGill University and has been a judge at the John Molson School of Business International MBA Case Competition for more than 10 years. He is the author of a number of books on small business management and contemporary history. He has written widely on business topics for magazines and newspapers in Canada and has edited books on health care and business strategy as well as works of fiction.

Margaret Kerr and **JoAnn Kurtz** are lawyers with experience in dealing face-to-face with clients' questions and concerns. They have written a number of books, including *Make It Legal: What Every Canadian Entrepreneur Needs to Know About the Law, Facing a Death in the Family, Wills and Estates for Canadians For Dummies,* and *Canadian Small Business Kit For Dummies.* (All their bio information is joint as they co-author everything together.)

Henri Charmasson is an attorney with a 35-year career in the field of intellectual property (IP) law. He has been a naming adviser to major corporations. Henri is also an inventor with his name on 15 U.S. patents and an entrepreneur who sits on the board of several small business corporations. In his early engineering career, Henri designed computer hardware. Henri has authored several articles and delivered lectures on patent, copyright, trademark and trade secret topics, and written an authoritative treatise about the art of naming companies and branding new products. Born, raised, and educated in sunny Provence, France, he's found in California the ideal place to exert his enterprising spirit.

John Buchaca, also an Intellectual Property law attorney, is a former software engineer and occasional inventor, and has worked with Henri for more than 15 years. Indeed, when Henri wrote the first edition of this book, John regarded himself as the "first dummy." Before becoming a lawyer, he worked in ocean acoustics analysis and modeling and computer programming. His undergraduate degree is in applied mathematics. But his highest claim to fame (according to Henri) is being married to Henri's daughter and to be the father of two of Henri's grandchildren. He lives in San Diego, California where he is a partner at Charmasson, Buchaca & Leach, LLP, an IP law firm.

Neil Milton is Canadian lawyer with 20 years' experience in intellectual property strategy and intellectual property transactions (licenses, purchase/sales, financings), for all manner of organizations: large established businesses, entrepreneurs, start-ups, charities, not-for-profits, and governments.

Diana Byron is a Toronto-based freelance writer and editor.

Paul Tiffany, PhD, is a professor of management at the Haas Business School, UC Berkeley, and an Adjunct Professor at the Wharton School, University of Pennsylvania. He is a management consultant to numerous firms and agencies all over the world focusing on the art and science of business strategy, planning, and management concepts.

Steven D. Peterson, PhD, is the founder and CEO of Strategic Play, and is an expert in the application of sophisticated computer models to business strategy and planning. He is the designer and developer of The Protean Strategist, a business simulation which recently received Human Resource Executive magazine's "Best New Training Product" award. Dr. Peterson is an Executive Education Lecturer at the UC Berkeley Haas School of Business and the IMD Business School in Lausanne, Switzerland.

Nada Wagner, MBA, is one of the Principals of Next Wave Marketing and held positions such as Director of Centre of Entrepreneurship and Corporate Development with Centennial College, Toronto; General Manager of Canadian Business Resource Centre, Toronto; General Manager of a manufacturing firm in East York; Controller of the Canadian subsidiary of a German-based multinational manufacturer. Nada has a Master of Business Administration degree from Richard Ivey School of Business, University of Western Ontario, and studied adult education with St. Francis Xavier University, Antigonish, Nova Scotia.

Lita Epstein, MBA designs and teaches online courses on topics such as investing for retirement, getting ready for tax time, and finance and investing for women. She earned her MBA from Emory University's Goizueta Business School, and is the author of *Streetwise Retirement Planning* and the co-author of *Teach Yourself Retirement Planning in 24 Hours.* Lita was the content director for a financial services website, MostChoice.com. She also wrote TipWorld's Mutual Fund Tip of the Day in addition to columns about mutual fund trends for numerous web sites.

Cécile Laurin is a Chartered Accountant and teacher based in Ottawa. In addition to teaching in Algonquin College's Professional Accounting Program and coordinating the college's distance education accounting program, she has adapted a number of U.S. higher education accounting titles for Wiley Canada.

Harold Messmer is chairman and CEO of Robert Half International Inc. the world's largest specialized staffing firm. He is one of the foremost experts on human resources and employment issues. His entire business is built on the promise that the success of any company is based on the extent to which attracting and keeping outstanding talent is top priority.

Barbara Schenck is the author of several Dummies books, including *Small Business Marketing For Dummies*, *Branding For Dummies*, and *Business Plans Kit For Dummies*, as well as marketing and training materials for the Microsoft Small Business Relationship Program and the marketing specialist for the VISA-sponsored Business Breakthrough program.

John Arnold has established himself as a leading online marketing expert. His primary work revolves around his job as Director of Customer Training & Certification for eMail marketing firm Constant Contact. He also writes a Marketing Tools & Technologies column for *Entrepreneur* magazine. His authoring credits include *e-Mail Marketing For Dummies* and *Web Marketing All-in-One For Dummies* along with *Mobile Marketing For Dummies.*

Ian Lurie started his Internet marketing company, Portent Interactive, in 1995. He is a long-time Internet marketing geek, with a blog, a book, and occasional speaking gigs on the subject. If you care about this kind of stuff, Ian's been interviewed and/or written for *The Seattle Times,* the *Puget Sound Business Journal, Direct Magazine,* DMNews, and *Visibility Magazine.*

Marty Dickinson launched his first website — `http://MusicMates.com` — in 1996 as a hobby. Today, Music Mates is one of the largest musician referrals in the country. Marty soon began helping other business owners with their Internet strategies through services, writing, and workshop-style training. Someone once asked him, "We'd like to hire you, but how do we know you will be around in six months?" So, Marty formalized his Internet marketing–services company by calling it HereNextYear, Inc. (`www.HereNextYear.com`). Since then, he has produced and managed nearly 100 of his own websites and has assisted with more than 200 client projects.

Elizabeth Marsten is the PPC Manager at Portent Interactive, a full-service Internet marketing agency based in Seattle, WA. She oversees all the pay per click (PPC) operations and staff and is also learning the ropes in affiliate marketing and managing many of the affiliate efforts at Portent Interactive, as well. She is a regular contributor of PPC best practices on the Portent Interactive blog, along with the worst practices on the PPC spoof blog: `www.ppcvillain.com`.

Michael Becker is a leading voice in the mobile world. He heads up the business development arm for iLoop Mobile, an industry-leading mobile marketing solutions provider. He is also on the board of directors for the Mobile Marketing Association.

Publisher's Acknowledgments

We're proud of this book; please send us your comments at http://dummies.custhelp.com. For other comments, please contact our Customer Care Department within the U.S. at 877-762-2974, outside the U.S. at 317-572-3993, or fax 317-572-4002.

Some of the people who helped bring this book to market include the following:

Associate Acquisitions Editor: Anam Ahmed

Production Editor: Pauline Ricablanca

Copy Editor: Heather Ball

Editorial Assistant: Kathy Deady

Cover Photo: © iStock / Willie B. Thomas

Cartoons: Rich Tennant (www.the5thwave.com)

Composition Services

Project Coordinator: Kristie Rees

Layout and Graphics: Sennett Vaughan Johnson, Lavonne Roberts

Proofreaders: Lindsay Amones, The Well-Chosen Word

Indexer: BIM Indexing & Proofreading Services

John Wiley & Sons Canada, Ltd.

  Deborah Barton, Vice President and Director of Operations

  Jennifer Smith, Publisher, Professional and Trade Division

  Alison Maclean, Managing Editor

Publishing and Editorial for Technology Dummies

  Richard Swadley, Vice President and Executive Group Publisher

  Andy Cummings, Vice President and Publisher

  Mary Bednarek, Executive Acquisitions Director

  Mary C. Corder, Editorial Director

Publishing for Consumer Dummies

  Kathleen Nebenhaus, Vice President and Executive Publisher

Composition Services

  Debbie Stailey, Director of Composition Services

Contents at a Glance

Introduction *1*

Book I: From Start to Finish and Everything in Between ... 7

Chapter 1: Small Business Essentials 9
Chapter 2: Getting Started..29
Chapter 3: Operating Your Business 57
Chapter 4: Looking to the Future of Your Business 87

Book II: Intellectual Property 121

Chapter 1: Introducing Intellectual Property.....................................123
Chapter 2: Mastering Patents, Trademarks, and Copyrights.............137
Chapter 3: Profiting from Intellectual Property 181

Book III: Business Planning........................... 201

Chapter 1: Knowing Where You Want to Go 203
Chapter 2: Describing Your Marketplace 231
Chapter 3: Weighing Your Business's Prospects 273
Chapter 4: A Sample Business Plan 301

Book IV: Bookkeeping 323

Chapter 1: Basic Bookkeeping: What It Is and Why You Need It 325
Chapter 2: Reporting Results 347
Chapter 3: Computer Options for Your Bookkeeping........................373

Book V: Human Resources 381

Chapter 1: The People Picture 383
Chapter 2: Recruiting the Right People...395
Chapter 3: Retention: Critical in Any Business Environment.............435
Chapter 4: Monitoring Ongoing Performance 463

Book VI: Marketing..................................... 483

Chapter 1: Getting Started in Marketing 485
Chapter 2: Sharpening Your Marketing Focus 509
Chapter 3: Creating and Placing Ads...519
Chapter 4: Reaching Your Market in More Ways..................................533

Book VII: Online Marketing 549

Chapter 1: Creating an Online Presence for Your Business 551
Chapter 2: Getting Started with Mobile Marketing....................................563
Chapter 3: Getting Ready to Use SEO and Web Analytics 571

Index 599

Table of Contents

Introduction 1
  Foolish Assumptions 1
  How This Book Is Organized 2
    Book I: From Start to Finish and Everything in Between 2
    Book II: Intellectual Property 3
    Book III: Business Planning 3
    Book IV: Bookkeeping 4
    Book V: Human Resources 4
    Book VI: Marketing 4
    Book VII: Online Marketing 5
  Icons Used in This Book 5
  Where to Go From Here 6

Book 1: From Start to Finish and Everything in Between 7

Chapter 1: Small Business Essentials 9
  Weighing the Pros and the Cons 10
    The pros 10
    The cons 11
  Choosing Your Business 12
    Looking for a business start-up 13
    Avoiding a difficult business start-up 13
  Determining If You Have the Small Business Personality 14
  Knowing If and When to Give Up Your Day Job 17
  Seeking Out General Business Information 18
    Canada Business — Services for Entrepreneurs 18
    Provincial/territorial government websites 20
    Bank and trust company websites 21
    Small business or entrepreneurship centres 21
    Business incubators 22
  Getting Information Geared to Your Specific Business 22
    Industry Canada 23
    Trade and professional associations 23
  Obtaining Essential Business Skills 24
    Skills for your particular business 24
    General business skills 25
  Finding Professional and Other Help 26
    Determining whom you need 26
    Finding peer support 28

Chapter 2: Getting Started 29

Developing Your Product or Service with a Market in Mind 30
    Is this idea right for you? 30
    Does anyone want the product or service? 31
    Who's the competition? 31
    How much money can you put behind this idea? 32
Finding a Route to the Target Market 32
Pricing Your Product or Service 33
    Deciding on the minimum price you can charge 33
    Deciding on the maximum price you can charge 34
    Setting your price 34
Considering an Off-the-Shelf Business 35
    Buying an existing business 35
    Looking carefully at existing businesses 36
    Why is the owner selling the business? 36
    What is the reputation of the business? 37
    What is the reason for the success of the business? 37
    How's the neighbourhood? 37
    What do the financial statements tell you? 38
    What is the "corporate culture"? 40
Deciding on a Price for a Business 40
    What's a business worth? 40
    Sources of information for valuing a business 42
Considering a Franchise 42
    Checking out the advantages of a franchise 43
    Investigating the disadvantages of a franchise .43
    Finding a franchise 44
    Evaluating the franchises you find 44
    Doing due diligence before you sign 45
Deciding On a Place of Business 46
    Working from home 46
    Working from real business premises 46
    Space-sharing arrangements 47
    Renting business premises 47
Looking at Ownership Issues 50
    Going alone 50
    Taking on a co-pilot 50
Should You Incorporate? 51
    Checking out your options 51
    Understanding the difference 51
The Corporation: A Form of Business with a Life All Its Own 52
    Understanding corporations 52
    Owning a corporation 53
    Running a corporation 53
    Setting up a corporation 54
Protecting Your Assets without Incorporating 54

Chapter 3: Operating Your Business............................57

Minimizing Business Risks and Troubles..57
    Injury to others 58
    Injury to your business 60
    Injury or death of a key person...62
Insuring against Your Risks...63
    Do you already have insurance?...63
    Do you need insurance?...63
    Choosing an insurance agent or broker...................................64
    Examining different insurance policies.....................................64
Working Well with Customers and Clients..64
    Reviewing a typical business transaction.................................65
    Making the sale 65
Documenting Your Agreement 66
    Contracts for the sale of goods or services..............................67
    Speaking to your lawyer about your contracts.........................68
Doing the Work..69
    Keeping customers happy...69
    Dealing with unhappy customers...69
    Getting repeat business and referrals......................................70
Getting Paid...71
    Planning to get paid..71
    Looking at credit...71
    Getting paid online 72
Addressing Customer Privacy...72
Getting Fired and Getting Sued...73
    If you get fired for no good reason 73
    If you really screw up 74
Dealing with Suppliers and Advisors..76
    Determining what goods and services you need.......................76
    Finding suppliers 77
    Choosing a supplier...78
    Establishing credit with your suppliers....................................79
    Entering into contracts with your suppliers 80
    Establishing good relationships suppliers 81
    Avoiding problems in the first place 82
    Considering problems that can arise 82
    Knowing what to do if you suffer loss or damage
        because of a supplier...83
    Using suppliers of professional services 84

Chapter 4: Looking to the Future of Your Business 87

No Money, More Problems...87
    Your business can't make a payment that's due.......................88
    You've personally guaranteed a debt for your
        business and your business can't pay...................................90
    Your business can't pay its rent..91
    Your business can't pay a mortgage on real property 91

Your business can't pay its taxes 92
Your business is insolvent... 92
Bankruptcy 93
Disputes 94
Negotiating a settlement 94
Alternative dispute resolution (ADR).. 97
Litigation 98
Closing Up Shop... 99
Parting from your business may be a joint venture...................... 99
Considering taxes when going out of business............................ 100
Dealing with the tax bill 101
Selling Your Business as a Going Concern 101
Knowing what your business is worth.. 102
Dealing with prospective buyers 102
Putting the deal together 103
Going Out of Business.. 106
Finding buyers for your business's assets 106
Unloading leased equipment.. 107
Paying off your debts 107
Notifying your clients or customers.. 107
Notifying your suppliers 108
Negotiating with your landlord 108
Being Put Out of Business 108
How your secured creditors can put you out of business 108
How your unsecured creditors can put you out of business....... 109
Dying to Get Out of Business 109
Short-term planning versus long-term planning.......................... 110
Keeping it in the family 111
Selling to an outsider... 112
Getting Bigger.. 112
What "doing more business" means 112
Finding more business 113
Financing Your Expansion.. 115
Managing a Bigger Business... 116
Using personal management techniques...................................... 117
Using business management techniques...................................... 119

Book II: Intellectual Property *121*

Chapter 1: Introducing Intellectual Property. .123
Explaining Intellectual Property 123
Defining IP rights.. 124
Types of IP 124
Considering the Benefits of Protecting Your IP Rights........................ 125
Keeping your competitors at bay 126
Developing a new revenue source 126
Adding value to your business.. 127

Bringing in the Pros..128
    Getting the help you need...128
    Identifying the right person for the job 129
    Keeping it secret 130
    Finding an IP professional...130
    Qualifying an IP professional...130
    Retaining an IP professional 131
    Working with foreign IP professionals 132
Paying the Piper...132
    Assessing the costs 133
    Managing the expenses 134
Coordinating with Other Professionals 135

Chapter 2: Mastering Patents, Trademarks, and Copyrights 137
Presenting Patents..137
    Defining patents 138
    Investigating what your patent can do for your country.............138
    Discovering what your patent can do for you...............139
    Understanding your rights and limits as a patent owner............139
Considering the Pros and Cons of Patents.................................140
Testing Patentability — 1, 2, 3 141
    Making yourself useful 141
    Developing a novel approach..142
    Avoiding the obvious 143
Assessing Your Rights 143
    Defining the invention in writing.....................................143
    Qualifying the invention..144
    Coming up with an inventor 144
Figuring Out Ownership..144
Applying for Patent Rights 145
    Provisional applications 146
    Searching and surfing...146
    Proceeding with the patent application..........................148
    Prosecuting the patent application 149
Patenting Internationally 151
    Pursuing patents in the United States............................151
    Going global..152
    Benefitting from treaties 152
Looking at the Services of a Patent Professional 154
Exploring Alternatives to Patents..155
    Keeping trade secrets...155
    Publishing to poison the well..156
Tackling Trademarks 157
    Making your mark..157
    Distinguishing yourself from the competition 158
Taking the Next Steps in Trademarking 159
    Deciding whether to register...160
    Clearing the way...161
    Finding registered trademarks...162

Seeking out adopted trademarks 162
Applying for registration 162
Retaining your registered mark 164
Going international 164
Enforcing Your Mark 165
Infringing on your rights 166
Passing it off 167
Asserting Your Copyrights 168
Defining copyright 168
Untangling ownership issues 170
Making Your Copyright Official 171
Infringing Copyright 172
Reading Your Rights 173
Forbidding copies 173
Prohibiting preparation of derivative works 173
Preventing unauthorized distribution 174
Barring public performances 174
Protecting your artistic reputation 174
Exceptions to the Rules 175
Dealing fairly 175
Claiming exemptions and privileges 176
Protecting Industrial Designs 176
Defining designs 176
Registering Your Design 177
Introducing the basics 178
Ensuring you're entitled to apply 178
Completing the application 179

Chapter 3: Profiting from Intellectual Property 181
Catching the Copycats 181
Violating copyright 182
Running afoul of a patent 182
Taking a trademark 182
Determining whether your copyright's been violated 182
Infringing on an industrial design 183
Pursuing the Infringers 184
Firing a warning shot 184
Proceeding to court 185
Fighting for Your Rights 185
Questioning the scope of your rights 186
Questioning the ownership of your IP 187
Exhausting your rights 187
Claiming you failed to act promptly 187
Getting to the Finish Line 188
Cashing In on Your IP Rights 188
Selling and Licensing 189
Understanding Licences 190
Granting Licences 190

Inspecting the Basic Elements of a Licence 191
    Getting it in writing.. 192
    Getting paid: Remuneration.................................... 193
    Reporting 194
Assigning Rather Than Licensing 194
Developing a Commercialization Strategy 195
Benefitting from Someone Else's IP................................. 196
    Being a licensee.. 196
    Using licensing with trademarks............................... 196
Using IP Filings as a Research Tool............................... 197
    Technically speaking.. 198
    Tracking your competitors..................................... 198
    Partnering up... 199

Book III: Business Planning 201

Chapter 1: Knowing Where You Want to Go 203

Preparing to Do a Business Plan.................................... 203
    Identifying your planning resources 204
    Setting steps and schedules 207
Planning Each Part of a Business Plan............................. 207
    Executive summary 208
    Business overview 209
    Business environment.. 209
    Business description.. 210
    Business strategy... 210
    Financial review 210
    Action plan... 211
Defining Values and Principles 211
    Understanding why values matter............................... 212
    Facing tough choices.. 212
    Applying ethics and the law 213
    Understanding the value of having values 213
    Clarifying your business's values 214
    Focusing on existing beliefs and principles 215
    Putting together your values statement 217
    Following through with your values............................ 218
Creating Your Business's Vision Statement......................... 219
Mapping Out a Mission Statement 221
    Crafting an effective mission statement....................... 221
    Answering questions 222
    Capturing your business (in 50 words or less)................. 223
Zeroing In on Goals and Objectives 224
    Goals versus objectives 225
    Setting goals and objectives.................................. 227
    Avoiding business-planning pitfalls........................... 228
    Timing is everything.. 230

Chapter 2: Describing Your Marketplace **231**

Understanding Your Business 232
Analyzing Your Industry 232
  Solidifying the structure 234
  Measuring the markets 235
  Remembering the relationships 236
  Figuring out the finances 237
Recognizing Critical Success Factors 239
  Adopting new technologies 240
  Getting a handle on operations 240
  Hiring human resources 240
  Minding your organization 240
  Cultivating customer loyalty 241
  Looking for a great location 241
  Benefiting from branding 241
  Dealing with distribution 241
  Getting along with government regulation 241
Preparing for Opportunities and Threats 242
  Enjoying the clear sailing ahead 242
  Watching for clouds on the horizon 243
Slicing and Dicing Markets 243
  Separating customers into groups 244
  Identifying market segments 244
  What customers buy 249
  Why customers buy 252
Finding Useful Market Segments 255
  Sizing up the segment 255
  Identifying the customers 255
  Reaching the market 256
Becoming Market Driven 256
  Researching your market 257
  Defining personality types 257
Checking Out Your Competition 258
  Understanding the value of competitors 259
  Identifying your real competitors 261
  Tracking your competitors' actions 266
  Predicting your competitors' moves 269
Competing to Win 271
  Organizing facts and figures 271
  Choosing your battles 272

Chapter 3: Weighing Your Business's Prospects **273**

Identifying Strengths and Weaknesses 274
  Getting other points of view 274
  Defining capabilities and resources 275
  Monitoring critical success factors 284

Measuring Your Business against Competitors...........................285
   Getting a glance at competitors........................285
   Completing your SWOT analysis 286
Evaluating the Value Chain and What You Do Best 287
   Describing what you do best...........................288
   Looking at the links in a value chain 288
   Forging your value chain 289
   Creating your value proposition.....................292
Putting Together a Business Model 293
   Where's the money? 293
   How's your timing? 294
Making Your Business Model Work 295
   Searching for a competitive advantage...........295
   Focusing on core competence 297
   Sustaining an advantage over time.................298
   Earmarking resources 299

Chapter 4: A Sample Business Plan **301**

Network Components, Inc. (NCI)
Business Plan — CONFIDENTIAL!......................................301
   Executive Summary 301
   1. NCI Business Plan 303
   2. Markets and Competition 306
   3. Marketing and Sales....................................312
   4. The Products 314
   5. Risk Analysis..317
   6. Financial Data 317

Book IV: Bookkeeping *323*

Chapter 1: Basic Bookkeeping: What It Is and Why You Need It . . .325

Bookkeepers: The Record Keepers of the Business World....................326
Wading through Basic Bookkeeping Lingo..............................326
   Talking about the balance sheet.......................327
   Speaking about the income statement..............327
   Knowing other common terms 328
Pedalling through the Accounting Cycle 329
Exploring Cash and Accrual Accounting 331
   Cash-basis accounting.....................................331
   Recording by using accrual accounting............332
Seeing Double with Double-Entry Bookkeeping 333
Differentiating Debits and Credits........................335

Outlining Your Financial Roadmap with a Chart of Accounts 335
    Starting with the balance sheet accounts....................336
    Tackling assets...336
    Laying out your liabilities 339
    Eyeing the equity 341
    Tracking the income statement portion of the
        chart of accounts 341
Setting Up Your Chart of Accounts 346

Chapter 2: Reporting Results 347

Developing a Balance Sheet 347
    Dividing and listing your assets.......................348
    Acknowledging your debts 351
    Naming your investments................................352
Ta Da! Pulling Together the Final Balance Sheet 353
    Account format 354
    Report format 354
    Financial position format................................355
Putting Your Balance Sheet to Work...........................356
    Testing your liquidity......................................357
    Assessing your debt 358
Producing an Income Statement.................................359
    Classifying accounts in the income statement.............360
    Formatting the income statement 361
    Preparing the income statement 362
    Drawing remaining amounts from your worksheet.......363
    Gauging your cost of goods sold 364
    Deciphering gross profit 365
    Monitoring expenses.......................................366
Using the Income Statement to Make Business Decisions 366
Testing Profits..369
    Return on sales...370
    Return on assets 371
    Return on equity 371

Chapter 3: Computer Options for Your Bookkeeping. 373

Surveying Your Software Options 373
    Simply Accounting Pro....................................374
    QuickBooks Pro..375
Setting Up Your Computerized Books 376
    Customizing software to match your operations 378
    Converting your manual bookkeeping to a
        computerized system 379

Book V: Human Resources *381*

Chapter 1: The People Picture .... .383
Managing Human Resources 384
Scoping Out Your HR Duties 384
    Thinking strategically 385
    Adapting to the changing workplace 386
    Easing the work/life conflict 387
    Keeping pace with technology and new skills 388
    Rules and regulations: Ethics first 388
Being Strategic in Your HR Efforts 389
Staying Ahead with HR Software 390
    Becoming an educated buyer 391
    Checking off the software features you need 392

Chapter 2: Recruiting the Right People .... .395
Thinking about Hiring in a New Way 396
    Grasping the big picture 397
    Reassess goals annually 398
Finding New Employees 398
    Inner peace: Filling jobs from within the organization ... 398
    New horizons: Looking for staff outside the company ... 399
    Outsourcing: The role of HR 399
Building Competency Models 400
The ABCs of Job Descriptions 401
    Sample job description 402
    Keeping tasks and qualifications straight 403
    Being flexible 404
    Considering soft skills 404
    Being specific 404
    Setting a salary range 405
    Determining a job title 405
Resourceful Recruiting 405
Recruiting from Within Your Business 406
    Creating a successful internal hiring process 407
    Developing an employee skills inventory 407
Writing a Good Job Ad 408
Using the Internet as a Recruitment Tool 408
    Receiving (too?) many responses 409
    Using your website to attract candidates 409
Using Recruiters 410
    Looking at the types of recruiters 410
    Knowing when to use a recruiter 411
    Finding the "right" recruiter 411
    Recruiting on campus 412
    Other recruiting sources 412

Assessing Potential Employees 412
    Evaluating candidates systematically...................................413
    Establishing an evaluation process.....................................413
Reading Resumes Effectively 413
    Mastering the basics 414
    Reading between the lines 414
    Watching out for red flags 415
Performing Short Phone Interviews 415
Interviewing Effectively Face to Face..416
    Knowing the goals..416
    Setting the stage...417
    Meeting the candidate...417
    Minding the Q&As...418
    Varying the style of questions...419
    Knowing what you can't ask..420
Fifteen Solid Questions to Ask and How to Interpret the Answers.......421
Ending the Interview on the Right Note...424
Making the Final Hiring Decision 424
    Coming to grips with the decision-making process 425
    Using the "tools" of the trade...425
    Using a system to make your selection................................426
    Setting up your own scale...427
    Factoring in the intangibles 428
    Hiring right..429
Checking References 429
    Discovering the truth behind background checks 430
    Checking out kinds of background checks 430
Making Offers They Can't Refuse..430
    Avoiding delays...431
    Putting your offer on the table...431
    Setting a deadline...431
    Staying connected..431
    Negotiating salary..432
    Knowing when to draw the line 433
    Clarify acceptance details...433
    Checking in 433

Chapter 3: Retention: Critical in Any Business Environment.......435
Ensuring an Effective Compensation Structure.................................436
    Speaking the language of employee compensation......................436
    Being consistent and flexible..437
    Basing compensation and benefits on a scale 437
Setting the Foundation for an Effective Compensation System 438
    Setting pay levels in your organization...............................439
    Accounting for individuals 441
    The bottom line on overtime..441

Reviewing the Basics of Raises, Bonuses, and Incentives.....................442
Pay raises...442
Bonuses..442
Incentives...443
What's fair versus what works?...444
Communicating Your Compensation Policies 444
Creating an Employee-Friendly Work Environment......................445
Saying Goodbye to Nine to Five: Alternate Work Arrangements 446
Looking at options for alternate work arrangements 446
Making alternate arrangements work 447
Telecommuting 447
Identifying prime candidates for telecommuting 447
Setting up an agreement for a telecommuter...............................449
Avoiding Burnout 450
Recognizing employee burnout...450
Being sensitive to extended periods of excessive workload........451
Giving employees more day-to-day job autonomy.......................451
Providing help 451
Keeping Tabs on Morale 452
Conducting an employee survey 452
Conducting exit interviews...453
Training and Development 453
Providing training for the good of the business 453
Knowing the benefits of training..454
Assessing your training needs 454
Tying training needs to strategic goals..456
Deciding whether to train or not to train 457
Evaluating training options 457
Mentoring as a training tool 459
Deciding on a training program 460
Measuring results of training efforts 460

Chapter 4: Monitoring Ongoing Performance 463
Assessing Employee Performance 463
Reaping the Benefits of Performance Appraisals 464
Deciding on a Performance Appraisal System.................................465
Goal-setting, or management by objectives (MBO) 466
Essay appraisals..466
Critical incidents reporting 467
Job rating checklist...467
Behaviourally anchored rating scale (BARS) 467
Forced choice..468
Ranking methods 468
Multi-rater assessments..469
Launching an Appraisal Program 469

Getting the Most Out of the Performance Appraisal Meeting 470
Preparing for the meeting..470
Conducting the session..470
Giving constructive feedback..471
Preparing for a negative reaction 472
Choosing areas for further development................................472
Making appraisal followup ongoing................................473
Handling Difficult Situations..474
Establishing an ethical culture..475
Staying out of court 475
Developing Disciplinary Procedures................................476
Firing Employees Is Never Easy..477
Following post-termination protocol 478
Using a waiver of rights..479
Easing the trauma of layoffs 480

Book VI: Marketing 483

Chapter 1: Getting Started in Marketing 485

Describing the Marketing Process 486
Making marketing your key to success................................486
Going around the marketing wheel of fortune................486
Distinguishing marketing from sales................................488
Starting Your Marketing Program 488
Marketing a start-up business..488
Marketing to grow your business..489
Marketing to compensate for lost business 489
Scaling your program to meet your goal................................489
Considering Your Customers..490
Looking at customer segments 490
Collecting information about your customer................................491
Seeing your business from the customer's perspective................492
Giving the Facts about What You Sell..493
Tallying your sales by product line..493
Using the cash register to steer your business................................494
Realizing Why People Buy What You Sell..494
Understanding the importance of value 495
Looking at the value formula..495
Riding the price/value teeter-totter................................496
Pricing considerations 496
Presenting your prices..497
Increasing Your Sales..497
Enhancing the appeal of existing products 498
Following the product life cycles..498
Sizing Up Competitors and Staking Out Market Share 499
Direct competitors..499
Indirect competitors..499
Phantom competitors..500
How businesses compete..500

Winning Your Share of the Market 500
    Defining your direct competition...501
    Climbing the competitive ladder 501
    Calculating your market share 501
    Increasing your market share 502
Making Your Marketing Plan and Budget 503
    Knowing where you're going 503
    Having a vision 504
    Developing your statement of purpose 504
    Defining goals 505
    Setting strategies 506
    Taking action 506
    Planning..506
    Budgeting to reach your goals 507

Chapter 2: Sharpening Your Marketing Focus **509**
Projecting the Right Image 509
    Making first impressions...510
    Taking an impression inventory 511
    Rating your marketing communications................................513
Establishing Your Brand and Position...513
    Having a powerful brand..514
    Staying consistent to build your brand 514
    Following six steps to brand management 514
Filling a Meaningful Market Position..515
    How positioning happens 515
    Creating a positioning statement...515
Conveying Your Position and Brand through Tag Lines 517
Advancing Your Brand through a Creative Strategy.............................517
    Writing your creative strategy 517
    Using your creative strategy 518

Chapter 3: Creating and Placing Ads **519**
Advertising Basics 519
    Using the image-plus-product advertising approach....................520
    Identifying your prospective customer 520
Creating Ads That Work 521
Sampling the Mass Media Menu 521
    Capturing Prospects with a Media Plan and Schedule 523
Evaluating Your Advertising Efforts..524
    Generating ad responses 524
    Keying responses 525
Writing and Designing Your Ads..525
    Packing power into headlines 525
    Writing convincing copy 527
    Making design decisions 527
Looking at Ad Placement 527
    Newspaper ads 527
    Placing magazine ads 528
    Out-of-home advertising 528

Broadcasting Ads on Radio and TV 529
  Buying airtime 529
  Achieving broadcast reach and frequency.....................................529
  Establishing your own broadcast identity.....................................530
  Overseeing the writing of your broadcast ad 530

Chapter 4: Reaching Your Market in More Ways................533

Reaching Your Market Directly...533
  Exploring direct sales strategies...534
  Direct mail success factors...534
  Building your direct mail list..535
  Deciding on a direct mail offer..536
  Writing direct mail messages 536
  Following up 537
Written Materials, Trade Shows, and Promotions 538
  Producing and using marketing literature....................................538
  Types of marketing literature...539
  Writing and designing brochures 539
  Launching and maintaining newsletters 540
  Converting business material to marketing opportunity 541
  Choosing and using trade shows...541
  Building sales through promotions...542
Looking at Public Relations...543
  Focusing on publicity...543
  Orchestrating media coverage...543
  Getting real with your expectations 544
  Circulating your news with a new release 544
  Writing news releases 545
  Establishing media contacts...545
  Managing media interviews 545
  Dealing with bad news 547

Book VII: Online Marketing..................................... 549

Chapter 1: Creating an Online Presence for Your Business........551

Putting a Website to Work for You..552
  Types of websites 552
  Building your website...553
  Creating website content..553
  Setting up website navigation 553
  Knowing the attributes of a good site 554
  Generating traffic to your website 554
Making Money Online 555
  Promoting affiliate products...556
  Monetizing traffic 556
  Developing your own online products and services.....................556

Blogging 557
   Choosing a topic to blog about 558
   Introducing blogging tools 559
Using Social Media 559
   Connecting via social networks 560
   Microblogging 561
   Media sharing sites 562

Chapter 2: Getting Started with Mobile Marketing **563**
   Understanding and Weaving Mobile into Marketing 563
      Direct mobile marketing 564
      Indirect mobile marketing 564
      Adding mobile to your marketing strategy 564
   Understanding the Many Paths within the Mobile Channel 564
      Understanding SMS capabilities 565
      E-mailing your messages 565
      Humanizing your messages with IVR 566
      Making connections through Bluetooth 566
   Running Mobile Communication Campaigns 567
      Planning your communication flow 567
      Providing text promotions 568
      Using quizzes to gather information and entertain 568
      Gathering input with open-
         ended survey questions 569
      Offering incentives 569
      Applying user-generated content 569

Chapter 3: Getting Ready to Use SEO and Web Analytics **571**
   Understanding Why Search Engines Exist 572
   Knowing What Makes a Website Relevant 573
   Setting Up Your SEO Toolbox 575
      Downloading and installing Firefox 575
      Installing add-ons 576
      Setting up and using Webmaster tools 576
   Creating Your SEO Worksheet 577
   Choosing the Right Keywords 578
      Thinking like your visitors 578
      Understanding the long tail 578
      Using the right tools to develop keywords 579
   Eliminating Search Engine Roadblocks 582
      Ensuring search engine visibility 582
      Eliminating registration forms 583
      Eliminating login forms 584
      Avoiding all-Flash pages 585
   Structuring Your Site for Search Engines and People 585
      Creating content clusters 585
      Creating deep links 586
      Keeping the structure clean and clear 586

Getting Started with Analytics 588
   Discovering the traffic report...588
   Collecting data and what it can tell you.........................589
   Choosing your reporting tool..590
   Setting up Google Analytics...591
Tracking Traffic Volumes 592
   Seeing why hits are a lousy metric 593
   Understanding the five basic traffic metrics 593
   Tracking sessions (visits)..594
   Tracking unique visitors 594
   Tracking pageviews 595
   Tracking time on site..595
   Tracking referrers...595
Measuring Visit Quality 596
   Setting quality targets 596
   Setting benchmarks for pageviews per visit and time on site 597
   Calculating your loyalty benchmark 597
   Learning more with bounce rate......................................597

Index *599*

Introduction

• •

*T*his is the book I wanted — and more importantly needed — some 30 years ago when I started out in business. Of course, in those days there was no such thing as laptops, the Internet, smartphones, tablets, digital cameras, Google, YouTube, Facebook, LinkedIn, Netflix, and other innovations that have changed the way we live, work, and play. Even the fax machine was a decade or more away when I started. But one thing has remained the same: Businesspeople have to tackle (or get tackled by) any number of issues and overcome any number of obstacles to get started, keep going, and, with a little luck, grow and thrive.

What I needed, and you need, too, is a guide to some of the important dimensions of a business that haven't changed much at all: getting started; planning and acting strategically; managing customers, employees, suppliers, and others; keeping the books; protecting your intellectual property; marketing the enterprise; and profiting from the latest tools and technological advances. *Starting & Running a Small Business For Canadians All-in-One For Dummies* is a mouthful — but it is **it**: The point of reference that every businessperson starting or sustaining a business needs.

As a starting point, this guide even leads you to the more complete *For Dummies* titles on the issues discussed briefly in this compendium. It can also help you decide where you need more help and more information — so you can find it by doing further research and reading, hiring consultants, or adding expertise in-house by hiring employees with the skills, interests, and experience you lack.

The breadth of topics covered in this book, combined with easy-to-follow tips, make this book perfect for your business, organization, or association. Keep this book on a nearby bookshelf or on your desk so you can reference it often.

Foolish Assumptions

We wrote this book for people who want to go into business for themselves. You have aspirations of being an entrepreneur, but that's all we know about you. We don't assume that you know where your business will be located, or even what it will be. We don't assume that you have any background knowledge about law or income tax or insurance or marketing or anything else for that matter. We do assume that you have a computer with Internet access, although we don't assume that you're a techno-nerd. We assume that you are intelligent and self-motivated. And we assume that you're aware that this book is just the start of a long journey that will entail a lot of work, but will hopefully confer great rewards, too.

How This Book Is Organized

This book is really seven minibooks, each covering a topic related to starting and running a small business. Each minibook provides an overview of the subject and more in-depth coverage of specific areas at the core of the subject matter.

The content of each minibook and each chapter stands alone, so you don't have to read all the minibooks — or even all the chapters — in order. You can use this book like an entire series of books on the subject of small business. Scan through the table of contents to find a single topic to refresh your memory or to get a few ideas before beginning a task, or you can read an entire chapter or a series of chapters to gain understanding and gather ideas

The following sections offer a quick overview of what each minibook contains.

Book 1: From Start to Finish and Everything in Between

This minibook introduces you to the topic of starting and managing a business, beginning with helping you determine whether you're made to have a small business or not. After all, maybe the most helpful thing we can do is to make sure you know what you're getting into and understand whether you've got what it takes to succeed.

Some entrepreneurs are pure entrepreneurs who go looking for a business — any business — where they can succeed. Others have a specific set of skills and experience. They may have worked in a large business or a smaller one and decide to branch out on their own. Regardless, if you are one type or another, or somewhere in between, you need to know how to choose a product, whether to buy a franchise, where to locate your business — and a slew of other things as well. They're covered in Book 1.

Beyond the startup phase we look at the operational side, working with customers and clients, dealing with suppliers and creating an environment that brings in repeat business.

Finally we look at the future and growth and getting out of business, through sale to someone else, preferably, but also your options if it comes down to closing your business when it is no longer viable.

If you're about to start a new business, start with this minibook. If you're about to retire, are thinking about selling, or think you may want to close your business, Chapter 4 of the minibook is the one for you.

Book II: Intellectual Property

This minibook is a primer on your intellectual property rights, what they are, how to protect them, and how to make money from them by gaining the rights to other people's intellectual property or, alternatively, contracting the rights to your own property to someone else.

We go into some detail about patents, trademarks, and copyrights, how they may apply to your business and to the intellectual property you create. We also go into how they are different and how they are same. Then we close the minibook on how to enforce your rights, how to profit from licences, and more.

While this minibook won't make you into a lawyer or a patent agent, it will give the knowledge you need to deal with intellectual property issues effectively if and when you have to.

Book III: Business Planning

A wise person once told me that there are lots of ways to get there if you don't know where you want to go. Business planning is all about assessing where you are on a given dimension, establishing where you want to go, and plotting out the strategy or route to get there.

In this minibook we show you how to prepare to do a business plan, how to establish your values and vision, how to set your mission, and how to translate those into goals and objectives.

We look at critical success factors such as the competitive environment, the markets, customer needs, and more to help you assess what next steps will move your business forward toward financial sustainability.

Book IV: Bookkeeping

Especially with inexpensive, easy-to-use small business bookkeeping systems available today, every business owner must know how the business is doing on a monthly or even a weekly basis.

We start you off with the bookkeeping basics and what they mean, then we go over what you can tell about your business from creating a balance sheet, an income statement, and other basic reports using the standard small business software systems available.

This minibook will unleash your inner accountant!

Book V: Human Resources

All businesses depend on customers, but most businesses depend on people on the inside, too. Chances are, your biggest business expense will be paying your people and getting value from them that exceeds the cost of paying them.

Sounds simple, but it isn't. This minibook shows you how. We take you through the basics of building a staffing strategy; go through the hiring process; and make a brief stop at competency models, job descriptions, and job titles.

We then take a look at the art and science of recruiting; writing employment ads that work; and using the Internet to attract, qualify, and help select the best candidate.

The minibook then takes you through the interviewing process and making your final selection, ensuring you get the right person for the job.

Finding the right employees is only half the story. Keeping them is another story, so we cap off the minibook with a discussion of compensation, creating a productive and happy work environment, training and development, and performance evaluation.

Book VI: Marketing

You can have the best product in the world, but if the right people don't know about it, you'll go bust just as fast as the guy who has a lousy product. Maybe even faster. So this minibook gives you what you need to be your own product manager and to get what you need from your advertising and promotions.

We start off with helping you think about your customers and look at things from their point of view. We then take you through the integrated communications mix, including print and broadcast advertising, direct mail through public relations, and documentation such as brochures and websites.

Book VII: Online Marketing

Remember when we said that the fundamentals of small business management hadn't changed much? Well, one thing is certain: the tools certainly have.

The website has replaced the corporate brochure and is giving the retail store and the cash register a run for their money. In this environment, creating a Web presence is no longer an option, it is a necessity for most businesses. So this minibook takes you through Internet business basics; making money online; and understanding how you can use a website, blogs, and social media such as Facebook, LinkedIn, and Twitter to your advantage.

We also take a look at mobile applications, and where they fit into the mix, and we close with a look at search engine optimization (SEO, that is) because at the risk of sounding like a broken record — oops, there really aren't any records left to break anymore and CDs are going the way of the dodo bird too — what's the point of running a business if no one can find you?

Icons Used in This Book

The Tip icon marks tips (duh!) and shortcuts that you can use to make your business life easier.

Remember icons mark the information that's especially important to know. To siphon off the most important information in each chapter, just skim through the paragraphs marked with these icons.

The Technical Stuff icon marks information of a highly technical nature that you can normally skip, if you want to.

The Warning icon tells you to watch out! It marks important information that may save you headaches.

The Ask A Lawyer icon points out where it's best to consult with a professional on things like contracts and other written agreements.

The Example icon marks real-world scenarios that small businesses encounter.

The Investigate icon gives you some suggestions for further research, and points out some good questions you should ask.

Where to Go From Here

You don't have to read this book in order. Each minibook and each chapter are self-contained, so you can pick up some information here and some information there about a topic that's of particular interest to you.

The *For Dummies* series also includes dozens of reference books that are pertinent for the small-business owner and that go into many of the topics covered in this All-in-One guide. They can take you into the level of detail you require.

If you're really thinking of starting a business and you haven't been in business before, you really should read all the minibooks before you commit to the perilous, but rewarding, journey that running your own business can be.

Book I

From Start to Finish and Everything in Between

The 5th Wave   By Rich Tennant

OUT OF BUSINESS

Main Street CHINA SH

"What made you think you were the one to own and operate a china shop, I'll never know."

In this book . . .

Chapter 1: Small Business Essentials 9

Chapter 2: Getting Started 29

Chapter 3: Operating Your Business 57

Chapter 4: Looking to the Future of Your Business................87

Chapter 1

Small Business Essentials

. . . .

In This Chapter

▶ Knowing the pros and cons of becoming a small business owner

▶ Deciding on the right business for you

▶ Assessing your entrepreneurial spirit

▶ Deciding if you should keep your day job

▶ Getting general business information

▶ Getting information specific to your business

▶ Acquiring the right skills

▶ Knowing the professionals who can help

. . . .

So you're thinking of starting your own business! Every year, lots of people get the entrepreneurial urge and start businesses. Some of those businesses become very successful. But every year lots of new businesses fail.

Business success or failure isn't the result of fate, or random chance, or (usually) acts of God. A business does well for good reasons — like a great product or service, a solid marketing plan, and the owner's good management skills.

Likewise, when a business goes under, you can often identify the reasons — lack of money to get properly started, poor timing or location for entering the market, or a wipeout on the customer service front. Whatever the reason for a business failure, it usually boils down to this: The business owner didn't look carefully before leaping.

In this chapter, we help you think about going into business before you spend a lot of time, money, and effort. We also point you toward some valuable resources and professionals so you can find out more about business in general, or the specific business you're considering.

Weighing the Pros and the Cons

People start up their own businesses for different reasons. One of the best reasons is that they've found a business opportunity that's too attractive to pass up. A good reason is that they want to work for themselves rather than for someone else. A depressing — but still valid — reason is that their other job options are poor (the number of small business start-ups always rises when the economy sinks).

Whatever your reason is for wanting to become an entrepreneur, you should know that life as an entrepreneur is a mixed bag. Running your own business has some great advantages, but it also has some hefty disadvantages.

The pros

Here are some of the advantages of going into business for yourself:

- **You're free!** You'll have the freedom to

    - Make your own decisions — you're in charge now. Only investors, customers and clients, government regulators, and so on will tell you what to do.

    - Choose your own work hours — in theory, anyway. You may not be able to get away with sleeping in until noon or concentrating your productive hours around 3 a.m. But you're more likely to be able to pick up the kids from school at 3 p.m., or exercise from 10 a.m. to 11 a.m., or grocery shop during normal office hours.

    - Create your own work environment — surround yourself with dirty coffee cups and overflowing ashtrays if you feel like it.

- **You can be creative!** You can build your business from scratch following your own ideas rather than following someone else's master plan.

- **You'll face new challenges!** Every day. And twice as many on days that end in a *y*. You'll never be able to say that work is always the same old boring routine.

- **Your job will be secure . . . as long as you have a business!** Your business may fail — but no one can fire you. (You can ask yourself to resign, though.)

- **You'll have increased financial opportunities!** If your business is successful, you have the potential to make more than you could as an employee.

- **You'll have tax advantages!** This is especially true if your business is not incorporated (a sole proprietorship or a partnership), but it's also true in a different way if your business is incorporated.

The cons

Do you think we used enough exclamation marks in the exuberant pros section? Bet they got you all enthused and excited about entrepreneurship. But calm down for a minute — being an entrepreneur has plenty of disadvantages, too. For some people, they outweigh the advantages. Here are some examples:

- ✔ **You may not make a lot of money.** You may make enough money to live on, but it may not come in regularly like an employment paycheque, so you'll have budgeting problems. Or you may not make enough money to live on. You may not even make any money at all. You may go bankrupt and lose not only your business, but most of your personal possessions as well.

- ✔ **You lose easy and inexpensive access to employment benefits if you don't hang on to employment elsewhere.** These may be benefits that you have come to count on — extended health and dental benefits, disability insurance, life insurance, a pension plan, and so on.

- ✔ **You'll have to work really hard.** That is, if you want to succeed — and you won't just be working at the business your business is about. You'll also have to do stuff you may not be trained to do, such as accounting, sales, and collection work.

- ✔ **You may not have a lot of free time.** You may see less of your friends, family, and pets (even if you're working at home) and have less time for your favourite activities. Getting a business up and running takes more than hard work; it also takes your time and commitment. Don't scoff that you won't let that happen to you, at least not until you've put in hours filling out government paperwork (GST/HST for example) on a beautiful sunny day that would be perfect for, well, almost anything else. By the way, you don't get paid for your sacrificed time, either.

- ✔ **You may have to put a lot of your own money into starting up the business.** And even if you can borrow the money, unless the lender is your mother and your mother is a sweet, trusting soul rather than a financial shark, you'll have to give personal guarantees that the money will be repaid (with interest) within a certain time. Pressure! And not to add to the pressure or anything, but you might lose your own money or not be able to repay borrowed money because of factors beyond your control. You could get sick (and now you probably don't have disability insurance), be flattened by a competitor, squashed by a nose-diving economy, or whacked by a partner who pulls out on you.

- ✔ **You are the bottom line.** No excuses — success is up to you, and failure is your fault. You'll have to keep on top of changes in your field, the impact of new technology, economic fluctuations. . . .

- ✔ **Your personal life can stick its nose into your business life in a major way.** If you and your spouse split up, your spouse may be able to claim a share of your business under equalization provisions in the family law of some provinces. You might have to sell your business or your business assets (property) to pay off your spouse.

Choosing Your Business

After you're aware of the upside and the downside to running your own business, start considering how people choose a business to go into.

Five main kinds of businesses exist:

- **Service:** Doing things for others, including the professions (doctors, lawyers, dentists, architects, accountants, pilots); skilled trades (plumbers, electricians, carpet installers, bookkeepers, renovators, truckers, carpenters, landscapers); and a huge range of other things for which you might need a lot of training and skill, or at least some talent and willingness. We're talking about music teachers, financial planners, real estate agents, painters, insurance brokers, management consultants, taxi drivers, travel agents, dry cleaners, caterers, event planners, hairstylists, equipment repairers, commercial printers, photographers, gardeners, snow removers . . . this list could go on.

- **Retail:** Selling things to the general public, such as jewellery, groceries, clothing, appliances, books, furniture, antiques and collectibles, toys, hardware, cards and knick-knacks, garden accessories, plants, cars . . . this list could also go on.

- **Wholesale:** Buying large quantities of goods from manufacturers at a discount and selling in smaller quantities to others — usually retailers — for a higher price. For example, you could buy nails in bulk from a manufacturer and resell them to hardware stores. Wholesalers sometimes also sell to the general public, usually without the frills of a retail establishment (for example, bulk food, carpets, and clothing).

- **Manufacturing:** Making things from scratch — from designing and sewing baby clothes for sale through a local children's clothing store to making furniture in a workshop to manufacturing steel ingots in a mammoth industrial plant.

- **Extraction:** Harvesting natural resources, including agriculture, fishing, logging, and mining.

Note that e-commerce is not a new and separate kind of business — that kind of thinking got it into trouble in the first place and caused the dot-coms to crash in the first years of this century. E-commerce is simply a tool to use in business.

Small businesses are most likely to concentrate in service and retail. Service, in particular, is usually the cheapest business to start up, which attracts a lot of entrepreneurs.

Now, most people don't look at a list of the five kinds of businesses and wonder, "Service or extraction? Retail or manufacturing? What best expresses my personality?" Instead, they have an idea that happens to fit into one of the five categories. At least, having an idea helps. And most people do, but others don't.

Looking for a business start-up

To begin with, try to aim toward something you'll enjoy doing. Starting a business is hard enough without choosing a business that you're pretty sure you'll loathe, even if you think it could make a lot of money.

Next, look for something people want . . . as opposed to something they don't want, or that they'll have to be carefully educated to want. It should also be something they'll want tomorrow and next week as well as today — in other words, don't base your business on a product or service that's going out of use or out of style. Ideally, your product or service is something that people want often, rather than occasionally or only once.

Especially in Canada, consider offering a product or service that isn't completely seasonal like skate sharpening or outdoor ice cream stands. Choose something with a good distribution and advertising system in place: For example, a product you manufacture should be one that established retailers will be happy to carry; a product you sell should be one that already benefits from a national marketing campaign by the manufacturer; a service you offer should be positioned within a network that will bring you lots of referrals.

Look for a business with a high profit margin. You'd like your direct cost of performing the work or supplying the product to be a small percentage of what you charge the client or customer. (The service industry is good for high profit margins; manufacturing and extraction aren't.)

Avoiding a difficult business start-up

While you're searching for a business with lots of advantages, you also have to avoid a business with too many disadvantages.

Stay away from a business that will be immediately overwhelmed by the existing competition. If the field is competitive (as are most fields worth going into), look for a niche where you have a competitive advantage (say, because you have a lot of natural talent or you've acquired great skills and experience; or because you have exclusive manufacturing or distribution rights). Don't go head-to-head with the established players and imagine you'll knock them down!

You also don't want a business that will be overwhelmed by regulation — by the federal, provincial, or municipal government — or by the governing body of a professional or skilled trade. Regulations exist in any type of business, but some businesses are more heavily regulated than in others. For example, food and drug manufacturing are heavily regulated by the federal government, as are telecommunications and commercial aviation. If you open a restaurant or bar, municipal food inspectors and provincial liquor inspectors will visit you regularly. Look into the extent of regulation when you research the area of business that interests you. We tell you about getting information geared to your specific business later in this chapter.

You might prefer to avoid a business that requires expensive insurance from the start (this describes most of the professions, and the manufacture of products that are potentially harmful).

Unless you've got guaranteed access to a big wad of cash, you'll certainly also want to avoid a business with high start-up costs. You may think you can build a better steel mill, but you can't do it on a $25,000 loan. Consider how much you have to invest in starting up a business, or how much you can raise by borrowing. If you have almost nothing to invest and realistically don't expect anyone else will want to invest a lot in you and your business, choose a business that requires almost no initial investment (that's usually service).

Consider steering clear of a business with immediate high labour needs. Paying employees isn't just a matter of cash flow (although that's pretty important). Employers also have to deal with a lot of regulations and paperwork — such as income tax, Employment Insurance, Canada or Quebec Pension Plan, provincial workers' compensation, and occupational health and safety rules — and you may already have enough on your plate. (See Book 3 for more about the responsibilities of being an employer.)

Determining If You Have the Small Business Personality

Whatever your reason for wanting to go into business for yourself, and whatever the business you choose, stop and check whether you have the right personality for the adventure before you start. This is true whether you really want to go into business for yourself or whether you think you have no choice but to do so. And it gives you an excuse to put off figuring out your finances.

Realizing that you don't have the right stuff to run your own business is better done *before* you sink a lot of time, effort, and money into a business. You can always pursue other options.

Book I

From Start
to Finish
and
Everything
in Between

And if you find you're not the perfect entrepreneur, but you're determined to go ahead anyway, then a self-assessment will tell you where your weaknesses lie and show you where you need to improve or get outside help.

An entrepreneur needs most of the following qualities — whether you were born with them, or developed them, or are about to get working on them now:

- ✔ **Self-confidence:** You have to believe in yourself and your abilities . . . no matter what other people think. You have to believe that your success depends on the good work you know you can do and not on matters beyond your control. Just make sure your self-confidence is realistic and not induced by the weird stuff they put in the coffee at your current workplace.

- ✔ **Goal-orientation:** You have to know what you want, whether it's to revolutionize a particular industry or to be home when your children return from school. However, if your main goals are money, power, and prestige, you probably need to reorient yourself toward something a little more attainable in the small business sector.

- ✔ **Drive to be your own boss:** If you need or even want direction about what to do next, you won't make it in your own business. You have to be able to make your own plans and carry them out.

- ✔ **Independence:** You must be able to work independently rather than as part of a team. You've probably had propaganda pounded into your head since you were a kid that teamwork is really important, and maybe even better than working on your own. It isn't if you're an entrepreneur.

- ✔ **Survival skills:** The ability to survive without a social group is handy. When you start up your own business, you'll probably be working by yourself for some time. If you need people around you to chat with, or else you start to go crazy . . . then you may go crazy.

- ✔ **People skills:** Even though you have to be okay with being alone a lot, you still have to get along with people. You'll be dealing directly with customers and clients, investors, suppliers, associates, and employees, and you need their willing cooperation.

- ✔ **Determination and persistence:** You have to want to succeed, and you have to plan to succeed and keep working at succeeding. It's that "fire in the belly" stuff you hear about from people who look like they haven't slept in eight months.

- ✔ **Self-discipline:** You can't get distracted from your work by nice weather, phone calls from family and friends, earthquakes, or wrestling matches on TV.

- ✔ **Reliability:** You'll build most of your important business relationships by always meaning what you say and doing what you promise.

- ✔ **Versatility:** You have to be prepared to do many different things in short periods of time, probably constantly switching from task to task.

- ✔ **Creativity:** You have to want to do something new or something old in a new way. If copying what someone else is already doing is the best you can manage, you may not go far.

- ✔ **Resourcefulness:** Creativity's country cousin, resourcefulness, means being prepared to try different ways of doing things if the first way doesn't work.

- ✔ **Organizational talents:** You'll be plunged into chaos if you can't organize your goals, your time, or your accounts, to name just a few things.

- ✔ **Risk-management instincts:** You have to be able to spot risks, weigh them, and come up with a plan to steer around them or soften their impact in case of a collision.

- ✔ **Nerves of steel in a crisis:** Nerves of granite, titanium, oak, and so on are acceptable. Nerves of rubber, talc, or pasta al dente are not. Crises won't necessarily be frequent, but they will occur. Don't count on gin or prescription drugs to stiffen your spine during a crisis. And you can't collapse until the crisis is over.

- ✔ **Pick-yourself-up-itiveness — a combination of optimism and grit:** You're going to have failures, some of them caused by your own mistakes; and you have to see failures as valuable experiences rather than as signs that you and your business are doomed.

- ✔ **Opportunism:** You need to not only recognize opportunities when they come along, but you also need to seek them out — and even create them yourself.

- ✔ **Success-management instincts:** You can't let yourself be bowled over or lulled by success. You have to be able to see each success as a platform on which you can build your next success.

- ✔ **Objectivity:** Business owners are always doing reality checks. You need the courage to stare down reality's throat and acknowledge your own mistakes. You also have to corner reality by getting feedback about your business and how you run it from customers and clients, suppliers, professional advisors, competitors, employees, and even your mother-in-law. Then you need the strength to make necessary changes.

That's a long list! And you'll also need a Zen-like calm about not having a regular paycheque. Not only will you not get a bank deposit once a month, but you won't get paid for sick days, personal days off, or days when you show up at the office but are too zonked to work.

In addition, having parents (or close relatives or close friends) who are or were in business for themselves is helpful. You may have absorbed some business know-how from them, plus they can give advice.

And to finish you off, good health and physical stamina can do an entrepreneur no harm.

Knowing If and When to Give Up Your Day Job

Should you start a business and keep your day job (if you've got one)?

Conventional wisdom says don't give up your day job until absolutely necessary (when you have to devote the time to your business or give it up) or until you don't need a day job (when you're making a living from your business). Conventional wisdom also urges entrepreneurs not to go it alone until they've saved up about six months' salary. That's a good joke! It would take most of us years to save six months' salary, unless we were offered a fantastic buyout package.

Even if you're dying to tell your current employer "I quit!", think about the following questions:

- ✔ **Do you need the money from employment?** Even if your business turns out to be a success, you may not have much, or even any, income when you first start your business.

- ✔ **Do you want to keep your employment contacts?** The business you're starting might be something your employer or fellow employees could assist or patronize.

- ✔ **Do you have the time to hold down a job and start a business (and still have time to eat and sleep)?**

- ✔ **Would starting your own business and keeping your day job be problematic because of**

  - Your employer's requirement (in your employment contract) that you not carry on any kind of a competing business while you're an employee?

  - Your employer's requirement (in your employment contract) that you put your full effort toward your employment work?

  - Suspicious superiors and co-workers who would assume you were goofing off by focusing on your own business instead of doing what you were paid to do?

- ✔ **Do you want to be able to fall back on your day job if your business venture doesn't work out?** Remember, if you quit to start a business, you might not get hired back.

Seeking Out General Business Information

The amount of information available about business can seem infinite. How do you zero in on what's useful to you? The following sections give you some pointers on where to get helpful and reliable business information.

Getting general information about starting and carrying on a business is a good starting point. Our advice is to find a fairly comprehensive and self-contained start-to-finish source, such as a book — hey, this book is a great choice! — or a business resource centre, or a website. You've already got the book, so coming up are our suggestions for resource centres and websites. We start with the superstars, the Canada Business network, but we also tell you about provincial and private-sector resources.

Canada Business — Services for Entrepreneurs

Canada Business is a cross-jurisdictional government organization that provides access to both government and general business information, for both start-up entrepreneurs and established, small- to medium-sized businesses in any field. It delivers its services through an organized network of service centres across Canada, one in each province and territory. In addition, each provincial service centre works with partners in many other communities in their regions providing numerous service access points. The services of the Canada Business network are available on the Web, by phone, and in person.

Looking at Canada Business network services

The Canada Business network provides information on government services, programs, and regulations pertaining to business. Each centre also has an extensive and up-to-date reference collection of general business information from government and non-government sources — topics include starting a business, writing a business plan, finding financing, marketing, exporting, and being an employer. The service centres have information officers to help you navigate your way through everything they offer.

In addition, you can get products, services, publications, and referrals to experts. Here are some examples of the products and services the service centres provide:

- ✔ **Info guides:** These free guides on different topics provide brief overviews of services and programs.

- ✔ **How-to guides:** These guides provide information about the potential licence, permit, and registration requirements for specific types of businesses.

Book I

From Start
to Finish
and
Everything
in Between

✔ **Fact sheets:** These fact sheets contain information about starting and running a business and are available online.

✔ **BizPaL online business permits and licences service:** This online service provides information about business permits and licence requirements from all levels of government.

✔ **Specialized Research Service:** This limited business research service is free and provides access to information on topics such as business associations, Canadian demographics, company data, consumer spending, and sample business plans.

Some of the service centres also offer low-cost seminars and workshops on a variety of business topics.

Accessing Canada Business services

You can get in touch with your provincial or territorial service centre in five ways:

✔ **Website:** The Canada Business website (www.canadabusiness.ca) contains information about business-related programs and services of federal and provincial agencies. The site allows you to input your province, industry, and/or demographic group and receive information tailored to the location and nature of your business, and provides links to the individual websites maintained by some provinces. The main site contains information on such topics as

- Starting a business

- Looking at growth and innovation in your business

- Getting financial assistance through grants, loans, and financing

- Managing federal and provincial taxes

- Complying with business regulations

- Obtaining licences and permits

- Exporting and importing

- Hiring and managing staff

- Creating a business plan

- Managing and operating a business

- Conducting market research and getting access to statistics

- Doing marketing and sales

- Exiting your business

Some of the provincial sites also provide information about and let you register for business workshops and seminars, as well as links to other useful websites.

- ✔ **Phone:** Call the Canada Business toll-free Business Info Line at 1-888-576-4444 between 9:00 a.m. and 5:00 p.m. in every Canadian time zone. (TTY service for the hearing-impaired is also available from 8:30 a.m. to 6:00 p.m., Eastern Time, by calling 1-800-457-8466.) A business information officer will direct you to the best sources of information or refer you to programs and services relevant to your business situation.

- ✔ **Fax:** Contact Canada Business by fax at 1-888-417-0442.

- ✔ **E-mail:** Send questions to Canada Business by e-mail from the main website under "Contact Us."

- ✔ **In person:** At the offices of your provincial/territorial service centre, you can use the resource materials on your own or with the help of a business information officer. The provincial service centres also have arrangements with existing business service organizations in communities across Canada to provide Canada Business information. Contact your provincial/territorial service centre for the location nearest you.

Provincial/territorial government websites

Each provincial and territorial government maintains a website. Some of the provincial sites contain good general business information that you can use to get started.

Here are the websites:

- ✔ Alberta: www.alberta.ca
- ✔ British Columbia: www.gov.bc.ca
- ✔ Manitoba: www.gov.mb.ca
- ✔ New Brunswick: www.gnb.ca
- ✔ Northwest Territories: www.gov.nt.ca
- ✔ Nova Scotia: www.gov.ns.ca
- ✔ Nunavut: www.gov.nu.ca
- ✔ Ontario: www.gov.on.ca
- ✔ Prince Edward Island: www.gov.pe.ca
- ✔ Quebec: www.gouv.qc.ca
- ✔ Saskatchewan: www.gov.sk.ca
- ✔ Yukon: www.gov.yk.ca

Book I

From Start
to Finish
and
Everything
in Between

Bank and trust company websites

The major banks' and trust companies' websites have information about the products and services they provide to small businesses. Some have information about general business topics, as well.

Small business or entrepreneurship centres

A number of small business or entrepreneurship centres provide support and training to start-up and small businesses, for example:

- **Centennial College Centre of Entrepreneurship:** This Toronto-based centre provides entrepreneurial training, business plan development, analysis of proposed acquisitions, as-needed business advice and consulting, and international business training. It also offers a 30-day New Business Starter Program, designed to provide entrepreneurs with the basic principles and practices of business, along with the skills to market, operate, and control a business. Visit www.centennial college.ca/coe/home to find out more.

- **Centre for Entrepreneurship Education and Development Incorporated (CEED):** This Nova Scotia not-for-profit society is devoted to helping people discover and use entrepreneurship as a vehicle to become self-reliant. Its services include technical assistance, entrepreneurship consulting, and entrepreneurship courses. CEED's website (www.ceed.ca) has more information.

- **Ontario Small Business Enterprise Centres:** These Ontario government centres are located throughout the province and provide entrepreneurs with support to start and grow their businesses. They offer a wide variety of support resources, including consultations with qualified business consultants, workshops and seminars, and mentoring and networking opportunities. Visit www.ontariocanada.com/ontcan/1medt/ smallbiz/en/sb_sbec_en.jsp for more information.

- **The Stu Clark Centre for Entrepreneurship:** The University of Manitoba's Asper School of Business (http://umanitoba.ca/ faculties/management) operates this centre. It aims to encourage the development of new businesses and entrepreneurial thinking among Canadians. The centre supports a variety of programs aimed at youth, as well as undergraduate students and adults. Its Manitoba Venture Challenge (www.manitobaventurechallenge.ca) is a province-wide competition open to new and established businesses in Manitoba whose owners are seeking outside investment or need advice to start or grow their businesses.

✔ **Youth Employment Services (YES)**: Among other services, this not-for-profit organization based in Montreal provides English language services to help entrepreneurs start and run businesses. Services include business coaching, seminars on topics of interest to small business, a mentorship program, and more. Visit www.yesmontreal.ca for more information.

Business incubators

A *business incubator* is a business-mentoring facility that nurtures small- and medium-sized businesses during the start-up period. Business incubators provide management assistance, education, technical and business support services, and financial advice. They may also provide flexible rental space and flexible leases.

For more information about Canadian business incubators, including a list of business incubators in Canada, contact the Canadian Association of Business Incubation (www.cabi.ca).

Getting Information Geared to Your Specific Business

After you find out about starting and carrying on a business in general, you can find out more about your field of business in particular. For example, you might want to know these facts:

✔ What skills you need for this business

✔ What government regulations apply to this business

✔ How much it will cost to run this kind of business

✔ What the demand is for the goods or services you'll be supplying

✔ Who the likely customers are for the goods and services you'll be providing

✔ What the competition is like for this type of business

✔ What supplies and equipment you require for this type of business

You need a good gateway into the sector you're interested in. Here are our recommendations.

Industry Canada

Industry Canada's website (www.ic.gc.ca) is particularly useful at the preliminary stage of starting a business because, in addition to general business information, it contains information on a wide variety of businesses, organized by sector. Each type of business has its own page, with additional pages on a number of subtopics. The subtopics vary for each business category, but they cover areas such as the following:

- ✔ **Company directories:** With links to lists of Canadian companies carrying on business in the field

- ✔ **Contacts:** With links to major trade associations in the field

- ✔ **Electronic business:** With links to a variety of information about e-business and e-commerce

- ✔ **Events:** With links to major trade shows in a particular business field

- ✔ **Industry news:** With links to Canada and U.S. trade periodicals

- ✔ **Regulations and standards:** With links to relevant government regulations and standards organizations

- ✔ **Statistics, analysis, and industry profiles:** With links to North American Industry Classification definitions and to selected Canadian statistics on topics such as the Canadian market, imports, and exports

- ✔ **Trade and exporting:** With links to relevant international trade agreements and export information

Trade and professional associations

Trade and professional associations are another great source of information about particular fields of business. Thousands of associations exist in North America. Whatever your field of business, a related association probably exists. A good association will give you access to industry-specific information. Most associations maintain a website, setting out the services the association provides and membership information. You'll find many benefits to trade and professional associations:

- ✔ **Trade and professional journals:** Many trade and professional associations publish journals or newsletters with current information about the field. They also contain ads for equipment and supplies that the business uses, and some list business opportunities (businesses for sale, partners wanted, premises for lease, equipment for sale, and so on). You may be able to get information about trade and professional journals on the Industry Canada website by following the Industry News link offered for some industry sectors.

✔ **Workshops and seminars:** Many trade and professional associations hold seminars and workshops on topics of specific interest to members. Some offer courses leading to a designation or certification in the field.

✔ **Trade shows:** Most trade associations hold an industry-wide trade show at least once a year. Trade shows are good places to make contacts in the industry and learn about the latest trends in the field.

Obtaining Essential Business Skills

After you research your chosen business field, you may realize that you need some training before you can start your business. You may need skills specific to your chosen business field (such as how to frame a picture if you're going into the framing business, or how to mediate if you're going into family counselling), or you may want to pick up some general business skills and knowledge such as simple bookkeeping, basic computer skills, or how to prepare a business plan.

When people think of education, they usually think of universities, community colleges, career colleges, vocational schools, and boards of education. But in fact, many different places offer business education and skills training. You may be able to pick up the skills you need from a trade association, a Canada Business service centre, or the little place in your local mall that teaches keyboarding. In fact, you may want to avoid many of the educational institutions, because they often offer certificate or diploma programs more suited to people looking for a job, rather than individual courses focused on the specific skills an entrepreneur needs.

Where you go to get your training will depend on the kind of skill you're trying to acquire.

Skills for your particular business

You may be able to pick up the special skills required for your particular business in a day, a weekend, or a week. Or you may need a certificate or diploma in the field that will take months or years to get.

You may be able to find out not only what skills you need, but also where to get them, from Industry Canada or from the relevant trade or professional association. Or you can use an online search engine (such as Google, Bing, or

Yahoo!) and type in the name of the specific field you're interested in plus the word "education" or "training."

If you're not required to have a degree, diploma, or certificate offered by a university or community college, consider programs offered by privately run career colleges or vocational schools. These programs tend to be shorter than university and community college programs, but be warned — these courses are usually more expensive, sometimes much more expensive!

The trade or professional association in your field may offer short workshops or seminars on individual topics of interest to you, as well as complete training programs specifically for your field.

General business skills

To acquire in-depth business skills, you can enroll in degree, diploma, or certificate programs offered by colleges and universities. These programs run over the course of a year, or from two to three years. You probably won't be able to take one course of interest to you without taking another course as a prerequisite or without signing on for the entire program.

If you want to acquire some business skills as quickly as possible, look for *continuing education* courses offered by your local university. For example, the University of Toronto School of Continuing Studies (http://learn. utoronto.ca) offers courses (usually with classes held once a week for about three months) in a wide variety of business-related areas, including Accounting Fundamentals, Business Law and Insurance, Business Management, Business Strategy, Social Media Starter, Taxation for Canadian Business, and Understanding and Resolving Conflict. University of Calgary Continuing Education (http://conted.ucalgary.ca) has seminars on numerous topics, including Time Management, Accounting for Non-Financial Managers, Building Great Customer Relationships, Writing Skills for Business, and Creative Negotiating.

Your local board of education may offer courses in business skills as part of its continuing education programs, and you should have no problem enrolling in individual courses rather than in programs. Classes will probably be scheduled once a week over several months.

You may also be able to find weekend workshops or evening seminars offered by your trade or professional association, or through your provincial Canada Business service centre.

Finding Professional and Other Help

Planning a business start-up takes a lot of work. But you don't have to do it all alone. You can and should get professional help with many of the tasks involved. In this section, we help you determine who you need on your team, and how to find the best candidates.

Determining whom you need

At the very least, you need a lawyer, an accountant, and an insurance agent or broker. We also offer suggestions for other professionals you might find useful.

Lawyer

Almost everything that happens in the business world has legal implications. A lawyer can help you navigate through every stage of your business odyssey.

When you're setting up your business, a lawyer can

- Help you decide whether or not to incorporate
- Help you form a corporation or partnership
- Review start-up documents such as loan agreements, leases, and franchise agreements
- Draft standard forms for contracts to use in your business

When you're in business, a lawyer can be of further assistance by

- Helping you negotiate contracts
- Giving you advice about hiring and firing employees
- Helping you collect your unpaid accounts
- Acting for you in a lawsuit if you sue or are sued

Even if you decide to get out of the business, you'll still need a lawyer to help you sell it, or give it to your children, or wind it up.

Accountant

In Canada, anyone can claim to be an accountant. What you want is a professional accountant — a chartered accountant, certified general accountant, or certified management accountant. Professional accountants are licensed and regulated.

An accountant can help you

- ✔ Buy an existing business
- ✔ Set up a bookkeeping system
- ✔ Prepare budgets and cash-flow statements
- ✔ Prepare financial statements
- ✔ Prepare your income tax returns
- ✔ Deal with the Canada Revenue Agency (CRA) from time to time

Insurance agent or broker

You'll need insurance for your business, including

- ✔ Property insurance to cover loss or damage to your business property
- ✔ Business interruption insurance to cover your loss of earnings if your business premises are damaged
- ✔ General liability insurance to cover claims made if you cause injury to a customer, supplier, or innocent bystander
- ✔ Key person insurance to tide over your business in case you, a partner, or an important employee dies or becomes disabled

An *insurance agent* (a person who deals with and sells the policies of only one insurance company) or *insurance broker* (a person who deals with and sells the policies of several insurance companies) can give you advice about what kind of insurance you need and how much. Both agents and brokers are regulated and licensed by provincial governments.

Other assistance

Depending on the nature of your business, you may also want help from any of the following professionals (in no particular order):

- ✔ **Advertising firm and/or media relations firm:** To help you get the word out about your business
- ✔ **Business coach:** To help you acquire presentation skills, get pointers on power dressing, pick up business etiquette, and even improve your table manners (for those four-fork lunches with potential investors and customers)
- ✔ **Business evaluator:** To help you decide on the value of a business you are thinking of buying
- ✔ **Computer systems consultant:** To help you choose and set up your computer equipment and choose and install your software

- ✔ **Graphic designer:** To help you design a business logo, your business cards, and letterhead

- ✔ **Human resources specialist (also known as a headhunter):** To help you hire staff

- ✔ **Interior designer:** To help you set up your business premises attractively

- ✔ **Management consultant:** To help you polish your management skills

- ✔ **Marketing consultant:** To help you identify the market for your product or service and determine how best to reach that market

- ✔ **Website designer:** To help you create a great website for you business

Finding peer support

Even though you're going it alone in the business universe, you may want to seek out the companionship of fellow travellers for sharing experiences and getting advice. Whatever demographic group you fall into, you'll likely find a business organization for you. These organizations provide opportunities to network and get advice geared to your demographic.

Here's a sampling:

- ✔ **Canadian Association of Women Executives & Entrepreneurs:** An organization that provides networking, support, mentoring, and professional development to businesswomen at all stages of their careers (www.cawee.net).

- ✔ **Canadian Council for Aboriginal Business:** A national, non-profit organization that promotes the full participation of Aboriginal individuals in the Canadian economy (www.ccab.com).

- ✔ **Canadian Gay & Lesbian Chamber of Commerce:** An organization designed to improve opportunities for gay, lesbian, bisexual, transgender, transsexual, two-spirited, and intersex owned/operated/friendly businesses (www.cglcc.ca).

- ✔ **Canadian Youth Business Foundation:** A national charity whose mandate is to support business owners age 18 to 34 (www.cybf.ca).

Chapter 2

Getting Started

. . . .

In This Chapter

▶ Thinking about your target market as you develop a product or service

▶ Getting your product or service to the right people

▶ Pricing your product or service

▶ Buying an existing business instead of building your own business

▶ Deciding on a fair price for a business

▶ Considering a franchise

▶ Finding the right location and business premises

▶ Understanding incorporation and partnerships

▶ Knowing the rights and responsibilities of a corporation

▶ Safeguarding assets without incorporating

. . . .

Your business will be in big trouble if you offer a product or service that not a soul wants, or that your chosen customer group is not interested in. In this chapter, we help you avoid those problems and give you hints on how to develop a product or service tailored for your target customers or clients, and at a reasonable price. And don't forget that starting a business from the ground up isn't your only option. This chapter also gets you thinking about existing businesses and franchises.

Where you do business is a big factor in your future success, so we point out what to remember when finding your ideal business location. We also get into the ins and outs of different forms of ownership, and what you should know about incorporating a business.

Developing Your Product or Service with a Market in Mind

To start a business, you need a product or service to sell. And it needs to be something that customers or clients want to buy.

Developing a product or service requires quite a chunk of your time and energy. You'll need to take on some tasks that may seem challenging, such as researching potential customers and existing competition.

If your idea is new and innovative, you may be able to get assistance with the evaluation, for example from The Canadian Innovation Centre (CIC) (www.innovationcentre.ca) in Waterloo, Ontario, an organization that grew out of the invention commercialization activities of the University of Waterloo. Their website has information for inventors as well as links to other useful organizations such as the (U.S.) National Inventor Fraud Center (www.inventor-fraud.com), which offers advice on how to steer away from invention marketing companies that are set up only to scam inventors.

Don't get mixed up with a company that combines high-pressure sales tactics with a low success rate.

Is this idea right for you?

Or is this a good idea at all? Before choosing a product or service, play a little Q and A with yourself:

- ✔ **Is it legal?** And if it's legal now, will it become illegal after it takes off? Remember radar detectors for the travelling public?
- ✔ **Is it hands-off?** The idea may already be patented and the patent owner doesn't want to license to you. (Go to Book II for more about intellectual property, such as patents.)
- ✔ **Are you legal?** Some products and services can be provided only by a licensed individual or business.
- ✔ **Is the product or service safe?** Could you cause harm to someone and end up getting sued?
- ✔ **Do you have the right reputation or expertise?** You may need both to develop the idea into a business and reel in customers or clients.

Does anyone want the product or service?

Book I

From Start to Finish and Everything in Between

Your idea may seem wonderful to you, but to prosper, your market must be slightly larger than one person. So you have to do some *customer research* — identify a target market for the product or service and estimate the size of the market. Here's a brief guide to doing customer research.

First, think generally about who your customers or clients might be (keep in mind that you could be wrong about this, though). For example, are they

- ✔ **Other businesses?** A whole bunch of them or just one or two? Are the businesses service providers or retailers or manufacturers?

- ✔ **Individuals?** Do the individuals live in a particular neighbourhood or geographic area, or do they live all over the country or around the world? Are they men only? Women only? The young? Older people? The well-to-do, or just anyone with a buck to spend?

Who's the competition?

And what are they up to? This information is known as *competitive intelligence.* Your competitors may already have claimed all of the customers or clients you identified by doing your market research. Or they may not. You can find out by assessing your potential market share.

To start with the question we just asked (Who's the competition?), your competition is made up of the following:

- ✔ **Direct competitors** — who offer exactly the same product or service

- ✔ **Indirect competitors** — who offer an alternative product that more or less meets the same need as your product

- ✔ **Who-was-that-masked-man? competitors** — who offer something completely different that potential customers will spend their money on instead of on your product or a similar product, much to your regret and amazement

- ✔ **Inertia** — the tendency of customers and clients to do nothing at all when brought face-to-face with your wonderful product or service

Look carefully at your direct and indirect competitors and see if you can find out whether

- They've cornered the market and are doing such a good job at such a good price that you haven't much hope of taking market share away from them. Or whether you should be able to relieve them of market share because you can offer better value — for example, a lower price, a higher-quality product or service, a more convenient location, greater expertise, friendlier service, and so on. Sometimes the first competitor into the market may just have collected and educated your potential clients for you!

- Their business is profitable — are they growing or shrinking?

- They're big enough and mean enough to run you out of town if you show your face on the street (have you noticed how small airlines regularly get eaten?).

How much money can you put behind this idea?

You likely can't get your idea off the ground for free. So you've got to crunch a few numbers to find out the following:

- **The approximate cost of launching your business.** This involves adding up your start-up costs plus bridge financing for your operating expenses until your business is generating income.

- **The approximate amount of money available to you for a business start-up.** The cash you have on hand or can raise through family contributions may be enough to get your particular business up and running; or you may need a bank loan for a larger amount; or you may need a significant investment from an angel investor or venture capital firm.

How much you'll be able to raise (especially from outsiders) is linked to the likely return on investment for your idea. So just because it will take $1 million to build a plant to produce your product doesn't mean you should scrap the idea. It could be full steam ahead if an investor believes that your business could generate profits of $2 million annually after a couple of years or that the business might be worth $50 million in five years.

Finding a Route to the Target Market

Okay, so you think you've got a product or service that can go the distance. Now you have to figure out how to get it from you to the person who will actually use it — so you have to decide on one or more distribution channels. You have two basic choices:

- ✔ **Distribute directly:** The product or service goes from your business to your buyer (most services and products take this route).

- ✔ **Distribute indirectly:** The product or service goes from your business to another business to the buyer. Although your target market is the buyer, your customer is the "middleman" business.

Pricing Your Product or Service

You can make a profit in different ways — for example, by combining a small profit on each item or service provided with high sales volume, or by combining a low sales volume with a big profit on each transaction. (Best, of course, is high profit on each unit and high sales volume, but not many businesses are that lucky.) But if you underprice, you'll lose money on every sale even if you sell a gazillion units; if you overprice, no one will buy at all. How do you figure this whole thing out? In this section, we talk about how to settle on the right price to charge.

Deciding on the minimum price you can charge

Minimum price is not all that difficult to figure out. As a rule, you don't want to charge less for your product or service than it costs to produce. (An exception is offering the product or service as a loss leader, to lure customers in — but you can't keep that up for long, and certainly not on an important part of your line.) The formula below tells you, as the owner of a start-up business, your cost to produce (your *break-even cost*):

$$\frac{\text{Total direct and indirect costs over a given period (say, one to three months)}}{\text{Total number of products or services that it would be reasonable for you to provide over the given period}} = \begin{array}{l}\text{Your break-even cost} \\ \text{for that period}\end{array}$$

Your break-even cost for the period is the amount you need to charge for each unit of your product or service to pay your direct and indirect costs.

Deciding on the maximum price you can charge

Now over to the other end of the price scale. Here, the ceiling for your price is the value of your product or service to the customer or client. Value is what the customer perceives that he or she is getting in exchange for the cost of the product, and includes things such as quality and reliability of the product or service, image or prestige associated with the product or service, uniqueness of the product or service, backup from your business such as support and guarantees, convenience of dealing with your business (such things as good location or inexpensive delivery or the helpfulness of your staff), and incentives such as rebates (money back following a purchase), discounts (money off the purchase price), and other freebies.

If a customer believes that your price is greater than the value of your product or service, the customer won't buy from you.

Setting your price

Setting a price comes down to supply and demand. If a product is essential or useful and hard to find, the price can be higher and the product will still sell (until people run out of money). If a product is not a must-have or is readily available, the price has to be lower if you want to sell. Higher or lower than what? The competition's price.

So see what your competition is charging. When you know that, then you can implement one of the following three strategies:

- ✔ **Charge more than the competition.** This will work only if your product is seen as more valuable than the competition's. You can increase the value of the same product or service offered by the competition by (for example) creating a higher-end image for your business or by trading on your reputation as an expert.

- ✔ **Charge the same as the competition.** But you still need to increase the value of your product over the competition's. You could do this, for example, by offering a more convenient location to your target customers.

- ✔ **Charge less than the competition.** Just be careful not to undercut your own cost of production, and keep in mind that you'll acquire a "reputation." Whether it's true or not, customers and clients will tend to associate lower prices with lower value. Only in rare cases will people think they've made a marvelous discovery of a business that carries exactly the same product as the competition, but at a lower price.

Considering an Off-the-Shelf Business

Book I

**From Start
to Finish
and
Everything
in Between**

Building your own business is a lot of work. In addition to coming up with a business concept, you have to find a good location, prepare your business premises, buy equipment, and find and attract clients or customers (see Book VI). And when you custom-build your business, you have no one to give you on-the-job training or to pass on wisdom gained from experience about what works and what doesn't.

But custom-building a business is not the only way to go into business. You can buy an existing business instead. In the next few pages, we weigh the advantages and disadvantages of each approach.

Buying an existing business

You might want to buy an existing business for a number of reasons:

- You already know of a business that you want to own.
- You'll be able to eliminate a lot of the difficult, early work involved in building a business.
- You may be able to tap into a source of advice from the original owner.
- You may be able avoid some of the risks of starting a new business:
    - You know that the product or service already has a market.
    - Your immediate money situation may be better — borrowing money may be easier, because banks know that the risks of failure are lower for an established business than for a start-up.
    - You may be able to get rights such as the right to distribute a specific product in a particular area, or the licence to manufacture a particular item.

But before you go rushing off to buy a business, know that buying a business has disadvantages, as well:

- A successful business isn't cheap.
- A successful business may not continue to be successful for you. The success may have been based on the personality and/or skill of the current owner.
- The business's problems become your problems.

Looking carefully at existing businesses

Before the owner agrees to answer your questions, show you around the business premises, and let you see documents, he or she may ask you to sign a *confidential disclosure agreement.* By signing the agreement you agree not to tell anyone else what you find out about the business, and usually you also agree not to use the information for any purpose but assessing the business for a possible purchase.

Take a very careful, even cynical, look at any business before deciding to buy. In the upcoming sections, we set out some questions to guide your examination of a business that's up for sale.

Why is the owner selling the business?

This may be the most important question to ask. Many reasons exist for selling a business, but from the buyer's point of view, some are better than others.

These reasons shouldn't set off alarm bells for you:

- ✔ The owner is retiring (. . . as long as the business didn't cause the ill-health).
- ✔ The owner wants to pursue a different career or business opportunity (unless a problem with this business triggered that desire).
- ✔ The owner is having marital problems.

These reasons may signal trouble:

- ✔ The business is not profitable.
- ✔ The owner cannot raise enough money to finance the business.
- ✔ Competition for the business is heating up.
- ✔ Markets for the business's product or service are drying up.
- ✔ The work hours are too long and/or the work is unpleasant.

The owner may be very forthcoming about the reasons for selling, or may be reluctant to talk. Even if the owner does talk, don't believe everything you hear. Try to get information from others in the same industry — business owners, employees, suppliers, and customers.

What is the reputation of the business?

A major reason for buying an established business is to get the benefit of its reputation. Speak to the business's customers and suppliers to find out what they think of the business. Contact the Better Business Bureau, industry associations, and any licensing bodies to see if any complaints have been made against the business. Search online for reviews of the business.

Book I

From Start to Finish and Everything in Between

What is the reason for the success of the business?

You want to make sure that the business has been successful because of a lasting reason. So here are some areas to check out:

✔ Does the business have a great product or service — or was it built on a fad that's now fading?

✔ If the business was built on a small number of enthusiastic clients or customers, are they likely to stay on with you?

✔ If the business was built on exports, what's the economic and political outlook for the countries where the exports go?

✔ If the business has done well because it had little competition, is competition likely to increase in the future?

How's the neighbourhood?

Perhaps your main reason for buying the business is that it has a wonderful location that draws customers like a magnet, or it's perfectly placed for receiving supply deliveries and shipping out products. If so, be sure to check the terms of the lease for the location:

✔ Is the rent reasonable?

✔ How much time is left on the lease — and does the lease contain any rights to renew?

✔ If the business is located in a mall, does the lease protect you from competition by other tenants?

✔ Does the lease affect the hours you can or have to work?

If the location of the business is not the main reason you want the business, then make sure that the location is not a reason you'll come to regret your purchase:

  ✔ Does the municipality or landlord have any plans for the property that will affect traffic, parking, or access to the property? A major renovation of the building or major road construction or anything else that limits customer or supplier access could be bad news for you.

What do the financial statements tell you?

When you're looking over a business, you should ask to see its financial statements for the preceding three to five years.

The financial statements of a business contain information that will be very useful to you in deciding whether the business is worth buying at all, and, if it is, in deciding on the price you should pay. But you have to be able to understand the financial statements. We talk about financial statements in Book IV.

Have a professional accountant or business evaluator review the financial statements before you make a final decision to buy — even if you think you've got the business's financials all figured out.

The income statement

The *income statement*, also called a profit and loss statement, sets out a business's revenues and expenses over a stated period of time (a month, quarter, or year). The *revenues* (also called sales) refers to money paid by customers or clients for products or services. The *expenses* are the costs of doing business. A business's *profit* (also called income) equals revenues minus expenses.

Look at the revenues of the business, and ask

  ✔ How profitable is the business?

  ✔ Have revenues increased over the past while?

  ✔ Will the profits give you a reasonable return on your investment?

Look at the expenses, and ask

  ✔ Have expenses as a percentage of revenues gone up, remained steady, or gone down over the past while?

  ✔ Could you cut some expenses? Would you want to increase any expenses?

  ✔ How much has the owner been paying himself or herself?

The balance sheet

The *balance sheet* lists and shows a value for everything a business owns (its *assets*) and everything it owes (its *liabilities*) as of a specified date, usually the last day of the company's *fiscal* year.

Assets fall into two categories, current assets and fixed assets. *Current assets* are cash, and assets that are intended to be and can be turned into cash easily. *Fixed assets* are assets the business intends to hold onto for a long time.

With the balance sheet in one hand and the income statement in the other, have a look at the business's assets to find out more about the financial shape the business is in.

Look at the expenses, and ask

- ✔ Are the accounts receivable, the money that customers owe you, over time, becoming a larger percentage of the business's revenue? High amounts of accounts receivable that are over 90 days old are a sign of problems.

- ✔ Have inventory levels been going up or down over the past years? You should be concerned if the inventory levels are going up more than revenues.

- ✔ Does the equipment appear to be worth its book value? Does the business have too much equipment? Does the business lack equipment or have obsolete equipment?

Look at the *liabilities* and ask

- ✔ Who actually owns the business — the owner or the creditors? To find this out, divide the total amount of debt (current and long-term) by the net worth of the business. Calculate net worth by subtracting everything the business owes from everything the business has (cash, equipment, real estate, etc., etc.)

- ✔ How easily could you borrow money? Lenders look at the debt-to-equity ratio to decide whether or not to cough up the cash when a business asks to borrow. If the ratio is too high (2:1 or higher), you may find it hard to persuade a lender to part with its money.

- ✔ How quickly could the business get cash without borrowing, if it needed to? Divide the business's current assets by its current liabilities to get the business's current ratio. The *current ratio* measures the business's *liquidity* — its ability to raise cash by disposing of assets that are fairly easy to sell.

What is the "corporate culture"?

In some businesses, management, staff, suppliers, and customers may treat each other like family. (We mean like family who like each other.) In others, they may treat each other very formally and follow a rigid structure. In a few, they may be engaged in guerrilla, or even open, warfare. Do you like what you see of the corporate culture? If you don't, do you think you will be able to change the culture — and still keep the business's staff, customers, and suppliers?

Deciding on a Price for a Business

If you've checked out the business and are pleased with it, don't just say, "I'll take it!" You must first decide what the business is worth and what price you're willing to pay. Buying a good business for the wrong price can be as big a mistake as buying a bad business. In this section, we tell you about different approaches to valuing businesses and where to find information on the value of a business.

Don't make a final decision to buy a business without getting professional help — from an accountant and/or a business evaluator and/or a lawyer — perhaps from all three.

What's a business worth?

When you buy a business as a going concern, you're buying more than the physical assets of the business. You're also buying the business's *goodwill* — the likelihood that the business will be successful in the future. So in arriving at a price for a business, you have to find a price that includes both.

Valuing assets

You can value physical (or "tangible") assets in different ways, including the following:

- ✔ **Fair market value** — the price you would have to pay on the open market for equipment or inventory of the same age and condition

- ✔ **Replacement value** — the price you would have to pay for new inventory and equipment to replace what the business currently has

- ✔ **Book value** — the value at which the assets are shown in the business's balance sheet. It may be higher or lower than the fair market value of the assets

Another is *liquidation value* — the price for which the equipment and inventory could be sold if the business were liquidated (turned into cash), for example in a bankruptcy. However, liquidation value is not normally used when the business is a going concern, because it's lower than fair market value.

Note that if you will be taking over the debts of the company (and that's the usual scenario if you buy a going concern), to arrive at a value for the assets you have to deduct the amount of debts from the value of the assets.

Valuing goodwill

If you're buying a business as a going concern, you're not just shopping for some equipment and inventory. You also want the business's goodwill, which is an "intangible" (untouchable) asset of the business. *Goodwill* is often defined as the likelihood that customers will keep coming back.

All of the following affect a business's goodwill:

- ✔ The customer base it has established
- ✔ The business's age and reputation, including its name and any trademarks or trade names
- ✔ The location
- ✔ The exclusive rights the business might hold
- ✔ The quality of its employees
- ✔ The reliability of its suppliers
- ✔ The amount of competition the business faces

How do you place a value on goodwill? Most valuation methods involve examining the past earnings of the business as the best indicator of what future earnings are likely to be.

One common valuation method is the *multiple of earnings* method. With this method, the business's earnings (its revenues less its expenses) over the past three to five years are averaged, and then that average is multiplied by a given number to arrive at a value for the business. The given number (known as a "multiple") varies from industry to industry.

After you come up with a proposed purchase price, check how reasonable it is by calculating the return you would likely get on your investment if you bought the business for that price. Take the average annual earnings of the company over the past three to five years and divide them by the proposed purchase price. That will give you the rate of return you may reasonably expect from your investment. (For example, if you're thinking about paying

$250,000 for a business that has had average earnings of $15,000, the rate of return is 6 percent.) How does the rate of return compare to what you might earn on the same sum put into a different investment? Is the rate of return worth your investment when you take into account the work and risk involved in this particular business?

Sources of information for valuing a business

The best way to figure out what a business is worth is to find out how much comparable businesses have sold for. Unfortunately, getting sales information about businesses is harder than getting it about homes. Here are some possible sources of information about sale prices, and also about valuing businesses generally:

- ✔ Trade publications
- ✔ Businesses that you've looked at
- ✔ Accountants, lawyers, and consultants
- ✔ Business brokers
- ✔ A professional business appraiser

Using a professional business appraiser is probably your best bet. Your lawyer, accountant, or business consultant may be able to refer you to an appraiser or valuator. Or you can contact the Canadian Institute of Chartered Business Valuators (www.cicbv.ca) for a list of members in your province.

Considering a Franchise

A *franchise* isn't exactly an off-the-shelf business. It's more like a pre-packaged business — you add water and stir. The *franchisor* (the company that created and developed the original business) owns the business name and trademarks and practices and procedures; the *franchisee* (the buyer of the franchise) gets a licence to use them. The franchisee pays an up-front franchise fee and then also makes continuing payments (royalties) based on the franchise's earnings. The franchisee sets up his or her own business, but sets it up as if it were part of a chain with one name and with standardized products, design, service, and operations.

Checking out the advantages of a franchise

Buying a franchise provides the benefits of belonging to a large organization, while still being your own boss, including

- ✔ A business concept that has been thought out, and a product or service that has been researched and developed
- ✔ A recognized business name, centralized advertising, and sophisticated marketing
- ✔ Assistance, training, and support in management and production
- ✔ Economies of scale in buying supplies and services, because purchasing is centralized
- ✔ Assistance in choosing a business location (reputable franchises check out the strength of the local market before selling a new franchise in an area)

Investigating the disadvantages of a franchise

Buying a franchise can sometimes lead to trouble for the franchisee because

- ✔ Franchises are standardized operations, and standardization can be stifling to a business owner who is very independent.
- ✔ Successful franchises are expensive — and new franchises are a gamble because costs may be higher than expected and/or profits lower than expected.
- ✔ Franchise agreements are always drafted by the franchisor and they favour the franchisor over the franchisee.
- ✔ The franchisor may promise training and support, but they may not be as good or thorough as promised.
- ✔ Franchisees may be charged more than the going market rate for supplies if they have to be purchased through the franchisor or specified suppliers.
- ✔ Franchisees are often required to pay substantial amounts for advertising and they may not see that they're getting anything in return.

✔ Sometimes the franchisor leases premises for a franchise location and subleases them to the franchisee. Then the franchisor can use its rights as a landlord to lock the franchisee out of the premises without notice if the franchisee doesn't make all the payments required under the franchise agreement.

✔ If the franchisor opens too many franchises in one area, or starts distributing products through the Internet or mail-order catalogues, it can drastically reduce the profits of franchisees.

✔ Franchisees often don't have special legislation to protect them against franchisors, because fewer than half of the provinces have passed franchise statutes, although legislation is under discussion in some other provinces.

Finding a franchise

Franchises are available in just about any business area, from accounting and tax services to pet care to lawn services to funeral homes. So the first step in finding a franchise is to decide on the kind of business you want to be in. We talk about choosing your business in Chapter 1 of this book.

After you decide on the kind of business you want to be in, find out whether any franchises exist in that kind of business, and if so, whether any franchises are being offered in locations that interest you.

You can look for franchises that are available in Canada in a number of ways:

✔ Read franchise magazines

✔ Check a franchise directory

✔ Search the Internet

✔ Visit franchise shows

✔ Use a franchise advisor

Evaluating the franchises you find

A franchise is a very expensive purchase. Many require an investment of at least $100,000. And when you buy a franchise, you're not just purchasing a product and walking away; you're entering into an ongoing relationship, somewhat like a partnership. So you should be confident that you want to go into business with the franchisor. Make a list of the franchises you find, and then investigate each of them thoroughly and carefully.

Knowing what you're looking for

You should know a number of things about a franchise opportunity before you buy:

- ✔ How does the franchisor make most if its money?
- ✔ What is the franchisor's business record?
- ✔ How much will the franchise cost, and does the franchisor offer any financing?
- ✔ How much can you expect to earn?
- ✔ What is the term of the franchise agreement?
- ✔ Where will your franchise be located?
- ✔ Will the franchisor train you?
- ✔ What rights do you have to sell the franchise?

Knowing where to find it

You can get your franchise information from several sources:

- ✔ The franchisor
- ✔ Other franchisees
- ✔ The Internet
- ✔ The Better Business Bureau and trade associations

Doing due diligence before you sign

Get advice from your accountant and your lawyer before you agree to buy a franchise:

- ✔ Have your accountant review the franchisor's financial statements to see if they disclose any problems, and to tell you whether the financial projections are based on reasonable assumptions.
- ✔ Have your lawyer review the franchise agreement. At the very least, your lawyer should make sure that you understand the agreement fully. If appropriate, your lawyer should try to negotiate necessary changes to the agreement.

Deciding On a Place of Business

Finding a location for your business (if you're able to choose a location) is an important step. When choosing your business premises, aim to spend as little as possible while making sure that your place of business satisfies the needs of your newly launched enterprise.

Working from home

Working from home is the cheapest way to go. With computers, high-quality printers, e-mail, fax, and voice mail, a home-based business doesn't have to look like an amateur operation. And the Internet allows even the smallest company to have worldwide exposure. You can project a big business image even if your head office is the kitchen table.

In addition to cost, working from home has other advantages, too:

✔ You'll be able to claim an income tax deduction for a portion of the expenses of running your home.

✔ You won't have to commute to and from work.

✔ You'll have more flexibility to deal with your children, aging parents, or pets.

Working from home does have some disadvantages as well:

✔ You may have little, if any, room for expansion as your business grows.

✔ You may find accommodating employees difficult or impossible.

✔ You may find that you need facilities and services that you can't have at home.

✔ You may feel isolated from business associates.

✔ You may find yourself not isolated enough from family and friends!

Working from real business premises

If you can't work from your home, you'll have to look for business premises elsewhere. Different types of premises are available, and the type you choose will depend on the nature of your business:

Book I

From Start
to Finish
and
Everything
in Between

✔ Retail

✔ Office

✔ Industrial

Space-sharing arrangements

If you can't work from home, you don't necessarily have to rent and equip your own retail store, suite of offices, or industrial space. You have other options for premises that may be of modest size, and cheap to rent and equip, and that may be available on a short-term basis. One of these arrangements may be right for you:

✔ If you need office space, you may be able to sublet a single office from another business, or rent an office in a business centre or executive suite — the landlord provides reception services and use of a boardroom and office equipment (as part of your monthly rent) and access to secretarial and other support services (usually for an additional fee).

✔ If you need retail space, you may be able to operate from a booth or cart in a shopping mall or in a pedestrian area. If your goods are seasonal, this may allow you to operate on a seasonal basis. A booth is also a good way to test your product before investing in a traditional store.

✔ If you need industrial space, you may be able to use a self-storage unit for your warehousing needs and maybe even for some light manufacturing or assembly of merchandise.

After you finalize arrangements for the space, you will be entering into a contract. Make sure that the contract is in writing, that you understand it, and that it sets out all the terms that are important to you.

Renting business premises

Most small businesses that need permanent retail, office, or industrial space rent the space (rather than buy). You should consider a number of factors before you rent space.

Knowing what you need

Before you start to look for rental premises, stop and think about your business needs:

✔ What kind of space are you looking for?

✔ What kind of image are you trying to project?

✔ What location is most accessible to your potential clients or customers and employees?

✔ What kind of parking do you need?

✔ Is it best to locate near competing businesses or away from them?

✔ How much space do you need now and in the future?

✔ What kind of layout or floor plan do you need?

✔ What are your electrical and plumbing requirements?

✔ Will your suppliers need special access to make deliveries to you?

✔ Are you willing to pay for improvements to the property you rent?

✔ How long do you want to rent these premises for?

✔ How much rent are you willing and able to pay?

Finding the right premises

To find commercial rental space, you can look at classified ads in the newspaper or on online classified websites such as Craigslist (www.craigslist.org) or Kijiji (www.kijiji.ca) under headings such as Commercial, Industrial Space, Office Space, or Stores for Rent. You can also search for those terms on the Web, or you can drive around areas that seem suitable and look for For Rent signs. But your best bet is probably to use a real estate or leasing agent who specializes in industrial, commercial, and investment properties.

When you rent business space, you sign a contract called a *commercial lease*. Commercial tenancies are very different from residential tenancies. Commercial tenants don't have the legal protection from their landlords that residential tenants have.

As you look at different premises, and before you start negotiating with a landlord, focus on the following matters:

✔ Size of the space

✔ Cost of the space

✔ Leasehold improvements

✔ Insurance coverage

Book I

**From Start
to Finish
and
Everything
in Between**

- ✔ Term of the lease
- ✔ Your right to terminate the lease before the term is up
- ✔ Date the premises will be available
- ✔ Use of the space
- ✔ Protection against competition
- ✔ Hours of business
- ✔ Facilities
- ✔ Unforeseen problems with the premises

Negotiating a lease

When you've found premises that you'd like to take, you will negotiate the terms of the lease with the landlord by discussing some or all of the matters set out in the previous section. You may negotiate with the landlord directly or through a leasing agent, and you may negotiate with or without help from a lawyer. When you and the landlord reach an agreement in principle, you will be asked to sign one or more legal documents.

You may be given a standard form lease to sign right away, or the landlord may ask you to sign a written offer in which you agree to sign the landlord's standard form lease at a later time.

Don't sign an offer agreeing to sign the landlord's standard form lease unless you have seen the lease itself and are in fact willing to sign it and be bound by its terms. Once you sign the offer, you're legally obligated to go through with signing the lease.

The landlord's standard form lease will be long, difficult to understand, and written to benefit the landlord. Most commercial landlords are not willing to make many, if any, changes to their standard form lease.

Because commercial leases are so long and complicated, you should have a lawyer look at the lease and explain it to you before you sign it. But don't spend a lot of money to have the lawyer try to negotiate changes for you, because the landlord is likely to tell you and your lawyer to "take it or leave it."

You should also go over the lease with your insurance agent or broker before you sign it so you're sure about the coverage you'll need and what it will cost.

Looking at Ownership Issues

Before you can start your business, you need a vehicle for carrying on your business — a "form of business" or a "business organization." Only a few forms of business exist, and we take you around to each one of them and help you kick the tires. After you've looked at all of them and thought about your own business circumstances, you can decide which form of business is right for you.

Going alone

If your new business is a team effort, you can skip ahead to "Should You Incorporate?" now. If your new business is a one-person show, stick around and read this section.

Certainly, being the only owner of a business has its advantages. Here are just a few of them:

- The profits of the business will be yours alone.
- You have the only say in what the business does.
- Setting up a business with just one owner is usually easier, faster, and cheaper.

Taking on a co-pilot

But here are reasons that you might want to, or have to, have a co-owner:

- You may want someone else to share the financial risks.
- You may want company — being in business all by yourself can be lonely.
- You may need someone else to provide skills or knowledge that you don't have.
- You may want someone to share the workload.

If you're considering sharing ownership of your business with someone else, think about these questions:

- Are you capable of working well with a co-owner?
- Is the business likely to be able to generate enough revenue to support two (or more) owners?

✔ Does the business have roles for two (or more) owners?

✔ Does your potential co-owner have skills and knowledge that will add to yours?

Ultimately, whichever form of ownership gives your business the best chance of success should be the reason you decide to go on alone or take a co-pilot.

Should You Incorporate?

"Should I incorporate?" is a very common first question that entrepreneurs ask, whether they're working alone or in a team. But it's not the right first question. It can't be answered in a vacuum. And before you even ask the question, you need to know about the alternatives to incorporation.

Checking out your options

When you ask whether or not you should incorporate, what you're really asking is "What form of business organization should I choose?" You have choices, and the choices available to you depend on whether your business will have only one owner, or two or more owners.

If you will be the only owner of the business, you have two choices:

✔ To operate as a sole proprietor

✔ To operate as a corporation that is owned by you

If two or more people will own the business, you also have two choices:

✔ To operate as a partnership

✔ To operate as a corporation that is owned by you and your co-owner(s)

Understanding the difference

The main distinction between a business that's incorporated and one that's not is that an *incorporated business* is a legal being separate from the owner of the business. (Visit the next section for more about corporations.)

What many people don't know is that, in practice, keeping the business debts of your corporation away from your personal assets is not always possible.

Many people are also unaware that you can protect your personal assets without incorporating your business.

Here are two other main differences between an incorporated and an unincorporated business:

- ✔ The profits of a corporation are taxed differently than the profits of a business operated as a sole proprietorship or partnership.
- ✔ The amount of paperwork increases greatly when you're setting up and running a corporation.

Incorporation should not be an automatic step, because it may or may not make sense for you and your business.

The Corporation: A Form of Business with a Life All Its Own

A corporation is probably as close as most people will get to an alien life form, barring abduction by extraterrestrial beings for bizarre medical experiments. And we're not kidding when we call a corporation a "life form."

Understanding corporations

A *corporation* is a legal being that is created by the process of incorporation, and that has a separate legal identity from that of the individuals who create it and own it as shareholders.

Even though a corporation is not human, it has many of the legal powers, rights, and duties of a Canadian resident. But because it is not human, it must act through its human directors and officers.

Corporations can be public or private. A public corporation, or offering corporation, can sell its shares to the public. A private, or non-offering, corporation is very limited in its rights to sell its shares. Whether you know it or not, if you're thinking about incorporating a new business, you're thinking about a private corporation. When we talk about corporations in this chapter, we're talking about private corporations. Very few private corporations ever become public.

Owning a corporation

The shareholders of a corporation own the corporation through their owner-ship of shares in the corporation. The shareholders acquire their shares for a set price and they pay for them by giving money, goods, or services to the corporation. (The money and goods become the property of the corporation. Shareholders are not the legal owners of the corporation's property.) If the corporation is a failure, the shares will go down in value — maybe even down to zero — and the shareholders' investment will diminish and disappear. But the shareholders will not usually lose more than what they already gave in exchange for the shares, because they are not ordinarily responsible for paying any debts the corporation has.

A corporation can have several classes of shares, each of which has different rights. Common shares usually give a shareholder the right to elect directors, receive a portion of the corporation's profits in the form of dividends, and receive a share of the corporation's property if the corporation closes down. Preferred shares (also called preference or special shares) always have the right to receive dividends before the common shares do, and can have other special privileges attached to them.

Running a corporation

Every private corporation must have at least one director, whose role it is to manage the corporation's affairs. No upper limit exists on the number of directors a corporation can have, but even big public corporations don't usu-ally have more than 10 or 20. A director has a duty to be reasonably careful in running the corporation's affairs, to act in the corporation's best interests, and to carry out his or her duties honestly and in good faith. If a director doesn't fulfill these duties, the shareholders can take the director to court.

A director must be at least 18 years old, of sound mind, and not bankrupt. In federal corporations and in most provincial corporations, a majority of the directors must be Canadian citizens who reside in Canada; and in some prov-inces, at least one director must also be a resident of the province.

In many corporations, the director(s) and shareholder(s) will be the same people, so the people who own the corporation also run the corporation.

Setting up a corporation

You incorporate a business by filling out and filing incorporating documents with the government and paying government fees. You can incorporate your business as a federal corporation (in which case you file with the federal government) or as a provincial corporation (in which case you file with your provincial government).

In most provinces the incorporation forms are available on the government website, and the forms themselves look relatively simple to fill out. You don't legally need a lawyer to incorporate your business, but if you do it yourself you may make mistakes that will be difficult to correct later. We strongly suggest using a lawyer.

After the documents are filed and the fees paid, the government will issue a certificate of incorporation or, in Prince Edward Island and Quebec, a charter by letters patent. This is the moment when your corporation is "born." Before it can actually start to carry on business, though, it has to have a first directors' meeting. At this meeting, the first directors pass the corporation's by-laws — the rules about how the corporation will be run — and make resolutions appointing officers of the corporation (such as the president, treasurer, and secretary, who will run the corporation day-to-day according to the directors' orders), among other things. You can buy standard printed bylaws and standard forms for the first directors' resolutions if you don't have a lawyer help you with the incorporation and this initial organization.

Protecting Your Assets without Incorporating

Most people incorporate to protect their personal assets in case their business has debts that it can't pay — but that strategy doesn't always work. The classic method for protecting personal assets from business debts is to put those assets in the name of a spouse or other family member who is not an owner of the business.

For this method to work, you must change ownership before your business runs into trouble. If you wait until your business starts to encounter financial problems, transferring your property to another person is considered a form of fraud, and anyone trying to collect money from you is entitled to have the property transfer set aside.

After you put property into someone else's name, the property belongs to that person. So this approach involves risk. If your marriage or relationship with your family member falls apart, your property may disappear with the relationship. You have to decide what you're more worried about financially — the failure of your business or the failure of your relationship.

Chapter 3

Operating Your Business

- -

In This Chapter

▶ Investigating the risks a business can run

▶ Ensuring your business is insured

▶ Finding out how to work with customers

▶ Checking out contracts

▶ Keeping customers happy and dealing with dissatisfied customers

▶ Getting paid for the product or service you provide

▶ Prioritizing privacy laws

▶ Losing customers and coping with lawsuits

▶ Dealing with suppliers and advisors

- -

Running a business involves risks, sometimes extremely important ones. One of your important jobs as a business owner is to minimize the risk to your business, anticipating problems before they occur and making contingencies for when things go wrong—because they will. Insurance and contracts are not the sexiest aspects of running a business, but you've got to deal with them. Rare is the business that has not to deal with unhappy or angry customers. Sometimes that unhappiness is justified; sometimes it is not. But it doesn't really matter.

This chapter takes you through some important troubleshooting aspects to deal with the situations will inevitably occur.

Minimizing Business Risks and Troubles

Operating a small business is no bed of roses. Your business might encounter a lot of troubles, which fall broadly into three categories:

✔ Your business may cause injury to others.

✔ Your business itself may be injured.

✔ You and your business associates and employees may be injured.

You can't make all risks associated with your business vanish, but you can try to cut them down to size. We tell you how in the upcoming sections.

Injury to others

To avoid lawsuits against your business by people or other businesses that have been injured . . . don't let anyone get injured in the first place! That's not as tall an order as it sounds. You can take sensible precautions so that your business doesn't pose too much (unintended) danger to others.

Preventing physical injuries and damage.

If you own or lease business premises, take a tour of them and look for problem areas (refer to Chapter 2 of this book for more about finding your business premises). Here are some of the most common problems and some suggestions for avoiding them.

To prevent slip-and-fall or trip-and-fall incidents:

✔ Clean up spills of any kind as soon as you discover them.

✔ Regularly check for and mop up water and slush that accumulates inside entrances; put mats down at entrances to soak up the water; put out "Caution: Slippery Floor" signs.

✔ Level off uneven flooring.

✔ Make sure carpets and mats can't bunch up and turn into a trip hazard.

✔ Close off areas where you're doing repairs or renovations.

✔ Clear snow and ice off sidewalks outside your premises, and keep walkways and parking areas free of snow and ice and wet leaves.

✔ Fill in any holes in walkways or parking areas, and call the municipality to have uneven sidewalks repaired.

✔ Don't leave things lying around where people will walk into them.

✔ Install handrails on stairs with three or more steps; mark the edges of the steps to make them more visible.

✔ Make sure ramps aren't too steep and that they have rails if necessary; put non-slip material on the ramp and mark the ramp edges.

✔ Keep your premises well lit, inside and outside.

To prevent people from getting whacked or felled by doors, windows, signs, and so on:

✔ Mark glass doors and other large areas of glass so that people won't try to walk through them.

✔ Check that outdoor seating is stable.

✔ Make sure that awnings and outdoor signs are securely fastened to the building or to some other firm anchorage.

✔ Trim back overhanging tree branches.

✔ Check the roof and flashing to make sure that nothing is loose and might fall off.

To prevent injuries involving business equipment and business vehicles:

✔ Maintain all your equipment and vehicles properly.

✔ Make sure that anyone who is operating business equipment or a business vehicle is properly trained and licensed, and that they understand that safety comes first.

✔ Don't serve alcohol to your associates or employees and don't allow anyone to drink while at work.

To prevent injuries caused by manufacturing or selling defective products:

✔ If you're manufacturing a product, know all safety measures required and best manufacturing practices — and follow them; have quality assurance professionals review the product for potential defects that could cause injury.

✔ If you're manufacturing or selling a product, make sure that it's licensed or approved by the proper government authorities.

✔ Keep informed about the potential dangers of any product you manufacture or sell, and put warning labels about the dangers on the product; notify in writing any customers who have already bought the product (you need to keep good records to do that).

Preventing damage caused by giving careless advice

Sometimes just opening your mouth can pose a danger to others. So before anyone in your business says a word, consider the following advice:

✔ Make sure that you and your associates and employees are properly educated and/or trained and/or licensed to give advice or recommendations in any particular area.

✔ Stay current in your field.

✔ Use care when you give advice

✔ Include disclaimers of liability in the documents you provide to customers and clients.

✔ Keep detailed documents showing exactly what information your clients or customers have provided, what advice you have given, and what work you have done.

Preventing damage caused by not fulfilling a contract

Contracts are the daily stuff of business. Take your contracts seriously:

✔ Read and understand every contract you enter into — before you enter into it! That's not easy if you're not a lawyer (and even lawyers don't always understand contracts, especially if the contracts are in an unfamiliar field or if they're badly written). Don't just sign a contract and assume everything will be all right. Get advice from a knowledgeable lawyer about the contract's meaning and its consequences for you.

✔ Make careful note of all the things you're required to do under the contract, so that you don't accidentally fall short of the requirements.

✔ Set up a "tickler" system to remind you in plenty of time about contract deadlines, so that you don't miss them.

✔ If you think you may not be able to fulfill a contract, speak to your lawyer right away. It may be possible to build a bridge, legally speaking, to keep you from falling into a pit.

Injury to your business

If your business is damaged through someone else's fault, you may be able to sue for financial compensation. But that could be a long time coming — so protecting your business is better than counting on getting paid for any trouble you suffer. And anyway, the damage might be inflicted by you, or by someone you can't sue.

Damage to premises

You can take several steps to safeguard your premises against damage:

✔ Install approved fire alarms and fire extinguishers, and maybe even sprinkler systems and emergency lighting.

✔ Be a good housekeeper.

✔ Check out building maintenance.

✔ Lock or fasten securely all doors and windows

✔ Install burglar alarms.

✔ Cut down trees and shrubs that grow around entrances and windows.

✔ Keep the premises well lit outside at night.

✔ Fence the premises if necessary.

✔ Consider hiring a security guard.

✔ Keep vehicles in a secure area, with doors locked. Don't leave valuable equipment inside vehicles unless absolutely necessary.

Non-payment of accounts receivable

As a businessperson, what you'd like best is to be paid in advance for your work, or have an absolute guarantee of payment. That way you don't have to worry about clients and customers who ignore your bills.

✔ If you're a professional such as a lawyer or accountant, you can ask clients for a *retainer*, an advance payment that is put into a trust account. (Although you have the money safely in hand, you cannot legally touch it until the work has been done and a bill has been sent to the client.)

✔ In any business you can ask for partial payment in advance for the work you're going to do. If a job can be divided into stages, you can ask for payment in advance for each stage.

✔ In any retail business you can insist on payment in full before delivering the item you're selling.

But if you have to deal with people who can't or won't pay in advance, here are some ways to avoid being left holding the bag:

✔ Don't extend credit yourself. Make arrangements to accept certain credit cards and tell clients they can use those cards.

✔ Make sure customers and clients understand, before you do the work or supply the product, how much it's going to cost. (If they're not taken by surprise, they're more likely to pay the bill quietly.)

✔ Do your work properly; supply good products; provide guarantees. Clients balk at paying bills if they're dissatisfied.

✔ Bill regularly if you're supplying a product or doing work on an ongoing basis. If one month's bill isn't paid, consider not doing any more work or providing any more supplies until it is. That way you'll limit the damage to your business.

✔ Send regular reminders of unpaid bills, and start collection proceedings (small claims court, or handing the matter over to a collection agency) within a reasonable time.

Theft and embezzlement

To prevent theft and embezzlement by employees or associates, you need to have control systems for handling cash and cheques. (For example, require that all cheques bear your own signature, or the signatures of two people. Don't keep large sums of cash on the premises.) You also need to hire carefully in the first place, and not allow employees (or associates) to handle money unless you're sure you can trust them.

Loss of paper records

To avoid losing your important paper records — even temporarily — take these precautions to keep paper records safe:

- Store written records in fireproof filing cabinets.
- Store valuable written documents in a safety deposit box in a bank or in a fireproof safe on your premises.
- Keep photocopies of your most valuable paper documents off-site.
- Scan paper documents into your computer and store them off-site using a CD, DVD, portable hard drive, or online storage service.

Computer and Internet hazards

To avoid losing or sending astray electronic data, take the following precautions:

- Maintain your computer equipment properly, and protect it from harm — with surge protectors and humidity control, for example.
- Protect against sudden power failures by installing a UPS (uninterrupted power supply — a battery backup system).
- Don't let untrained or unauthorized people mess around with your computer systems.

Injury or death of a key person

If you're the one who dies or leaves, you may not care that much about what happens to the business. But if it's a partner or business associate who dies or leaves, that's a different matter. How are you going to get along without them — especially if they were storing important information in their heads? And what if the person (if he or she is alive) or the person's family (if he or she is dead) is demanding the return of an investment in the business?

Don't let any one person be the only person with access to essential business information. Make sure important information is written down and stored carefully. Have key personnel "cross-train" so that two or more people have at least some familiarity with essential operations. Or have an associate or employee act as an "understudy" for each key person.

Insuring against Your Risks

You can't eliminate every possible risk, even if you try. So you also need to pass at least some of your risks off to somebody else, which is where insurance comes in.

Most people think insurance is boring. But it's really quite exciting! When you start thinking of all the dreadful things that can happen to your business and you and the people you deal with, you'll feel as though you're living in an adventure serial! You'll realize that you're constantly surrounded by danger, and that a wily mind and constant vigilance are your only protection.

Do you already have insurance?

You may think you've already got enough insurance to cover your business, but you probably don't. For example, if you're going to run your business out of your home, your home insurance probably doesn't cover your business. Most home insurance policies exclude or limit coverage for business activities. If you're going to use your car as a business delivery vehicle, your existing car insurance probably doesn't cover that kind of business use. Key people in your business may already have life insurance — but the beneficiary is unlikely to be your business: it's probably their family members or their estate.

Do you need insurance?

Some businesses need certain kinds of insurance, whether they want it or not, because they're required to be insured under legislation governing their field, or under a contract they've entered into. (Commercial leases typically require the tenant to have insurance.)

But if you don't have to have insurance, do you need to have insurance? You don't need insurance against every risk. But insuring against certain risks makes a lot of sense.

Having insurance protects you from going out of business if you're sued and the court rules against you. And it also ensures that anyone you injure receives compensation for the damage you've caused.

Choosing an insurance agent or broker

You need to talk to an insurance agent or broker (agents work for just one company, brokers deal with several companies) about your business's needs. An agent or broker will help you evaluate the risks in your business and suggest what insurance coverage you need and in what amount.

Choose someone who is knowledgeable about your kind of business. Ask business associates for recommendations, and then make an appointment to talk to two or three of the agents or brokers recommended, before choosing one who seems best able to give you advice and find the coverage you need. Make sure the one you choose has errors and omissions insurance. Then, if the agent or broker makes a mistake in getting the right coverage, you'll be able to sue for compensation for any damage you suffer as a result.

You may need different insurance from year to year, so you should review your coverage annually with your agent or broker.

Examining different insurance policies

Various kinds of insurance policies are available. You can often get a package policy geared to your particular kind of business. For a home-based business you may be able to get a home business insurance package that provides coverage for things such as your business property (inventory, samples, supplies, filing cabinets, computers and software, tools, customers' goods) on and off the premises, loss of cash, business interruption if your home is uninhabitable, and legal liability (for products or services, or business-related accidents on the premises). Alternatively, you may be able to get an extension of your existing home insurance policy to cover your business. You may also be able to find packages for retail businesses, skilled trades, manufacturing, day care, or office-based businesses.

Working Well with Customers and Clients

If you're in business, you're going to have to deal with customers or clients to provide your product or service. Customers and clients need special care. On

Book I

From Start
to Finish
and
Everything
in Between

the one hand, you have to satisfy them — by providing good quality products or services and by treating them well. On the other hand, you have to get them to satisfy you — principally by paying you in full and in good time.

Your potential customers must know that you exist, what you have to offer, and where to find you. (Creating knowledge of and interest in your product or service is called *marketing*. We tell you about marketing in Book VI.)

Customers and clients must also be interested enough in you and your product or service to seek you out — in person, by telephone, or on your website — or (if you have to seek them out instead) to sit through your sales pitch. But making contact is just the beginning. When you have your customers' attention, you want them to do several key things:

- Take the plunge and actually agree to buy your product or service.
- Allow you to make a profit by paying a reasonable price for your goods or services (including delivery).
- Pay you promptly.
- Come back for more and refer other customers to you.

Reviewing a typical business transaction

After you know what you want from your customers, you have to think about how to get it. Your business transactions should be designed with this in mind. Here's what you want to happen:

- You make contact with the customer and make your pitch.
- You close the deal.
- You document your agreement.
- You perform your work and/or deliver your product.
- You invoice (bill) your customer.
- You get paid.
- Your customer comes back again and/or refers other customers.

Making the sale

Don't make the mistake of thinking that if a customer is interested in you and your product or service, you've already made the sale. You've still got some work to do.

The pitch and the close

Briefly, here's what you or your staff should do to make a sale and close the deal:

- ✔ Know your product or service thoroughly so that you're prepared to answer all questions about it and not have to give lame answers like "That's a good question," or "I can look that up for you."

- ✔ Listen to the customer or client so you know what the customer really wants, and gear your sales pitch to the customer's needs.

- ✔ Propose a deal that you think will meet the customer's needs (and yours too, of course, which we tell you about earlier in this part), and close the deal if the customer is willing to accept the offered terms. (And try again if the customer isn't willing.)

When your customer agrees to buy the product or service you're offering, you have entered into a contract. After you have a contract, you have a legal obligation to deliver your product or service, and your customer has a legal obligation to pay you for it.

First impressions and customer service

Customer service is an important part of any business and of every stage of contact with your customers or clients. (For more about customer service than we can cover in this chapter, check out *Customer Service For Dummies*, written by Karen Leland and Keith Bailey and published by Wiley.)

Your customers will get the first taste of your customer service when they make contact with your business and while you're making your pitch. Treat them properly. Don't keep them waiting. Greet them politely and then pay attention to them. They do not want to be ignored in favour of other customers or, even worse, your personal business. Listen to their concerns and show that you're interested in solving their problems rather than in simply making a sale. If customers or clients come to your place of business, make sure your premises are always clean, organized, and well maintained.

Customer service doesn't end after the customer agrees to buy your product or service. You may still lose the sale if you take your customer for granted while processing the sale — for example, by taking too long to complete the paperwork or by failing to be attentive to the customer while the customer is waiting.

Documenting Your Agreement

One of the keys to good customer relations is to make sure that both you and your customer or client have a clear understanding of exactly what

Book I

From Start
to Finish
and
Everything
in Between

each of you is expected to do. What goods or services must you provide and when? What is the customer to pay? Does the customer have to do anything to enable you to do your work and/or deliver your product (for example, remove the old kitchen cabinets so that you can install the new ones, or provide certain documents for you to review), or does he just sit back until it's time to pay you?

The way to ensure clear expectations on both sides is to have a contract that both of you understand and are reasonably happy with. A contract doesn't have to be a pages-long document filled with small print and incomprehensible language. Contract documents and their contents vary from business to business. (In fact, a contract doesn't have to be in writing at all.) In this section, we tell you about the things you should be aware of, no matter what form your contracts take.

Contracts for the sale of goods or services

Every time you make a sale, you and your customer or client are entering into a contract for the sale of goods or the provision of services.

The terms of the contract

When you and your customer enter into a contract, you come to terms on many matters. All contracts for the sale of goods involve agreement about the following points, whether or not the contract is put in writing:

- ✔ **The parties to the contract:** One party (you) agrees to provide the goods or services; the other party (your client) agrees to pay for them. Your client may be an individual, a partnership, or a corporation. If it's a partnership or a corporation, make sure you're dealing with a person who has the legal authority to contract on behalf of the partnership or corporation.

- ✔ **The goods or services being sold:** Include quantity, name, model number, services to be performed, or any other important details.

- ✔ **The price:** Any amounts for GST and PST, or HST, should also be identified, but separately from the basic purchase price.

- ✔ **The date(s) payment(s) is to be made; how payment is to be made:** Will you be paid in full at the beginning, or paid in full at the end, or paid in instalments as you do your work or after you complete the work?

- ✔ **The quality of the goods or services:** If your contract says nothing about the quality of the goods, provincial sale of goods legislation implies a promise on your part that the goods are of reasonable quality.

✔ **The timeframe in which the goods or services are to be delivered:** If your contract doesn't address the place, provincial sale of goods legislation says that your customer must pick up the goods at your place of business. If your contract addresses the place but not the date, the legislation says that the goods must be delivered within a reasonable period of time.

✔ **The right of the buyer to return the goods:** In the absence of a problem with the quality of the goods, a buyer has no right to return the goods unless the seller agrees to give that right. Your business should have a returns policy set out in the contract — for example, no returns; or returns for exchange or credit only; or full returns, no questions asked.

✔ **The rights to change or end the contract:** You may want to give yourself the right to end the contract for certain reasons, and you may want to limit the customer's right to end the contract due to some sort of wrongdoing on your part. You may also want to give yourself the right to change the contract in certain circumstances — for example, the right to raise the agreed price if the cost of materials rises.

✔ **Injury to someone or cause damage to property:** You may want to include in your contract an exemption or *exculpatory clause* that limits your liability if you cause damage or injury. (With or without an exemption clause, you should make sure that you have proper insurance in place, so refer to the earlier section "Insuring against Your Risks.")

Consider the customer relations aspects of your contracts:

✔ Think about how your customers will feel about your contract terms before you finally decide on them. (For example, having a strict no-returns policy may cost you business.)

✔ Make sure that your customers are aware of your contract terms (whatever they are) when they enter into the contract. (You may lose repeat business from a customer who doesn't notice that you don't take returns until the customer is standing in your store asking for money back.)

Speaking to your lawyer about your contracts

Before you open for business, have your lawyer prepare your standard documents, such as sales order forms and invoices, and standard form contracts.

If a customer presents you with a purchase order form or standard form contract that you don't understand clearly and agree with fully, have your lawyer review it before you fill the order. Ditto if a customer wants to make a change to your standard sales order form or standard form contract. If the terms of the customer or client are unfavourable to you, you may be able to negotiate changes.

You may also want to consult your lawyer if you are negotiating a contract that involves a lot of money or a long-term commitment.

Doing the Work

After you enter into a contract with a customer, you have to do what the contract says you will do. If you don't carry out your promises, even if you don't get sued, you won't stay in business very long.

Keeping customers happy

The first step in keeping your customers happy is to do what you agreed to do.

 However, just doing the work isn't enough if you want to be paid promptly and get repeat business and referrals from your customers. You must also keep an eye on customer service:

- Don't make promises you can't keep.
- Keep the promises you make.
- Document all changes.
- Communicate.
- If you make a mistake or miss a deadline, deal with it

 Especially don't admit in writing that you did something wrong. Your words could come back to haunt you if you get sued over the mistake.

Dealing with unhappy customers

What do you do with customers who are unhappy or who may be downright difficult? We give you some pointers in this section.

Even if you do everything right, you're still going to encounter unhappy customers. Sometimes things go wrong, and sometimes it's not even your fault. Sometimes you'll have a customer who is simply impossible to please. But you must be able to deal with complaints, whether or not they're justified.

Here are the keys to dealing with a difficult customer:

✔ Listen to what the customer has to say.

✔ Show that you understand the customer's problem.

✔ Try to solve the customer's problem.

Even if you decide that you never want to have anything to do with a particular customer again, and you doubt that the customer will ever refer any business to you, try not to send the customer away angry. You don't want him or her badmouthing you to potential customers.

Getting repeat business and referrals

If you want your customer to use your business again and refer other customers to you, you've got to do your work right. But your relationship with your customers isn't over just because you've done your work and you've been paid. You have to go on paying attention to your customers.

Your customers may have questions or problems that come up days or weeks after you've provided the product or service, and even at that point they still need good service. If your customers think that you don't care about them after you've got their money, they're less likely to deal with you again or refer other customers to you.

And if your customer doesn't contact you, you should contact your customer. After delivering a product or performing a service, call to say thank you for the business and to ask whether the customer is happy with your work or product. As time goes by, contact your customers about new products or developments in your field that may be of interest to them. (Of course, you can do all of this only if you have permission to use a customer's contact information for these purposes. See the section later about customer privacy.) Send holiday greeting cards, and, depending on how personal your relationship with your customers or clients is, perhaps birthday and anniversary cards as well (but only if you have collected birth dates and anniversary dates with consent, naturally).

Getting Paid

Often you won't get paid until after you do your work or deliver your goods, but that doesn't mean that you should put off thinking about payment until then. In fact, you must lay the groundwork at the time you and your customer make your deal.

Book I

From Start
to Finish
and
Everything
in Between

Planning to get paid

The best way to make sure that you get paid is to avoid situations in which you risk not getting paid. Here's how to avoid these problems:

- Turn customers away if you can't do the job or you know they'll have trouble paying.
- Make sure your agreements are fair to your customers.
- Get paid up front if you can.
- Don't be sneaky when you bill customers.
- Don't extend credit automatically.
- Protect yourself if you do extend credit.
- Do what you promised to do.

Looking at credit

Before you extend credit, you may want your accountant to help you assess the creditworthiness of a customer. In the credit agreement, make sure that you establish terms for payment, including the amount and date of the payments, and the interest rate being charged.

If you are extending credit to a corporation that does not have significant assets, think about asking for *personal guarantees* from the shareholders and/ or directors. That way, if the corporation doesn't pay you, you can demand payment from the guarantors.

If you decide to ask for a guarantee, get your lawyer to prepare the document.

If you are selling goods on credit, think about taking a security interest in the goods until they are fully paid for (for example, sell the goods under a conditional sales contract). A *security interest* allows you to take back and sell the goods if you are not paid. If you take a security interest, you will have to register it under your province's Personal Property Security Act. If you take security, get your lawyer to prepare the documents and register the interest.

Getting paid online

If you'll be selling goods through your website, you should have a way to get paid before you process your customer's order. You can either set up a credit card merchant account with a credit card company, or you can use a third-party credit card processing company.

If you use a third-party processor, you are not responsible for the security of your customers' credit card information, but you must still comply with the privacy provisions of PIPEDA, by making sure via a written contract that the third-party processor complies with PIPEDA. For more information about PIPEDA, see the next section "Addressing Customer Privacy."

Addressing Customer Privacy

In the good old days, you could keep extensive files about your customers' birthdays, wedding anniversaries, and tastes in scotch and lingerie. You could harass your customers by cold-calling their homes at dinnertime, sell your customer lists to another business so *it* could harass your customers at dinnertime, and much more — all without asking your customers' permission or risking more than a telephone receiver being slammed down. Alas, the good old days ended on January 1, 2004, which was the date that the federal Personal Information Protection and Electronic Documents Act (PIPEDA) came into force across Canada for all commercial activities.

If you want to collect, keep, and use or disclose any personal (factual or subjective) information about an identifiable individual, you have to get that individual's consent beforehand, and even then you can use the information only for the purpose for which consent was given. And even then you can collect, use, or disclose the information only for purposes that a reasonable person would consider appropriate in the circumstances. The customer can call the Privacy Commissioner of Canada on you if you violate PIPEDA. (However, the Commish isn't necessarily a heavy, and will work toward finding a solution to privacy problems and complaints, rather than immediately throwing you in jail . . . even if you deserve it.)

Book I

From Start
to Finish
and
Everything
in Between

Personal information includes

- Name, address, phone numbers, identification numbers (like a social insurance number or a driver's licence number)
- Age, social status, ethnic origin, medical information and records
- Income, or credit or loan records
- Existence of a dispute between a customer and a business
- Opinions, intentions, and comments (even the printable ones)

(We'll throw you a crumb here — personal information does not include the name, title, business address, or business telephone number of an employee of an organization.)

Individuals have a right to look at the personal information that your business holds about them, and to correct any inaccuracies.

For quite a lot of useful information about privacy in the commercial sector, and how a business goes about complying with PIPEDA, go to the Privacy Commissioner of Canada's website at www.priv.gc.ca. Or you can call 1-800-282-1376. And no, this is not the Privacy Commissioner's home phone number.

Getting Fired and Getting Sued

Your relationship with your customers and clients will not be undiluted sweetness and light. In particular, two nasty things could happen:

- You could be fired, without having done anything wrong.
- You could totally screw up (and very likely get fired).

This is the end of the business relationship. But it may not be the end of the entire relationship — you could run into the customer or client again . . . in court.

If you get fired for no good reason

It's one thing never to get any repeat business or referrals from an unhappy customer. But it's another to be told you're through while you're in the process of providing services or goods. No doubt the customer or client has reasons for booting you off the job. Some may have something to do with you, and others may not have a thing to do with you (the client's nephew's girlfriend just set up a competing business and the client wants to patronize it instead).

If your agreement with the customer or client gives him or her the right to terminate the agreement for no reason (usually on a few days' or weeks' notice), then you just have to put up with this injustice.

If your agreement doesn't give the customer or client the right to terminate for no reason (or for the reason that the client has stated), then you may be entitled to sue the customer or client for the full amount that's still outstanding under the contract. If the outstanding amount is a large sum, you may look upon this as an attractive idea. On the other hand, you may be concerned about what suing a customer or client will do to your business's image and reputation.

Talk the situation over with your lawyer before you make a decision to sue or not to sue.

If you really screw up

It's always desirable, but it's not always possible, to avoid making mistakes. Sometimes fixing a mistake can inspire as much customer loyalty as doing it right in the first place. But that's not the kind of mistake we're talking about here. We're talking about a situation where a simple apology and a small gift are not going to get you off the hook. You've got an excellent chance of being fired and a pretty good chance of being sued.

You can be sued if

- ✔ You don't finish your work (on time or at all), or you do the work poorly.
- ✔ You don't deliver the goods, or deliver the goods late.
- ✔ You provide damaged or defective goods.
- ✔ You injure someone or damage their property, either directly or by providing defective goods.

Anticipate screwing up — and protect yourself beforehand

One way of protecting yourself is to put an exemption or exculpatory clause in your contract. (We talked about this earlier in the chapter. An exemption clause may work with business customers, but may not work with consumers.) This

Book I

From Start
to Finish
and
Everything
in Between

clause limits your responsibility if you do a bad job. Such a clause could say the following:

- ✔ You are not responsible at all (for a particular kind of loss such as non-delivery, or for any kind of loss, period).
- ✔ You're responsible only for correcting the mistake, or repairing or replacing the goods.
- ✔ You're responsible only to the extent of reducing the contract price by a fixed maximum amount, or of refunding the amount the customer or client paid.

The most important way of protecting yourself is to have third-party liability insurance. Your insurance company will defend the lawsuit and pay any compensation you are required to pay. (Refer to the section "Insuring against Your Risks" for more about insurance.) You can't insure against deliberate screw-ups, only careless screw-ups.

But if you aren't protected . . .

So. You couldn't or didn't prevent the screw-up from happening. And you either didn't get insurance for this kind of risk, or you can't get insurance for this kind of risk.

But all is not lost. Just because you screwed up doesn't mean you'll get sued. The larger the amount of money involved or the madder the client or customer, the more likely it is that you'll get sued. If the customer hasn't suffered a big financial loss because of your mistake, suing you probably won't be worthwhile.

Suppose, though, that you do get sued. If you have insurance coverage, your insurer will defend the lawsuit on your behalf, and will pay compensation on your behalf. Notify your insurer as soon as you realize you have a problem (even before you get served with legal documents, if possible). They'll let you know whether you're covered.

Keep in mind that if you make a claim against your insurance, your premiums will rise.

If you don't have insurance coverage, speak to your lawyer right away so you can take the proper steps to defend the lawsuit.

And just because you get sued doesn't mean you'll have to pay a lot of money, or even any money . . . even if you have no insurance. The person who suffered the loss has to prove the loss and has to *mitigate damages* (take reasonable steps to reduce the loss). Sometimes people mitigate their damages right out of existence. For example, if you failed to deliver a computer system that a customer had ordered, but the customer was able to get a very similar one from another business immediately and for less money, the customer may not have suffered any damages at all. And if the customer didn't bother to try to get a computer system to replace the one you didn't deliver but just let her business go to pot, a court won't award her compensation to cover all the losses she suffered — it will order compensation only for the loss she would have suffered if she had bought a computer system from someone else.

In addition, even if you get sued, someone else may be more responsible than you. For example, if as a retailer you sold defective goods, you can sue the manufacturer in your turn. You may not have to pay any money or may get reimbursed for the money that the court orders you to pay.

Dealing with Suppliers and Advisors

If you read the previous section you may think that customers and clients aren't all that much fun to deal with, although they are admittedly essential to your business. But the tables are turned — you're somebody else's customer!

In this section, we ease you into the supplier universe. We talk about deciding what products or services you need from providers, how to make up a list of providers of those products or services, and how to choose a suitable provider from your list.

Determining what goods and services you need

Some of the purchases you make for your business simply support your business — for example, furniture for your office or office supplies or courier services. When you buy these goods and services you're essentially a consumer, and you'll make your purchases the way you'd make any consumer purchase — such as groceries or an oil change — by looking for a supplier with the best combination of price, selection, quality, service, and convenience. If you're not happy with the supplier, just go to someone else the next time.

But your business may (also) need specialized products, and their providers may be choosy about the businesses they deal with or the terms on which they deal with them. They may also not be easy to find.

Reviewing essential goods and services

Goods and services that don't just support your business, they are vital to your business. Here are a few examples of essential good and services:

- ✔ The things you sell, called *inventory*, such as shoes for a shoe store, greeting cards and wrapping paper for a card store, ready-made desserts for a food shop

- ✔ Parts and materials you use to make your product, such as the leather for making shoes if you're a shoe manufacturer, the paper for printing cards if you run a printing shop, fresh fruit and baking supplies if you have a dessert

- ✔ Ongoing services you need for your business operations, such as an Internet service provider for a Web-based business, a pest-control service for a restaurant, or a window display service for an upscale clothing store

Determining what you need

Before you decide on what your particular business needs, do some research to find out what businesses in your field generally need. You can get help from the following sources:

- ✔ Trade associations
- ✔ Trade publications
- ✔ Trade shows

Finding suppliers

After you have an idea of what goods and services you need, you have to find a business that offers them.

You can locate suppliers in a number of ways:

- ✔ Speak to colleagues in your field.
- ✔ Contact your trade association.
- ✔ Read trade publications.
- ✔ Go to trade shows and conventions.
- ✔ Use a searchable Internet database.
- ✔ Search the Internet.
- ✔ Search www.yellowpages.ca to find the locations and phone numbers of suppliers in your area.

Choosing a supplier

After you figure out what you need and see who's selling it, you have to narrow your list of suppliers down to the supplier who's right for you. Take care, because this is a supplier with whom you'll be dealing on a regular basis and on whom you'll depend to keep your business in business.

If you rely on a single supplier for any of your important needs, you can run into serious problems if deliveries are interrupted for any reason. Sometimes you may have no choice about whom you deal with because only one supplier has what you need. Other times, you may be seduced into committing to a supplier because you're offered very good terms if you agree to deal with that supplier exclusively.

If you do deal with just one supplier, try to stay informed about other available suppliers, just in case you need them.

Inventory and parts suppliers

When you're deciding on a supplier of inventory or parts for your business, be sure to consider all of the following:

- ✔ Does the supplier have the full range and selection of products that you need?

- ✔ How competitive are the supplier's prices? Does the supplier ever offer any specials? Do large or standing orders receive discounts?

- ✔ How reliable is the supplier? What is the supplier's track record for filling orders completely and on time?

- ✔ What is the supplier's delivery time from the date an order is received until the date it's shipped? How are goods shipped? Who pays for shipping?

- ✔ Will you be able to return or exchange defective, damaged, non-selling, or overstocked merchandise? If so, who pays for shipping, and will you have to pay a restocking charge?

- ✔ Does the supplier provide good customer service? Will the supplier give reliable advice about what you should purchase? If you're buying complicated equipment, either for your own use or for resale to your own customers, does the supplier offer training in the operation of the equipment to you and your employees or to the customer? Does the supplier have a good reputation for responding to customer complaints?

- ✔ Does the supplier extend credit? What do you have to do to establish credit? When you're granted credit, can you get a discount for cash payments on delivery or for early payment?

- ✔ If you're buying goods for resale, does the supplier offer any advertising support?

Ask potential suppliers for names of customers you can contact for references.

Book I

**From Start
to Finish
and
Everything
in Between**

Service suppliers

With some service suppliers you may have a close working relationship — that might be the case with a pest control company or a security firm or a window dresser. But some of your service suppliers may almost end up living in your back pocket — they'll be more like employees of your business than independent businesses themselves. If you hire a business that provides secretarial or bookkeeping services or provides support for your hardware and software, you may be dealing with your supplier almost every day.

Take special care in choosing a supplier who will become an integral part of your business.

To avoid unpleasantness, when you're deciding on a supplier, consider the following:

- ✔ Does the supplier offer what you need?
- ✔ How competitive are the supplier's prices?
- ✔ How reliable is the supplier?
- ✔ Does the supplier stand behind his or her work?
- ✔ Who will be your company representative?
- ✔ Does the supplier extend credit?

Ask for names of customers you can contact for references.

Establishing credit with your suppliers

Most businesses like to have some flexibility in paying their bills. When you're the supplier, cash on delivery is very nice. But when you're the customer, you'd much rather have time to make your payments. You may need the time to collect your own accounts receivable so that you'll have money in the bank when the supplier cashes your cheque.

As a new customer, you may not be able to get credit from a supplier immediately. You may have to put up with being a *COD* (cash on delivery . . . and you already knew that, so stop making fish noises) customer until the supplier has had a chance to look you over and decide that you won't take the goods or services and then skip town without paying. After the supplier stops being suspicious of you, you may be granted a line of credit so you no longer have to pay on delivery. The supplier may first ask for financial statements and credit references. (If your business is just starting, you'll show your supplier your projected statements and you'll offer personal credit references instead of references for your business.)

After you've got credit, the supplier will still invoice you for the product when it's delivered or for the services when they are provided. But you'll be allowed a grace period (usually 30 days) in which to pay the bill without interest being charged. If you pay the bill before the 30 days are up, you may be given a discount. Suppliers commonly give a discount of 2 percent if a customer pays within ten days.

When you first get your credit, make sure that you pay your bills on time. (Just like when you first get the keys to your parents' car, make sure that you don't crash it.) Then you'll be able to use the supplier as a credit reference for new suppliers. Over time, you'll acquire a good credit rating and suppliers will be able to get credit information about you from credit rating agencies instead of from your suppliers.

Entering into contracts with your suppliers

Every time you agree to buy goods or get services from a supplier, you are entering into a contract. In theory at least, your contracts with your suppliers will be the product of give and take on both sides, so that you negotiate an agreement that both of you are equally happy with. (In actual fact, however, you may not have a great deal of negotiating power, especially when your business is new and small and your suppliers are large and powerful.)

After both sides have agreed to the contract (whether or not they're blissfully happy with it), both sides have to do what the contract says. Both you and your supplier must understand clearly what you are to do. If one party doesn't do what the contract says, the other party may have the right to sue and/or end the contract.

Contracts

Unless you're making a purchase at a retail store, you should have some form of written contract with a supplier of goods. The contract may be

- ✔ A sales order form or invoice created by your supplier
- ✔ A purchase order form created by you
- ✔ A formal written contract signed by both parties

See the previous section on "Documenting Your Agreement" for what should be included in agreements. The only difference is that you're now the client.

Speak to your lawyer

Get your lawyer to advise you about the contracts you enter into with suppliers:

✔ Have your lawyer prepare a standard purchase order form for you to use if you regularly order goods.

✔ Have your lawyer review invoices or contracts for goods before you agree to them if you don't understand them and the supplier cannot explain them to your satisfaction. If different terms need to be negotiated, your lawyer may be able to do a better job at negotiations than you can. (See the heading "Using suppliers of professional services.")

✔ Consult a lawyer if you're negotiating a contract that involves a lot of money or a long-term commitment.

Establishing good relationships suppliers

When you find suppliers you're happy with, you want to make sure that you do what you can to establish a good working relationship. Here are some tips:

✔ Be clear about what you need and when you need it.

✔ Communicate with your supplier.

✔ Don't squabble over every invoice, or try to get price reductions on everything you buy.

✔ Pay your bills promptly.

✔ Treat the supplier's sales and service representatives courteously, even if you have a complaint.

✔ Ask for special service only when you need it. Don't ask for last-minute deliveries or extra goods or services unless you're in an unusual situation.

In return, you expect quality goods or services, reliably delivered. Over time, as a valued customer you should expect some extra service. You would like your supplier to

✔ Tell you about new products that become available.

✔ Tell you about discounts, rebates, or special deals.

✔ Advise you of any possible delays in delivery before they happen.

✔ Help you out if you occasionally need extra inventory or immediate delivery.

✔ Be flexible if you have an occasional problem paying a bill on time.

As a new, and perhaps small and rather insignificant customer, you can't immediately expect the same kind of service a long-standing customer would get. Building that kind of relationship takes time, so be patient.

If a supplier does not meet your expectations of quality, price, service, and reliability, don't fume, don't fight . . . just find another supplier. Keep your bases covered — even if things are going well with your suppliers, try to stay informed about other suppliers in case you need them one day.

If you ditch a supplier with whom you've had a long-term or important relationship, show good business etiquette and inform the supplier that you're moving on.

Avoiding problems in the first place

When you're the supplier, you run into problems with your customers. So as a customer, you'll likely run into problems with your suppliers.

The best way to deal with problems is not to have them in the first place. So may we suggest you take the following steps:

- ✔ Choose your suppliers wisely.
- ✔ If you're buying goods, choose the product carefully.
- ✔ Don't automatically accept your supplier's contract terms.
- ✔ Try to arrive at an agreement that's fair to both sides (even if you're the one with the bargaining muscle).
- ✔ Put your deal in writing.
- ✔ See a lawyer if you need to.

Considering problems that can arise

Even if you do everything right, problems can still arise. We go over some typical problems you may encounter, and some solutions.

Suppliers of services

If your supplier is providing a service, here are a few scenarios that can cause you grief and what you can do about them:

- ✔ **The supplier doesn't finish the work.** You'll have to find someone else to finish the work. Before you hire someone else, notify the first provider in writing that you consider your contract to be at an end.

Book I

From Start
to Finish
and
Everything
in Between

✔ **The supplier does the work badly.** If you realize that the work isn't satisfactory as the services are being provided, ask the service provider to correct the problems. If the supplier does not correct the problems, you may have the right to end the contract and refuse to pay

✔ **The supplier injures you (or your associate or employee) or damages your property.** The injured person or the property owner can sue for compensation for personal injury or property damage.

Suppliers of goods

If your supplier is providing goods and something goes wrong, you can take steps to address problems such as these:

✔ **The supplier doesn't deliver the goods.** Don't pay for goods that are not delivered. To protect yourself, try to keep the amount you pay before delivery as low as possible.

✔ **The supplier delivers the goods late.** Unless your contract states that "time is of the essence," you have to accept late delivery and pay for the goods in full. You may, however, be able to sue the supplier for compensation for any loss you suffer because the goods were not delivered on time.

✔ **The supplier delivers the wrong goods or damaged goods.** You do not have to accept or pay for wrong or damaged goods. Inspect your shipments upon receipt and refuse to accept them if you spot a problem.

Knowing what to do if you suffer loss or damage because of a supplier

If your supplier breaches its contract with you (doesn't perform the contract as promised — for example, by not delivering the goods you ordered), you can sue the supplier for damages, which we've been referring to as "compensation" for losses you've suffered. If you win your lawsuit, the court will order the supplier to pay you money for your losses. The amount you receive in damages is supposed to put you in the position you would have been in if your supplier had performed the contract properly (and your business affairs had sailed on smoothly).

If you suffer loss or damage, you can't just sit back and let your losses pile up. You have a legal obligation to *mitigate* your damages — that is, to take all reasonable steps to keep your losses as low as possible. For example, if a supplier fails to deliver parts that you need to manufacture your product, you have to try to find an alternative supply of the parts. If you don't take steps to mitigate your damages, the court will not give you an award for your total loss, only for what you would have lost if you had made an effort to reduce your losses.

Consult a lawyer immediately if your supplier doesn't do what it promised under the contract and you suffer a loss as a result. Your lawyer can give you advice about steps to take immediately to improve your chances of recovering damages from the supplier.

Using suppliers of professional services

Suppliers of professional services — that is, professional *advisors* — are somewhat different than other suppliers. So you have to approach them a bit differently.

In the way of professional advisors, you'll need a lawyer, an accountant, and an insurance agent or broker. Depending on the nature of your business, you may also want help from one or more of the following individuals:

- A publicist or media relations expert
- A marketing consultant
- An interior designer
- A graphic
- A computer systems consultant
- A management consultant
- A human resources specialist (also known as a headhunter)
- Business coaches

You should have a contract in writing with your professional advisors, as you would with any other service provider.

Finding professional help

You'll be looking for professional advisors with experience in small business matters, with whom you'll feel comfortable working, and who will charge you a reasonable fee. In hiring any kind of professional help, you should

- Get recommendations.
- Investigate possible candidates.
- Interview the best candidates.

Book I

From Start
to Finish
and
Everything
in Between

Working with professional advisors

Whether you're dealing with a lawyer, accountant, or consultant, you should expect your professional service provider to do the following:

- ✔ Perform the services competently and promptly.

- ✔ Act honestly, and not behave in a sneaky way either with you or with the people the advisor is dealing with on your behalf.

- ✔ Keep confidential any information you share with the advisor about your business (or personal life, for that matter, because PIPEDA applies to these advisors too).

- ✔ Avoid any conflicts of interest (for example, not take your direct competitor on as a client).

- ✔ Keep you thoroughly and regularly advised of all work being done for you.

- ✔ Act only on your instructions, and not make independent decisions about what's best for you and then carry them out without your permission.

Chapter 4

Looking to the Future of Your Business

In This Chapter

▶ Coping with money problems

▶ Dealing with disputes, in and out of court

▶ Deciding to go out of business

▶ Being put out of business

▶ Planning in the event of your death

▶ Expanding your business

▶ Finding money to expand your business

▶ Managing a bigger business

*Y*ou can't know what the future of your business will be. No matter how careful you to try to be with your business affairs, problems can — and do — arise from time to time. You might find your business can't make its payments on time, or you may find yourself in a dispute with a customer. You may also have to deal with the decision to close up shop, or someone else could put you out of business, or (worse-case scenario) you could die. But hey, maybe your business will become so successful that you'll decide to expand.

In this chapter we help you anticipate situations that the future may hold (some bad, some good) for your business. We help you face your issues head-on, make an objective assessment of the situation, and try to come up with a plan of action.

No Money, More Problems

So your creditors are after you. They want their money and you haven't got it at the moment. You may find yourself in one of these situations:

> ✔ You can't repay a loan.
>
> ✔ You can't pay for equipment you're buying on credit.
>
> ✔ You can't pay your rent.
>
> ✔ You can't pay off a mortgage.
>
> ✔ You can't pay your taxes.
>
> ✔ You are insolvent.
>
> ✔ You are about to go bankrupt.

What's going to happen and what can you do?

Even though you may be broke, consider talking to your lawyer (if your lawyer will talk to someone with as little money as you have). Borrowing and lending are subject to legal rules and you may be in a better position than your creditor thinks (and your creditor may be in a worse position). Your lawyer may be able to help you negotiate an extension of the deadline for repayment, or more favourable repayment terms.

Don't fight your creditors out of sheer pig-headedness. If you lose the fight, you'll owe even more money — because creditors are usually allowed to pass on the cost of collecting their debts to you, the debtor. (And you'll still have to pay your own legal fees.)

Your business can't make a payment that's due

If you borrow money, you're expected to repay it. If you don't repay, the lender is liable to get a little upset. But what the lender can do depends on the nature of the lender and the loan.

A payment on a loan from a non-commercial source

You got *love money* from a family member or friend to set up your business, but the lender doesn't feel so loving now. The lender can sue for return of the money. This is true whether or not you have a written contract.

So don't ignore the lender or tell him to buzz off. If you have no money to pay now, try to reach an agreement:

> ✔ See if the lender will agree to wait a few weeks or months.
>
> ✔ See if the lender will agree to accept smaller payments over a longer term.

Book I

From Start
to Finish
and
Everything
in Between

✔ Offer something other than money in full or part payment of the loan — something you own or the business owns, or your services for free.

✔ Offer security for the loan, such as a mortgage on property you own; or offer a share in your business.

Then put into writing the agreement you've reached, and sign it and have the lender sign it.

A payment on a loan from a commercial source

If you have a commercial loan, you probably agreed to pay it off in instalments, so you may think that not being able to pay one instalment is no big deal. You're wrong. Most commercial term loans have an *acceleration clause*. That means that the lender can demand that you repay the entire loan as soon as you miss one payment by more than a few days.

If a lender demands repayment and you can't repay, the lender has the right to sue you for the outstanding amount of the loan, plus interest owing, plus the lender's costs of collecting the debt from you. That means that the lender, after demanding repayment of the loan and waiting a few days for payment,

✔ Can take property you offered as security and either keep it or sell it (or start a lawsuit for possession of the secured property if you won't let the lender have it)

✔ Can demand that a person who guaranteed the loan pay back the loan (plus interest)

✔ May be able to appoint a receiver/manager to take possession of the secured property and sell it, depending on the terms of the loan

If you know that you don't have the money to make a payment, but you think that you'll have money soon to get back on track, do the following:

✔ First, try to find the money for the payment from another source.

✔ Then, if you can't get money from another source, talk to your lender before the due date of the payment that you're going to miss. The lender may agree to overlook your default for a short time, especially if you offer some additional security.

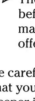

Be careful about borrowing more money and offering more security for a loan that you're already having trouble repaying! You may be digging yourself deeper into a hole and you may lose more in the long run.

If you're in a really bad financial position and you don't think that a little extra money or a little extra time is going to do anything but delay bigger trouble, you should think about making a proposal to all of your creditors or even going bankrupt (see the heading "Your business is insolvent").

A payment for an asset bought on credit

If you've bought assets (such as equipment or vehicles or furniture) for your business and are paying for them over time, you've almost certainly entered into a financing agreement such as a *chattel mortgage, conditional sales agreement, purchase money security interest,* or a *lease with an option to purchase.* If you stop making your payments, the other party to the financing agreement can

- ✔ Sue you for the full amount still left to pay (plus interest)
- ✔ Seize the asset and sell it (and account to you after the sale)

The best you can do is see if the financer is willing to give you more time to pay (and then try to find some money).

A payment under an equipment lease

If your business leased assets instead of buying them outright or on time, you're not in any better position if you stop making your regular payments. The terms of a commercial asset lease normally don't allow you to stop making your lease payments for any reason — including the fact that the asset is broken or defective and the fact that you have no money. You have to make all the payments for the full term of the lease. If you miss a payment, the lessor can

- ✔ Sue you for the full amount owed under the lease
- ✔ Seize the asset (and, if you have an option to purchase, sell it and account to you)

Again, the most you can do is try to negotiate more time to pay, and look for some money to pay with.

You've personally guaranteed a debt for your business and your business can't pay

If you've given a personal guarantee for a business loan and your business can't make a payment, the lender can demand payment from you. If you don't pay, the lender can sue you for the full outstanding amount of the loan, plus interest. If you gave security (such as a mortgage on your home) as well as guaranteeing the debt, the lender can realize on the security.

If you've co-signed a loan with your business, the lender doesn't even have to wait for your business to miss a payment — it can demand that you make the payment instead, because you're equally responsible for the loan from the get-go.

Book I

From Start
to Finish
and
Everything
in Between

Note that if you're a member of a partnership, in most provinces the partners are individually responsible for paying debts of the partnership if the partnership itself can't pay.

Your business can't pay its rent

If you can't pay the rent owing under your commercial lease, your landlord can do a variety of nasty things to you, including

- ✔ Sue you for *arrears of rent* (rent owing) or for *damages* (money compensation) for breach of the lease, while letting you stay on under the lease
- ✔ Retake possession of the premises and terminate the lease
- ✔ Retake possession of the premises and terminate the lease with notice for future loss of rent
- ✔ Retake possession of the premises without terminating the lease, and re-let the premises acting as your agent (you remain responsible for the rent, minus whatever the landlord collects from the new tenant)
- ✔ *Distrain* (seize and sell your property on the premises) to satisfy arrears of rent

If your landlord terminates your lease, retakes possession of your premises, or distrains, consider seeing a lawyer to find out whether doing so is within the landlord's rights. Landlords sometimes ignore the fine print of the law, and you may have some rights of your own.

Your business can't pay a mortgage on real property

If you took out a mortgage to buy real property for your business and you can't make your payments, the *mortgagee* (the lender) has the right in many provinces to *foreclose* on the mortgage (become the legal owner of the property), or to sell the property — under court supervision in a *judicial sale*, or privately under a *power of sale*.

If the mortgagee starts a legal action for foreclosure or judicial sale, you can stop it by paying off the entire mortgage, or in some cases by paying the payment(s) you missed plus a penalty. If you can't pay the entire mortgage immediately, you can ask the court for a delay (from about two to six months) to come up with the money. You can also stop foreclosure by asking for judicial sale.

If the mortgagee wants to sell the property, see if it will let you try to sell the property yourself first. Buyers may think they can get a good deal and may offer a lower price when they see it's a judicial sale or sale under a power of sale. The more money the property sells for, the less you'll owe the mortgagee or the more you'll get to keep.

Your business can't pay its taxes

The Canada Revenue Agency (CRA) has a *statutory lien* against the personal property (as opposed to real property, or real estate) of a taxpayer who does not pay taxes or remittances that are due. This lien lets the government seize your business's personal property — which is your personal property, if you're a sole proprietor or partner — after giving 30 days' notice. (During the notice period you can pay up and avoid the seizure.)

If you own real property in a municipality and you don't pay your property taxes, the municipality will add interest charges and penalties to your property tax bill. If you still don't pay your taxes, the municipality has the right to sell your real property.

Your business is insolvent

Your business is insolvent if it owes at least $1,000 and cannot pay its debts as they become due. Being insolvent in itself isn't so wrong (apart from the fact that you have no money), but if you're insolvent, you're in danger of being forced into bankruptcy. A creditor to whom you owe more than $1,000 and who has no security from you for the debt can petition your business into bankruptcy.

If you're dealing with unsecured creditors

If you're insolvent, what can you do before someone petitions you into bankruptcy? You can try to reach some kind of agreement with your creditors — for example, that they'll give you more time to pay, or accept part payment of your debt. Put any agreement into writing. By the way, your creditors won't likely be interested in cutting you any slack unless your business has decent prospects.

If you're dealing with secured creditors

If you're insolvent and a secured creditor notifies you that it's going to realize on its security, consider making a formal proposal under the Bankruptcy and Insolvency Act. If you do nothing, your secured creditors are going to make off with the secured property, and you probably need it to keep your business

Book I

From Start
to Finish
and
Everything
in Between

running. You should get a trustee in bankruptcy to advise you and to file in bankruptcy court a *notice of intention to make a proposal.*

After you file your notice of intention, you have to file the actual proposal, and then your creditors meet within about three weeks to vote on it. Here's another downside to the proposal process: If your secured creditors reject the proposal (even if your unsecured creditors don't), they can immediately realize on their security. In addition (as if you needed an addition at this point), your business is deemed to have made an *assignment in bankruptcy* (a transfer of its property to the trustee in bankruptcy) and will be officially declared bankrupt.

Choosing to go bankrupt

You can be forced into bankruptcy, but you can also choose to go into bankruptcy by making an assignment in bankruptcy. Why would you actually want to go bankrupt? Well, when a court declares you bankrupt, your trustee in bankruptcy deals with your creditors. You don't have to look at their ugly faces anymore. Your trustee will make arrangements to sell the business's property to pay the debts. And you'll be able to start over again.

If you're carrying on business as a sole proprietorship or a partnership, you'll go bankrupt as an individual. If you're carrying on business as a corporation, the corporation will go bankrupt. As an individual you'll probably be discharged from bankruptcy after nine months, and if you receive an absolute discharge, almost all of your debts are cancelled. (If you receive a conditional discharge, you'll still be responsible for repaying certain debts — income taxes for example.) A corporation can't be discharged until it has paid all its debts, but you can always start up a new corporation (however, you may find that the creditors you stiffed won't be very anxious to deal with your new corporation).

See the next section for more (hooray!) about bankruptcy.

Bankruptcy

After the bankruptcy court has made an order that your business is bankrupt, it appoints a trustee in bankruptcy. The trustee becomes the legal owner of all the unsecured property that formerly belonged to your business and it uses the property to pay off debts. Your secured creditors keep their rights over secured property — the property doesn't go to the trustee.

If your business is a corporation and you're a director, you may not escape having to make some payments personally if your business goes bankrupt. You'll be held responsible for up to six months' worth of unpaid wages for employees, for unpaid amounts owed to the CRA for income tax and GST/HST,

Canada Pension Plan and Employment Insurance, and for unpaid provincial sales tax owed to your provincial department or ministry of finance. And that's on top of paying any business loans for which you gave a personal guarantee.

If your business disposed of any property to save it from creditors, you can be personally charged with a criminal offence. And your trustee in bankruptcy can sue to get his hands on property that was improperly transferred away from the business, so that it can be distributed among the creditors.

If a person or business is an undischarged bankrupt, the person or business can't borrow more than $500 without telling the lender about the state of bankruptcy (and not telling is an offence punishable by a fine or imprisonment). If a person is an undischarged bankrupt, he or she cannot be the director of a corporation.

Disputes

Talking about money troubles is depressing. Let's talk about something more cheerful, like fighting with your customers, suppliers, and neighbours.

Disputes can escalate and end up in court, but they don't have to. (On the other hand, some disputes belong in court.) In this section, we lead you gently through the mechanisms available for resolving a dispute. They range from negotiating a settlement through mediation and arbitration, all the way to litigation. We won't get into the messy illegal stuff like baseball bats and cement overshoes.

But before we go any further, we want you to remember two things about any dispute you get into:

- ✔ Wrap up the dispute in writing.
- ✔ Learn from the experience.

Negotiating a settlement

The traditional way to negotiate a settlement is for each side to state what it wants and then use whatever power it has to persuade or force the other side to agree. The sides sometimes exaggerate what they want so they'll have maneuvering room if they're forced to make a compromise. The purpose of traditional negotiation is to win, not necessarily to solve the problem effectively.

Book I

From Start
to Finish
and
Everything
in Between

We give you some help to know how to be a successful negotiator without upsetting the traditional negotiation pattern too much. We do this by showing you various negotiation techniques, including how to focus not on what you want (or on what the other side wants) but on interests that you and the other side may have in common.

Preparing for negotiations

If you want to negotiate successfully, you can't just rush in punching as soon as the bell sounds — first, you have to prepare to negotiate. Preparation involves two steps: studying the situation and planning your moves. When you study the situation, you will

- ✔ Gather information about the matter in dispute.
- ✔ Separate your *position* in the dispute from your short-term and long-term business *interests*.
- ✔ Think about what are the other party's business interests.
- ✔ Think about your goals in this negotiation.
- ✔ Gather information about the other party in the dispute.
- ✔ Think about the side problems you may encounter in the negotiating process and how you might deal with them.
- ✔ Think about the leverage you can use to argue for your interests.

Having a plan

Next, you plan — but if you did all that preparation, the planning is easy. Here are the steps:

1. Create a list of alternatives to the position the other side is taking or is likely to take.

2. Choose your own opening position.

3. Marshal the arguments you think you can use to persuade the other party of the strength of your position.

Opening discussions

Don't let discussions get underway until you're ready. If you haven't finished your planning and preparation when the other side announces that it's ready to negotiate, tell them that you have to look into the matter and will be back in touch as quickly as possible. If they won't go away, encourage them to chat about the problem. If the issue is personal to the other party, he or she can blow off a little steam; and you may be able to get valuable information about the other party's position, interests, and side issues just by listening to the person talk.

But after you're ready to discuss the problem via a meeting or phone call,

- ✔ Start by getting personal, if possible.
- ✔ Don't be in a hurry to state a position or describe your interests.
- ✔ Be courteous to the individual you're dealing with.
- ✔ Do your best not to get angry or upset.
- ✔ Really listen to the other side.
- ✔ Admit that the other side has reason to be annoyed with you and/or your business, if the reason is legitimate.
- ✔ Focus on your interests and champion them.
- ✔ Look for ways of putting your interests and their interests into the same basket.
- ✔ Deal with solvable issues.
- ✔ Avoid using threats or pressure tactics against the person or organization.
- ✔ Offer the other side ways of moving from its original position toward your position.

Calling it quits

Quit while you're ahead. But how will you *know* when you're ahead?

- ✔ Use the objective criteria you dreamed up in the planning stage.
- ✔ Ask yourself what your alternatives are if you don't agree to the other side's offer.
- ✔ Ask yourself whether you and/or the other side will be able to or will want to go through with the terms of the deal.

Looking further into negotiation

You might like to read these books on negotiating:

- ✔ *Getting to YES: Negotiating Agreement Without Giving In*, by Roger Fisher, William L. Ury, and Bruce Patton (published by Penguin). This is the famous book about negotiating that grew out of the Harvard Negotiating Project and that everyone has heard about. We based a lot of our advice about negotiating on this classic. If you want to know more about the Harvard Negotiating Project, you can go to its website at www.pon. harvard.edu.

Book I

From Start
to Finish
and
Everything
in Between

✔ *Swim with the Sharks Without Being Eaten Alive*, by Harvey Mackay (published by William Morrow and Company).

✔ *Negotiating For Dummies* by Michael C. Donaldson (published by Wiley).

Alternative dispute resolution (ADR)

The "alternative" in alternative dispute resolution means alternative to going to court. Litigation is expensive and usually leads to bad feelings between the parties — and just because you're facing a dispute doesn't mean you want to spend as much money as possible to resolve it or end up never doing business again with the other side.

Mediation

Mediation is quite simply settling a dispute by setting up an independent third party to help arrive at a settlement.

Mediation is *not useful* if

✔ One of the parties does not want mediation — the parties both have to have some desire to settle the matter and must both be willing to meet with a mediator.

✔ One of the parties has a lot more power than the other and is going to use it to impose a solution on the weaker party.

In some provinces, the parties to a lawsuit are required to go to mediation shortly after the lawsuit starts, to see if the matter can be settled without going any further through the court system.

Arbitration

Arbitration gets closer to court proceedings. In *arbitration*, a neutral third person (the *arbitrator*, but sometimes three arbitrators are involved) is chosen by the parties to hear both sides' stories.

These are the advantages of arbitration:

✔ Arbitration can be faster and cheaper than a lawsuit (although the bigger and more complex the dispute, the closer arbitration costs get to litigation costs).

✔ Parties can choose an arbitrator who has expertise in the area of the dispute (instead of just hoping that the judge they draw knows something about it). This can be very important in specialized areas of business.

✔ Arbitration proceedings are private and confidential — unlike court proceedings, which are public.

✔ Arbitration decisions do not *set precedents* (establish examples that have to be followed in later cases) the way court decisions do.

Litigation

When disputes arise, the parties often think of a lawsuit as the first option. A lawsuit is just one of several options and may even be the last option.

Should you sue?

If you're the injured party, you decide whether to take the dispute to court. You need to talk to a lawyer about deciding whether to sue. Your lawyer will help you make the decision, based on the following matters:

✔ What are your chances of winning the lawsuit?

✔ What will you get if you win?

✔ What's this going to cost?

✔ Where's the lawsuit going to take place?

✔ What are your chances of making the other party carry out the court order if you win?

What should you do if you're sued?

If you are sued, your options are narrower than if you're the one deciding whether to sue. You can put in a statement of defence and then defend the action vigorously, or you can put in a statement of defence and then try to negotiate a settlement. In some cases you can put in a statement of defence and a *counterclaim* (a lawsuit against the other side) or a *third-party claim* (a lawsuit against other people who were really responsible for causing the problem in the first place — hey, the more the merrier, right?). Or you can do nothing.

Doing nothing is a poor choice. If you don't defend, and the other side continues with its lawsuit, the court will quickly enter judgment against you and the other side can start trying to enforce the judgment right away.

In the no man's land between doing absolutely nothing and responding formally to the lawsuit, you could see a lawyer and try to

✔ Settle the matter before the deadline for putting in a defence has passed (the defendant usually has several weeks after being notified of the lawsuit to file a statement of defence, but sometimes the allowed reaction time is much shorter)

✔ Persuade the other side to call off the lawsuit even if the dispute can't be settled right away

Closing Up Shop

You've had your Big Bang (when you started up your business). Things didn't work out quite the way you expected . . . and now your business could be heading for the Big Crunch.

It may seem strange in a book about starting a business to talk about getting out of business. But you may have good reasons to get out of business sooner than you planned:

✔ Someone wants to buy you out.

✔ You want out.

✔ You have to get out.

✔ You keel over and die.

In the next few sections, we tell you about what's involved in selling your business as a going concern, going out of business voluntarily, being put out of business by your creditors, and making arrangements about your business in the event of your death.

Parting from your business may be a joint venture

What happens to your business if you want out will not be yours alone to decide unless you are in business by yourself, either as a sole proprietor or as the only shareholder of a corporation.

If you have associates, either as partners or as fellow shareholders, they will have something to say about what happens. You won't be able to sell the entire business to an outsider or hand it over to family members without their agreement. Actually, if you have associates, they're the real market for your share of the business if you want out, because outside buyers aren't likely to want a share in someone else's business. But just because you want to sell to your associates doesn't mean they have to buy — unless you have a partnership agreement or shareholders' agreement that covers this situation.

Considering taxes when going out of business

Closing a business is never as simple as locking the door and walking away. If you sell the business you will likely be liable for capital gains taxes. It's the same principle as most taxes: if you make money, the government wants a piece of it.

Taxation of capital gains

When you sell your business, either by selling the assets (property) of the business or by selling your shares in the corporation that carries on the business, you are selling *capital property*, which is property with long-term value. The profit you make from selling capital property is called a *capital gain*. A capital gain is not taxed the same way as the profits you make from running your business. The entire profit you make from running your business is taxed as income. But only one-half of a capital gain is taxed. (If you have a *capital loss*, one-half of it can be used to reduce your capital gains, although it can't be used to reduce your other income.)

Calculating capital gains

A capital gain or loss is calculated by comparing how much you get when you sell the property to how much it cost you when you bought the property. If you sell property for more than it cost you, you have a capital gain. You don't use just the raw sale price and the raw purchase price when you're making this calculation, though. You use the *adjusted sale price* — which is the sale price of the property minus the expenses associated with selling it, and the *adjusted cost base* — which is the purchase price of the property plus the expenses associated with buying it.

The calculation gets a bit more complicated (What? You thought it was already complicated?) if you sell capital property against which you have claimed *capital cost allowance* (*CCA*). You can't claim the full cost of capital property as a business expense in the year of purchase because its usefulness to your business lasts for more than one year. However, its usefulness doesn't last forever, so you can claim a percentage of the cost as an expense every year over a period of several years until the entire cost has been claimed. The

Book I

**From Start
to Finish
and
Everything
in Between**

amount you are allowed to claim on capital property each year as an expense is called capital cost allowance.

If you've claimed CCA on property that you then sell, you have to take the CCA you've claimed into account when you calculate the adjusted cost base of the capital property. If you sell the property for more than its *undepreciated capital cost* (its value on your business's books after you've claimed CCA) — and this is quite possible to do because an asset's book value is not necessarily the same as its market value — then you've claimed too much capital cost allowance, and you have to pay back the excess to the tax authorities.

The excess capital cost allowance is taxed fully as income of your business, not just one-half as a capital gain. (That's because you used the CCA as an expense to reduce the income of your business, and now the government wants to collect the tax you should have paid.) Taxing excess capital cost allowance is called a *recapture* of capital cost allowance . . . picture the tax officials chasing the capital cost allowance around with a net. On the other hand, if you sell capital property for less than its undepreciated capital cost, you did not claim enough capital cost allowance over the time the business owned the property, and you may be able to deduct the entire loss — called a *terminal loss* — as an expense from the income of the business.

Dealing with the tax bill

When you sell your business — especially if it's been successful and has increased in value — you may have to pay tax on half of the money you get from the sale (and on all the excess capital cost allowance you claimed on assets purchased for your business). So the sale proceeds aren't pure profit to you. Don't go on a spending spree until you've figured out how much belongs to the Canada Revenue Agency (CRA). We talk further along in this section, however, about ways of reducing the tax consequences of a sale. See the heading "Putting the deal together," a bit later in this chapter.

Selling Your Business as a Going Concern

If someone approaches you about taking over your business, or if you want someone to take over and run the business, you're looking at selling your business as a *going concern*.

Knowing what your business is worth

If you are selling your business, you need to have a good idea of what it's worth, both to set a reasonable asking price and to decide whether or not to accept any offer that a buyer might make.

When you sell your business as a going concern, its value is based not only on what its physical assets are worth, but also on the value of its *goodwill*. Goodwill, which can be defined as the likelihood that the business's customers will come back, is usually valued by looking at the business's past earnings. (Chapter 2 of this book has a section on how assets and goodwill are valued.)

The best way to figure out what your business is worth is to find out how much comparable businesses have recently sold for. You may be able to get this information from industry publications, your accountant, lawyer or other consultants, a business broker, or a professional business appraiser.

Dealing with prospective buyers

No one is going to show up at your door and say, "I'll take it! Show me where to sign." Any prospective buyer is going to have lots of questions about your business, and you have to be prepared to answer them.

For example, a buyer might want to

- ✔ Know why you are selling the business
- ✔ See the lease for your business premises
- ✔ Know whether you're aware of any plans by the municipality or landlord that will affect traffic, parking, or access to the premises
- ✔ See the business's financial statements for the past three to five years

You may or may not be asked to give a lot of information about your business to a prospective buyer, but if a buyer asks you a question, you must answer it honestly. Don't make any false statements about your business. A buyer who decides to buy your business based on your false statements may be able to set the sale aside or sue you for financial compensation if he or she suffers losses after the deal goes through.

Don't agree to show a prospective buyer around your premises, answer questions about your business, or let the buyer see any business documents, unless the buyer first signs a *confidential disclosure agreement*. Signing the document means that the buyer agrees not to tell anyone else what he or she

Book I

From Start
to Finish
and
Everything
in Between

finds out about your business and not to use the information for any purpose other than assessing the business for possible purchase.

Putting the deal together

If you find someone who wants to buy your business, you'll have to negotiate a deal with the buyer. That will involve deciding between a sale of assets and a sale of shares if your business is incorporated, deciding on a purchase price for individual assets if you go for an asset sale, arranging to pay off the business's debts out of the sale price, and working out the terms of a noncompetition agreement and possibly a consulting agreement.

Get advice from your lawyer and accountant before entering into any agreement to sell your business.

Sale of assets or sale of shares

You can sell a business in two ways — by selling the property the business owns (the assets) or by selling ownership of the whole business.

If your business is a sole proprietorship or partnership, you have no choice — you must sell the business by selling its assets.

If your business is a corporation, you have a choice between selling the assets of the business and selling ownership of the corporation by selling the shares of the corporation:

- ✔ If you sell all the shares of the corporation, the buyer will become the owner of the corporation.
- ✔ If you sell the assets of the corporation, the buyer will be the owner of the assets, but you will continue to be the owner of the corporation because you still own the shares.

The choice between a sale of shares and a sale of assets will be based mainly on the tax consequences. Consult your lawyer and accountant to help you decide between the two and to find out how to reduce your taxes as much as possible.

If you sell the shares of your corporation, you are the seller and you receive the sale proceeds personally. The sale proceeds will be taxed in your hands as a capital gain (or loss). If you sell the assets of your corporation, the corporation, not you, is the seller. The corporation receives the sale proceeds, and pays tax on any income or capital gains resulting from the sale. You get your money from the corporation in the form of a dividend on which you will pay tax as income (subject to the dividend tax credit).

Owners of a corporation usually prefer to sell shares for these reasons:

✔ The sale of shares (rather than assets) doesn't involve the recapture of capital cost allowance (CCA). In the section "Calculating capital gains" we talk about how recaptured CCA gets added to the seller's income and is 100 percent taxable — whereas capital gains are only 50 percent taxable.

✔ The capital gain (if any) on the sale of your shares may be tax-free up to $500,000 because of the capital gains deduction available for some small business corporations (and no equivalent deduction is available on the sale of assets).

✔ The buyer has to buy all the corporation's assets and can't just pick and choose the assets he wants.

✔ The buyer takes over the debts and liabilities of the business.

Keep in mind, though, that the buyer may well prefer an asset sale for the following reasons:

✔ The buyer will have a better chance of rejecting unwanted assets.

✔ The buyer doesn't have to take over the debts and liabilities of the business.

Allocating the purchase price if you sell assets

If you sell the assets of your business, negotiating the price has two parts. First, you have to decide on an overall price. Second, you must *allocate* the amount of the purchase price among the various assets included in the sale (in other words, you must assign a price to each asset).

The way you allocate the purchase price among the assets will affect the amount of tax you pay on the sale:

✔ You will want the price allocated to each asset to be less than its *undepreciated capital cost* (its value on your books after deducting the capital cost allowance you have claimed). If you allocate a sale price to an asset that is higher than its undepreciated capital cost, the recaptured capital cost allowance (the extra amount of CCA that you claimed over the years) will be taxed as income in your hands.

✔ You will also want to allocate as little of the purchase price as possible to the business's inventory. That's because 100 percent of any amount allocated to inventory will also be taxed as income.

As it turns out, the buyer will want to allocate a higher price to the very assets to which you want to allocate a lower price, because that allocation saves the buyer taxes down the road.

Book I

From Start
to Finish
and
Everything
in Between

Paying the debts of the business (if you sell assets)

When you sell all the assets of your business, your business remains responsible for its debts. Your business is you personally if it's a sole proprietorship or partnership, or your corporation if your business is incorporated.

After a business sells off its assets, it has no way of earning money to pay off its debts. So creditors of a business can get the short end of the stick when a business sells off all or substantially all of its assets. For that reason, every province has legislation to protect creditors. This legislation — called the Bulk Sales Act in most provinces — requires the buyer and seller to make arrangements to pay the creditors out of the proceeds of the sale. Usually that means that the proceeds of the sale will be paid directly to the business's creditors, and the owner who sold the assets (the corporation or the sole proprietor or partner) will get only what's left over. So if your business has debts, be prepared to see the sale proceeds shrink or even vanish.

Non-competition agreements

When you sell your business as a going concern, whether by share sale or asset sale, the new owner will want to make sure that you don't set up a competing business nearby and take away all the business's customers. To keep you from doing this, the buyer (if he or she is on the ball) will want you to sign a *non-competition agreement* — an agreement not to enter into a competing business within a specified distance for a fixed period of time. A cautious buyer is likely to want an agreement that prevents you from opening a business anywhere in Canada and anytime for decades.

If you sign a non-competition agreement and then start up or join a competing business, the buyer's remedy would be to sue you, either for compensation for the business he loses to your competing business, or for a court order to stop you from competing. But a court will enforce only a reasonable non-competition agreement — in other words, one that keeps you from setting up a similar business for a reasonable period of time and within a reasonable distance of the business location. What's "reasonable" will depend on the nature of the business. It's usually much less than the buyer would like.

Consulting agreements

A consulting agreement keeps you on as a consultant with the business for a limited time after the sale, and allows you to turn some of the purchase price of the business into consulting fees spread out over the period of the contract. You'll pay tax on the part of the purchase price that's paid in consulting fees as income rather than as a capital gain — so you'll pay tax on 100 percent of the amount rather than on 50 percent — but you'll get to spread the tax payable out over two or more years.

Going Out of Business

If business is bad, you may not be able to find a buyer to take over your business as a going concern. Then your only choice is to close down and try to sell off as many of assets as you can. You'll need to find buyers for the business's inventory, fixtures, and equipment. If you're lucky, you'll raise enough cash to pay off the debts of the business before you close the door and turn off the lights.

In the upcoming sections, we give you some advice on how to go out of business with your head held high.

Finding buyers for your business's assets

If you are in a retail business, you can have a "going out of business" sale to sell off your inventory, and perhaps some of your store fixtures.

Speak to your landlord and your municipality before holding any sort of liquidation sale. Most commercial leases state that the landlord's permission is required, and many municipalities require a permit or licence before a going out of business sale may be held. Also check your lease to make sure that your store fixtures don't belong to your landlord.

Speak to your lenders before holding any sort of liquidation sale. Most commercial loan agreements state that a going out of business or liquidation sale is a breach of the loan agreement. If you hold a sale without first getting permission, your lender may demand immediate payment of all your loans. And if you have given security for the loans, the lender may seize the property that is the security.

When it comes to your machinery, computers, office furniture, office supplies, and so on, you can try offering them to business associates, or family and friends. If you don't get any takers, you can place ads in the newspaper or Internet classifieds, or try to find a dealer who buys used equipment. Businesses sometimes end up giving their assets to charity for a tax credit, or simply giving them away to anyone who's willing to remove them from the premises.

If you don't have the heart to sell off the bits and pieces of your business personally, you can hire a business liquidator to sell your inventory, equipment, and supplies for you.

Book I

From Start
to Finish
and
Everything
in Between

Unloading leased equipment

If your business has leased equipment, you can't just return the equipment and stop paying. Your obligation to make the lease payments continues for the full term of the lease.

Speak to the *lessor* (the business that leased you the equipment) to find out whether you can arrange for someone to take over your lease.

Paying off your debts

If you sell all or almost all of the assets of your business, you will have to comply with your province's Bulk Sales Act, which is designed to protect the creditors when a business sells all or substantially all of its assets. You will have to make arrangements to pay your creditors out of the proceeds of the sale. Usually the proceeds of the sale will be paid directly to the business's creditors, and the business will get only what's left over.

If nothing is left over from the sale proceeds but more debts, you're in trouble. How much trouble will depend on whether or not your business is incorporated. If your business is a sole proprietorship or partnership, your business's debts are your personal debts and you will have to use your personal assets to pay off any debts left over after you use up the assets of the business. If your business is incorporated, you won't have to use your personal assets to pay the business's debts unless you gave a personal guarantee for the debts of the business. Earlier in this chapter, we talk more about what happens when you can't pay your business's debts.

Notifying your clients or customers

Let your customers and clients know that you are shutting down your business. If you are a service provider, finish off whatever work you are doing and send your customers a final bill. If you have property belonging to your customers in your possession, tell them to come and pick it up. As a final act of customer relations, thank your customers and clients for their business over the years, and, if possible, refer them to another business that can offer them similar goods or services.

In some professions, you must find another professional in the field to take over your clients. Speak to your professional organization to find out what your obligations are when you close down your business.

Notifying your suppliers

Tell your suppliers that you are closing down your business. Return any goods that you have on consignment. If you have purchased supplies or inventory outright, ask if your suppliers will take anything back and give you a refund.

Pay off your outstanding accounts if you are able. You may not be able to pay off your accounts until you sell off the assets of your business. In that case, let your suppliers know what you are doing to see that they are paid.

Negotiating with your landlord

If you have leased business premises, you can't just close up shop and walk away. Your obligation to pay rent continues to the end of your lease, and your landlord can sue you if you don't keep on paying. So you'd better have a chat with your landlord. See the heading "Your business can't pay its rent," earlier in this chapter.

Being Put Out of Business

If business is really bad, you won't be able to pay your debts. When that happens, your creditors may decide to put you out of business.

When you started your business you probably borrowed money. In fact you probably took out several different loans. You may have other debts as well: an outstanding balance on your business's credit cards or money owing to your business's suppliers.

When you borrowed money, you entered into a contract to repay the money. If you don't repay the money as promised, the lender has the right to take steps to collect the money that you owe.

Earlier in this chapter, we told you about all the nasty things your lenders can do to you if you don't repay your loans. Here we tell you about only those things they can do that will put you out of business.

How your secured creditors can put you out of business

Your secured creditors are the lenders to whom you gave *security* (which is the right to take specified property from you if you don't repay the loan).

When you borrowed money and gave security, you may have signed a *general security agreement* or given a *debenture*, both of which give the lender security over all your business assets, including equipment, vehicles, machinery, inventory, and accounts receivable. Under a general security agreement or a debenture, the lender has the right to take possession of all this property (including the right to collect your accounts receivable) if you don't repay your loan. Many general security agreements and debentures give the lender the right to appoint a *receiver/manager* to take possession of the secured property if the loan is not repaid.

After your lender appoints a receiver/manager, you are effectively out of business. The receiver/manager will take over your business and either liquidate it or run it for the sole purpose of taking possession of the secured property, which will then be sold to pay off your loan.

How your unsecured creditors can put you out of business

If your business can't pay its debts as they become due, and it owes at least $1,000, your business is *insolvent*. If your business is insolvent, any *unsecured creditor* (a lender who has no security from you for the debt) to whom you owe more than $1,000 can *petition* your business into *bankruptcy* if your business commits an *act of bankruptcy*. Not paying a debt when it's due is an act of bankruptcy. (See the earlier headings "Your business is insolvent" and "Bankruptcy.")

If the court makes an order that your business is bankrupt, it will appoint a *trustee in bankruptcy*. The trustee becomes the legal owner of all the unsecured property that belongs to your business and will use the property to pay off your debts. Once the court appoints a trustee in bankruptcy, you are (again) effectively out of business. The trustee will take over your business and liquidate it or run it for the sole purpose of taking possession of the unsecured property, which will then be sold to pay the business's debts. If you're a sole proprietor or partner, the trustee will take over your personal property as well as your business property (with some exceptions, so that you don't freeze to death) and sell it to pay your debts.

Dying to Get Out of Business

Thinking about dying is not very pleasant. We cover this topic quite briefly, so you're probably not in danger of having an emotional breakdown before you get to the end of the chapter. If, however, you're keen to know more about how to arrange your business and personal affairs before you pass on, you should read *Wills and Estate Planning For Canadians For Dummies* (published by Wiley)— which we also wrote.

If your business is worth anything, you'd probably like to pass its value on to your family when you die. You can do that by leaving it to family members to run or by making arrangements to sell it to someone outside the family and leaving the proceeds to your family.

Deciding whether to keep your business in the family or to sell it is complicated. If you're thinking of keeping it in the family, you have to consider the nature of the business, the abilities and interests of your family members, and your own temperament:

- Is your business one that can be passed successfully on to family members?

- Can your family run the business without running it into the ground?

- Can you do whatever is necessary to ensure a smooth transfer of control of your business to your family?

- Will all hell break loose in the family?

Short-term planning versus long-term planning

You're just starting up your business at this point. Practically speaking, you're probably not yet thinking about whether your family should take over and run the business or whether it should be sold to an outsider. But, again practically speaking, you should still make some sensible short-term plans about what should be done with your business if you were to die suddenly (or even if you were to become seriously ill).

Whatever your long-term plans for your business, you should have someone on tap who can step in and run your business, at least temporarily. (The best way to maintain the business's value is to keep it running; and even if it's not going to run for much longer, it still needs to be properly shut down.) That person can be your spouse, your adult child, another family member, a trusted employee, or a manager hired by the *executor* of your will (the person you name in your will to handle your estate).

The person, whoever it is, will need access to enough information about your business to be able to operate it on short notice for a period of time. If the person you have in mind is a family member or employee, you should keep him or her informed about the business's activities. You should also keep your business's books and documents in good order and together in an obvious (but secure) place.

In addition, consider whether you need life insurance so that you have enough money to do the following in the event of your death:

- ✔ Pay the debts of your business.
- ✔ Pay for someone to help your family run the business.
- ✔ Help cover the business's expenses if its income goes down because of your death.
- ✔ Pay any capital gains tax that result from your death.

Finally, you'll need a properly drafted will so that the assets of a sole proprietorship (or partnership) or the shares of a corporation are passed on to the appropriate person or people to allow the business to continue to operate or to close down in an orderly fashion. If you don't have a will, provincial legislation determines who gets your property after your death. Speak to your lawyer about drafting a will.

Keeping it in the family

If you want to pass your business on to your family, you must plan how and when to do it. If you want family members to run your business successfully after you die, you may have to transfer ownership or part-ownership of your business to them while you're still alive. When the time comes, you'll have to consider whether you can afford to retire from the business and/or whether you can afford to pay the tax on any capital gain that results from a full or partial transfer of ownership. (Even if you don't take any money for handing over a share of the business, the CRA says this is another "deemed disposition" or pretend sale that triggers capital gains.) If you can't afford to transfer ownership of your business before you die, think about bringing your family into the business anyway (as employees, for example), so that they can have the opportunity to learn about the business from you and to get to know your clients or customers.

Bringing your family on board has a legal side, too. For example, if you're a sole proprietor and you want to share ownership of your business during your lifetime, you'll have to transfer legal ownership of all the assets of the business jointly to yourself and to the person or people you have in mind as successor(s). If you want to hand over full ownership of your corporation, you'll have to transfer legal ownership of all the shares of the corporation to your intended successor(s). If you want your family to take things over only when you die, you will need a properly drafted will leaving the assets of the business or the shares of the corporation to your intended successor(s).

Seek the advice of both your lawyer and your accountant about bringing your family into the business.

Selling to an outsider

If you want to sell your business to an outsider — so that when you die your family gets the proceeds of the sale of the business instead of getting the business itself — you have two choices about when to sell. You can sell while you're still alive, or you can let your executor sell after you die. If your business is worth more as a going concern than as a collection of assets, its sale value will probably be greatest while you're in the land of the living. But you may not be able to afford to retire from business, or to pay the tax on the capital gain, if you sell the business while you're alive.

If you want to sell your business during your lifetime, you'll have to find a buyer and then legally transfer ownership of all the assets of the business, or the shares of the corporation, to the buyer. (We talk about selling your business earlier in this chapter.) If you don't want to sell your business until you die, you need a properly drafted will directing your executor to sell your business and then leaving the proceeds of the sale to your family. Either way, your lawyer and other professionals need to help you sell your business.

Getting Bigger

A lot of this chapter talks about problems your business could run into that might force your business to shut down. Well, let's stop with the doom and gloom and get to the exciting possibility of growing your business.

You launched your business some time ago, and now your business is expanding, or you'd like it to expand. In any case, you have to have some idea of what you're getting into when your business expands, and how you can finance an expansion and manage a bigger, busier business. And if you aren't expanding but want to, you have to know how to find more business.

What "doing more business" means

If you think that "doing more business" means "making bigger profits," "having access to more opportunities," or "becoming a more important player," you're right. But that's not all. They say that every action has an equal and opposite reaction — well, in this case the reaction can seem bigger than the action! Here are some of the things that go along with doing more business:

Book I

**From Start
to Finish
and
Everything
in Between**

✔ You'll probably do even more work than you're doing now.

✔ You may have to travel more.

✔ You may have to create new lines of products or services.

✔ You'll probably need new accounting and bookkeeping and/or inventory control systems.

✔ You'll need employees, or more employees, to help you.

✔ Your employees will need training, or more training.

✔ You'll need more equipment.

✔ You'll need more inventory if you're in the retail or wholesale business.

✔ You'll need bigger premises.

✔ And last but not least, you'll need more money.

Haven't we been here before? Most of these issues look strangely familiar.

Expanding a business will upset its equilibrium. You and your business will probably have trouble coping, at least in the beginning. In fact, you may never be ready to cope. Sometimes expansion is just not the best thing for you, and you and your business will be happier if things stay the way they are.

Finding more business

If you're reading this section, you probably want to expand your business and you believe that expanding won't lead to disaster. So how do you go about increasing the amount of business you do so you can get on with the expansion process?

Some enterprises are born with more business, others have more business thrust upon them. But some have to achieve more business. If you're not flooded with work but you'd like to be, you can proceed in four ways:

✔ Do more of what you're already doing for the customers you already have.

✔ Find new customers for the work you already do.

✔ Do new work for the customers you already have.

✔ Find new customers for new work.

Doing more of the same work for existing customers

This is the most cost-effective way to expand. You already know your product and your customers. Doing more for the customers you have costs a lot less than going out and finding new customers or hunting down or creating new products.

The first place to start in your quest to do more work for your customers is to review your customer turnover rate and, if it's significant, to find out why customers aren't coming back to you. Speak to non-returning customers, if you can. Ask what they like about the business they're dealing with instead of you, and if they'd be interested in doing business with you again if you made some changes. If you can't talk to the lost sheep, chat with the customers who're still with you and try to get a sense of what they like and don't like about your business. Make reasonable changes as required.

Next, go to work on the customers you've got. Try to "generate new demand" by getting them to use more of your products or services, or use the same amount but more frequently. Apart from persuading your customers or clients that they'll benefit from using more of your products or services (for example, be healthier, smell cleaner, save money), try out these moves on them:

- Make sure they know everything you can do for them.
- Reward your customers.
- Bundle your products or services.
- Make your product or service more appealing.
- Come up with new uses for the product or service.
- Automate delivery.

Overall, one of the most important things you can do is to develop a good relationship with your customers. Make them your friends. Listen to them — and give them lots of convenient ways of talking to you, such as regular opportunities to meet face to face. If they have complaints or concerns, respond. If they have suggestions, pay attention.

Don't waste or lose any information from your clients. Keep a customer information file for each client (or at least for the best ones or up-and-coming ones) that includes notes and records of the following information:

- Which products or services the customer buys, how frequently the customer buys, and how much the customer spends
- How the customer makes the purchase and payment (and any interesting collection history) and takes delivery

Book I

From Start
to Finish
and
Everything
in Between

✔ Any complaints the customer has made, and what you did in response

✔ Which products or services you provide that your customer buys from someone else, and why; and which products or services you provide that your customer doesn't buy at all, and why

✔ Any notes about the customer's plans (that might tie in with your goal of providing more to the customer)

✔ Any of the customer's special interests and important dates (these may not involve flogging any of your products or services; remembering them is just good customer relations)

✔ Any ideas you have about how you might persuade the customer to buy more of your products or services

Customers and clients will be pleased that you consider them important enough to remember details of past transactions, and they'll be thrilled if you remember something about them that isn't immediately linked to making a sale.

Finding more customers for the same work

If you're sure that your current customers are satisfied with the work you're doing, then you can go out and look for new customers. You can look for them in a new geographic area or in a new target group. When you go into a new area or after a new group, focus on it and make a good job of capturing it before you move on to another area or group. Don't try to expand on too many fronts at once.

Doing new and additional work for existing customers

Don't go wild if this is the route you decide to take! Just because your customers love what you're doing with their stock portfolio doesn't mean they'll also be eager to buy pedicures and facials from your business. The best way to proceed is simply to ask your customers what more they'd like from you — or even just listen to what they're saying in your regular contacts with them. You'll probably find that your customers and clients are your best sources for new ideas.

Finding new customers for new products or services

If you're looking for new customers and new products, it almost means you're starting over again! So you'd better go back and read Chapter 1 of this book.

Financing Your Expansion

As an established business, you've got a track record, so prying money out of your initial sources of financing — especially the commercial sources —

should be easier now than when you first started your business. In addition, you have some new sources of financing. Here are possible sources you can turn to for funding the growth of your business:

- ✔ **Sale or sale and leaseback of equipment:** If you already own equipment, you can sell it to a leasing company and then lease it back. Or you can sell one thing, and then lease something else. Or you can sell and not buy anything. Whichever way you go, you free up some cash for other purposes.

- ✔ **Retained earnings:** *Retained earnings* are money you've set aside out of the profits of your business. As soon as you can, you should start building a fund from your profits for unforeseen problems and for expansion.

- ✔ **Equity investment:** An *equity investment* is capital for your business in exchange for partial ownership of your business.

- ✔ **Venture capital and angel capital:** You're no longer a start-up, but you're still eligible for an investment from an angel or from a venture capital firm. In fact, you may be more eligible because you've been in operation for a while an investor can tell more easily whether your business is going places (or not). Venture capitalists will probably see you as looking for *first stage financing* (to increase production) or *second stage financing* (to increase production and expand your markets).

- ✔ **Investment from within your business:** If you bring in new people who are going to run the business with you, you'll usually ask them to buy a partnership share (if your business isn't incorporated) or to buy shares in the corporation (if it is incorporated). This gives you some fresh capital to play with. The new guy may have to take out a loan to make the purchase; the interest payable on the loan is deductible from his or her income.

  If your business is incorporated, you can set up a stock plan that allows employees to buy shares in the business. However, to get much money via employee investment, you'll probably have to sell a significant percentage of shares, and even though you make sure you keep at least 51 percent of the shares, you can still end up with conflict about control of the corporation.

- ✔ **Investment from outside the business:** Under provincial securities laws in Canada, up to 50 people who are not employees of the corporation can own shares in a private corporation. So you can go looking for a few individual investors.

Managing a Bigger Business

The bigger a business grows, the more managing, and the more expert managing, it needs. Poor management is probably the most common reason for a business to fail.

Book I

From Start
to Finish
and
Everything
in Between

 Before you manage others effectively, you must manage yourself. If you can't manage your own time and work efficiently, you're going to have a lot of trouble managing anybody else. And because you're the most important person in the business at this point, you won't have a business to manage if you can't keep it together personally.

Using personal management techniques

As your business expands, you're going to have more and more to do and less and less time to do it. So you're going to have to make the time you do have go further. Here's some advice about managing your time and work.

Schedule your time wisely

 Don't rely on your memory! You haven't got one anymore — it drowned in the sea of details that a business floats in. So plan ahead in writing. Plan your year, your month, your week, your day. Keep a calendar or daybook — just one, if possible!

 Remind yourself what you're supposed to be doing now or next — have a tickler (reminder) system. Use your calendar or organizer to enter reminders of what you have to do in a day, week, or month, such as following up on an e-mail you just sent. Get into the habit of glancing frequently at your tasks for the month, week, and day. Every night before you close up shop (or before you go to sleep, whichever comes first), look over your schedule and to-do list for the following day. If you don't, you'll end up missing a morning meeting or phone call.

Whenever you do something, keep a record. Otherwise, a day or two later you won't remember whether or not you've done something, and what you did. And when a matter has been finally disposed of, put documents relating to it in your storage area, not in your active files area, so you won't be wondering if you're *still* supposed to do something.

Meetings can be terrible time wasters. So always make sure that a meeting is necessary, and that a phone call or an e-mail can't replace it. Then make sure that you're properly prepared for the meeting . . . and that everyone else is too:

- ✔ Before the meeting, review your files, gather any additional information that's necessary, and make notes about what you've done and what you want to talk about.
- ✔ If you're hosting the meeting, send around a detailed agenda.
- ✔ At the end of a meeting, prepare *minutes* (a summary of what was said or what happened) of the meeting.

Screen and bundle

Don't let your phone and e-mail and faxes and mail and drop-in associates or employees rule your time. Organize your day so that you have blocks of time when you give your full attention to matters that require thought and concentrated effort, and other blocks of time when you read and answer your mail and return phone calls. Let customers or clients and suppliers know that you return phone calls and e-mails within 24 hours, but that they should not necessarily expect an instant response.

Put off procrastinating

Putting off work that must be done is one of the biggest thieves of your time. So no matter how much you DON'T WANT TO DO IT, start your work right away — and finish it, too.

Here are some tips for the hard-core procrastinator who's looking to reform:

- Divide up complex work into smaller segments.
- Don't avoid starting something just because you won't be able to finish it in one sitting.
- Set a deadline.
- Reward yourself for accomplishing a task.
- Get an employee or business associate or family member to nag you.
- Live in fear of what might happen if you don't do the work.

Delegate

Do what you do best, and delegate the rest. Your time is better spent doing what you're expert in. Try outsourcing this work, or hiring a temp or a part-time worker, before you hire a full-time employee.

While we're on the subject of delegation, don't let people you've hired delegate to you! "Upward delegation" is a sneak attack. If someone you've delegated to isn't doing the work right, don't do it for him. Provide more training, or give guidelines for correcting the work and have the person try again until it's right. Otherwise you'll end up doing the work *and* paying someone else to do it.

Just say no

The word *no* has a lot of power. Sometimes you have to use it to keep other people from hijacking your time and your energy.

> ✔ Whenever someone makes a demand on you, consider what's in it for you.
>
> ✔ Don't hold or attend useless meetings.
>
> ✔ Discourage drop-in visits from colleagues and clients.
>
> ✔ Tell your family and friends not to call you all the time to chat.

Using business management techniques

As your business expands, it's turning into an enterprise that needs professional management. You may be able to turn yourself into a professional manager, or you may need to bring managers on board. While you wait to discover whether you have what it takes to be a professional manager (management may be something you left your employed life to avoid), think about the issues we talk about in this section.

Giving up control (at least a little)

Giving up control isn't something you want to hear about — unless, of course, someone's buying you out for an obscenely large amount of money. One of the reasons you went into business for yourself was so you could run things the way you wanted to! But you can't do everything yourself, so you're going to have to share some of the responsibilities with others or even hand responsibilities over entirely.

Start off slowly, if you like:

> ✔ Have brainstorming sessions to solve problems.
>
> ✔ Take your time to think about important matters, and gather information and get advice before you make a decision.
>
> ✔ Make yourself redundant.
>
> ✔ Set up formal systems to make business decisions.

Setting goals

You've probably had goals all along. But do they still match the direction your business is taking? Are you following the right strategies to reach them? Review your goals, and set new ones if that makes sense. Rethink your strategies if your goals are fine but you're not making headway in reaching them.

Your goals should take into account the underlying values of your business (such as fairness, honesty, reliability) and the purpose of your business. They shouldn't focus purely on making money, or you'll find yourself going astray pretty quickly.

When setting your goals, keep in mind that they should be

- ✔ Realistic
- ✔ Specific
- ✔ Measurable
- ✔ Time limited
- ✔ Well communicated

Focusing on your strengths

Focus on your areas of strength. Have you heard of the "80/20" rule? It says that the most significant areas of your business (whether significant for good or bad reasons) actually make up a small percentage of your business. For example, about 20 percent of your customers give you about 80 percent of your business, about 20 percent of your products bring in about 80 percent of your revenue, and about 20 percent of your employees do about 80 percent of the work. (And about 20 percent of your clients and employees give you about 80 percent of your headaches.)

So concentrate on your best customers, your top-selling products, and your best employees.

Living with change

In fact, go beyond living with change and embrace it. Change brings you opportunities as well as challenges, so keep these ideas in mind:

- ✔ Keep your eyes open at all times.
- ✔ Be ready to act on a change.
- ✔ Assume change will happen even when things look pretty stable.
- ✔ Learn from your mistakes.

Making good use of employees

You're the boss. If you hire people to work for you, make sure you help them do a good job by following these guidelines:

- ✔ Communicate clearly.
- ✔ Encourage, don't discourage, employee input.
- ✔ Run a tight ship — but not too tight.
- ✔ In fact, try not to be a control freak in general.
- ✔ Don't let the sun set on employee conflicts.

Book II
Intellectual Property

The 5th Wave — By Rich Tennant

"What'll we do with all this inventory?"

In this book . . .

Chapter 1: Introducing Intellectual Property 123

Chapter 2: Mastering Patents, Trademarks,
and Copyrights 137

Chapter 3: Profiting from Intellectual Property 181

Chapter 1

Introducing Intellectual Property

In This Chapter

▶ Discovering the IP basics

▶ Understanding the benefits of IP

▶ Knowing how and why to select a professional to guide you

▶ Checking out tips on how to manage the costs

▶ Incorporating your IP program into your business strategy

*W*elcome to the world of intellectual property, which is abbreviated IP. If you've ever created, invented, or named something that you're selling, then congratulations — you already have intellectual property. And, even better, that IP may be quite valuable. Think about the people who created the Segway scooter or wrote the first For Dummies book. Imagining cashing in on your IP, just like they did? In this chapter we introduce you to the basics of IP, and discuss how a professional can help you make the most of your IP.

Explaining Intellectual Property

So, what exactly is intellectual property? Through the years, we've encountered many definitions, including "information that has commercial value," "a proprietary product of the mind," and "things protected by patents, copyrights, and trademarks." Although each of these is true, none is quite complete. Here's our favourite definition:

Intellectual property is an intangible creation of the mind that can be legally protected. Not all intangible creations can be protected; the ones that can are considered IP.

Because it has no physical form, IP can be a confusing concept. Explaining IP is easier by providing some contrasts of what it is and isn't. Intellectual property is not

✔ The new and wondrous machine you developed in your garage, but the invention embodied in that machine

✔ The marvelously efficient cholesterol-reducing pill you see advertised on TV, but the formula and the process used in manufacturing that pill

✔ The physical portrait that an artist made of you, but the right to reproduce the image in the painting

✔ The riding mower you reluctantly start up every Saturday, but the brand name that embodies the reputation of the product and its manufacturer

That's what IP isn't. In the rest of this section, we focus on what it is.

Defining IP rights

Intellectual properties are rights, not things. The owner of the rights can enforce them against any third party. The two most fundamental rights belonging to an intellectual property owner are

✔ The right to use the property without interference from others, and

✔ The right to exclude others from using the property.

Established under a framework created by the state, IP rights vary from time to time, and country to country.

IP rights differ from other property rights, as the following examples illustrate:

✔ IP rights can be used simultaneously by multiple different users. Many people can use Windows software at once, but only one person can use a chair at one time.

✔ IP rights don't wear out. With most IP rights, the more they're used, the greater their value.

✔ IP rights, as a general rule, aren't enforced by anyone else, such as the police or the government. You must enforce them yourself, in the country where the infringement takes place.

Think of intellectual property rights as similar to a call option on a stock — you don't have to sue someone for infringing on your right, but the option is yours if you want to enforce it (see Chapter 3 of this book for more on enforcing your rights).

Types of IP

Several core categories of IP exist, with each category protecting different rights in different ways. (We tell you more about each category in Chapter 2 of this book.) You can use one or more of the following to secure your IP rights:

- ✔ **Patents:** Obtaining a patent protects your invention from outright thievery.
- ✔ **Trademarks:** Adopting a trademark as a brand name keeps it, and its reputation, all yours.
- ✔ **Copyrights:** Holding a copyright shields your artistic expression from copying.
- ✔ **Industrial designs:** Registering an industrial design protects the non-functional design features of a product.

Two other categories of rights are relevant to IP: trade secrets and contractual rights. Unlike the rights we describe above, these can be enforced only against people with whom you have a contractual relationship. So, strictly speaking, they're not property rights because they can't be enforced against third parties. But they are important to understanding IP, so we introduce them here:

- ✔ **Trade secrets:** Keeping a formula or manufacturing process confidential safeguards it against imitators. (Chapter 2 reveals trade secrets.)
- ✔ **Contractual rights:** Licensing the right to use someone else's invention.

Book II: Intellectual Property

Consult with a professional to determine the best way to use IP rights to your advantage. If you don't protect your IP assets by securing your rights, you're out of luck. Without protection, anyone can copy, steal, or change your IP asset. The bottom line is that your unprotected IP gives the bad guys a chance to fatten their bottom line.

Considering the Benefits of Protecting Your IP Rights

Developing and protecting your IP rights is important for at least three good reasons:

- ✔ Gaining an edge over your competitors
- ✔ Creating a revenue source
- ✔ Enhancing the value of your business

When properly secured, IP rights offer benefits similar to those of real property: they can be sold, licensed (see Chapter 3 of this book), or used by you or your company.

In some businesses, specific rights convey enormous value. For example, having a patent (see Chapter 2 of this book) provides pharmaceutical companies a head start of up to 20 years during which competitors can't manufacture or sell the same drug. Aspirin, Tylenol, and Advil all benefitted from this protection. Ultimately, their patents did expire, but the businesses that launched these products endure because of the power of their trademarks.

In other businesses, such as those dependent on relationships rather than patentable products, a patent may not be valuable but a client list could be priceless. IP comes into play there, too. You can protect a client list through trade secrets.

An IP professional can help you determine what IP protection your business will benefit from most.

Keeping your competitors at bay

Almost every IP right gives you a way of excluding others from doing something that interferes with or competes against a vital part of your business.

You may think IP protection isn't for you — that you can tolerate competition and still maintain a reasonable income — so instead of paying for IP protection you spend your resources on marketing or some other activity you consider more productive and lucrative. However, we can't conceive of a business that wouldn't benefit from acquiring at least some IP rights.

At a minimum, your business can capitalize on the protection afforded by a trade secret program. This can prevent, or at least deter, former associates or employees from using your manufacturing or marketing methods or stealing a customer list. At the other end of the spectrum, acquiring a patent, copyright, and/or trademark can give you a huge competitive advantage in the marketplace, and the legal clout to stifle copycats.

 Consider what your competitors can do if you decide not to protect some IP rights. Without a barbed-wire fence, your neighbours' cattle would come and drink from your well. After those strays deplete your meager water resources, your ranch isn't worth its tumbleweeds. Don't let your competitors deplete your IP resources.

Developing a new revenue source

Many businesses think that the only way to monetize their IP is to sell their own product or service directly to customers, from behind a barbed-wire fence of IP protection. However, after you acquire IP rights, you can also generate substantial income by

- ✔ Licensing someone to manufacture your protected product

- ✔ Leasing your commercial identifier to another organization to market products under your brand name

- ✔ Franchising other folks to manufacture or sell your goods and services under your guidelines

All too often these benefits are overlooked, but remember that under these arrangements you earn money any time someone makes, sells, or uses your goods or services. As we discuss in Chapter 3 of this book, IP rights can be licensed to many people (including to competitors), in many places, at the same time. In addition, generally the more you license, the more valuable your rights become.

**Book II:
Intellectual
Property**

 Licensing IP rights is like renting out real estate. You maintain title to the property (the IP assets and rights) while collecting "rent" in the form of royalties (see Chapter 3 for more on selling and licensing IP rights.)

Some business ventures limit themselves to securing solid protection for a product or technology and then licensing the IP rights to others. Say a young entrepreneur launches a new line of sporting or casual garments, enhances his product line with an attractive brand name and logo, and then licenses the brand to other manufacturers after it's established. He then gets out of the business — except, of course, for opening envelopes containing quarterly royalty cheques and laughing all the way to the bank.

Alternatively, many businesses choose to focus on their core activities and license out their name for others to use as a way to extend their brand. For example, we recently saw a Revlon hair dryer for sale, but closer inspection revealed that it wasn't manufactured or distributed by Revlon. Revlon was licensing its mark to a third party in the hair dryer business, and collecting royalties on this brand extension. When they're planned and marketed well, IP rights can be an essential part of your product line.

If you want to generate extra income but don't want to give up the business completely, you can maintain the right to continue manufacturing your product by granting non-exclusive licences. However, the royalty rate is lower than for an exclusive licence (see Chapter 3 for more).

Adding value to your business

When the time comes to sell your business, you can get more for it if your

- ✔ Products are protected by patents

- ✔ Proprietary computer programs are covered by copyrights

- ✔ Brand names are unique, motivating, and not copyable by competitors

✔ Goodwill — the reputation of the business — is transferable under the business name (that is, it's not your family name)

✔ Customer list has remained secret

Generally, you'll get the most from IP when the acquirer can put the IP to bigger or wider use than you can. But you don't have to sell your business to capitalize on its IP-enhanced value. If you need to raise more capital or borrow money, your IP can help boost your net worth, making your stock more attractive to investors and offering additional collateral security for the lender to consider.

Bringing in the Pros

If you're like most people, the idea of hiring a professional, especially one with the tag "LL.B.," sends cold shivers down your spine, puts goosebumps on your arms, and sets your heart palpitating.

Yes, attorneys are expensive, probably even more so than you think, especially if they specialize in intellectual property cases. But hang on, don't panic — we show you ways to mitigate the high cost of professional services.

First, you have to accept that you'll need a professional's services sooner or later. What counts is that you know what kind of help you need and how to get it, and that you know as much as you can about what you're getting (and not getting) from the IP process.

Getting the help you need

Let's face it, you need professional help — and no, we're not questioning your mental fitness. You need professional help when diving into IP waters because acquiring and using IP rights to protect and exploit IP assets are essentially legal procedures. And, as you know, laws are full of nuances, exceptions, and loopholes. IP laws are no exception. Although saving money by doing it yourself is tempting, we equate this approach with do-it-yourself dentistry — possible, but the results are seldom satisfactory.

An IP professional spends years studying this stuff, bringing a level of expertise to the table that others can't easily duplicate. By steering you clear of legal pitfalls, the IP professional saves you the time, grief, aggravation, and expense of having to refile a defective application or other paperwork. More important, a professional makes sure that you don't miss any critical deadlines and lose the opportunity to acquire the IP protection you need.

This book, helpful as it is, is no substitute for engaging the services of a competent IP specialist.

Identifying the right person for the job

Because IP is such a vast and complex field, many professionals limit their practice to narrow specialties, such as patent applications, trademark cases, IP litigation, or entertainment copyright cases. You need to retain the professional most qualified to handle your particular case.

**Book II:
Intellectual
Property**

Registered patent and trademark agents

Individuals who specialize in "prosecuting" IP can be accredited by the Canadian Intellectual Property Office (CIPO) as either patent or trademark agents. Prosecuting is a fancy word for "going through the application process to get the rights from the government."

Qualifying as a patent agent involves passing a rigorous four-part examination on patent application procedures. Becoming a trademark agent means either passing an exam or, if the individual is a lawyer, swearing an affidavit that the individual has practised under a trademark agent for two years.

Patent and trademark agents can be lawyers, but what matters for prosecution purposes is that they are agents, and many very good agents aren't lawyers. What agents don't do is help with enforcing IP rights (suing people), or licensing or buying and selling IP rights after they have been secured through prosecution. IP lawyers can help you with these things.

For the purposes of this book, we use the phrase IP professional to refer to an individual with the appropriate skills and accreditation to assist you with the specific task at hand.

Nonregistered IP attorneys

Certain well-intentioned business and corporate lawyers won't hesitate to tackle IP matters (other than patent applications) — which indeed they are authorized to do but not necessarily competent to handle. Many are very knowledgeable and do their best, but may not be current in the latest developments in IP law.

Be especially careful if you approach someone who's not a specialist in the particular area of IP that's relevant to your current needs, whether it's patents, trademarks, or copyrights; prosecution; enforcement; or licensing. Ask lots of questions about the IP professional's competence and experience in dealing with issues like yours — something you should do whenever consulting a lawyer.

Keeping it secret

You may worry that consulting an IP professional jeopardizes the secrecy of your creation, but rest assured that the IP professional has a fiduciary duty to retain your confidences, and this duty is of *indefinite duration* (it never expires). If your IP professional spills the beans, in addition to being in breach of duty to you, the IP professionals can be in very serious trouble with the profession's licensing body (for instance, the provincial Law Society). For this reason, the fiduciary duty is usually considered "longer and stronger" than any contractual duty of nondisclosure.

In Canada, communications with lawyers are privileged, but communications with patent and trademark agents are not. Privileged communications are ones that you can't be compelled to reveal to your opponent in litigation.

 If you want to discuss something sensitive, such as whether your business infringes on someone else's IP, make sure you do it with an IP professional who is a lawyer and make sure you keep the communication private. If you hold a conversation in a crowded restaurant, or in a room with your accountant, you may be deemed to have waived privilege.

Finding an IP professional

The best and safest way to find a competent IP professional is by getting a referral from someone who has used that professional's services and been satisfied. You do have some other options, though (listed here in order of our preference):

- ✔ Ask for a referral from an attorney you know and trust.

- ✔ Consult an attorney referral service, such as your local Bar Association.

- ✔ Check the Canadian Intellectual Property Office's list of agents in your area, available online at www.cipo.ic.gc.ca.

- ✔ Sift through listings of IP professionals in the phone book under Intellectual Property Law, Patent Attorneys or Patent Lawyers, Patents or Patent Searches, and Trademarks and Copyrights.

Qualifying an IP professional

To ensure the person you hire is right for the job, interview several candidates and ask some hard questions before you make your final decision.

Lawyers and agents will gladly supply you with references and samples of their work and answer these questions:

- ✔ What is your technical background?
- ✔ How long have you been practising in this field?
- ✔ Who else, besides you, will be working on my case?

When interviewing patent agents, ask these questions:

- ✔ Are you familiar with my area of technology?
- ✔ Have you assisted clients in obtaining patents related to my invention?
- ✔ How many patent applications have you handled?
- ✔ How many patents have you obtained?

Ask trademark agents these questions:

- ✔ How many applications have you handled?
- ✔ Do you have experience dealing with Examiner's Reports?
- ✔ Have you dealt with oppositions?

When interviewing licensing lawyers, be sure to ask the following:

- ✔ Do you draft licences and other IP contracts?
- ✔ Have you dealt with this industry?
- ✔ Do you issue infringement or non-infringement opinions?

Ask a prospective litigation lawyer these questions:

- ✔ Have you conducted cases in similar areas?
- ✔ Have you conducted trials?
- ✔ What is your approach to mediation?
- ✔ How do you resolve cases?

Retaining an IP professional

When you're ready to retain or hire an IP professional, insist on an engagement contract or retainer agreement that clearly spells out all the services, terms, and conditions of your professional relationship.

Here is a partial checklist of the most important things to include:

- ✔ What the IP professional will do for you
- ✔ Which professional in the firm will handle your case
- ✔ How much and when you have to pay for the services
- ✔ What additional costs and fees you may encounter
- ✔ How you can terminate the agreement and hire another professional
- ✔ Whom the IP professional will represent: you, your associate or partner, your company, or the man in the moon

This last point is particularly important. You may ask your IP professional to do something that isn't beneficial to your associate or your company. An eventual conflict of interest that wasn't properly anticipated can lead to, at best, additional time and expense and, at worst, a nasty legal fight.

Working with foreign IP professionals

You must have a representative in every foreign jurisdiction in which you file a patent application, and often for every application to register a mark. Most patent attorneys and agents maintain working relationships with IP professionals in industrialized foreign countries.

In all cases, you need to pay the foreign IP professionals' fees and government charges. Usually, neither you nor your attorney has any control over these costs, but always ask for a rough estimate when you file overseas. Because foreign costs tend to be substantially higher, don't forget to take those expenses into account when preparing your IP budget and laying out your IP protection strategy. (For more about costs, check out the next section.)

Paying the Piper

Legal services are expensive and eat up the lion's share of the money you spend to protect your intellectual property. We give it to you straight here (you may want to sit down), but don't panic — we also give you some advice on keeping your IP protection expenses within your budget.

Giving up a piece of the action

Fledgling entrepreneurs are often short of cash and eager to offer their IP professional a part of their business, technology, or invention as payment for services. If you're tempted to do so, think about a few things first:

✔ If the IP professional acquires shares, as part owner of your company or its assets the IP professional may have some say about how the business is run. Have a clear, written understanding about these matters to prevent a costly dispute.

✔ You don't yet know what your business or IP is worth, so you may be giving up too much for the services you're trying to secure. Later, you may find yourself without enough remaining assets or ownership of the business to obtain the capital and resources you need. Don't sell yourself short; make sure to evaluate the services and IP properly, and make a fair tradeoff.

✔ A part-of-the-action fee arrangement is different from ownership of shares of a company; you may be able to pay your agent a royalty from revenue. But, as with any commercial arrangement, get the entire financial arrangement in writing and get an opinion from a business lawyer.

✔ Giving a piece of your invention or company to someone must be done in a legal business framework. As with any business relationship, ensure you clearly document the rights and responsibilities of each party. Any payments must comply with applicable laws, including income tax and securities laws. Remember, IP professionals are not business or securities lawyers, and deals of this nature require review by a professional with relevant experience.

**Book II:
Intellectual
Property**

Assessing the costs

Here's the skinny on some hefty prices. Don't be surprised if your IP specialist quotes you hourly rates between $200 and $500. Keep in mind that fees and costs, including government charges, often change and may not be the same everywhere.

Despite the temptation to save money, please remember our earlier advice about not flexing your DIY muscles. Our experience tells us not to rely on what the client has done on his or her own. An IP pro would rather start from scratch than try to unravel the mangled mess of an inadequate patent application.

You can pay for IP professional services in one of three common ways:

- An hourly fee
- A fixed amount for the whole job
- A combination of the two

If you agree to an hourly fee, request a complete estimate of all the costs over the life of the project, such as filing fees, copying and mailing costs, foreign agent charges, and maintenance fees. Maintenance fees, also called annuities, are paid to patenting authorities during the life of a patent. In some countries, the annuities are due from the date of filing the application. Be prepared for an estimate having a wide range of costs, because you can't predict what will happen over the life of the project.

If you're going to pay a fixed fee, ask about other expenses that may not be included, such as government charges, drawing costs, and copying charges. In all cases, clarify how and when you must make the payments.

Managing the expenses

Informing yourself about IP (by reading this book, for instance) and being organized, efficient, and clear about your goals and expectations will dramatically improve the quality of the service you receive from your IP professional, while also keeping costs down.

Your IP professional can help you properly allocate your resources and minimize IP-related expenses. The following is a short list of what your IP professional can do for you:

- Give you short-term and long-term estimates of all fees and costs.
- Show you how to strategically spread the protective measures over a number of years so you don't have to blow the entire budget all at once, and give you time to figure out whether your product really is as good as the famous Tea Kettle whiskey of yesteryear.
- Devise the least expensive approach for protecting your intellectual property — such as applying for a copyright, configuration mark, or design patent application instead of a more expensive patent, or by implementing a trade-secret protection program using confidentiality agreements and other procedures.
- Tailor your IP protection program to suit your basic needs.
- Give you some peace of mind and a bill for her services — not necessarily in that order.

Coordinating with Other Professionals

Don't forget to keep your other advisers informed about your IP program:

✔ Keep your business or corporate attorney aware of all your IP activities. Give the attorney copies of all your major correspondence with IP
professionals. Your patents and marks may be put to good use in some
distributorship and representative agency agreements.

✔ Inform your CA, comptroller, and other bean counters about your IP
expenses. Acquiring a patent or developing a trade secret can have
important tax implications, and you don't want to miss lucrative amortization or depreciation deductions. Proceeds from the sale of licensing
of an invention may benefit from special taxation rules, and your technological acquisitions and research program may qualify for tax credits.

✔ Make your PR and advertising agency fully aware of the marks you
acquire and register. Those marks can be effectively put to work in your
promotional campaigns. Your advertising and marketing people can play
an important role in selecting your commercial identifiers.

**Book II:
Intellectual
Property**

Chapter 2

Mastering Patents, Trademarks, and Copyrights

In This Chapter

▶ Understanding the purpose of patents

▶ Determining what rights you have to your invention

▶ Exploring international patents

▶ Touring the world of trademarks

▶ Taking the steps of trademarking

▶ Enforcing your trademark

▶ Checking out copyright

▶ Knowing how copyright works

▶ Avoiding copyright infringement

▶ Protecting your industrial design assets

▶ Investigating IP exceptions and alternatives

*M*ost business people use the terms patent, trademark, copyright without fully knowing the significance of these words to their business. As a result some businesses worry too much about protecting things that don't need or can't be protected. Still others miss important opportunities to protect their innovations or derive revenues from them. If you think you may fall into either category, this chapter is for you!

Presenting Patents

A patent is perhaps the best-known IP right, but it also happens to be the most misunderstood. In this section, we untangle for you — one step at a time — the knotty complexity of patents so that you have no doubts about what a patent is and whether you can get one.

Defining patents

A patent is a *temporary*, limited legal right granted to an inventor by a government to prevent others from manufacturing, selling, or using his invention. It's a loaded definition. Read it again, focusing on the most important parts:

- ✔ **Temporary:** Patents last for 20 years, not forever.

- ✔ **Limited:** The right associated with a patent isn't absolute, but very specifically limited. It's also subject to the right of any other person who happens to own a dominant patent related to the same subject matter.

- ✔ **Right . . . to prevent:** A patent allows its owner to go to court and ask a judge to stop someone from doing something. But remember, what's good for the goose is good for the gander. An inventor isn't immune from a superior right to prevent held by another patent owner, as illustrated in the "Understanding your rights and limits as a patent owner" section in this chapter.

- ✔ **By a government:** Patents are granted country by country. If you patent an invention in only one country, then the invention is free for use in most of the world. Canada is a member of two important treaties, the Paris Convention and the Patent Cooperation Treaty, which make filing patents in foreign countries easier.

Patenting your invention doesn't give you the right to do anything with the invention. Instead, think of the patent as veto power over someone else trying to do something with your invention. A patent allows the owner to stop others from using, manufacturing, selling, licensing, or otherwise exploiting the specifically covered invention. And that may require going to court and paying large legal fees if the infringer isn't deterred by your threat of litigation.

Investigating what your patent can do for your country

The Canadian Intellectual Property Office (CIPO) controls Canada's patent system. Because it gives one person sole control of a possibly important technological application, the patent system is a limited exception to the principles of free competition that underline our body of laws. Yet, in a roundabout way, patents still promote competition among all citizens. A patent gives the inventor incentive to disclose his or her invention, which contributes to general scientific and technological knowledge.

A patent applicant publishes the nuts and bolts of the invention, giving the public knowledge of the invention very early on — as soon as 18 months from the earliest filing date. In return, the owner gets a 20-year head start in exploiting it. When the patent expires, the owner can no longer prevent anyone from using the invention or manufacturing and selling anything that falls within that previously taboo area of technology — free competition reigns again, and the country is richer for the technology.

Discovering what your patent can do for you

A patent can be a powerful legal tool that gives you, as an inventor, business-person, or entrepreneur, the sole right to your technology and a competitive edge in the market.

After your patent is granted, you can go into business yourself to practise the invention, free of competition in respect to what you have patented. You can also license your patent rights to someone else. (A *licence* is a lease that allows another party to exploit your invention. In most cases, it's just a promise by the patent owner not to sue the holder of the licence.) If you've invented something really valuable, potential licensees will be lining up for the opportunity to pay you handsome royalties for the right to profit by your invention. Or you can *assign* (sell) the patent outright for a bundle, giving the new owner the patent's exclusive benefits for the remaining term of the patent.

You don't have to register your patent before going into business. If you prefer, you can start a business armed only with your new idea (so long as it doesn't infringe on someone else's IP rights). You'll just be subject to potential competition without the protection of a patent.

Understanding your rights and limits as a patent owner

Under your patent, you can sue anyone who manufactures, sells, markets, or even uses the invention without your permission. Remember, however, that receiving your patent does *not* give you the right to make or sell your product. Your product may still infringe someone else's patent, and you will have to deal with that problem separately.

Here's an example. Say that Jane has a patent covering a bicycle that happens to have upright handlebars, but Jane's patent is on a bicycle without reference to the type of handlebars. By developing new under-slung handlebars, you've made it more efficient as a racing bike and have been granted a patent covering the improvement. Jane wants to modify her bike according to your invention, but can't do so without your permission. You, on the other hand, can't make or sell the improved bike without her permission (Jane's patent covers all bikes). The solution is to get together and strike a deal. Here are your options:

- ✔ One of you gives the other exclusive permission to use both inventions, paying a fee for such use to the one who withdraws.
- ✔ Each of you agrees not to sue the other and goes into business using the other's invention without exchanging money.
- ✔ Some other combination of terms on which you can both agree.

Considering the Pros and Cons of Patents

So you think you have a patentable invention. Just remember that applying for a patent is a long, expensive, and uncertain undertaking. We set out some of the advantages and disadvantages of patents, to help you consider whether pursuing a patent is right for you.

Here are the advantages a patent offers:

- ✔ **Broad scope of protection:** Properly drafted by an IP professional, your patent can extend to other ideas and uses beyond your original one. Frequently, you'll find that your invention has broader applications than you first realized.

  Consider that lasers were originally invented for scientific research. The original creators never imagined lasers would become so widespread they'd be used to scan a carton of eggs at the grocery store.

- ✔ **Powerful anti-competition tool:** Businesspeople are wary of infringing patents because of high litigation costs and significant damages awards.

- ✔ **Increase in the value of your business:** A patent portfolio is a must if you want to raise capital.

Not to be ignored, the disadvantages of a patent are the following:

- ✔ **High costs:** The costs of patenting are high and difficult to predict. Patenting is a continuous process often requiring multiple applications to cover all aspects of the invention and subsequent improvements. And that's without even thinking about enforcing your patent against an infringer.

A very rough guesstimate of costs is $10,000 to $25,000 to draft and prosecute the application in the first country, and $5,000 to $10,000 for each additional country.

✔ **Your secret is out:** You must bare it all in your application, making it easy for others to use your invention as soon as the patent expires or to design around the manner you have claimed in your application.

✔ **Long wait for (relatively) short-lived protection:** The protection lasts, at most, 20 years from your earliest application filing date, but patent offices can take three, four, and even more years to grant a patent.

The first patents for compact fluorescent light bulbs were filed in the early 1970s, but not many were sold until after 2000, when those patents had expired. Of course, later patents on improvements may still be valid or pending.

Testing Patentability — 1, 2, 3

To qualify as patentable, a patent application not only must be drafted correctly, but the law also requires the invention to pass through a three-pronged *patentability test:*

✔ **Utility:** Practical usefulness — it needs to have a useful function.

✔ **Novelty:** Innovativeness — it's gotta be new.

✔ **Non-obviousness:** Something that isn't immediately apparent to a knowledgeable but uninventive person.

In the following sections, we explore each hurdle the invention must clear patent.

Making yourself useful

The *utility test* determines whether your invention has any use in the real world. This is an easy one. As long as you can dream up some kind of application for your invention, you won't have any problem passing the utility test. Proving before you apply that your invention actually works satisfactorily is a wise move — if it doesn't, your application is invalid. Furthermore, when applying you must include a complete description of how to make your invention work or your patent application will fail.

Developing a novel approach

The *novelty test* confirms that you've developed an original way to solve a problem. Your invention will be compared to everything that has already been created, disclosed, or proposed anywhere in the world, which is called the *prior art*. Each claim that you have made in your patent will be denied if a prior art device, machine, or process includes *all* the basic components of that claim. As a result, claims are often drafted like Russian nesting dolls, starting with a very broad claim and successively narrowing with more specific claims.

The novelty requirements vary from country to country. In Canada, the rule is absolute novelty, with a 12-month grace period to file. This means that no one in the world, with the possible exception of you, can have disclosed the invention before you file your patent application, and that you can file a patent claim up to 12 months after you first publicly disclose the invention.

The United States has a *first-to-invent* system, with a 12-month grace period. (In the first-to-invent system, if two inventors file competing patent applications for an invention, the patent goes to the first to make the invention, not the first to file the patent.) Many other countries have an absolute novelty requirement, and are first-to-file jurisdictions with no 12-month grace period.

Be careful if you want to apply for international patent rights. In many countries you must file a patent application somewhere in the world *before* you make any public disclosure of your invention (see the "Patenting Internationally" section later in this chapter).

A key component of the novelty test is the disclosure of the invention. The rules for what constitutes disclosure differ from country to country, especially if the invention isn't obvious from just looking at your product. In Canada, you aren't considered to have disclosed your invention unless the observer can understand it, but this isn't the case in the United States, where even casually showing your prototype to your neighbour may constitute disclosure.

Generally, you don't lose the patent rights to your invention when you disclose it to someone who owes you a duty to retain the invention in confidence. This includes your lawyer and patent agent (who both owe a fiduciary obligation of confidentiality, which is stronger and longer than any contract) and others who have signed nondisclosure agreements with you. However, note that if someone breaches an obligation of confidence and discloses your invention, your patent rights against the world may be lost, and all you'll be left with is a claim for damages against the discloser.

Avoiding the obvious

To pass the non-obviousness test, the difference between your invention and the prior art must not be obvious to a person with ordinary skill in the relevant field. The problem with this test is defining this mythical person with ordinary skill in your field, who knows everything but isn't inventive. For example, this person isn't a typical weekend do-it-yourselfer or a Nobel Prize winner, but an uninventive technician who magically knows, or has access to, all prior art information in the field of the invention.

Your invention probably isn't obvious if it provides a solution to a long-standing problem in an offbeat way or, as the courts like to put it, by teaching away from the prior art.

**Book II:
Intellectual
Property**

Assessing Your Rights

The first step in attempting to protect an invention or other technological breakthrough is determining what rights you have to it. Be prepared for some surprises.

Defining the invention in writing

At first glance, preparing a written description of your invention may seem like a childish exercise — but it's what the pros do to sharpen their understanding of the invention, so follow their lead. Go over your notes, drawings, and models and write down an accurate description of what's new about your invention. Be as concise as possible — 15 lines at the most. Keep your focus on what makes the invention new and unique. Help yourself by sketching the essential aspects of your invention with cross-reference numbers that refer back to the written description.

Focus on describing the nuts and bolts of the invention — how it's made and how it operates, rather than its advantages and commercial applications. Keep in mind that you're not drafting a brochure or technical paper; you're drafting a definition that will become the cornerstone of your patent application. So make sure it's technically accurate and complete. This description is also exactly what a professional needs to conduct your novelty search (see "Searching and surfing" in this chapter).

Qualifying the invention

Determining whether your invention qualifies for a patent is as easy as apply-ing the three-part patentability test and reviewing the checklist of patentabil-ity criteria. Check out "Testing patentability — 1, 2, 3" for details.

If your innovation ticks all the boxes favourably, then you're in good shape; otherwise, it's back to the drawing board.

Coming up with an inventor

Be brutally honest in assessing whether you alone conceived the invention, or whether someone else made suggestions or contributions to the concept. Did anyone else refine or improve the device when you built the prototype or model? Maybe a co-worker or your 10-year-old whiz kid helped out.

Regardless of the circumstance, make sure you acknowledge any helpful out-side contribution now. Any contributor may have rights equal to yours, and therefore must (by law) be listed as a co-inventor on your application.

If you fail to name co-inventors on your patent application you run the risk, especially in the United States, of having your patent invalidated.

Figuring Out Ownership

Determining ownership of a patent is related to, but still separate from, inventorship. Patent rights can be bought and sold, both before and after a patent is granted, so often the owner is different from the inventor. The first owner of the patent is named as the applicant on the patent application, and the inventors are named separately. Basically, the inventor owns the rights in an invention if no other circumstances exist. If you have co-inventors, then you have co-owners. If you were employed to create the invention with the understanding that the rights would belong to your employer or customer, then the employer or customer is entitled to own the rights.

Having clear paperwork that establishes ownership and any other rights and obligations in relation to a patent is crucial. Your IP professional can draft an invention and patent transfer agreement for your particular circumstances. The document will be valid regardless of whether it's registered with the Patent Office. However, registering it while your application is pending is wise, because then the patent will issue in your name only.

If you're an employer, take care that your employees don't end up patenting concepts you'd like to use yourself. See an IP professional, generally a lawyer, for guidance, and make sure to consider the following:

- You can tailor your employment intake forms to include invention-assignment clauses. With these agreements, even an invention outside of your technological field that's made entirely at home with the employee's own resources can be captured by the boss.

- All contracts signed with independent entities that are going to develop products for your company should address the issue of ownership of any resulting inventions. If you don't do this, the contractor will own the patent rights. The terms of any contract should address ownership expressly, as well as the terms of any cross-licences, if one of the parties insists.

- If the invention was developed as part of a university project or under a government grant, the government may be due a piece of the action. Accordingly, you should carefully explore the role of government at the outset.

Addressing ownership issues early in the game lessens the likelihood that you'll run into problems later. When your patent is a success, you may find your consultant or former employee will claim a piece of the action.

**Book II:
Intellectual
Property**

Applying for Patent Rights

Absolute novelty is a big deal around the world, and the sooner you file a patent application the better, because this establishes your priority date. The *priority date* is the earlier of either the date that you first file a patent application, or the date when you disclose your invention. Your priority date is important for

- Proving you've filed a patent application in time,

- Establishing the relative priorities between competing applications that disclose the same invention, and

- Determining numerous different international deadlines for filing and paying fees that you must meet in the patent application process.

Two schools of thought exist on the proper approach to applying for patent registration: The first advocates filing as quickly as possible and then conducting a search for prior art; the second prefers conducting a thorough search and then filing.

Although both approaches have pros and cons, we believe that the best approach is a hybrid, which we outline here:

1. File a provisional patent application as quickly as possible, with or without a prior search.

2. Conduct a search if you haven't done so already. (The "Searching and surfing" section in this chapter provides more details on the prior art search.)

3. File a complete patent application before the first anniversary of your priority date.

Provisional applications

Canadian patents are awarded on a *first-to-file* basis, which means that submitting your application as early as possible is essential. CIPO allows you 12 months from your initial application date to revise your application. We encourage you to file a *provisional patent application* as soon as you can. This quick and dirty application essentially marks your spot in line and allows you to preserve your patent rights from the earliest possible filing date. You can use the 12-month window to polish your final specification.

Be aware, however, that real limits to the quality of your rights exist under a provisional patent application. For example, in Canada, failing to amend the application within the first 12 months means that your provisional application will proceed to examination as filed, and will likely lead to weak or narrow rights; in the United States, it leads to your application expiring.

Provisional patent applications are gaining popularity. You can expect to pay approximately $2,500 to $5,000 for yours. Having your IP professional conduct a search before you file your patent application will help to improve the quality of the application and focus the claims, but conducting one before filing a provisional application is not necessary.

Searching and surfing

Because novelty is hugely important, searches of prior art are a key component of the patent system. Performing a prefiling search before you apply for registration isn't mandatory, but it's certainly prudent. By reviewing existing patents, technical books, and other relevant publications, you can save yourself a lot of money and potential embarrassment. And your search results will help you and your IP professional submit a better (and cheaper) application.

We strongly recommend that you put some time and energy into conducting searches by yourself. This will help you gain an understanding of the relevant prior art, patenting and the patent system generally, and how you can use other people's IP to your advantage. The best place to begin your search is at the U.S. Patent Office website (www.uspto.gov). Both the tools and records found at the USPTO site are more extensive than those accessible at the CIPO website (www.cipo.ic.gc.ca). Don't worry, though: Both sites are user friendly.

Searching on both sites is keyword based, which sounds good at first but often yields spotty results. You see, unfortunately most patents aren't written by normal people. Eccentric IP professionals write them, so instead of describing a spring as . . . well . . . a *spring*, these wacky characters are more likely to call it a *resilient biasing member*. Make sure to include a lot of synonyms in your keyword search (keep a thesaurus handy). And remember, you're not looking for a prior patent showing every detail of your invention, but something that is similar or that suggests one of its main features.

**Book II:
Intellectual
Property**

Although you should conduct a preliminary search, relying solely on the results of your DIY searching is a bad idea. We strongly recommend using qualified IP professionals to

- ✔ Conduct fulsome searches before you file a full patent specification,

- ✔ Interpret the results of the search, and

- ✔ Correlate the results with your invention.

A reasonable estimate of the cost of a properly conducted prior art search is $1,500 to $3,000, which includes a modest amount of interpretation and analysis.

Our preferred approach is to conduct a search either immediately prior to, or — when time is tight — immediately after, filing a provisional patent application. The search may confirm that your invention isn't patentable, and save you a lot of grief. Often, the information you gain from the search will substantially improve the quality and focus of the application that you file. In fact, sometimes a search conducted immediately after a provisional application discloses enough information that filing another provisional application is worthwhile.

Your prefiling search must look at everything you disclose, teach, or suggest in your claim. And anything that even partially anticipates your invention is a problem.

Proceeding with the patent application

Applying for a patent is a complex process, and if you take our advice you'll let your IP professional guide you through most of it. You're not off the hook, though; after all, no one knows your invention better than you, so you should be an active co-participant in preparing the application.

Being at the front of the line

The CIPO employs a first-to-file priority system to deal with competing applications. If someone else files for the same invention before you do, you're out of the game. Apply for a patent as soon as possible. Indeed, avoid waiting until you work out all the minute details; the CIPO allows you an entire year after your initial filing date to upgrade and consolidate all your ideas into a single, final application, so long as you didn't publish your idea before the initial filing date. Starting with a provisional patent application in the United States gives you the same benefit there.

Filing early is particularly important if you believe that others are working on the same area of technology. Your application filing can serve as a spoiler that prevents theirs from advancing.

Drafting the document

Completing a patent specification (application) involves providing a great deal of detailed information about your invention. Your IP professional can guide you in respect to most of the details, including the following:

- **Title:** This'll be short and to the point, and should relate to the article that incorporates the invention.

- **Field of invention:** Lists the area of technology that applies to your invention (used for indexing purposes).

- **Background of invention:** Sets the stage for your genius by describing the problem your invention overcomes.

- **Summary of invention:** Here's where you get to brag about your achievement, and explain your advance over what others have done.

- **Summary of drawings/figures:** Briefly outlines any attachments that facilitate the understanding of your invention.

- **Description of preferred embodiments:** Provides one or more examples of the best ways to practise your invention.

- **Abstract:** Summarizes what your invention is all about.

- **Drawings or figures:** These complement and support your description of the preferred embodiments.

- **Claims:** This section defines your rights under the patent. (See more in "Defining your claim" next.)

Focus on assisting your patent professional with the three most important areas of the application — creating your claim, explaining your invention, and providing a detailed description.

Defining your claim

As the inventor, you (with the guidance of your IP professional) are responsible for defining your exclusive rights. A *claim* defines the exclusive rights granted to a patent owner. Completing your claim involves creating a numbered list of features that collectively specify your contribution to humanity. Functioning as a sort of checklist for infringement, the claim identifies the presence of your invention and specifies what you want to claim as your exclusive rights.

Keep it short and sweet. When drafting your application, you're allowed to make as many claims as you like; however, we recommend you make some of these claims as concise as possible. A claim defines what others can't do, and you can pursue only those infringers who violate every feature listed in a claim. The shorter the claim, the broader the coverage. Don't go any further until you have fully grasped this concept. Please, repeat after us:

> Short claim = more coverage = broad patent
>
> Long claim = less coverage = narrow patent

Keep in mind that your patent coverage may be broader or narrower than you anticipate. Determining what a patent actually covers requires a complex, expert analysis by your IP professional.

Summarizing your invention

Explain what's new and special about your invention. Maintain focus on your specific innovation; don't describe the entire object if you adapted only a portion of it.

Describing your invention

Provide a detailed description of your invention, including figures or drawings whenever they'll be helpful.

Prosecuting the patent application

After you've applied for a patent, you begin the process of prosecuting the patent application. *Prosecution* may sound scary, but it simply means following through on your application.

In Canada, filing a Declaration of Entitlement within three months of submitting your application is one of the first steps in prosecuting the application.

This process establishes the claim of the applicant, as owner, to the patent application. Then, assuming you've completed your application correctly, little will happen for a number of years unless you press the action (you know — push the examiner forward rather than waiting patiently for your turn).

If you've filed in Canada, then on the second anniversary of your filing date you must begin to pay annual maintenance fees, and you'll have to keep paying them yearly during the remaining 20 years that your patent is active. Other countries also require maintenance fees. In the United States, the fees are due less frequently but are in larger amounts.

You must request an examination within five years of filing your application in Canada. Given the current number of pending applications, you'll wait about two years for the results of your examination. Taking advantage of the five-year window is often a good idea. You likely have applications pending in other jurisdictions, particularly the United States. You and your patent agent will learn a great deal from your experiences with these other patent offices. You can use this knowledge to amend your Canadian claims to conform with claims that have been approved by foreign offices. Generally, if you inform the examiner of foreign approvals, you'll have an easier time obtaining Canadian approval.

During the examination process, the examiner issues a Patent Office Search Report and an Examiner's Report (commonly known as the *office action*) containing objections and commentaries from the patent examiner. The office action advises you what's required for your patent to be granted. Often, some objections from the examiner will be simple technical concerns as to general wording in the patent specification. Other objections will be directed to the claims with reference to the prior art, accompanied by a requirement that the claims be made more specific. Every applicant also has an opportunity to amend his application to make grammatical corrections to the story and to refine the scope of the claims.

In Canada, this procedure of responding to the examiner's objections frequently goes through two or three cycles, so be patient. Remember, in principle you have to go through the same examination process in each country where you have filed a patent application, so develop a streamlined and efficient response process.

If you overcome all of the examiner's objections, your application will be allowed; if you can't overcome them all, your application will be rejected. In Canada, for a successful application you'll have six months to pay the final government fee and to record any assignments that you want in place at the time the Canadian patent is issued. The patent will be issued in the name of the assignee on record at the time of issue.

Patenting Internationally

Filing international patent applications is important for Canadians. It's a big world, and for many products Canada and the United States represent only a small portion of the potential market. Protecting your rights internationally is vital. You may choose to patent in countries where you expect to sell your product, in countries where you think you have a prospect of licensing your patent rights, or in countries where infringement is common.

Pursuing patents in the United States

Book II:
Intellectual
Property

Consider applying for protection in the United States, because it's a major market for many Canadian businesses. The U.S. economy is more than 10 times larger than ours, and if you do business there your U.S. patent could be correspondingly more valuable than your Canadian one.

Canadians often choose to file their U.S. patent application prior to filing in Canada, and as a result many Canadian patent agents are also licensed to practise before the USPTO and can assist Canadians by filing and prosecuting applications there. Your IP professional will guide you through the U.S. patent process, but we'd like to point out one of the key differences between Canadian and U.S. patent law so you can prepare accordingly:

United States patent law reserves patents for the first inventor. To preserve U.S. rights in the event of a conflict with another applicant, it's essential that you make records of your invention(s) as you proceed. (We use the expression *invention(s)* because you'll be surprised at how the nature of the invention grows over time.)

As you develop your product or process, take copious notes and plenty of illustrative sketches, preferably in a bound notebook with numbered pages — after all, that's what Edison did. Use a pen, not a pencil, and don't erase your mistakes, cross them out. Once in a while, ask a trusted relative or friend to review your notes and date and sign the last written page, stating that on the specified date she or he read the notes and understood the invention. This will serve you well if you have to defend against potential interference in respect to your U.S. application.

Because Canada is a first-to-file country, keeping these kinds of records isn't necessary to obtain a Canadian patent. Effectively, the law here treats an invention as not yet invented until an application has been filed at the Canadian Patent Office, or at some other Patent Office in the world from which priority is claimed. However, be aware that if your Canadian patent ever goes into litigation, your opponent will want to know the history of the idea's development. They'll investigate every nook and cranny in the hope that they might discover you're not the true inventor of the idea — because that would invalidate your Canadian patent. Therefore, keeping good records that are up to the U.S. standard is in your best interest, whether or not you file there.

Going global

Patenting is expensive, but protecting your rights is essential if you do business globally. Patent applications must be filed in each country where you want protection, and your costs increase with each application filed. So, determining where to file is one of the most vexing capital allocation decisions the management of an innovative company can face.

As you try to decide whether or not to apply for a patent in Lower Slobovia, ask yourself two key questions:

- ✔ Will the patent make a difference to how much revenue we can generate in Lower Slobovia?
- ✔ Will we (or a licensee) have the money and desire to enforce the patent in Lower Slobovia?

If Lower Slobovia is a small market, or has a weak judicial system, you might decide to spend your IP resources elsewhere. Also, don't feel that you have to file a patent in a country where you fear infringers may create knock-offs of your products. If the real market for those products is elsewhere, then you should pursue patent protection where the products will be sold, not where they're created.

Benefitting from treaties

Canada is a member of two treaties that make it easier for you to apply for international patents: the Paris Convention of 1883 and the Patent Cooperation Treaty. The Paris Convention allows member countries from around the world to accept patent applications from citizens of other member countries. With close to 200 members, this opens up a world of possibilities. The Patent Cooperation Treaty (PCT) doesn't produce patents, but rather is a central processing system you can use during an interim stage of the patent application process. Rather than applying to many different countries, you can initially make a single filing in the PCT system, which reserves your right to file that application in any member nation.

As a Canadian, you can enter the PCT when you submit your original patent application, or just before the end of the priority year, claiming the benefit of your first priority filing date. Either way, you must exit from the PCT system by filing your patent applications in the desired foreign countries within 30 (or 31) months of the earliest priority date associated with your filing (meaning you can't use the PCT as an indefinite placeholder).

Filing a single PCT application allows you to postpone filing overseas while still retaining a priority date from your initial PCT application — key in any first-to-file jurisdictions. PCT applications also provide a number of other benefits:

- ✔ **Receiving a well-done international search report as of 16 months from your earliest priority date.** (Actually, this can take a little longer in countries with large backlogs, such as the United States.)

- ✔ **Having an opportunity to amend your claims within two months of receiving the international search report.** This means you can make one amendment that will count for all destination countries. Imagine the time and financial costs you'll incur if you file separately and have to amend multiple applications.

- ✔ **Obtaining a preliminary examination.** For an extra fee, a PCT examiner will produce a Preliminary Examination Report. The report is nonbinding in any of the destination countries, but it provides you, and your investors, with feedback about your prospects for obtaining patent protection. The deadline for filing for Preliminary Examination is month 22 from your priority date. You are allowed to amend both the claims and the disclosure (to correct grammatical errors) during Preliminary Examination.

- ✔ **Retaining the right to operate in English or French while you're within the PCT system.** This means that if your Preliminary Examination reveals your chances of obtaining a patent are slim and you decide not to go ahead, you've saved yourself the cost of translating your patent application (which can be very expensive). If you do decide to file in a particular country, you must file in its native language.

  Your application will be published in printed form and then distributed around the world as of 18 months from your earliest priority date. It will also be available over the Internet at the PCT website, `www.wipo.int/pctdb/en`. You may be concerned that publication of your application will end its secrecy. However, applications filed in most countries around the world are now published as of 18 months from the earliest priority date, so the PCT system is no different. If you wish to preserve your first priority date, you'll have to accept that your PCT application is going to be published.

✔ **Using the PCT to defer your patent application while maintaining your priority date allows you to keep your rights alive and your options open, while delaying expenditures as much as possible.** Additionally, your knowledge of both your invention and the potential market for your product will improve over time, so deferral allows you to submit a better application.

Taking advantage of the PCT process is a complex but worthwhile endeavour that's best left to the pros. Consult an IP professional about your situation.

Looking at the Services of a Patent Professional

Patent professionals don't simply file patents for new inventions — they also use their relevant expertise to provide different *IP opinions*, including the following:

✔ **Infringement opinion:** If you're concerned about infringing on someone else's turf by selling your own thingamajigs, or if you're concerned that someone else is infringing your patent, ask an IP professional to provide an infringement opinion.

Determining whether you're infringing someone else's patent involves predicting what invention you might be infringing upon — which is no easy task. Your IP professional will search all unexpired patents and pending applications for any claims that potentially overlap with your product or process. If this infringement search locates a patent with an independent claim that you appear to be infringing upon, you must either change your product or challenge the validity of the patent. Similarly, you require an infringement opinion before suing anyone for infringement of your own patent.

✔ **Validity analysis:** If you're accused of violating a patent, you may be able to defend yourself by disputing the *validity* — the legal soundness — of the patent. Your IP professional scrutinizes the patent that you're violating, and its application, for errors, but validity searches mainly focus on the role of the examiner — did the examiner do a good job? If your IP professional can challenge the validity of the patent, then you may be in luck. For instance, perhaps prior art exists that predates the patent in question, which invalidates the patent.

If you can't invalidate the patent, you may need to change the configuration of your product or approach the patent owner for a licence.

✔ **Freedom-to-operate analysis:** Your IP professional attempts to establish that you can conduct your business as you intend to, without infringing anyone else's patent rights. This is an expensive and time-consuming analysis and, unfortunately, conclusively proving that you're free to operate is impossible, so this analysis can only reduce your risk, not eliminate it.

But remember, just because something's difficult or expensive doesn't mean it's not worth doing. Research In Motion encountered difficulty with NTP when the BlackBerry e-mail software inadvertently infringed on a pre-existing patent belonging to NTP. A freedom-to-operate analysis might have disclosed the existing NTP patent and helped prevent costly litigation.

✔ **State-of-the-art search:** Inventor-initiated research and development programs often use these searches to gain expertise in a technical field. Your IP professional conducts very detailed and technical searches of electronic databases, websites, and literature from technical libraries. A state-of-the-art search nearly always produces interesting information to help you improve your understanding of your own invention.

✔ **Patent title search:** If you need to find the name of a patent owner, a patent title search is helpful. Although recording an ownership interest in a patent isn't a legal requirement, many people do. The CIPO keeps track of all recorded assignments and other recorded transactions relating to patents or pending applications.

Exploring Alternatives to Patents

Given the length and expense of the patent application process, you should understand some alternative, less-taxing approaches for protecting your invention. You may want to use one or more of those approaches rather than, or in addition to, the patent application.

Keeping trade secrets

If you're dealing with a chemical or process invention, or other invention that you don't have to expose to your customers or the general public, and can keep it under your hat, then a patent application may not be the best approach for you.

Instead, consider the option of a *trade secret strategy*. If your invention is to be protected as a trade secret, then it must genuinely be a secret, even within your own organization. Employees must sign secrecy or confidentiality agreements, and the techniques or technologies involved with your invention must not be apparent to visitors at your facilities.

If someone takes advantage of you and improperly acquires knowledge of your concept, you must satisfy a court that you were trying to maintain a trade secret. If you do, the court issues a restraining order, preventing the bad guys from exploiting your idea. However, if the secrecy is spoiled and anyone can understand your technology, then you lose control over the secret. Your only recourse is to seek compensation in the form of damages from whoever broke their duty of secrecy.

Another risk of trade secrets is that someone else may independently discover the same invention that you've been keeping secret. They're free to compete with you. In fact, they might even file a patent application and cause you considerable grief by shutting you down.

Generally, pursuing the trade secret route is a good idea if the useful life of your invention is relatively short: less than seven years. The odds of anyone discovering and patenting the same invention during that timeframe are small, and you'll have achieved a head start on the competition.

Backing up your trade secret with a covert patent application isn't common, but it can be an effective strategy if you think your invention will give you a competitive advantage for more than seven years. Patent applications are initially held in secrecy for up to 18 months from the date of your initial filing. If you've managed to keep your invention a secret for those 18 months, you can withdraw the patent application so that it's not published. You can then begin the process again.

Publishing to poison the well

Publishing your invention without filing a patent application means you'll likely lose your right to patent, but because prior art now exists you also can bar anyone else from ever filing a patent on the same invention. This technique relieves you of the cost of patenting, and puts everyone on a level playing field.

Publishing the invention can be as simple as putting it on your website. Another very effective method is filing a provisional Canadian patent application, which allows CIPO to publish the invention. After it's been published, you can abandon the application. This tactic allows you to produce a publication that every competent patent searcher in the world will find when searching for prior art.

In certain circumstances, other alternatives to patenting exist, including industrial design protection and copyright protection. Knowing the best option for you depends greatly on your specific circumstances — consult an IP professional.

Tackling Trademarks

When you start a business or introduce a new product or service, you have an opportunity to create value out of nothing. By selecting a strong and effective identifier, you gain protection for your enterprise and the chance to catapult your products or services into a dominant market position.

Book II: Intellectual Property

In this section, we bring you the basics of trademarks, including valuable advice on choosing a distinctive, legally protectable name.

Making your mark

Everyone's familiar with brands. You probably even have your own favourites: names that make you reach out for a particular product instead of the others on the shelf. That's the power of a brand — it lends personality to products and services, and creates an association in the mind of the consumer. Trademarks allow you to harness the power of that association so that only you can benefit from it.

Trademarks are symbols, words, logos, or shapes that differentiate your ware (in the trademark business, products are referred to as *wares*) or service from its competitors. When you've established your trademark, you're entitled to defend it from imitators (see the "Enforcing Your Mark" section in this chapter).

The following categories of trademarks exist:

- **Ordinary marks** are the words, logos, or symbols that make your product or service stand out from the competition. For example, the word Nike and the swoosh logo make Nike shoes noticeable on the shelf.

- **Distinguishing guise** is the packaging or design of a product that helps to distinguish it from others — such as the unique shape of a Coca-Cola bottle.

- **Certification marks** single out products or services meeting a particular standard (for example, CSA stickers on a bike helmet or a professional designation such as CMA or CFP). The owner of a certification mark doesn't make wares or services available directly to the public; instead it certifies the quality of a ware or service provided by a third party. The owner of the mark (the *licensing body*) controls the use of the mark by its licensees.

✔ **Official marks** are owned by entities under government control.

✔ **Geographic indications** control the use of specific geographic locations as trademarks. Only products originating from a certain region can bear a trademark of that region. For example, sparkling wine can be called Champagne only if it originates in the Champagne region of France. As globalization continues to expand and cheap imitations arise, this area of trademark protection grows more important.

Although they sound similar, a trademark is not the same thing as a trade name. Your *trade name* is the name under which you carry out your business. Contrary to popular belief, registering your trade name doesn't protect it from use by others. The good news is that you can also register it as a trademark, but only if you're using it as one. (For more about registering trademarks, see the section "Taking the Next Steps in Trademarking.")

Distinguishing yourself from the competition

Creating a distinctive brand makes your business more valuable and your trademark rights easier to enforce. The name you create will fall into one of five main categories; we list them below, in order from best to worst.

✔ **Invented marks** are the best kind to have for your business. They didn't exist before you made them up, so they are inherently distinctive. (Examples include Kodak, Exxon, Cisco.)

✔ **Arbitrary marks** exist in the dictionary because they're genuine words. They're considered arbitrary in this case because they don't refer specifically to the character or quality of your product. (Examples include Indigo, Apple, Roots.)

✔ **Suggestive marks** allude to the nature of the product or service, without fully describing it. (Examples include Whirlpool for washing machines, Chapters for book stores.)

Personal names are very common, and yet they aren't a good choice for a trademark. Remember, the key to a good mark is distinctiveness — likely nothing is unique about your name, so it's very hard to register.

✔ **Descriptive marks** are the weakest kind you can adopt. Terms such as "click" for a camera or "clean and fast" for a dry cleaner are difficult if not impossible to register, and may not be enforceable; after all, almost everyone in your industry could lay claim to the same terms.

When choosing your trademark, don't pick something that someone else will object to. Don't select "Orange Crash" for your new soft drink — you're only asking for trouble from the good people at Orange Crush. Even if you're able to defend your choice of mark, who needs the distraction and expense of litigation? You've got a business to run and products to launch.

The key feature of a trademark is that it makes your product or service stand out from others available on the market. Your reputation develops over time, as the combination of a good product and a memorable trademark generate goodwill with your customers. Customers continue to buy your products and spread the word about your services, and this goodwill (see Book I for more about goodwill) brings in additional customers. The first step in developing this reputation is creating a quality product or service. A close second is choosing your mark carefully. Make sure to select something that reflects your identity and highlights your uniqueness.

Book II: Intellectual Property

Selecting your mark is a little like flirting — you want to be suggestive, not obvious. Anything too descriptive is a no-no. You can't call your ice cream "Cold & Tasty" because the courts won't take away the freedom of others to use these basic descriptors. And if you're hoping to stand out from the crowd, calling your new hotel "Sandy Beach Resort" won't do. Potential customers immediately know what and where you are, but what's the difference between your hotel and all the others that are located on sandy beaches? You'd never be able to claim trademark rights because the name is so broad and descriptive that it lacks distinctness.

Writing some sample advertisements is a good exercise that can help you avoid this pitfall. Remember, your mark should identify your product and make it stand out from the competition; it shouldn't describe it. Consider the difference between "use Turtle wax next time you shine your car" and "use Glossy wax next time you shine your car." See how easily you can spot potential trouble this way?

Taking the Next Steps in Trademarking

As with all IP rights, establishing ownership is crucial. Business owners commonly make the mistake of hiring a contractor to assist with developing a trademark, especially logos and designs, and then failing to get an assignment of the copyright from the contractor. The technical term for this situation is *a mess*, and it can be easily avoided by obtaining clear paperwork upfront.

After you carefully craft your trademark and ensure you have ownership of it, you need to get moving. Canadian law operates on a first-come, first-served basis with respect to trademarks. In other words, priority goes to the first person to adopt the trademark.

As we're sure you know, laws are often complicated and confusing — why should trademark laws be any different? Below we explain the basic steps involved, but we can't possibly cover all the complex aspects of registering and protecting a mark. We encourage you to spend some of your branding budget on consulting with an IP professional who specializes in trademark law. He or she will be able to guide you through the intricate legal issues that lie ahead.

Deciding whether to register

In Canada registering your trademark isn't necessary in order to lay claim to it; you can choose to just *adopt the mark* instead. Adopting the mark is as simple as displaying it with the wares when they're sold or advertising your services so that the public understands the mark represents the product. After you have made your first Canadian sale, you have adopted the trademark.

Use is an important concept in trademark law. Using your trademark in Canada establishes your unregistered common-law right to defend it within the geographic area where you're doing business and enjoying a reputation. Advertising your *wares* doesn't count — you must actually make a sale before you can claim your trademark is in use. Advertising your *services,* however, is enough to establish a common-law trademark for them. But remember, the service must actually be available — "coming soon" isn't good enough.

Registered trademarks are indicated by the symbol ®, and marks that have been adopted but not registered can use the symbol ™.

Although adopting a mark is easy, we highly recommend you also take the time to register your mark. Indeed, the best-run companies apply to register trademarks based on *proposed use*, before they actually begin using the mark. Applying based on proposed use lets you define a range of wares and services that you have a bona fide intention of selling in association with your trademark. Applying based on proposed use is more efficient and offers much better potential protection than applying to register the trademark in association with a limited number of wares and services after you've begun selling them.

For example, if you're launching a new soft drink called Chug, you may also plan to sell related merchandise. Filing an application based on the proposed uses of the mark Chug is smart, including uses associated with soft drinks and all sorts of other things you might sell emblazoned with the Chug mark — such as T-shirts, hats, jackets, bags, and golf accessories. In Canada, you must sell each of these items for the trademark registration to issue for that item. If you don't use an item on your application within a reasonable time, that part of the application for registration will lapse.

Registering a mark provides you with several advantages, including the following:

- ✔ **The exclusive right to use your mark across Canada.**

- ✔ **An effective legal tool to prevent others from imitating your mark.** Registration provides you with clear ownership, which means that in the event of a legal dispute, the onus of proof will be on the other party — your registered mark is presumed to be valid. If you simply use your trademark, you need to prove entitlement to your rights before you can establish the defendant is violating them — a long, cumbersome process.

- ✔ **Additional value to your business.** A great way to expand your business and make more money is franchising or licensing out your trademark, which is much more easily done with a registered mark.

Clearing the way

Before adopting or registering the mark, you must *clear* it. This means searching, searching, and still more searching to ensure no one else is using your proposed mark in association with wares or services that are similar or related to the wares and services you propose to sell. The last thing you want is to go to the expense of printing up packaging, labels, and advertisements, only to discover that someone else has beaten you to the punch. A good search can also help you learn more about your competitors and strengthen your mark.

Lexus is a well-known mark associated with cars made by Toyota, and it co-exists with a registration of Lexus used in association with canned tomatoes. This is possible because the wares are very different and the channels of trade for cars and food are very different. Conversely, when an import company applied to register the mark Jaguar in association with luggage, the application was refused because the carmaker Jaguar successfully challenged it. The carmaker had previously made branded luggage available to its customers, and the court decided that luggage is a natural extension of wares associated with the brand.

Hunting for a trademark is a peculiar kind of search because you're actually hoping to not find anything. A similar mark or business name used on similar wares and services or used in a similar channel of trade may cause confusion in the marketplace. Finding such a mark is known as a *knockout*. And it's going to knock you all the way back to the drawing board. Be warned that the probability of a knockout is quite high. It's wise to have a few options to search, because you'll likely go through at least three before you stumble upon one that's available for your use.

Finding registered trademarks

Hiring a qualified trademark searcher who has access to all the relevant databases is the best way to do a trademark search. Your IP professional can order and review a search for you. The cost of the search will depend on how comprehensive it is, but remember that no amount of searching can prove conclusively what is or isn't actually out there.

In Canada, trademark searches start with the Trademark Register in Ottawa. The Canadian Intellectual Property Office (CIPO) maintains the Register, and you can find the database online at www.ic.gc.ca. People on the Trademark Register are serious about their marks. They've gone to the trouble and expense of registration, and they mean business. In all likelihood they have retained a registered trademark agent to help with the application and with monitoring and policing the efforts of others attempting to register a potentially conflicting mark. If you find a mark here that reminds you of your own, you might have trouble.

While you're at it, checking out the U.S. trademark site at www.uspto.com is a good idea. Some companies operate in both Canada and the United States, but go to the expense of registering their trademark only in the United States. This site will help alert you to any such cases before it's too late.

Seeking out adopted trademarks

If you make it over the first hurdle, and aren't knocked out by any registered marks, it's time to expand your search to adopted but unregistered trademarks.

Checking the Government of Canada name search database (http://nuans.com) is a great next step. The system includes information on corporate names issued federally and by the provinces of British Columbia, Alberta, Ontario, New Brunswick, Nova Scotia, and PEI. You can also search for names and marks that aren't exact matches but that are similar enough to cause confusion to the public (and consternation to you).

Additionally, searching telephone books and business registers will help you to weed out any unregistered names.

Applying for registration

If you choose to follow our advice to register your trademark, you're in for a long but worthwhile journey. The application process can take 12 to

18 months, but after your trademark is registered — and if the registration remains unchallenged — your trademark will be valid for 15 years. Processing your registration is a six-stage process:

✔ **Formalities:** First you (or your IP professional) fill out an application form, complete with your name and address, a description or drawing of your mark (as appropriate), and a statement indicating details of your first sale in Canada or your plan to introduce your mark to Canada — including a list of the wares and/or services used, or to be used, in association with your mark. After it's complete, the application form and, of course, your application fee are forwarded to the Trademark Office (TMO). The TMO reviews your application to ensure it's been completed satisfactorily. After the TMO is satisfied your paperwork is in good order, it opens your application file and sends you an application number and filing date.

✔ **Examination:** An examiner at the TMO goes over your application with a fine-toothed comb. And, ideally, the examiner confirms that your proposed mark doesn't conflict with any existing ones and that the product or service to be covered is described appropriately. The findings of this stage are sent to you in an official Examiner's Report.

Promptly responding (in writing) to any objections raised in the Examiner's Report will keep your application active.

If you don't convince the examiner to withdraw the objections raised, your application will be rejected — and if you don't respond at all, your application will lapse into abandonment.

✔ **Advertisement:** The TMO publishes applications that successfully pass through the examination stage in the *Trademarks Journal.* This official publication of the Canadian Intellectual Property Office allows third parties, usually other people with marks to protect, to review your mark and register their opposition if they feel it potentially conflicts with their own.

✔ **Opposition:** If your mark meets with opposition, it is removed from the normal processing cycle and placed on hold until the opposition proceedings are complete.

✔ **Allowance:** After your application successfully passes through the process, the TMO issues you a Notice of Allowance and (you guessed it) a request for payment of the registration fee.

✔ **Registration:** After you submit the appropriate fee, your trademark proceeds to registration and you receive an official certificate. This is your proof that you are the registered owner of the mark.

Retaining your registered mark

Like most good things, having a registered trademark comes with some responsibilities. To keep the trademark valid, you must do a number of things:

- ✔ **Renew it every 15 years.** So long as you remember to renew it regularly, it'll be yours in perpetuity.

- ✔ **Use it.** The mark must be used for all the wares and services for which it was registered. You have a free ride for the first three years of registration. After that, if you don't use the mark for a period of three years or more, your competitor(s) can apply to have it removed from the register. So, use it or lose it.

  Before and after registration, you must use your trademark in a manner that shows you intend to treat it as a trademark, and not just as text. For example, use a distinctive font or colour when you write it down, so that it stands out from ordinary text, and use the ® symbol (or ™ before it's registered).

  Removing a registered but unused mark is called an *expungement* under section 45 of the Trade-Marks Act. If your searches turn up a registered mark that is in the way of the one you want to apply for, and it's not being used, you can apply to have the old mark expunged.

- ✔ **Keep it the same.** Your mark should be used in the manner in which it was registered. Companies often make modifications to their mark or logo, but this can cause difficulties with enforcement, because the trademark you are using may not be the same as the one you registered. Consult your IP professional as your company evolves — you may need to reapply with a new mark.

Going international

Acquiring foreign trademark rights is done on a country-by-country basis, and registering your trademark is vital when you're launching a new product or service into a new market where you don't have the benefit of established goodwill. Applying all the principles of searching and establishing good trademark protection is key as you expand abroad.

Filing your first application in association with specific wares or services establishes an *international priority date*. When you file foreign applications in the subsequent six months, you can claim the priority date — your foreign applications will be treated as if they were filed on the same date as your first one. Taking advantage of your priority date allows you to defer the costs of filing foreign applications without compromising the date of adoption. If you don't file internationally within this six-month period you don't automatically lose your right to file. But because you've lost your priority you do run the risk that someone else will file before you.

Trademark applications are prosecuted as a fresh application in each country, and local rules apply. Be aware that many countries are "first to file" jurisdictions, and don't have the examination process that Canada does. This makes it important to establish priority and to get your foreign application on file as quickly as possible.

Canada is unusual because trademark applications here aren't "class-based"; instead, you describe your wares and services in detail. In other countries, the application you file and the filing fee(s) you pay will depend on the number of classes you designate. Be warned that designating many classes will cause costs to rise rapidly!

Book II: Intellectual Property

Enforcing Your Mark

A trademark can be a very valuable asset to your business, and you need to look after it.

You must control the use of your mark. If third parties begin using your mark without your control, then by definition the mark is no longer a signifier that the wares and services originate from you, and it ceases to be a trademark. This means that you must

- ✔ Prevent third parties from using your mark without authorization,
- ✔ Clearly control the use of the mark when you authorize a third party to use it, and
- ✔ Stop third parties from registering marks that are confusingly similar to your mark.

Opposing confusing registrations is essential. Just as third parties had the right to oppose your trademark application, you can (and should) oppose applications by third parties if you believe their mark will create confusion with yours.

If you permit a third party to use your mark, make sure that they adhere to proper licensing standards and that they clearly acknowledge your ownership of the mark and right to control its use. If you mention the trademark of a third party in your advertising (as happens when, say, Future Shop has a sale on iPods), identify the proper owner of the trademark (that is, not you).

As with so many other things in IP law, you must protect the rights to your good name — no one else will do it for you.

Infringing on your rights

Infringement occurs when a competitor uses a mark similar enough to your registered trademark to cause confusion. Whether or not the competitor intended to piggyback on your good reputation, if common sense tells you that your customers (or potential customers) might mistake this product for yours, then infringement has occurred. If you discover someone is using your mark without your permission, you can bring an infringement action against that person or organization and ask the court to stop it. Your lawyer has to prove only two things:

✔ You're the registered owner of the mark (your certificate of registration will come in handy here), and

✔ The mark is confusingly similar to your registered trademark, and is being used without your permission.

After you satisfy both requirements, the court will order the infringer to stop immediately. Depending on circumstances, the bad guys may also be forced to change their name or brand, to destroy current inventory, and/or to pay compensatory damages. See what a powerful tool a registered trademark can be?

What's a trademark worth?

All this talk about spending time developing a unique mark, searching out potential conflicts, applying for registration, and defending it against misuse may have you wondering if it's really all worthwhile. Pinpointing the exact value of a trademark is impossible because each one is unique, but consider this story for a glimpse into how valuable trademarks can be.

Polaroid was famous for its Land cameras that produced instant photos, but in an era of digital cameras the instant print business died

and Polaroid went bankrupt twice. Recently, Polaroid's remaining assets — little more than the worldwide trademark rights and associated goodwill — were sold for nearly $100 million to a private equity firm that saw enduring value in the name.

Now, we're not saying that registering your mark will lead you to millions; we're simply pointing out that your rights can be quite valuable and they are worth defending.

Be vigilant about potential infringers, and shut them down quickly. Owners of famous marks, like Harley-Davidson, need to watch the marketplace constantly, taking to task knock-off artists and infringers.

Sometimes, if the marks are not identical, or the wares and services are different, determining infringement is a judgment call. Saying with certainty that a reasonable consumer would be confused is difficult. If you have evidence that actual confusion has already occurred, make sure you document it; it'll make your life in court much easier. For example, keep track of any mistaken calls or inquiries you've received that were meant for the other guys. Note any instances that have come to your attention where one of your customers has purchased goods or services from the infringer, thinking they were from you.

A related problem that arises with successful trademarks is *genericide*. The public becomes so familiar with a mark that the rights associated with it become diluted. For example, a mark may be used in an inappropriate way, such as being turned into a verb — "Xeroxing" a document instead of photocopying it, or going "Rollerblading" instead of inline skating. Marks may also become so common that they no longer distinguish the product from its competition. For example, people use the phrase Q-Tips for all cotton swabs, regardless of the manufacturer. The same can be said for Escalator, Kleenex, Hoover, Scotch tape, and many, many more.

Some companies believe a high level of generic use is a benefit, as it shows how popular their product has become. Don't fall prey to this assumption — allowing such (mis)use by the public to continue makes it much more difficult to enforce your trademark rights. You don't want the courts to think you have abandoned the mark and allowed it to fall into the public domain.

Book II:
Intellectual
Property

Passing it off

If you've ignored our advice and haven't registered your trademark, don't despair; you can still defend your rights. Because your mark is unregistered, it's not covered under the trademark statute and, therefore, you have a smaller set of rights to defend. However, if you think someone is imitating your mark, you can have your lawyer seek relief through the common-law remedy known as *passing off*. This common-law tort prevents others from misrepresenting their products as being associated with yours — that is, it stops them from passing off their products as yours.

Bringing a passing-off action against your competitor is onerous, because your side bears the burden of proof. Your lawyer needs to convince the court that

 ✔ You have adopted the trademark and enjoy a reputation with the mark.

 ✔ The third party has been using your mark with the intention of cashing in on your reputation (passing it off as yours).

 ✔ Damages have occurred as a result of the unauthorized use.

Although the upfront effort of registering your mark may seem like a pain, registration provides you with more robust rights to prevent unauthorized use of your mark. If you need to enforce your rights, the burden on you, your business, and your legal team is much less taxing if you've registered.

Asserting Your Copyrights

Of all the types of intellectual property rights, copyrights are probably the easiest to understand. Certainly they're the easiest to acquire. However, for all its apparent simplicity, the concept of copyright is like a fish underwater: easy to see, but hard to get a grip on — and this fish is worth grabbing.

In the past, copyrights have been treated like the ugly duckling of IP rights (largely because IP professionals don't make much money helping you acquire or file copyrights). But copyright law is rapidly turning into the swan of IP and is becoming very important for many industries, especially software and entertainment. Whether applied to open source software, downloading and sharing music, video games, or movies, copyrights often determine who can do what — and who makes money. If you intend to create a new ringtone, or simply have someone design a new website for your business or charity, you need to understand copyrights. To help you get a handle on copyrights, in this section we look at the various kinds of works protected by copyright, who owns these works, and the rights the copyright owner holds.

Defining copyright

A *copyright* is primarily an exclusive right allowing the owner of the rights in a qualifying work to prevent others from making copies of the protected work for an extended period of time.

In Canada copyrights generally last for life of author plus 50 years. (In the United States, it's life of author plus 70 years.) When you consider how little it costs to get the rights in the first place, this makes obtaining copyright protection the single best deal in IP. Conversely, however, it means that if you want to reproduce a work, you need to track down the copyright owner — and you can't assume the owner won't enforce the copyright just because the work is old.

To qualify for copyright, a work must be substantial — copyright isn't available for bumper stickers or titles. Eligible works fit into one of these broad categories:

- **Literary works:** A written or recorded sequence of words, numbers, or symbols, including books, pamphlets, and computer programs.

- **Musical works:** Compositions that include music or a combination of music and lyrics (lyrics alone would be covered under literary works).

- **Dramatic works:** Works that incorporate the spoken word to be performed by one or more characters, including plays, films, scripts, and videos.

- **Artistic works:** Two- and three-dimensional works of fine, graphic, or applied art, including paintings, photographs, sculptures, maps, and architecture.

Book II: Intellectual Property

Three other categories are eligible for protection, and although they aren't strictly works of authorship, creating them entitles you to prevent unauthorized duplication:

- A performer's performance
- A sound recording
- A communication signal

If you write it, they will come

Here's some good news — copyrights come to you automatically. That's right: They arise upon authorship of your work. Writing the next book-club bestseller or recording the next chart-topping song? As soon as you do, it's copyrighted.

Just to be clear, though, the bestseller still germinating inside your head isn't covered. A work isn't accepted as existing unless it's been fixed in some form. For instance, if you give a brilliant off-the-cuff speech (without prepared notes) it isn't protected unless you are recording it in some way, perhaps with a stenographer or a video recorder.

Being an original

To be eligible for copyrights, the work must be original. This doesn't necessarily imply that it's new, unusual, or innovative — it simply means that the work is the result of creativity and hasn't been copied from a pre-existing source.

Copyright doesn't protect the *idea* behind your original work; it protects the *original expression* of the idea. For example, taking a photograph of someone else's photograph doesn't qualify as original work. However, if you travel to the same location, look down the same valley, place your camera in the same spot as the original photographer and take your own photo, then you've made an original work.

Untangling ownership issues

Generating an original work, whether it's a musical recording, graphic, promotional material, textbook, or photograph, raises ownership and protection issues. Generally, the author of a work is the first owner of the copyright. However, any original creation is potentially valuable, and when money's involved you know things won't remain simple for long.

Creating ownership

If you've been plugging away in your basement and are finally finishing up the next bestseller, the ownership of the manuscript's copyright is likely pretty simple: You're the creator, so you own the copyright. However, paying someone to create a work muddies the waters. Consider the following situations:

- ✔ **Employees' creations:** If you're an employee creating a work as part of your employment, then you don't own copyright, your employer does.

- ✔ **Works created on a for-hire basis:** Hiring someone under contract to provide you with some sort of deliverable creates a stickier situation. Because the person you hire isn't considered an employee, as the original author the copyright will revert to them if you don't specify otherwise. Consider this example: You hire a firm to create some ad copy for your business. Although you have freedom to use the agency's materials as per your contract, you don't own copyright to the text or artwork. That means if someone else copies your ads, you can't go after them for infringement — you have to get the advertising agency to pursue them. And, to make things more complicated, you — not the agency — may own the trademark rights to the logo in the same ads.

Each work-for-hire situation is different, and you can tailor it to suit your specific needs. For example, you can specify in the hiring contract that copyright will be assigned to you. Have a competent IP professional review your contract before signing to make sure you've protected your rights.

Be aware that anyone contributing to an original work may have a partial interest in the ownership of that work. Be careful if you're downloading online software and incorporating it into your next great application. Other people may be lining up for payment after it becomes a smash hit. Many costly copyright litigations involve questions over ownership. The usual participants in the great ownership debate are associates, employers and employees, collaborators, and contractors. Consulting an IP professional will help you understand the legalities of ownership.

Joining forces

If you work (on your own, not as an employee) with a co-author, then you jointly own the copyright, unless you have an agreement to the contrary. Drafting a *co-ownership agreement* is wise in these cases. Similar to a shareholder agreement, these address many of the issues that may arise in the future, including derivative uses (such as creating a revised edition of the work) and succession planning.

Transferring ownership

Determining that you are in fact the owner of the copyright can open up opportunities for you beyond simply defending your work from infringers. As the owner, you can license or assign your work. *Licensing* your work to a third party allows it to use your work while allowing you to maintain ownership of the work and copyrights. *Assigning* your work to one, or more, third parties transfers both the right to use the work and the copyrights.

Entire industries, like movies, music, gaming, and software, are premised on the licensing of copyrights, so be sure to have your ownership ducks in a row. If you can't prove that you either own the copyright in a work, or have a licence that permits you to re-license it, then your commercialization of a work will get stopped in its tracks. For businesses that hire contractors and employees to help develop any form of copyrighted work, having clear paperwork that specifies ownership of the copyrights (and any waivers of moral rights) is absolutely crucial. Consult your IP professional.

**Book II:
Intellectual
Property**

Making Your Copyright Official

Registering your work is not necessary in Canada. Because copyrights arise automatically (refer to the previous section for more), pursuing infringers all the way to court is possible without any official certification. You can even mark your work with a © without registering it. However, applying for copyright registration is a quick and easy process, and we recommend that you do so. Arriving at court armed with a certificate of registration makes your life much easier, because the onus of proof will now be on your opponent.

Applying is as easy as completing an application form and sending it to the copyright department at the Canadian Intellectual Property Office (CIPO), along with your application fee, of course. Applying for copyright registration is much easier than applying to register other types of IP. You'll just need to include the title of your work, determine which category it fits into — literary, dramatic, musical, or artistic — note the publication details (date and place of publication) if applicable, and name the author of the work and the owner of the copyright.

Including a copy of the work with your application is not necessary; CIPO will just review your application for completeness. If everything is in order, you'll be hanging your certificate on the wall within a matter of weeks.

If you have several works to protect you need to file separately for each one, because no blanket protection exists.

With any luck, creating and registering your work hasn't left you too tired, because policing your rights is up to you. CIPO registers the copyright and sends you a certificate, but it doesn't enforce your rights. (Check out the next section for more about protecting your copyright.)

Infringing Copyright

Someone is *infringing* on your rights if they do anything that the Copyright Act says only an owner can do. Common violations include copying, performing, importing, or selling a work without authorization from the copyright owner.

The golden rule of copyright is simple to define, but it's not always easy to interpret. Copyright doesn't protect the *idea* behind a work. It only protects the *original expression* of the idea. Consider this example:

You write a nifty iPhone application for your employer, and decide to quit your job and write the same application to run on a BlackBerry. No copyright exists in the idea of your application, but copyright does exist in the code, so you must make sure you start entirely from scratch and don't use any of the same code. And remember, if someone in the Ukraine, who has never seen your iPhone application, writes the exact same application from scratch, they're not infringing on your copyright because the idea of the application isn't protected.

Computers and the Internet have made copyright infringement a much bigger problem than in the past, and a much easier trap to accidentally fall into.

The fact that you *can* copy something doesn't mean that you *have the right* to copy it.

Consider that the founders of Pirate Bay, a popular website for the sharing of music files, were recently sentenced to lengthy prison terms in Sweden for copyright infringement. And, closer to home, the Law Society of Upper Canada (Ontario) was involved in lengthy (read, expensive) litigation that went all the way to the Supreme Court of Canada. The case involved the making of photocopies of case law for lawyers without the permission of the book publishers. So be forewarned that everyone can get into trouble.

Whether you're hunting for photographs to use on your website, handing out materials to students in your class, or downloading music to your MP3 player, you need to be attentive to copyright issues. Businesses or institutions that are using copyrighted materials in their products or services must be particularly careful, because copyright owners are more likely to sue an infringer who profits from the infringement. For instance, if your business uses, modifies, or distributes any form of software, you should invest a significant amount of energy into making sure you clear copyright in any software that you bring in or send out.

Reading Your Rights

Being the author of an original work means having some exclusive rights to control how your creation is used, and these extend beyond the right to simply prevent others from copying your work. The following sections discuss the nature and scope of these exclusive rights.

Forbidding copies

The primary and most important right that the creator or owner of a work holds, regardless of the work's category, is to exclude others from duplicating the work. The mere copying is what's forbidden, even if the copy is never used:

- ✔ Copying your own portrait bought from a photographer infringes on the photographer's copyright. The fact that you paid good money for the original and some copies of the portrait doesn't automatically transfer the copyright to you.

- ✔ Downloading a pirated copy of a song or computer program onto your hard drive is committing an act of copyright infringement.

- ✔ Installing or downloading a legitimate copy of software without a licence to do so is considered infringement.

- ✔ Using copyrighted popular music as background for your home video production is a violation of the composer or songwriter's rights.

Prohibiting preparation of derivative works

A *derivative work* arises when a further creative contribution is overlaid onto a pre-existing work. This includes recasting, transforming, or adapting the previous work. Nobody has the right to make a derivative work based on your work without your permission. Here are some examples of derivative works:

- ✔ Translating a book into a different language
- ✔ Creating new lyrics for an old song
- ✔ Photographing a statue
- ✔ Modifying a computer program to make it compatible with a different hardware or software product

Preventing unauthorized distribution

Distributing copies or adaptations of a work, whether by public sale, free distribution, rental, lease, or loan, is an infringement, even if you didn't actually make the copies. For example, copying a clipping from a newspaper or magazine about the impact of secondhand tobacco smoke and giving copies to all your chain-smoking relatives is a no-no. So is passing a copy of a spreadsheet program, licensed only to you, to one of your associates.

Barring public performances

You can prevent the public performance, for profit, of a copyrighted work at a theatre or other place of entertainment.

If you own a copyright on a piece of popular music, you can prevent anyone else from playing a recording of it in public, such as in the background at your favourite martini bar

A radio or TV station can't broadcast any copyrighted music or video program without a licence from the copyright owner.

Protecting your artistic reputation

Moral rights are a special brand of copyrights, giving you the ability to maintain credit for your work and protect your reputation. Even if you transfer your copyrights to someone else, moral rights remain with you. This means you can still do the following:

- ✔ Claim authorship of the work
- ✔ Prevent the work from being associated with a product or cause that's detrimental to your honour or reputation
- ✔ Stop the modification of your work if it interferes with the integrity of the work

Canadian artist Michael Snow created a sculpture based on a flock of geese, which were suspended by wires from the ceiling of Toronto's Eaton Centre. Some years later, a decorator decided to place Christmas ribbons around the necks of the geese. The artist objected, claiming that the ribbons interfered with the integrity of his work. The court agreed that his moral rights had been violated, and the ribbons were removed.

You might think that moral rights apply only to the artistic community, and don't concern you as a businessperson. However, consider this scenario: You commission an artist to create a logo for your company and the artist transfers the copyright to you. Years later, a cigarette company offers to buy your logo for big bucks, but the deal falls apart because the artist refuses to have the work associated with cigarettes.

Although moral rights cannot be transferred to another owner, they can be waived, either in whole or in part. Having your IP professional include a full waiver of moral rights when you arrange the copyright transfer is a good idea.

Book II:
Intellectual
Property

Exceptions to the Rules

Of course, for every rule an exception exists, and copyrights are no different. Certain activities that would ordinarily infringe on a copyright are allowed in particular circumstances. We discuss some of the common exceptions, but you should know that the exceptions are narrower in Canada than in other countries. For instance, a parody of an original work is much more likely to be guilty of infringement here than in the United States.

Dealing fairly

The concept of *fair dealing* allows others to use your copyrighted work (published or unpublished) without your permission for the purposes of research or private study. Of course, fairness is one of those subjective criteria about which you and the user of your work may disagree — so the law spells out what's fair use of copyrighted material:

- Reviews or criticism of the work
- News reporting
- Teaching
- Scholarship
- Research

Claiming exemptions and privileges

Some activities that would otherwise infringe on a copyright are allowed for specific non-profit, charitable, or educational purposes.

- ✔ **Copies for the blind:** Literary works may be reproduced or distributed as copies or recordings in specialized formats exclusively for use by blind or other disabled persons. Braille copies of a text or talking books are examples of this type of exemption.

- ✔ **Libraries and archives:** Public libraries, archives, and museums may reproduce and distribute one copy or phonorecord of a copyrighted work for study or research purposes. Copying is also permitted to assist in managing their collections (making a copy for insurance purposes, for example).

- ✔ **Teachers:** Teachers can perform or display a copyrighted work for their students in a face-to-face teaching activity in the classroom of a non-profit educational institution.

- ✔ **Ephemeral recordings:** Radio and TV studios may make temporary recordings of their programs for internal use, under certain conditions.

- ✔ **Personal use:** Finally, an exemption familiar to everybody. You may record a radio or television program while it's played on the air for later listening or viewing by you and the members of your household. You may not, without permission from the copyright owner, copy, sell, lend, or publicly play your recording.

The most important feature of these exceptions is that they are relatively narrow and apply to a relatively small range of acts. Copyrights are routinely violated, either knowingly or unwittingly (see the "Infringing Copyright" section). But assuming that you won't get caught is poor business, and pleading ignorance is a poor defence. When in doubt, consult your IP professional.

Protecting Industrial Designs

Even though industrial designs are lesser known than the other types of IP we discuss in this book, such as patents and copyrights, they can be an effective IP tool.

Defining designs

An *industrial design* is a decorative, nonfunctional part of a finished article that you mass produce. It can refer to shape, arrangement, pattern, or decoration —

for example, the shape of the arm on a chair, a decorative pattern applied to the product you are selling, or a piece of ornamentation on a set of cutlery. Designs protect just the cosmetic features that are visible to the eye. Only features that are both new and nonessential to the function of the article are eligible for protection.

If you make an original work of art or craft — such as a chair — the design elements are protected by copyright. But when you make more than 50 of these "articles," you lose copyright protection in the design. And, if you fail to secure industrial design rights, your design will be open for all to copy.

The range of possible articles that can be protected by industrial designs is very wide, and includes almost anything: car parts, motor boat hulls, shoes, or furniture, to name just a few. Whether your product is sexy, cool, or just plain good looking, you should investigate design rights.

Imagine you've gone to the trouble and expense of launching your great new product and it becomes known for its fabulosity. Consumers recognize the distinctive whatchamacallit on the package and equate it with your superior product. Harried shoppers don't always have time to focus, and they reach for what they recognize on the shelf. A design registration allows you to stop your copycat competitors from putting a similar whatchamacallit on their product and diverting sales that should, rightfully, be yours.

Book II: Intellectual Property

Registering Your Design

Industrial design rights don't arise upon creation. You must register your creation with the Industrial Design Office (a branch of CIPO) in order to exercise your rights and you must file separately in each country where you want to protect your design rights.

Like patent rights, a novelty requirement for design rights exists. The rules vary greatly from country to country

Applying for industrial designs is relatively inexpensive. Generally, the applications are much easier to draft and prosecution is not particularly complex — therefore, designs often cost less than trademarks.

In Canada, design rights last for 10 years from the date of registration, provided you remember to pay the maintenance fee at the five-year mark. The Industrial Design Office registers your design and issues your design certificate.

After you register your design, mark it with the industrial design symbol — the letter D inside a circle — and the name of the proprietor. Although this isn't a requirement, it's in your best interest. Without the mark, a court can only grant an injunction that forbids the bad guys from using your design on their product in the future; if they establish that they didn't know they were infringing, the courts will excuse their past behaviour. However, if you've taken the time to mark your design, then in addition to banning the bad guys the court may also award you financial compensation for your troubles.

Introducing the basics

Before you leap into applying for registration, keep a few important things in mind:

- ✔ **Your design registration must be new.** You can't take away the freedom of the public to use something that previously existed.

- ✔ **Although the design must be applied to a completed article, it mustn't be involved with the function of the article.** Remember, it's just for show.

- ✔ **Keep quiet about your design.** No time restrictions exist for filing an application, so long as the design has remained private. That means it has never been sold, in Canada or internationally. It also means that it has never been seen by the public. Someone who owes you an obligation of confidence (like your lawyer, an employee, or a contractor who has signed a nondisclosure agreement) isn't considered a member of the public. Be sure to keep track of your disclosures. When it's gone public the clock starts running.

Ensuring you're entitled to apply

Canadian design rights are unique because the proper party — the owner of the design, *not* the design's creator — has to apply for registration. Usually a design's proprietor is the creator, although the design can be assigned to someone else, who becomes the proprietor.

Be sure the proprietor files for the design registration. If an application is granted based on misinformation (such as an incorrectly named proprietor), the registration becomes invalid and can't be corrected.

Particular care should be taken when a design has been created by

- ✔ **An employee:** In this case, even though the author is the employee, the employer remains the proprietor, because he mandated and paid for the creation of the design. The employer must apply for registration.

- ✔ **A group of people:** If several people collaborate on a design, then they should all apply as joint proprietors, unless they're working as a team for an employer — in which case the employer applies as a single applicant.

✔ **Two companies working together:** They should file jointly as co-applicants.

✔ **An outside contractor:** The person who paid for the work should file. But it's best to get a clear assignment of all rights — in writing — just to be safe.

Completing the application

When identifying the design, give some thought to what you want to protect. You can choose to protect just a portion of the article (the shape of the back of a chair) or the whole thing (the shape of a kettle). The scope of what you choose to protect is a delicate balancing act, because if you make your description too wide your design may become impossible to enforce, and if you make it too detailed or specific you may make it easy for someone to evade your design.

**Book II:
Intellectual
Property**

Title

You need to give your application a title. Your title should be concise and should identify the article to which you've applied the design — for example, "set of cutlery." Your title's important, because it determines the scope of protection you'll receive.

Description

In your application, you need to describe the article and the features that make up the design. Clarity is key. Identify the features and their placement on the article.

Drawings

The application needs to be supported by at least one visual depiction of the design. Either a photo or a drawing is acceptable.

If you end up in court, the judge will use the visual aid you included in your industrial design registration application to determine the outcome of your case.

Chapter 3

Profiting from Intellectual Property

In This Chapter

▶ Figuring out whether infringement is taking place

▶ Going after IP infringers

▶ Ending IP disputes

▶ Making money off of your IP

▶ Looking at licensing your IP

▶ Assigning your IP

▶ Taking a commercial approach to IP

▶ Capitalizing on other people's IP as a licensee

▶ Researching with IP findings

*F*rom a legal point of view, your patent, copyright, trademark, or industrial design gives you permission to control who uses your intellectual
property. But this permission has many limits and restrictions. You can't just
put the meddler under citizen's arrest or seize any counterfeit merchandise;
instead, enforcing your rights involves time, money, and lawyers. In this
chapter, we explain some of the procedures particular to IP litigation and
point you toward the most expeditious and least expensive approaches.

And we don't stop there. We also tell you how you and your business can cash
in on IP — yours or someone else's — through licences and assignments.

Catching the Copycats

Determining whether your IP right has been violated requires careful legal
analysis of all circumstances. Here we introduce some common infringement
issues that you may run into.

Violating copyright

Your copyright can be infringed upon by any of the following methods:

- ✔ Copying or adapting the protected work
- ✔ Distributing or displaying copies or adaptations of the protected work
- ✔ Publicly performing a musical or dramatic work
- ✔ Transmitting the work

Running afoul of a patent

Proving patent infringement is a costly and complex process, requiring expert legal analysis. We don't expect you to get into the nitty gritty details — after all, that's what you pay your IP professional for.

The bad guys are infringing on your patent only if their device or process includes *all* of the elements listed in any one of your patent claims. Refer to Chapter 2 for our advice on drafting an effective claim.

Taking a trademark

To determine whether your trademark rights are being violated, you and your legal team must assess whether a likelihood of confusion exists between your trademark and the alleged infringer's. Keep in mind that *likelihood* doesn't mean possibility, it means probability. Reasonable expectation must exist that the public will be confused between your trademark and another's.

Proving the likelihood of confusion in court can be a challenge, because it's really a judgment call. Giving your lawyer proof that actual confusion has already occurred will help your case. Be sure to document any instances that come to your attention.

Determining whether your copyright's been violated

Some forms of copyright infringement are straightforward and easy to detect. Either a recording of your song aired on the radio, or it didn't. Your paper got published, or it didn't. Period. However, determining infringement isn't always so easy. Say you wrote articles on a freelance basis years ago, and now the newspaper that bought them wants to put the old articles online. Does the newspaper have a right to do something neither side even considered when the articles were first purchased?

Many of the most contentious issues in copyright law involve the role of intermediaries who operate between the copyright owner and a blatant infringer. For example, is an Internet service provider liable for illegal downloading by a subscriber? Or consider illegal uploading or file sharing — is someone who hosts a directory of files available for illegal sharing, like Pirate Bay, liable for copyright infringement? Is this different from a search engine that makes it possible to find illegal files?

Knowing whether or not your copyright's been violated requires a little bit of analysis. We summarize the infringement test in four words: access, expression, and substantial similarity. If you suspect infringement, ask yourself these questions:

- ✔ Did the alleged infringer have access to my work?

- ✔ Does part of my work constitute a protected expression rather than a pure idea or material already in the public domain?

- ✔ If I've answered yes to the preceding questions, do the similarities between the part of my work containing the protected expression and the infringer's work indicate that partial or whole copying occurred?

Finally, make certain that the suspected infringement doesn't fall under the fair dealing rules, or one of the copyright exemptions. (Refer to Chapter 2 of this book for a partial listing.)

In most cases, IP owners (or the appropriate licensee) are responsible for enforcing their rights through civil remedies. However, many forms of copyright infringement are considered criminal offences in much of the world. This means that in many countries the state may help you pursue the infringers. Canada's relative lack of criminal sanctions for copyright enforcement is an anomaly and rapidly becoming a major irritant to our trading partners, especially the United States.

Infringing on an industrial design

Enforcing your industrial design rights is similar to enforcing both a patent and a trademark. First you must establish that the infringer copied your design, and then you must defend your registration as the infringer tries to establish that it doesn't cover its activity (or, as we explain a bit later, that your registration is invalid).

Pursuing the Infringers

You've done your homework. You're certain that your competitor is selling a bike that includes a pedal-activated whistle, contrary to your patent. What now? First up is a trip to your lawyer. You need an IP professional who is a litigator to help you. Your business lawyer may be willing to help, and so may your patent agent, but it's unlikely that either has the IP and litigation expertise necessary for these complex cases. (Refer to Chapter 1 of this book for advice on how to find a good IP pro.) Just as you acquire IP rights country-by-country, you must enforce them country-by-country — so if someone is infringing your copyright in Brazil, you need a Brazilian IP pro to go after them.

Firing a warning shot

Instead of heading directly to court, first have your lawyer send the bad guys a stern *cease and desist letter.* This letter advises them that you believe they are infringing on your rights, and demands an immediate stop to all acts of infringement.

Ideally, your lawyer should end the letter with a request for an explanation and an offer of a meeting. After all, your key objective is to have the infringer stop, not to endure the time and financial costs of a lawsuit. It pays to be reasonable.

Meeting with the other side can be very beneficial. For example, could you possibly be wrong about the violation? Talking with your competitor helps you gain valuable insight even if you are correct about the infringement. For example:

- Are they dug in and refusing to comply with your IP rights?
- Do they seem the type to fight rather than admit they are wrong?
- Do they seem amenable to some sort of compromise?

Even after you've proceeded to court, always remain open to meeting with the opposition. You may be surprised how perspectives change as time goes by and legal fees grow.

Be aware that trials can go on for weeks, and are exceptionally expensive. Cases that involve experts cost well into the hundreds of thousands of dollars, and sometimes more. Take every opportunity to settle. Keep in mind the case of Waterloo-based Research In Motion, which lost a patent case in the United States to the tune of $615 million. At the beginning of the case they had the chance to settle for a very small amount. (Remember that settlement costs add up, but so does the diversion of management time and energy, which could be much better spent driving your business.) In most situations, the sensible approach to resolving an infringement issue is skillful negotiation.

Proceeding to court

If you're unable to reach an out-of-court settlement with your infringer, your lawyer will initiate court proceedings.

When you get to court, the *burden of proof* — who must prove what — often affects who wins and who loses. Keep in mind that registering your copyrights and trademarks, although optional, provides you with a big advantage — your rights are presumed to be valid. Your opponents bear the burden of proving that your rights should be invalidated. Unregistered rights can be defended, but you must first prove you're entitled to the rights, which complicates and lengthens your trial.

Book II: Intellectual Property

You begin your journey to trial by exchanging *pleadings* with the opposing side; as the plaintiff you declare your claim against the defendant, and the defendant states a defence. Then the parties exchange all relevant documentation — and we do mean *all* relevant documentation. Providing full disclosure is essential, even if some of the papers hurt your case. Relevant papers that disappear count heavily against you. Next, a representative from each side answers questions, under oath, during a pre-trial discovery examination. Finally, it's on to court, which we cover in the section "Fighting for Your Rights."

IP trials often involve highly complex subject matter. In some patent cases, educating the judge about the technology takes up the first days of the trial. You're responsible for providing an expert witness who understands the subject matter and who presents your version of events. Your legal team will help you secure a qualified candidate, but you'll have to pay the expert's fees. Your opponent will provide an expert witness with the defendant's perspective on the events.

Fighting for Your Rights

After you arrive in court, the defendant is entitled to use any of a number of defences recognized by the law. We introduce you to a few of the major ones in the upcoming sections.

Questioning the scope of your rights

Your opponent claims that no infringement is taking place, because your protection isn't broad enough to cover what the opponent is doing. The opponent's actions exceed the *scope of your rights*.

Patents

You define the exclusive rights that will be protected when you draft your claim. Within the claim, you create a list of the innovations for which you are seeking protection. In court, the judge checks the alleged infringements against the list in your claim, and if you include something on your claim that your opponent has omitted, they're not guilty of infringement. (Refer to Chapter 2 for advice on drafting an effective claim.) For example, if your patent claims a whistle fastened to the front wheel of a bicycle, and your opponent fastens a whistle to the back wheel, you have no case. The opponent's use doesn't fall within the scope of your claim.

Trademarks

If the copycat uses your exact trademark on the same type of product you sell, then the case is fairly clear cut and is unlikely to go to court. However, if the marks are merely similar to yours and the wares are slightly different, you need to prove that customer confusion over whose product is whose is likely to arise. If confusion is unlikely, then you can't prevent the use of your trademark.

Copyright

Violating a copyright involves copying; coming up with a similar creation independently doesn't count as infringement. You are responsible for proving to the court that copying has occurred. The court makes a judgment call based on the balance of probabilities — is it more or less likely that copying occurred? If copying didn't occur, then the creation exists beyond the scope of your copyright.

Generally, providing proof that the opposition had access to your work and that a similarity exists between the works will cause the court to rule in your favour.

Industrial designs

Submitting a drawing that depicts the look of your product defines your exclusive design rights, and selecting the title of your registration defines the type of product you're protecting. If you choose "bottle" as your title and the infringer is using a similar design on a lamp, that falls outside the scope of your rights.

Invalidating your claim

The bad guys may try to claim that your right is invalid. If they can prove that you aren't in fact entitled to the rights you are defending, the rights will be ruled invalid. Invalidity arguments are usually asserted by way of a counterclaim in response to your claim. If the invalidity claim is successful, this can end your IP rights — which can be a disaster for you, your business, and your licensees. In Chapter 2 we discuss the requirements you must meet to secure valid IP rights — and you can rest assured that a defendant will probe each possible requirement to challenge the validity of your rights.

Questioning the ownership of your IP

**Book II:
Intellectual
Property**

Proving you own your IP right may be necessary, particularly if you acquire the rights through an assignment or transfer. For your own protection, set everything in writing. Registering the transfer of rights with the Canadian Intellectual Property Office (CIPO) isn't a requirement, but it's in your best interest. For example, in the case of a disputed patent (perhaps the original owner sold the patent twice), the first to register wins. Instead of twisting your ankle racing to the patent office at the first sign of trouble, register as soon as the transfer takes place.

Exhausting your rights

Defendants commonly claim you gave them permission, and if it's true, it's a pretty good defence. If the infringer buys whistles from one of your distributors who's going bankrupt — and they really are your whistles — you can't complain. Selling something gives the buyer the implied right of use; your rights become exhausted by the sale. You've used them up and can't assert them a second time.

Claiming you failed to act promptly

Sitting on your IP rights and then leaping out of the bushes to sue an infringer isn't allowed. Knowing about infringement and failing to act is called *acquiescence*. Your opponent may claim that he believed you had waived your rights because you had already been allowing the use of your right for a period of time.

Getting to the Finish Line

Although visions of multi-million dollar settlements may dance in your head when you think of court cases, remember that your main goal when bringing an IP infringement case to court is simply to end the infringement. Reaching the end of an IP case allows you to breathe a little easier. In this section, we consider some of the other potential outcomes of an IP case.

Settlements

Settling is the best, fastest, and least expensive way to end an infringement dispute. Aim to settle if it's at all possible. Here are a couple possible settlements:

- You and the infringer negotiate a compromise where the other person continues to use your right on an ongoing basis, in exchange for making payments to you.

- The infringer agrees to pay you a fee for permission to continue using your right until existing inventory is cleared out. The infringer will then stop the infringing activity.

Rulings

If you're unable to reach a settlement, the court will make a ruling based on the information presented at trial. A few possible outcomes include the following:

- **The court issues an *injunction*:** This is an order directing the defendant to stop selling the infringing article. Usually the court also orders that existing inventory be delivered to the holder of the IP right or destroyed. Injunctions can be either *interlocutory* (before the trial) or permanent. In the RIM vs. NTP litigation, the possibility that the court might grant an injunction that shut down all BlackBerry service in the United States was front-page news.

- **You may receive a pay-over of the profits arising from the infringing activities.** Doing so means that you are, legally, condoning the activities, therefore no injunction would be granted.

- **The court may award you compensation for damages.** You could receive an amount comparable to lost profits or a royalty, reasonable for the amount of infringement that took place.

Cashing In on Your IP Rights

IP rights offer much more value than simply allowing you to prevent copycats from using your creations. Sure, selling the product that embodies your IP right is a good start, but other opportunities to monetize your IP also exist. Always develop your IP assets with an eye toward letting these assets, and your IP rights to them, work like a lucrative investment. You can profit from your IP rights just like you can with a good investment in real estate — you can sell them after they go up in value, retain ownership and collect the royalties they generate (similar to rent), or both.

That dream is a reality for many astute entrepreneurs who took advantage of the opportunities that rewarded their creativity. In the upcoming sections we suggest some of the different ways you can maximize the benefit of your IP.

Selling and Licensing

Commercializing your IP — getting people to pay for it, whether by selling the IP or licensing it — can be quite different from selling your product or service. However, commercializing IP has some real similarities to other business activity: it requires preparation, persistence, marketing, and selling.

IP doesn't commercialize itself. It must be sold, and every ad you've ever seen for a Microsoft product proves this. Not all IP is valuable. Only IP that provides a right to exclude others from doing something that they want to do, and can't get around quickly and cheaply, is valuable. People buy or license IP because it's cheaper and easier to buy or license it than to develop an alternative in-house. For example, if you use Microsoft Word, you likely do so because buying a licence is cheaper and easier than writing your own word processing program.

Most successful IP rights sales depend on the buyer having easier and quicker access to customers than the seller. You may have a great idea for a computer networking device, but chances are Cisco is going to be able to take it to a bigger market faster and with more marketing muscle than you can. If Cisco buys your IP, it steps into your shoes, and can use the IP to protect its product. For the same reason, most successful IP licensing involves vastly expanding the use of the IP through distribution channels that the original creator can't reach directly as easily as the licensee(s) can.

Commercializing IP successfully requires you to adjust your thinking, because IP isn't like tangible property. IP can have

- **More than one owner.** Although co-ownership can be complex, it can also solve many thorny problems.

- **More than one simultaneous user,** and can increase in value the more it's used. IP doesn't wear out, and costs nothing to ship.

- **More than one exclusive licensee,** if the licensees are in different markets.

Here's an example: You're in charge of fundraising for a major university. Chances are, your trademark is one of your most valuable assets, and if you proceed carefully you can license it to more than one third party in exchange for valuable revenue that enhances your brand: affinity credit cards, insurance services, travel packages for seniors, and so on. Many universities are already exploring precisely this sort of trademark licensing strategy as a fundraising tool.

Understanding Licences

Your driver's licence gives you the permission to do something that you previously couldn't — take your car out for a spin on the highway. The government, which owns the highway, gives you this permission as part of a deal. For your licence to remain in effect, you have to uphold your end of the deal: Drive responsibly and follow the rules of the road — otherwise they'll take your licence away. An IP licence follows the same principle.

A *licence* is a contract between two parties. The *licensor* owns an IP right. The *licensee* is an individual or company willing to use the IP right in exchange for paying royalties or other valuable considerations. For example, if the IP right is a patent, the licensee can practise the invention without being sued for infringement by the patent-owning licensor.

A licence doesn't actually transfer the IP right — it just gives the licensee permission to use the IP, backed by the licensor's promise not to cancel that authorization as long as the licensee keeps up her end of the bargain. A licence is like the lease on a house, where the landlord gives the tenant permission to live there as long as the tenant pays the rent on time. A licence differs from an *assignment,* which is an outright transfer of an IP right, similar to selling a house. (See "Assigning Rather Than Licensing".)

Granting Licences

Because all IP can be licensed, many different types of licences exist. To get you thinking about the possibilities, we list a few of the common ones below, according to the type of underlying IP right:

- ✔ **Patent licence:** You can license your patent rights, whatever they may be, as soon as they arise. That means you can license them from the time of invention — before any patent is granted — and benefits of this can include having the licensee assume the costs of prosecuting and maintaining the patent in its territory. In situations such as these, consider who enforces the patent, and what the consequences will be if the patent is deemed partially or wholly invalid.

✔ **Trademark licence:** This licence authorizes someone else to operate under one or more of your commercial identifiers. The law requires you to keep some quality control over the activities of your licensee so that the customers who relied on the quality of your goods or services in the past will not be deceived into buying substandard products.

Nowadays, many products aren't made by their original manufacturers but by firms that use the trademark under licence from the original manufacturer and strict quality control conditions. A Mountain Equipment Co-op jacket likely isn't manufactured by employees of the Co-op.

✔ **Copyright licence:** A copyright licence allows the licensee to use the copyrighted work. Often these licences are named for their use — such as a publication licence, broadcast licence, or recording licence. Technically, you don't buy software or ringtones — you buy a licence to use the software or ringtone, and the scope of what you're allowed to do with it is set by the precise terms of the licence.

Registering your copyright before granting a licence isn't a prerequisite, but we highly recommended doing so. Registered rights are much easier to enforce, making the terms of a licence easier to enforce. Additionally, a registered copyright offers better protection against third-party infringers, making it more attractive to licensees, and more valuable to you.

✔ **Trade-secret licence:** The licensor discloses proprietary and confidential information to the licensee in exchange for payment and a promise to keep the information under wraps. Trade secret licences are particularly common in the chemical field, where keeping formulae and manufacturing processes secret is relatively easy.

✔ **Merchandising licence:** Certain marks are so strong, recognized, and widely accepted that they can be rented out for use on a wide variety of goods. Merchandising licences allow the use of a copyright or trademark, or a combination of both, on a range of goods that goes beyond the original purpose of the mark. For instance, a movie studio may license the use of a cartoon character on a variety of children's products, from toys to book bags.

**Book II:
Intellectual
Property**

Inspecting the Basic Elements of a Licence

In these sections, we highlight the key issues you should address when exploiting your IP assets, and offer some actual text that you can use in legal documents and other legal observations. (That text appears in italics.)

This outline of the basic make-up of a licence agreement isn't exhaustive; you must seek the assistance of a competent IP professional to negotiate and draft the licence agreement.

Getting it in writing

Before negotiating any type of licence agreement, you should understand the important parts of the agreement. Here are some key things that you and your lawyer need to cover in the agreement:

- ✔ **Clearly define the IP right you're licensing.**

- ✔ **Grant permission to use your IP.** This is a critical part of the licence agreement, because here you define the scope of the permitted activities. Be very specific here in order to avoid future disputes.

- ✔ **Determine the level of exclusivity** — who gets to use the rights.

  - • **Exclusive:** The licensor waives any right to use the rights or to authorize anybody else to do so.

  - • **Sole:** The licensor reserves the right to use the rights himself or through his company, but agrees to license only the licensee.

  - • **Non-exclusive:** The licensor reserves the right to use the rights and can also license third parties in competition with the licensee.

    In general, an exclusive licence carries higher royalties than the other two types.

- ✔ **Outline the territory and field of use.** An IP owner can divide and parcel the geographical areas and commercial fields where the invention can be practised or applied.

  For example, say you hold a patent on energy-efficient window frames. Because they're reasonably priced and work well, you sell a number of them. You'd like to expand your territory and sell more, but because windows are heavy and fragile, they don't travel well. Licensing your patent to window makers in other markets is a perfect option for this situation; you can continue to service your home territory, while your licensees pay you royalties to use your invention in theirs.

- ✔ **Define the duration.** Fix the term of the licence and any renewals, and deal with what happens if the IP right is lost or is no longer enforceable against third parties.

- ✔ **Address enforcement.** Determine who has what rights and obligations to enforce the IP and to shut down infringers. Paying a royalty to the licensor is no fun if your competitor is using the IP for free.

- ✔ **Specify termination.** State when the licence can be terminated, and what happens if it is. Software licences often require the licensor to place the source code in escrow, for release to the licensee in certain circumstances. If you are the licensee of any IP right, protecting yourself against arbitrary termination if the licensor goes bankrupt is very important and can be very difficult, even for the most experienced IP professionals.

If the licence authorizes the licensee to use or operate under your trademark, include a clause allowing you to control the quality of the goods or services provided to the customer under your identifier. This allows you to maintain quality and service standards, and therefore the value of your trademark.

Getting paid: Remuneration

You have great flexibility when setting up the payment for the licence. Payments may comprise

✔ One or more lump sums

✔ Royalties based on net proceeds, number of items made or sold, costs of goods, or any other readily verifiable parameter

✔ A combination of the above

Advances against royalties, delayed payments, stepped-up or stepped-down royalty rates based on sale proceeds or number of items sold, and guaranteed remittances can be used to fine-tune the agreement to your circumstances:

**Book II:
Intellectual
Property**

Licensee shall pay Licensor each of the following:

A non-refundable lump sum of $5,000.00 on each anniversary of the effective date of this agreement.

During the first 10 years of the term of this agreement, royalties at the rate of $10.00 per camera manufactured under the exclusive and co-exclusive licences, and at the rate of $3.00 per camera manufactured under the non-exclusive licence; plus 1% of the net proceeds from the sales of all types of cameras.

After the 10th anniversary of the effective date of this agreement, these royalty rates shall be reduced by one half.

A royalty advance of $25,000.00 upon execution of this agreement by all parties.

The details of the remuneration clause are usually dictated by the business circumstances — the financial status and marketing clout of the licensor, the anticipated sales, the required investment in tooling and marketing, and so on.

Think carefully about what the royalty is applied to. If you charge the licensee a royalty as a percentage of revenue from one product, but it also sells to the same customers another product or service that isn't under licence, the licensee has an incentive to under-price your product and mark up the other service.

Including a minimum performance clause with an exclusive licence agreement is wise because you depend entirely upon the licensee's performance to exploit your IP asset. Such a clause may use a sliding scale to keep the licensed company on its best behaviour. For example:

> *Licensee shall pay Licensor:*
>
> *In the first calendar year, $50,000.00.*
>
> *In each subsequent year, the greater of $150,000.00 or one half of the total monetary remuneration received by Licensor during that year.*

Reporting

Except when licence fees are fully paid upfront or by a fixed payment schedule, requiring the licensee to periodically report its production and/or sales figures is smart, as royalties are based on these numbers:

> *Within thirty days from the end of each calendar year, Licensee shall provide Licensor with a report of the number of cameras manufactured and net proceeds collected by Licensee during that calendar year.*

Assigning Rather Than Licensing

When IP is transferred outright, whether from employee to employer, or from company to company, it's done using a written document called an *assignment.*

When your lawyer drafts the assignment document, make sure your lawyer includes a complete and readily identifiable description of what's being transferred (attach a copy or photograph if necessary). And if the buyer is paying you a royalty rather than a lump sum payment up front, also include in the agreement all the payment and reporting clauses usually found in a licence agreement. (See the "Inspecting the Basic Elements of a Licence" section, earlier in this chapter.)

If you're buying the assignment of rights, record the assignment as soon as possible in the Canadian Intellectual Property Office (CIPO), or any other appropriate agency. In general, recording the transfer cuts off the transferor's right to assign the same asset or right to another person. If you don't record the assignment, any subsequent assignment takes precedence over yours if it's recorded first.

Developing a Commercialization Strategy

Many inventors and other developers of IP assets and rights don't have a clue about how to find a buyer or licensee to bring their creations to the market. No magic formula will work for everybody, but planning your commercialization strategy before you pursue IP rights is the best way. Don't panic if you haven't; all is not lost. As long as you understand the marketplace, you can develop an effective and lucrative strategy.

Understanding market realities is the first step to a good commercialization strategy. To help you begin your planning, we offer a few observations based on many years serving entrepreneurs:

Book II: Intellectual Property

- ✔ **The more you develop your project, the more you get for it.** You generally can't sell an idea or concept. A patented but unproven invention may sometimes be sold or licensed, but not for much. If you can show that you have an ongoing business with real customers, built around a product, process, or method protected by IP rights, it can be sold more readily and lucratively than the same business without IP rights.

- ✔ **Few large companies respond to an unsolicited licence offer or proposal.**

- ✔ **The most promising buyers and licensees are companies that can increase their existing sales by owning/licensing a little of your IP,** especially if they're trying to catch up with a market leader and can use your IP to give them a new edge. For example, a company that sells furnaces may want to buy your latest and greatest Internet-enabled thermostat to gain market share in the furnace business. They might even give the thermostat away for free to furnace buyers.

  Another very attractive potential group of licensees are people who do what you do, but for a different market. Say you sell diagnostic tools to Canadian dentists. Potential licensees of some of your IP include people who sell diagnostic tools to dentists in other countries, or perhaps veterinarians in Canada and elsewhere.

- ✔ **Commercialize your IP early, often, and aggressively.** Start commercializing as quickly as you can and don't wait for the IP to be formally granted. This gains you customers, and with customers come revenue and feedback. Revenue keeps you in business, and feedback leads to further improvements. Don't keep your IP in the dark — it grows better in the light of day.

Getting sophisticated help to design and roll out an IP commercialization strategy isn't easy. Most IP professionals are not business experts, and many businesspeople are not IP experts. This leaves a void of people who speak both languages; this book is our attempt to start a dialogue across this void.

Benefitting from Someone Else's IP

IP provides benefits not only to its owners, but also to outsiders — especially licensees, who can acquire new products, processes, materials, and brands much more efficiently through the use of licences than by developing them from scratch.

Licensing used to be an exotic way to conduct business, but it's rapidly becoming mainstream. The key to successful licensing is to ensure that it's win-win: both the licensor and licensee must gain by contributing something the other doesn't have or can't easily reproduce. Here we consider some of the key benefits of licensing IP into your business. (We talk about the basics of licensing and being a licensor earlier in this chapter.)

Being a licensee

If you've ever bought software, you've benefited from licensing someone else's IP. For example, accounting software offers specific applications for all sorts of different markets, such as lawyers, dentists, municipal governments, and so on. To gain access to a high-quality solution at a reasonable cost, users license these applications rather than building them from scratch. This also provides them the assurance that the costs of supporting and maintaining the product will be spread over many users.

Acquiring an exclusive right to use or distribute someone else's IP in your market can give you a substantial boost. Say you're in the business of selling products and services to pig farmers in Manitoba, and you've heard about ways to cut down on methane emissions while generating electricity and heat from pig manure. Many alternative energy technologies are far more advanced in Europe than they are in Canada. As a result, a possible strategy is to approach European companies that have good technology. Chances are good they don't consider Canada their biggest or most important market (they may not have even considered Manitoba), and they may license their world-leading technology to you for modest royalties. If they do, this will quickly and cost-effectively get you right to the front of the line as a leader in your market.

Using licensing with trademarks

All sorts of reasons to license someone else's trademark exist, including trying to benefit from the goodwill inherent in the trademark. Maybe your product would have an easier time in the market if it were under the halo of a well-known brand rather than your own unknown one. After all, which are you more likely to buy on a whim: *Joe's Guide to Beekeeping,* or *Beekeeping For Dummies?*

To pursue this strategy, you may have to actively pursue the licensor and convince them that you will add to, not detract from, their brand. Trademarks are powerful things that can have a huge impact on sales. If you have a good product or service but not much market awareness, licensing a well-known trademark can pay off in spades.

Sometimes, you can co-brand your product with both your own trademark and someone else's, so that some of their goodwill rubs off on your trademark. Consider the Pink Ribbon associated with breast cancer research. This trademark has been licensed extensively by a wide range of companies that see value in being associated with this cause. Licensees pay a royalty for the right to apply the Pink Ribbon to their regular packaging because they believe they'll enjoy enhanced sales and goodwill from the positive association.

Licensing isn't an easy way to riches. It requires keen attention to detail. Work closely with your IP professional to ensure you understand the precise terms of your rights and to address potential challenges before they arise.

You need to consider the following when considering becoming a licensee:

✔ Can you sub-license?

✔ Was the royalty a one-time payment, or must you pay ongoing royalties based on time or use?

✔ If you, the licensee, improve upon the licensor's technology so it better suits your market, who will own the IP in those improvements, and who will pay to protect them?

✔ What will happen to you if

- The licence is ever terminated?

- Ownership or control of the licensor changes?

- The licensor goes bankrupt or is sold to your competitor?

Using IP Filings as a Research Tool

If you're willing to invest some time and effort into research, you can find lots of information in IP databases, just waiting for you to exploit it. Here's a list of some of the material you may find particularly worthwhile:

✔ Technical information to help you improve production, distribution, or sale of your product

✔ Inspiration for new initiatives or improvements on your existing devices

✔ Legitimate competitive information on your rivals

✔ Leads on potential foreign partners

These sections suggest ways to use this information to your advantage, such as spurring on innovation in your own company, exploiting lapsed patents, or making international connections.

Technically speaking

Patent offices around the world are great sources of technical information. Fortunately, you don't have to search each of them to find useful information. Most significant innovations in the world are registered in the United States as well as their home country. Patent applicants disclose their invention when filing for registration with the United States Patent and Trademark Office (USPTO). Searching its website at www.uspto.gov gives you access to virtually unlimited technical information.

Use the information from patent disclosures to stimulate ideas with your own team — creating a new device or tweaking an existing one. However, you must be careful to avoid infringing on a patent; indeed, you may need to consider licensing. Refer to Chapter 2 of this book for information on patent violations.

Additionally, you may find patents that are expired, either because they're more than 20 years old or because the owner has neglected to pay maintenance fees. These inventions are no longer entitled to protection, and you're free to use them.

Tracking your competitors

Using the patent office websites (www.cipo.ic.gc.ca and www.uspto. gov), you can track the activities of your rivals. Regularly searching the CIPO and USPTO websites will keep you up to date on your competitors' latest inventions. It will also alert you to potential opportunities arising from neglect. For example, are your rivals keeping their maintenance payments current, or has their registration lapsed? Perhaps they registered their invention in the United States but not in Canada, leaving the invention in the public domain — and free for anyone to use in Canada.

Swimming with the fishes

Keeping an open and inquisitive mind will lead you to find opportunities. Consider the success of Marineland in Canada. The owners were well aware of the Marineland in Florida and California — they even hired dolphin trainers from the U.S. operation, and they copied the name for their Canadian venture. They seized the opportunity to legally establish a similar business with the same name in Canada.

Even though the Americans had advertised in Canada, their failure to register in Canada meant that the Canadians got the Canadian trademark. Although the Canadians' tactics might seem sneaky, that doesn't matter — the test is not who's a nice guy, but who uses the trademark first in Canada.

**Book II:
Intellectual
Property**

Partnering up

If you're interested in expanding your business beyond Canadian borders, international IP databases can provide a wealth of information. Using IP office websites, you may find a potential distributor for your product, or perhaps discover some IP that you can license in this country.

Many possibilities exist to expand your business. Make sure you — and your IP professional — are creative, curious, and always on the lookout for new opportunities.

Book III
Business Planning

The 5th Wave   By Rich Tennant

"It's quite a business plan, Ms. Strunt. It's the first
one I've read whose mission statement says,
'...keeps me out of trouble.'"

In this book . . .

Chapter 1: Knowing Where You Want to Go 203

Chapter 2: Describing Your Marketplace..............................231

Chapter 3: Weighing Your Business's Prospects 273

Chapter 4: A Sample Business Plan 301

Chapter 1

Knowing Where You Want to Go

. . . .

In This Chapter

▶ Assembling your business-planning resources

▶ Preparing for each part of a business plan

▶ Identifying your business's values and principles

▶ Declaring your business's vision

▶ Putting together a mission statement

▶ Setting goals and objectives that make good business sense

. . . .

*F*or any initiative, from a winter vacation to starting a business or developing a new way to operate some aspect of an existing business, there are lots of good reasons to have a plan and no good reasons not to have one. Plans can take a global view of the business or be very specific. They can be used simply to guide your decision making or they can help others, like lenders, make decisions relating to things such as giving you a line of credit, joining your business as a partner or otherwise help you fund growth. This chapter looks at the fundamental values, the objectives and the goals of your business to help chart what you stand for and where you want to go.

Preparing to Do a Business Plan

Planning is serious business. For many companies, a solid business plan is the difference between success and failure. Many people going into business for the first time want to rush right in, print business cards, hang up the sign, and start making money — a natural response for anyone excited about a new business idea. But taking a little extra time up front to prepare pays off down the line; especially when it comes to writing a business plan. Face it, after your business is up and running, you won't have much time to write the major pieces of your plan.

Identifying your planning resources

Having the right resources at the right time can make business planning easier and more successful. Fortunately, you can now find more useful and usable business-planning resources than ever before, from books and software to Internet websites and professional experts. Of course, you may also find plenty of stuff that isn't worth looking at — much less paying for. And you can't always judge a book (or software program) by its cover.

As you begin to put together your business plan, you may discover that you need some additional tools — a book devoted to marketing, for example, or business-planning software that can help you create and maintain your written document.

Hitting the corner bookstore

Obviously, you already selected one of the best hands-on, business-planning books around. But okay, you can also find other useful business-planning books — particularly books that concentrate on specific areas, such as marketing or financial planning, and books that focus on particular kinds of businesses, such as non-profits or sole proprietorships. (See Chapter 4 of this book for a sample business plan.)

You can find out a lot about a book by reading through its table of contents. You should also dip into the first chapter.

The basic principles of business planning may be timeless, but certain subjects — Internet marketing, for example — change rapidly. A book that was published three years ago may already be ancient history. If you want to find timely information, such as details about tax considerations for a small business, be sure to check the book's publication date.

For the timeliest info, turn to magazines, newspapers, and journals. They are terrific for keeping up with the business world, in general — and your industry, in particular. The business press also provides an efficient way to routinely scan for trends or new developments that may affect your business plan. If you're not sure what periodicals focus on your particular industry or your region, do a quick online search (see the following section for more details).

Surfing the Internet

Today, hundreds of websites offer information on business planning. You can access the information on some of these sites for free; other sites tease you with a sample and then charge you for more details. In our experience, some of the freebies can be just as helpful as the subscription sites, so we suggest that you check first to see what's free for the asking before you plunk down your hard-earned cash. In particular, the federal government offers heaps of solid information on planning, starting, and operating your own business through its Canada Business site (www.canadabusiness.ca) and its network of provincial and regional sites. Even the Canada Revenue Agency (CRA) has helpful planning tips, which you can find at www.cra-arc.gc.ca.

 Beyond sharing some basic business-planning tools, the Internet is also a great place for the latest information about competitors, markets, business trends, and new technologies — all the things you need to put together a complete picture of your business environment.

Internet hotspots for business-planning info

You can find a treasure trove of business-planning information and resources online. To help you sort through all the riches, we put together a list of popular sites that provide useful and reliable tips, tools, and examples — including dozens of real-life business plans:

✔ www.canadabusiness.ca: The Canada Business site is far and away the best source of information about planning, funding, starting, and running a small business. You can find useful FAQs, as well as counselling help and shareware software programs.

✔ www.ic.gc.ca: Industry Canada's website has a wealth of information. Check out the Programs and Services menu by subject and look for Business Tools and Resources. The site offers a number of diagnostic and benchmarking tools, as well as useful financial figures comparing the performance of other small businesses.

✔ www.statcan.ca: Statistics Canada is our nation's statistical agency. It has the most current information, including statistics and data on population, economy, industry, import/export activity, and special subject areas. You can also find links to other useful sites here.

✔ www.cra-arc.gc.ca: A useful site if you run a small business or are self-employed. The CRA provides all kinds of bookkeeping, accounting, and tax information. The site also includes links to other helpful non-CRA business resources on the Web.

✔ www.cfib.ca: The Canadian Federation of Independent Business (CFIB) calls itself the big voice for small business, representing small and independent businesses in Canada. Its website features tools, tips, and research reports that small business owners may find useful.

✔ www.bdc.ca: The Business Development Bank of Canada website has a number of business tools, from planning templates to e-business diagnostics. The Ask a Professional section enables you to post your own questions and review previous Q&As.

✔ www.legalline.ca: You can't find a better place than Legal Line to turn for basic information on the legal aspects — federal and provincial — of key business issues. The website also offers free information in 35 areas of law, including info on insuring your home business, independent contractor arrangements, trademarks and copyrights, debts, bankruptcies, and employment law.

**Book III:
Business
Planning**

The Internet may be a gold mine of business information, but you may also find plenty of fool's gold.

Follow three simple rules when you use the Web for business research:

- ✔ **Make sure the material is current.**
- ✔ **Know your sources.**
- ✔ **Double-check key facts and statistics.**

Installing business-planning software

Business-planning software allows you to automatically assemble all the components of a business plan, turning them into a printer-ready, spiffy-looking document. The best programs also make easy work of the financial parts of business planning — creating income statements and cash-flow statements, for example, or making financial projections.

Business-planning software programs can sometimes make the job of business planning *too* easy. Remember, the best software-planning tools guide you through the important aspects of business planning and then keep track of your words, sentences, and paragraphs. But they don't think for you. You do the serious mental work yourself.

Investors and bankers who make a living reviewing and funding business plans are all too familiar with the look and feel of the most popular software-generated, business-planning documents. If you use one of these programs, customize your plan to make it unique.

Seeking professional help

No one knows the ins and outs of planning and running a business better than people who have done it. And most business people are happy to share their experience and expertise, as long as you don't plan on becoming a competitor! Many will even mentor first-time entrepreneurs. Don't be afraid to turn to a grizzled veteran for advice if you run into questions that you can't answer or run out of ideas to get your business off the ground.

Finding expert advice is surprisingly easy. The first place to look is in your own address book. Ask your friends and colleagues for suggestions. Other good places to look for help are the Chamber of Commerce, provincial government business centres, a local college or university, or the business section of your newspaper.

Choose experts with experience in a business similar to the one you're planning. After you identify a person, decide exactly what kind of assistance you need. You can't ask someone to plan your whole business for you, after all. But you can ask them to fine-tune your marketing strategy, for example, or review and critique your financial projections.

Finding friendly advice

Many communities have organizations of business people who convene to share ideas, exchange contacts, help each other out, and socialize. Some organizations focus on helping specific groups, such as women, Aboriginals, immigrants, youths, gay/lesbian/transgendered, or freelancers; other organizations, made up of local people across the business spectrum, are open to the public. Thanks to the Internet, you can find business groups that regularly schedule online support meetings.

Business networking organizations are an invaluable resource for help in planning and running your business. For information about what's available in your community, check with your local Chamber of Commerce. Ask whether they have a mentoring program. Because websites change so fast, look for a networking organization online by using a search engine.

Setting steps and schedules

Putting together a business plan resembles any project that involves teamwork, from building a house to running a relay race. The clearer the ground rules, the smoother the process — and the happier your team. Make sure that your ground rules do three things:

- **Identify key steps.** Typically, the process of writing a business plan includes five distinct steps: research, first draft, review, revised draft, and final review.

- **Clearly assign duties.** Everyone involved needs to know exactly what you expect from them. You can use the key steps to create separate sets of tasks, and then you assign each task to members of your team.

- **Establish a schedule.** Although writing a business plan is a big job, the process doesn't need to be a long and drawn-out affair. After you complete the preliminary research, the rest of the steps are fairly straightforward. To keep your project on track, set due dates for each component of the plan and each step in the process.

Book III: Business Planning

Planning Each Part of a Business Plan

When you first set out to create a business plan, the task may seem overwhelming. Right off the bat, you need to answer fundamental and sometimes difficult questions about your business and what you see for the future. You have to decide what targets to aim for when you look ahead and set business goals and objectives. To succeed, you have to take the time to know your

- ✔ Industry
- ✔ Customers
- ✔ Competitors
- ✔ Business resources
- ✔ Business's unique qualities
- ✔ Business's advantages
- ✔ Basic financial condition
- ✔ Financial forecast and budget

You also need to prepare for changes that you make to this list down the road. That means thinking through other options and alternatives, and being on the lookout for new ways to make your business prosper.

You don't want to scare people — yourself included — with a giant written plan. The longer your plan is, in fact, the less likely people are to read it. Ideally, your written plan should be 15 or 20 pages, maximum. We give you a sample business plan in Chapter 4.

To avoid becoming overwhelmed, and to keep the business-planning process in perspective, break the plan up into the basic sections that every good business plan needs to include. The following sections outline the sections of a business plan.

Executive summary

Your executive summary touches on every important part of your business plan. It's more than just a simple introduction; it's the whole plan, only shorter. In many cases, the people who read your plan don't need to read any further than the executive summary; if they do, however, the summary points them to the right place.

You don't need to make the executive summary much longer than a page or two, and you can wait until you complete the rest of the business plan before you write it; that way, you only have to review the plan to identify the key ideas that you want to cover.

If you want to make sure that people remember what you tell them, summarize what you're going to say, say it, and then reiterate what you've just said. The executive summary is the place where you summarize what your business plan says.

Business overview

In the overview, you highlight the most important aspects of your industry, your customers, and the products and services that you offer or plan to develop. Although you should touch on your business's history and major activities in the overview, you can leave many of the details for later sections.

To put together a general business overview, you need to draw on several key planning documents, including the following:

- ✔ **Values statement:** The set of beliefs and principles that guide your business's actions and activities

- ✔ **Vision statement:** A phrase that announces where your business wants to go or paints a broad picture of what you want your business to become

- ✔ **Mission statement:** A statement of your business's purpose; what it is and what it does

- ✔ **Goals and objectives:** A list of all the major goals that you set for your business, along with the objectives that you need to meet to achieve those goals

Later in this chapter, we tell you how to begin constructing these statements.

Book III:
Business
Planning

Business environment

Your business environment section covers all the major aspects of your business's situation that are beyond your immediate control: the nature of your industry, the direction of the marketplace, and the intensity of your competition. Look at each of these areas in detail to come up with lists of both the opportunities and the threats that your business faces. Based on your observations, you can describe what it takes to be a successful business.

Pay special attention to how your industry operates. Describe the primary business forces that you see, as well as the key industry relationships that determine how business gets done. Talk about your marketplace and your customers in more detail, perhaps even dividing the market into sections that represent the kinds of customers you plan to serve. Finally, spend some time describing your competition: their characteristics, how they work, and what you think you may see from them in the future.

For more information on how to explore your business circumstances and the overall environment that your business competes in, check out Chapter 2 of this book.

Business description

In this section, go into much more detail about what your business has to offer. Include information about your management, the organization, new technology, your products and services, operations, and your marketing potential — in short, anything special that you bring to your industry.

In particular, look carefully and objectively at the long list of your business's capabilities and resources. Separate the capabilities that represent strengths from the ones that show weaknesses. In the process, try to point out where you have real advantages over your competitors.

Examining your business through your customers' eyes helps. With a consumer viewpoint, you can sometimes discover something of value to the customer that you didn't know you provide, and find additional long-term ways to compete in the market.

Business strategy

Business strategy brings together everything that you know about your business environment and your business to come up with future projections.

Map out your basic strategies for dealing with the major parts of your business, including the industry, your markets, and competition. Talk about why your strategy is the right one, given your business situation. Describe how you expect the strategy to play out in the future. Finally, point out specifically what your business needs to do to ensure that the strategy succeeds.

You need to talk about the ways your business world may change. List alternative possibilities for action, and in each case, describe what your business is doing to anticipate the changes and take advantage of new opportunities.

Financial review

Your financial review covers both where you stand today and where you expect to be in the future.

Describe your current financial situation by using several standard financial statements. Reference your financial statements in the text so that they support the assumptions and arguments that you make in the other sections of the business plan. The basic financial statements include the following:

- ✔ Income statement
- ✔ Balance sheet
- ✔ Cash-flow statement

Your projections about your future financial situation use exactly the same kind of financial statements. But for projections, you estimate all the numbers in the statements, based on your understanding of what may happen. Make sure to include all the assumptions that you made in other sections of your business plan to come up with your estimates in the first place.

Action plan

Your action plan lays out how you intend to carry out your business plan. It points out proposed changes in management or in the organization, for example, as well as new policies or procedures that you expect to put in place. Also, include any new skills that you, your managers, and your employees may need to make the plan work. Finally, talk about how you plan to generate excitement for your business plan inside your business, creating a culture that supports what you want to accomplish.

Book III: Business Planning

Defining Values and Principles

A successful business plan must start with a statement of business values, as well as a vision for the future. *Values* and a *vision* give your business a moral compass that guides you if you encounter trouble along the way. The two Vs also keep everybody in your business — even if that means only two of you — on course and heading in the same direction. What if you're a business of one? Taking time to establish your values and vision still guides you as your business grows.

In the upcoming sections, we point out why values are so important in the first place. We help you identify your business's values by evaluating the beliefs and business principles that you already hold. We show you how to put together a values statement, along with a set of rules to work by. Finally, we encourage you to create a vision statement for your business.

Understanding why values matter

Your business faces all sorts of options, alternatives, and decisions every day. If you take the time to define your business's values, your principles and beliefs can guide your managers, employees, or just you (if you're in business for yourself) as your business wades through complicated issues that sometimes don't have easy answers. When the unexpected happens, you can react quickly and decisively, based on a clear sense of what's important. Even when your business is sailing along just fine, a strong sense of value helps motivate you and your employees.

Facing tough choices

Consider one scenario. Frank Klein is an independent consultant working for a large Canada-based petrochemical firm that we'll call Canuck Oil. Frank conducts market analysis for one of the business's largest divisions and is involved in an important project concerning the development of new overseas business.

Frank sketches out several options for the production, distribution, and pricing of petrochemicals in three countries.

In one of his most promising scenarios, the numbers for a country that we'll call Friedonia yield substantially higher short-term profits than the other two — primarily because the nation doesn't yet have expensive pollution-control procedures in place. The other two nations have environmental laws similar to those in Canada.

Here's Frank's dilemma: By introducing the Canuck Oil product line into Friedonia, Frank's client could make huge profits. Sure, the resulting pollution may cause ecological damage that environmentalists could possibly trace back to Canuck Oil. But the business would do nothing illegal, according to Friedonia's current laws, and Frank stands to get a lot more business from Canuck Oil if the project goes ahead.

He agonizes over the situation and his report. What should Frank recommend to senior management? His options include

- ✔ Going for the short-term bucks
- ✔ Voluntarily enacting procedures to control pollution, even though the business isn't legally required to do so
- ✔ Forgetting Friedonia until the country has stronger environmental laws

Maybe you can relate to Frank's quandary, having faced similar kinds of ethical questions and tradeoffs in your own business.

If Frank has taken the time to set out his core values in advance, those values can help him out of his quandary. Values provide a framework to guide people who confront difficult choices, especially as a business grows and more people have to face tough decisions. Also, research suggests that principled companies with strong values tend to attract and retain better employees, and those companies are often more successful as a result.

Applying ethics and the law

A *values statement* is a set of beliefs and principles that guide the activities and operations of your business, no matter what its size. To make the statement mean anything, the people at the top of your business must exemplify your stated values, and your business's incentive and reward systems should lead all employees to act in ways that support your business's values.

Having a values statement can keep you and your colleagues on the right side of the law. After a spate of stunning financial scandals in the United States, Canada moved to protect and build confidence with investors. The Canadian Security Administrators developed new rules that include stringent standards of disclosure. The rules require senior managers of publicly traded companies to certify the accuracy of their financial statements and take responsibility for internal financial controls. Failing to do so can land you in jail. No longer can top-level executives say they don't really know what's going on in the companies that they run. Now, the executives are responsible for every number on a financial statement.

Book III: Business Planning

If your business isn't big enough to be publicly traded, you're still certain to come up against the law every time you file a tax return, whether you run a corporation, a partnership, or a sole proprietorship (refer to Book I for more about forms of business). Having a clear set of values can keep you from getting too well acquainted with the Canada Revenue Agency (CRA).

Understanding the value of having values

A clear values statement can be most important when the unexpected happens.

In the late 1980s, the United States experienced what many consider a terrorist attack. Someone in the Chicago area tampered with bottles of Tylenol, the best-selling pain reliever from McNeil Laboratories, a subsidiary of the health-care giant Johnson & Johnson. An unknown number of Tylenol capsules were laced with cyanide, and eight people died. The tragedy created a business crisis for Johnson & Johnson.

Johnson & Johnson reacted quickly and decisively to the threat against its customers. The business pulled every bottle of Tylenol from retail shelves throughout America — a massive undertaking that ultimately cost the business more than $100 million — and it did so immediately upon discovering the problem.

When the crisis was over, Johnson & Johnson became a corporate role model. Its lightning-fast response to the Tylenol incident earned it a reputation as one of the most responsible companies in the world, one that takes its civic duties seriously and puts the public good ahead of its profits. Johnson & Johnson's many businesses benefited accordingly.

Why did Johnson & Johnson behave so well when so many other companies act paralyzed in sticky situations? The reasons are summed up in the business's statement of values, an extraordinary document called the Johnson & Johnson Credo. (You can read this document at www.jnj.com/connect/about-jnj/jnj-credo.)

For more than half a century, the Credo has successfully guided behaviour and actions across the sprawling Johnson & Johnson empire, currently a $53 billion worldwide corporation with more than 122,200 employees.

The Johnson & Johnson Credo works so well because each employee takes it seriously. With the active encouragement and involvement of top management, from the chairperson on down, the Credo is invoked, praised, and communicated throughout the company. Old-timers and new hires alike are reminded of the importance of the message. Promotions depend, in part, on how well managers live up to and disseminate the values of the Credo within their areas of responsibility. The Credo is a significant factor in Johnson & Johnson's continued performance near the top of its industry — and an indication of why the company is so well regarded by so many people.

Clarifying your business's values

Values statements often address several audiences. The Johnson & Johnson Credo that we talk about in the previous section speaks to doctors, patients, customers, suppliers, distributors, employees, stockholders, and the community and world at large.

Strong coffee and high principles

Second Cup has grown from a single java kiosk selling whole bean coffee in a Toronto shopping mall, opened in 1975, to an international company with more than 360 cafés across Canada and 15 in the Middle East. Second Cup is Canada's largest specialty café franchisor and second largest retailer of coffee. Its tag line proudly boasts, "Independently owned; uniquely Canadian." The company owes its success to many savvy decisions. But it also credits its guiding principles, which allow the company to measure the appropriateness of everything it does. Here are Second Cup's guiding principles:

✔ Work in harmony with both the environment and people.

✔ Treat our coffee-growing environment with the utmost respect and dignity.

✔ Ensure that no coffee purchased from Second Cup is harvested from child or forced labour.

✔ Provide a safe and healthy work environment.

✔ Provide fair and equitable compensation.

✔ Offer financial payment for quality coffee beans to directly benefit the farmers, workers, and mills.

You put together a values statement primarily for the benefit of your employees, of course (or just for yourself, if you operate a business alone). But your business's values have an obvious impact on all your stakeholders, including the owners, investors, bankers, customers, suppliers, regulators — and heck, even your mother if she loaned you $10,000 to start your business. When you start to identify your business's most important values, you have to consider different viewpoints, including the following:

**Book III:
Business
Planning**

✔ The demands of your investors (if you have any)

✔ The interests and expectations of all your stakeholders

✔ The beliefs and principles that you and your business already hold

After you come up with a preliminary list of values that you feel are most important, you're in a good position to create your values statement.

Focusing on existing beliefs and principles

Drawing up a list of beliefs and principles is one thing; putting those beliefs to the test is another. Tough choices are bound to come along, and they force you to examine your beliefs closely. If you run a one-person business, you already know something about what you stand for. In a bigger business, certain beliefs and values are inherent in the ways that the business operates. The best way to get to the heart of your business's beliefs and principles is to imagine how you'd respond to dilemmas.

Think about the situations described in the Beliefs and Principles Questionnaire (see Figure 1-1). Ask other people in your business, or trusted colleagues from outside your business, to do the questionnaire to see how they'd react to each scenario. Include a box on the questionnaire labelled Other or Don't Know. And remember, the whole point of situations that put your values to the test is that they're not always easy.

Keep in mind that answers aren't right or wrong; you don't have to send a note home or give anyone a bad grade. You're simply trying to identify the basic values with which your business already feels comfortable. Completed questionnaires give insights into the general beliefs and principles that your business considers important.

Beliefs and Principles Questionnaire

Situation	Possible Response
A disgruntled customer demands a full sales refund on a product. The product isn't defective but can't be resold. The customer insists that it just doesn't work right. Would you be more inclined to	❑ Send the customer away, keeping the sale on the books ❑ Refund the customer's money, absorbing the loss but betting on repeat business and loyal customers
You're faced with filling a key position in your company. Would you be more inclined to	❑ Hire a person from the outside who has the necessary job skills but little experience in your industry ❑ Promote an experienced and loyal employee, providing job-skills training
You're forced to let one of your employees go. Would you tend to dismiss	❑ The young, recently hired college grad, inexperienced but energetic ❑ The 55-year-old manager with 20 years at the company, solid and hard-working but somewhat set in his or her ways
You find out that a long-term supplier has been routinely under billing you for services, increasing your own profit margins. Would you be inclined to	❑ Let the matter pass, assuming that it's ultimately the supplier's mistake and responsibility ❑ Take the initiative to correct the billing error in the future ❑ Offer to not only correct the mistake, but also pay back the accumulated difference

Situation	_Possible Response_
You have a brilliant and creative employee. Unfortunately, this employee continually flouts the rules and disrupts the entire company. Would you tend to	❏ Tolerate the behaviour ❏ Work on ways to correct the situation ❏ Terminate the employee
An employee is faced with a personal dilemma. To meet a deadline on an important project, the employee must work overtime and miss a child's birthday celebration. Which do you tend to think of as the better employee	❏ The one who willingly agrees to work overtime ❏ The one who declines to come in and instead attends the birthday party
To meet your profit target for the coming quarter, you're faced with reducing costs. Would you lean toward	❏ Cutting back on customer-service expenses ❏ Reducing current investment in new product development ❏ Missing the quarterly target, concluding that the long-term investments are both necessary and justified
When developing the compensation packages for managers in your company, would you support	❏ Incentives based primarily on rewarding individual effort ❏ Compensation systems that promote attainment of group or team-based goals
You discover that one of your products doesn't quite meet its published specifications. Would your likely response be to	❏ Immediately alert your customers to the discrepancy ❏ Invest some time and effort into understanding the problem before informing customers ❏ Quietly correct the error, assuming that if customers were having problems, they would have already come to you
Rank the following in terms of their importance to you in your business	❏ Maximize profits ❏ Satisfy customers ❏ Create jobs ❏ Promote new technologies ❏ Win product-quality awards ❏ Beat the competition ❏ Maintain long-term growth ❏ Dominate markets

Figure 1-1:
Answers to the questionnaire point to beliefs and principles.

Book III: Business Planning

Putting together your values statement

Your business's values statement represents more than a quick to-do list. The description of your values reaches beyond quarterly goals or even yearly targets. Your values should guide you through tough decisions while you build a sustainable business that lasts and grows.

Maybe your business has some sort of values credo in place. If so, you're a step ahead of the game. (You lose points, however, if you have to glance at the dusty plaque on the office wall to remember it.) If you can't dig up a ready-made values statement to start with, begin putting together your own.

You may not have the luxury of spending weeks or months developing a values statement, so we show you a quick way to create one that sets your business on the right track. If your business is small, you can follow the steps yourself or with one or two of your colleagues — no need for long meetings and careful review.

You can't create a values statement quickly, but you *can* quickly begin a process to help capture and articulate the values intrinsic to your business.

Follow these steps to start creating a value statement:

1. **Gather your business's decision-makers (you, your partners and your trusted advisors) to talk about the general business values that should (and do) guide employee behaviour.**

2. **Prepare a first-draft list of all the values discussed in the meeting and circulate copies for review.**

3. **Schedule one or two follow-up meetings to clarify and confirm a final set of values.**

4. **Create a values statement that captures the agreed-upon values clearly and concisely, and get it approved by the senior managers and chief decision-makers.**

5. **Meet with managers at all levels to make sure that they understand the importance of, and the reasoning behind, the business values statement.**

6. **See that every employee gets a copy of the statement.**

   If you're in business for yourself, place a framed copy of the values statement near your desk at work or in your home office. Don't let it gather dust. For a bigger business, print the values statement on wallet-size cards to hand out, and don't forget to include the statement in the annual report. Post it on the business website and make sure it reaches all the stakeholders. Refer to and rely on the business values and let them be a guiding force in the actions and activities of every person who represents your business.

Don't forget to include two other important groups — customers and shareholders. Both can help you figure out what values are essential to your business.

Following through with your values

A values statement can sometimes turn out to be a bit too simplistic, using words that sound good on paper but that are difficult to put to practical use.

We recently looked through a stack of values statements from some of the biggest companies around. Over half of them included the word "integrity" or something close ("ethical conduct," "doing the right thing"). The next most popular value showing up was "respect for others," followed by "teamwork," "excellence," and "customer service."

To make your values statement really useful, you need to take the next step and link your values to basic, sensible rules. If you have employees, a good place to start is to ask them employees to fill out a questionnaire similar to the Beliefs and Principles Questionnaire shown in Figure 1-1. And if you have enough employees, you may also want to create an anonymous suggestion box in which employees can express their own ideas about values and about how your business is fulfilling its stated values.

The values statement of the infamous Enron Corporation, by the way, boasted four key words: "respect," "integrity," "communication," and "excellence." Nice words. But Enron went from one of the highest-flying businesses in the country to bankruptcy and scandal in months. The lesson of its fall is a simple one: Values must matter. And you must integrate those values into the way your business operates day-to-day and week-to-week.

Creating Your Business's Vision Statement

Book III:
Business
Planning

Your business's *vision statement* should be a precise, well-crafted document announcing where your business wants to go and painting a picture of what your business wants to become. To people on the inside and outside of your business, your vision statement is a compass, showing the whole world the direction in which your business is heading.

A vision statement not only points the way to the future, it also makes you want to get up and go there. It represents your business's best hopes and brightest dreams. Now, we know that Karl Marx and his vision of socialism seldom come up in conversation at cocktail parties, even in Moscow. But when you hear his message

> *Workers of the world, unite! You have nothing to lose but your chains!*

it's hard not to be roused, even today. Effective vision statements are, in part, inspirational calls to action. What if Marx had come up with this:

> *Hey, guys, let's all get together over here! Maybe we can figure out how to make you more dough!*

You'd say, "Karl who?" And Marx could forget that place in history.

Companies with vision

Check out these vision statements to see how some companies look toward the future:

Ballard Power Systems' vision is power to change the world. Our mission is to make fuel cells a commercial reality.

— Ballard Power Systems, Burnaby, B.C.

A manufacturer of zero-emission fuel cells

To offer the best service and the right product at the right price to North American consumers of housing and home improvement products.

— RONA Inc., Boucherville, Q.C.

A distributor and retailer of hardware, home renovation, and garden products

To make Sobeys the most worthwhile shopping experience in the marketplace by accurately identifying customers' preferences and efficiently meeting their needs.

— Sobeys Inc., Stellarton, N.S.

A grocery retailer and food distributor

A complete commitment to helping clients achieve results.

— CGI Group Inc., Montreal, Q.C.

An international IT and business-process service provider

Don't panic if the makings of a dynamic, charismatic leader aren't in your back pocket. An insightful corporate vision is much more likely to develop out of a diverse team of hard-working folks than to spring mysteriously from an inspired moment in the life of a leader.

The best way to create a meaningful vision statement resembles the best way to create a values statement. Just follow these steps:

1. **Select a small group of partners and trusted advisors.**

2. **Have the group reread your business's values statement and review the list of stakeholders who have an interest in your business.**

3. **Begin a verbal free-for-all where each volunteers opinions and ideas.**

4. **When you feel comfortable with the results, add the finishing touches to the wording and choice of medium to get your vision ready for prime time.**

Although you may end up with only a couple of sentences or even just a phrase, the vision statement is the compass that provides your business's direction into the future. Spend enough time with your statement to make sure that the north on your business compass truly is north — that it does indeed point in the direction in which you want to go.

Assume that your vision statement could serve the business for the next decade. Does this mean that you can never change the statement? No — but you should change a vision statement only if business conditions truly warrant a new course of action. Keep in mind that no one should cross out or rewrite the ideas that you capture in your business's vision statement on a whim; those ideas represent the lasting themes that guide your business at any time and under any circumstance.

But only diamonds are forever. If a changing environment throws you an unexpected curve, by all means, alter your vision to reflect the new reality. You should craft your statement in such a way that it's flexible enough to respond to a changing environment. If the words on paper no longer have meaning for your business, they become useless. Again, the vision statement is useful only to the extent that it has the power to move your business into the future.

Mapping Out a Mission Statement

You probably have a good idea of what you want your business to become. But how do you make your idea a reality? You start by defining the business activities that your business plans to engage in, the goals that you expect to meet, and the ways in which you're going to measure success.

In this section, we help you create a basic overview of your business and its activities, and we guide you as you shape your expectations into a mission statement. We introduce business goals and objectives and show you how to use them to measure the results that you expect to achieve. We also help you prepare to set your business's goals and objectives, and we look at how you can use those goals and objectives to improve the overall efficiency and effectiveness of your future business.

**Book III:
Business
Planning**

Crafting an effective mission statement

Mission statements have become very popular with business types in the last few years. Many of us remember the days when you'd find a business's mission statement turning yellow on the cafeteria bulletin board, completely ignored by everyone but the people who wrote it. That's no longer the case.

More and more companies, in fact, post their mission statements for everyone to see. Some put mission statements in their brochures, on letterheads, or feature them prominently on their websites.

Many businesses are finding out that they can use a mission statement as a powerful tool to communicate the purpose of the business to people both inside and outside the organization. It establishes who you are and what you do.

To be effective, your mission statement must

- ✔ Highlight your business activities, including the markets that you serve, the geographic areas that you cover, and the products and services that you offer.

- ✔ Emphasize what your business does that sets it apart from every other business.

- ✔ Include the major accomplishments that you anticipate achieving over the next few years.

- ✔ Convey what you have to say in a clear, concise, informative, and interesting manner (a little inspiration doesn't hurt, either).

Answering questions

A mission statement doesn't need to be long. In fact, the shorter, the better. Even so, the task of creating one can seem daunting — the Mount Everest of business-planning chores. A mission statement has to sum up some pretty grand ideas in a few sentences. Also, writing a mission statement requires you to ask yourself some fundamental questions — and come up with solid answers. And don't forget, your mission statement should closely reflect the values and vision that you set for your business (we talk about values and vision earlier in this chapter).

A little preparation up front can make the process a bit easier. Ask yourself some background questions when you get ready to work on your business's mission statement. Don't worry if the answers are fairly general at this point because you're only interested in the basics right now. Research your goals and the practices of the competition, and then answer these questions:

- ✔ Which customers or groups of customers do you plan to serve?

- ✔ What needs do you want to satisfy?

- ✔ What products or services do you plan to provide?

- ✔ How will your business's products differ from competitive items?

- ✔ What extra value or benefits will customers receive when they choose your business over the competition?

- ✔ How fast do you expect these answers to change?

In other words, a mission statement answers the basic question:

> *What is your business?*

Need some help? You should enlist managers who are familiar with all the aspects of your business. Follow these steps to begin the process:

1. **Get together with a small group including your partners and trusted advisors.**

2. **Ask them to prepare for the meeting by coming up with their own answers to the background questions we list earlier in this section.**

3. **Review the reasons for having a business mission in the first place and go over what the mission statement should include.**

4. **Meet so group members can present their perspectives, brainstorm, and form a consensus.**

5. **Create, revise, and review the business's mission statement together until you are satisfied with the final product.**

A well-crafted mission statement is clear, concise, and easily understood. You should also make it distinctive (from the competition) and up-to-date (give the business's current situation).

Capturing your business (in 50 words or less)

Your business's mission statement has to draw a compelling picture of what your business is all about. We often refer to drawing this picture as creating a *tangible image* of the business. Begin with a first stab at a mission statement:

> *Our gizmos bring unique value to people, wherever they may be.*

Not a bad start. This statement says a little something about geography and a bit about being different. But you're far from done. To work toward communicating the business's activities, accomplishments, and capabilities with more clarity and punch, we suggest expanding the statement:

> *We provide the highest-quality gizmos with unmatched value to the global widget industry, which allows our customers to be leaders in their own fields.*

This statement conveys what the business does (provides the highest-quality gizmos), who it serves (the global widget industry), and what sets it apart from its competitors (unmatched value, which allows customers to lead their own fields). The energy makes it a far more compelling mission statement than the earlier version.

How do other companies go about capturing their purpose clearly and concisely, in 50 words or less? The following examples provide useful insights:

- ✔ **Delta Elevator** (an Ontario manufacturer of elevators): "Our mission is to develop and manufacture leading-edge elevating devices and provide dependable and honest service, while giving lifelong satisfaction and employment for our people."

Book III: Business Planning

- ✔ **Cooper Virtual Office Services** (a small Saskatchewan administrative support service): "Our mission is to offer affordable, efficient services to professionals and students locally and around the globe."

- ✔ **ZENN Motor Business** (an Ontario car manufacturer): "As a leading developer, manufacturer, and supplier of electric vehicles, our goal is to provide drivers with a quality urban transportation solution that positively impacts our environment and greatly reduces operating costs. Working with our internationally respected partners, we bring the world's zero-emission vehicles to you, setting the standard for what electric vehicles can be. The culmination of this passion for quality is the ZENN Neighbourhood Electric Vehicle."

- ✔ **Strategic Leadership Forum** (a professional association): "Our mission is to provide our community of members with an independent and intellectually challenging forum that delivers practical insights and interactions on strategic management and leadership."

- ✔ **Canadian Humanitarian** (an Alberta humanitarian organization): "Our mission is to provide the basic necessities of life such as nutrition, shelter, health care, and education, to disadvantaged children everywhere."

- ✔ **Magnetic Hill Zoo** (a New Brunswick zoological park): "The Magnetic Hill Zoo is committed to safeguarding animal species and raising public awareness of endangered species. The zoo is designed with the well-being of the animals, as well as the safety of the public, in mind."

- ✔ **Cognos Incorporated** (an Ontario-based software business; prior to the purchase by IBM in 2008): "As enterprises around the world move to adopt performance management, Cognos will continue to direct our products, support, and services toward helping our customers deliver on its promise."

Zeroing In on Goals and Objectives

Your mission statement is a giant step forward; in it, you articulate the purpose of your business by defining the business that you're in. But the definition is just the beginning. When Canada decided to assist the United States with its space shuttle program, it set its sights on building robotic arms (now known as Canadarm 1 and 2). Stating the nature of the mission was the easy part. Actually figuring out, step by step, how to get there was the trick. It involved carefully formulated goals and objectives.

You don't have to be planning a trip to outer space to know that goals and objectives are important. If you've ever planned a long car trip, you know that choosing the destination is essential (and often painful, especially if the kids want to go to Canada's Wonderland and you want to go to the West Edmonton Mall). But the real work starts when you begin to work out an itinerary, carefully setting up mileage goals and sightseeing objectives so that your three-week getaway doesn't turn into a *National Lampoon* vacation. Goals and objectives are vital to successful business planning.

We know you're eager to get going with your business plan. But allow us, in the following sections, to introduce some important ideas that you can take advantage of when you begin setting your own goals and objectives.

If your business opportunities are so obvious and so overwhelming that you don't need to define a particular course of action to reach your ultimate destination, you've won the business planner's lottery. You're more likely, however, to run into one hazardous crossroad after another, and a lack of careful planning can be dangerous. Just look at the following examples:

✔ The manufacturing breakdown of the sports car Bricklin in 1976, which cost taxpayers close to $23 million, resulted from a failure to create sound processes and quality assurance.

✔ Monumental planning blunders have been partly blamed for fiascos involving certain infamous product introductions, including the Ford Edsel in the 1950s and New Coke in the 1980s.

Not setting goals and objectives created financial chaos in the situations discussed in the preceding list, and not knowing customers and competitors, and how they play into the business mission resulted in product failure. Setting goals and objectives provides an important insurance policy for your business: the opportunity to plan a successful course of action and keep track of your progress.

Book III: Business Planning

Goals versus objectives

After you complete a mission statement, your business goals lay out a basic itinerary for achieving your mission. *Goals* are broad business results that your business absolutely commits to attaining.

Goals are typically stated in terms of general business intentions. You may define your business's goals by using phrases such as "becoming the market leader" or "being the low-cost provider of choice." These aims clearly focus the business's activities without being so narrowly defined that they stifle creativity or limit flexibility.

In working toward set goals, your business must be willing to come up with the *resources* — the money and the people — required to attain the intended results. The goals that you set for your business should ultimately dictate your business choices and may take years to achieve. Goals should forge an unbreakable link between your business's actions and its mission.

Simply setting a general goal for your business isn't the end of the story; you also need to spend time thinking about how to get there. So, your business must follow up its goal with a series of *objectives:* operational statements that specify exactly what you must do to reach the goal. You should attach numbers and dates to objectives, which may involve weeks or months of effort. Those numbers help you realize when you reach a given objective.

Objectives never stand alone. They flow directly from your mission and your values and vision (as we discuss earlier in this chapter), and outside the context of their larger goals, they have little meaning. In fact, objectives can be downright confusing.

The goal "Improve employee morale," for example, is much too general without specific objectives to back it up. And you can misinterpret the objective "Reduce employee grievances by 35 percent over the coming year" if you state it by itself. (One way to achieve this objective is to terminate some employees and terrorize the rest of the workforce — effective, but not really the way to run a good business.) When you take the goal and objective together, however, their meanings become clear.

Want an easy way to keep the difference between goals and objectives straight? Remember the acronym GOWN: G for goals, O for objectives, W for words, and N for numbers. For goals, we use words — sketching in the broad picture. For objectives, we use numbers — filling in the specific details.

Ford Motor Company and its China goal

One hundred years ago, the Ford Motor Company had a simple mission statement: "We will democratize the automobile." The company's efforts extended around the world, and in 1913, Ford sold its first Model T in mainland China.

But the turbulent events of the twentieth century ended Ford's bid to democratize the automobile in one of the world's most populous countries. To this day, Ford has been slow to re-enter the vast and booming modern Chinese market. With just one car-manufacturing plant in China, Ford lags far behind its rivals, General Motors and Japan's Toyota Motor Corporation.

However, Ford still wants to achieve its original mission in the People's Republic. So, the company announced a new strategic business goal in 2004 to increase its market share and close in on its competitors in China. The company planned to achieve its goal through a set of targeted objectives. One objective was to build a second car plant in Nanjing, close to the bustling eastern provinces, which launched operations in 2007. Another objective was to expand output seven-fold at its existing plant in Chongqing, located in western China.

These key objectives are supported by initiatives that should help Ford make up for lost time. These initiatives include

- Partnering with solid local companies
- Taking advantage of a strong local labour pool
- Developing human resources in the region
- Leveraging its global operations expertise

Whether Ford's new goals and objectives will win it the lion's share of the Chinese market or force the company out of the market for good remains an open question.

If you already use different definitions for goals and objectives, don't worry; you're not going crazy. What we find crazy is the lack of any standard definition of terms when it comes to business planning. The important task is to settle on the definitions that you want to use and stick with them in a consistent manner. That way, you prevent any unnecessary confusion within your business.

Setting goals and objectives

Your business's goals and objectives reflect your primary business intentions, and they determine both the itinerary and timetable for fulfilling your intentions. In other words, your goals and objectives focus the business on the important work at hand and provide a mechanism for measuring your progress.

Goals and objectives are ultimately meant to make your business more efficient and effective. But how do you ensure that setting them is an efficient and effective process? Here are some guidelines to get you started.

Creating your business goals

Goals are the broad business results that your business commits to achieving. To jump-start the process of setting your business's goals, use this useful list of guidelines:

✔ Determine whom to involve in setting your business's goals. Because goals are the core of your business, the group members should include the people who are responsible for all your major business activities. If you're going it alone in business, try to develop a core group of advisers who can meet with you periodically to set goals.

✔ Develop a procedure for monitoring your business's goals on a routine basis, revising or reworking those goals as business circumstances change.

✔ Create individual goals that clarify your business activities without limiting flexibility and creativity.

✔ Confirm that your business's goals, taken together, provide an effective blueprint for achieving your broad intentions.

✔ Make sure that your business's stated goals closely tie in to your mission statement (see the section "Mapping Out a Mission Statement," earlier in this chapter).

✔ Rely on your goals when you communicate your business intentions to people both inside and outside your business.

**Book III:
Business
Planning**

Laying out your objectives

Objectives are the statements that fill in the details, specifying exactly how you plan to reach each goal.

As much as possible, you should tie your objectives to cold, hard numbers: the number of new customers you want to serve, products you want to sell, or dollars you want to earn.

This list of guidelines provides a useful template when your business starts to develop objectives:

- Determine who should set business objectives in your business. (If you're on your own, that would be you.)
- Develop a system for reviewing and managing business objectives throughout your business.
- Make sure that objectives are achievable and verifiable by including numbers and dates where appropriate.
- Create business objectives that can clearly advance and achieve larger business goals.
- Confirm that your business's objectives, taken together, result in an efficient use of *resources* — money and people — in pursuit of broader business intentions.

Matching goals and objectives with your mission

We say it over and over throughout this book, but this statement is so important that it deserves repeating: Your business's goals and objectives must be closely tied to your mission statement.

Avoiding business-planning pitfalls

Goals and objectives are meant to motivate everyone in your organization. They also help channel every employee's efforts in the same direction, with the same results in mind. When human nature is involved, nothing is certain. But you can improve the odds that your actions will produce the results you expect by avoiding several common pitfalls while your business works toward specific goals and objectives:

- **Don't set pie-in-the-sky goals for yourself.** If you don't have a prayer of achieving a particular goal, don't bother setting it. The best goals are *stretch goals:* goals large enough to propel your business forward without causing you to stumble along the way.
- **Don't sell your organization short.** Although trying to reach too far with your goals can be dangerous, you don't want to wimp out, either. Goals

often become self-fulfilling prophecies. If anything, try to err a bit on the high side, creating goals that expand your organization's capabilities.

✔ **Be careful what you aim for.** Your goals should clearly state what you want to see happen with your venture. If your goals contradict the intentions of the business, you may end up pursuing misguided aims.

✔ **Beware of too many words or too many numbers.** Remember — a goal is a broad statement of a business intention that flows directly from your business's mission. Objectives are more narrowly defined and always tie in to a specific goal; they fill in the details, specify time frames, and include ways of verifying success. You define goals in words, and you define objectives in numbers.

✔ **Don't keep your goals and objectives a secret.** If you want goals and objectives to focus and direct your organization's behaviour, every employee has to know about them. Prominently display your business goals and objectives in your business newsletter or website.

How goals can keep a mission on track

Norco Product Ltd. began producing bikes in Vancouver in 1964. It started with a man, a garage, and a dream of a western Canadian–based bicycle manufacturing company committed to quality products and outstanding customer service. Today it has a staff of 150 in three offices across Canada, domestic manufacturing facilities, and 25 international distributors.

Success hasn't always been easy, though. The industry has taken a number of turns. Bikes have changed dramatically from the simple 3-speed or 10-speed roadsters of the mid-1900s to the complex metal-matrix composite, shock-absorbing, extreme sport versions of today. Cheaper foreign imports lured customers away. Market demand declined.

Norco has managed to ride out these changes by keeping its goals and objectives closely aligned to the company's mission statement. Here's its mission statement:

We are dedicated to building rewarding, long-term relationships with our Employees, our Customers, and our Suppliers. We are driven by our Customers to supply innovative cycle products, outstanding service, and marketing support that will promote their growth and success.

Fine words, of course. Making progress can be challenging, however, when competition threatens and markets change. On its website, Norco shares its strategic business goals for meeting these challenges:

✔ To provide a rewarding and challenging environment where our Employees and the company can grow together on a progressive basis

✔ To be the number one supplier to our Customers, partnering with them in the adventure of cycling

✔ To be an industry leader in developing and delivering innovative performance products

✔ To maintain the financial stability of the company and ensure an adequate return on investment for our Shareholders.

The language of these goals and objectives may not be as stirring as the mission statement, but they represent the wheels and gears that turn the company mission into a reality.

Book III: Business Planning

Timing is everything

What's the proper time frame for you to reach your goals and objectives? How far out should you place your planning horizon — one year, three years, maybe five? The answer is . . . it depends on the pace of your industry.

Certain industries remain tortoise-like in their pace. Many plastics companies in Canada, for example, operate today much the same as they did 30 years ago, with perhaps the addition of a website. The needs of plastics end-users have changed slowly, and the types of materials used and levels of materials required have stayed pretty much the same. But change is definitely on the horizon, with producers overseas adopting leading-edge innovations, investing in research and development, and delivering quality plastics at significantly lower costs.

Change is perhaps the only constant for other industries. Take health care, for example. The world of doctors and hospitals was at one time a predictable universe in which organization goals and objectives could be developed years in advance. In the last decade, the Canadian health-care system has gone through a sea change. Changes in government regulation, new technology, outdated facilities, labour shortages, and increasing demand from an aging population have all conspired to create a very uncertain world. If you're in hospital management today, you don't worry about five-year horizons; you're now pressured to measure your planning cycles and reviews in months.

When dealing with change, business planners have to maintain a balancing act between moving too fast and not fast enough. You need to set business goals and follow them up with verifiable objectives, basing time frames on your comfort level with what you expect to happen down the road. Build in some flexibility so that you can revisit your goals and objectives and account for the changes you see.

Chapter 2

Describing Your Marketplace

. . . .

In This Chapter

▶ Defining the business that you're in

▶ Performing industry analysis

▶ Knowing the keys to success

▶ Watching out for opportunities and problems

▶ Creating market segments that you can use

▶ Shaping your business around the segments you serve

▶ Unveiling your real competitors and keeping tabs on them

▶ Predicting what your competitors are going to do next

▶ Being serious about the competition

. . . .

*O*ne of the most important questions you can ask yourself as you prepare to create a business plan (refer to Chapter 1 of this book for help with planning, and Chapter 4 to see a sample business plan) is "What business am I really in?" You also want to know what part of the market you serve and where you stand with the competition. If you can answer these basic questions correctly, you take the first giant step toward creating an effective business plan.

In this chapter, you can find out how to capture your big picture by defining the business that you're really in. We help you analyze your industry and search for critical success factors, and then we give you some pointers on preparing for the opportunities and threats that may appear on your business horizon.

Understanding Your Business

Okay, so what business are you *really* in? Don't say that you're in the widget business, if widgets are what you produce; go beyond the easy answer that you base simply on what you do or what you make. You have to dig a bit deeper and ask yourself what makes your marketplace tick:

- ✔ What basic customer needs do you fulfill?
- ✔ What underlying forces are at work?
- ✔ What role does your company play?

Analyzing Your Industry

No business operates alone. No matter what kind of business you're in, you're affected by forces around you that you must recognize, plan for, and deal with to be successful over the long haul. Ivory-tower types often call this process *industry analysis*.

How much do you already know? Take a moment to complete the Industry Analysis Questionnaire (see Figure 2-1). If you're unsure about an answer, check the ? box.

Your answers to the questionnaire in Figure 2-1 provide a snapshot of what you think you know. The ? boxes that you check highlight the areas that need a closer look. Now you can roll up your sleeves and make a serious stab at completing your industry analysis.

The good news is that many smart people have already worked hard at analyzing all sorts of industries. Although no two businesses are exactly the same, basic forces are at work across many industries (see Figure 2-2).

The following sections describe the most important of these forces — those factors in your industry — and provide some hints on how you can think about these forces in terms of your business planning.

Industry Analysis Questionnaire

Number of competitors in your industry:	❏ Many	❏ Some	❏ Few	❏ ?
Your industry is dominated by several large firms:	❏ Yes	❏ No		❏ ?
The combined market share of the three largest companies in your industry is:	❏ <40%	❏ In between	❏ >80%	❏ ?
New technologies change the way your industry does business every:	❏ 1 year	❏ 5 years	❏ 10 years	❏ ?
The barriers that stop new competitors from entering your industry are:	❏ High	❏ Medium	❏ Low	❏ ?
The barriers that prevent competitors from getting out of your industry are:	❏ High	❏ Medium	❏ Low	❏ ?
Overall market demand in your industry is:	❏ Growing	❏ Stable	❏ Declining	❏ ?
There's a large, untapped market that your industry can take advantage of:	❏ Yes	❏ Maybe	❏ No	❏ ?
Your industry offers a selection of features and options in its product lines that's:	❏ Extensive	❏ Average	❏ Limited	❏ ?
Customers buy products in your industry based almost entirely on price:	❏ Yes	❏ No		❏ ?
Customers can find other alternatives to take the place of your industry's products:	❏ Easily	❏ With difficulty	❏ No	❏ ?
Suppliers to your industry have a lot of influence when it comes to setting terms:	❏ Yes	❏ No		❏ ?
Customers have a lot of bargaining power when buying your industry's products:	❏ Yes	❏ No		❏ ?
Distributors have a lot of power and play a major role in your industry:	❏ Yes	❏ No		❏ ?
Overall costs in your industry have been:	❏ Declining	❏ Stable	❏ Rising	❏ ?
Profit margins in your industry are:	❏ Strong	❏ Average	❏ Weak	❏ ?

Figure 2-1:
Use the Industry Analysis Questionnaire to test your industry knowledge.

Book III

Business Planning

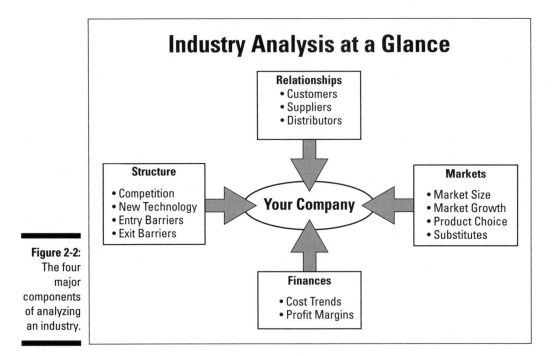

Industry Analysis at a Glance

Relationships
- Customers
- Suppliers
- Distributors

Structure
- Competition
- New Technology
- Entry Barriers
- Exit Barriers

Your Company

Markets
- Market Size
- Market Growth
- Product Choice
- Substitutes

Finances
- Cost Trends
- Profit Margins

Figure 2-2:
The four major components of analyzing an industry.

Solidifying the structure

Every industry, from fresh-flower shops to antique stores, has a unique shape and structure. Here are a few tips on how to recognize the particular structure of your industry.

The number of competitors, taken by itself, has a major impact on the shape of an industry. An industry can be a *monopoly* (one monster company with no competitors), an *oligopoly* (a small number of strong competitors), or a *multiopoly* (many viable competitors). Actually, we made up the word multiopoly because we figure that you need a word to represent the vast majority of industries in this competitive world. In addition to the number of competitors, check out how many of the companies are big and how many are small, as well as how they carve up the various markets that they compete in.

Make a list of all the major competitors in your industry. Find out their sizes, based on revenue, profits, or some other readily available measure, and estimate their relative market shares for the markets that you want to explore. Take advantage of the extraordinary range of information on the Internet to gather as much data as you can find. Use patience and persistence as you sift through all the raw data to find the gems.

Measuring the markets

Competition comes down to customers, and customers make up markets. Ideally, the customers you intend to target represent a market that you feel is ripe for new goods or services. Here we give you tips to help you judge for yourself.

How big is big?

The size of a market tells you a lot about what's likely to happen to it over time, especially when it comes to competition. Large markets, for example, are always big news and can't help but attract competitors. Smaller markets don't get the same attention, however, and because competitors can easily overlook them, they often represent business opportunities. You hit the real jackpot if you can turn a small market into a bigger market by discovering a *usage gap* — finding a new use for your product or service that no other company has thought of before.

Try to work out some estimates of the overall size of your market based on current usage patterns. Try your luck at coming up with novel approaches or applications that have the potential to redefine your market. Make some market projections based on the new uses that you're thinking about.

Growing or shrinking?

If large markets are good news, rapidly growing markets are great news, and competitors are going to come crawling out of the woodwork. A growing market offers the best odds for new players to gain a foothold and unseat the existing competition. As for shrinking markets, you can bet that the old competitors get leaner, meaner, and fiercer. So, as markets change size in either direction, the competition is likely to heat up.

Identify changes in the size of your market over the past five years, in terms of both units sold and revenue generated. If the market is changing rapidly in either direction, look for opportunities and predict the likely effect on both the numbers and the intensity of the competition. Business journals and the Internet are good places to start gathering data. Also, try talking to customers, suppliers, and even other competitors in the market.

What choices do customers have?

A quick survey of the similarities and differences among products or services in a market measures something called *product differentiation*. If each product looks pretty much like every other product (think sugar or drywall), you can bet that price is important to customers in what's known as a *commodities marketplace*. However, if each product is different and offers customers something unique or special — from laptop computers to hot little roadsters — product features are likely to determine long-term success or failure in the market.

Book III

Business Planning

Take a hard look at the products or services that the top three competitors in your market offer. How similar are they? In what ways are they unique? Think about what you can do to differentiate your business — adding special features to products or offering value-added services — so that you can compete in ways beyond simply raising or lowering your price. Your competitors' websites can offer a wealth of inside information.

What about something altogether different?

Sometimes, a completely new type of product or service suddenly makes a debut in a market and crashes the party. The product often comes out of another industry and may even be based on a different technology. The new product becomes an overnight rival for the affections of existing customers — the rise of e-mail to challenge fax machines and snail mail, for example, or the proliferation of digital cameras to overtake film-based cameras. The threat of *product substitution* — new products taking the place of existing ones — is real, especially in fast-changing, highly competitive markets.

Think about what your customers did 5, 10, or even 20 years ago. Did they use your product or a similar one back then, or did a completely different kind of product serve their needs? What about 1, 5, or 10 years from now? What types of products or services may satisfy your customers' needs? Although you can't predict the future, you can envision the possibilities.

Remembering the relationships

Business is all about connections. Connections aren't just a matter of who you know — they involve who supplies your raw materials, distributes your product, and touts your services. Connections are about who your customers are and what kind of relationship you have with them. The tips in the following sections can help you spot the key connections on which your business depends.

Recognizing supply and demand

One obvious way to think about products and services is how a business puts them together. Every business relies on outside suppliers at some stage of the assembly process, whether for basic supplies and raw materials, or for entire finished components of the product itself. When outside suppliers enter the picture, the nature of what they supply — the availability, complexity, and importance of that product or service to the company — often determines how much control they have over the terms of their relationship with a company. That means everything from prices and credit terms to delivery schedules.

Think about your own suppliers. Are any of them in a position to limit your access to critical components or to raise prices on you? Can you form alliances with key suppliers or enter into long-term contracts? Can you turn to alternative sources? Are any of your suppliers capable of doing what you do, transforming themselves into competitors? How can you protect yourself?

Keeping customers happy

You've probably heard the expression "It's a buyers' market." As an industry becomes more competitive, the balance of power naturally tends to shift toward the customer. Because customers have a growing number of products to choose among, they can afford to be finicky. As they shop around, customers make demands that often pressure businesses to lower prices, expand service, and develop new product features. A few large customers have even greater leverage as they negotiate favourable terms.

The last time that you or your competitors adjusted prices, did you raise or lower them? If you lowered prices, competitive pressures no doubt are going to force you to lower them again at some point. So think about other ways in which you can compete. If you raised prices, how much resistance did you encounter? Given higher prices, how easy is it for customers to do what you do for themselves, eliminating the need for your product or service altogether?

Delivering the sale

No matter how excited customers get about a product or service, they can't buy it unless they can find it in a store, through a catalogue, on the Internet, or at their front doors. *Distribution systems* see to it that products get to the customers. A *distribution channel* refers to the particular path that a product takes — including wholesalers and anyone else in the middle — before it arrives in the hands of the final customer. The longer the supply chain, the more power the channel has when it comes to controlling prices and terms, not to mention smart marketers who partner with channel members to create a superior delivery network. The companies at the end of the chain have the greatest control because they have direct access to the customer.

Think about what alternatives you have in distributing your product or service. What distribution channels seem to be most effective? Who has the power in these channels, and how is that power likely to shift? Can you think of ways to get closer to your customers — perhaps through direct-mail campaigns or online marketing?

Figuring out the finances

Successful business planning depends on you making sense of dollars-and-cents issues. What are the costs of doing business? What's the potential for profit? The following sections give you some tips that can help get you started.

Book III

Business Planning

The cost side

With a little effort, you can break down the overall cost of doing business into the various stages of producing a product or service, from raw material and fabrication costs to product-assembly, distribution, marketing, and service expenses. This cost profile often is quite similar for companies competing in the same industry. You can get a handle on how one firm gains a cost advantage by identifying where the bulk of the costs occur in the business and then looking at ways to reduce those costs.

Economies of scale usually come into play when major costs are fixed up front (think of large manufacturing plants or expensive machinery, for example); increasing the number of products sold automatically reduces the individual cost of each unit. *Experience curves* refer to lower costs that result from the use of new technologies, methods, or materials somewhere during the production process.

Separate your business into various stages and ask yourself where the bulk of the costs occur. Can you take any obvious actions to reduce these costs immediately or over time? How does the doubling of sales affect your unit costs? How are your competitors toying with new cost-saving ideas?

The profit motive

Businesses typically have their own rules about expected *profit margins* — how much money they expect to end up with after they subtract all the costs, divided by all the money that they expect to take in. In certain industries, these profit margins remain fairly constant year after year. A look at the history of other industries, however, points to cycles of changing profitability. These cycles often reflect changing *capacity levels* — how much of a product or service an industry sells and delivers compared to what it can actually produce.

Knowing where an industry stands along the cycles of profit margin and capacity, as well as the direction in which the industry is heading, tells you a lot about the competitive pressures that may lie ahead. Ideally, you want to be in an industry without much excess capacity — now or in the near future. Try to answer the following questions:

✔ Is your industry one that has well-known business cycles?

✔ Traditionally, how long are the business cycles?

✔ If you've been in business for a while, have your profit margins changed significantly in recent years?

✔ In what direction do profits appear to be heading?

✔ Do you think that these changes in profitability may affect the number of competitors you face or the intensity of the competition over the next one to five years?

Don't stop with our list here. No doubt we've missed one or two industry forces that may be important and perhaps unique to your business situation. Spend a little extra time and creative effort coming up with other forces while you work on your own industry analysis.

After you give some thought to the many forces at work in your industry, put together a written portrait. If you're stuck, imagine that someone who has no experience in your industry has come to you for advice, asking if you recommend a substantial investment in your industry. How would you respond? If you get your arguments down on paper, you've made real progress in assembling a serious industry analysis.

Recognizing Critical Success Factors

Time spent doing careful industry analysis rewards you with a complete picture of the major forces at work in your business: the basic structure of your industry; your core markets; key relationships with suppliers, customers, and distributors; and costs and changing profit margins. The analysis can also point out trends in your industry and show you where your company is in terms of general industry and business cycles.

This information is all well and good. But how do you interpret your industry landscape and use it to improve your business planning? Take a fresh look at your industry analysis (as we describe earlier in this chapter). Ask yourself what your company must do to succeed against each powerful force that you identify. Again, what special skills, organization, and resources do you need to survive and conquer? In the business world, such an asset is called a *critical success factor* (CSF) or *key success factor* (KSF). Critical success factors are the fundamental conditions that you absolutely, positively have to satisfy if you want to win in the marketplace. These factors are different for every industry because they depend so directly on the particular forces that work in each industry.

The CSFs (or KSFs) for your company should be rather specific — a one-of-a-kind set of conditions based on your industry analysis and the forces that you see shaping your business. You probably don't want to juggle more than three or four CSFs at any one time. But no matter how many factors you believe are important, your CSFs are likely to fall into several general categories. In the following sections, we provide a starting point for creating your own CSF list.

Book III

Business Planning

Adopting new technologies

When jet engines became available in the late 1950s, commercial airlines knew they had to adopt this technology to remain competitive. When fax machines replaced couriers and mail for many kinds of business correspondence, business had to adapt to the new standards and expectations of the business environment. When the fax machine was replaced by the scanner and email, and when the corporate brochure was displaced by the website, the same thing happened. Most businesses can't afford to lag behind in technology. Other businesses have to always be at the forefront.

Getting a handle on operations

For commodity products, such as steel or oil, large-scale mills or refineries are often the critical factors that lead to low-cost production and the capability to compete on price due to economies of scale. In high-tech industries, however, automation and efficient, clean rooms may be the critical ingredients that allow the production of competitively priced consumer electronics products.

Hiring human resources

Consulting firms usually recruit only at the top business schools because those firms sell the expertise of their consultants, and clients often equate skill with educational background. In the same way, software companies are nothing more than the sum of the talent, creativity, and expertise of their programmers. In each case, people themselves are the CSFs.

Minding your organization

The long-term success of movie companies that consistently produce hits and make money often hinges on logistics — the capability to evaluate, organize, and manage independent writers, actors, site scouts, and production companies, as well as the media and distribution outlets. In the health care industry, insurance companies must excel at record-keeping, efficiently steering patients, suppliers, and insurance claims through the system. Even a simple bookstore that sells used books can gain an advantage by offering a quick, easy-to-use inventory of what's available and a system for reserving bestsellers when they appear on the shelves.

Cultivating customer loyalty

Businesses that offer services sell rather abstract products that customers can't hold or touch, and those services are difficult to copyright or patent. Success often goes to service companies that enter the market first and then work hard to cultivate a following of loyal customers. Chartered Accountants (CAs), Certified General Accountants (CGAs), and accounting firms, for example, build impeccable reputations one step at a time.

Looking for a great location

Profitable mills tend to be located in agricultural areas and brick works crop up near rock quarries; after all, transportation of the raw materials is extremely expensive. But transportation costs aren't the only reason why location matters. At the other end of the spectrum, fast-food restaurants and gas stations also live or die based on their locations.

Benefiting from branding

Manufacturers of cosmetics, clothing, perfume, and even sneakers all sell hype as much as they do physical products. In these cases, CSFs depend on the capability of companies to create and maintain strong brands. Customers often consider the name, the logo, or the label attached to a product before they buy the lipstick, jeans, or shoes that represent the brand.

Book III

Business Planning

Dealing with distribution

Packaged foods, household products, snacks, and beverages often sink or swim depending on how much shelf space the supermarkets or local grocery stores allot to them. Speed of delivery and logistics can also be critical success factors, especially when freshness matters.

Getting along with government regulation

Companies that contract directly with public agencies, such as waste-management firms and construction companies, often succeed because of their unique capability to deal directly with bureaucrats and elected officials. Government regulation plays a role in many industries, and the capability to navigate a regulatory sea is often the critical factor in a company's success.

Preparing for Opportunities and Threats

After you have a handle on the major forces that shape your industry and you can point out the critical success factors for coming out on top (we help you with these things earlier in this chapter), you can begin to look ahead.

You can find no end to the number of potential opportunities and threats in an industry. A *situational analysis* is a process of analysis for a company's internal and external environmental factors, successes and failures, as well as past and present resources and abilities. A winning business plan should include a situational analysis that points out both the biggest opportunities and the clearest threats to your company so that you can anticipate ways to deal with both the good and the bad as part of your planning process. Opportunities and threats come from the forces, issues, trends, and events that exist beyond your control as a business planner and owner.

Enjoying the clear sailing ahead

Opportunities don't always knock; sometimes, you have to find the door and know when to open it. Consider the following situations. They can all lead to business opportunities, so see if any of them can generate new possibilities in your industry:

- ✔ Major shifts in technology
- ✔ Availability of new materials
- ✔ New customer categories
- ✔ Sudden spurts in market growth
- ✔ New uses for old products
- ✔ Access to highly skilled people
- ✔ Additional locations
- ✔ Fresh organization models
- ✔ New distribution channels
- ✔ Changing laws or regulations

Watching for clouds on the horizon

Business is risky. For every big opportunity in an industry, you find an equally powerful threat to challenge the way in which you currently do business. Consider the following examples of how fundamental changes can dramatically alter the business environment and see if any of them apply to your industry:

- ✔ Market slowdowns
- ✔ Costly legislation
- ✔ Changing trends
- ✔ New and aggressive competition
- ✔ Substitute products
- ✔ Exchange-rate volatility
- ✔ Shortages of raw materials
- ✔ Loss of patent protection
- ✔ Labour agreements
- ✔ Laziness and complacency
- ✔ Disasters, natural and otherwise

Book III

Business Planning

Slicing and Dicing Markets

As you put together your business plan (refer to Chapter 1 of this book), it may seem nice to view each of your customers — the Tom, Dick, and Mary who regularly walk through your doors — as individuals with unique personalities and distinct likes and dislikes. You may also be tempted to make things simple: Lump everyone together and view all your customers in exactly the same way — after all, the whole world should want your products and services, right? Unfortunately, neither of these tactics is very helpful when it comes to creating a business plan that you can use.

Luckily, you have a simple alternative. When you think about who your customers really are, one of the first things you notice is that many of them have a great deal in common. That simple fact gives you a golden opportunity to divide customers into specific groups, based on their similarities. Eureka! By planning your business around these customer groups, you can serve each group's particular needs almost as effectively as if they were individuals. As the saying goes, you get to have your cake and eat it, too.

In the upcoming sections, we show you how to create practical market segments that you can use in your business plan. We explore various ways to identify market segments based on who's buying, what they buy, and why they buy. Finally, we talk about things you can do to make sure that your business practices reflect who your customers are and why they come to you in the first place.

Separating customers into groups

Although each individual customer is unique, groups of customers often look a great deal alike. When you make sense of your marketplace by grouping customers together, you create *market segments*.

To be of any real use in your business planning, however, market segments should describe groups of customers that you can easily identify and that respond to your products and services in similar ways — ways that appear distinct from those of other customer groups. A successful market segment allows you to satisfy the particular needs and wants of an entire group of customers.

Good strategy not only identifies what you are and who you serve, but also what you are *not* trying to do. Similarly, identifying market segments allows you to choose those customers that are *not* a good fit with your business and that you shouldn't spend resources on.

You may remember a time when running shoes (also known as runners or sneakers, depending on where you lived) were simple, rubber-soled canvas shoes that kids played in and maybe used for school sports. Back then, most of the buyers were parents, and most of the wearers were boys. If you wanted to play in the running-shoe market (Keds and Converse, for example, produced black high-tops that parents bought in droves), you kept your eye on what those boys needed and what those parents looked for.

Look at the market for athletic shoes today. The difference is phenomenal. Young males still wear the shoes, of course, but so do girls, toddlers, cool teenagers, serious runners, senior citizens, and everyone else — all demanding athletic shoes in various shapes and colours, with different features and options, and in a wide range of prices. Athletic shoes are designed especially for walking, running, tennis, skateboarding, and even fashion.

Identifying market segments

Despite what the marketing gurus may tell you, you can't find one right way to divvy up your market. You need to view your customers from various angles and describe them based on several factors. The more you can apply your imagination and creativity in this area, the more successful you're likely to be in coming up with unique and effective market segments. One dimension isn't enough. As Figure 2-3 shows, you can come up with ways to create market segments by asking three basic questions:

- ✔ Who buys your product or service?
- ✔ What do they buy?
- ✔ Why do they buy?

Who buys

A good way to begin carving out your market segments is by researching who buys your product or service. If you focus on individual consumers, discover a bit about how they live their lives. If your customers are other companies, find out about their business operations. Think about your customers in these terms:

- ✔ **Geography:** Where do they live?
- ✔ **Profile:** What are they like?
- ✔ **Lifestyle:** What do they do?
- ✔ **Personality:** How do they act?

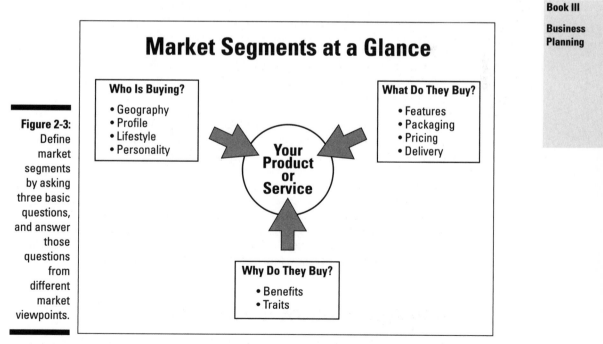

Figure 2-3:
Define market segments by asking three basic questions, and answer those questions from different market viewpoints.

Market Segments at a Glance

Who Is Buying?
- Geography
- Profile
- Lifestyle
- Personality

Your Product or Service

What Do They Buy?
- Features
- Packaging
- Pricing
- Delivery

Why Do They Buy?
- Benefits
- Traits

Where do they live?

Perhaps the simplest and most widely used way to describe your customers is based on where they are, beginning with a simple geographic breakdown by these factors:

✔ Country

✔ Region

✔ Province

✔ City

✔ Neighbourhood

But geography can also lead to more specialized groups. For example, you may find it useful to describe customers based on factors such as

✔ How close their nearest neighbours are

✔ How hot or cool their summers are

✔ How long their trips to the airport take

You can divide customers into groups based on geography to separate them according to regional taste — which often is a significant factor in the distribution and delivery of a product or service. Ethnic foods, for example, tend to sell better in certain regions of Canada. Indian food is hottest in the Toronto area, kosher products are most popular in central Canada, and Asian food is everywhere. Per-capita wine consumption is far higher in Montreal than it is in Edmonton.

Speaking of regions, instead of trying to sell heavy coats throughout the country, you may want to concentrate sales efforts in regions that have cold winters, taking advantage of market differences based on weather patterns. By looking at the geographic characteristics of consumers as they relate to your product or service, you begin to create market segments that you can use.

What are they like?

A profile of your customers includes all the attributes that you may expect to find in a national census. Marketing gurus call these attributes *demographic data,* which include the following:

✔ Age

✔ Gender

✔ Family size

✔ Education

✔ Occupation

- ✔ Income
- ✔ Ethnicity
- ✔ Nationality
- ✔ Religion

Company profiles, of course, are somewhat different. These profiles can include basic characteristics, such as the following:

- ✔ Industry
- ✔ Size of company
- ✔ Number of employees
- ✔ Years in business

You can often use customer profiles to spot market trends and take advantage of potential opportunities. Why is the market for health-care products booming today? Because the fabled baby boom generation — those 10 million Canadians who were born between 1946 and 1964 — is coming face to face with its own mortality. And where can you find a growing market for housing and home loans? In regions of the country with plenty of recreation, where people can enjoy their retirement years.

Book III

Business Planning

What do they do?

Lifestyle is an awfully tired word these days. People use it to describe anything and everything that you do in the modern world. But when applied to your customers, *lifestyle* has a particular meaning; it captures characteristics that go deeper than what's available in plain old census data. Customer lifestyle factors include the following:

- ✔ Hobbies
- ✔ Television viewing habits
- ✔ Social groups and activities
- ✔ Club memberships
- ✔ Vacation preferences

All this information is sometimes called *psychographic data* (no relation to the Psychic Friends Hotline) because you can use it to map out the psychology of the customer.

When applied to business customers, lifestyle factors include such things as what companies do when it comes to

- ✔ Protecting the environment
- ✔ Donating to charitable causes

  ✔ Investing in employee training

  ✔ Offering employee benefits

  ✔ Promoting people from inside the company

You can use these characteristics to understand how you may better serve a particular segment of your business market.

How do they act?

Your customers are individuals who have their own ways of acting and interacting with the world. But imagine if you could create market segments based on general personality types? Luckily, you don't have to start from scratch. Some behavioural scientists (the spooky folks who always have their eyes on us) have come up with five basic personality types, which we describe in Table 2-1.

Table 2-1	Customer Personality Types
Type	**Description**
Innovators	Risk-takers of the world
	Young and well educated
	Comfortable with new ideas and technologies
	Mobile and networked
	Informed by outside sources
Early adopters	Opinion leaders in their communities
	Careful evaluators
	Open to well-reasoned arguments
	Respected by their peers
Early majority	Risk avoiders whenever possible
	Deliberate in their actions
	Unlikely to try new products until those products catch on
Late majority	Skeptics
	Extremely cautious
	Disappointed by other products
	Reluctant to try new products
	Respond only to pressure from friends
Laggards	Hold out until the bitter end
	Wait until products are old-fashioned
	Still hesitate!

Personality type has a great deal to do with how eager people are to try new products and services. Although some people are adventurous and willing to try new things, others are quite the opposite, never using anything until it has made the rounds. In general, the laggards among us simply take longer to adopt new ideas than the innovators do. Experts make all this stuff sound like rocket science by calling it the *diffusion of innovation* (see Figure 2-5, a bit later).

Over the years, marketers have accumulated plenty of data on the typical person in each of the five groups we highlight in Table 2-1. You can use this information in your planning efforts. Identify which personality types are most likely to have a positive response to your product or service. You can begin to assemble a description of your target customers and create a business plan that enables you to reach them efficiently and effectively. (Check out Chapter 4 of this book for a sample business plan.)

What customers buy

A description of your customers in terms of their geography, profiles, lifestyles, and personalities tells you a lot about them (see the preceding sections for more information on customer research). To begin to understand how customers make choices in the marketplace that you compete in, you need to consider not only who they are but also what they buy.

A description of customers based on what they buy enables you to view them from a perspective that you're very familiar with: your own products and services. After you come up with market segments based on what your customers purchase, you can address the needs of each group by making changes in the following aspects of your product or service:

> ✔ Features
>
> ✔ Packaging
>
> ✔ Pricing
>
> ✔ Delivery options

What can your product do?

Features refer to all the specifications and characteristics of a product or service — things that you often find listed in a product brochure, users' manual, or the company website. When you group customers based on the product features that they look for, the customers themselves turn out to have a great deal in common. Their similarities include the following:

> ✔ **How much they use the product:** Light, moderate, or heavy use
>
> ✔ **How well they use the product:** Novice, intermediate, or expert
>
> ✔ **What they do with the product:** Recreation, education, or business
>
> ✔ **What kind of customers they are:** Adviser, reseller, or user

WestJet Airlines is a major player in the so-called *no-frills* segment of the airline business. The company caters to price-sensitive people who travel relatively short distances and who often have to pay for travel out of their own pockets. You can usually find a cheap ticket to fly WestJet, but don't expect a seat assignment in advance (except do-it-yourself online seating 24 hours before departure) or more than a package or two of munchies after you board. You do get an easygoing, fun airline that respects you, however.

WestJet Airlines customers tend to be different from those of Air Canada, a global, full-service carrier at the opposite end of the airline spectrum. Air Canada offers service to every major airport around the globe. The company targets business customers, frequent flyers, and global travellers who expect a hot meal on a ten-hour flight, help with their international connections, and their luggage to arrive when they do, no matter where they are in the world.

How do you sell the product?

When marketing types talk about *packaging,* they refer to much more than cardboard, shrink wrapping, and plastic. Packaging means everything that surrounds a product offering, including the following:

- ✔ **Advertising:** Radio and TV, magazines, billboards, T-shirts, and the Internet
- ✔ **Promotions:** In-store sales, coupons, and sweepstakes
- ✔ **Publicity:** Book reviews, telethons, and celebrity endorsements
- ✔ **Product service:** Warranties, help lines, and service centres

The market segments that you identify based on packaging criteria often reflect customer attributes similar to the ones based on product features: frequency of use, level of sophistication, product application, and the type of user.

As we discuss in the preceding section's example, WestJet Airlines focuses on the no-frills end of the airline market, and Air Canada caters to a different market segment altogether. WestJet Airlines keeps its costs low by offering single class service and ticket offices at airports only. It doesn't offer baggage-transfer service, in-flight meals, or business-class lounges. If you want to book a ticket on Air Canada, on the other hand, you can use your favourite travel agent or travel website, as well as the company's representatives, and you get a lot of frills — but at a higher price, of course.

What does your product cost?

The pricing of a particular kind of product or service creates different groups of customers. Price-sensitive customers make up one camp; financially free customers who are willing to pay for a certain level of quality make up the other. If you've ever had to endure a course in microeconomics (yuck), you might remember two facts: Price is a major market variable, and the price/

quality trade-off is a fundamental force in every marketplace. People who buy Timex watches at their local drug store tend to be price sensitive, whereas shoppers acquiring a Rolex timepiece at a classy downtown jewellery store want luxury, craftsmanship, elegance — and the chance to make a personal statement.

In general, the *mass market* tends to be price sensitive, and the so-called *class market* buys more on the basis of quality, high-end features, and status. But price isn't the only financial factor that can lead to different market segments. Here are other criteria:

- ✔ **Available financing:** Offered by home-furnishings companies
- ✔ **Leasing options:** Offered to airlines that buy airplanes
- ✔ **Money-back guarantees:** Offered regularly on TV
- ✔ **Trade-in arrangements:** Offered by automobile dealerships

Where can consumers find your product?

Distribution and delivery determine how customers actually receive your product or service. In this case, market segments are often based on where your customers shop:

- ✔ Factory outlet stores
- ✔ Discount centres
- ✔ Department stores
- ✔ Boutiques
- ✔ Catalogues
- ✔ On the Internet

Mary Kay Cosmetics reaches its customers directly at home through independent sales consultants, and its products aren't available in any store. The company believes that beauty aids are personal in nature and require highly personalized selling for its lines to be successful. With the same aim in mind, other cosmetic companies strategically place consultants (you can easily spot them by their white coats, perfect faces, and expensive aromas) in department stores.

Market segments based on delivery also may rely on additional criteria:

- ✔ Anytime availability (convenience stores)
- ✔ Anywhere availability (gas stations)
- ✔ Guaranteed availability (car rental)
- ✔ Time sensitivity (florists)

Why customers buy

When it comes to satisfying customers' needs over the long haul, you can't forget the basics. Perhaps the most difficult — and useful — questions that you can ask yourself about customers deal with *why* they buy in the first place. These include questions such as the following:

- ✔ What do customers look for?
- ✔ What's important to them?
- ✔ What motivates them?
- ✔ How do they perceive the world?
- ✔ How do they make choices?

When you group customers by using the answers to these questions, you create market segments based on the benefits that customers look for. Because these market segments describe your customers from *their* point of view, rather than your own, these segments provide the best opportunity for you to satisfy the particular needs of an entire customer group.

What do they get?

When you try to figure out exactly why customers buy products and services in your marketplace, start a list of the benefits that you think they look for. Product benefits may sound an awful lot like product features, but in subtle, yet crucial ways, product benefits and product features are really quite different.

Features are defined in terms of products or services. A car, for example, may have a manual transmission (as opposed to an automatic) and may come with power windows, anti-theft locks, or a dashboard GPS. *Benefits,* on the other hand, are defined by the customer. Depending on the customer, the benefits of a manual transmission may be in handling and responsiveness, or in improved gas mileage. A dashboard GPS may represent an added luxury for the weekend driver or may be an absolute necessity for the travelling sales representative. Again, the benefits are in the eyes of the customer.

Perceived benefits can change over time. Consider the newest generation of cars equipped with hybrid engines, which combine gas and electric power. A customer may buy a hybrid because it pollutes less than a regular engine, satisfying a customer's sense of social conscience. But when gasoline prices soar — like they almost always do — savings at the gas pump may begin to seem like the more important benefit.

You must understand the difference between benefits and features if you plan to use the market segments that you come up with to create an effective business plan. Take a moment to think about the business situations sketched out in Figure 2-4.

Which of the benefits listed represent genuine benefits to the customers of each company? A trick question, of course: *You* don't define benefits — the *customers* do.

To identify the benefits that your products offer, choose one of your products or services, and follow these steps:

1. **Draw a mental image of the product or service, based on its features, attributes, and options.**

2. **Put that picture completely aside for a moment.**

3. **Place yourself in your customers' shoes.**

4. **Now create a new description of the product or service from your customers' viewpoint that focuses on the benefits that they want.**

Grouping customers based on the particular benefits that they look for when they select a product or service is the key to satisfying individual customers and keeping them happy over the long run.

Book III

Business Planning

Choose the Customer Benefits

Situation	Potential Customer Benefits
A boutique offers upscale bath and beauty products imported from Europe, tasteful gift wrapping, and hassle-free delivery anywhere in the world.	❏ A nice place to go after lunch when you've extra time to kill ❏ The opportunity to impress relatives back in Sweden ❏ An alternative to divorce after discovering that today's your anniversary ❏ Aromatherapy after an ugly day at the office
A franchised quick-printing outlet provides self-service copy machines; sells custom stationery and business cards; and offers two-hour rush jobs on flyers, posters, and newsletters.	❏ The ability to look like a big company — at least on paper ❏ A money-saving alternative to buying a copier ❏ A threat used to keep the printing and graphics supplier in line ❏ A job-saver when the printed brochures don't arrive at the trade show
A semiconductor manufacturer sells customized chips to high-tech companies for use in brand-name consumer products, including home-electronics gadgets, computers, and games.	❏ An extension of the in-house research and development department ❏ An easy way to expand the product line ❏ A weapon in the cost/price wars ❏ A way to reduce a new product's time to market

Figure 2-4: Consider these business situations.

The benefits of toothpaste

For many years, the toothpaste market defied successful analysis, until a team of market researchers applied the concept of customer benefits. Their research resulted in the discovery that four principal benefits — seen by toothpaste users themselves — describe the toothpaste market. Customers seek out one or more of the following benefits when they make their purchase decisions:

✔ **Dental health:** One group of customers seeks perceived dental benefits. Mothers, for example, hope to deny the dentist an opportunity to buy yet another yacht.

✔ **Taste appeal:** Another group looks for good-tasting toothpaste. Children, of course, don't particularly like to brush, unless it tastes good.

✔ **Sex appeal:** A third group desperately hopes to appeal to the opposite sex. This group, of course, includes teenagers, who struggle through the rigors of adolescence and want fresh breath.

✔ **Basic hygiene:** The final group seeks basic dental hygiene at a good price. Many men, for example, view all toothpaste as being essentially the same.

As a result of the new research, toothpaste suppliers began to market their offerings around the defined benefit categories. Crest ("recommended by nine out of ten dentists!") targeted mothers, for example; Aim went after kids; Close-Up targeted teenagers; and the low-price house brands appealed to men.

How do they decide?

Different customers approach your market in different ways, and you can often identify market segments based on certain customer traits as they relate to your product or service category. Some of the conditions that guide customer buying decisions include the following:

✔ **Speed of the purchase decision:** The *decision-making process* (DMP) that customers go through before they purchase a product or service varies, depending on the product or service's complexity and price tag. People may buy chewing gum at a drugstore without much thought. But car dealerships and real estate agents face a completely different DMP.

✔ **The actual decision-maker:** Families represent a common *decision-making unit* (DMU) that buys various consumer goods. But who in the family has the final word?

✔ **Customer loyalty:** The way that companies relate to their customers can easily define a set of market segments. Service industries, for example, go out of their way to identify and encourage customers based on their loyalty. You've probably been asked to join more than one frequent-flyer program or to keep track of frequent-caller, frequent-diner, or frequent-you-name-it points.

> ✔ **Level of product use:** In many industries, a small percentage of consumers account for a large percentage of sales. If you want to sell beer, for example, you may not want to ignore the heavy-beer-drinking population — an estimated 10 million Canadians. Keeping this high-consumption group of customers satisfied can be profitable indeed.

Finding Useful Market Segments

A market segment is useful only if it allows you to deliver something of value to the customers you identify — and to do so profitably. Not all the market segments that you come up with are going to be practical ones. What should you look for if you want to find a really useful market segment? In general, you want to make sure that it has the following characteristics:

> ✔ A size that you can manage
>
> ✔ Customers that you can identify
>
> ✔ Customers that you can reach

Sizing up the segment

Identifying useful market segments requires a delicate balance between defining your markets so broadly that they don't offer you any guidance, and planning and defining them so narrowly that you make them impractical and unprofitable. A useful market segment has to be manageable. The right size depends on your particular business situation, including your resources, the competition, and your customers' requirements.

You can bet that your customers are going to become more demanding over time and that your competitors are bound to become more adept at serving smaller markets. When you choose the manageable market segments in which you want to compete, make sure that you factor in ways to use information technology in your business.

Identifying the customers

While you piece together a complete picture of your customers, take advantage of the many different ways to categorize them (see the section "Identifying market segments," earlier in this chapter, to check out the ways we describe them). In particular, market segments based on why customers buy are often the best because they define groups of customers who have similar needs. Whenever possible, come up with market segments that take into account your customers' viewpoints — the benefits that they look for, as well as their buying behaviour.

Suppose that while searching for a hot new business opportunity, you discover a group of people who have the same general attitude about their jobs and work. Members of this group want to be more productive on the job, yet they feel neglected and frustrated with their working conditions and office environment. You may have come up with a potential market segment. But what next? How do you identify these potential customers? Well, maybe you go on to discover that many of these workers are left-handed and would feel more comfortable with their numeric keypads on the left side of the computer keyboard and with their handsets on the right side of the telephone. Now, you've taken a major step toward defining a useful market segment because the segment is based on customer wants and needs and is made up of customers who you can describe, observe, and identify.

Given this situation, you may have the urge to take a planning shortcut and base your new market segment entirely on what you observe: left-handers, who, after all, constitute about 10 percent of the population. Bingo! You decide to design and produce office equipment exclusively for left-handed customers. But wait; control that urge. Before you identify a really useful market segment, you need to satisfy one more requirement, which we talk about in the following section.

Reaching the market

After you define a promising market segment based on customer wants and needs, and including customers that you can describe, you have to develop ways of communicating with those customers. You must be able to set up affordable ways to contact them through advertising, promotions, and the delivery of your product or service.

Becoming Market Driven

Remember back in school when you were told to check your homework before handing it in — especially if the teacher was going to grade it? Well, the marketplace is a difficult class to tackle (as difficult as, say, calculus or physics), and the stakes are high. Before you commit to a particular market segment scheme, look back over your homework. Pose these review questions to yourself:

✔ What benefits are customers in the market segment looking for?

✔ Will product features, options, and packaging satisfy customers' needs?

✔ Is the size of the segment manageable?

✔ Can you describe, observe, and identify your customers?

> ✔ Can you reach your customers efficiently through advertising and promotion?
>
> ✔ Will distribution and product service be effective?

Researching your market

At some point, you may want to use a more sophisticated approach to answer some of the questions in the preceding list. *Test marketing* tests your ideas on a carefully selected sample of potential customers in your market segment. Using a test market, you can often gauge how well your product plan is likely to work before you spend *beaucoup* bucks going forward. The bad news is that, like all market research, test marketing can be expensive and time-consuming, especially if you bring in big guns from the outside. So, you may want to start by conducting some preliminary customer interviews on your own.

Customer interviews produce a snapshot of who buys your product, as well as what they think they're buying. You can conduct interviews on an informal basis. Just follow these steps:

1. **Select customers in your market segment.**

2. **Arrange to meet with them individually or in small groups.**

3. **Get them to talk a bit about themselves.**

4. **Have them tell you what they like and don't like about your product.**

5. **Ask them why they buy your product and what they would do without it.**

One word of caution: Use common sense. These interviews aren't meant to be rigorous pieces of market research, so be careful to confirm what you see when you start drawing conclusions about customer behaviour from them.

Defining personality types

After you come up with a market segmentation scheme and a useful description of your customers (refer to the section "Identifying market segments," earlier in this chapter, for more info), you're in a good position to say something more about their buying behaviour toward the products and services that you plan to offer. So, look back over your notes and review what you know about your customers and their likely personality types. (If you need help, flip to the section "How do they act?" earlier in this chapter.)

Why are personality types so important? They have a great deal to do with how eager people are to try out new products and services. Although some of us are adventurous and willing to try anything new, others are quite the opposite, never using anything until it's been around for quite a while. In general, the laggards among us simply take longer to adopt new ideas than the innovators do (refer to Table 2-1).

In Figure 2-5, the percentage of people who represent each personality type is just an estimate, of course. But you get a rough idea of the relative size of each personality group in your own marketplace.

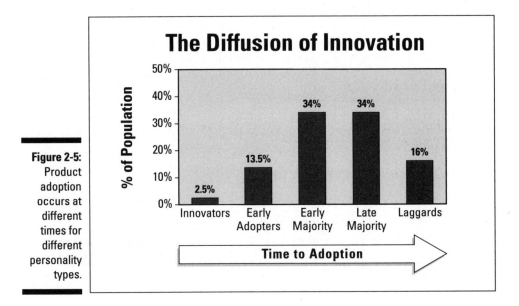

Figure 2-5:
Product adoption occurs at different times for different personality types.

The important thing to remember is that if you bring a brand-new kind of business, product, or service to the marketplace, the innovators and early adopters are going to be easier to capture than most consumers. The longer your kind of product or service has been on the market, the more effort you must spend focusing on your customers and understanding their wants, needs, and motives.

Checking Out Your Competition

Spending time with the competition isn't anyone's idea of fun. Think they're out to get you? You bet they are. But the more you know about the competition, the more easily you can figure out their next move — and set a strategy to stay one step ahead.

When the Japanese decided to become global players in the automobile industry in the late 1960s, their car manufacturers planned very carefully. They knew what they had to do because the Western business experts had taught them. First, they needed to understand the consumer markets in Canada, the United States, and Europe; second, they needed to know everything about the worldwide competition.

So, Japanese car-makers came to Canada and the United States to analyze and learn from their competitors-to-be. They visited General Motors, Ford, and Chrysler. They asked questions, taped meetings, took pictures, measured, sketched, and studied. While they did all their research, the Japanese were amazed by the Canadian and American hospitality. When they got back home, of course, they hatched their plans. By finding out as much as possible about their marketplace and the competition in advance, Japanese auto firms were able to successfully penetrate the North American market and other world markets.

North American car companies never knew what hit them, even though the blow was a decade or more in coming. They simply failed to track their competition and take their competitors seriously. Over the last 35 years, the automobile industry has dealt with waves of competition, not only from the Japanese, but also from European and Korean car makers. And who knows, your next sedan may just be made in China or India.

We show you why you need to have competitors in the first place. We help you identify your current competitors and your potential competitors. We look at competition from the viewpoint of customers and the choices they make in the marketplace. And we examine your competitors in relation to their strategies and company structure, introducing the idea of strategic groups. After identifying your competitors, we help you understand them better by looking at what they do; by forecasting their future plans; and by checking out their capabilities, strategies, goals, and assumptions.

Understanding the value of competitors

Competitors are almost always portrayed as the bad guys. At best, they annoy. At worst, they steal customers away and bank the cash — your cash. In short, they make your business life miserable. Is this picture unfair? You bet.

Look up from the fray, and we can point out another way to look at your competitors: They invent new technologies, expand market opportunities, and sometimes create entire industries . . . and believe it or not, they also bring out the best in you. Competitors force you to sharpen your strategies, hone your business plans, and go that extra mile to satisfy customers. After all, your real goal is satisfying customers and developing long-term, rewarding relationships with them.

Competition is a force to be reckoned with because of the power of customers. Customers are always making market choices, deciding what to buy and where to spend money based on their needs and willingness to pay. How do they do it? The process is based on the *value equation,* which looks like this:

Customer value = Benefits ÷ Price

Figure 2-6 illustrates this equation.

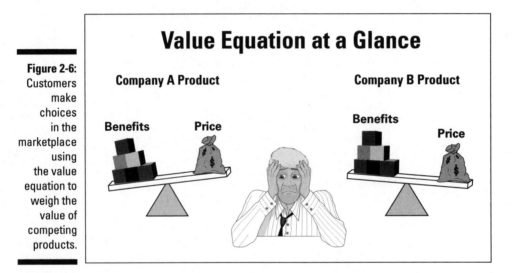

Value Equation at a Glance

Company A Product

Company B Product

Benefits   Price

Benefits

Price

The equation points to a simple truth: Today's consumers are awfully good at making complex choices. Think about the last time you ran errands. You probably stopped by the grocery store, where you used the value equation to make all sorts of trade-offs. Maybe you chose a certain cut of meat, weighing what you were in the mood for and what looked fresh against the price per kilogram. Maybe you decided that you didn't have time to drive to the warehouse store, so you bought cereal in the more expensive 375-gram box. On your way out, you picked up organic tomatoes for your salad at three times the conventional price. Driving home, you put fuel in the car. You opted for the most conveniently located station, even though its fuel prices were a little higher.

Competition encourages each player in your industry to figure out how to provide customers with the best value possible. Competition can often create a win-win situation, so don't try to avoid it by ignoring your competitors. Don't ever think that you're immune to it, either. Instead, take advantage of competition and what it can do for your company.

Identifying your real competitors

Two boys go hiking in the woods. They suddenly come across a bear. One of the boys immediately sits down and tightens his shoelaces. The other kid looks down at him and says, "There's no way we can outrun that bear." The first kid replies, "I'm not interested in outrunning the bear. I just want to outrun you!" Like the boy in the story, you need to know who you're really competing against.

You can come up with a list of possible competitors based on any number of factors. The problem is finding the method that most successfully identifies the competitors who impact your business.

To really understand your competition, you need to know the following things:

- ✔ How customers make choices
- ✔ How customers use products
- ✔ The capabilities of your competitors
- ✔ Your competitors' strategies
- ✔ Where future competition may come from

Considering competition based on customer choice

Customers choose to buy certain products based on a value equation, weighing the benefits of several products against their relative prices (refer to Figure 2-6 for more equation info). But which products do customers actually compare? If you want to know who your real competitors are, you need to know how many products — and which products — your customers typically look at before they decide to buy.

If you identify your customers and their *selection criteria* — that is, what they look for in a product or service — you can divide a list of competitors into groups based on how intensely they compete with you.

- ✔ **Head-to-head competitors:** Together, these businesses represent your most intense competition. Their products always seem to be on customers' *short lists* (those three or four competing products that they plan to compare very carefully).
- ✔ **First-tier competitors:** These businesses are direct competitors, but perhaps not quite as fierce as the head-to-head kind.
- ✔ **Indirect competitors:** These competitors are the ones that you don't often think about. Their products surface as alternatives to yours only occasionally. But this group deserves a periodic review because indirect competitors always have the potential to surprise you with competing products out of the blue. Many health-related magazines find themselves competing indirectly with sites on the Internet that can provide much of the same updated medical information.

Parable of the Corvette and the Sundancer

The Corvette is still a car with an image. General Motors has made the two-seater since 1953, and even today the 'Vette conjures up fond memories of the muscle cars of the '50s and '60s. But, in the last two decades, the Corvette has faced increasing competition, so General Motors decided to find out exactly what it was up against.

Now, you may assume that the typical 'Vette buyer is a young, restless male longing for a cool, fast car — and if he could afford it, you'd probably be right. But GM discovered that the profile of the typical Corvette buyer is actually a man reaching middle age. This typical buyer, who grew up in the '60s and '70s, now has some disposable income, a few grey hairs, and an empty nest, and is approaching retirement.

When the company asked these Corvette buyers about other ways that they could have spent their money, customers came up with the usual suspects: a BMW Z4, an Audi TT, maybe a low-end Porsche. But something else appeared on the radar screen: the Sea Ray Sundancer. What? Isn't that a boat? In fact, the Sundancer is a fast, sporty cabin cruiser that sleeps six. How in the world did a boat get into the running with the Corvette, BMW, Audi, and Porsche?

To find out, GM asked customers how they plan to use their Corvettes — in what kinds of situations and for what purposes. The answers made it clear that a Corvette was worth the big bucks because it offered these buyers a ticket back to their youth — a way to cope with getting older. And they could punch that ticket just as easily on a Sundancer as in a Corvette. Either vehicle seemed to fit the bill when it came to showing off, getting away for a weekend escape, or just feeling young again. By asking the right questions about the context of this purchase, GM identified an indirect competitor — one that also had some muscle.

You should be able to count your head-to-head competitors on one hand. You may have twice as many first-tier competitors to track and an equal number of indirect competitors. Be careful to keep the number of competitors that you track manageable. Your head-to-head competition deserves much more attention than your indirect competitors, obviously, but do set up a schedule for reviewing companies in each of the three competitor groups.

Paying attention to product usage and competition

Looking at products and services in the context of how customers use them gives you another viewpoint from which to eye the competition. In this case, follow these steps:

1. **Ask customers to think about situations, applications, or occasions in which they may use your product.**

2. **Ask customers to come up with other kinds of products or services they think are appropriate and may be just as satisfying in the same situations.**

3. **Ask customers to identify two things they would change about the product that they use.**

Spotting strategic groups

If you step back and look at the competitors around you, their differing appearances may amaze you. In certain industries, for example, companies that have a full product line compete with companies that offer a single product. In other industries, companies that gain recognition for their innovative R&D (research and development) compete with companies that don't develop anything on their own.

How can competitors in the same industry be so different? Over time, doesn't every business figure out the best strategies, as well as the most efficient and effective ways to do business? Shouldn't all businesses end up looking pretty much alike? These good questions have two possible answers:

✔ Businesses don't always discover a best way to do things. Markets and industries are complex, and different ways of doing business can exist side by side and be equally successful.

✔ Businesses that do things one way can't always easily change and start doing things another way.

A *strategic group* is a set of businesses in a particular industry that look alike and tend to behave in similar ways. In particular, firms in the same strategic group have the following traits:

✔ They display similar characteristics (size, geography, rate of growth).

✔ They operate in similar ways (degree of risk-taking, level of aggressiveness).

✔ They demonstrate similar capabilities (people, skills, image, money in the bank).

✔ They pursue related strategies (customer segments, distribution, marketing, and product-line decisions).

You can apply all sorts of business criteria to identify the most useful strategic groups. Although every industry is different, you need to consider these general variables:

✔ Businesses that manufacture most of their product components versus those that assemble or resell products

✔ Businesses that produce name-brand products versus those that produce generic or private-label brands

✔ Businesses that rely on their own R&D versus those that license or buy technology

✔ Businesses that have a full product line versus those that have limited or specialized products

Book III

Business Planning

✔ Businesses that emphasize marketing versus those that focus on production

✔ Businesses with diverse endeavours versus those that thrive in only one industry

Strategic groups fall somewhere between an individual company and the entire industry. Lumping your competition into groups is helpful because all the businesses in a strategic group tend to be affected by, and react to, changes in the marketplace in the same ways. But grouping works only if those businesses stay put in their assigned groups long enough to be analyzed. Fortunately, they usually do.

As part of your industry analysis, you may have already discovered a few *entry barriers* — factors that make getting into your business tough, such as high capital costs, expensive distribution systems, new technology, and regulation. You also may have come up with some *exit barriers* — factors that keep competitors from getting out of the business, such as expensive factories, specialized equipment, and long-term agreements. Strategic groups can have the same kind of *mobility barriers,* which tend to keep competitors where they are, in one group or another.

Strategic groups can be a great timesaver in business planning because, when you put all your competitors in strategic groups, you know where to focus your energies. You can spend most of your time analyzing the businesses in your strategic group and deal with the rest of the companies in clusters instead of tracking each business separately.

To divide your list of competitors into strategic groups, follow these steps:

1. **Put your competitors in a small number of groups, based on their similarities.**

2. **Add your business to one of the groups.**

3. **Looking at each group carefully, try to come up with the basic criteria that you used to make your selections.**

4. **Take a hard look at the group in which you put your business.**

   Are these competitors really closest to you in terms of their characteristics and the criteria that you identify?

5. **Ask a few trusted customers to look over your groups and see whether they agree.**

   Viewing the world through your customers' eyes is always worthwhile and can sometimes be a real eye-opener.

6. **Adjust the groups, if necessary, and work on additional criteria that may point to other strategic groupings.**

A strategic circle of friends

The Canadian communication sector is so complex that keeping track of competitors would be tough without the help of strategic groups. Fortunately, players can use several criteria to break the communication world into more manageable industry segments.

When Rogers Communications Inc. looks out over the competitive landscape, the competitors that loom the largest are Bell and Telus. The following traits, which these companies have in common, place them in the same strategic group:

✔ They're extremely large companies.

✔ They have a hand in many aspects of the telecommunication process.

✔ They boast a full line of offerings with many services, bundles, and prices.

✔ They distribute services on a national scale.

These companies need to know about one another in terms of resources, capabilities, goals, and strategies. Although Rogers keeps a close eye on CTVglobemedia and CanWest Communications (after all, Rogers has broadcasting, content, and publishing holdings), the company tracks those media with different criteria and intensity of effort than it tracks Bell and Telus. By identifying the members of its own strategic group, Rogers focuses on the competitors that have the greatest impact on its strategic business units.

Strategic groups are relevant and useful in many industries; they often provide a means of organizing competitors in ways that can simplify the competitive landscape. But keep in mind that all industries don't play by the same rules. If the mobility barriers aren't very high, for example, businesses can adjust their capabilities and change strategies quickly, limiting the usefulness of long-term strategic groups. In addition, acquisitions and alliances between companies can change the composition of groups very rapidly. Make sure that the groups you identify in your industry are real and won't dissolve before you have a chance to analyze them.

Focusing on future competition

Always remember that new competition can come from anywhere. So keep an eye out for emerging competitors. Determine who they are and how seriously to worry about them. The following are the most likely sources of new competition:

✔ **Market expansion:** For example, a business that operated successfully for years outside your geographic region decides to expand into your territory.

✔ **Product expansion:** For example, a business decides to take advantage of its brand name, technology, or distribution system and creates a new product line in direct competition with yours.

Book III

Business Planning

- ✔ **Backward integration:** In-house grocery store brands, such as President's Choice, are a perfect example of a packaged goods customer becoming a direct competitor.

- ✔ **Forward integration:** Your business buys many products from many suppliers. One day, one of those suppliers decides that it can bring all the pieces together as well as you can.

- ✔ **Change in fortune:** Out of the blue, a major company purchases a minor competitor. With access to new resources (financing, marketing, and distribution), the minor competitor becomes a major player.

Keeping track of your future competitors is as important as tracking your current ones. So, keep your eyes and ears open, and don't be shy about asking your customers and suppliers about competitors on a regular basis.

Tracking your competitors' actions

Suppose that you're armed with a fresh, up-to-date list of competitors. You rank which of those competitors you have to watch most carefully and tag them as head-to-head competitors, first-tier competitors, or indirect competitors. (We discuss separating companies into groups in the section "Identifying your real competitors," earlier in this chapter.) Maybe you even put them into strategic groups, singling out the competitors in your group for special attention.

So, what's next? First, decide which competitors on your list to spend more time with. Remember — you probably can't find out everything about each competitor. Keeping track of competitors' actions involves looking at both what the companies are capable of doing and what they plan to do.

Determining competitors' capabilities

The capabilities that you're most interested in tell you something about your competitors' ability to react when your industry changes. How quickly they can react — and how much they can do to change themselves — says a great deal about the competitive danger they pose.

To determine your competitors' capabilities, start with this list of important business functions and areas. Get going with the following questions:

- ✔ **Management:** What do you know about the background and experience of the competitor's chief bigwigs? What about the board of directors? Do any managers hail from another industry? If so, what are their past track records?

- ✔ **Organization:** How structured and centralized is the competitor's organization? Does it promote from within or hire from the outside? How would you describe the corporate culture?

- ✔ **Customer base:** What's the competitor's share of the market? Is it growing? How loyal are its customers? Are customers concentrated in one segment, or do the competitor's products appeal to several segments?

- ✔ **Research and development:** Is the competitor known for innovation and technology? Is it even involved in R&D (research and development)? How often does it come out with new products? Does it have patents and copyrights to rely on? How stable and committed are the members of its technical staff? Does the competitor draw on outside expertise?

- ✔ **Operations:** How modern are the competitor's facilities? What about capacity? Can the company count on its suppliers? What's the general attitude of the workforce? Does the competitor have a history of labour disputes?

- ✔ **Marketing and sales:** How strong are the competitor's products? How broad is the product line? Does the competitor have a reputation for quality? How about brand-name recognition? Does the competitor put a large amount of its resources into advertising and promotion? Is it known for its customer service? Are the salespeople aggressive and well trained?

- ✔ **Distribution and delivery:** How many distribution channels does the competitor sell through? Does it have a good relationship with its distributors? Is it quick to take advantage of new distribution opportunities?

- ✔ **Financial condition:** Is the competitor's revenue growing? How about profits? Does it manage costs well? Are profit margins steady or growing? What's the cash-flow situation? Is its long-term debt manageable? Does the competitor have ready access to cash?

Jot down a half-page corporate bio on each competitor. Each bio should capture the competitor's defining traits, including the following:

- ✔ Capability to respond quickly

- ✔ Willingness to change

- ✔ Determination to compete

- ✔ Capacity to grow

Assessing competitors' strategies

Your competitors' capabilities tell you something important about their capacity to get things done right now in your business. But what about the future?

To answer that question, you need to assess their capabilities strategically. The following three strategies are sometimes called *generic strategies* because they've been tried many times before and because they work well in almost any market or industry:

Book III

Business Planning

- **Low cost:** The first generic strategy comes from a basic economic principle: If you can offer a product or service at the lowest price in the market, customers are naturally going to buy from you. This strategy assumes, of course, that you can also produce your product at a low-enough cost so that the company makes a profit over time. The strategy also assumes that your product or service is similar enough to the competition's that a lower price can entice customers and clinch the sale.

- **Something different:** This strategy is based on the simple notion that if you can come up with something different or unique in the products you offer or the services you provide, customers will beat a path to your company door. These customers are likely to become good customers, loyal customers, and customers that aren't terribly sensitive to price because you offer them special benefits that they can't find anywhere else.

- **Focus:** The last generic strategy is about the kinds of customers you decide to serve. Instead of positioning yourself everywhere in the market and trying to sell products and services to everyone, carefully choose your customers. You win these customers over as a group by focusing on understanding their needs better than the competition does and by providing them with the benefits that they look for, be it cost savings or something unique.

Competitors often combine strategies. A business that follows a focused strategy may find success in serving a particular market segment simply because its products or services are different from those of the competition.

Put together a short summary of what strategies you think your competitors may be coming up with. Review their capabilities and past actions, considering the following questions:

- What generic strategies has each competitor adopted in the past?

- Have the strategies generally been successful?

- Are changes in the industry forcing competitors to change their strategies?

- What kinds of change is each competitor capable of making?

- How fast can each competitor change?

Usually, you find that a long-term strategy requires time and the total commitment of the business. So knowing a little about your competitors' history is very useful in understanding their strategies. It also helps you keep in mind what you think your competitors are capable of in the future. Remember, you can use the concept of strategic groups to simplify this process. (See the section "Spotting strategic groups," earlier in this chapter, to find out more about this concept.)

Winner's circle of stocks

When Frank Stronach first dabbled in horse racing, business leaders and racing pundits thought the results-oriented entrepreneur would give up after a number of disappointing outcomes. However, Stronach had something else in mind — owning the winner's circle. He was pretty clear about his goals in media interviews. Under Magna Entertainment Corp. (MEC), he had his senior people move quickly to expand his herd of thoroughbred horses, buy up a number of racetracks in the United States, and branch out into breeding.

MEC's competitors should have paid attention. If past performance is an indicator of future performance, then clearly Stronach's passion for taking risks and capturing market leadership would mean swift and aggressive action. Competitors who saw the early warning signs had the opportunity to adjust their strategies to meet a changing landscape.

Predicting your competitors' moves

Trying to predict where your competitors are headed isn't easy, of course; looking into the future never is. But where your competitors plan to be in the months and years to come certainly depends on where they are today, as well as on their capabilities and the strategies that they've set in motion.

Many companies intentionally (or accidentally) send market signals about how they may behave. Some businesses, for example, always lower their prices in response to a competitor. Looking at the past actions of competitors can provide you with an indication of what they may do next. Predicting your competitors' actions also requires a little insight into what they think and how they think — their goals and the assumptions that they make about the industry.

Figuring out competitors' goals

Your competitors' mission, vision, and values statements tell you a great deal about what they expect of themselves in the future. (Chapter 1 of this book talks about these statements.) These documents aren't top-secret; they communicate a business's intentions to all its stakeholders, and you should take advantage of them. You don't have to read your competitors' minds. All you have to do is read what they say about themselves and what they plan to do.

To discover the details about your competitors' plans, take the following steps:

1. **Select a short list of competitors.**

2. **Dig up as much information as you can find on each competitor's values, vision, and mission statements, as well as any stated business goals and objectives.**

3. **Ask customers, suppliers, your salespeople (if you have any), and maybe even your competitors' former employees for information about each of your competitor's long-term plans.**

4. **Write down your educated estimation of your competitors' financial and strategic goals.**

   Don't forget to read between the lines. In particular, look for the following:

   - Market-share goals

   - Revenue targets

   - Profitability targets

   - Technology milestones

   - Customer-service goals

   - Distribution targets

   - Changes in leadership or senior management

Uncovering competitors' assumptions

What your competitors plan to do is usually related to their assumptions about themselves, about you and other businesses like you, and about your industry — how they think and the way in which they see the world. Sometimes, you can get important clues about your competitors' assumptions by going back over their goals and objectives. Businesses can't easily make a statement about where they want to go without giving something away about where they think they are today. You can often come up with valuable insights by comparing your competitors' assumptions about the industry with what you know (and think) is true.

Assumptions aren't always true — which is what makes them assumptions in the first place. False assumptions can be very dangerous for business, especially when they lead to so-called conventional wisdom or blind spots:

- ✔ **Conventional wisdom:** Prevailing assumptions in an industry often become so ingrained that businesses mistake them for the gospel truth. Conventional wisdom is almost always proved wrong when an unconventional competitor comes along. Watch your competitors for signs that they take their assumptions too seriously and have forgotten the importance of asking, "Why?"

- ✔ **Blind spots:** Missing the significance of events or trends in an industry is all too easy, especially if they run counter to prevailing notions and conventional wisdom. A competitor's worldview often dictates what that company sees and doesn't see. While you track your competitors, look closely for actions and reactions that may point to blind spots and a misreading of what's happening in the marketplace.

Competing to Win

The more you get to know your competitors, the better off you are when it comes to understanding their actions and anticipating their moves.

But remember — the more you discover about your competitors, the more they probably discover about you. You probably put out as much information about your company and its intentions as your competitors do, so listening to yourself is just as important as listening to your competition. Put yourself on your list of competitors. Interpret your actions from a competitor's point of view. That way, you understand the implications of your competitive behaviour in the industry as well as you understand your competitors' behaviours.

If you're serious about the competition, you can't do all this analysis one time, wash your hands, and be finished. You have to monitor your competitors in a systematic way. If you're good at observing your competitors, you can choose the competitive battles that you want to win. You don't get ambushed in competitive situations where you're bound to lose.

Organizing facts and figures

To find out what really makes your competitors tick, take advantage of data from all sorts of places. Start your search by using the power of the Internet. You can usually find facts and figures on the competition included in the following resources:

- ✔ Business, trade, and technical publications
- ✔ Trade shows
- ✔ Company documents
- ✔ Stock-market analyses
- ✔ Management speeches
- ✔ Suppliers and distributors
- ✔ Customer feedback
- ✔ Your employees

The last item on the list deserves a special note. Your employees (if you have any at this point) are an invaluable source of data when it comes to the competition. When you look inside your business, start with your salespeople, who are smack-dab in the middle of the information stream. They talk with customers, deal with distributors, and occasionally run into competitors. They hear all the gossip, rumours, and news flashes that flow through your industry. Take advantage of their position and figure out how to capture what they know — and how to use it to your advantage.

You have to be a little careful about gathering information from employees other than your salespeople. In many industries, people move from job to job and company to company. Brainstorming about what a competitor may be up to is harmless, but warning flags should go up if someone pulls out documents marked Top Secret. Such behaviour isn't only wrong, it's illegal. You can't use certain pieces of information that a former employee may have about a competitor — anything that may be construed as proprietary information or trade secrets. (Read more about trade secrets in Book II.) High-tech companies are forever exchanging threats and lawsuits over alleged violations of trade secrets laws.

You need a way to organize the facts and figures that you collect from your many sources so that you can turn the pieces into useful competitive information. Long ago, filing cabinets and file folders did the trick nicely. Now, however, setting up a computer-based system to keep track of the data probably makes more sense. When you set up the system, keep in mind that information about your competitors won't fall in your lap in the next two days — instead, it trickles in over weeks, months, and years.

More than likely, you already have bits and pieces of data about your key competitors stashed away. You just need to develop a procedure that keeps the bits and pieces coming in and brings them together to create a useful, up-to-date profile of the competition. The following steps help you develop such a procedure:

1. **Start with a pilot procedure for tracking competitors.**

2. **Set up a company-wide system for tracking competitors.**

3. **Make someone responsible for competitor analysis.**

4. **Make it your priority to see that the system is carried out.**

Choosing your battles

The more thoroughly you understand your competitors — what they did in the past, what they do now, and what they may do in the future — the better you can plan for and choose the competitive battles that you want to take part in.

Naturally, you want to go after markets in which you have a strategy and the capability to succeed. But you have to keep your eyes wide open because you're never alone in any marketplace for long. By embracing the competition, rather than ignoring it, you have the added advantage of knowing where the competition is weakest. Choose each battleground by pitting your strengths against areas where the competition has weaknesses so that you win half the battle before it begins.

Chapter 3

Weighing Your Business's Prospects

....

In This Chapter

▶ Spotting business strengths and weaknesses

▶ Recognizing opportunities and threats

▶ Using SWOT to analyze your business landscape

▶ Stringing together the value chain

▶ Creating your business model

▶ Putting your business model into action

....

*W*e've all looked at a snapshot of ourselves or listened to our voices on the outgoing voice mail messages and said, *That sure doesn't look like me!* or *Is that what I really sound like?*

If your business is already up and running, you likely have difficulty seeing clearly and objectively when you take on the task of measuring your business's internal strengths and weaknesses. If you're just starting up a business, this chapter shows you what to think about soon enough because successful business planning absolutely requires that you always know where you stand.

In this chapter, we help you get a handle on your business's strengths and weaknesses in relation to the opportunities and threats that you face. We show you how the critical success factors (CSFs) in your industry come into play to determine which of those capabilities and resources are strengths and which aren't. We help you pull all the pieces of the puzzle together into a SWOT analysis to create a complete picture. We also create a strategic balance sheet so you can track where you stand, what you should do, and when you should do it. And while we're at it, we show you how to develop and sustain a business model so you can make money now and in the long term.

Identifying Strengths and Weaknesses

Assessing yourself isn't easy. You have to measure strengths and weaknesses relative to the situations at hand; a strength in one circumstance may prove to be a weakness in another. Leadership and snap decision-making, for example, may serve you well in an emergency. But the same temperament may be a liability when you're a part of a team that must navigate delicate give-and-take negotiations.

Your business's *strengths* are the capabilities, resources, and skills that you can draw upon to carry out strategies, implement plans, and achieve the goals that you set for the business. Your business's *weaknesses* are any lack of skills or a deficiency in your capabilities and resources relative to the competition that may stop you from acting on strategies and plans or from accomplishing your goals.

To capture your first impressions of your business, complete the Business Strengths and Weaknesses Questionnaire (see Figure 3-1). On the right side of the questionnaire, assess your capabilities and resources in each area. On the left side, rate the importance of these elements to your industry.

Getting other points of view

Completing the questionnaire in Figure 3-1 gives you a beginning list of your business's strengths and weaknesses. To be objective, however, you need to go beyond first impressions and look at your business assets from more than one point of view. Different frames of reference offer the advantage of smoothing out biases that creep into a single viewpoint. They also offer the best chance of making your list as complete as it can be. Consider these three independent viewpoints:

✔ **Internal view:** Draw on the managerial experience inside your business (use your own experience or that of your friends and former co-workers if you're self-employed) to come up with a consensus on your business strengths and weaknesses.

✔ **Outside view:** Perhaps you identify business strengths as assets only because your competitors haven't reacted yet, or maybe you ignore real weaknesses because everybody else has them, too. You need an objective outside assessment of what's happening in your business, and consultants can assist.

✔ **Competitive view:** Beware of becoming too self-absorbed in this analysis. Step back and look around, using your competitors as yardsticks, if you can. Your competitors do business in the same industry and marketplace, and they show strength or weakness in all the key areas that interest you. If your list is going to mean anything when the time comes to apply it to your business situation, you have to measure your strengths and weaknesses against your competitors'. (Refer to Chapter 2 of this book for more about how sizing up your competitors helps you.)

Figure 3-1:
Fill out the questionnaire to get a quick take on your business's strengths and weaknesses in major business areas.

Company Strengths and Weaknesses Questionnaire

Importance to Industry			Business Area	Your Capabilities and Resources			
Low	Moderate	High		Poor	Fair	Good	Excellent
❏	❏	❏	Management	❏	❏	❏	❏
❏	❏	❏	Organization	❏	❏	❏	❏
❏	❏	❏	Customer base	❏	❏	❏	❏
❏	❏	❏	Research and development	❏	❏	❏	❏
❏	❏	❏	Operations	❏	❏	❏	❏
❏	❏	❏	Marketing and sales	❏	❏	❏	❏
❏	❏	❏	Distribution and delivery	❏	❏	❏	❏
❏	❏	❏	Financial condition	❏	❏	❏	❏

Book III

Business Planning

If you don't have a management team that can conduct a situation analysis, bring together one of the informal groups that you rely on for some of your other planning tasks. Ask the group members to analyze strengths and weaknesses. Make sure that the group looks at your business's situation from various perspectives, using the different frames of reference in the preceding list.

Defining capabilities and resources

In putting together a list of your business's capabilities and resources, cast your net as widely as possible. Start by reviewing all the business areas we introduce in the Business Strengths and Weaknesses Questionnaire (refer to Figure 3-1). In each area, try to identify as many capabilities and resources as possible by using different frames of reference (refer to the bulleted list in the preceding section). At the same time, assess how relevant each capability or resource is in helping you carry out your plans and achieve your business goals.

Management: Setting direction from the top

Your business's management team brings together skills, talent, and commitment. You want team members to find their direction from your business's mission, values, and vision statements, as well as from the business goals and objectives that you plan to achieve. Top-notch managers and owners are particularly important in industries that face increasing competition or fast-changing technologies. Try to think of an industry that doesn't fit into one of these two categories.

Management determines what your business does in the future. Senior managers are officially charged with setting the direction and strategy for your business and laying the foundation for a new business, but all managers indirectly set a tone that encourages certain activities and discourages others. Frank Stronach, the founder of automotive-parts giant Magna International, has always believed employees should own a piece of the business, share in its profits, and receive excellent benefits without the help of a labour union. Therefore, Magna International employees receive this vested involvement in the business, and the business has the speed and flexibility of much smaller rivals. Edmonton-based BioWare Corp, a world leader in video-game design, ranks close to the top of the Best Employer list when it comes to providing a healthy workplace and recognizing good performance. Because of this culture, the business attracts highly qualified people who want to work in a business environment that values both personal and corporate responsibility. These capabilities point to great strengths of both companies.

The following list gives you some key questions to ask about the management and/or ownership of your business:

- ✔ How long have managers been around at various levels in your business? (Alternatively, what variety of experiences do you have as an owner?)
- ✔ Does your business plan to hire from the outside or promote from within?
- ✔ What's the general tone set by you and your business's management?
- ✔ Do you have a management-development program in place? (Alternatively, how do you plan to develop your own skills, if you're a sole proprietor?)
- ✔ What background do you or your managers have?
- ✔ How do you measure management performance in your business?
- ✔ How would you rate the general quality of your skills or those of your management team?

Organization: Bringing people together

The people who make up your business and its workforce represent a key resource, both in terms of who they are and how you organize them. Although human resources are important to all companies, they play an especially key role for companies in service industries, in which people are closely tied to the product.

Your organization starts with who your employees are, and that characteristic depends first on how well you select and train them. Beyond that, the work environment and your business's incentive systems determine who goes on to become a dedicated, hard-working employee and who gets frustrated and finally gives up. The setup of your organization (its structure and how it adapts) can be just as important as who your employees are when it comes to creating a business team — even a small one — that performs at the highest levels, year in and year out.

Many industries, such as financial services, experience high employee turnover at a cost of millions of dollars a year. So, it's no wonder that the key expressions of employee engagement and retention dance on the lips of human resources managers. The National Quality Institute (NQI) knows this and not only provides a menu of solutions for its members, but also recognizes outstanding results through its Canada Awards of Excellence (CAE). By implementing healthy workplace programs, some award winners have reduced employee turnover by an outstanding 99 percent — obviously becoming "employers of choice." A recent NQI study showed CAE recipients experienced a whopping 143-percent total growth between 1990 and 2005, outperforming the TSX Composite index by 55 percent for the same period.

Book III

Business Planning

The following list includes some key questions about your organization that you may want to consider:

- ✔ What words best describe the overall structure of your organization?
- ✔ How many reporting levels do you have between a front-line employee and your CEO?
- ✔ How often does your business plan to reorganize?
- ✔ What are your employees' general attitudes about their jobs and responsibilities?
- ✔ How long does the average employee stay with your business?
- ✔ Does your business plan to have ways to measure and track employees' attitudes and morale?
- ✔ What does your business plan to do to maintain morale and positive job performance?

Customer base: Pleasing the crowds

Your business success depends, to a great extent, on the satisfaction and loyalty of your customers. In Chapter 2 of this book, you discover who those customers are and what makes them tick. Understanding your customers and satisfying their wants and needs are critical to the future of your business.

Nordstrom is a Seattle, Washington–based department store chain that appeals to upscale shoppers. The business bases its reputation on the simple idea that the customer is always right. And the business means it. As one story goes, some time ago, a disgruntled customer stormed into the back loading dock of a Nordstrom store, demanding the immediate replacement of defective tires that he recently purchased. The store managers were extremely polite. They quickly discovered that the man was indeed one of their best customers, and they arranged an immediate reimbursement for the full price of the tires. In a better mood, the customer decided that he'd rather have a new set installed. When he asked where he should take the car, the managers informed him that Nordstrom doesn't sell tires. Obviously, this man became a satisfied customer — and a Nordstrom advocate for life.

Is the story true? Maybe, maybe not. The point is that this often-repeated account highlights the customer-focused mentality of the department store chain. Nordstrom customers receive thank you cards for shopping. A knowledgeable sales staff handles unusual request with aplomb. Employees have hand-delivered special orders to customers' homes and even obtained specialty merchandise from competing stores to satisfy customer requests. And merchandise returns are never challenged when the items clearly have not come from Nordstrom stock.

The following list gives you some key questions to consider when you study your customer base:

- ✔ What does your business do to create loyal customers?
- ✔ How much effort do you put into tracking customers' attitudes, satisfaction, and loyalty?
- ✔ What do you offer customers that keeps them coming back?
- ✔ How easy and economical is it for your business to acquire new customers?
- ✔ How many years does a typical customer stay with you?
- ✔ How many markets does your business serve?
- ✔ Are you either number one or number two in the markets in which you compete?

Research and development: Inventing the future

Research and development (R&D) often plays an important role in the long-term success of a business. R&D is particularly critical in industries where new and better products come along all the time. But your research and product-development efforts must align with your business strategy and planning to make the investments pay off.

Operations: Making things work

The operations side of your business is obviously critical if you're a manu-facturing business. The products that you make (and the way that they work, how long they last, and what they cost) depend entirely on the capabilities and resources of your production facilities and workforce. But you can easily forget that operations are equally important to businesses in the service sector. Customers demand value in all markets today, and they simply won't pay for inefficiencies. Whether you make autos or anoraks, produce cereal boxes or serial ports, run a bank, or manage a hotel, operations are at the heart of your enterprise.

Operations in your business are driven, to some extent, by costs on one side and product or service quality on the other. The tension between controlling costs and improving quality has led many companies to explore new ways to reduce costs and increase quality at the same time. One way is to involve outside suppliers in certain aspects of your operations, if those suppliers have resources that you can't match. Another way to achieve both goals is to streamline parts of your operations (through automation, for example).

Automation can also be a source of growth and may even create new busi-ness opportunities for your business. The airline industry is as big as it is today because of the computer revolution: Computers enable airlines to track millions of passenger reservations and itineraries at the same time. Imagine the lines at airports if airlines still issued tickets by hand and com-pleted passenger flight lists by using carbon paper.

Business operations are often at the heart of major corporate success stories. Wal-Mart's relentless rise to become the world's largest company is based largely on its continuously improving ability to handle, move, and track mer-chandise. Wal-Mart uses its operations efficiency for one strategic goal: to bring the lowest possible prices to its customers. And the company now does more business than HBC, Sears, Zellers, and a number of major U.S. retailers combined.

Airlines have tried to streamline their business operations by offering online reservations systems and installing do-it-yourself check-in kiosks at major airports. They even want to do away with the hassle and expense of paper tickets, so they now offer electronic tickets, which customers can print out themselves.

Book III

Business Planning

The following list gives you some questions to mull over about the operations side of your business:

- ✔ Does your business have programs for controlling costs and improving quality?
- ✔ Has your business taken full advantage of new technologies?
- ✔ Are your production costs in line with those of the rest of the industry?
- ✔ How quickly can you boost production or expand services to meet new demand?
- ✔ Does your business use outside suppliers?
- ✔ Is your operations workforce flexible, well trained, and prepared for change?
- ✔ Can you apply your operations expertise to other parts of the business?

Sales and marketing: Telling a good story

The best product or service in the world won't take your business far if you don't successfully market and sell it to all the potential customers. Your sales and marketing people are your eyes and ears, giving you feedback on what customers think about and look for. They're also your voice, telling your business's story and putting your products in context, offering solutions, satisfying needs, and fulfilling wants in the marketplace.

What could a marketing department possibly do to package and promote a boring old chemical such as sodium bicarbonate? It turns out that such a department can do quite a bit, if it happens to be part of Arm & Hammer, which markets sodium bicarbonate as Arm & Hammer baking soda. Their marketing strategy created an indispensable product for baking, cleaning, bathing, and even medicinal purposes. The familiar yellow box is in thousands of refrigerators, open and ready to remove unpleasant odours. The business also created a successful market for baking soda–based toothpaste. And in another pitch, Arm & Hammer now touts baking soda as the best way to ensure that your fresh fruits and vegetables are as clean as they can possibly be. All this from a common, readily available chemical salt.

Lately, drug makers have also begun to tell good stories about their products to polish up their images and to encourage patients to ask their doctors about specific drugs. Some tell the inspirational stories of patients whose lives have been saved by cancer treatment and support programs, such as *Canada AM's* Beverly Thomson, whose photograph was included in the global Breast Friends initiative that was sponsored by a pharmaceutical business. Others show happy families enjoying a summer picnic, thanks to new allergy medicines.

The following list includes a few key questions to ask about the marketing of your product line:

- ✔ How broad is your business's product or service line?
- ✔ Do consumers identify with your business's brand names?
- ✔ Are you investing in market research and receiving continuous customer feedback?
- ✔ Are you using all the marketing resources you have at your disposal?
- ✔ Is your business's sales force knowledgeable, energetic, and persuasive?

Distribution and delivery: Completing the cycle

To be successful, you have to get your products and services to their final destinations and into your customers' hands. Distribution and delivery systems must come into play. No matter how good your products are, your customers have to be able to get them when and where they want them.

Your business most likely distributes its products and services through *traditional channels* — time-tested ways in which you and your competitors have always reached customers. On top of that, your distribution and delivery costs may represent a significant part of your total expenses. The standard costs often include warehouse operations, transportation, and product returns. If you operate in retail, you can end up paying for expensive shelf space, as well. Supermarkets routinely ask for money up front before they stock a new item, and you pay more for the best locations. After all, supermarkets control what customers see — and buy — as harried shoppers troop down the aisles with kids and carts in tow.

Book III

Business Planning

How — and where — customers shop is often just as important as what they buy, so when a different way to deliver products and services comes along, the new system revolutionizes a marketplace or even an entire economy. The Internet offers companies a new and powerful way to reach out to their customers more directly, increasing business clout and, at the same time, lowering distribution costs. So consider *alternate channels* and *multichannels* (more than one type of channel) as you plan your distribution and delivery strategy going forward.

Many innovative products and companies succeed because of their novel approaches to the costs and other hurdles associated with traditional distribution networks. In the '80s, Canada Post was mandated by the federal government to improve its operations, reduce losses, and perhaps (just perhaps) make a profit, despite being a Crown corporation. Canada Post revisited its mission and values (refer to Chapter 1 of this book), and claimed its vision prepared it to be a world leader in providing innovative physical and electronic delivery systems, creating value for customers, employees, and all Canadians. One approach was to cut cost and improve service. It accomplished that by franchising some of its postal outlets, increasing their number, and making them more accessible to customers through new locations, such as in convenience stores. These privately owned outlets have longer hours and a wider range of services than government-owned locations. Canada Post also increased the number of stamp retailers by 75 percent and provided electronic postage service through its website. Along with implementing other changes, Canada Post now boasts 11 years of profits and a spot on Canada's Top 100 Employers list.

The following list gives you some questions about the distribution and delivery of your product or service:

- ✔ What are the costs associated with your business's inventory system?
- ✔ Can you reduce inventories by changing the way that you process orders?
- ✔ How much time does it take you to fill a customer order, and can you reduce the time?
- ✔ How many distribution channels does your business use?
- ✔ What are the relative costs in various channels, and which are most effective?
- ✔ How much control do your distributors have over your business?
- ✔ Can you use any new channels to reach your customers more directly?

Financial condition: Keeping track of money

The long-term financial health of your business determines the overall health of your business, period. You simply can't survive in business for long without having your financial house in order. Come to think of it, the expenses that you have to track when looking at business finances aren't all that different from the issues that you face in running your own household.

If you're just starting in business, for example, how much money your business can get its hands on up front (your *initial capital*) is a key to survival. (Does this sound like trying to buy and furnish your first house?) When your business is up and running, you need to make sure that more money comes in than goes out (a *positive cash flow*) so that you can pay all your bills. (Remember those times when the mortgage and utility bills were due, but payday hadn't come yet?)

Figuring out how to keep your business financially fit is critical to planning your business. When you take the time to look over your important financial statements periodically, you give your business the benefit of a regular financial checkup. The checkup is usually routine, but every once in a while, you uncover an early warning — lower-than-expected profits, for example, or an out-of-line promotional expense. Your financial vigilance pays off.

The lonely shopping cart

Imagine going into a store, taking the time to fill a shopping cart with all sorts of things, and then abruptly walking away, abandoning the cart, and leaving the store without buying anything. Strange? Well, it happens from time to time at almost every grocery or department store. And it happens too many times at Internet stores. At `http://Chapters.indigo.ca`, for example, customers routinely prowl around the online aisles, select this and that, fill up their shopping carts — and then suddenly vanish. Poof.

Believe it or not, this phenomenon has wheeled out more than one research study by global firms trying to understand why online shopping carts get abandoned between 25 and 75 percent of the time. It turns out that researchers don't really know much about how people interact with websites while they surf around the Net, but those researchers are figuring it out quickly. Some have identified that a multiple-page checkout process is too complicated;

shoppers don't want to pay shipping costs, especially if shipping costs more than the item itself; and if the total cost of the purchase is more than expected, the shopper gets cold feet. Some shoppers just look.

Companies noticed the lonely shopping cart phenomenon and are finding ways to turn it into an asset. Many of the biggest Internet retailers now set up their systems so that if you fill your cart and then log off without buying anything, you get an e-mail within five minutes asking what's wrong. Weeks later, you might receive an e-mail stating that your filled cart is still waiting for you if you want to log in again. Some retailers (or e-tailers) allow you to manage your cart, deleting items, saving others, or setting up wish-list carts filled with items you want to buy — or have someone buy for you — at a later date. The smart e-retailers calculate the total price as a continuous process and have streamlined checkout to one page for you.

Book III

Business Planning

The following list includes questions to ask about your business's financial health:

- ✔ Are your revenue and profits growing?
- ✔ Are you carefully monitoring your business's cash flow?
- ✔ Does your business have ready access to cash reserves?
- ✔ Does your business — and every business unit or area — have a budget for the coming year?
- ✔ Do you consistently track key financial ratios for the business?
- ✔ How does your business's financial picture compare with that of the competition?

If you don't know how to answer the questions in the preceding list, carve out some time to spend with Chapter 2 of this book, and Book IV.

Monitoring critical success factors

Not all your capabilities are equally important. Some may be critical to success. Others may be nice to have but not especially relevant to your business. You must decide whether your capabilities and resources represent business strengths that you can leverage or weaknesses you have to correct as you plan for the future. To make those decisions, you have to be clear about what's important to your industry and the marketplace. The *critical success factors* (CSFs) are the general capabilities and resources that absolutely have to be in place for any business in your industry to succeed over the long haul.

You may have already prepared a list of CSFs (if you haven't, take a look at Chapter 2). Along with a CSF list, you need a list of your business's capabilities and resources. You can use the two lists to construct a grid, which in turn allows you to compare your capabilities and resources with those that your industry thinks are important. In a perfect world, the lists match up exactly, but that seldom occurs. The completed grid helps you identify your business's current strengths and weaknesses (see Figure 3-2).

Figure 3-2: Compare your capabilities and resources with the critical success factors (CSFs) in your industry.

To complete a grid similar to the one in Figure 3-2, remember the following:

> ✔ The capabilities and resources that you place on the left side of the grid are in your industry's must-have category. They represent CSFs.

> ✔ The capabilities and resources that you place in the top-left corner of the grid are CSFs in which your business is good or excellent. They represent your strengths.

> ✔ The capabilities and resources that you place in the bottom-left corner of the grid are CSFs in which your business is only fair or even poor. They represent your weaknesses.

You can easily find value in the capabilities that your business already excels in, and you can just as easily underestimate the importance of things that your business doesn't do very well. Admitting that you devote valuable resources to areas that don't affect you as much is hard, as is admitting that you may neglect key business areas. Try to be as objective as you can.

Measuring Your Business against Competitors

You must be prepared to take advantage of your business's strengths and minimize its weaknesses, which means that you have to know how to recognize opportunities when they arise and prepare for threats before they overtake you. Timing is everything here, and it represents another major dimension that you need to think about.

Getting a glance at competitors

Create strengths-and-weaknesses grids for two or three of your most intense competitors. (Refer to Figures 3-1 and 3-2 for grid info and Chapter 2 for a refresher on exactly who your competitors are and what information you have about them.) You don't know as much about your competitors as you know about yourself, of course, so the grids can't be as complete as they may be for your business. But what you *do* know tells you a great deal.

Comparing the strengths and weaknesses of competitors with your own can help you see where competitive opportunities and threats to your business may come from. Opportunities often arise when your business has a strength that you can exploit in a critical area in which your competition is weak. And you can sometimes anticipate a threat when you see the reverse situation — when a competitor takes advantage of a key strength by making a move in an area where you're weak. Because the competitive landscape always changes, plan to monitor these grids on a regular basis.

Book III

Business Planning

Completing your SWOT analysis

A *SWOT* analysis (an analysis of your strengths, weaknesses, opportunities, and threats) allows you to construct a strategic balance sheet for your business. In the analysis, you bring together all the internal factors, including your business's strengths and weaknesses. You weigh these factors against the external forces that you identify, such as the opportunities and threats that your business faces due to competitive forces or trends in your business environment. How these factors balance out determines what your business should do and when it should do it. Follow these steps to complete the SWOT analysis grid (and check out Figures 3-1 and 3-2 for info on coming up with a strength/weakness grid):

1. **Divide all the strengths that you identify into two groups, based on whether you associate them with potential opportunities in your industry or with latent threats.**

2. **Divide all the weaknesses the same way — one group associated with opportunities and the other with threats.**

3. **Construct a grid with four quadrants.**

4. **Place your business's strengths and weaknesses, paired with industry opportunities or threats, in one of the four boxes (see Figure 3-3).**

SWOT analysis provides useful strategic guidance, mostly through common sense. First, fix what's broken and address imminent threats. Next, make the most of the business opportunities that you see. Only then do you have the luxury of tending to other business issues and areas. Be sure to address each of the following steps in your business plan:

Figure 3-3:
The SWOT grid balances your business's internal strengths and weaknesses against external opportunities and threats.

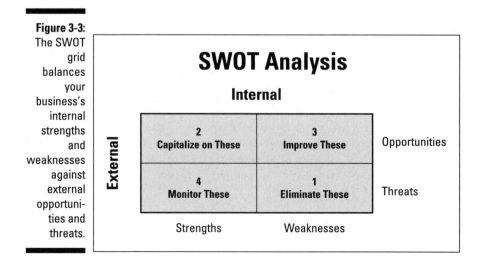

SWOT Analysis

Internal

	Strengths	Weaknesses	
External	2 Capitalize on These	3 Improve These	Opportunities
	4 Monitor These	1 Eliminate These	Threats

1. **Eliminate any business weaknesses that you identify in areas in which you face serious threats from your competitors or unfavourable trends in a changing business environment.**

2. **Capitalize on any business opportunities that you discover where your business has real strengths and your competitors may have weaknesses.**

3. **Work on improving any weaknesses that you identify in areas that may contain potential business opportunities.**

4. **Monitor business areas in which you're strong today so that you aren't surprised by any latent threats that may appear.**

Change is the only constant in your business, your industry, and your marketplace. Constant change means that you have to revise the grid regularly while your business grows and the environment around you changes. Think of your SWOT analysis as a continuous process — something that you do repeatedly as an important part of your business-planning cycle.

Evaluating the Value Chain and What You Do Best

When customers are making decisions on what to buy and where to shop, they continually weigh various combinations of product or service benefits against price. This calculation is referred to as the *value equation* (refer to Chapter 2 of this book). But what does having the best value actually mean? If you want to be successful in your marketplace, you need to know exactly where and how your products add value in the eyes of your customers. In the customers' minds, their perception is reality.

In the upcoming sections, we look at creating customer value around products and services. The approach is called the *value chain,* and you use it to identify which parts of your business are responsible for adding the greatest value for customers. We look at how to put together a value proposition for your customers and how you can use it as the basis for your *business model,* or plan for making money. We also show you how to use your value chain to help explain why you may have a competitive advantage in the marketplace, and we talk about how you can maintain that competitive advantage over the long term. Finally, we show you how to make the most of your business's human and financial resources while you put your business plan and business model to work.

Describing what you do best

Describing what your business does best — summarizing your key business activities in a few well-chosen sentences or in a clear diagram — should be easy, shouldn't it? It's not. (Refer to Chapter 1 of this book for help capturing your business in 50 words or less.) From the inside of your business looking out, you may have difficulty pushing away the everyday details and getting at the core of what actually keeps you in business from one day to the next.

Due to this difficulty, business consultants do a bang-up business. They may have fancy names for the services they offer, but the essence of what they do is simple: They help you describe what you do. Their little secret, of course, is that they don't really possess more valuable knowledge than you. Consultants seem to have a clearer view of your business because they view it from the outside looking in.

You have a built-in understanding of your business and what really makes your business successful — you just need to unlock what you already know.

Looking at the links in a value chain

A business constructs its *value chain* from the sequence of activities that it engages in to increase the value of its products and services in the eyes of its customers (see Figure 3-4). The chain shows where a business may have an advantage over its competitors, and it connects a business to the market-place, making sure that it doesn't stray too far from the customers it plans to serve.

The links in a value chain help you better understand your business activities.

Primary links in the value chain are the business functions representing the heart of what your business does. Primary links are usually sequential. They're the essential stages that your business goes through in developing, producing, and getting products to market, and they often involve the following:

- ✔ Research and development
- ✔ Operations
- ✔ Marketing and sales
- ✔ Distribution and delivery
- ✔ Service

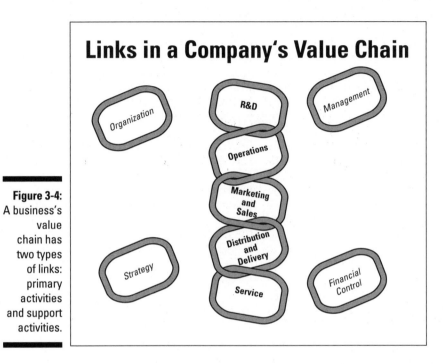

Figure 3-4:
A business's value chain has two types of links: primary activities and support activities.

Links in a Company's Value Chain

Organization
R&D
Management
Operations
Marketing and Sales
Strategy
Distribution and Delivery
Service
Financial Control

Supporting links in the value chain contribute to the overall success of the business by strengthening your business's primary links. Supporting links are often spread throughout an organization. They assist and tie together all the primary business functions, as well as support one another. The activities often involve the following:

- ✔ Management
- ✔ Organization
- ✔ Strategy and planning
- ✔ Financial control

Forging your value chain

To develop your business's value chain — the sequence of activities that you go through in the process of adding value to your products and services — you need a list of your business's capabilities and resources. Read the earlier sections of this chapter if you need help.

The great U.S. Steel conundrum

Created in 1901 out of the combined steel holdings of J. P. Morgan and Andrew Carnegie, U.S. Steel was a giant corporation on the day it was born. The firm started with 70 percent of the U.S. basic steel-making capacity and became the world's first billion-dollar business. For the next half-century, however, U.S. Steel saw its share of the market erode until it fell down to 20 percent by the mid-1960s. Thus, the riddle of U.S. Steel: How did the business manage to keep its profits consistently high over this 60-year period while losing almost three-quarters of its market share?

The answer: U.S. Steel's share of the market didn't really matter.

How that could possibly be the case? Well, the first head of U.S. Steel, Judge Elbert Gary, started out worrying about his business's market share, too — but he worried that it was too big. He feared that Teddy Roosevelt and the U.S. government would think that U.S. Steel looked a lot like a monopoly and would break the business up into much smaller pieces.

Judge Gary turned out to be one smart capitalist. Although he didn't have a name for it at the time, he created a value chain for U.S. Steel. He discovered that one of the most important links in the steel-making value chain was the mining of its basic ingredients: iron ore, coal, and limestone. Coincidentally, U.S. Steel owned vast land holdings and pretty much controlled the source of all these raw materials. So, the good judge decided to invite competitors to join him in making steel — the more, the merrier. In fact, he demanded competition, and the industry recognized him as an industrial statesman for his efforts at the time. He never stopped making tons of money for U.S. Steel, of course. He knew that the real value in his business was in the sale of raw materials to any and all competitors on an equally profitable basis.

Even U.S. Steel's recent purchase of Canada's largest steel producer, Stelco Inc., is consistent with Gary's strategy. Along with the acquisition came part ownership in three Canadian iron ore mines that supply domestic, as well as international, competitors.

You can construct a framework for your value chain by creating a grid that divides your business into value-creating areas (see Figure 3-5). You place activities in the grid based on whether they act as part of your primary business functions or you associate them with supporting areas.

Follow these steps to create the grid that shapes your value chain:

1. **List all the key business areas that work to put together your business's products and services and get the products and services out to customers.**

   Include such departments as R&D (research and development), operations, marketing, sales, distribution, delivery, and service. (Refer to the earlier section "Defining capabilities and resources" for more details on these areas.)

2. **Arrange a list of key business areas in order, from the first good idea R&D produces to the finished product or service.**

3. **List the general business areas in your business that support the primary business functions.**

   Include such supporting areas as management, organization and human resources, strategy and planning, and financial control.

4. **Construct a grid similar to the one you see in Figure 3-5, using your lists of primary and supporting business areas.**

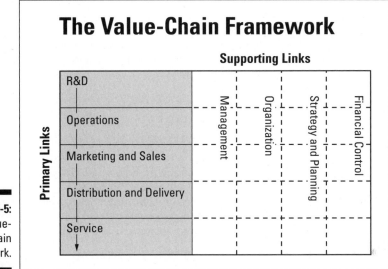

Figure 3-5:
The value-chain framework.

Book III

Business
Planning

Your value chain may not look exactly like all those organization charts you see floating around your business. The primary and supporting business functions that add customer value may be framed differently, depending on whom you ask, so you should talk to customers and co-workers. Ask your customers to describe your business as they see it — they may have a better vantage point.

To fill in the value-chain grid, you have to fill in all the specific value-adding activities — the capabilities and resources that your business uses to increase the value of your products and services. Follow these steps:

1. **Go through the lists of capabilities and resources, and make a first pass at placing them in the value-chain grid.**

2. **In the boxes on the left side of the value-chain grid, place value-adding activities that directly contribute to your primary business functions.**

These activities make up the primary links in your value chain.

3. **Place value-adding activities that you associate with supporting functions in grid boxes to the right of the primary functions that they support.**

These activities make up the supporting links in the value chain.

4. **On the grid, include a description of the customer value that the various links add, as well as how they add that value.**

 The value chain offers you a unique look at your business through your customers' eyes. Every link in the value chain is something that you do as a business. Every link is an activity that you spend money on. The value chain allows you to see exactly what value customers get out of each link. It gives you a relatively clear picture of why you stay in business, as well as where you could do a better job.

Creating your value proposition

During a recent business trip, a colleague of ours pulled into a small town to look for a gas station. She had two choices, and the gas prices were exactly the same. One station had several cars at the pumps; the other was empty. When she asked the manager of the busy station whether he could explain the popularity of his station compared with the one across the street, the man didn't miss a beat:

> *Oh, they're in a different business. They're a filling station; we're a service station.*

This canny businessman had a real feeling for why his station was successful. You can develop that same feeling by taking the value chain that you put together for your business (see the preceding section) and boiling it down into a clear statement of what benefits you provide your customers and what real value your customers place on those benefits.

Business people refer to the preceding statement as the *value proposition* — fancy jargon for a simple idea. A value proposition may be similar to your business's mission statement (flip to Chapter 1 of this book for the details on mission statements), but the proposition is more narrowly focused on customers — what you provide them and what they take away. At first glance, a business's value proposition seems pretty obvious:

✔ Giant Tiger Discount Stores offer the cheapest prices around on a wide range of merchandise.

✔ Canadian Tundra Diamonds offers unparalleled luxury and the ultimate in snob appeal in the world of jewellery.

> ✔ Canadian Automobile Association (CAA) offers travel and motoring services at home and around the world.

But companies often provide their customers with more value than first meets the eye — even more value than the businesses themselves may realize.

Putting Together a Business Model

Business models don't have to be complex or elaborate. In fact, when management types talk about them — as in, "So what's your business model?" — they intend to ask a very direct and basic question: How do you plan to make money? Your answer should be at the very heart of your business plan and reflected in each of its sections.

Where's the money?

Whether you like it or not, at some point, you have to get down to the nitty-gritty details of your business's finances — income statements, balance sheets, cash flow, budgeting, and all that stuff. (Check out Book IV.) In this chapter, you need to ponder something much more basic: coming up with the money. Not literally, of course (just yet). But you need to know how you expect to make money in your business.

Simple, you say. Your customers give you money in exchange for the valuable products and services you provide, right? Well, much like the value chains that support them (refer to the section "Evaluating the Value Chain and What You Do Best," earlier in this chapter, for more on value chains), business models aren't always that obvious or straightforward. Businesses often make a profit on areas outside the main product or service — areas that customers don't focus on. These areas can bring great success. Here are some surprising examples:

> ✔ Given the price of a good meal out, you may think that successful restaurants rake in the dough. And many of them do. But they make the bulk of their profits not on those delicious appetizers and entrees, but on the mixed drinks and wine that they serve before, during, and after the meal.

> ✔ Luxury vacation fractional ownership is all the rage for the about-to-be-retired set. The prices sound reasonable, and who wouldn't enjoy owning a piece of a condo or villa overlooking the Rockies, the ocean, or a pristine Muskoka lake? It turns out that fractional-ownership real estate companies make their profits not on that primo real estate, but on all the maintenance fees they tack on to the contract — fees that every fractional owner must pay on an ongoing basis.

Book III

Business Planning

✔ Some companies happily sell their products at break-even prices — and then make their real money on the so-called *consumables* (products you use up). Hewlett-Packard, for example, doesn't mind selling its printers at close to cost, knowing that the business makes its real profits on ink and toner cartridges. As long as HP can keep customers satisfied with their total printing experience, the money flows in month after month, year after year.

How's your timing?

How you expect to make your money is only one part of your business model. An equally important piece relates to *when* you get the cash. You may like the idea that the loonies are going to start pouring in tomorrow; however, reality suggests that your business may begin incurring costs and spending money months (or maybe even years) before a revenue stream begins to flow. In the case of pharmaceuticals, for instance, a company can spend years and millions of dollars developing and testing a drug before the first patient — or insurance company — pays a penny to buy it. If your business must spend money before it starts sending out those invoices, your business model must include a timeline that takes the following factors into account:

✔ The up-front costs you expect when you set up your business

✔ The source of funds to pay for your up-front costs

✔ A schedule showing when you expect cash to pour in (For more information on cash flow, see Book IV.)

The question of timing is as important for both small and large businesses. Many retail businesses that operate year-round actually take in most of their revenue during one season — the Christmas holiday rush, for example. In some cases, retailers rake in half of their annual revenues during late November and December. Timing for these establishments is quite literally a make-or-break affair.

At Harris Hatch Inn, a bed and breakfast in St. Andrews-by-the-Sea, New Brunswick, the tourist season begins on May 24 and ends in September. Except for a few hardy souls who go there for holiday weekends — Thanksgiving, Christmas, and New Year's — virtually all Harris Hatch's revenue comes in during those three summer months. The inn's business model must ensure that the money coming in during that short period is enough to pay for fixed costs — mortgage, utilities, taxes, salaries, and upkeep — throughout the entire year. If not, the innkeeper could wake up one morning to the sound of creditors knocking on the door.

Making Your Business Model Work

Companies don't stay in business year after year by accident. Oh, maybe a manager somewhere gets lucky occasionally, making a brilliant move without knowing its significance. But that kind of luck never lasts long, especially when the competition is intense. Companies succeed over the long haul because they understand what their customers value the most, and they figure out how to make money by providing products and services that consistently meet or exceed customer expectation, often at the expense of unsuspecting competitors. By capturing this information in your business plan, you improve the odds of your business model continuing to work in the future.

Searching for a competitive advantage

Most people who take car trips have a special produce stand, a favourite diner, or a certain ice-cream place along the way that they never miss. Why do these travellers develop such affection for specific stops on their route when hundreds of other places are available? What makes particular establishments so unique?

These travellers could come up with all sorts of reasons. They may tell you that they've stopped at the same places for years, they love the food, they like the atmosphere, they know the owners, they can count on the service . . . whatever. No doubt, all these things are true. But if you take a careful look at the value chain for many of these businesses, one important link likely jumps right out at you: location. (Distances and driving times likely are the major reasons why many customers find these businesses in the first place; the storefronts literally happen to be in the right place at the right time. Customers choose the business based on location and stay for the value added in other business areas. Location provides a significant competitive advantage in this on-the-move marketplace.

Competitive advantage means exactly what it says; a business has some sort of advantage over the competition. Where does it come from? Usually, out of the distinct and special value that the business can offer its customers — and from the premium that customers place on that value. Ask yourself this basic question:

> *Why do customers choose my business and its products when other competitors in the industry have more-or-less similar offerings?*

You can find the answer in the strongest links of your value chain (refer to earlier in this chapter) — the links that produce the bulk of your customer value. Location, service, image, and product features are some of the links that create a competitive advantage in the marketplace.

In 1975, Microsoft was a partnership of two: Bill Gates and Paul Allen. They started out competing against a host of bright young entrepreneurs like themselves and eventually had to go head-to-head with IBM. Today, Microsoft has 79,000 employees and $51 billion in revenue, and it offers a wide array of software products, ranging from word processing programs and spreadsheet applications, to language tools and operating systems, to games and smartphone applications. You can find Microsoft's competitive advantage in these areas:

- ✔ **Standards:** Microsoft's programs pretty much set standards in the PC world. Microsoft offers the standard operating system and the standard suite of office applications. Although other companies sell better products here and there, customers see Microsoft as the safe and sensible choice across the board, a distinctive image advantage over the competition.

- ✔ **Compatibility:** Microsoft programs promise to work with one another and with the operating system. You don't have to worry about your favourite application becoming an outcast or somehow misbehaving on your computer.

- ✔ **Product range:** You name it, and Microsoft probably has a product that can do it — from word processing to picture editing, from managing your money to keeping track of your e-mail. The company continues to aggressively develop new software to meet the needs of rapidly changing markets. The company even targeted Internet users with a host of new products, including its flagship Internet site, www.msn.com.

- ✔ **Service and support:** With Microsoft, you know what you're getting. If a product doesn't work, the company tries hard to fix it quickly. Microsoft devotes tremendous resources to product support and provides a wide range of service options, including online knowledge bases, news groups, chat rooms, e-mail, and (of course) telephone support.

Discount Car & Truck Rentals is by far Canada's largest privately owned international car-rental agency. The company has more than 300 rental locations in Canada and Australia. But Discount faces competition at all levels, from the mom-and-pop rental outlets at popular vacation spots to regional agencies and global companies, including Avis, Hertz, and National. Here's how Discount finds a competitive advantage:

- ✔ **Free pickup and return:** When you call Discount to book a vehicle, a representative picks you up at your home, office, or travel location. Discount also takes you where you need to go after you return the rental unit.

- ✔ **National presence:** No matter which major Canadian city you visit, Discount can rent you what you need.

- ✔ **Peace of mind:** With Discount, you don't have to worry about the car not being there, the rate doubling, or that you'll end up paying for an old rent-a-dent.

- ✔ **Rewards for loyalty:** As a loyal Discount customer, the company rewards you with membership in a club that provides notification of low-rate specials; a rent two weekends, get one free deal; and frequent-user points that you can redeem toward free rental days.

Focusing on core competence

You create your competitive advantage in the marketplace. Your advantages have everything to do with your customers — with the relative value that they place on your products and services, and with the purchase decisions that they finally make. What internal capabilities and resources do you have, and what business activities do you engage in that lead directly to your competitive advantage? You must make sure to capture these in your business plan.

Go back to your business's value chain (which we discuss in the section "Evaluating the Value Chain and What You Do Best," earlier in this chapter) and focus on the links that provide your competitive advantage. When you do, you come face to face with something that the gurus call your core competence. Simply defined, *core competence* is your business's special capability to create a competitive advantage in the marketplace. In almost all cases, this gift is specific to your business. Think of core competence as being corporate DNA. Unlike your personal genetic code, however, your business's core competence is something you can build on — or lose, depending on how attentive you are to your marketplace and your business.

Book III

Business Planning

The preceding section examines two well-known companies: Microsoft and Discount.

Microsoft's core competence consists of

- ✔ **Visionary executives:** The executive team has a broad vision of the future, enabling the company to forge today's software standards and shape tomorrow's.

- ✔ **Top-notch development team:** The company supports a dream-team corps of developers and programmers who create and maintain a state-of-the-art product line.

- ✔ **Management of complexity:** Microsoft manages a complex related set of software products that all have to behave and work together.

> ✔ **Capability to change direction:** The company has the capacity to redirect resources and energies when the fast-moving marketplace shifts course and the rules of the game suddenly change.

Microsoft's first two core competence factors lead to the others because success and profit allow for more capabilities and value.

Discount's core competence includes

> ✔ **Information systems:** A sophisticated computer database allows the company to keep track of customer profiles and match them against an ever-changing supply of rental cars and special rates.
>
> ✔ **National logistics:** The company can track, distribute, arrange, and rearrange a huge fleet of vehicles in all shapes and sizes on a regional and national basis.
>
> ✔ **Scale of operations:** The company uses its sheer size and business volume to negotiate favourable terms on new-car purchases and even insurance premiums.
>
> ✔ **Relationships and tie-ins:** Discount has the resources to work closely with corporate clients, travel agencies, and the travel industry to create new business by expanding car-rental options and opportunities.

A business's core competence can point the way toward new market opportunities. Honda, for example, used a core competence in designing engines to expand its markets. The company created product lines in lawn mowers, snow throwers, snowmobiles, motorcycles, and all-terrain vehicles, to name just a few of its motor-based businesses. Honda benefits from a related competitive advantage (state-of-the-art engines) in each of these distinct markets. Take another look at your business's core competence to see if you can come up with any new business directions based on your already successful business areas.

Sustaining an advantage over time

Every organization that manages to stay in business has some sort of competitive advantage and core competence to draw upon; otherwise, it simply can't exist. But here comes the million-dollar question: How can you renew and sustain that competitive advantage over years and even decades? Customers and their needs shift over time, competition gets more intense, and industries evolve, so your competitive advantage and the core competence that supports it aren't guaranteed to stay around. You rent them; you don't own them. You want to make sure that you keep a long-term lease on both.

Sustained competitive advantage — the business world's Holy Grail — is a business's capability to renew competitive advantages over and over again in the face of a constantly changing business environment and marketplace. But, if you want to sustain competitive advantages over time, you need a long-term strategy.

Think about ongoing strategies that your business can use to see that you preserve your core competence. How can you sustain the competitive advantage that your business already has? Get a blank sheet of paper and jot down answers to these key questions:

- ✔ Where will changes in your business most likely come from?

- ✔ How will those changes likely affect your business's competitive advantage?

- ✔ What can your business do to maintain core competence in the face of change? Is it consistent with your values and mission statements? (Refer to Chapter 1 of this book for more about values and for information about your mission statement.)

Focus on each of the major forces that fuel change in your industry:

- ✔ Your customers and their changing needs and requirements

- ✔ Your competitors and their changing capabilities, strategies, and goals

- ✔ Your business, its value chain, and its shifting strengths and weaknesses

When you create your business plan, make sure that you continue to track these forces so that they don't threaten the core competence that you work so hard to achieve.

Earmarking resources

The value chain paints a portrait of your business as your customers see it. (We talk about the value chain in the section "Evaluating the Value Chain and What You Do Best.") Links in the chain reflect the value that customers place on aspects of your products and services. The strongest links capture your competitive advantage in the market and define your core competence as a business.

Because the value chain is so good at helping you weigh the importance of your business decisions, it comes in handy when you put together your business plan. In particular, the value chain is invaluable for earmarking scarce resources toward specific business activities.

Book III

Business Planning

At almost any major racetrack, a group of regulars hangs around the stands or clusters at the fence. These people are serious about horse racing. They spend time poring over track sheets and newspapers — circling this, checking that, and pacing back and forth.

When they finally place bets, they don't rely on Lady Luck alone. They use all the information available — the condition of the track, the horse's racing history and bloodlines, the jockey's record, and the betting odds — to place their cash on the wagers most likely to result in the best payoffs and the biggest winnings.

Betting on the horses is a serious business for these committed professionals. And they can show you something about how to divvy up your working assets. Is it sensible to spread your business's limited resources equally among all the areas that make up your business? Probably not. Each time you set aside time and money for a particular business activity, you place a bet on your business plan. You bet that the resources you commit are going to contribute to your business, add value to what you do, and eventually come back around to generate revenue and profits.

So, how do you know where to place your bets? You guessed it: You go back to your business's value chain. Follow these simple steps to check your resource allocation based on your value chain:

1. **Look at where your business currently spends money.**

   Make a quick-and-dirty estimate of how you divvy up yearly expenses among business activities — from R&D to delivery and service — and jot the numbers down on your value-chain grid (refer to Figure 3-5). To keep things simple, use percentages. Make sure that the numbers add up to 100 percent.

2. **Look at where your customers think that you provide them value.**

   Take the total value that customers think you provide and divvy it up among your business activities. If customers pay $100 to buy your widget, for example, how much of that do they pay for features, how much for service, and how much for convenience? Again, use percentages and jot the numbers on the same value-chain grid. Make sure that the numbers add up to 100 percent.

3. **As a reminder, highlight the boxes on the value-chain grid that represent your core competence and account for your competitive advantage in the marketplace.**

4. **Analyze the completed grid.**

   If the percentages line up and are concentrated in the highlighted boxes, you're in good shape. But if you find a glaring mismatch in where you spend money, what your core competence is, and where your customers think that your products give them value, you need to reassess where you direct your resources.

Chapter 4

A Sample Business Plan

In This Chapter

▶ Viewing a sample business plan

▶ Following a business-plan template

Sometimes, you have to see something up close and personal before you really understand what it's all about. Viewing a real live business plan should get you much closer to putting your own plan on paper.

Your written business plan says something about all the important parts of your business. After all, you want to convince people — and yourself — that your business knows what it's doing. If you want to persuade people of anything, however, they have to actually sit down and read what's in front of them. So you want to be clear, concise, and to the point, and spending some time on your prose doesn't hurt, either.

In this chapter we show you a sample business plan. (We changed some names and of the numbers to protect the innocent.) By reviewing the plan in some detail, you can understand how to construct a business plan of your own.

Network Components, Inc. (NCI) Business Plan — CONFIDENTIAL!

Executive Summary

Company Overview

With the proliferation of client/server architecture and the use of online transaction processing (OLTP), online analytical processing (OLAP), as well as Internet/intranet servers in corporate enterprise computing, increased server capacity has become necessary to handle the expanded processing load — that is, processing power, memory, data storage, and so on. In turn, this has led to the computer cluster as a means to meet this need.

A computer cluster is a group of compute nodes (single, SMP, and so on) that are connected by a network and act together as a single system. The cluster architecture provides increased fault-tolerance and the ability to grow processing power by simply adding new compute nodes to the cluster (they are highly "scalable"). For such scalable cluster systems to be constructed, a new network, called System Area Network (SAN), must be implemented. Necessary features of these SAN systems include high bandwidth, low latency, low overhead, and scalability. Our firm, **Network Components, Inc. (NCI),** has developed a proprietary high-performance network architecture that possesses these features, based on completely open technologies. We believe that cluster computing will become the next dominant architecture for the expanding server market over the next three to five years — as do many other informed industry analysts.

Technology and Products

NCI is developing a SAN architecture called *Tera*Net©, which consists of an SCI-PCI network interface (*Tera*Link©), an SCI-based switch (*Tera*Switch©), and an SCI interface to mass storage devices such as RAID, magneto-optical farms, tape libraries, and so on. NCI hardware and driver software will be compatible with all major software Mbytes/throughput on the SCI network with 2.1GB/node-to-node bandwidth and latencies of 2–5 μs.

This architecture uses two proprietary technologies developed by NCI founder Dr. Fritz von Honecker. These technologies include a novel approach to resource management and intelligent network interface architecture. A critical feature of *Tera*Net© is the use of an intelligent I/O system that handles all intra-node traffic, alleviating costly compute node processor intervention — and that, in turn, provides complete scalability for adding nodes to the cluster. Full production prototypes are expected by November 2008, with initial *Tera*Link© tests completed by December 2009.

The Market Opportunity

Initial customers for NCI will be server manufacturers who provide volume and mid-range server systems for corporate enterprise computing. Each of the principal network operating system developers has announced the updated release of clusterable operating systems, including Microsoft Windows Vista, Linux BProc, and Sun Solaris Cluster. Initially, the now-defunct Zona Research projected an $8.9 billion market for corporate intranet server systems and $1.95 billion in Internet server sales by 1998. However, intranet server revenues grew at >200 percent CAGR, while IDC reports that NT-based server unit sales increased at 85 percent CAGR from 2002 to 2005. Worldwide revenues in 2006 for the x86-based server market reached $25.8 billion with shipments of 6.9 million servers and will continue to expand by 7 percent annually to reach 10 million units by 2011.

When valued-added resellers (VARs) become involved in cluster-server development, NCI expects to use both a push and a pull marketing strategy. The key to the push strategy will be the development of strategic relationships with the larger VAR firms. The pull strategy will be implemented through advertising to IT/IS managers/developers to raise their awareness levels of the underlying cluster network. The corporate end-user market will be supplied through the use of both direct sales and distributors.

Competition

Two key vendors are currently providing or planning to provide SAN architecture hardware and software within the coming year. These competitive technologies include Dolphin's Express SCI-PCI interconnect and Myricom's Myrinet. In each case, NCI's *Tera*Net© technology will outperform competitors. More importantly, Dolphin Express and Myrinet are proprietary technologies, whereas NCI will provide completely open network architecture. We believe that NCI will have a distinct competitive advantage over these rivals.

Funds Requested

The company is currently at the seed stage of financing, with an initial $150,000 investment completed from a group of private individuals. This current investment provides capital for the development and production of alpha production prototype hardware. NCI is seeking additional Stage One financing of $1.5 million by Q4 2008. Use of these funds includes completion of both 2- and 64-bit versions of our product and the development and fabrication of an SCI Link Controller ASIC. Within 9 to 12 months of closing on Stage One financing, NCI anticipates the need for an additional $3 million in Stage Two financing; we project a positive cash flow from Q3–Q4 2010.

Book III

Business Planning

Exit Strategy

NCI projects that it will either be acquired or that it will implement an IPO. This choice will be determined by the board of directors based on market developments and the firm's competitive situation. It is not possible to predict at this time when either of these options might occur.

1. NCI Business Plan

The Company

With Microsoft, Linux, and Sun each developing a clusterable operating system, producers of volume and mid-range servers are beginning to provide cluster-based server systems. Cluster servers are single or Symmetric Multi-Processor (SMP) systems that, when connected, act as a single system. There are two classes of these systems: (1) fail-over and (2) fully scalable.

Simple fail-over systems provide a mechanism for the migration of active processes from one node to another. This provides increased uptime for the server by being tolerant against single-node system crashes, as well as system hardware and software upgrades. These fail-over systems can be connected by standard high-speed networking technologies, for example, Fast Ethernet, Fibre Channel, ATM, and so on. Beyond a few compute nodes, these types of systems yield little or no performance enhancement.

Scalable systems not only provide fault tolerance, but also enhanced performance as nodes are added to the cluster. Applications can be distributed over multiple compute nodes, providing superior performance when compared with single nodes. In order for applications to communicate/coordinate activities in this distributed environment, high-speed, low-latency, scalable networks must be implemented. Traditional networking technologies cannot provide these features. Therefore, a new class of network must be used. NCI has developed a novel network architecture based upon open standards, which will enable scalability in these clustered systems.

The mission of Network Components, Inc., is to become the leading provider of high-performance network systems for use in computer clustering, enabling the construction of powerful, scalable, fault-tolerant server systems from low-cost, commodity hardware. NCI's network architecture called *Tera*Net© consists of a node-to-node interconnect (*Tera*Link©), a switch (*Tera*Switch©), and connectivity to mass storage devices, such as RAID, tape, magneto-optical systems, and so on. *Tera*Net© has several major advantages over competitive technologies, including performance, scalability, versatility, and openness. Currently, no available SAN systems outperform *Tera*Net©. The use of a proprietary (patent-filed) intelligent I/O system allows *Tera*Net© to handle all inter-node I/O traffic, alleviating I/O overhead on the process nodes. Because the additional traffic from added compute nodes does not provide additional overhead on other compute nodes in the cluster, *Tera*Net© systems are completely scalable.

Current Company Status

NCI is a start-up company with superior technical expertise. An early prototype of the SAN *Tera*Link© interface board, connecting a PCI bus to an SCI network, has been evaluated in a system test at Lawrence Berkeley National Laboratory. The prototype implements a patent-pending proprietary resource management technology (this was invented by the founder of NCI), which has been found to be fully functional and verified.

NCI Objectives

NCI's full SAN architecture will be delivered to the market within 12–18 months. In order to reduce the overall capital necessary for this extended period, NCI plans to initially market the product to producers of proprietary cluster-server systems. By providing these customers with a solution to their requirements for a high-speed interconnect, NCI will be able to profit from high-margin products in the early stages of the company's development. In order to attain positive cash flow as early as possible, as well as complete development of the product, NCI plans to implement the business in three phases, described below.

Phase I

NCI is currently in the early stage of Phase I development and expects to complete this phase no later than December 2008. Product development for this phase is expected to provide proof of principal for the interconnect product. Potential strategic partners will also be identified during mid-Phase I. By allowing customers to provide software support for integration of NCI products into their proprietary systems, NCI will significantly reduce overhead and manpower costs. Organizationally, NCI anticipates recruiting a chief executive officer (CEO) during this first six months. Prior to Phase II, the CEO will provide strategic consulting, industry networking, and so on.

Phase II

Phase II development will be implemented in quarter-based stages. Several iterations of board development are expected during the first two quarters of Phase II.

Quarter 1

By Q1, a small customer/strategic partner base is expected to have been identified. NCI anticipates further testing and development of the *Tera*Link© product, which will be made available to strategic partners. By mid/late Q1, 50 *Tera*Link© boards will be produced. *Tera*Link© sales will be made to customers interested in a solution in which they provide much of the software development. Development of the NCI SCI ASIC will begin by early Q1 2009. NCI plans to hire six additional employees during Q1 2009, including two software developers and one each of a firmware developer, hardware engineer, business development manager, and administrative assistant.

Quarter 2

During Q2, NCI expects to sell the first working *Tera*Link© interface boards. Working system prototypes of customers' cluster servers, using the NCI interconnect product, should be available during this period. An additional 100 *Tera*Link© interface cards will be produced. Hiring during this period will include a second software/firmware developer and a product quality control/ assembly/customer-support technician.

Quarter 3

Development and refinement of the complete SAN product line will also be pursued. NCI anticipates additional sales of 100 *Tera*Link© boards to a small customer base, while late in Q3, NCI plans production of an additional 200 *Tera*Link© cards. Strategic alliances and relationships with OEM customers should also be developed in this time period. An additional support technician will be hired during Q3 2009.

Quarter 4

NCI anticipates completion of development and fabrication of the NCI SCI ASIC in early Q4 2009. Development of the *Tera*Switch© product line will begin by early Q4. Additional *Tera*Link© board sales are expected to rise to 200 during this final quarter of Phase II. Late in Q4, NCI plans to have a fully operational and functional *Tera*Net© solution available for customers. Ramping of *Tera*Link© production will begin in Late Q4. Complete full *Tera*Net© systems integration should occur at this time. Additional hiring during this phase, including engineers and marketing personnel, will bring total NCI employee headcount to 19.

Phase III

Within 18 months of initial seed funding, NCI plans to have a full release of *Tera*Net©. The hardware and software components of the architecture will be fully developed, allowing integration of the NCI open SAN technology in NT-based cluster server systems. Product expansion and *Tera*Net© enhancements will be ongoing during this period. First year full production sales are expected to be 8,500 *Tera*Link© units and 600 *Tera*Switch© units. It is expected by the end of Phase III (Q4 2010) that NCI will employ 28–32 people.

2. Markets and Competition

The Enterprise Server Market

International Technology Group reports that the typical Fortune 500 firm had 8 gigabytes (GB) of corporate data in 1979. In 1990, the number had grown to 28,000GB; to 400,000GB by 1999; and to 161 billion GB (exabytes) by 2006. Between 2006 and 2010, data added annually will increase to 988 exabytes. In order to access and utilize this information, new classes of powerful business applications have been developed. These new applications require huge amounts of processing power, storage capacity, and communication bandwidth. Database-driven servers able to run on-line analytical processing (OLAP) applications, as well as serve interactive Internet and intranet sites, are quickly becoming the staple in corporate enterprise computing.

One architectural implementation of these systems uses symmetric multi-processors (SMP). These computers have a global view of system resources, including memory, disk space, tape storage, and so on. Therefore, as the number of processors in a given system is increased, eventually the performance rises only slightly due to competition for access to the resource; thus, these systems do not scale well with the number of users or as increasing processing power becomes necessary. Also, this architecture leads to single points of failure, minimizing fault tolerance in the system.

One type of multi-processor server system gaining attention in the enterprise market is the clustering of single and multi-processor computers. By clustering computers in a share-nothing environment (meaning each computer has its own memory, disk space, and so on), systems can scale by simply adding compute nodes to the cluster. A mechanism can be implemented in which, if a compute node or process fails, the process being executed can be migrated to another processor in the cluster, allowing for a completely fault-tolerant system. Separate servers can also be assembled into a single computing facility, making these systems more easily managed while affording IT groups the flexibility to grow beyond single machines. By providing fail-over services, clustered systems can be utilized as extremely high-availability corporate Internet/intranet servers, allowing for nearly continuous service or "Web tone." Additionally, as the number of accesses or "hits" increases, Internet/intranet server performance can be enhanced by simply adding nodes to the cluster, providing nearly unlimited scalability.

The Cluster Interconnect Market

For simple fail-over solutions, any number of network protocols and architectures can be used, but to build truly performance-scaleable cluster server systems, a new class of network technology must be employed. These would be high-speed, low-latency, low-overhead networks that can facilitate message passing from CPU to CPU to coordinate processor activities, as well as CPU-to-I/O and I/O-to-I/O communications. The network framework used in clustering has been called the "system area network" (SAN). Currently, all commercially available multi-processor cluster systems are based on proprietary SAN technology. Clustering multiple processors to build servers for corporate enterprise applications is a market with a tremendous growth potential if an open SAN technology is made available. NCI intends to provide an industry-standard open SAN technology to meet this need.

According to a survey of 400 large companies conducted by Oracle Corporation, the average computer downtime event results in a $140,000 loss in the retail industry and $400,000 in the securities industry. Yet clusters can provide 99.99 percent uptime, yielding average downtime costs of only $84,000 per year. By reducing system management needs and providing fault-tolerance against costly downtime while increasing system performance, cluster servers — and ultimately the NCI SAN technology used to construct these architectures — can pay for themselves within 6 to 12 months.

Book III

Business Planning

Alternative Network Technologies (Fail-Over)

It might appear that cluster interconnect technologies would be compatible with high-end networking protocols, Fast or Gigabit Ethernet, Fibre Channel, or Asynchronous Transfer Mode (ATM). Although useful as possible client-server components, traditional networking is insufficient for clustering interconnects. For example, one very important aspect of a cluster interconnect is its message passing latency and overhead. The NCI network allows extremely low-latency message-passing (typically less than five microseconds) with zero processor overhead. This compares with several hundred microseconds to millisecond latency and processing overhead per message for LAN (local area network) and WAN (wide area network) architectures.

In Table 4-1, we compare standard networking technologies with NCI's *Tera*Net©. Note that although several of these networks claim to have similar throughput, the complex protocols involved in using them for data transport significantly reduces the throughput.

Table 4-1	Comparison of Standard Networking Technologies with NCI's *Tera*Net©				
	Fast Ethernet	**Gigabit Ethernet**	**ATM-155**	**Fibre Channel**	**NCI *Tera*Net©**
Throughput	12 MB/s	100 MB/s	155 MB/s	2.13 Gbps	2.1 Gbps
Latency	ms	ms	100 µs	100 µs	2–5 µs
Processor Overhead	Large	Large	Large	Large	N/A
NIC Cost	$25	not required	615	$940	$800
Switch Cost	$80	$150 (8)	$15,000 (4)	$3,925 (8)	$3,000 (8)

(The numbers in parentheses are the number of ports)

For each of the standard technologies listed in Table 4-1, the processing overhead is very large, with similarly large latencies. For environments where distributed applications must communicate between the various processors, this latency will severely impede performance and scalability.

Market Size and Development

Market reports and projections for an open SAN market segment are difficult to obtain due to the market infancy. However, by providing a general overview of the current and projected number of NT server sales, Intel-based application servers, and the projected revenues for Internet/intranet servers, we can provide a plausible scenario for NCI revenue projections.

Microsoft has recently announced a schedule for deploying Windows Server 2008 (formerly Windows Server 2003), which will eventually provide clients with a single system image of the clustered server and enhance cluster management. The release is scheduled for February 2008. Windows Server 2008 shares much of the same architecture and functionality of Windows Vista, with a variation called Server Core. Server Core is a scaled-back installation, which does not include many features that are not core server features such as .NET Framework or Internet Explorer. Beta 1 has been in the market since 2005, and Beta 2 with WinHEC was released in spring 2006, followed by Beta 3 in spring 2006. Sun's Solaris Cluster Technology was released in late 2000. Capabilities to cluster 8 and 16 nodes were anticipated by 1998 and 1999, respectively; however, the technology today supports from 2 to 100 nodes.

As Windows Server 2008, Linux BProc, Sun's Solaris Cluster, and so on become increasingly accepted, corporate IT managers will begin migrating enterprise server systems from proprietary SMP architectures to open clusters of single processor and SMP systems. This new technology will enable smaller to mid-sized businesses to begin using some of the more processor-intensive applications and fail-safe features, which have historically been cost prohibitive. Therefore, along with crossover from the SMP market, a significant portion of the low-end x86-based server market has adopted cluster systems and clustering technology. Prices for the major categories of servers are displayed in Table 4-2.

Table 4-2	Category Pricing of Servers
Category	*Unit Price*
Volume servers	< $25,000
Midrange Enterprise servers	$25,000–$499,999
High-end Enterprise servers	$500,000 or more

It is expected that the majority of these servers will be application servers, where fault tolerance and scalability are essential. Table 4-3 displays the forecast shipments of x86-based servers worldwide. Industry analysts predict that when scalable clustering becomes fully available, 20–30 percent of the x86-based server market will use clustering capabilities.

Table 4-3   Forecast Shipments of x86-Based Servers (Worldwide)

Year	Units Shipped
2006	6,900,000[1]
2007	7,383,000
2008	7,900,000
2009	8,450,000
2010	9,000,000
2011	9,680,000

([1]Actual shipments; source: DataCenter.com [Feb. 27, 2007])

Since the greatest volume of clusterable computers will be used by corporations for application and Internet/intranet servers, we forecast revenues for the server market for Internet/intranet and higher-end servers worldwide in Table 4-4. Notice that while the annual growth rate is 7 percent in shipment of units, revenue AGR is lower at 5 percent due to competitive pricing and production cost reductions.

Table 4-4   Forecasted Revenues Worldwide Server Market (in Billions)

Year	x86	Other	Total
2008	$28.4	$29.7	$58.1
2009	$29.9	$31.1	$61.0
2010	$31.4	$32.7	$64.1
2011	$32.9	$34.3	$67.3

(Forecast based on worldwide revenues in 2006 of $52.7 billion; source: DataCenter.com, [Feb. 23, 2007])

Revenue Projections

In 2009, NCI plans to market and sell to the segment of the cluster-server market that needs high-speed interconnects for proprietary server systems, thus integrating *Tera*Link© into their overall system design. NCI estimates board sales to these customers of 350 units (150 in FY09), with the majority of these in Q4. Assuming the NT server market continues to grow at 7 percent AGR, we estimate 29.9 million x86-based servers sold in 2009. During 2009, we expect only 5 percent of the total x86 server market will use clustered systems. Because the majority of clusters in 2009 will be simple fail-over systems, NCI projects that only 10 percent of the cluster market will use high-speed interconnects. We also expect that in 2009, the average number of nodes in a cluster will be two. Therefore, the projected 350 interface cards sold in 2009 represents a 0.8 percent market share for NCI.

It is expected that the open x86-based cluster server market will become mature with the Phase II release of Microsoft's Windows Vista software, due in early 2008. Initial discussion with several large multi-processor server suppliers indicates, conservatively, an initial market of *Tera*Link© interface boards to be 12,000 units. NCI estimates that on average for every 16 *Tera*Link© boards sold, a *Tera*Switch© will be implemented. In 2010, the projected number of x86 servers sold is 9 million. Conservatively, we estimate that 15 percent of these will be clustered systems with two nodes. We also expect that the number of cluster systems with high-speed interconnects will increase to 25 percent. Assuming that NCI can double its market share to 5 percent in 2010, NCI projects the sale of 8,500 *Tera*Link© (32- and 64-bit) units and 600 *Tera*Switch© units. With an average price of $1,612 for *Tera*Link© and $800 for *Tera*Switch©, NCI expects to generate revenues of $14.0MM in FY10 (see Table 4-5, below).

Table 4-5	Expected Revenues of NCI for FY 2010
Est. Number of x86 Servers Sold =	9,000,000
X % That Are Clusters	15%
= Number of Clusters	1,356,674
X % That Are High-Speed	25%
= Number of Clusters	339,168
X Average Number of Nodes	2
X % Est. NCI Market Share	2.5%
= *Tera*Link© Revenue	8,360 @ $1,612 ea = $13,476,320
+ *Tera*Switch© Revenue	555 @ $800 ea = 444,000
= Projected Total NCI Revenue	$14,238,000

Competition

There are currently two competitors providing non-SCI-based system area network (SAN) interconnect technologies: Myricom, Inc.'s *Myrinet* technology and Dolphin Interconnect Solutions' Express.

Myricom, a privately held corporation located in California (currently with 50 employees), introduced its high-speed, low-latency SAN technology called Myrinet in 1994; it claimed 60 MB/s point-to-point for large message sizes (10KB) and at least 40 μs latencies. It later released its second product, Myri-10G. It is operating in numerous clusters in over 50 countries and in 20 percent of the Top 500 supercomputer list of 2005. Myrinet PCI cards cost $750, while 8-port switches are $3,500–$3,990, yielding $850 per port to implement a Myrinet system. NCI expects Myricom will continue to dominate the demanding scientific and engineering market, but will likely only be a niche player in the open Intel-based server market.

Dolphin Interconnect Solutions is a privately held company that emerged out of an ASIC design house in Oslo, Norway. Currently, Dolphin is the principal provider of CMOS SCI chips. It has announced that it has perfected the Dolphin Express interconnect technology with the innovative Dolphin Express Supersockets software. It boasts that it can enable users of MySQL Cluster to achieve superior database performance. Although Dolphin will be a prominent competitor in the SAN interconnect marketplace, NCI's patented flow control and resource management architecture will provide an edge over this competitor in price and performance. Additionally, NCI expects the initial clustering methodologies to vary widely. Because NCI provides a CPU at the network interface, while Dolphin does not, it will take Dolphin much longer to adapt to the changing environment, giving NCI a significant edge in system implementation.

Response of Competitors to NCI Entry into Market

Dolphin could potentially be very competitive and possibly underbid NCI products. It has established sales channels and has several critical strategic alliances, which provide a reasonable lead time. One principal concern is Dolphin's SCI link controller chips, necessary for any SCI-based network products. Dolphin could essentially starve the entire market of these chips in hopes of capturing greater market share. This is the principal reason NCI believes the development of an alternative SCI link controller ASIC will be necessary, not only for NCI but also for the SCI-based market, in general.

Myricom is expected to remain a niche player in this market. It will primarily continue to supply research institutions and governmental customers with its product. Currently, however, Myrinet does not have enough market share to impact NCI's strategy.

3. Marketing and Sales

Customers

Initially, NCI products will be sold to providers of enterprise-class server systems who wish to add a clustering option to their portfolio of products. Providers of these systems and market size are shown in Table 4-6.

Table 4-6	Market Share of Server Shipments Worldwide (2006)	
Company	**% Market Share**	**Revenue (Billions)**
IBM	37.9	$19.9
HP	26.8	$14.1
Dell	9.7	$0.5

Company	% Market Share	Revenue (Billions)
Sun Microsystems	9.7	$0.5
Fujitsu/Fujitsu-Siemens	4.1	$0.2
Others	11.8	$0.6

NCI Market Strategy

Initial customers will be providers of volume to mid-end x86-based server systems looking to provide a cluster solution, without developing in-house SAN technology. Many of these principal customers have the resources to develop a SAN technology. However, the availability of an open SAN architecture that is ready to integrate into their server systems, is affordable, and meets their performance requirements is clearly a better solution. NCI expects that the cluster and subsequent SAN market will evolve in three distinct phases.

Phase 1

Phase I is expected to dominate the sale of clusters until Q3–Q4 2010. Although VARs will begin cluster development and integration in Q1 2010, volume sales to these customers is not expected until 2011. Sales to top-level server companies require this to be an executive sales strategy, as each sale will entail multi-hundred-thousand- to multi-million-dollar transactions, and the decision to use a given SAN system will be made by senior executives and senior engineers at the given server company. Direct contact and in-house demonstration with test systems integrated into the company's full cluster-server systems will provide the bulk of market communication during the first 12–18 months. Trade show participation will be limited to one to two shows per year, initially, because primary sales will be through direct executive channels.

Phase 11

During 2010, NCI expects an increase in the number of VAR's building cluster-server systems for clients. This will coincide with the release of Microsoft's Cluster Server software, which provides improved system-management tools and initial development of a single system image for the cluster. During the increase in the number of VAR cluster-server providers, NCI expects to engage additional sales personnel. For the VAR market, NCI plans to use both push and pull marketing strategies; push strategies will again be implemented as direct sales channels from both executives and sales associates. Demonstrations will also be provided both in conjunction with server manufacturers and NCI sponsored cluster-server conferences. NCI plans to tightly integrate customer support with customer education programs during the early phases of this market development.

Book III

Business Planning

On the pull side, NCI plans promotion in the principal business journals, which cover enterprise/corporate computing topics. These magazines include *Computer Reseller News (CRN), VAR Business, EE Times, Computer World, PC Week, Network World, INFOWorld, Ent,* and *Information Week,* among others. Because corporate end-users typically have more intimate relationships with VAR suppliers than manufacturers, NCI will attempt to raise the awareness of the IT/IS specialists at the enterprise level in an effort to have them contact/question their VAR product providers concerning NCI products.

During this market development, NCI expects to participate in three to six trade shows per year. These shows will include Hot Interconnects, Storage Networking World, INFOWorld, LISA, and Massive Technology Show. During this phase, a customer support manager and team will be developed in order to handle the assumed increased customer volume.

Phase III

Finally, during 2011–2012 — when Microsoft Windows Vista is expected to become truly scalable — NCI expects to develop direct corporate accounts as end-users. Not only will these corporate customers be developing and integrating new cluster systems, but they will also be using NCI hardware/ software to upgrade their current scalable systems. Advertising will be expanded to include all relevant enterprise/Intel/Internet/intranet trade magazines.

4. The Products

NCI intends to supply open System Area Network (SAN) interface and switch products in the form of an initial product called *Tera*Net©. *Tera*Net© consists of several independent components, including *Tera*Link©, the PCI-SCI interface card, and *Tera*Switch©, an SCI switch product.

*Tera*Link© provides the interface between the local bus of a given host system and the SAN interconnect fabric. NCI expects to initially offer this product in a PCI form factor, allowing it to be used in PC/Intel-based computer systems. Both 32- and 64-bit versions of this interface card will be produced. Because development from PCI to the PMC (embedded [VME] computer systems) form factor is trivial, NCI expects to eventually offer this product, as well. Despite the large market segment of PCI-based computers, there are also other systems not using PCI as the local bus standard (for example, SGI). NCI intends to eventually produce follow-up products that interface to those buses, as well.

The second product is a scalable network switch, *Tera*Switch©. This switch allows the construction of any architectural compute fabric in the clustered system. Even with a 500 MB/s network link, as additional nodes are clustered, intra-cluster communication will begin to suffer. The *Tera*Switch© product allows the construction of clusters much larger than eight nodes.

A third product, expected to be completed 9–12 months after Stage One funding, is the generic SAN SCI ASIC (Application Specific Integrated Circuit). This SCI interface chip will be used in both the NCI *Tera*Link© interface card and the NCI *Tera*Switch© product. This ASIC provides the chip-level interface between the *Tera*Link© board and the SCI network. NCI will make this ASIC commercially available as a stand-alone chip product and logic core, in order to further promote an open SCI-based SAN architecture.

Applications

*Tera*Net© will be used in clustered server environments where continuous, fail-safe operations and applications and performance are critical issues. The SCI network implements a shared memory approach to all I/O. This means any processor or agent in the system can directly access any other resource in the system by simply reading from or writing to it. This concept grants minimum latency access to any system resource. This low-latency, high-bandwidth network will provide the environment for applications to be fully parallelized to enhance performance, similar to Massively Parallel Processor (MPP) type systems. Supercomputer-level performance will be attainable by clustering individual and multi-processor nodes. Large enterprise-level Internet/intranet server installations will be the primary application environment; this technology can also be utilized as a high-speed, point-to-point interconnect in any application where high throughput is necessary.

Product Advantages

The most important feature of the NCI SAN bridge architecture is the combination of the data transfer controller with a micro-controller CPU. The firmware for this processor can be updated in the field by downloading new update/configuration software. The availability of the CPU to system vendors allows offloading time-critical parts of higher-level network or clustering protocols from the host CPU onto the appropriate network bridge. Complex self-test and monitoring functionality can be implemented with minimal cost. Customized server configurations are also more easily implemented because the I/O controller is a programmable CPU.

The most important feature of the SCI network is its scalability, meaning that the aggregate bandwidth of a switched SCI network scales linearly with its size. Therefore, as more nodes are added to the network, the aggregate bandwidth becomes higher.

Book III

Business Planning

Present Product Status

A prototype SCI–PCI interface was completed in January 2007 and has been tested for one year. Dr. von Honecker, the founder of NCI, was the principal investigator of the R&D project leading to the implemented design. The basic flow control concept has been implemented and its functionality completely verified. The second hurdle, the micro-controller or the full data transfer controller, was not implemented in this prototype.

The full design of the *Tera*Link© product is currently under way. The design of the data transfer controller is 80 percent finished and completely simulated at this point. There are very few design risks remaining with respect to its overall functionality. The implementation of Commercial-Off-The-Shelf (COTS) chips in the architecture has been discussed in detail with various chip designers. The architecture described was well within the design limits of these devices. Fully functional and tested alpha prototype boards will be ready in Q4 2008.

Product development is also ongoing. With $150,000 in capital in place, it is expected that alpha prototype production boards will be available in December 2008. Further development will continue as the boards are installed in the clustered systems of NCI's initial customers. Given adequate funding, beta products are expected to be available by May 2009.

Manufacturing

NCI expects that all SAN components will be manufactured off-site, as a volume of 200,000 *Tera*Link© interface cards does not warrant the creation of an independent production facility. NCI expects to have a two-to-three person production team that oversees the production process at the fabrication house. Outsourcing these products allows costly resources to be more effectively utilized, along with significant savings in time-to-market. Later, some of the COTS chips on the *Tera*Link© board will be merged into a proprietary ASIC in order to reduce production costs. Unit production costs for the *Tera*Link© interface boards and *Tera*Switch© are projected as shown in Table 4-7.

Table 4-7	Unit Production Costs (FY 2009 - 2013)				
	FY 2009	*FY 2010*	*FY 2011*	*FY 2012*	*FY 2013*
*Tera*Link©	$1,200	$960	$700	$580	$400
*Tera*Switch©	$500	$500	$320	$280	$250

5. Risk Analysis

In evaluating an investment in NCI, a prospective investor must particularly consider the risks involved. NCI believes the primary risk in the overall venture is the current lack of experience in the management team. A senior management team that has successfully taken a product from inception to market will be needed for success of the venture. As mentioned earlier, NCI is currently searching for a CEO with a proven track record in the computer/networking industry. Another risk factor involves NCI's markets and competition. A principal concern has been the widespread establishment of Tandem's ServerNet in the industry prior to full release of NCI's product line. Although Tandem had a significant head start in this market, NCI expects that only early pioneers purchased this product. Also, with the acquisition of Tandem by Compaq and then Compaq acquisition by Hewlett-Packard (HP), NCI expects competitors of HP to become reluctant to using ServerNet as their primary SAN architecture. Software for clustering more than two Intel-based processors will not be available from Microsoft, Novell, or IBM until Q3 2009. NCI believes few end-users will have developed preferences of clustering interconnect technology by NCI's product release date. Additionally, the NCI SAN product provides a significant performance increase over Tandem, Digital, and Dolphin SAN systems.

6. Financial Data

Financial projections have been developed for FY 2009–2013 (FY for NCI is October 1–September 30). The financial projections for Pro-Forma Revenues, the Pro-Forma Income Statement, the Pro-Forma Balance Sheet, and the Pro-Forma Cash-Flow Statement are shown in Tables 4-8 through 4-11.

The company is currently seeking an additional $1.5MM in Stage One capital investment for the purpose of reaching the beta stage of product development for the *Tera*Link© interface board (both 32- and 64-bit versions), as well as for developing the NCI SAN ASIC. Following seed and State One investments, NCI expects to obtain an additional $3MM in order to complete prototype development for the *Tera*Switch© product, complete development of the *Tera*Net© system, attain full integration for the components in the *Tera*Net© system, and bring the technology to market.

Any purchase of securities of NCI will not be registered under the Securities Act of Ontario or other applicable securities laws and regulations. Accordingly, such securities of NCI may not be resold unless they are subsequently registered under the Securities Act or other applicable laws, or an exemption from registration is obtained. NCI has no current plans to register any of its capital stock under the Securities Act or any other applicable laws.

Book III

Business Planning

In addition, in the event that NCI should register its capital stock, there is no assurance that a purchaser of such securities would be able to include any securities owned in such initial registration or any subsequent registration. In the absence of such registration, there is no existing public or other market for the NCI securities, and it is not anticipated that any such market will develop. Moreover, the transferability of the stock is subject to certain restrictions. Consequently, investors may be unable to liquidate their investment when they desire, or anytime in the near future.

Table 4-8   NCI Pro-Forma Revenues by Product (FY 2009–2013)

Units	FY 2009	FY 2010	FY 2011	FY 2012	FY 2013
PCI-32 NT	150	6,475	9,500	7,500	0
PCI-64 NT	0	1,885	22,000	67,500	175,000
s.k.u. 3	0	0	0	0	0
SCI Switch	0	556	2,520	6,000	14,000
Total Units	**150**	**8,916**	**34,020**	**81,000**	**189,000**
Prices:					
PCI-32 NT	$2,000	$1,500	$1,250	$1,000	$750
PCI-64 NT	0	2,000	1,250	1,000	750
s.k.u. 3	0	0	0	0	0
SCI Switch	0	800	700	600	500
Revenue:					
PCI-32 NT	$300,000	$9,712,500	$11,875,000	$7,500,000	$0
PCI-64 NT	0	3,770,000	27,500,000	67,500,000	131,250,000
s.k.u. 3	0	0	0	0	0
SCI Switch	0	444,800	1,764,000	3,600,000	7,000,000
Total Revenue	$300,000	$13,927,300	$41,135,000	$78,600,000	$138,250,000

Table 4-9	Pro-Forma Income Statement (FY 2009–2013)				
	FY 2009	**FY 2010**	**FY 2011**	**FY 2012**	**FY 2013**
Revenue:					
NT Product Sales	$300,000	$13,927,300	$41,139,000	$78,600,000	$138,250,000
Total Revenue	$300,000	$13,927,300	$41,139,000	$78,600,000	$138,250,000
CGS	162,110	8,356,380	23,860,620	43,230,000	74,655,000
Gross Margin	137,890	5,570,920	17,278,380	35,370,000	63,595,000
(% of Revenue)	46%	40%	42%	45%	46%
Operating Expenses:					
R&D	1,148,841	1,671,276	5,348,070	8,646,000	13,825,000
(% of Revenue)	383%	12%	13%	11%	10%
Sales & Marketing	280,489	974,911	2,056,950	7,074,000	12,442,500
(% of Revenue)	93%	7%	5%	9%	9%
Gen'l. Admin.	197,117	835,638	1,645,560	2,358,000	2,765,000
(% of Revenue)	66%	6%	4%	3%	2%
Total Operating Exp (% of Revenue)	1,626,447	3,481,825	9,050,580	18,078,000	29,032,500
	542%	25%	22%	23%	21%
EBIT	($1,488,557)	$2,089,095	$8,227,800	$17,292,000	$34,562,500
(% of Revenue)	496%	15%	20%	22%	26%
Tax Expense	0	417,819	2,303,784	4,716,000	9,677,500
Net Income:					
(% of Revenue)	($1,488,557)	$1,671,276	$5,924,016	$12,576,000	$24,885,000
	496%	12%	14%	16%	18%

Book III

Business Planning

Table 4-10 Pro-Forma Balance Sheet (FY 2009–2013)

	FY 2009	FY 2010	FY 2011	FY 2012	FY 2013
Assets:					
Current Assets					
Cash	($1,488,121)	($4,998,668)	($1,558,853)	$5,228,216	$23,804,616
Net A/R	148,500	5,878,125	7,328,475	12,969,000	22,811,250
Inventory	66,000	1,996,367	3,577,500	6,331,003	7,193,688
Total Current Assets	(1,273,621)	2,875,804	9,347,122	24,528,219	53,809,554
Gross Fix Assets	77,500	185,500	327,000	506,500	651,500
Less Accum Dep	12,492	57,517	153,717	282,783	431,250
Net Fixed Assets	65,009	127,983	173,283	223,717	220,250
Total Assets	**($1,208,612)**	**$3,003,787**	**$9,502,405**	**$24,751,936**	**$54,029,804**
Liabilities					
Short-Term Liab.					
Acct Payable	87,768	2,153,072	2,508,939	4,485,902	7,550,743
Salaries	48,750	106,750	185,358	260,872	348,524
Taxes	0	417,819	575,946	1,179,000	2,419,375
Total S-T	136,518	2,677,641	3,270,243	5,925,774	10,318,642
Long-Term Liab.	0	0	0	0	0
Total Liab.	**$136,518**	**$2,677,641**	**$3,270,243**	**$5,925,774**	**$10,318,642**
Equity:					
Preferred Stock	138,000	138,000	138,000	138,000	138,000
Common Stock	5,427	5,427	5,427	5,427	5,427
Ret. Earnings	(1,488,557)	182,719	6,106,735	18,682,735	43,567,735
Total Equity	**($1,345,130)**	**$326,146**	**$6,250,162**	**$18,826,162**	**$43,711,162**
Liabilities + Equity	**($1,208,612)**	**$3,003,787**	**$9,520,405**	**$24,751,936**	**$54,029,804**

Table 4-11	Pro-Forma Cash-Flow Statement (FY 2009–2013)				
	FY 2009	**FY 2010**	**FY 2011**	**FY 2012**	**FY 2013**
Beginning Cash	$0	($1,488,121)	($4,998,688)	($1,558,8534)	$5,228,216
Sources of Cash:					
Net Income	(1,488,557)	1,671,276	5,924,016	12,576,000	24,885,000
Add Depr/Amort	12,491	45,026	96,200	129,066	148,467
Issu. of Pref Stock	138,000	0	0	0	0
Issu. of Com Stock	5,427	0	0	0	0
Plus Changes In:					
Acct. Payable	87,768	2,065,304	355,867	1,976,963	3,604,841
Salaries Payable	48,750	58,000	78,608	75,514	87,652
Taxes Payable	0	417,819	158,127	603,054	1,240,375
Total Src of Cash	**($1,196,121)**	**$4,257,425**	**$6,612,818**	**$15,360,597**	**$29,426,335**
Uses of Cash					
Less Changes					
Net Acc/Rec	148,500	5,729,625	1,450,350	5,640,525	9,842,250
Inventory	66,000	1,930,367	1,581,133	2,753,503	862,685
Gross Fixed Assets	77,500	108,000	141,500	179,500	145,000
Total Uses	**$292,000**	**$7,767,992**	**$3,172,983**	**$8,573,528**	**$10,849,935**
Changes/Cash	($1,488,121)	($3,510,567)	$3,439,835	$6,787,069	$18,576,4000
Ending Cash	($1,488,121)	($4,998,688)	($1,558,853)	$5,228,216	$23,804,616

Book IV
Bookkeeping

The 5th Wave   By Rich Tennant

I'm mathematically dyslexic. But it's not that unusual — 100 out of every 15 people are.

In this book . . .

Chapter 1: Basic Bookkeeping: What It Is
and Why You Need It 325

Chapter 2: Reporting Results 347

Chapter 3: Computer Options for Your Bookkeeping 373

Chapter 1

Basic Bookkeeping: What It Is and Why You Need It

In This Chapter

▶ Being a bookkeeper

▶ Learning the language of bookkeeping

▶ Navigating the accounting cycle

▶ Choosing cash or accrual accounting

▶ Deciphering double-entry bookkeeping

▶ Knowing your debits from your credits

▶ Charting a course with the chart of accounts

*A*ll businesses need to keep track of their financial transactions — that's why bookkeeping and bookkeepers are so important. Without accurate records, how can you tell whether your business is making a profit or taking a loss?

In this chapter, we cover the key parts of bookkeeping by introducing you to the language of bookkeeping, familiarizing you with how bookkeepers manage the accounting cycle, and showing you how to understand the most difficult and most prevalent type of bookkeeping — double-entry bookkeeping. We also tell you about the difference between debits and credits (it's not as simple as you'd think!), and show you how to plot out a roadmap for your business with a chart of accounts.

Bookkeepers: The Record Keepers of the Business World

Bookkeeping, the methodical way in which businesses track their financial transactions, is rooted in accounting. *Accounting* is the total structure of records and procedures used to record, classify, and report information about a business's financial transactions. Bookkeeping involves the recording of that financial information into the accounting system while maintaining adherence to solid accounting principles.

Many small-business people who are just starting up their businesses initially serve as their own bookkeepers until their businesses grow large enough to hire someone dedicated to keeping the books. Few small businesses have accountants on staff to check the books and prepare official financial reports; instead, they each have a bookkeeper on staff who serves as the outside accountants' eyes and ears. Most businesses do seek an accountant who has a professional designation to perform all of the necessary duties and responsibilities as required by the business owners and by the different Canadian laws.

In many small businesses today, a bookkeeper enters the business transactions on a daily basis while working inside the business. At the end of each month or quarter, the bookkeeper sends summary reports to the accountant, who checks the transactions for accuracy and completeness, and then prepares financial statements.

In most cases, an accountant initially helps set up the accounting system so that the business owner can be sure it uses solid accounting principles. That accountant periodically stops by the office and reviews how the business uses the system to be sure the business is handling transactions properly.

Accurate financial reports are the only way you can know how your business is doing. The business develops these reports by using the information you, as the bookkeeper, enter into your accounting system. If that information isn't accurate, your financial reports are meaningless. As the old adage goes, "Garbage in, garbage out."

Wading through Basic Bookkeeping Lingo

Before you can take on bookkeeping and start keeping the books, you must get a handle on some key accounting terms. The following sections list basic terms that all bookkeepers use.

Talking about the balance sheet

Here are a few terms you need to know to understand the common elements of all balance sheets:

- **Balance sheet:** The financial statement that presents a snapshot of the business's financial position (assets, liabilities, and equity) as of a particular date in time. It's called a *balance sheet* because the things owned by the business (assets) must equal the claims against those assets (liabilities and equity). Sometimes, accountants call this statement the *statement of financial position*, which emphasizes the fact that the amounts presented are a snapshot of a particular point in time.

  On a proper balance sheet, the total assets should equal the total liabilities plus the total equity. If your numbers fit this formula, the business's books are in balance. (We discuss the balance sheet in greater detail in Chapter 2 of this book.)

- **Assets:** All the things a business owns to run successfully run, such as cash, inventory, buildings, land, tools, equipment, vehicles, and furniture.

- **Liabilities:** All the debts the business owes, such as bank loans and unpaid bills.

- **Equity:** All the money invested in the business by its owners. In a small business owned by one person, the owner's equity appears in a Capital account named after the owner. In a partnership, you need several Capital accounts. In a larger business that's incorporated, owners' equity appears in shares of stock. Another key Equity account is *Retained Earnings,* which tracks all business profits that the business has chosen to reinvest into the business, instead of paying out to the business's shareholders. Small, unincorporated businesses track money paid out to owners in Drawings accounts, whereas incorporated businesses dole out money to owners by paying *dividends* (a portion of the business's profits paid by share of common stock for the quarter or year).

Speaking about the income statement

The *income statement* (or *statement of earnings*) is the financial statement that presents a summary of the business's financial activity over a certain period of time, such as a month, quarter, or year. The statement starts with revenue earned, subtracts out the costs of goods sold and the expenses — terms we define below — and ends with the bottom line — net profit or loss. (We show you how to develop an income statement in Chapter 2 of this book.)

Book IV

Bookkeeping

✔ **Revenue:** All money collected in the process of selling the business's goods and services. Some businesses also collect revenue through other means, such as collecting rent, selling assets that the business no longer needs, or earning interest by offering short-term loans to employees or other businesses. (We discuss how to track revenue in Chapter 2.)

✔ **Costs of goods sold:** All money spent to purchase or make the products or services that a business plans to sell to its customers. (We talk about purchasing goods for sale to customers in Chapter 2 of this book.)

✔ **Expenses:** All money spent to operate the business that's not directly related to the sale of individual goods or services. (We review common types of expenses later on in this chapter.)

✔ **Net profit or loss:** What is left or the deficit once all the costs have been subtracted from the first line, the revenue.

Knowing other common terms

Some other common bookkeeping terms include the following:

✔ **Accounting period:** The time during which you track financial information. Most businesses track their financial results on a monthly basis, so each accounting period equals one month. Some businesses choose to do financial reports on a quarterly basis, so the accounting periods are three months. Other businesses only look at their results on a yearly basis, so their accounting periods are 12 months. Businesses that track their financial activities monthly usually also create quarterly and *annual reports* (a year-end summary of the business's activities and financial results) based on the information they gather.

✔ **Accounts receivable:** The account used to track all customer sales that are made on credit (or on account). The terms *credit sales* and *sales on account* refer not to credit card sales, but rather to sales in which the customer receives credit directly by the store or business and for which the business needs to collect payment from the customer at a later date. (We discuss how to monitor accounts receivable in Chapter 2.)

✔ **Accounts payable:** The account used to track all outstanding bills from vendors or suppliers, contractors, consultants, and any other companies or individuals from whom the business buys goods or services. (We talk about managing accounts payable in Chapter 2.)

✔ **Depreciation:** An accounting method used to track the aging and use of property, plant, and equipment assets. Accountants use the term *property, plant, and equipment* for a category of assets that the business finds useful for more than one year. For example, if you own a car, you know that each year you use the car, its book value is reduced. Every major asset a business owns ages and eventually needs replacing, including buildings, factories, equipment, and other key assets. (We tell you more about depreciation throughout this chapter.)

✔ **General ledger:** Where all the business's accounts are summarized. The general ledger is the granddaddy of the bookkeeping system.

✔ **Interest:** The money that a business needs to pay if it borrows money from a bank or other business, in addition to the original sum borrowed. For example, when you buy a car by using a car loan, you must pay not only the amount you borrowed, but also additional money (interest), based on a percent of the amount you borrowed.

✔ **Inventory:** The account that tracks all products that you plan to sell to customers.

✔ **Journals:** Where bookkeepers keep records (in chronological order) of daily business transactions. Each of the most active accounts — including cash, accounts payable, and accounts receivable — has its own journal.

✔ **Payroll:** The way a business pays its employees. Managing payroll is a key function of the bookkeeper and involves reporting many aspects of payroll to the government, including taxes and benefits to be paid on behalf of the employee, such as payments to the Canada Pension Plan, for Employment Insurance, and for worker's compensation.

✔ **Trial balance:** How you determine whether the books are in balance before you pull together information for the financial reports and close the books for the accounting period.

Pedalling through the Accounting Cycle

As a bookkeeper, you complete your work by completing the tasks of the accounting cycle. It's called a *cycle* because the workflow is circular: entering transactions, manipulating the transactions, closing the books at the end of the accounting period, and then starting the entire cycle again for the next accounting period.

The accounting cycle has eight basic steps, which you can see in Figure 1-1.

Here's a breakdown of each step in this cycle:

1. **Transactions:** Financial transactions start the process. Transactions can include the sale or return of a product, the purchase of supplies for business activities, or any other financial activity that involves the exchange of the business's assets, the establishment or payoff of a debt, or the deposit from or payout of money to the business's owners.

2. **Journal entries:** You list the transaction in the appropriate journal, maintaining the journal's chronological order of transactions. (Accountants also call the journal the *book of original entry*, and it's the first place you record a transaction.).

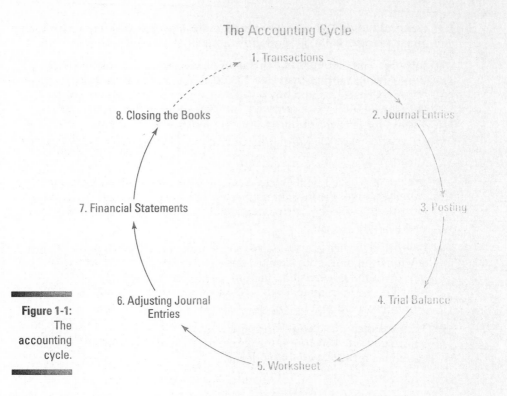

1. Transactions

2. Journal Entries

8. Closing the Books

3. Posting

7. Financial Statements

4. Trial Balance

6. Adjusting Journal Entries

5. Worksheet

Figure 1-1:
The accounting cycle.

3. **Posting:** You post each transaction to the account that it impacts. These accounts are part of the general ledger, where you can find a summary of all the business's accounts.

4. **Trial balance:** At the end of the accounting period (which may be a month, quarter, or year, depending on your business's practices), you calculate a trial balance. (Your accounting software might produce this trial balance automatically.)

5. **Worksheet:** Unfortunately, many times, your first calculation of the trial balance shows that the books aren't in balance. If that's the case, you look for errors and make corrections called *adjustments*, which you track on a worksheet. After you make and record adjustments, you take another trial balance to make sure the accounts are in balance.

6. **Adjusting journal entries:** You post any necessary corrections to the affected accounts after your trial balance shows the accounts are balanced and in the correct amounts when you make the adjustments to the accounts. You don't need to make adjusting entries until you complete the trial-balance process and identify all needed corrections and adjustments.

7. **Financial statements:** You prepare the balance sheet and income statement by using the corrected account balances.

8. **Closing:** You close the books for the Revenue, Expense, and Drawings accounts, and then begin the entire cycle again with zero balances in those accounts.

As a businessperson, you want to be able to gauge your profit or loss month by month, quarter by quarter, and year by year. Therefore, Revenue, Expense, and Drawings accounts must start with a zero balance at the beginning of each accounting period. In contrast, you carry over Asset, Liability, and Equity account balances from cycle to cycle because the business doesn't start each cycle by getting rid of old assets and buying new assets, paying off and then taking on new debt, or paying out all claims to owners and then collecting the money again.

Exploring Cash and Accrual Accounting

Small businesses often run their operations on a *cash basis,* meaning they never buy or sell on credit (often referred to as *on account*) and essentially measure their financial performance based on how much money they have in the bank. Although cash basis provides a very simple business model, it quickly becomes impractical. When the business starts to send out invoices on account, or when it starts to deal with suppliers on credit, we suggest that your business adopt accrual accounting. In the following sections, we look at both methods.

Cash-basis accounting

With *cash-basis accounting,* you record all transactions in the books when cash actually changes hands, meaning when the business receives cash payment from customers or pays out cash for purchases or other services. Cash receipt or payment can be in the form of cash, cheque, credit card, debit card, electronic transfer, or other means.

You can't use cash-basis accounting if your store sells products on account and bills the customer later. The cash-basis accounting method has no provision to record and track money due from customers at some time in the future.

With the cash-basis accounting method, the business records the purchase of supplies or goods that you plan to sell only when you actually pay cash for those supplies or goods. If you buy goods on credit, which you plan to pay later, you don't record the transaction until you actually pay out the cash.

Book IV

Bookkeeping

Although cash-basis accounting is easy, the Canada Revenue Agency (CRA) doesn't like it, and allows only certain businesses to use it for reporting taxable income. Businesses involved in the farming and fishing industries can report income on a cash basis. All other businesses must follow the accrual accounting method.

Cash-basis accounting does a good job of tracking cash flow, but it does a poor job of matching revenues earned with money laid out for expenses. You may find this deficiency a problem if, as it often happens, your business buys products one month and sells those products the next month.

If you choose to use cash-basis accounting, don't panic: You can still find most of the bookkeeping information in here useful, but you don't need to maintain some of the accounts we list, such as accounts receivable and accounts payable, because you don't record transactions until cash actually changes hands. If you're using a cash-basis accounting system and you sell things on credit, though, you need to have a way to track what people owe you — particularly for tax-reporting purposes.

Recording by using accrual accounting

With *accrual accounting,* you record all transactions in the books when those transactions occur, even if no cash changes hands. For example, if you sell on account, you record the transaction immediately and enter it into the Accounts Receivable account until you receive payment. If you buy goods on account, you immediately enter the transaction into the Accounts Payable account until you pay out cash.

Accrual accounting is based on the *generally accepted accounting principles* (GAAP), the authoritative standards and rules that govern financial accounting and financial reporting. We don't go into all the technical jargon of the rules, but we need to point out that GAAP is very important to businesses that are incorporated and intend to have their shares traded on a stock market, such as the Toronto Stock Exchange (TSX).

Like cash-basis accounting, accrual accounting has its drawbacks. It does a good job of matching revenues and expenses, but it does a poor job of getting you to pay attention to cash. Because you record revenue when the transaction occurs and not when you collect the cash, your attention may be diverted from the all-important cash collection. If your customers are slow to pay, you may end up with a lot of revenue and little cash.

Many businesses that use the accrual accounting method monitor cash flow on a weekly basis to be sure that they have enough cash to operate the business. If your business is seasonal, such as a landscaping business that has little to do during the winter months, you can establish short-term lines of credit through your bank to maintain cash flow through the lean times.

Seeing Double with Double-Entry Bookkeeping

All businesses use double-entry bookkeeping to keep their books. A practice that helps minimize errors and increases the chance that your books balance, *double-entry bookkeeping* gets its name because you enter all transactions with two sides, using a minimum of two accounts.

When it comes to double-entry bookkeeping, the key formula for the balance sheet (Assets = Liabilities + Equity) plays a major role. Accountants call this formula the *accounting equation*.

In order to adjust the balance of accounts in the bookkeeping world, you use a combination of debits and credits. You may think of a *debit* as a subtraction because debits usually mean a decrease in your bank balance. On the other hand, you've probably been excited to find unexpected *credits* in your bank account or on your credit card, which mean you've received more money in the account. Now, forget all that you've ever heard about debits or credits. In the world of bookkeeping, their meanings aren't so simple.

The only definite thing about debits and credits in the bookkeeping world is that a debit is on the left side of a transaction and a credit is on the right side of a transaction. Everything beyond that can get muddled. We show you the basics of debits and credits in this chapter.

Before we get into all the technical mumbo jumbo of double-entry bookkeeping, here's an example of the practice in action. Suppose you purchase a new desk that costs $1,500 for your office. This transaction actually has two parts: You spend an asset — cash — to buy another asset — furniture. So, you must adjust two accounts in your business's books: the Cash account and the Furniture account. Here's what the transaction looks like in a bookkeeping entry:

Account	Debit	Credit
Furniture	$1,500	
Cash		$1,500

To purchase a new desk for the office with cash.

In this transaction, you record the accounts affected by the transaction. The debit increases the amount of the Furniture account, and the credit decreases the amount in the Cash account. For this transaction, both affected accounts are asset accounts, so if you look at how the balance sheet is affected, you can see that the only changes are to the asset side of the balance sheet equation:

Book IV

Bookkeeping

Assets = Liabilities + Equity

Furniture increase = No change to this side of the equation

Cash decrease

In this case, the books stay in balance because the exact dollar amount that increases the amount of your Furniture account decreases the amount of your Cash account. At the bottom of any journal entry, you should include a brief explanation of the purpose for the entry. In the first example, we indicate this entry was "To purchase a new desk for the office with cash."

To show you how to record a transaction if it affects both sides of the balance sheet equation, here's an example that shows how to record the purchase of inventory. Suppose that you purchase $5,000 worth of widgets on credit. (Haven't you always wondered what widgets are? We can't help you there. They're just commonly used in accounting examples to represent something that's purchased.) These new widgets add more costs to your Inventory Asset account and also add to your obligations in your Accounts Payable account. (Remember, the Accounts Payable account is a Liability account in which you track bills that you need to pay in the future.) Here's how the bookkeeping transaction for your widget purchase looks:

Account	*Debit*	*Credit*
Inventory	$5,000	
Accounts Payable		$5,000

Purchase on account widgets for sale to customers.

Here's how this transaction affects the balance sheet equation:

Assets = Liabilities + Equity

Inventory increases = Accounts payable increases + No change

In this case, the books stay in balance because both sides of the accounting equation increase by $5,000.

You can see from the two preceding example transactions how double-entry bookkeeping helps to keep your books in balance — as long as you make sure each entry into the books is balanced. Balancing your entries may look simple here, but sometimes bookkeeping entries can get very complex when the transaction affects more than two accounts.

Don't worry, you don't have to understand it totally now. Flip to Chapter 2 of this book for more information about balance sheets and income statements, which use the accounts we explain in this chapter.

Differentiating Debits and Credits

Because bookkeeping's debits and credits are different than the ones you're used to encountering in everyday life, you're probably wondering how you're supposed to know whether a debit or credit will increase or decrease an account. Believe it or not, identifying the difference becomes second nature when you start making regular entries in your bookkeeping system. But to make things easier for you, Table 2-1 gives you a chart that's commonly used by all bookkeepers and accountants. Yep, everyone needs help sometimes.

Table 1-1	How Credits and Debits Impact Your Accounts	
Account Type	*Debits*	*Credits*
Assets	Increase	Decrease
Liabilities	Decrease	Increase
Equity	Decrease	Increase
Drawings	Increase	Decrease
Revenue	Decrease	Increase
Expenses	Increase	Decrease

Copy Table 1-1 and post it on an index card at your desk when you start keeping your own books. We guarantee it can help you keep your debits and credits straight.

Outlining Your Financial Roadmap with a Chart of Accounts

Keeping the books of a business means recording each business transaction to make sure that it goes into the right account. This careful bookkeeping gives you an effective tool for figuring out how well the business is doing financially.

As a bookkeeper, you need a roadmap to help you determine where to record all those transactions, and this roadmap is called the *chart of accounts*. In the upcoming sections, we tell you how to set up the chart of accounts, which includes many different accounts. We also review the types of transactions you enter into each type of account in order to track the key parts of any business — assets, liabilities, equity, revenue, and expenses.

Book IV

Bookkeeping

Starting with the balance sheet accounts

The first part of the chart of accounts is made up of balance sheet accounts, which break down into the following three categories:

- **Asset:** These accounts track what the business owns. Assets include cash on hand, inventory, furniture, buildings, vehicles, and so on.

- **Liability:** These accounts track what the business owes, or more specifically, claims that lenders have against the business's assets. For example, mortgages on buildings and lines of credit are two common types of liabilities.

- **Equity:** These accounts track what the owners put into the business and the claims that the owners have against the business's assets. For example, shareholders are business owners who have claims against the business's assets.

The balance sheet accounts, and the financial report they make up, are so called because they have to *balance* out. The book value of the assets must be equal to the claims made against those assets. (Remember, these claims are liabilities made by lenders and equity belonging to owners.)

We discuss the balance sheet in greater detail in Chapter 2, including how you prepare and use it. The following sections, however, examine the basic components of the balance sheet, as reflected in the chart of accounts.

Tackling assets

First on the chart are always the accounts that track what the business owns — its assets. The two types of Asset accounts are Current Assets and Long-Term Assets.

Current assets

Current assets are the key assets that your business uses up during a 12-month period, so those assets likely won't be available the next year — or, at least, will be replaced by new assets by that time. The accounts that reflect current assets on the chart of accounts are

- **Cash in Chequing:** Any business's primary account is the chequing account used for operating activities, to deposit revenues, and to pay expenses.

- **Cash in Savings account:** This account is used for surplus cash. Any cash for which the business has no immediate plan is deposited in an interest-earning savings account.

✔ **Cash on Hand:** This account tracks any cash kept at retail stores or in the office. The Cash on Hand account helps you keep track of the cash held by the business outside a bank.

✔ **Accounts Receivable:** If you offer your products or services to customers on account (meaning on *your* credit system), then you need this account to track the customers who buy on your dime.

You don't use accounts receivable to track purchases made on other types of credit cards because your business gets paid directly by banks, not customers, when customers use credit cards from sources other than your business.

✔ **Inventory:** This account tracks the cost of products that you have on hand to sell to your customers.

✔ **Prepaid Insurance:** This account tracks insurance you pay in advance, which you reduce each month with a credit to represent that month's insurance coverage. For example, if you own a building and prepay one year in advance, each month, you reduce the amount that you prepaid by ¹⁄₁₂ because your business essentially uses up the prepayment.

Depending on the type of business you're setting up, you may have other Current Asset accounts that you decide to track. For example, if you're starting a service business, you might want to have a Supplies account.

Long-term assets

Long-term assets are assets that your business plans to use for more than 12 months. This list includes some of the most common long-term assets, starting with the key accounts related to buildings and factories owned by the business:

✔ **Land:** This account tracks the land owned by the business. The value of the land is based on the cost of purchasing it. Land value is tracked separately from the value of any buildings standing on that land because land doesn't depreciate in the books, but buildings do. *Depreciation* is an accounting method that shows an asset is being used up.

✔ **Buildings:** This account tracks the value of any buildings that a business owns. Like with land, the value of the building is based on the cost of purchasing it. The key difference between buildings and land is that the accountant depreciates the building's value, as discussed in the preceding bullet.

✔ **Accumulated depreciation — buildings:** This account tracks the cumulative amount the accountant has recorded as depreciation for a building over its useful lifespan.

Book IV

Bookkeeping

- ✔ **Leasehold improvements:** This account tracks the value of improvements to buildings or other facilities that a business leases, rather than purchases.

- ✔ **Accumulated depreciation — leasehold improvements:** This account tracks the cumulative amount the accountant depreciates leasehold improvements.

Your business might also have extra cash invested in the shares of other businesses, in long-term investments in land, or in other types of assets that might earn some interest income. If your business intends to hold these assets for long periods of time, as part of the required classification of accounts inside your balance sheet, you need to add another title and subtotal for long-term investments. You also need to create and track additional accounts in the general ledger.

The following list includes the types of accounts for small long-term assets, such as vehicles and furniture:

- ✔ **Vehicles:** This account tracks any cars, trucks, or other vehicles owned by the business. You list the initial book value of any vehicle in this account based on the total cost paid to put the vehicle in service. Sometimes, this book value is more than the purchase price if you needed to make additions to make the vehicle usable for your particular type of business. Vehicles depreciate through their useful lifespan.

- ✔ **Accumulated Depreciation — Vehicles:** This account tracks the depreciation of all vehicles owned by the business.

- ✔ **Furniture and Fixtures:** This account tracks any furniture or fixtures purchased for use in the business. The account includes the value of all chairs, desks, store fixtures, and shelving the business needs to operate. You base the value of the furniture and fixtures in this account on the cost of purchasing these items. These items depreciate during their useful lifespan.

- ✔ **Accumulated Depreciation — Furniture and Fixtures:** This account tracks the accumulated depreciation of all furniture and fixtures.

- ✔ **Equipment:** This account tracks equipment that you purchased for use for more than one year, such as computers, copiers, tools, and cash registers. You base the value of the equipment on the cost to purchase these items. Equipment also depreciates to show that over time, the asset reaches the point where you must replace it.

- ✔ **Accumulated Depreciation — Equipment:** This account tracks the accumulated depreciation of all the equipment.

The following accounts track the long-term assets that you can't touch, but that still represent things of value owned by the business, such as patents and copyrights (refer to Book 2 for more about intellectual property). These assets are called *intangible assets,* and the accounts that track them include

✔ **Patents:** This account tracks the costs associated with *patents,* grants made by governments that guarantee to the inventor or the owner of the patent of a product or process the exclusive right to make, use, and sell that product or process over a set period of time. You base the value of this asset on the expenses that the business incurs to get the right to patent the product or the cost of purchasing that patent.

✔ **Amortization — Patents:** This account tracks the accumulated amortization of a business's patents.

✔ **Copyrights:** This account tracks the costs incurred to establish *copyrights,* the legal rights given to an author, playwright, publisher, or any other distributor of a publication or production for a unique work of literature, music, drama, or art.

✔ **Goodwill:** You need this account only if your business buys another business for more than the fair value of its *net assets* (assets minus liabilities). Goodwill reflects the intangible value of this purchase for assets not on the seller's balance sheet, such as business reputation, store locations, customer base, and other items that increase the value of a business bought as a going concern.

Laying out your liabilities

After you cover assets, the next stop on the bookkeeping highway is the accounts that track what your business owes to others. These others can include vendors and suppliers from which you buy products or supplies; banks from which you borrow money; and any other individuals or groups that lend money to your business or to which the business needs to make a payment to settle an obligation, such as employees or the Canada Revenue Agency. Like assets, you lump liabilities into two types: current liabilities and long-term liabilities (sometimes also called *long-term debt*).

Current liabilities

Current liabilities are debts due in the next 12 months. The following are some of the most common types of Current Liabilities accounts that appear on the chart of accounts:

✔ **Accounts Payable:** This account tracks money owed that the business must pay in less than a year to vendors, contractors, suppliers, and consultants.

Book IV

Bookkeeping

✔ **Goods and Services Tax Payable and Retail Taxes Payable:** You may not think of Goods and Services Tax or Harmonized Sales Tax (GST/HST) and Provincial Sales Tax (PST) as liabilities, but because your business collects taxes from your customers and doesn't pay those taxes immediately to government entities, the taxes collected become a liability tracked in these accounts. A business usually charges the sales tax throughout the month, and then pays the tax to the appropriate provincial or federal government on a monthly basis.

✔ **Accrued Payroll Taxes:** This account tracks payroll taxes collected from employees to pay combined federal and provincial income taxes, as well as Canada Pension Plan (CPP) and Employment Insurance (EI) contributions. Businesses don't have to pay these taxes to government entities immediately, so depending on the size of the payroll, businesses may pay payroll taxes on a monthly or quarterly basis.

✔ **Credit Cards Payable:** This account tracks all accounts with credit card companies to which the business owes money. Most businesses use credit cards as short-term debt and pay them off completely at the end of each month, but some smaller businesses carry credit card balances over a longer period. Because credit cards often have a much higher interest rate than most lines of credits, most businesses transfer any credit card debt that they can't pay entirely at the end of a month to a line of credit at a bank. When it comes to your chart of accounts, you can set up one Credit Card Payable account, but you may want to set up a separate account for each card your business holds to improve your ability to track credit card usage.

How you set up your current liabilities and how many individual accounts you establish depends on how detailed you want to make each type of liability tracking.

Long-term liabilities

Long-term liabilities are debts due in more than 12 months. The number of long-term liability accounts you maintain on your chart of accounts depends on your debt structure. These are the two most common types of long-term liability accounts:

✔ **Loans Payable:** This account tracks any long-term loans, such as a mortgage on your business building. Most businesses have separate Loans Payable accounts for each of their long-term loans.

✔ **Notes Payable:** Some businesses borrow money from other businesses using *promissory notes,* a method of borrowing that doesn't require the business to put up an asset as collateral, which you need to do with a mortgage on a building. This account tracks any notes due.

Eyeing the equity

Every business is owned by somebody. *Equity accounts* track owners' contributions to the business, as well as their share of ownership. For a corporation, you track ownership by the sale of individual shares of stock because each shareholder owns a portion of the business. In smaller businesses that are owned by one person or a group of people, you track equity by using Capital and Drawings accounts. Here are the basic Equity accounts that appear in the chart of accounts:

- ✔ **Common Shares:** This account reflects the book value of outstanding shares sold to investors. The amount in this account corresponds to the amount paid by the investors. Only corporations need to establish this account.

- ✔ **Retained Earnings:** This account, exclusive to corporations, tracks the profits or losses accumulated since a business opened. At the end of each year, the profit or loss calculated on the income statement is closed to this account. For example, if your business made a $100,000 profit in the past year, you increase the Retained Earnings account by that amount; if the business lost $100,000, then you subtract that amount from this account.

- ✔ **Capital:** Only unincorporated businesses need this account. The Capital account reflects the amount of initial money the business owner contributed to the business, as well as owner contributions made after initial start-up. You base the book value of this account on cash contributions and other assets contributed by the business owner, such as equipment, vehicles, or buildings. If a small business has several different partners, then each partner gets a separate Capital account to track individual contributions.

- ✔ **Drawings:** Only businesses that aren't incorporated need this account. The Drawings account tracks any money or other assets that a business owner takes out of the business. If the business has several partners, each partner gets a separate Drawings account to track what each partner takes out of the business.

Book IV

Bookkeeping

Tracking the income statement portion of the chart of accounts

Two types of accounts make up the income statement:

- ✔ **Revenues:** These accounts track all money coming into the business, including sales, rents, dividends from investments, interest earned on savings, and any other methods used to generate income.

- ✔ **Expenses:** These accounts track all money that a business spends in order to earn revenues.

The bottom line of the income statement shows whether your business made a profit or suffered a loss for a specified period of time. We discuss how to prepare and use an income statement in greater detail in Chapter 2.

The following sections examine the various accounts that make up the income statement portion of the chart of accounts.

Recording the money you make

First up in the income statement portion of the chart of accounts are accounts that track revenue coming into a merchandising business. If you choose to offer discounts or accept returns, that activity also falls within the revenue grouping. Three types of income accounts are most common:

- ✔ **Sales and Service Revenue:** These accounts, which appear at the top of every income statement, track all the money that the business earns by selling its products, services, or both.

- ✔ **Sales Discounts:** Because most businesses offer discounts to encourage sales or quick payments, this account tracks any reductions to the full price of merchandise.

- ✔ **Sales Returns and Allowances:** This account tracks transactions related to *returns,* when a customer brings a product back to your business because the customer is unhappy with it for some reason, and *allowances,* which are reductions to the price of goods that you make because of a defect in the product. With allowances, the customer doesn't return the goods.

When you examine an income statement from a business other than the one you own or are working for, you usually see the following accounts summarized as one line item called Revenue or Net Revenue. Because sales of products or services don't generate all income, other income accounts that may appear on a chart of accounts include the following:

- ✔ **Other Income:** If a business takes in income from a source other than its primary business activity, you record that income in this account.

- ✔ **Interest Income:** This account tracks any income earned by collecting interest on a business's savings accounts or long-term investments. If the business loans money to employees or to another business, and earns interest on that money, you record that interest in this account, as well.

- ✔ **Rent Revenue:** Occasionally, a business may have extra office or warehouse space that it rents out to tenants. Although this source of cash might not represent a large amount of revenue, you need to track it in its own account in your bookkeeping.

✔ **Gain or Loss on Sale of Fixed Assets:** Any time your business sells a fixed asset, such as a car or furniture, you record any gain or loss made from the sale in this account. A business should record only revenue remaining after subtracting the accumulated depreciation from the original cost of the asset.

Tracking the cost of sales

Of course, before you can sell a product, you must spend some money to either buy or make that product. The type of account used to track the money spent is called a Cost of Goods Sold account. The most common Cost of Goods Sold accounts are as follows:

✔ **Purchases:** This account tracks the purchases of all items you plan to sell.

✔ **Purchase Discount:** This account tracks the discounts you may receive from vendors if you pay for your purchase quickly. For example, a business may give you a 2-percent discount on your purchase if you pay the bill in 10 days, rather than wait until the end of the 30-day payment allotment.

✔ **Purchase Returns and Allowances:** If you're unhappy with a product you buy, record the cost of any items you return in this account. You also use this account to record any *purchase allowances* — reductions in the purchase price you pay for defective goods that you're willing to keep.

✔ **Freight-In Charges:** You track any charges related to shipping items that you purchase for later sale in this account.

Acknowledging the money you spend

Expense accounts take the cake for the longest list of individual accounts. Any money you spend on the business that you can't tie directly to the sale of an individual product falls under the Expense account category. For example, advertising a storewide sale isn't directly tied to the sale of any one product, so the costs associated with advertising go into an Expense account.

The chart of accounts mirrors your business operations, so you decide how much detail you want to keep in your expense accounts. Most businesses have expenses that are unique to their operations, so your list is probably longer than the one we present here. However, you also may find that you don't need some of the accounts we suggest.

On your chart of accounts, the expense accounts don't have to appear in any specific order, so we list the most common expense accounts here, alphabetically:

Book IV

Bookkeeping

✔ **Advertising:** This account tracks all expenses involved in promoting a business or its products. You record money spent on newspaper, television, Internet, magazine, and radio advertising in this account, as well as any money spent to print flyers and mailings to customers. Also, when your business participates in community events, such as cancer walks or craft fairs, you track associated costs in this account.

✔ **Bank Service Charges:** This account tracks any charges made by a bank to service a business's bank accounts.

✔ **Depreciation and Amortization:** These accounts track the cost of property, plant, and equipment, as well as intangible assets, that the business has used up.

✔ **Dues and Subscriptions:** This account tracks expenses related to business club memberships, professional associations, or subscriptions to magazines for the business.

✔ **Equipment Rental:** This account tracks expenses related to renting equipment for a short-term project. For example, a business that needs to rent a truck to pick up some new fixtures for its store records that truck rental in this account.

✔ **Interest:** This account tracks all the interest paid by the business on borrowed money.

✔ **Insurance:** This account tracks any money paid to buy insurance. Many businesses break insurance costs down into several accounts, such as Insurance — Casualty, which tracks the coverage for any damages to property, or Insurance — Officers' Life, which tracks money spent to buy insurance to protect the life of a key manager or officer of the business. Businesses often insure their key executives because an unexpected death, especially for a small business, may mean facing many expenses in order to keep the business's doors open. In such a case, you can use the insurance proceeds to cover those expenses.

✔ **Legal and Accounting:** This account tracks any money that a business pays for legal or accounting advice.

✔ **Maintenance and Repairs:** This account tracks any payments to keep the property, plant, and equipment, or the rented premises, in good working order.

✔ **Miscellaneous Expenses:** A catch-all account for expenses that don't fit into one of a business's established accounts. If certain miscellaneous expenses occur frequently, a business may choose to add an account to the chart of accounts and move related expenses into that new account by subtracting all related transactions from the Miscellaneous Expenses account and adding them to the new account. If you do this shuffle, you need to carefully balance out the adjusting transaction to avoid any errors or double counting.

✔ **Office Expenses:** This account tracks any items purchased in order to run an office. For example, office supplies (such as paper, pens, or business cards) fit in this account. Like with Miscellaneous Expenses, a business may choose to track some office expense items in their own accounts. For example, if your office uses a lot of copy paper and you want to track that separately, you set up a Copy Paper Expense account. Just be sure you really need the detail because the number of accounts can get unwieldy and hard to manage.

✔ **Payroll Benefits:** This account tracks any payments for employee benefits, such as the employer's share of Canada Pension Plan (CPP), Employment Insurance (EI), and worker's compensation.

✔ **Postage and Delivery:** This account tracks any money spent on stamps, express package shipping, and other shipping. If a business does a large amount of shipping through couriers such as UPS or Federal Express, it may want to track that spending in separate accounts for each vendor. This option is particularly helpful for small businesses that sell over the Internet or through catalogue sales. Don't confuse the delivery costs tracked here with the freight costs paid to purchase inventory for resale. We explain in the preceding section that freight-in costs get grouped with purchases to become Costs of Goods Sold.

✔ **Rent Expense:** This account tracks rental costs for a business's office or retail space.

✔ **Salaries and Wages:** This account tracks any money paid to employees as salary or wages. You might want a separate account to track vacation pay.

✔ **Supplies:** This account tracks any business supplies that don't fit into the category of office supplies. For example, you track supplies needed for the operation of retail stores, such as shopping bags, by using this account. You can also create separate Supplies accounts for services that your business provides. An example would be grease used by a business providing oil changes for vehicles.

✔ **Travel and Entertainment:** This account tracks money spent for business purposes on travel or entertainment. Some businesses separate these expenses into several accounts, such as Travel and Entertainment — Meals, Travel and Entertainment — Travel, and Travel and Entertainment — Entertainment, to keep a closer watch.

✔ **Telephone and Internet:** This account tracks all business expenses related to using telephones and the Internet.

✔ **Utilities:** This account tracks money paid for utilities, such as electricity, gas, and water.

✔ **Vehicles:** This account tracks expenses related to the operation of business vehicles.

Book IV

Bookkeeping

Setting Up Your Chart of Accounts

You can use the lists upon lists of accounts provided in this chapter to get started setting up your business's own chart of accounts. You don't need to know a secret method to make your own chart — just make a list of the accounts that apply to your business.

When first setting up your chart of accounts, don't panic if you can't think of every type of account you may need for your business. You can very easily add to the chart of accounts at any time. Just add the account to the list and distribute the revised list to any employees that use the chart of accounts for recording transactions into the bookkeeping system. (Even employees not involved in bookkeeping need a copy of your chart of accounts if they code invoices or other transactions that need to indicate to which account you should record those transactions.)

The chart of accounts usually includes at least three columns:

- ✔ **Account:** Lists the account names
- ✔ **Type:** Lists the types of accounts — Asset, Liability, Equity, Revenue, Cost of Goods Sold, or Expense
- ✔ **Description:** Contains a description of the type of transaction that you should record in the account

Many businesses also assign numbers to the accounts that you can use for coding charges. Computerized bookkeeping systems (which we talk about in Chapter 3 of this book) automatically assign account numbers.

Chapter 2

Reporting Results

In This Chapter

▶ Breaking down the balance sheet

▶ Pulling together your balance sheet accounts

▶ Drawing conclusions from your balance sheet

▶ Preparing an income statement

▶ Analyzing income statement data

▶ Testing if you're making a profit

*O*wning and running a business involves a lot of reports and statements, particularly about your business's financial situation. In this we chapter, we get into a couple of key documents and provide you with a delicious example so you can see how these statements work and how you can use them. We explain the key ingredients of a balance sheet and tell you how to pull them all together. You can also find out how to use ratios to see how well your business is doing. And you'd never know for sure whether your business made a profit without an *income statement,* to give you periodic pictures of how well the business is doing financially. We also show you a few ways to check your business's profitability.

Developing a Balance Sheet

Periodically, you want to know where your business stands. So at the end of each accounting period, you take a snapshot of your business's condition. This snapshot, which is called a *balance sheet,* gives you a picture of where your business stands — how much it has in assets, how much it owes in liabilities, and how much the owners have invested in the business at a particular point in time.

Basically, creating a balance sheet is like taking a picture of the financial aspects of your business. You put the business name, the title of the statement, and the ending date for the accounting period on which you're reporting at the top of the balance sheet.

Insert the proper name of the business in the titles of your financial statements. When outside readers look at your reports, they want to know whom they're dealing with, and your business's name tells them a lot. For example, an incorporated business has one of the following at the end of its name: Limited (Ltd.), Corporation (Corp.), or Incorporated (Inc.).

Although a balance sheet doesn't tell the whole story about a business, it gives outside readers some idea of the business's financial position and how it's financed at a particular point in time. For example, a bank needs to decide whether to lend your business money. Your balance sheet reveals that you already owe a lot of money to other banks and mortgage companies, and so the bank decides that your business is too high a risk and refuses you a loan request. Or, say, an outside reader might be someone interested in buying your business. In this case, the reader looks at the balance sheet to determine the value of the assets to decide on a fair purchase price.

The rest of the report summarizes the following information:

✔ **The business's assets:** Including everything the business owns in order to stay in operation

✔ **The business's debts:** Including any outstanding bills and loans that the business must pay

✔ **The owner's equity:** Basically, how much the business owners have invested directly and indirectly in the business

Assets, liabilities, and equity probably sound familiar — they're the key elements that show whether your books are in balance. If your liabilities plus equity equal assets, your books are in balance. All your bookkeeping efforts are an attempt to keep the books in balance based on this equation, which we talked about in Chapter 1 of this book.

Dividing and listing your assets

The first part of the balance sheet is the Assets section. The first step in developing this section involves dividing your assets into two categories: current assets and non-current assets.

Placing the accounts from your balance sheet (refer to Chapter 1 for explanations of various accounts) into groups onto your balance sheet is called *classification*. After you give the proper classification to the individual accounts, you can organize the financial statements into groups of accounts, which enables you to create subtotals (such as current assets) on your balance sheet. These key subtotals allow you and your readers make a quick comparison to other figures within a financial statement or with another financial statement.

For example, an owner might compare the amount of profit on the income statement to the total equity appearing on the business's balance sheet to decide whether the business is getting enough of a financial reward (profit) for the owner's investment (equity).

The grouping of current and non-current assets and liabilities on the balance sheet is the most valuable classification provided to outside readers. The reader can compare current assets to current liabilities to quickly and easily measure your business's liquidity.

Current assets

Current assets are things your business owns that you can easily convert to cash and that you expect to use in the next 12 months to pay your bills and your employees. Current assets include cash, *accounts receivable* (money due from customers), trading securities (including stocks and bond investments), inventory, and prepaid expenses.

The Cash line item on a balance sheet includes what you have on hand in the register and what you have in the bank, including chequing accounts, savings accounts, and possibly also money market accounts. In most cases, you simply list all these accounts as one item, Cash, on the balance sheet.

H.G.'s Cheesecake Shop's current assets are

Cash	$2,500
Petty Cash	$500
Accounts Receivable	$1,000
Inventory	$1,200

The bookkeeper totals the Cash and Petty Cash accounts to equal $3,000, which the bookkeeper lists on the balance sheet as a line item called Cash.

Non-current assets

Non-current assets are things your business owns that you expect to have for more than 12 months. Non-current assets include land, buildings, equipment, furniture, vehicles, and anything else that you expect to have for longer than a year.

H.G.'s Cheesecake Shop's non-current assets are

Equipment	$5,050
Vehicles	$25,000
Furniture	$5,600

Most businesses have more items in the Property, Plant, and Equipment category in the non-current assets section of a balance sheet than H.G.'s Cheesecake Shop. For example, a manufacturing business that has a lot of tools, dies, or moulds created specifically for its manufacturing processes would have a line item called Tools, Dies, and Moulds in this asset group on its balance sheet.

Similarly, if your business owns one or more buildings, you should have a line item labelled Land and another labelled Buildings. And if you lease equipment under certain conditions that resemble a purchase, you classify that equipment as Equipment under Capital Lease.

Some businesses lease their business space and then spend a lot of money fixing that space up. For example, a restaurant may rent a large space and then furnish it according to a theme. Money spent on fixing up the space becomes an asset called Leasehold Improvements that you list on the balance sheet in the Property, Plant, and Equipment category of non-current assets.

Everything we've mentioned so far in this section — land, buildings, capitalized leases, leasehold improvements, and so on — is a *tangible asset,* which is an item that you can actually touch or hold. Another type of non-current asset is the intangible asset. *Intangible assets* aren't physical objects; common examples are patents, copyrights, and trademarks (all of which are rights granted by the government, and you can find out more about them in Book II), as well as goodwill:

- ✔ **Patents:** Give businesses the right to dominate the markets for patented products. When a patent expires, competitors can enter the marketplace for the product that was patented, and the competition helps to lower the price for consumers. For example, pharmaceutical companies patent all their new drugs so they are protected as the sole providers of those drugs. When your doctor prescribes a brand-name drug, you're getting a patented product. Generic drugs are products whose patents have run out, meaning that any pharmaceutical business can produce and sell its own version of the same product.

- ✔ **Copyrights:** Protect original works — including books, magazines, articles, newspapers, television shows, movies, music, poetry, and plays — from being copied by anyone other than their creators. For example, this book is copyrighted, so no one can make a copy of any of its contents without the permission of the publisher, Wiley Publishing, Inc.

- ✔ **Trademarks:** Give companies ownership of distinguishing words, phrases, symbols, or designs. For example, check out this book's cover to see the registered trademark, *For Dummies,* for this brand. Trademarks can last forever, as long as a business continues to use the trademark and files the proper paperwork periodically. Consequently, because this type of asset can have a limitless useful life, you don't depreciate it.

- ✔ **Goodwill:** This category of intangible asset can exist only in relation to a business as a whole. A bookkeeper records goodwill in the books only if someone has purchased the business. Goodwill is somewhat of a specialized asset and has some unique accounting rules surrounding it. If it comes up in your chart of accounts, consult your business's accountant to find out what you need to know to properly deal with it. (For more about goodwill, see Book II.)

For financial statements to show that the book values of non-current assets reduce over time, you either depreciate or amortize them. You depreciate tangible assets in the category of Property, Plant, and Equipment, with the exception of land; you amortize intangible assets, such as patents and copyrights (amortization is very similar to depreciation). Each patent, copyright, or trademark asset has a lifespan based on the number of years the government grants the rights for it. After recording an initial cost for the intangible asset, a business then divides that cost by the number of years it has government protection and writes the resulting amount off each year as an amortization expense, which appears on the income statement. If, for some reason, the business doesn't feel like the asset will be useful during all of its legal life, then you reduce the amount of years used in the calculation to a lower, more reasonable number. You place the total amortization or depreciation expenses that your business has written off during the life of the asset on the balance sheet in a line item called Accumulated Depreciation or Accumulated Amortization (whichever is appropriate for the type of asset).

Acknowledging your debts

The Liabilities section of the balance sheet comes after the Assets section (refer to the heading "Dividing and listing your assets," earlier in this chapter) and shows all the money that your business owes to others, including banks, vendors, contractors, governments, financial institutions, or individuals. Like assets, you divide your liabilities into two categories on the balance sheet:

- ✔ **Current liabilities:** All bills and debts that you plan to pay within the next 12 months. Accounts appearing in this section include any demand Bank Loan for an operating line of credit, Accounts Payable (bills due to vendors, contractors, and others), Credit Card Payable, all the Payroll Withholding Liability accounts, and the current portion of any long-term debt (for example, if you have a mortgage on your store, the payments due in the next 12 months appear as current liabilities).

  Whenever a business has a demand bank loan, the business has to include the unpaid principal balance of this loan with current liabilities. (With a *demand bank loan,* if at any time the bank doesn't feel comfortable with your financial position or if you overstep the limits set down in the loan agreement, the bank can demand a full principal repayment within an extremely short period of time.) Because the business has the looming possibility that it could have to repay this loan balance quickly, accountants require that the business groups the loan with current liabilities.

Book IV

Bookkeeping

> ✔ **Non-current liabilities:** All debts you owe to lenders that your business is required to pay over a period longer than 12 months. Mortgages Payable, Loans Payable, and Notes and Bonds Payable are common accounts in the non-current liabilities section of the balance sheet.

Most businesses try to minimize their current liabilities that carry interest charges because the interest rates on short-term loans, such as credit cards, are usually much higher than those on loans that have long terms. While you manage your business's liabilities, always look for ways to minimize your interest payments by seeking long-term loans that have lower interest rates than you can get on a credit card or short-term loan.

H.G.'s Cheesecake Shop's balance sheet has only one account in each liabilities section:

Current liabilities:

Accounts Payable $2,200

Non-current liabilities:

Loans Payable $29,150

Naming your investments

Every business has investors. Even a small mom-and-pop grocery store requires money upfront to get the business on its feet. You report investments that individuals or other businesses make into the business on the balance sheet as *equity*. The line items that appear in a balance sheet's Equity section vary, depending on whether the business is incorporated.

If you're preparing the books for a sole-proprietorship business, the Equity section of your balance sheet should contain a single Capital account for the owner. If the business is a partnership, you need to record a Capital account for each partner, with the partner's name as part of the name of the account. *Capital accounts* record all money invested by the owners to start up the business, as well as any additional contributions they make after the start-up phase. You also have a *Drawings account* for each owner, which tracks all money that each owner takes out of the business.

For a business that's incorporated, the Equity section of the balance sheet should contain the following accounts, at a minimum:

> ✔ **Common Shares account:** Portions of ownership in the business, purchased as investments by business owners. The units of ownership are *shares*. Each share carries a voting right for the owner of the share.

> ✔ **Retained Earnings account:** All profits that shareholders have reinvested in the corporation.

Sorting out stock investments

You're probably most familiar with the sale of shares of stock on the open market through the various stock market exchanges, such as the Toronto Stock Exchange (TSX). However, not all corporations sell their stock through public exchanges; in fact, most corporations aren't public companies, but private operations.

Whether public or private, you obtain ownership in a business by buying shares of stock. If the business isn't publicly traded, you buy and sell shares privately. In most small companies, family members and close friends make these exchanges, as well as outside investors the business has approached individually to raise additional money.

Because H.G.'s Cheesecake Shop is a sole proprietorship, a single account appears in the Equity section of its balance sheet:

Capital $9,500

H.G.'s Cheesecake Shop has a balance of $5,000. This amount represents the balance in the owner's Capital account, exclusive of the profit results for the year. After you close the income statement accounts at the end of the year, the Capital account increases by the net profit for the year. The worksheet shows H.G.'s Cheesecake Shop had a net profit for the year of $4,500. Because the profit ends up in the Capital account, this account increases to the ending balance of $9,500.

Ta Da! Pulling Together the Final Balance Sheet

After you group together all your accounts, you're ready to produce a balance sheet. Private businesses usually choose between two common formats for their balance sheets: the account format or the report format. The same line items appear in both formats; the only difference is the way in which you lay out the information on the page. Publicly held corporations in Canada now use a third option, the statement of financial position format (as do corporations in Europe, Australia, and elsewhere in the world) because of the implementation of the International Financial Reporting Standards (IFRS).

Book IV

Bookkeeping

Account format

The account format is a two-column layout that shows assets on one side, and liabilities and equity on the other side. Here's how the balance sheet of H.G.'s Cheesecake Shop on May 31, 2012, looks by using the account format:

H.G.'s Cheesecake Shop
Balance Sheet
May 31, 2012

Current Assets		*Current Liabilities*	
Cash	$3,000	Accounts payable	$2,200
Accounts receivable	$1,000		
Inventory	$1,200		
Total current assets	$5,200	Total current liabilities	$2,200
Non-Current Assets		*Non-Current Liabilities*	
Equipment	$5,050	Loans payable	$29,150
Furniture	$5,600	Total liabilities	$31,350
Vehicles	$25,000	**Equity**	
Total Non-Current Assets	$35,650	Capital	$9,500
Total assets	$40,850	Total liabilities and equity	$40,850

Report format

The report format is a one-column layout that shows assets first, then liabilities, and then equity.

Here's the balance sheet of H.G.'s Cheesecake Shop on May 31, 2012, using the Report format:

H.G.'s Cheesecake Shop
Balance Sheet
May 31, 2012

Current Assets		
Cash	$3,000	
Accounts receivable	$1,000	
Inventory	$1,200	
Total current assets		$5,200
Non-Current Assets		
Equipment	$5,050	
Furniture	$5,600	
Vehicles	$25,000	
Total non-current assets		$35,650
Total assets		$40,850
Current Liabilities		
Accounts payable		$2,200
Total current liabilities		$2,200
Non-Current Liabilities		
Loans payable		$29,150
Total liabilities		$31,350
Equity		
Capital		$9,500
Total liabilities and owner's equity		$40,850

Financial position format

Although you can use the terms *balance sheet* and *statement of financial position* interchangeably in Canada, corporations that have stock traded on any of the public exchanges, including the TSX, must use the statement of financial position format. This format is consistent between countries around the world that have adopted the International Financial Reporting Standards (IFRS).

Here's the statement of financial position of H.G.'s Cheesecake Shop on May 31, 2012:

H.G.'s Cheesecake Shop
Statement of Financial Position
As of May 31, 2009

Assets		
Non-Current Assets		
Equipment	$5,050	
Furniture	$5,600	
Vehicles	$25,000	
Total non-current assets		$35,650
Current Assets		
Cash	$3,000	
Accounts receivable	$1,000	
Inventory	$1,200	
Total current assets		$5,200
Total assets		$40,850
Equity and Liabilities		
Equity		
Capital		$9,500
Non-Current Liabilities		
Loans payable	$29,150	
Current Liabilities		
Accounts payable	$2,200	
Total liabilities		31,350
Total equity and liabilities		$40,850

Putting Your Balance Sheet to Work

With a complete balance sheet in your hands, you can analyze the numbers through a series of ratio tests to check your cash status and track your debt. Because banks and potential investors use these types of tests to determine whether to loan money to or invest in your business, run these tests yourself before you seek loans or investors. Ultimately, the ratio tests we cover in the following sections can help you determine whether your business is in a strong cash position.

Testing your liquidity

When you approach a bank or other financial institution for a loan, you can expect the lender to use one of two ratios to test your liquidity position: the current ratio and the acid test ratio (also known as the *quick ratio*). A business has a good liquidity position when it can show that it has the ability to pay off its bills when they're due without experiencing a serious cash crunch.

Current ratio

The *current ratio* compares your current assets to your current liabilities. It provides a quick glimpse of your business's ability to pay its bills.

The formula for calculating the current ratio is

Current assets ÷ Current liabilities = Current ratio

The following equation calculates the current ratio for H.G.'s Cheesecake Shop:

$5,200 ÷ $2,200 = 2.36

Lenders usually look for current ratios of 1.20 to 2.00, so any bank would consider a current ratio of 2.36 a good sign. A current ratio less than 1.00 is considered a danger sign because it indicates the business doesn't have enough current assets to pay its current bills.

A current ratio over 2.00 may indicate that your business isn't investing its assets well and may be able to make better use of its current assets. For example, if your business holds a lot of cash, you may want to invest that money in some non-current assets, such as additional equipment, to help grow the business.

Acid test (quick) ratio

The *acid test ratio* uses only the financial figures in your business's Cash, Accounts Receivable, and Trading Securities accounts. Although the acid test ratio is similar to the current ratio in that it examines current assets and liabilities, the acid test ratio is a stricter test of your business's liquidity. The assets part of this calculation doesn't take inventory into account because you can't always convert inventory to cash as quickly as other current assets and because, in a slow market, selling your inventory may take a while.

Many lenders prefer the acid test ratio when determining whether to give you a loan because of this ratio's strictness.

Book IV

Bookkeeping

Follow these steps to calculate your business's acid test ratio:

1. **Determine your quick assets.**

   Cash + Accounts receivable + Trading securities = Quick assets

2. **Calculate your quick ratio.**

   Quick assets ÷ Current liabilities = Quick ratio

The following calculations give you an example of an acid test ratio:

$2,000 + $1,000 + $1,000 = $4,000 (quick assets)

$4,000 ÷ $2,200 = 1.8 (acid test ratio)

Lenders consider a business that has an acid test ratio around 1.0 to be in good condition. An acid test ratio less than 1.0 indicates that the business may have to sell some of its trading securities or take on additional debt until it can sell more of its inventory.

Assessing your debt

Before you even consider taking on additional debt, always check your debt condition. One common ratio that you can use to assess your business's debt position is the *debt to equity ratio.* This ratio compares what your business owes to what your business owns.

Follow these steps to calculate your debt to equity ratio:

1. **Calculate your total debt.**

   Current liabilities + Non-current liabilities = Total debt

2. **Calculate your debt to equity ratio.**

   Total debt ÷ Equity = Debt to equity ratio

The following calculations give you the debt to equity ratio for H.G.'s Cheesecake Shop on May 31, 2012:

$2,200 + $29,150 = $31,350 (total debt)

$31,350 ÷ $9,500 = 3.3 (debt to equity ratio)

Lenders like to see a debt to equity ratio close to 1.0 because it indicates that the amount of debt is equal to the amount of equity. Because H.G.'s Cheesecake Shop has a debt to equity ratio of 3.3, most banks probably wouldn't loan it any money until either it lowered its debt levels or the owners put more money into the business.

Generating balance sheets electronically

If you use a computerized accounting system (see Chapter 3 of this book for more), you can use its report function to automatically generate your balance sheets. These balance sheets give you quick snapshots of the business's financial position, but they may require adjustments before you prepare your financial reports for external use.

One key adjustment you likely have to make involves the value of your inventory. Most computerized accounting systems use the averaging cost formula to value inventory. This formula totals all the inventory purchased and then calculates an average price for the inventory. However, your accountant may recommend a different cost formula that works better for your business. So if you use a cost formula other than the default averaging cost formula to value your inventory, you need to adjust the inventory value that appears on the balance sheet that the computerized accounting system generates.

Producing an Income Statement

Did your business make any money? You can find the answer in your income statement, an important financial tool. An *income statement* is the financial report that summarizes all the sales activities, costs of producing or buying the products or services sold, and expenses incurred in order to run the business. Income statements summarize the financial activities of a business during a particular accounting period (which can be a month, quarter, year, or some other period of time that makes sense for a business's needs).

Analyzing the income statement and the details behind it can reveal a lot of useful information to help you make decisions for improving your profits and your business overall. The upcoming sections cover the parts of an income statement, how you develop one, and examples of how you can use it to make business decisions.

Normally, bookkeepers include three accounting periods on an income statement: the current period and two prior periods. So, a monthly statement shows the current month and the two previous months; a quarterly statement shows the current quarter and the two previous quarters; and an annual statement shows the current year and the two previous years. Providing this much information gives income statement readers a view of the business's earning trends.

Book IV

Bookkeeping

Classifying accounts in the income statement

Organizing the accounts from your balance sheet (refer to the earlier sections of this chapter) and placing them into groups in your income statement is called *classification*. Deciding which expenses belong in a particular group depends on what you want to emphasize and what the people looking at the income statement want to see. You classify a business's expenses either by their nature or their function.

The Employee Benefit Costs item on an income statement provides an example of the classification of an expense by its nature. Or, you could group this expense with others in the more general Administrative Expenses item, classifying the employee benefits costs as an expense, according to function.

The classification and grouping of accounts allows you to create subtotals that your readers can use to make easy comparisons within a financial statement or with another financial statement. These number comparisons often result in ratios, which managers or bankers, for example, use as tools to see quickly how the business is performing. We look at some key ratios in the section "Testing Profits," later in this chapter.

The following are the seven key lines that make up an income statement classified by function:

- **Sales/Revenues:** The total amount of money taken in from selling the business's products or services. You calculate this amount by totalling all the sales or revenue accounts. You label the top line of the income statement either sales or revenues; either is okay.

- **Cost of goods sold:** How much a business spent to buy or make the goods or services that it sold during the accounting period in review. We show you how to calculate cost of goods sold in the section "Finding cost of goods sold," later in this chapter.

- **Gross profit:** How much a business made before taking into account operations expenses; you calculate this line by subtracting the cost of goods sold figure from the sales or revenue figure. Gross profit is a subtotal and doesn't represent an account in the general ledger.

- **Operating expenses:** How much the business spent on operations; qualifying expenses include administrative fees, salaries, advertising, utilities, rent, and other operations expenses. You add all the expense accounts that appear on your income statement to get this total.

- **Other income:** How much a business has earned in rental revenue or interest income from savings or investments.

- **Other expenses:** How much the business spent on financing (in the form of interest costs).

> ✔ **Profit or loss:** Whether the business made a profit or loss during the accounting period in review. You calculate this line by subtracting the total expenses from gross profit and adding any other income.

Formatting the income statement

Before you actually create your business's income statement, you have to pick a format. You have two options: the single-step format or the multi-step format. They contain the same information, but present it in slightly different ways.

The *single-step format* groups all data into two categories: revenue and expenses. The *multi-step format* divides the income statement into several sections and gives the reader some key subtotals, which make analyzing the data easier.

The single-step format allows readers to calculate the same subtotals that appear in the multi-step format, but those calculations mean more work for the reader. Most businesses choose the multi-step format to simplify income statement analysis for their external financial-report readers.

Here's an example of a basic income statement prepared in the single-step format for H.G.'s Cheesecake Shop:

Revenues		
Net sales	$1,000	
Interest income	$100	
Total revenues		$1,100
Expenses		
Cost of goods sold	$500	
Depreciation	$50	
Advertising	$50	
Salaries	$100	
Supplies	$100	
Interest expense	$50	
Total expenses		$850
Profit		**$250**

Using the same numbers, here's a basic income statement prepared in the multi-step format:

Revenues		
Net sales	$1,000	
Cost of goods sold	$500	
Gross profit		$500
Operating expenses		
Depreciation	$50	
Advertising	$50	
Salaries	$100	
Supplies	$100	
Total operating expenses		$300
Profit from operations		$200
Other income		
Interest income		$100
		$300
Other expenses		
Interest expense		$50
Profit		$250

Preparing the income statement

Before you can prepare your income statement, you have to calculate net sales and cost of goods sold. We tell you how in the upcoming sections.

Finding net sales

Net sales is a total of all your sales minus any discounts, returns, and allowances. To calculate net sales, you look at the worksheet's line items regarding sales, discounts, and any sales returns. H.G.'s Cheesecake Shop's worksheet lists sales of $20,000 and $1,000 for sales discounts given to customers. To find your net sales, you subtract the sales discounts from your total sales amount; so, H.G.'s Cheesecake Shop has $19,000 net sales.

Finding cost of goods sold

Cost of goods sold is the total amount your business spent to buy or make the goods or services that you sold. To calculate this amount for a business that buys its finished products from another business and sells them to customers, you start with the book value of the business's *opening inventory* (the amount in the Inventory account at the beginning of the accounting period), add all purchases of new inventory (net of any purchase discounts or allowances), and then subtract any *ending inventory* (inventory that's still on the store shelves or in the warehouse; it appears on the balance sheet, which we explain earlier in this chapter).

The following is a basic cost-of-goods-sold calculation with imaginary amounts:

Opening inventory + Purchases = Goods available for sale

$100 + $1,000 = $1,100

Goods available for sale – Ending inventory = Cost of goods sold

$1,100 – $200 = $900

To simplify the example for calculating cost of goods sold, we assume that the book values for opening inventory (the book value of the inventory at the beginning of the accounting period) and ending inventory (the book value of the inventory at the end of the accounting period) are the same. So, to calculate H.G.'s Cheesecake Shop's cost of goods sold, we need only two key lines of its worksheet: the purchases made and the purchase discounts received to lower the purchase cost:

Purchases – Purchases discounts = Cost of goods sold

$8,000 – $1,500 = $6,500

Drawing remaining amounts from your worksheet

After you calculate net sales and cost of goods sold (see the preceding sections), you can use the rest of the numbers from your worksheet to prepare the income statement.

Showing three accounting periods on an income statement is standard practice, so Table 2-1 lists three months' worth of figures (but shows actual numbers for only one month).

Table 2-1	Monthly Income Statement for May 2012, H.G.'s Cheesecake Shop		
Months Ended	*May*	*April*	*March*
Revenues			
Net sales	$19,000		
Cost of goods sold	$6,500		
Gross profit	$12,500		

(continued)

Table 2-1 *(continued)*

Months Ended	May	April	March
Operating expenses			
Advertising expense	$1,500		
Bank service charges	$120		
Credit card fees	$125		
Insurance expense	$100		
Legal and accounting fees	$300		
Office expense	$250		
Payroll benefits expense	$350		
Postage expense	$75		
Rent expense	$800		
Salaries expense	$3,500		
Supplies expense	$300		
Telephone expense	$200		
Utilities expense	$255		
Total operating expenses	$7,875		
Profit from operations	$4,625		
Other expenses			
Interest expense	$125		
Profit	$4,500		

You and anyone else in-house are likely to want to see the type of detail the example in Table 2-2 shows, but most business owners prefer not to show all their operating details to outsiders. Remember, the more information you give to outsiders, the more they know about how your business operates and the more easily they can come up with strategies to compete with your business. So consider summarizing the expenses in income statements that you plan to distribute externally. For external statements, many businesses group all advertising and promotions expenses into one line item and all administrative expenses into another line item.

Gauging your cost of goods sold

Businesses that make their own products, rather than buy them for future sale, must track inventory at three different levels:

✔ **Raw materials:** This line item includes purchases of all items used to make your business's products. For example, a fudge shop buys all the ingredients to make the fudge it sells, so the cost of any inventory on hand that the business hasn't yet used to make fudge should appear here.

✔ **Work-in-process inventory:** This line item shows the book value of any products that your business is making but can't yet sell. A fudge shop probably wouldn't have anything in this line item, considering fudge doesn't take more than a few hours to make. However, many manufacturing companies take weeks or months to produce products, so they usually have some portion of the inventory book value in this line item.

✔ **Finished-goods inventory:** This line item lists the value of inventory that a business has ready for sale. (For a business that doesn't make its own products, finished-goods inventory is the same as the inventory line item.)

If you keep the books for a business that manufactures its own products, you can use a computerized accounting system to track the various kinds of inventory described in the preceding list. But your basic accounting system software won't cut it — you need an advanced package to track multiple inventory types.

Deciphering gross profit

Business owners must carefully watch their gross profit trends on monthly income statements. Gross profit trends that appear lower from one month to the next can mean one of two things: Sales revenue is down, or cost of goods sold is up.

If revenue is down month-to-month, you may need to quickly figure out why and fix the problem to meet your sales goals for the year. Or, by examining sales figures for the same month in previous years, you may determine that the drop is just a normal sales slowdown given the time of year.

If the downward trend isn't normal, it may be a sign that a competitor's successfully drawing customers away from your business, or it may indicate that customers are dissatisfied with some aspect of your products or services. Whatever the reason, preparing a monthly income statement gives you the ammunition you need to quickly find and fix a problem, minimizing any negative hit to your yearly profits.

In addition to sales revenue, cost of goods sold can also be a big factor in a downward profit trend. For example, if the amount you spend to purchase products that you then sell goes up, your gross profit goes down. As a business owner, you need to do one of five things if the costs of goods sold are reducing your gross profit:

- ✔ Find a new supplier who can provide the goods more cheaply.

- ✔ Increase your prices, as long as you don't lose sales because of the increase.

- ✔ Increase your volume of sales so that you can sell more products and meet your annual profit goals.

- ✔ Reduce other expenses to offset the additional product costs.

- ✔ Accept the fact that your annual profit will be lower than expected.

The sooner you find out that you have a problem with costs, the faster you can find a solution and minimize any reduction in your annual profit goals.

Monitoring expenses

The Expenses section of your income statement gives you a good summary of all the money you spent to keep your business operating that didn't directly relate to the sale of an individual product or service. For example, businesses usually use advertising both to bring customers in and with the hopes of selling many different types of products. So list advertising as an expense, rather than a cost of goods sold. After all, rarely can you link an advertisement to the sale of an individual product. You also can't directly connect the administrative expenses that go into running a business — such as rent, wages and salaries, office costs, and so on — with specific sales.

A business owner watches expense trends closely to be sure that costs don't creep upwards and lower the business's bottom line. Any cost-cutting that you can do on the expense side can definitely increase your bottom-line profit.

Using the Income Statement to Make Business Decisions

Many business owners compare their income statement trends by using percentages, rather than the actual numbers. You can calculate these percentages easily enough — simply divide each line item by the Net Sales appearing at the top of the income statement. Table 2-2 shows a business's percentage breakdown for one month.

Table 2-2	Monthly Income Statement for May 2012 with Percentage of Net Sales — H.G.'s Cheesecake Shop	
Month Ended	**May**	
Revenues		
Net sales	$19,000	100.0%
Cost of goods sold	$6,500	34.2%
Gross profit	$12,500	65.8%
Operating expenses		
Advertising expense	$1,500	7.9%
Bank service charges	$120	0.6%
Credit card fees	$125	0.7%
Insurance expense	$100	0.5%
Legal and accounting fees	$300	1.6%
Office expense	$250	1.3%
Payroll benefits expense	$350	1.8%
Postage expense	$75	0.4%
Rent expense	$800	4.2%
Salaries expense	$3,500	18.4%
Supplies expense	$300	1.6%
Telephone expense	$200	1.1%
Utilities expense	$255	1.3%
Total operating expenses	$7,875	41.4%
Profit from operations	$4,625	24.3%
Other expenses		
Interest expense	$125	0.7%
Profit	$4,500	23.7%

Looking at this percentage breakdown, you can see that H.G.'s Cheesecake Shop had a gross profit of 65.8 percent, and its cost of goods sold, at 34.2 percent, accounted for just over one-third of the revenue. If the prior month's cost of goods sold was only 32 percent, the business owner would need to find out why the cost of the goods used to make products likely went up. If the owner doesn't take action to change the trend of increasing cost of goods sold, the business will make a lot less profit.

Government assistance and small business

Industry Canada (www.ic.gc.ca) has a wealth of resources and information for small and medium-sized businesses (Small to Medium Enterprises, or SMEs). On Industry Canada's website, search for the keyword SME and click the link for SME Direct, which appears in the search results. Topics include valuation of businesses, succession planning, e-commerce, competitive intelligence, and government programs for financing.

You may want to see how your income statement results compare to industry trends for similar businesses with similar revenues; this process is called *benchmarking*. By comparing results, you can find out whether your costs and expenses are reasonable for the type of business you operate, and you can identify areas to improve your profitability. You also may spot some red flags showing where you spend much more than the national average.

You may find locating financial information truly comparable to yours that you can use for benchmarking is quite difficult. The vast majority of small businesses are privately owned, so their information isn't readily available. Some of the information that you can find concerns businesses that are much larger than yours and can consequently achieve huge economies of scale for some of their expenses. Take any information that you find with a grain of salt and use it only as a guide, rather than a rule.

To find industry trends for businesses similar to yours, visit www.bizminer.com to review reports for businesses in the same industry.

The income statement you produce for external use — banks and investors — may look very different from the one that you produce for in-house owners or managers. Most business owners prefer to provide the minimum amount of detail necessary to satisfy external users of their financial statements. For instance, they prefer to deliver summaries of expenses, rather than line-by-line expense details; a net sales figure without reporting all the detail about discounts, returns, and allowances; and a cost of goods sold figure without reporting all the detail about how you calculated that figure.

Internally, the contents of the income statement are a different story. With more detail, a business's managers can better make accurate business decisions. Most businesses develop detailed reports based on the data collected to develop the income statement. Bookkeepers commonly pull items such as discounts and returns out of income statements and break them down into further detail:

✔ **Discounts:** Reductions on the retail price as part of a special sale. Discounts may also be in the form of volume discounts provided to customers who buy large amounts of the business's products. For example, a store may offer a 10-percent discount to customers who buy 20 or more of the same item at one time. In order to put their net sales numbers in perspective, business owners and managers must track how much they reduce their revenues to attract sales.

✔ **Returns:** Transactions in which items are returned by the buyer for any reason — not the right size, damaged, defective, and so on. If a business's number of returns increases dramatically, a larger problem may be the cause. Business owners need to track these numbers carefully to identify and resolve any problems with the items that they sell.

Another section of the income statement that you're likely to break down into more detail for internal use is the cost of goods sold line item. Basically, you present the detail collected to calculate that line item, including beginning inventory, ending inventory, purchases, and purchase discounts and returns, in a separate report. (We explain how to calculate cost of goods sold in the section "Finding cost of goods sold," earlier in this chapter.)

You can generate an unlimited number of internal reports from the detail that goes into your income statement and other financial statements. For example, many businesses design a report that looks at month-to-month trends in revenue, cost of goods sold, and income. In fact, you can set up your computerized accounting system (if you use one — see Chapter 3 for more) to automatically generate this report and other custom-designed reports. Using your computerized system, you can produce these reports at any time during the month if you want to see how close you are to meeting your month-end, quarter-end, or year-end goal.

Many businesses also design a report that compares actual spending to the budget. On this report, each of the income statement line items appears with its planned budget figures and the actual figures. When you review this report, you flag any line item that's considerably higher or lower than expected, and then research that item to find a reason for the difference.

Book IV

Bookkeeping

Testing Profits

With a completed income statement, you can do a number of ratio calculations of your business's profitability. You certainly want to know how well your business did in comparison to other similar businesses. You also want to be able to gauge your return on your business.

Three common tests are return on sales (ROS), return on assets (ROA), and return on equity (ROE). These ratios have much more meaning if you can find industry averages for your particular type of business so that you can compare your results.

When you're looking at the profit of a small, owner-managed business, ask yourself, "Did the owner take a salary?" Many mom-and-pop operations have few, if any, employees. The owners don't take a salary from the business. Instead, they live off the profits of the business. If that's the case for your business, you need to make some adjustments to the numbers to make a comparison with another business that has employees (or vice versa). You want to level the playing field between the two businesses in your comparison. You can either add a salary to the non-salaried business or reduce the wages and salaries expenses from the business that has employees.

When looking at apparently comparable income statements, watch for income taxes. If one of the businesses is incorporated and therefore must pay income taxes, and the other business isn't incorporated (so it doesn't pay income taxes), you can't compare the results of the two businesses. If you want to compare your unincorporated business with an incorporated one, use that business's subtotal of profit before taxes to make your comparisons (or compare your incorporated business's subtotal with an unincorporated business's total profit).

Return on sales

The return on sales (ROS) ratio tells you how efficiently your business runs its operations. Using the information on your income statement, you can measure how much profit your business produced per dollar of sales and how much extra cash you brought in per sale.

You calculate ROS by dividing profit (before income taxes) by sales. H.G.'s Cheesecake Shop had profit of $4,500 and sales of $19,000. (If your business isn't a corporation, you don't have to factor in any business income taxes because only corporations pay income taxes.) Here's H.G.'s Cheesecake Shop's calculation of ROS:

Profit before income taxes ÷ Net sales = Return on sales

$4,500 ÷ $19,000 = 0.237 (23.7%)

As you can see from this calculation, H.G.'s Cheesecake Shop made 23.7 percent on each dollar of sales. To determine whether the ROS that you calculate for your business calls for celebration, find the ROS ratios for similar businesses.

Return on assets

The Return on Assets (ROA) ratio tests how well your business uses its assets to generate profits. If your business's ROA is the same as or higher than similar companies, you're doing a good job managing your assets.

To calculate ROA, you divide profit by total assets. H.G.'s Cheesecake Shop has on its balance sheet (which you can find earlier in this chapter) total assets of $40,850. H.G.'s Cheesecake Shop's profit was $4,500. Here's H.G.'s Cheesecake Shop's calculation of ROA:

Profit ÷ Total assets = Return on assets

$4,500 ÷ $40,850 = 0.11 (11%)

This calculation shows that H.G.'s Cheesecake Shop made 11 percent on each dollar of assets it held.

ROA can vary significantly, depending on your industry. For example, if your business requires you to maintain a lot of expensive equipment, such as a manufacturing firm, you have a much lower ROA than a service business that doesn't need as many assets. ROA can range from less than 5 percent for manufacturing companies that require a large investment in machinery and factories to as high as 20 percent or even higher for service companies that have few assets.

Return on equity

To measure how successfully your business earned money for its owners or investors, calculate the return on equity (ROE) ratio. This ratio often looks better than the ROA (refer to the preceding section) because ROE doesn't take debt into consideration.

You calculate ROE by dividing profit by shareholders' or owners' equity. H.G.'s Cheesecake Shop's equity (in the amount of $9,500) appears on its balance sheet, which you can see earlier in this chapter. The following shows H.G.'s Cheesecake Shop's calculation of ROE:

Profit ÷ Shareholders' or owners' equity = Return on equity

$4,500 ÷ $9,500 = 0.474 (47.4%)

Most business owners put in a lot of cash upfront to get a business started, so you often see a business whose liabilities and equities are split close to 50 percent each.

Book IV

Bookkeeping

Chapter 3

Computer Options for Your Bookkeeping

In This Chapter

▶ Finding the right accounting software for your business

▶ Getting your computerized books up and running

*V*ery few long-time small-business owners still do things the old-fashioned way — keeping their books in paper journals and ledgers. In this age of technology and instant information, most businesses computerize their books.

Not only is computerized bookkeeping easier than the pen-and-paper method, but also it minimizes the chance of errors, because most of the work that you do to a computerized system's ledgers and journals involves inputting data for transactions on forms that even someone without training in accounting or bookkeeping can understand. The person entering the information doesn't need to know whether something is a debit or credit (refer to Chapter 1 of this book for an explanation of the difference) because the computerized system takes care of everything.

In this chapter, we explore the two top accounting software packages for small businesses, discuss the basics of setting up your own computerized books, talk about how you can customize a program for your business, and give you some pointers on converting your manual bookkeeping system into a computerized one.

Surveying Your Software Options

More than 50 different types of accounting software programs are on the market, and all are designed to computerize your bookkeeping. The more sophisticated ones target specific industry needs, such as construction, food services, or utilities, and they can cost thousands of dollars. A quick Internet search unearths the options available to you. Several sites offer demos of their software packages.

Luckily, as a small-business person, you probably don't need all the bells and whistles offered by the top-of-the-line programs. Instead, two software programs that we review in this chapter can meet the needs of most small businesses. Using one of the two systems we recommend, you can get started with an initial investment of as little as $200. It may not be fancy, but basic computerized accounting software can do a fine job of helping you keep your books. And you can always upgrade to a more expensive program, if needed, as your business grows.

The two programs that meet any small business's basic bookkeeping needs are Simply Accounting Pro by Sage and QuickBooks Pro by Intuit. Each of these packages has an affordable (and practically identical) price. These software companies also offer simple systems that can take care of billing and cash transactions, but neither has full General Ledger capabilities — Sage has Simply Entrepreneur and QuickBooks has Simple Start. Either of these two software packages can get you started for as little as $100. But if you can afford it, we recommend that you step at least one notch above the basic levels to QuickBooks Pro or Simply Accounting Pro. These software packages offer a General Ledger module, which allows you to prepare a full trial balance and financial statements.

Accounting software packages are updated almost every year because tax laws and laws involving many other aspects of operating a business, such as payroll, change so often. In addition, computer software companies are always improving their products to make computerized accounting programs more user-friendly. So be sure that you always buy the most current version of an accounting software package.

Simply Accounting Pro

Simply Accounting Pro is a cost-effective choice for bookkeeping software if you're just starting up and don't have sophisticated bookkeeping or accounting needs. This program caters to the bookkeeping novice and even provides an option that lets you avoid accounting jargon by using words such as "purchase" and "vendor" in the icon list, rather than "accounts payable," when you want to record a purchase of goods from a vendor. The program includes more than 100 accounting templates for documents such as sales orders, quotes, receipts, and other basic needs for a variety of industries, including medical/dental, real estate, property management, and retail firms.

Simply Accounting Pro has an integrated feature that allows you to do employee direct deposit or electronic funds transfers (EFTs) for payroll, but for activities such as credit card processing or electronic payments, you need to install an add-on feature. However, the add-on feature doesn't work as well as one that's included in an original software package, such as the one included as part of QuickBooks.

If you're working with another software system to manage your business data and want to switch to Simply Accounting Pro, you may be able to import that data directly into Simply Accounting. (You can find information about how to import data included with the program.) You can import data from software such as Microsoft Excel (a spreadsheet program) or Access (a database program). If you're converting from QuickBooks or another accounting software program called MYOB, you can easily import your data to Simply Accounting.

QuickBooks Pro

QuickBooks Pro offers the best of both worlds: an easy user interface (for the novice) and extensive bookkeeping and accounting features (for the experienced bookkeeper or accountant). We chose to use QuickBooks to demonstrate various bookkeeping functions throughout this chapter because it's so user friendly. Yes, it's our favourite bookkeeping software, but we're not alone — more small-business owners today use QuickBooks than any other small-business accounting software packages. QuickBooks got better for the novice with the addition of its Learning Centre, which walks you through every type of key transaction with an interactive program that not only shows you how to do the function, but also explains the basics of bookkeeping. You don't have to use the tutorial, but the option pops up when you do a task for the first time, so the choice is always yours. You also can go back to the Learning Centre to review at any time. For additional information on this software, check out *QuickBooks 2012 For Dummies* (Wiley).

Most people have a love/hate relationship with Intuit support (Intuit's the company that makes QuickBooks). We've had good support experiences not only with QuickBooks, but also with its other popular software packages, such as TurboTax and Quicken. But we also know others who have complained loudly about support problems.

QuickBooks Easy Start, priced around $100, can meet most of your bookkeeping and accounting needs. If you want to integrate your bookkeeping with a *point-of-sale package*, which integrates cash-register sales, you need to get QuickBooks Pro, which sells for around $200 and allows up to five simultaneous users. You also need to upgrade if you want to do inventory management, generate purchase orders from estimates or sales orders, do job costing and estimates, automatically create a budget, or integrate your data so that you can use it with Microsoft Word and Excel programs.

QuickBooks is the most versatile software if you plan to use other software packages along with it. QuickBooks can share data with over 325 popular business software applications. You can easily share sales, customer, and financial data, too, so you don't have to enter that information twice. To find out if QuickBooks can share data with the business software applications you're currently using or plan to use, contact Intuit directly (www.intuit.ca).

Add-ons and fees

The accounting programs that we recommend in the section "Surveying Your Software Options," in this chapter, offer add-ons and features that you're likely to need, such as these three:

✔ **Tax updates:** If you have employees and want up-to-date tax information and forms to do your payroll by using your accounting software, you need to buy an update each year. The software suppliers or their distributors may instead charge you a monthly fee for the package, which gives you access to the updates when you need them.

✔ **Online credit card and debit card processing and electronic bill paying:** If you want

to perform these tasks, you have to pay additional fees. In fact, QuickBooks advertises its add-ons in these areas throughout its system; you can see the advertisements pop up on a number of screens.

✔ **Point-of-sale software:** This add-on helps you integrate your sales at the cash register with your accounting software. A more sophisticated version of the software helps you manage inventory at several locations.

Before you sign on for one of the add-ons, make sure you understand what fees you have to pay. Usually, the software supplier or a distributor advises you of the additional costs whenever you try to do anything that incurs extra fees.

Setting Up Your Computerized Books

After you pick your software, the hard work is done because actually setting up the package probably takes you less time than researching your options and picking your software. Both packages we discuss in this chapter (refer to the earlier section "Surveying Your Software Options") have good start-up tutorials to help you set up the books. QuickBooks even has an interactive interview that asks questions about all aspects of how you want to run your business and then sets up what you need based on your answers.

Simply Accounting Pro and QuickBooks Pro both produce a number of sample charts of accounts (refer to Chapter 1 of this book) that you can use as starting points to save time. Start with one of the charts offered by the software. You can then tweak the sample chart by adding and deleting accounts to suit your business's needs. If you want to, you can start from scratch.

Figure 3-1 shows you QuickBooks's EasyStep Interview screen, where we enter an income account as an example.

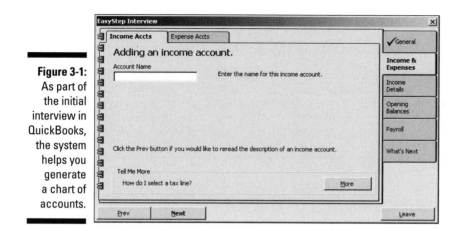

Figure 3-1:
As part of
the initial
interview in
QuickBooks,
the system
helps you
generate
a chart of
accounts.

After your chart of accounts appears, both programs ask you to enter a
company name, address, and business number (BN) to get started. You then
select an accounting period (see Figure 3-2). If the calendar year is your
accounting period, you don't have to change anything. But if your business is
incorporated, which means it can have a fiscal year other than the calendar
year (such as September 1 to August 31), you must enter that information.
After you enter this information, the software recognizes the fiscal year for
the part of the accounting cycle that involves closing the books.

If you don't change your accounting period to match your fiscal year, then you
have to delete the business from the system and start over.

Figure 3-2:
The
QuickBooks
EasyStep
Interview
asks your
taxation
year, the
province in
which you
operate,
and your
business
number
(BN).

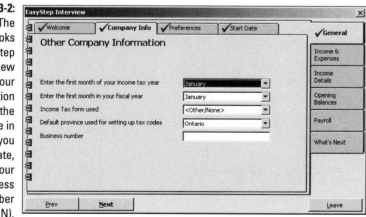

Book IV

Bookkeeping

Choosing your fiscal year

Many retail businesses don't close their books at the end of December because the holiday season isn't a good time for those businesses to close out for the year. Each year, because of gift cards and other new ways to give gifts, retail businesses can see very active purchases after the holidays. Therefore, many retail businesses operate on a fiscal year of February 1 to January 31 so that they can close the books well after the holiday season ends.

Customizing software to match your operations

After you set up the basics (see the preceding section), you can customize the software to fit your business's operations. For example, you can pick the type of invoices and other business forms that you want to use.

You can also input information about your bank accounts and other key financial data (see Figure 3-3). Then, you can add opening balances to accounts for customers and vendors so that you can track future cash transactions. Make your main business bank account the first account listed in your software program, labelled as either Cash in Chequing or just Cash.

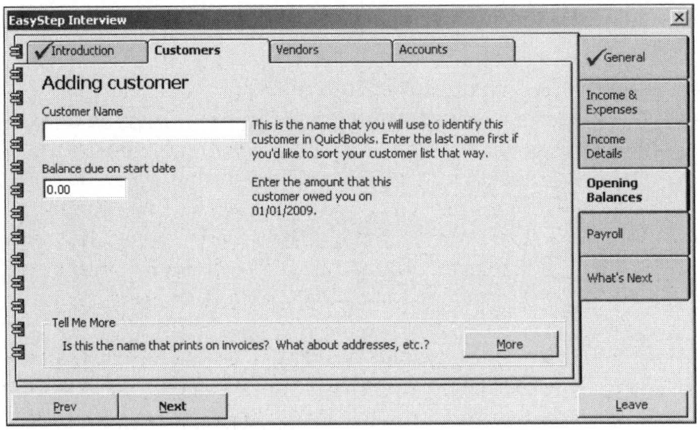

Figure 3-3: QuickBooks collects information about the beginning balance of key accounts as part of the initial interview for setting up a business.

After you enter your bank and other financial information, you can enter data unique to your business. If you want to use the program's budgeting features, you enter your budget information before entering other data. Then, you add your vendor and customer accounts (see Figure 3-3) so that when you start entering transactions, you already have the vendor or customer information in the system. If you don't have any outstanding bills or customer payments due, you can wait and enter vendor and customer information when the need arises.

If you have payments that you need to make or money that you need to collect from customers, be sure to input that information so that your system is ready when the time comes. Also, you don't want to forget to pay a bill or collect from a customer!

You may be able to import data about your customers, vendors, and employees from the software package that you're currently using to track that information, such as Microsoft Excel or Access. Full instructions for importing data come with the software program you choose.

Don't panic about entering everything into your computerized system right away. All programs make adding customers, vendors, and employees easy to do at any time.

You need to enter information about whether you collect GST/HST and provincial sales taxes from your customers and, if you do, the sales tax rates. Your software also lets you pick a format for your invoices, set up payroll data, and make arrangements for how you want to pay bills.

Converting your manual bookkeeping to a computerized system

If you're converting a manual bookkeeping system to a computerized system, your conversion takes a bit more time than just starting fresh, because you need to be sure that your new system starts with information that matches your current books. The process for entering your initial data varies, depending on the software you choose, so we don't go into detail about that process here. To ensure that you properly convert your bookkeeping system, use the information that comes with your software; read through the manual, review the start-up suggestions that the software makes while you set up the system, and pick the methods that best match your style of operating.

The best time to convert your pen-and-paper books to computerized versions is at the end of an accounting period. That way, you don't have to do a lot of extra work adding transactions that already occurred during a period. For example, if you decide to computerize your accounting system on March 15, you have to add all the transactions that occurred between March 1 and March 15 into your new system. You might even have to go back to the beginning of the fiscal year. You can make the process much easier by waiting until April 1 to get started, even if you buy the software on March 15. Although you can convert to a computerized accounting system at the end of a month, the best time to do the conversion is at the end of a calendar or fiscal year.

Book IV

Bookkeeping

Otherwise, you have to input data for all the months of the year that have passed.

Whenever you decide to start your computerized bookkeeping, use the data from the trial balance that you used to close the books at the end of the last fiscal year. (We explain how to prepare a trial balance in Chapter 2) In the computerized system, enter the balances in your trial balance for each of the accounts. Asset, Liability, and Equity accounts should have carry-over balances, but Revenue and Expense accounts should have zero balances.

Of course, if you're starting a new business, you don't have a previous trial balance. In that case, you just enter any balances you might have in your Cash accounts, any assets your business may own when it starts up, and any liabilities that your business may already owe relating to start-up expenses. You also add any contributions that owners made to get the business started in the Equity accounts.

After you enter all the appropriate data, run a series of financial reports, such as an income statement and balance sheet, to be sure you entered the data correctly and the software formats that data the way you want. If, for example, you need subtotals in financial statements, you can add that feature to your computerized financial statements or reports right away by using the Modify Report feature of any of the reports the software makes available. The software points you in the right direction for the summary of some subtotals into grand totals in certain reports and statements. You can change formatting more easily when the system isn't yet chock-full of data.

You need to be sure that you've entered the right numbers, so verify that the new accounting system's financial reports match what you created manually. If the numbers are different, now's the time to figure out why. Otherwise, the reports you do at the end of the accounting period will have the wrong information. If the numbers don't match, don't assume that the error can be only in the data entered. You may find that you made an error in the reports you developed manually. Of course, check your entries first, but if the income statement and balance sheet still don't look right, double-check your old trial balances, as well.

Book V

Human Resources

The 5th Wave — By Rich Tennant

A pie factory is no place to let motivation slip, Brad.

In this book . . .

Chapter 1: The People Picture 383

Chapter 2: Recruiting the Right People 395

Chapter 3: Retention: Critical in Any
Business Environment 435

Chapter 4: Monitoring Ongoing Performance 463

Chapter 1

The People Picture

In This Chapter

▶ Knowing what human resources means today

▶ Pinpointing key HR duties

▶ Taking a strategic approach to HR

▶ Considering investing in HR software

Most people in business agree that being sensitive to — and doing your best to meet — the "people needs" of your employees is in your best interest as an employer. But a good deal of debate exists over just how much responsibility a business needs to assume — and how much time (and money) a business must devote to the needs and priorities of employees, as opposed to the needs and priorities of its business operations and customers.

As a small-business owner, your job is to function as a human resources (HR) manager and focus on the practices and policies that directly affect the welfare and morale of your business's most important asset — its employees. You want to strike the optimal balance between the strategic needs of your business and the basic people needs of your workforce.

Striking this balance has never been easy, but most people in business agree that doing so is more important now than ever. In short, human resources has become a business unto itself. Throughout this chapter, we tell you what human resources management means in today's business world and explore the duties of HR professionals. We also get you thinking strategically about your HR endeavours, and give you tips on how to find the right HR software for your business. Remember, the way your business manages your employee base can make all the difference in your ability to stand out from the competition.

Managing Human Resources

Human resources management is the phrase that nearly everyone uses to describe a set of functions that once fell under the category of "personnel administration" or "personnel management." Regardless of the name, you can sum up this particular aspect of business as the decisions, activities, and processes that must meet the basic needs and support the work performance of employees.

The most common areas that fall under HR management include the following:

- Staffing
- Basic workplace policies
- Compensation and benefits
- Retention
- Training and developing employees
- Regulatory issues

Human resources management is all about people: finding and recruiting them; hiring them; training them; paying them; retaining them; creating an environment that's safe, healthy, and productive for them; communicating with them; and doing whatever is reasonably possible to find that delicate balance between what best serves the needs of employees and what best serves the market-driven needs of the business.

Scoping Out Your HR Duties

If you run a small business, you probably function as your own HR manager — that is, you personally oversee and conduct all the classic human resources functions of your company: You recruit and hire. You set up the compensation and benefits package. You write the paychecks and keep the appropriate records.

The chances are good, too, that you're the person responsible for training and developing the people you hire. And although you may not need to publish a newsletter to keep the people who work for you informed about what's going on in the business, you probably make a point to keep them in the loop.

Bigger businesses face the same basic challenges and carry out the same general activities. The only difference is that larger businesses employ individual specialists — or sometimes entire departments — to handle these same functions.

After most business reach a certain size, they feel virtually obligated to create a human resources department — even if it consists of only one person. Because of the increasing complexity of HR issues today, larger companies have boosted the size of their departments and typically employ specialists in areas such as benefits administration or RRSP retirement plans. But smaller firms that don't have the resources for such specialization must ensure that the people who handle their HR functions are solid *generalists* — that is, they possess skills in several areas of HR rather than in one particular specialty. If your business is on the smaller side and you want to meet the needs of your employees today, you'll need to know a lot about a lot of things— and the more you know, the better.

The human resources function in general has undergone enormous changes in the past 20 years. Some companies still take a highly structured, largely centralized approach to human resources management. The majority of companies today, however, take a far more decentralized approach, with HR practitioners and line managers working cooperatively to set basic policies and carry out programs.

The following sections tell you about key themes, trends, and issues that affect human resources management and that are likely to continue influencing the field in the near future.

Thinking strategically

We say it a lot in this chapter, but the most important asset a business has is not its products, factories, or systems, but its people. Businesses no longer take the "human" side of business for granted. And that's why the human resources function has become so important.

For several decades now, people responsible for the human resources function have ceased to be viewed merely as "personnel administrators" or strictly "support." The shift in terms from "personnel" to "human resources" reflects this thinking. But today's HR professionals are assuming an increasingly broad role in business as strategic advisors to the senior management team. Top managers now look to HR for help in formulating long-term staffing strategies, as well as introducing and following through on practices that help ensure that employees get the support and training they need to meet the increasing demands of their jobs. In short, senior management is looking to HR for insights on how to tap into the potential of every individual within a business.

This expectation creates many new opportunities for you. One key skill you need is the ability to think strategically. No doubt you've heard the term strategic thinkers. But what does it really mean?

Certainly, strategic thinkers spend plenty of time setting objectives and getting work done, but they also do much more. At heart, *strategic business thinkers* try to look ahead to anticipate which issues and information will be most relevant. They don't look at their work merely as a series of tasks or simply react to events; they also examine trends, issues, opportunities, and long-term needs — and shape what they discover into policies and recommendations. To borrow from the restaurant industry, strategic thinkers do more than cook; they help shape the menu.

How does the concept of strategic thinkers apply to the HR world? In effect, strategic HR professionals act as consultants to the rest of the business. They help set a path — that is, a vision of how to ensure HR effectively delivers on its mission. Deliberating when you're in a hurry to move forward isn't easy, but they know looking before they leap is wise, and this philosophy helps them offer valued counsel. Before merely saying "yes" to a proposed direction, HR professionals carefully examine and explain the long-term cost-benefit ratio. They expand the range of people they talk and listen to, drawing insights not just from departmental colleagues but from finance, marketing, legal counsel, manufacturing, sales, and other areas who can help them better understand what makes their company tick. And they do so with people at all levels, ranging from experienced senior managers to entry-level employees.

Taking this approach is not easy. Still, you've got a great opportunity — the chance to become an HR professional who is a vital source of counsel and a central part of your business's management team — even if you own the business. Even taking just 15 minutes a day of solitary "think time" and research time can make a big difference in effectively shaping your work.

Adapting to the changing workplace

Businesses today are smaller, leaner, and not as hierarchically structured as they were 20 years ago. But the most significant change in the organizational makeup of most businesses has less to do with the infrastructure and more to do with the fundamental *nature* of jobs — and the working arrangements of the people who hold those jobs.

You can no longer think of today's workplace as the specific building or piece of real estate where employees perform their jobs. Today is the age of the telecommuter and the virtual office. Thanks to wireless connections, the Internet, video conferencing, smartphones, and other technology, many businesses can run efficiently even though the key players never meet face-to-face.

Offering flexibility

Today is also the age of flexibility, with many businesses providing some or all of their employees with an opportunity to modify the normal nine-to-five schedule in ways that suit their particular family situations or lifestyles. Work hours vary greatly, as does the philosophical approach people take to their work.

Using contingent employees

Perhaps most important is the rise of the *contingent employee:* The man or woman who, instead of having one full-time job with a single employer, may work part-time or on a contract or project basis for a variety of companies in a given year.

The percentage of professionals in today's workplace who are working on a temporary or project basis is rising rapidly — and for a variety of reasons. The ability to call on contingent workers on an as-needed basis helps businesses to avoid the disruptive cycle of hiring and layoffs. Businesses can hire and develop a core team of full-time employees and then, as additional needs arise, bring in supplemental people temporarily.

Then, too, more and more professionals these days voluntarily choose to make their "full-time" job a series of temporary assignments. They like the flexibility, variety, and learning opportunities this option affords them.

Easing the work/life conflict

Is your business, or does it plan to be, employee-friendly? It had better be if you want to attract and keep top performers in today's job market. Being *employee-friendly* means that your scheduling and general operating policies consider the personal needs of employees — in particular, their desire to balance job responsibilities with family responsibilities. Most survey data today indicates that being able to maintain more control over schedules has become a priority for most workers, parents especially. And it has become increasingly apparent throughout the past decade or so that family-oriented policies do more than simply enhance a business's recruiting initiatives. They also produce a number of bottom-line benefits, such as reduced absenteeism, fewer disability claims, and fewer workplace accidents. Businesses may offer flexible scheduling, telecommuting arrangements, employee assistance programs (EAPs), and benefits programs that enable employees to select the benefits (child care support, for example) relevant to their needs.

Keeping pace with technology and new skills

As it has in many fields, technology has been a revolutionary development for people in HR management. E-mail has replaced the cork bulletin board as the primary communication between management and employees — and gone on to serve far more functions. Computers have streamlined the administrative aspects of every HR function. And, of course, the Internet, company intranets, and other online resources play a significant role in employee training.

But you still face a challenging side to this otherwise rosy picture. The software that enables companies to process large amounts of information is complex (and often expensive). Furthermore, it has introduced training and security issues that HR professionals didn't need to concern themselves with in the days of the typewriter.

Then, too, as work processes become more technically sophisticated, the need for skilled employees is intensifying. *Knowledge workers* describes employees who possess the skills and knowledge needed to perform the jobs and functions most affected by technological advances, tasks that in turn require significant levels of education. These positions include analysts, database administrators, programmers, systems analysts, technical writers, academic professionals, librarians, researchers, lawyers, and teachers, as well as scientists and students of all kinds. Businesses are looking more and more to their HR departments to simultaneously enhance the skills of existing employees and identify job candidates who possess the necessary level of expertise.

Rules and regulations: Ethics first

In the twenty-first century, a workplace that's free of hazards, sexual harassment, and discrimination is no longer considered a "benefit." It's something that employees have every right to expect. And federal, provincial, and local government agencies are using their powers of enforcement to ensure that workers are protected.

If you don't already have an HR background, one of your biggest challenges is to familiarize yourself with the many government-mandated regulations and programs with which your business must comply. Don't worry; you don't need to know the details of every one of them. But you do need to pay attention to the areas in your business that are covered by these regulations, as well as the laws you must keep track of to stay in compliance.

Government-mandated regulations touch almost every aspect of the human resource function, including safety and health, equal-employment opportunity, sexual harassment policies, and more.

You cannot underestimate the importance of ethics to an organization. We live in a dynamic business world that presents a great many challenges and opportunities. With all this flux and potential for reward, entire organizations may be tempted merely to pay lip service to integrity. In the HR role for your business, you have the chance to be front and centre in creating a corporate culture of accountability and personal integrity with a strong spirit of ethical behaviour at its heart. Helping your organization understand the importance of putting ethics first is a way in which you can begin to make HR more than a function as you take on the role of strategic counsellor.

Being Strategic in Your HR Efforts

The following list offers some general guidelines on how to be more successful overall in your HR efforts:

- ✔ **Become business savvy.** Make sure you know everything about your business, particularly in terms of revenues and profits (refer to Book 4 for more about that). Keep in mind that the more broad-minded you can be in how you approach everything you do in your job, the more credibility you will have as a strategic business professional — and the easier it will be to get everyone on board with new initiatives you recommend.

- ✔ **Don't ignore the basics.** Regardless of how committed you are to bringing new ideas to your business, don't overlook the traditional needs (such as policies regarding benefits, computers and the Internet, dress code, and privacy) that are all but universal among employees. At the very least, make sure that every employee is familiar with your business's basic practices. If you don't already have one, create an employee manual, and keep it up to date.

- ✔ **Make quality hiring a priority.** Make a personal commitment — and try to secure a similar commitment from others in your business — that you will devote the time and energy needed to ensure that each new employee you recruit and hire is the right person for that particular job. (See Chapter 2 of this book for more about hiring the right people.)

- ✔ **Keep your ear to the ground.** Keep your co-owners or senior managers apprised of all workplace issues and concerns that may affect your business's ability to meet the needs of customers. Taking on this role means that you always have your hand on the staffing pulse of your business. You're aware, for example, when morale is starting to slip, or when the workload is starting to burn out people. You smell the smoke before a big fire occurs.

✔ **Stay current.** Be aware of new developments in human resources administration, including technological advances and key trends in pay practices and benefits programs. When you come across new and promising ideas, consider implementing them and discuss them with your co-owners or senior managers. Be particularly diligent about keeping pace with what is going on in the legal and regulatory side of HR, making sure that you're aware of any laws or regulatory changes that apply to your business.

Staying Ahead with HR Software

Computer software has been very good to HR professionals over the last few decades. Many labour-intensive functions — time reporting, payroll calculation, tax computation, and tax reporting — are now processed quite rapidly.

The scope, flexibility, and versatility of HR-related software — formally known as Human Resource Information Systems (HRIS) — continue to accelerate at a dizzying pace. The new generation of training and development software, for example, not only tracks such aspects of training as scheduling, enrollments, vendor data, and costs, but it also integrates that data with information relating to career development and assessment.

The evolution of HRIS has not only enhanced the efficiency of HR operations in general, but it has also enabled HR departments to lower their administrative costs and make better and more timely use of data in strategic planning.

Unfortunately, however, an inherent challenge exists in this otherwise upbeat picture. The problem is that, with so many products and applications evolving so quickly (the number of HR-related software products on the market, according to WorldatWork, now exceeds 3,000 and shows no signs of ebbing), HR professionals have difficulty making basic buying decisions. This challenge is no small matter. Depending on the size of your business, the level of customization you require, and the number of functions you're interested in automating or integrating, the cost can run anywhere from just under $500 to more than $1 million. And that sum doesn't include what you may have to spend on additional computer hardware, the time your employees need to learn the new system, or the potential operational problems during the transition period.

The challenge you face when choosing an HR software application is not just deciding which product has the niftiest features or which vendor is the most supportive. It's also figuring out an overall strategy to ensure that the transition from the old way to the new way goes as smoothly as possible.

It's a given that all software decisions should be driven by the strategic and operational needs of the business — as opposed to the capabilities of the software. This axiom takes on special significance when you're considering buying software that will combine and integrate functions that currently operate as separate tasks. Regardless of how elegantly the software is designed, how easy it is to use, and how fast it runs, the system must ultimately produce a business payoff — whether it's through increased productivity, cost savings, quicker response time, or improved employee morale.

You may get so swept up in the remarkable capabilities of today's HRIS products that you lose sight of what the technology is meant to do: help your company operate more efficiently and profitably. So before you move ahead on any software initiative, be prepared to go through a rigorous and disciplined needs assessment, followed by a cost/benefit analysis.

Rather than think about this purchase as an administrative matter of implementation, step back and assess it strategically. A new HR application may not be the only way to achieve a business goal. You may be able to achieve the same result more cost-effectively through some other means, such as outsourcing or using contingent workers (refer to earlier in this chapter). So don't jump the gun on any major software decision. Think it through.

Ask the following key questions when you're going through this process:

- ✔ What benefits does your business stand to gain once the software is in place?
- ✔ How much does the software cost?
- ✔ How long will it take to recoup the investment?
- ✔ Do you expect any downtime or reduced productivity while employees are learning the new system?
- ✔ Is the new system compatible with the business's existing hardware and software, or will it need a complete upgrade?

Becoming an educated buyer

You don't need to be a computer programmer to make intelligent HRIS buying decisions. But if your business is seriously exploring a major software purchase, get a general idea of what products are meant to do and what features distinguish one system and one vendor from another.

No secret formulas ensure that your HRIS buying decisions will give you the results you seek. But the following suggestions stack the odds in your favour:

✔ Instead of taking on sole responsibility for making the final decision (or assigning it to your information technology department), put together a cross-functional team.

✔ Find out everything you can about vendors you're thinking of using.

✔ Insist that any vendor who wants your business demonstrate how the software you're considering performs those specific functions that you believe are most important to your business.

✔ Ask specific questions about how the product was developed.

✔ If the IT investment is significant, get the names and telephone numbers of at least five current users of any product you're considering to get a real-world perspective.

✔ Include as part of your overall strategy some mechanism that gets users excited about the system you're considering implementing. Identify those people who may be resistant and get them onboard first. Start training before the system is introduced and fully implemented.

Checking off the software features you need

When (and if) the time comes to compare two or more integrated software products on a feature-by-feature basis, focus on two considerations: the specific feature being compared and how important that feature is to your needs. The following list provides a general idea of features that normally differentiate one product from another, but you must determine how important each feature is to your business:

✔ Response time (How long does it take users to access information, especially during peak periods?)

✔ Scope of search capabilities

✔ Report and audit capabilities

✔ Internet and intranet compatibility

✔ Scanning and OCR capabilities

✔ Security and self-service capabilities (Can employees update it without compromising security?)

✔ Flexibility (Can it run in a variety of environments — local area network and stand-alone?)

✔ Ease of use

You can find a lot of information about HR software through directories, websites, and publications:

- ✔ **The Canadian Council of Human Resources Associations (CCHRA)** (www.ccarh.ca)**:** This website contains a full range of information, tools, and resources for human resource professionals in Canada.

- ✔ **Advanced Personnel Systems (**www.hrcensus.com)**:** An online directory of vendor-provided information specializing in providing objective information on most types of HR systems, this website typically monitors 2,500 products from 1,500 vendors.

- ✔ **The International Association for Human Resource Information Management (IHRIM) e-Journal (**www.ihrim.org/resources)**:** Published six times a year and available in a PDF format, this publication includes reviews of timely articles and books aimed at senior executives in HR and IT. Though primarily aimed at extremely large organizations ($1 billion or more in annual revenues), smaller businesses can often apply many useful principles by studying the approaches taken by larger companies.

- ✔ **Society for Human Resource Management (**www.shrm.org)**, WorldatWork (**www.worldatwork.org)**, and hrVillage (**www.hr Village.com)**:** These three websites contain a lot of useful information, such as case studies, tutorials, white papers, and information on vendors.

- ✔ **Workforce Online (**www.workforceonline.com)**:** Although much of the HRIS information on this website is vendor-provided, it is comprehensive and organized attractively into categories that list database compatibility, current clients, and price range. Each listing includes a link to the vendor's website.

Chapter 2

Recruiting the Right People

. . . .

In This Chapter

▶ Looking at the hiring process in a strategic way

▶ Searching for potential candidates

▶ Creating competency models

▶ Writing proper job descriptions and job ads

▶ Having a process for recruiting

▶ Filling a position with a current employee

▶ Using external recruiters

▶ Considering responses you receive and perusing resumes

▶ Getting the most out of phone and in-person interviews

▶ Knowing great interview questions to ask

▶ Making the final decision and checking references

▶ Presenting and negotiating the "offer"

. . . .

Recruiting and hiring good employees is arguably the most critical of all the areas you're responsible for overseeing in your business. And it's not a simple matter of filling job openings. More than ever, successful hiring is a multidimensional process. It is rooted, above all, in your ability to know your business's strategic needs; you may need to change the way you view the hiring process, and take a step back and take a long-term view of your specific business needs so you can find the right combination of resources.

A lot is riding on choosing the right candidate — but don't panic. Most bad hiring decisions are avoidable, assuming that you and others in your business approach the process with respect, understanding, and discipline. This chapter is full of information. It takes you through the steps of recruiting, from drafting the job description to conducting effective interviews and making the final offer of employment.

Thinking about Hiring in a New Way

The traditional hiring notion of "finding the best people to fill job openings" has been replaced by a much more dynamic concept. It's generally referred to as *strategic staffing,* which means putting together a combination of human resources — both internal and external — that are strategically keyed to the needs of the business and the realities of the labor market.

This hiring approach is based on the immediate and long-term needs of the business, as opposed to the specs of a particular job.

Table 2-1 shows the difference between the traditional approach to hiring and the strategic staffing model.

Table 2-1	Paradigms: Old and New
Old Staffing Paradigm	*Strategic Staffing*
Think "job."	Think tasks and responsibilities that are keyed to business goals and enhance a business's ability to compete.
Create a set of job "specs."	Determine which competencies and skills are necessary to produce outstanding performance in any particular function.
Find the person who best "fits" the job.	Determine which combination of resources — internal or external — can get the most mileage out of the tasks and responsibilities that need to be carried out.
Look mainly for technical competence.	Find people who are more than simply "technically" qualified but can carry forward your business's mission and values.
Base the hiring decision primarily on the selection interview.	View the selection interview as only one of a series of tools designed to make the best choice of hiring.
Hire only full-time employees.	Consider a blend of full-time and temporary workers to meet variable workload needs.

True, setting the strategic direction of your business is not normally an HR function, but as a small-business owner, you need to look at your business's overall priorities and determine their staffing implications. Equally important, you need to make sure that any staffing decision clearly supports these business priorities. You're not simply "filling jobs." You're constantly seeking to bring to your business the skills and attributes that it needs to meet any challenge. To do so, you must look beyond the purely functional requirements of the various positions in your business and focus instead on what skills and attributes employees need to perform those functions exceptionally well.

Grasping the big picture

Strategic staffing begins with an effort to reassess your human resources needs in the context of your business priorities. It's a mindset rather than a process. The idea is to begin thinking in terms of need rather than job, long term rather than short term, and big picture rather than immediate opening. This approach ties directly into the changing role of the HR professional from administrator to strategist (refer to Chapter 1 of this book). To succeed, you need to gain a firm understanding of your business's major goals and priorities.

Unless you head an extremely small organization, you can't adopt a strategic staffing approach all by yourself. Make it a priority to introduce the concept to managers in your organization. Get their input to better understand business and departmental priorities. In turn, you can help them through the process and adopting this mindset as well.

Together, you'll need to identify everything that may affect the efficiency and profitability of your business's operations — and not just in the short term, either. To get you started, here are some of the key questions that you and other people in your business should answer before you make your next move:

- ✔ What are your business's long-term strategic goals or those of departments seeking your assistance in hiring employees?

- ✔ What are the key competitive trends in your industry? (In other words, what factors have the greatest bearing on competitive success?)

- ✔ What kind of culture currently exists in your business? And what kind of culture do you ultimately want to create? What are the values you want the business to stand for?

- ✔ What knowledge, skill sets, and attributes (in general) are required to keep pace with those goals and, at the same time, remain true to your business values?

- ✔ How does the current level of knowledge, skill sets, and attributes among your present employees match up with what will be necessary in the future?

- ✔ How reasonable is it for you to expect that with the proper support and training, your current employees will be able to develop the skills they're going to need for your business to keep pace with the competition?

- ✔ What combination of resources (rather than specific people) represents the best strategic approach to the staffing needs you face over the near-term and the long-term?

Strategic staffing is not just about hiring more employees. It involves making the best staffing choices available to address core business needs. If you're thinking of filling an existing position, consider how the business's most critical needs have changed since the last time the job was open, rather than immediately searching for a candidate to fill the vacant position. Is a full-time individual still required in this role? And should a potential replacement have the same skills and experience as the predecessor? Or does the position need to be re-filled at all and the duties handled in other ways?

Analyze the business's daily activities to better understand how current resources are allocated. Identify the frequency and timing of workload peaks and valleys and look for predictable patterns. Consider the impact of shifts in business priorities and what eventual effect these are likely to have on your business. This thought process allows you to spot any shortfalls in human resources for upcoming initiatives.

Reassess goals annually

Change is the name of the game in business. Business priorities will undoubtedly shift over time as you seek ways to keep your business competitive. As a result, you and any managers should consider performing your needs assessments on an annual basis to ensure that you're still on track with the assumptions that are guiding your staffing strategy.

Finding New Employees

You can look for new employees in two general places: inside or outside your organization. Looking inside your business is the easier of the two approaches, simply because it's a finite universe (although if your business is still very small, this option won't work for you). But before you get into the specifics of your hiring strategy, you should have a general idea of what you stand to gain — or lose — when you focus your staffing efforts inside your organization or look outside for new talent.

Inner peace: Filling jobs from within the organization

The rule in successful staffing has always been to do your best to fill new job openings from within before looking for outside candidates. Here are the key reasons:

- ✔ Increased efficiency
- ✔ Increased morale
- ✔ Shorter period of adjustment

New horizons: Looking for staff outside the company

For all its virtues, a staffing strategy that's built almost entirely around promoting from within isn't always the best way to go — especially if your business has never taken the time and effort to develop a well-structured employee development program. Here are the basic arguments for looking outside the business to fill certain positions:

- ✔ A broader selection of talent
- ✔ The "new blood" factor
- ✔ The diversity factor

Diversity doesn't mean that you have to include employees from every possible background, which is impossible. However, a commitment to diversity means that you create a workplace environment supportive of a wide range of perspectives.

Outsourcing: The role of HR

Outsourcing is the practice of turning over an entire function (shipping, payroll, benefits administration, security, computer networking) to an outside specialist. In many cases, the outside firm's employees or consultants work side by side with a company's regular employees. In some cases, a function may be moved to a remote location away from your office — even occasionally out of the country. This latter approach, often referred to as *offshoring,* has grabbed headlines and generated much economic and political debate in recent years.

Of course, outsourcing is hardly a new concept. Small businesses and mom-and-pop businesses have been outsourcing for a long time. What's new is the emergence of outsourcing as an increasingly useful staffing strategy for businesses that have historically used their own personnel.

Businesses usually outsource to save time and money, either because of one of two factors:

✔ **Necessity:** This is the driving factor when a company's business demands outstrip its ability to handle a particular function without investing heavily in new equipment (or a new facility) or bringing in a large number of new employees.

✔ **Choice:** This is the driving factor when businesses want to focus all their internal energies on those operations that contribute directly to their competitive advantage — and outsource those that may only be necessary for a discreet period of time or specific function.

In your HR role, you need to grasp the implications of outsourcing so that you can help provide strategic counsel throughout any hiring process — and contribute to decisions about whether to use this alternative in the first place. After all, any outsourcing effort inherently carries a demand not just for one discreet hire, but for many people — and knowing how to conduct an effective search for skilled contractors or consultants is extremely valuable.

Another reason to be aware of the outsourcing trend is that it affects the HR function itself: Businesses are increasingly outsourcing some of their HR services. But no matter which business process is involved, your ability to apply hiring principles can play a major role in ensuring that any outsourcing effort is implemented as efficiently as possible.

Building Competency Models

Many businesses today are using a process called *competency modelling* to help target the characteristics that distinguish top performers. Businesses can then use this information in the hiring process to seek and evaluate prospective employees.

Competency modelling is a matter of determining, as accurately as you can, what particular mix of skills, attributes, and attitudes produce superior performance in those operational functions that have the most bearing on your business's competitive strength. This strategic recipe becomes the basis not only of your hiring decisions but also of your training and development strategies.

Suppose, for example, that your business sells home security systems. One way that you market your service is to solicit potential customers by phone. The basic job of a telemarketer, of course, is to generate leads by calling people on the phone. Some telemarketers, however, are clearly much better at this task than others. They're better at engaging the interest of the people they call. They don't allow repeated rejections to wear down their spirits. In other words, they possess certain attributes that contribute to superior performance in this job. And these attributes (as opposed to the actual tasks of the job) are the basis of the competency model.

You can apply the concept of competency modelling to virtually any function in your business. The basic objective is always the same: To determine as precisely as you can what combination of skills and attributes are required to excel at that function. You can then identify with greater precision any skill deficits — gaps between the requirements of the job and the qualifications of the candidate. And you can frequently close these gaps through training and coaching.

The following suggestions can help you gain insights on your own:

- ✔ **Interview your own "top" performers.** Sit down with your key people to determine what makes them so successful. Try to answer the following questions:

    - What special skills do these star performers possess that the others don't?

    - What type of personality traits do they share?

    - What common attitudes and values do they bring to their jobs?

- ✔ **Talk to your customers.** One of the best ways to find out who in your business can provide the basis for your competency modelling is to talk to your customers. Find out which employees your customers enjoy dealing with the most, and, more important, what those employees do to win the affection of these customers.

The ABCs of Job Descriptions

After you've determined the qualities that are most important to specific functions and positions in your business (see preceding section), you're ready to use these competency models to create hiring criteria. Your first stop is the job description.

Done correctly, a well thought-out job description delivers the following benefits:

- ✔ Ensures that everyone who has a say in the hiring decision agrees on what the job entails.

- ✔ Serves as the basis for key hiring criteria.

- ✔ Ensures that candidates have a clear idea of what to expect if, indeed, you hire them.

- ✔ Serves as a reference tool during the evaluation process.

- ✔ Serves as a benchmark for performance after you hire the candidate.

The job description needs to communicate as specifically but concisely as possible what responsibilities and tasks the job entails and to indicate the key qualifications of the job — the basic requirements (specific credentials or skills) — and, if possible, the attributes that underlie superior performance.

Following is a quick look at the categories that make up a well-written job description:

- ✔ Title of the position
- ✔ Department (if applicable)
- ✔ Direct report (to whom the person directly reports)
- ✔ Responsibilities
- ✔ Necessary skills
- ✔ Experience required

Sample job description

The following job description is a good model to follow, regardless of what job you're describing. Notice the following:

- ✔ A distinction exists between overall responsibility and specific areas of responsibility.
- ✔ The experience requirement is separated from skills and attributes.
- ✔ The language is easy to understand.

Position title
Senior Mailroom Clerk

Department
Operations

Reports to
Building Services Supervisor

Overall responsibility
Supervise mailroom staff and interface with all levels of management regarding mail and supply deliveries

Key areas of responsibility

- ✔ Maintain established shipping/receiving procedures
- ✔ Sort and distribute all mail on a timely basis
- ✔ Maintain all photocopiers, fax machines, and postage meters
- ✔ Order, store, and distribute supplies
- ✔ Facilitate all off-site storage, inventory, and records-management requests
- ✔ Document current policies and procedures in the COS Department as well as implement new procedures for improvement
- ✔ Oversee the use of a company van when needed
- ✔ Ensure that water and paper is available for customers on a continuous basis

Skills and attributes

- ✔ Strong sense of customer service
- ✔ Good organizational skills
- ✔ Ability to lift a minimum of 25 lbs.

Experience requirement

- ✔ Supervisory experience in a corporate mailroom environment
- ✔ Good driving record

Keeping tasks and qualifications straight

A *task* is what the person or people you hire actually do: take orders over the phone, deliver pizzas, keep your computer network up and running, and so on. *Qualifications* are the skills, attributes, or credentials a person needs to perform each task, such as possess a driver's licence, have an upbeat personality, be familiar with computer networking, and so on.

Do your best to avoid the common pitfall of blurring this distinction. Discipline yourself to clarify the actual tasks and responsibilities before you start to think about what special attributes the person needs to carry out those tasks and fulfill those responsibilities.

Being flexible

Credentials such as degrees and licences are formal acknowledgements that a candidate has passed a particular test or completed a specific field of study. Credentials are absolute necessities in some jobs. (The person who delivers pizza for you, for example, must have a driver's licence.) At the same time, stay flexible. What you prefer in a candidate — such as an advanced degree — may not necessarily be what's required for the position, particularly when you take into account a candidate's various work experiences and accomplishments. This advice is particularly true when hiring for middle and senior-level managers. The thing that you want to make sure of most of all is that the credentials you establish have a direct bearing on a candidate's ability to become a top performer.

Considering soft skills

Don't overlook those broad but telling aspects of a candidate known as *soft skills.* These skills include an aptitude for communicating with people; the ability to work well in teams; and other factors, such as a strong sense of ethics and a talent for efficient and creative problem-solving. Candidates who are weak in these areas may prove unable to grow with your business.

Being specific

You don't need to be William Shakespeare to write a solid job description, but you definitely need to appreciate the nuances of the language. And you want to make sure that the words you choose actually spell out what the job entails. Table 2-2 provides a handful of examples of task descriptions that are far too general, coupled with suggested rewrites.

Table 2-2	Good and Bad Task Descriptions
Too general	*Specific*
Handles administrative chores	Receives, sorts, and files monthly personnel action reports
Good communication skills	Ability to communicate technical information to nontechnical audiences
Computer literate	Proficient with Microsoft Word, Excel, and QuickBooks

Apart from everything else, a job description is generally regarded as a legal document. As such, any references to race, colour, religion, age, sex, national origin or nationality, or physical or mental disability can expose your company to a possible suit.

Setting a salary range

Before you start the recruiting process and look at options for how and where you'll find the ideal candidate for the job you're designing, you should establish a salary range for the position. See Chapter 3 of this book for details of salary and benefits and what constitutes an effective compensation structure.

Determining a job title

Now that so many jobs involve multitasking, job titles are no longer a reliable indicator of the responsibilities of any particular job and, as such, can be tricky to handle. Even so, you need to give some attention to what you're actually calling the job. An inaccurate or overblown job title can create false expectations and lead to resentment, disappointment, or worse.

Resourceful Recruiting

The obvious objective of a recruiting effort is to attract as large a pool of qualified candidates as possible. Two considerations, however, are less obvious but no less important. For one thing, the measure of a successful recruiting effort isn't only numbers; it's also about quality. Keep in mind as well that everything you do as a recruiter is making a statement about your business, and, in the process, shaping your company's reputation.

Clearly, recruiting is probably the most challenging stage of the hiring process. The following list covers some of the general guidelines that you want to bear in mind:

✔ **Make recruitment an ongoing process.** Businesses known for their ability to attract and hire good employees are always recruiting — even if they have no current openings. At the very least, keep an active database of the names and resumes of qualified people you've met, sent you letters, or contacted you online.

✔ **Create a plan.** Always have a general idea before you start any recruiting effort of how you intend to conduct and manage the process: various candidate sources, the deadline for filling the position, how you are going to post or advertise the position, etc.

✔ **Be systematic.** Before you start the search, set up a *protocol* for processing process applications, resumes, and cover letters. If you're using an outside recruiter (see the heading "Using Recruiters " later in this chapter), make sure that someone in your business has a direct line to the individual who's handling the search. If you're seeking candidates through the Internet, have secure and streamlined systems in place. If you intend to use a variety of publications or websites for your classified ads, think about setting up some sort of database of basic information so you don't need to re-educate yourself every time you run a new ad.

✔ **Keep tabs on your progress.** Monitor your recruiting efforts on a daily basis and evaluate your progress on the quality of inquiries.

✔ **Be flexible.** Be prepared to revisit the job description or even explore the possibility of restructuring the job — breaking it into two part-time jobs, perhaps — in an effort to attract more (or better) candidates.

Recruiting from Within Your Business

If your business has enough employees to fill a position from within, the advantages of doing so are well known and well documented. Promoting from within helps keep morale and motivation levels high. And, assuming that your internal search is successful, you don't need to worry about the employee fitting into your culture; that person already knows the territory.

The drawbacks? Only two, really. The most obvious one is that limiting your search to internal candidates limits the candidates to choose from, and you may end up hiring someone who's not up to the challenge of the job. The second drawback is that, whenever you recruit from within, you always run a risk that otherwise important and valuable employees who don't get the job may become resentful and even decide to quit.

Your only real defense is to go out of your way to ensure that everyone understands the scope and basic duties of the job plus the hiring criteria you're using. You also must make sure that everyone gets a fair shot at the opening.

Creating a successful internal hiring process

Following are the key procedures that you need to initiate in setting up a successful internal hiring process:

- ✔ Create a means to post jobs internally
- ✔ Spell out the criteria
- ✔ Establish procedures for applying

Developing an employee skills inventory

If you see yourself hiring internally, setting up an employee skills inventory can be a great help. This inventory is exactly what the name implies: a catalog of the individual skills, attributes, credentials, and areas of knowledge that currently exist. You may assume that this practice is one that is suitable for only big businesses and that the process isn't worth the bother. Even if your company is relatively small it still may be worth the time and effort to develop an employee skills inventory.

The key to developing a practical, user-friendly employee skills inventory lies in how you organize various categories of information. Try to keep the number of fields to a reasonable minimum and make sure that they're job-related. A typical employee skills inventory form may incorporate the following fields, including conventional job history data:

- ✔ Skills/knowledge areas
- ✔ Second-language skills
- ✔ Special preferences
- ✔ Educational background
- ✔ Job history at your business
- ✔ Previous job history
- ✔ Training courses and seminars
- ✔ Skills, aptitude, and other test results
- ✔ Licences, credentials, and affiliations

The preceding list is meant to be a set of recommendations. You can incorporate into your own employee skills inventory anything that you consider relevant.

Writing a Good Job Ad

Whether you plan to post a job ad in the newspaper, on your company website, or on a job board, you're not going to have much luck if it doesn't concisely convey what you're offering potential applicants. Writing a good job ad is a critical step in the hiring process. You're trying to attract the right candidates!

Keep in mind the following two considerations in writing a job ad:

✔ The goal of a job ad is not only to generate responses from qualified applicants, but also to prevent candidates who are clearly unqualified from applying for the position.

✔ You're advertising your company. Every aspect of your ad must seek to foster a favourable impression of the organization.

Your next step is to actually compose the ad. If you've done a good job of writing the job description (see the earlier section "The ABCs of Job Descriptions" for more about developing a quality job description), then you've already accomplished this task. In fact, think of the ad as a synopsis of the existing job description.

As for the ad itself, the following list describes the elements you need to think about as you compose the ad:

✔ **Headline:** The headline almost always is the job title.

✔ **Job information:** A line or two about the general duties and responsibilities of the job.

✔ **Company information:** Always include a few words on what your company does.

✔ **Qualifications and hiring criteria:** Specify the level of education and experience and relevant attributes and skills required to do the job.

✔ **Response method:** Let applicants know the best way to get in touch with you: e-mail, regular mail, phone, or in person.

Using the Internet as a Recruitment Tool

The Internet has revolutionized the recruiting process. It has created countless new opportunities for employers and job seekers alike. Specialized and general job sites abound, and today even the smallest of businesses has a website describing what the business does and, often, the advantages of working for the business.

Seeking great employee

This is an ad that takes into consideration the criteria of a good job ad.

ADMINISTRATIVE ASSISTANT, LAW OFFICE

Busy, growing law office specializing in entertainment and intellectual property seeks well-organized individual to support staff of five lawyers and two paralegals. Responsibilities include processing correspondence, maintaining schedules and client files, and updating publications. College diploma preferred. Must be bilingual and familiar with Microsoft Office. Competitive salary and benefits. AAjob@lawfirm.com or Bing, Bong, and Bang, P.O. Box 999, Overbrook, ON K1K M3P.

No doubt, you're already familiar with many of the benefits of the Internet as a recruiting tool: access to a much larger potential candidate base and a relatively low-cost way to manage the process of hiring and continually attracting future employees.

Receiving (too?) many responses

One of the Web's huge appeals is its ability to help you locate qualified candidates at extremely low costs. More candidates for less money? Sounds like a hiring manager's dream. But hang on. It can also become a nightmare if not managed properly. For starters, the Internet has the potential of dramatically increasing the number of responses to your job ads. Many HR managers report they have great difficulty even keeping track of submissions. Even small businesses can receive hundreds of resumes from a single ad, depending on the position and job market. Some HR professionals, or their staff members, still manually read through or at least scan each resume.

Using your website to attract candidates

The Internet has greatly facilitated applicants' research. Your website is a great place to communicate your unique culture and most appealing characteristics. Well executed, your site can give job seekers a glimpse into the employee experience — what it's like to work in your company.

In addition, the proliferation of social media such as Facebook and LinkedIn allow candidates to research and share information and perspectives on your company.

With information now so much more accessible then ever, you want to make sure that your company's website accurately showcases your firm's strengths and range of capabilities. Don't be surprised at how well prepared candidates are today when you get to the interview process. You'll also need to be prepared and raise your expectations for the discussion. The topics you cover can relate more specifically to business priorities and issues affecting your industry.

Establish a system to keep track of your recruiting success from various websites and publications. How many candidates did each source produce? How qualified and skilled was each applicant? These metrics can help you determine the return on your investment in a variety of recruiting channels.

Using Recruiters

Recruiters can be an invaluable part of your search arsenal. And if you know how to maximize their services, recruiters can more than pay for themselves. Using outside recruiters has several key advantages — namely, the following:

- ✔ Outside recruiters generally have access to a large pool of applicants — after all, continually locating quality candidates is their job.

- ✔ They handle such cumbersome administrative details of recruiting as placing ads, skills evaluation, and preliminary interviews.

 In the course of their evaluation process, staffing firms typically check selected references from their candidates' past employers to gather skill proficiency information and job performance history, but employers should perform their own reference checks as well.

- ✔ They're often a valuable source of staffing advice.

Looking at the types of recruiters

If you're not sure what makes a *headhunter* different from a *recruiter* and an *employment agency* different from a *search firm,* you're not alone. The difference between the various specialists in this large and growing industry is primarily how they charge and on which segment of the labour market they focus.

The following list offers you a rundown on how these players differ on the recruiting field:

✔ **Employment agencies, staffing firms, and contingency search firms:** These are companies you engage to find job candidates for specific positions. What they all have in common is that you pay them a fee — but only after they find you someone you eventually hire. These firms recruit candidates in virtually every industry, and businesses call on them to fill positions at all levels of the corporate ladder. They typically charge you a percentage of the new employee's first year's salary. It can range from 15 percent to 30 percent, depending on the level of the position you're filling and the skills required.

The trend toward specialization is good news for you because firms that specialize have a strong sense of the marketplace in a given field. Among other things, they make sure that the package you're offering is competitive. Many of the larger staffing firms offer an expanded variety of services, including preliminary reference checks, as well as refunds or replacement guarantees if the new employee doesn't work out.

✔ **Executive search firms, or headhunters:** These types of recruiters focus on higher-level executives, up to and including CEOs. Unlike employment agencies, most executive search firms charge a retainer whether they produce results or not. You can also expect to pay, in addition to expenses, a commission of 25 percent — or even a third — of the executive's annual salary if the firm's successful in its search. The main value comes into play if you're seeking someone for a high-level job that's most likely to be filled by an executive who's already working for another company.

Knowing when to use a recruiter

Most businesses that rely on outside recruiters to fill positions do so for one of two reasons:

✔ They don't have the time or the expertise to recruit effectively on their own.

✔ The recruiting efforts they've put forward to date have yet to yield results.

Finding the "right" recruiter

You choose a recruiter the same way that you choose any professional services specialist: You look at what services are available. You ask colleagues for recommendations. You talk to different recruiters. The following list provides some reminders that can help you make a wise choice:

✔ Check out recruiters personally.

✔ Be explicit about your needs.

> ✔ Clarify fee arrangements in writing.
>
> ✔ Ask about replacement guarantees.
>
> ✔ Express your concerns openly. If you aren't happy about any aspect of the arrangement you've struck with a recruiter, speak up. Tell the recruiter exactly what your concerns are. If you don't feel comfortable expressing your concerns with the recruiter you've chosen, you're probably dealing with the wrong company.

Recruiting on campus

If you're recruiting for an entry-level position, college or university campuses can be a good place to look. Smaller firms without well-organized college/ university recruiting programs have always been at something of a disadvantage. If you're one of the "smaller guys," get to know the folks in the placement office, because campus recruiting is usually coordinated by the college/ university placement office. The best way to build a strong relationship with placement office personnel is to pay them a personal visit — or better still, invite them to your company to see what you have to offer.

Other recruiting sources

Aside from some of the traditional recruiting options discussed earlier in this chapter, the following resources may help you in your search for qualified candidates:

> ✔ Employee referrals
>
> ✔ Job fairs
>
> ✔ Open houses:
>
> ✔ Professional associations and unions
>
> ✔ Non-profit employment services

Assessing Potential Employees

Just about everybody agrees that the job interview is the most important element of the hiring process. But what many otherwise savvy business people often forget is that one of the keys to effective interviewing is effectively evaluating candidates. You don't want to inadvertently weed out candidates who clearly deserve a second look. Just as bad, your process may fail to accomplish its fundamental purpose: making sure that you're not wasting your time and effort on candidates who are clearly unqualified for the position you're seeking to fill.

Evaluating candidates systematically

No set rules exist for evaluating job applicants — other than common sense. Having some kind of evaluation system or protocol in place is important — before resumes begin to arrive.

Keep in mind the following three key questions at all times:

- ✔ What are the prerequisites for the position?
- ✔ What are the special requirements for your business, such as certifications or special education?
- ✔ What qualifications and attributes are critical to performing well in this particular position?

If you haven't answered these three questions, you're not ready to start evaluating potential employees.

Establishing an evaluation process

Here's an overview of the evaluation process:

1. **Scan applications or resumes first for basic qualifications.**

2. **Look for key criteria.**

   Begin the evaluation process by setting a high standard (for example, the resume must meet a certain high percentage of the criteria), but if your reject pile is growing and you haven't "cleared" anyone, you may need to lower the bar somewhat.

3. **Flag and identify your top candidates.**

4. **Contact top candidates for a phone or in-person interview.**

Reading Resumes Effectively

Based on resumes alone, you'd think that all your candidates are such outstanding prospects that you could hire them sight unseen. And no wonder. People write their resumes to put themselves in the best light possible. And those who don't know how to write a great resume can hire people who do know.

Why, then, take resumes seriously? Because resumes, regardless of how "professional" they are, can still reveal a wealth of information about the candidate — after you crack the code.

Mastering the basics

Here's what you probably know already: Basically, job candidates submit only two types of resumes:

- ✔ **Chronological,** where all the work-related information appears in a timeline sequence.
- ✔ **Functional,** where the information appears in various categories (skills, achievements, qualifications, and so on).

In the past, the general rule was that candidates trying to hide something, such as gaps in their work history, wrote functional resumes. But because a well-rounded background (in conjunction with one's specialty area) can prove an asset in today's job market, the functional resume is now more acceptable. The key point is to be open to either type of resume.

Some applicants use a combination of the two formats, presenting a capsule of what they believe are their most important qualifications and accomplishments, together with a chronological work history. If a resume is short on work history, look for skills that may be transferable to your position. Identifying these skills will be much easier if you've weighted the application questions to tie certain types of experience or skills with success in the job.

Before diving into that pile of resumes, consider the following observations:

- ✔ No sane job applicant is going to put derogatory or detracting information on a resume.
- ✔ Many resumes are professionally prepared, designed to create a winning, but not necessarily accurate, impression.
- ✔ Reviewing resumes is tedious, no matter what. You may need to sift through the stack several times.
- ✔ If you don't review resumes yourself or delegate it to the wrong person, you're likely to miss that diamond-in-the-rough, that ideal employee who unfortunately has poor resume-drafting skills.

Reading between the lines

Now that more and more people are using outside specialists or software packages to prepare their resumes, getting an accurate reading of a candidate's strengths simply by reading a resume is more difficult than ever. Even so, here are some of the resume characteristics that generally (although not always) describe a candidate worth interviewing:

✔ **Lots of details:** Though applicants are generally advised to avoid wordiness, the more detailed they are in their descriptions of what they did and accomplished in previous jobs, the more reliable (as a rule) the information is.

✔ **A history of stability and advancement:** The applicant's work history should show a steady progression into greater responsibility and more important positions. Be wary of candidates who have bounced from one company to the next, but do be open to the possibility that these candidates had good reasons for the career moves.

✔ **A strong, well-written cover letter:** Assuming that the candidate wrote the letter, the cover letter is generally a good indication of the candidate's overall communication skills.

Watching out for red flags

Resume writing is a good example of the Law of Unintended Consequences. Sometimes what's not in a resume or what's done through carelessness or mistake can reveal quite a bit about a candidate. Following are some things to watch out for:

✔ Sloppy overall appearance

✔ Unexplained chronological gaps

✔ Static career pattern

✔ Typos and misspellings

✔ Vaguely worded job descriptions

✔ Potentially misleading wording

✔ Job hopping

✔ Overemphasis on hobbies or interests outside of work

Performing Short Phone Interviews

After sorting through resumes and selecting the most promising candidates, conducting a telephone interview can help you narrow down the list of individuals to interview in person. Before calling a candidate, review the resume and cover letter carefully, noting questions to ask. You'll likely see a pattern emerge among the applicants who are a good fit for your business. Here are a few good questions to ask:

✔ "Tell me a little about yourself and your work history."

✔ "What interests you about this job?"

✔ "What skills can you bring to the job?"

✔ "What sort of work environment brings out your best performance?"

Estimate how long you'll need to effectively conduct a telephone interview with job applicants, say 15 to 30 minutes.

Interviewing Effectively Face to Face

Conducting a job interview seems easier than it is. As a result, many people take interviewing for granted. They don't invest the time, effort, and concentration that effective job interviewing requires. And, above all, they don't prepare enough for interviews, so often little correlation exists between the "positive reports" that emerge from the typical job interview and the job performance of the candidates who receive those glowing reports. This correlation goes up dramatically whenever interviewing becomes a structured, well-planned process — one that's well integrated into a business's overall staffing practices.

The upcoming sections take a look at interviewing, with a focus on the things you need to know and do to get the most out of the interviewing process.

Knowing the goals

Job interviews enable you to perform the following four tasks that, combined with other steps you take, are essential to making a sound hiring decision:

✔ Obtain firsthand information about the candidate's background, work experience, and skill level that clarifies what you need to confirm from the resume or previous interviews.

✔ Get a general sense of the candidate's overall intelligence, aptitude, enthusiasm, and attitudes, with particular respect to how those attributes match up to the requirements of the job.

✔ Gain insight — to the extent possible — into the candidate's basic personality traits and motivation to tackle the responsibilities of the job and become a part of the business.

✔ Estimate the candidate's ability to adapt to your business's work environment.

Setting the stage

Your ability to get the most out of the interviews you conduct depends on how well prepared you are. Here's a checklist to follow before you pop the first interview question:

✔ Thoroughly familiarize yourself with the job description, especially its hiring criteria.

✔ Review everything the candidate has submitted to date.

✔ Set up a general structure for the interview.

✔ Write down the questions you intend to ask.

✔ Make arrangements to hold the interview in a room that's private and reasonably comfortable.

Try not to schedule job interviews in the middle of the day. The reason: You're not likely to be as relaxed and as focused as you need to be, and you may have a tough time fighting off interruptions and distractions. The ideal time to interview candidates is early morning, before the workday starts. You're fresher then, and so is the candidate. If you have no choice, give yourself a buffer of at least half an hour before the interview so that you can switch gears and prepare for the interview in the right manner.

Meeting the candidate

Your priority in meeting a candidate face-to-face for the first time is to put the candidate at ease. Disregard any advice anyone has given you about doing things to create stress just to see how the individual responds. Those techniques are rarely productive, and they put both you and your business in a bad light. Instead, view the first minutes of the meeting as an opportunity to build a rapport with the candidate. The more comfortable the candidate is, the more engaging the interview will be, and the more you'll learn about your potential employee.

If you're seated at your desk as the candidate walks in, a common courtesy is to stand and meet the individual halfway, shake hands, and let the candidate know that you're happy to be meeting. (Basic stuff, but easy to forget.) You don't need to cut to the chase right away with penetrating questions. Skilled job interviewers usually begin with small talk — a general comment about the weather, transportation difficulties, and so on — but they keep it to a minimum.

Multiple and panel interviews

It's not unusual for more than one employee to interview a candidate to provide a variety of opinions, especially if the candidate will play a key role in the organization. In fact, sometimes these meetings are carried out simultaneously through an interviewing panel made up of the hiring manager plus other members of the management team or work group, usually no more than three to five people.

Panel interviews are beneficial when you want to quickly get a promising hire through multiple interviews in a timely manner. It's best for the hiring manager to conduct one-on-one interviews with applicants first, however, choosing only a few finalists for panel interviews. This saves panelists' time and ensures that the hiring manager is presenting only those candidates that may ultimately be hired. Panel interviews are most successful when the hiring manager distributes job criteria to the interview team in advance along with specific questions. This ensures panel members will be able to compare candidates in a consistent way using the same criteria.

Minding the Q&As

The Q&A is the main part of the interview. How you phrase questions, when you ask them, how you follow up — each of these aspects can go a long way toward affecting the quality and usability of the answers you get. The following sections describe the key practices that differentiate people who've mastered the art of questioning from those who haven't.

- ✔ **Have a focus:** Even before you start to ask questions, you want to have a reasonably specific idea of what information or insights you're expecting to gain from the interview based on your research and the hiring criteria in the job description. Whatever the need, decide ahead of time what you want to know more about and build your interview strategy around that goal.

- ✔ **Make every question count:** Every question you ask during a job interview must have a specific purpose. The general rule: If the question has no strategic significance, think twice before asking it. Again, tie questions to the job criteria defined in the job description.

- ✔ **Pay attention:** In a job interview situation, you find yourself drawing conclusions before the candidate has finished answering a question, or begin rehearsing in your mind the next question while the candidate is still talking. Fight those tendencies. Write down your questions and then concentrate completely on the candidate.

✔ **Don't hesitate to probe:** Nothing's wrong with asking additional questions to draw out more specific answers. Too many interviewers let candidates "off the hook" in the interest of being "nice." That practice, however, can prove counterproductive — the candidate may give you valuable background on specific abilities if your questions are more penetrating.

✔ **Give candidates ample time to respond:** Give the candidate time to come up with a thoughtful answer. If the silence persists for more than, say, ten seconds, ask if the candidate would like you to clarify the question. Otherwise, don't rush things. Use the silence to observe the candidate and to take stock of where you are in the interview.

Tread carefully whenever you come across a candidate who seems flat and disinterested during the job interview. If a candidate can't demonstrate any real enthusiasm during the interview, don't expect any enthusiasm on the job.

✔ **Suspend judgments:** Try to keep your attention on the answers you're getting instead of making interpretations or judgments. You're going to have plenty of time after the interview to evaluate what you see and hear.

✔ **Take notes:** Memory can be tricky, leading people to ignore what actually happened during an interview and to rely instead on general impressions. Taking notes helps you avoid this common pitfall. Make sure that you give yourself a few moments after the interview to review your notes and put them into some kind of order.

Varying the style of questions

You can usually divide interview questions into four categories, based on the kinds of answers you're trying to elicit.

Closed-ended

Definition: Questions that call for a simple, informational answer — usually a yes or no.

Examples: "How many years did you work for the circus?" "Did you enjoy it?" "What cities did you tour?"

When to use them: Closed-ended questions work best if you're trying to elicit specific information or set the stage for more complex questions.

Pitfall to avoid: Asking too many of them in rapid-fire succession without tying them back to the job criteria makes candidates feel as though they're being interrogated.

Open-ended

Definition: Questions that require thought and oblige the candidate to reveal attitudes or opinions.

Examples: "Describe for me how you handle stress on the job." "Can you give me an illustration of how you improved productivity at your last job?"

When to use them: Most of the time, but interspersed with closed-ended questions. Because this approach requires candidates to describe how they've handled real tasks and problems, it can be very useful and revealing.

Pitfalls to avoid: Not being specific enough as you phrase the question and not interceding if the candidate's answer starts to veer off track.

Hypothetical

Definition: Questions that invite the candidate to resolve an imaginary situation or react to a given situation.

Examples: "If you were the purchasing manager, would you institute an automated purchase-order system?" "If you were to take over this department, what's the first thing you'd do to improve productivity?"

When to use them: Useful if framed in the context of actual job situations.

Pitfall to avoid: Putting too much stock in the candidate's hypothetical answer. (You're usually better off asking questions that force a candidate to use an actual experience as the basis for an answer.)

Leading

Definition: Questions asked in such a way that the answer you're looking for is obvious.

Examples: "You rarely fought with your last boss, right?" "You know a lot about team-building, don't you?" "You wouldn't dream of falsifying your expense accounts, would you?"

When to use them: Rarely, if ever.

Knowing what you can't ask

Employers must respect the dignity of their employees and must make sure that their actions and workplaces are free of harmful discrimination.

Human rights laws across Canada prohibit employers from discriminating against individuals in hiring, firing, or the terms and conditions of employment because of certain personal characteristics (unless it is for a valid job requirement). With some exceptions, workers in Canada are protected from discrimination based on the following factors:

- ✔ National or ethnic origin, race, ancestry, place of origin, colour

- ✔ Disability (physical and/or mental)

- ✔ Religion, creed, political belief, association

- ✔ Sex, sexual orientation, pregnancy

- ✔ Age (with exceptions for minors and seniors in some cases)

- ✔ Marital or family status

Become familiar with the rules and regulations in your province and avoid interview questions related to the above factors. If you ask any of these questions in an interview and do not hire the candidate, you are presumed to have discriminated against the candidate. This can lead to any number of unwanted outcomes such as having to offer the candidate a job, compensating the candidate, or being subject to a discrimination suit.

Fifteen Solid Questions to Ask and How to Interpret the Answers

What makes an interview question "good"? The answer, simply, is that a "good question" does two things:

- ✔ It gives you the specific information you need to make a sound hiring decision.

- ✔ It helps you gain insight into how the candidate's mind and emotions work.

Avoid timeworn, cliché questions, such as "What are your strengths and weaknesses?" or "Where do you see yourself in the next five years?" or "If you were an animal, which one would it be?" Instead develop a list of questions designed to elicit responses that will be most helpful in evaluating a candidate's suitability for the position and your business. You can ask hundreds of such questions, but following are 15 to get you started, along with ideas on what to look for in the answers:

✔ **Can you tell me a little about yourself?** Most interview strategy books describe this one as the "killer question." You can bet the farm that a well-prepared candidate has a well-rehearsed answer. A confident applicant can give a brief summary of strengths, significant achievements, and career goals. Your main job? To make sure that the answers are consistent with the applicant's resume.

✔ **What interests you about this job, and what skills and strengths can you bring to it?** Nothing tricky here, but it's a solid question all the same. Note that the question is not "What are your skills and strengths?" but "What skills and strengths can you bring to the job?" The answer is yet another way to gauge how much interest the applicant has in the job and how well prepared the person is for the interview. Stronger candidates should be able to correlate their skills with specific job requirements.

✔ **Can you tell me a little about your current job?** Strong candidates should be able to give you a short and precise summary of duties and responsibilities. How they answer this question can help you determine their passion and enthusiasm for their work and their sense of personal accountability. Be wary of applicants who bad-mouth or blame their employers.

✔ **In a way that anyone could understand, can you describe a professional success you are proud of?** This question is especially good when you're interviewing someone for a technical position, such as a systems analyst or tax accountant. The answer shows the applicant's ability to explain what they do so that anyone can understand it.

✔ **How have you changed the nature of your current job?** A convincing answer here shows adaptability and a willingness to "take the bull by the horns," if necessary. An individual who chose to do a job differently from other people also shows creativity and resourcefulness.

✔ **What was the most difficult decision you ever had to make on the job?** Notice the intentionally vague aspect of this question. It's not hypothetical. It's real. What you're looking for is the person's decision-making style and how it fits into your company culture. Someone who admits that firing a subordinate was difficult demonstrates compassion, and those who successfully decided to approach a co-worker over a conflict may turn out to be great team players. Individuals who admit a mistake they've made exhibit honesty and open-mindedness.

✔ **Why did you decide to pursue a new job?** This question is just a different way of asking, "What are you looking for in a job?" Some candidates come so well rehearsed they are never at a loss for an answer. Sometimes by phrasing the question in a different way, you can cause them to go "off script."

✔ **I see that you've been unemployed for the past few months. Why did you leave your last job, and what have you been doing since then?** This question is important, but don't let it seem accusatory. Generally speaking, people don't leave jobs voluntarily without another one waiting in the wings, but it happens. Try to get specific, factual answers that you can verify later. Candidates with a spotty employment history, at the very least, ought to be able to account for all extended periods of unemployment and to demonstrate whether they used that time productively — getting an advanced degree, for example.

✔ **Who was your best boss ever and why? Who was the worst, and looking back, what could you have done to make that relationship better?** These two are more penetrating questions than you may think. Among other things, the answers give you insight into how the candidate views and responds to supervision. A reflective, responsive answer to the second part of the question may indicate a loyal employee capable of rising above an unpleasant supervisory situation and/or learning from past mistakes, both highly desirable qualities. A bitter, critical answer may indicate someone who holds grudges or simply can't get along with certain personality types.

✔ **Which do you enjoy the most: working alone with information or working with other people?** The ideal answer here is "both." People who say they like working with information are obviously a good choice for technical positions, but it may be a red flag if they don't also mention that they like communicating and collaborating with others, which is increasingly a function of even technical jobs. An excellent candidate might say the different perspectives within a group produce more innovative ideas than one person working alone can, but without information, a team can't get very far.

✔ **What sort of things do you think your current (past) company could do to be more successful?** This one is a great "big picture" question. You're probing to find out whether the candidate has a clear understanding of a current or past employer's missions and goals and whether the candidate thinks in terms of those goals.

✔ **Can you describe a typical day at work in your last job?** Strong candidates can give you specific details that you can later verify, but the main point of this question is to see how the applicant's current (or most recent) routine compares with the requirements of the job in question. How interviewees describe their duties can prove highly revealing.

✔ **What sort of work environment do you prefer? What brings out your best performance?** Probe for specifics. You want to find out whether this person is going to fit in at your business. If your corporate culture is collegial and team-centred, you don't want someone who answers, "I like to be left alone to do my work." You may also uncover unrealistic expectations or potential future clashes. People rarely, if ever, work at their best in all situations. Candidates who say otherwise aren't being honest with themselves or with you.

✔ **How do you handle conflict? Can you give me an example of how you handled a workplace conflict in the past?** You want candidates who try to be reasonable but nonetheless stand up for what's right. While some people may be naturally easygoing, candidates who say that they never get into conflict situations are either dishonest or delusional.

✔ **How would you respond if you were put in a situation you felt presented a conflict of interest or was unethical? Have you ever had this experience in previous positions?** How individuals approach this question and anecdotes they relay can offer valuable insights as to how they may respond if faced with such a situation.

In addition to an opportunity to showcase their qualifications, savvy candidates also use the interview to find out as much as they can about the position and company, so don't be surprised if they come prepared with questions of their own. Don't interpret questions as disruptive to your agenda: They're a show of interest and professionalism. In fact, you can address many of their concerns by proactively "selling" your company during the interview. Just as candidates try to show how their skills are a match with the position, you can also point out programs and policies that fit the needs of promising applicants and promote your firm as a great place to work.

Ending the Interview on the Right Note

With only a few minutes to go, you can bring the session to a graceful close by following these steps:

1. **Offer the candidate a broad-brushstroke summary of the interview.**

2. **Let the candidate ask questions.**

3. **Let the candidate know what comes next.**

4. **End the interview on a formal, but sincere note.**

As soon as possible after the candidate's departure, take a couple of moments to collect your thoughts and write your impressions and a summary of your notes. You don't need to make any definitive decisions at this point, but recording your impressions while they're still fresh in your mind will help you immeasurably if the final choice boils down to several candidates with comparable qualifications.

Making the Final Hiring Decision

The moment of truth in the hiring process is choosing who will get the job. Because hiring mistakes can be costly, a lot is riding on your ability to select the best people for your available positions.

Coming to grips with the decision-making process

Stripped to its essentials, the decision-making process in the final stages of hiring is no different than buying a car or deciding on your vacation destination. You look at your options, weigh the pros and cons of each, and then you make a choice.

You can never be absolutely certain that the decision you make is right. You can improve your chances significantly, however, if you manage the decision-making process in a reasonably disciplined, intelligent way, which means that you consistently focus on the key hiring criteria you established at the outset of the process (refer to the earlier parts of this chapter) and perform the following tasks:

✔ You do a thorough job early on in the hiring process of identifying your needs and drawing up a job description that pinpoints the combination of skills, attributes, and credentials that a particular position requires.

✔ You gather enough information about each candidate — through interviewing, testing, and observation — so that you have a reasonably good idea of the candidates' capabilities, personalities, strengths, and weaknesses.

✔ You remain objective in evaluating candidates. Your personal biases don't steer your focus away from your hiring criteria.

✔ You develop methods to evaluate your strategies, such as using a particular recruiter or running a classified ad, so that, the next time around, you can repeat practices that produce good results and modify those that lead to hiring mistakes.

The simplest method is to think back on the process that led to the hiring of your top employees, and compare that process with how you handled things with candidates who were eventually let go.

✔ You "sell" the candidates on the job, and they're enthusiastic about the position.

Using the "tools" of the trade

Your available resources in making hiring decisions are usually fairly limited, so you need to use them well. The following list takes a brief look at those tools and what you need to keep in mind as you're tapping each one:

✔ **Past experience:** A long-time truism in successful hiring is the concept that the best indicator of a candidate's future performance is past performance.

The only caveat to this usually reliable principle: The conditions that prevailed in the candidate's last job need to closely parallel the conditions in the job the candidate's seeking. Otherwise, you have no real basis for comparison. No two business environments are identical.

✔ **Interview impressions:** Impressions you pick up during an interview almost always carry a great deal of weight in hiring decisions.

✔ **Test results:** Some people regard test results as the only truly reliable predictor of future success. The argument goes as follows: Test results are quantifiable. In most tests, results aren't subject to personal interpretation. With a large enough sample, you can compare test scores to job-performance ratings and, eventually, use test scores as a predictor of future performance.

✔ **Firsthand observation:** Call it the proof-in-the-pudding principle. Watching candidates actually perform some of the tasks for which you're considering hiring them is clearly the most reliable way to judge their competence.

Using a system to make your selection

Decision-makers in businesses with good track records of making successful hires use their intuition, but they don't use intuition as the sole basis for their judgments. The following list describes what such decision-makers rely on:

✔ **They have in place some sort of *system*** — a well-thought-out protocol for assessing the strengths and weaknesses of candidates and applying those assessments to the hiring criteria.

✔ **The system that they use, regardless of how simple or elaborate, is weighted** — that is, it presupposes that certain skills and attributes bear more on job performance than do others and takes those differences into account.

✔ **They constantly monitor and evaluate the effectiveness of the system** — always with an eye toward sharpening their own ability and the ability of others to link any data they obtain during the recruiting and interviewing process to the on-the-job performance of new hires. If a particular type of testing mechanism is used in the selection process, the validity of the test (how closely the test results correlate with successful on-the-job performance) is monitored regularly.

Decision-making tips

Your success as a hiring manager depends largely on your ability to make sound strategic decisions. Here are some additional tips:

✔ Gather all the facts.

✔ Brainstorm options.

✔ Ask the right questions.

✔ Take action.

✔ Evaluate your decisions.

Setting up your own scale

These are the fundamental steps you must go through for selecting your next hire:

1. **Isolate key hiring criteria.**

   By this point in the hiring process, you should know what combination of skills and attributes a candidate needs to perform the job well and fit your business's pace and culture.

2. **Set priorities.**

   You can safely assume that some of your hiring criteria are more important than others. To take these differences into account, set up a scale that reflects the relative importance of any particular skill or attribute.

3. **Evaluate candidates on the basis of the weighted scale you established in Step 2.**

   Instead of simply looking at the candidate as a whole, you look at each of the criteria you set down, and you rate the candidate on the basis of how the person measures up in that particular category.

Say, for example, that one candidate's strength is the ability to work as part of a team. The candidate's rating on that particular attribute may be a 5, but the relative importance of teamwork to the task at hand may be anywhere from 1 to 5, which means that the overall ranking may end up as low as 5 (5 times 1) or as high as 25 (5 times 5).

All in all, a weighted system gives you an opportunity to see how well candidates measure up against one another and how closely their skills and attributes match the job requirements. You must be careful, however. The effectiveness of this system depends on two crucial factors: the validity of your hiring criteria and the objectivity of the judgments that underlie any ratings you assign to each candidate.

Factoring in the intangibles

The really tough part of any evaluation procedure is attaching numerical ratings to the *intangibles* — those attributes that you can measure only through your observations. The following sections cover those intangible factors that you commonly find in the criteria for most jobs, along with suggestions on how to tell whether the candidate measures up.

Industriousness and motivation

Definition: Candidates' work ethic — how hard they're willing to work and how important they feel it is to perform to the best of their ability.

When important: All the time.

How to measure: Verifiable accomplishments in their last jobs. Evaluation of past employers and co-workers. Track records of successful jobs that go back to college/university or even earlier.

Intelligence

Definition: Mental alertness, thinking ability, capability to process abstract information.

When important: Any job that requires the ability to make decisions (and not just follow instructions).

How to measure: Evidence of good decision-making ability in previous jobs. Also through testing. (Make sure, however, that the tests aren't in any way discriminatory.)

Temperament and ability to cope with stress

Definition: General demeanour — whether the candidate is calm and level-headed or hyper or hot-headed.

When important: In any job where the stress level is high or in any work environment where people must interact and rely on one another.

How to measure: Personality testing can sometimes prove reliable, but the best way to measure these criteria is to ask during the interview about stress levels in candidates' previous jobs and how they feel they performed.

Creativity and resourcefulness

Definition: The ability to think *outside the box* — to come up with innovative solutions to problems.

When important: In jobs that require imagination or problem-solving skills that don't rely on set procedures.

How to measure: Examples of previous work (graphic-design work, writing samples, and so on). Specific examples of situations in which the candidate had come up with an innovative solution to a problem. Previous accomplishments or awards. Outside interests.

Teamwork abilities

Definition: The ability to work harmoniously with others and share responsibility for achieving the same goal.

When important: Any task with a strong need for employees to work closely and collaboratively.

How to measure: Previous work experience. (Did candidates work on their own or with groups?) Team successes mentioned during the interview. Evidence of ability to work within project team rules, protocols, and work practices. Support for co-workers. Willingness to ask for help.

Hiring right

Bad hiring decisions rarely happen by accident. In retrospect, you can usually discover that you didn't do something you should have. The following list covers the key principles to follow in order to hire the right person:

- ✔ Anchor yourself to the hiring criteria.
- ✔ Take your time.
- ✔ Cross-verify whenever possible.
- ✔ Get help, but avoid the "too many cooks" syndrome.
- ✔ Don't put a "good" employee in the "wrong" job.
- ✔ Avoid the "top-of-mind" syndrome, choosing the last interviewed candidate.

Checking References

References and other third-party observations are useful and necessary components of the hiring process. Selected references from past employers help you separate those with good employment records from others who have a less positive job performance history. Not taking these steps can increase your risk of making a hiring mistake and putting your business at a disadvantage. If you succeed in matching up the candidate and the credentials presented to you, however, you may have found a new productive and valuable member of your team. Conduct reference checks or other checks yourself if you'll be the one working with the employee.

Discovering the truth behind background checks

Many businesses, increasingly aware of the pitfalls of failing to adequately evaluate applicants before bringing them on board, are conducting background checks on candidates. *Background checks* take reference checks a step further, and businesses use them because they feel they're a way to gain more assurance that the people they hire are what they seem to be. In other words, where reference checks allow you to verify with former employers a potential hire's accomplishments and personal attributes (see preceding section), background checks attempt to delve into additional aspects of a candidate's activities and behavior.

Checking out kinds of background checks

Background checks can take many forms, depending on the position and what the employer considers most important in evaluating job candidates. The principal measures in use today include the following:

- ✔ Criminal background checks
- ✔ Education records/academic degree verification
- ✔ Certifications and licences (such as CPA)
- ✔ Credit checks
- ✔ Driving histories
- ✔ Medical exams
- ✔ Drug tests
- ✔ Workers' compensation reports

Making Offers They Can't Refuse

After you make your final choice, you may think that you and the other decision-makers can just sit back and relax. Not just yet. You still must make the offer official, and if you don't proceed carefully, one of two things can happen: You can lose the candidate, or, even if the candidate comes aboard, you can start the relationship off on a bumpy note. The following sections tell you what to bear in mind.

Avoiding delays

After you make up your mind about a candidate, make the offer immediately, especially if you're in a tight labour market. Remember, even a day or two delay can cost you the employee of choice.

Putting your offer on the table

Give the person you want to hire all the details about salary, benefits, and anything extra. Most businesses make job offers verbally by phone and then follow up with an official letter.

Never back down on anything you promise at any stage in the recruiting or hiring process. ("You misunderstood. I didn't say, 'We're giving you a car,' I asked whether you 'had' a car.") That's a sure way to scare off an employee, and it may land you in legal trouble as well.

You should establish a salary range for the position before you begin recruiting. In addition, make sure that you have a standard job offer letter as a template that you can customize and that you clear the template with legal counsel.

Also, remind the individual of the benefits of joining your business. Augment the discussion about the financial aspects of the offer by highlighting positives, such as a supportive work environment and the chance to work on a variety of assignments.

Setting a deadline

Give candidates a reasonable amount of time to decide whether to accept the offer. What's "reasonable" generally depends on the type of job. The time frame for an entry-level job may be a few days, but for a middle- or senior-level candidate in a competitive market or for a position that involves relocation, a week isn't excessive.

Staying connected

While a candidate is considering an offer, you, the hiring manager, or people from the interview panel should stay in touch with the candidate. The purpose is for you to reinforce your excitement about the candidate potentially joining your team. This could involve keeping in touch by phone or email, or even asking the candidate to have lunch with you or visit the office during work hours.

Negotiating salary

After receiving a candidate's response to your offer, you must be prepared to negotiate. Job seekers today have access to an abundance of information on salary negotiation through websites and books, so most will enter the meeting ready to haggle. To reach a fair deal, you need to be equally prepared.

Decide how far you're willing to go

If the candidate suggests a higher figure than you've offered, you can choose to raise the amount of your proposal and wait for the candidate to respond or give a counteroffer. Then, ideally, you arrive at an agreement that's within the salary range you've set for the position.

If the candidate keeps pushing, whether you want to exceed the established range generally depends on two factors: one, how badly you want the individual; and two, the policies and precedents in your company. Ask yourself these three questions before you bring in the heavy artillery:

- ✔ Are other, equally qualified candidates available if the applicant says no?

- ✔ Has the job been particularly hard to fill, or are market conditions making finding and recruiting suitable candidates difficult? If the answer is yes, the leverage rests with the candidate.

- ✔ Will a stronger offer be significantly out of line with existing pay levels for comparable positions in your business?

Recognize that if you decide to go beyond the firm's pay scale to win a really stellar candidate, you risk poor morale among existing staff if they learn that a new hire in the same role is making more money. And the best-kept secrets often do get out.

Think creatively

If you're not able to match a candidate's salary request, consider expanding other components of the package. Applicants are often willing to compromise on base compensation if concessions are made in other areas.

Flexible scheduling is one candidate-pleasing option that will cost you little to nothing. Providing additional time off or opportunities to telecommute may also be acceptable to a candidate in lieu of higher wages. Also consider a signing bonus or a performance-based bonus after a specified period of time.

Knowing when to draw the line

Some HR experts insist that you shouldn't push too hard if a candidate isn't interested. Probing a bit in order to find out why a candidate is being hesitant isn't a bad idea, though. Try to identify the source of the problem and make reasonable accommodations. But don't get so caught up in negotiations that you lose sight of what is appropriate for your business. Sometimes you just have to walk away.

Clarify acceptance details

Some businesses ask candidates to sign a duplicate copy of the job-offer letter to show they accept the offer. The signature confirms that the candidate understands the basic terms of the offer. If you're making a job offer contingent on reference checking or a physical examination and/or drug and alcohol testing, or background checks, make sure that the candidate understands and accepts this restriction.

Checking in

Even after a candidate accepts your offer and you agree on a starting date, keeping in touch with the new employee is still a good idea. Two to three weeks is the customary time between an acceptance and start date. Most people who are changing jobs give a standard two-weeks' notice to their former employer. For those who want to take a few days off before starting their new job, a three-week interval is not unusual. Use the transition period to mail off all those informational brochures and employment forms and to schedule a lunch or two, if appropriate.

Employment contracts: Should you or shouldn't you?

Consult your lawyer for advice on employment contracts and to create a contract template if you go in this direction. An employment contract doesn't need to be a 20-page legal document. It can take the form of a one-page letter that specifies the job title, duties, responsibilities and obligations, conditions of employment, and, most important, severance arrangements if things don't work out.

Chapter 3

Retention: Critical in Any Business Environment

In This Chapter

▶ Getting a handle on the concept of employee compensation

▶ Creating an effective compensation system

▶ Using raises, bonuses, and incentives effectively

▶ Letting employees know your business's policies

▶ Making a positive work environment

▶ Offering flexible working arrangements

▶ Telecommuting

▶ Preventing burnout

▶ Checking the pulse of your workforce

▶ Exploring training

*T*he compensation system you establish for employees is one of the main engines that drives your business. If your business is like most, payroll is an expensive engine to maintain — probably even your number one expense.

But payroll is not just an expense. How much you pay your employees and the factors you use to establish pay scales and award raises, bonuses, and incentives can profoundly affect the quality of your workforce. The way you compensate people plays a key role in your ability to attract and retain a productive, reliable workforce.

In this chapter, you find out about how to build well-planned compensation system so your employees will stick around. You also see how to be a people-friendly business, check out different work arrangements, and look at the benefits of training and developing your workforce for the benefit of your business and employees.

Ensuring an Effective Compensation Structure

Your business's compensation and benefits package should be competitive enough to keep your top employees from being wooed away by businesses that claim to offer better total compensation packages.

Get the sound advice of your lawyer when making decisions about compensation. A lawyer can assist you in setting up policies and wage structures that can help you avoid problems, legal and otherwise.

Speaking the language of employee compensation

Unless you specialize in employee compensation, terminology can get confusing. So, to start you out, the following list offers a quick rundown of key terms in the field, along with their definitions:

- **Compensation:** You use this term to define all the rewards that employees receive in exchange for their work, including base pay, bonuses, and incentives.

- **Base salary:** The base salary is simply the salary or wage — before deductions and incentives — that employees receive for the work they do.

- **Raises:** This term refers to increases in base salary, as opposed to one-time or periodic awards.

- **Bonuses and incentives:** These two terms may seem synonyms. To some degree, they are. What both have in common is the objective of making employees feel appreciated and valued.

  But the terms also have key differences. A *bonus* is a reward for a job well done. Though usually financial, bonuses also can include rewarding with time off, a free membership to a local health club, or discounts on merchandise. In contrast, an *incentive* is a tool used to boost productivity. In other words, an incentive program sets a goal — "Contact ten new customers within a month" — and rewards employees who attain it. An easy way to remember the distinction: An incentive comes *before* work is done; a bonus comes *after*.

✔ **Benefits:** Benefits are also items that you offer to employees in addition to their base wage or salary. Examples include health insurance, stock options, and retirement plans.

✔ **Commission:** This term refers to a percentage of the sales price of a service or product that salespeople receive in addition to (or in lieu of) salary. Commission arrangements are sometimes *straight commission* (with no salary), sometimes combined with a base salary, and sometimes part of an arrangement in which the salesperson receives a set amount (known as a *draw*) on a regular basis, regardless of how much commission is actually earned during that period, with adjustments made at set intervals.

Being consistent and flexible

When you're establishing total compensation packages, you need to be both consistent and flexible. The two may sound contradictory, but they actually go hand in hand.

Consistency means that you have a logical plan and structure for compensation and benefits so you don't inadvertently create employee discord by giving the impression that you're showing favoritism or acting capriciously. *Flexibility* means that you're doing your best — within reason — to adapt to the individual needs and desires of your employees.

By balancing these two factors, you get a wage-and-salary structure that not only gives your employees equitable compensation, but also focuses on the market realities of your business.

Basing compensation and benefits on a scale

The compensation and benefits aspect of the human resources function is very detail oriented. And the bigger the business, the more complicated maintaining the required paper trail can be. But benefits and compensation is also one of the more engaging areas of human resources. Businesses have become much more creative in the ways they reward employees, from performance-based pay to stock options. Your business's overall compensation package plays a major role in your ability to recruit and retain employees. You don't need an advanced degree in economics to know that your business could wind up in big financial trouble if you ignore compensation and benefits.

It's all about scale. For a one-person business, decisions regarding wages, private health coverage, sick leave, retirement, and educational assistance aren't likely to bring a flood of red ink to your bottom line. You can give yourself a raise, take a few extra vacation days, add special areas to your medical coverage without losing sleep over whether these extra expenditures will put you out of business.

You enter an entirely new phase of operation when you hire your first full-time or part-time employee. When you're responsible for someone else's well-being, you must become more structured in your basic approach to compensation and benefits — and, for that matter, to all HR issues.

And that's not particularly easy. Even a seemingly routine decision, such as whether or not to offer private health and dental insurance, becomes complex. The same principle holds true for all decisions regarding such benefits as overtime, holidays, vacations, and so on.

Setting the Foundation for an Effective Compensation System

When thinking about compensation, think *system*. Creating an effective compensation system requires thinking strategically — that is, with a constant eye toward the long-term needs and goals of your business. Your goal is to establish a well thought-out set of practices that helps to ensure the following results:

✔ Employees receive a fair and equitable salary (from their perspective) for the work that they perform.

✔ Payroll costs are in line with the overall financial health of your business.

✔ Your employees clearly understand your basic philosophy of compensation.

✔ The pay scale for the various jobs in the business reflects the relative importance of the job and the skills that those jobs require.

✔ Pay scales are competitive enough so that you're not constantly seeing competitors hire your top employees away from you.

✔ Compensation policies are in line with provincial and federal laws involving minimum wage, vacation pay, etc.

✔ Compensation policies are keeping pace with the changing nature of today's labour market — particularly in recruiting and retaining your business's top performers.

Federal and provincial laws require employers to pay employees on time and at regular periods. The laws also regulate what employers must and may deduct from an employee's paycheck.

Setting pay levels in your organization

One of the fundamental tasks in creating an equitable and effective wage and compensation system is to develop a consistent protocol for setting pay levels for each job in your organization. The more essential a job is to the fundamental mission of your business, the higher its pay range is likely to be.

The following procedure can help you come up with some preliminary guidelines:

1. **Make a list of all the jobs at your business, from the most senior to the least senior employee.**

2. **Group the jobs by major function — management, administrative, production, and so on.**

3. **Rank the jobs according to their relationship to your business's mission.**

   You wind up with two major categories — those jobs that contribute directly to the mission and those jobs that provide support for those mission-critical jobs. Ask yourself the following questions to help make this particular distinction:

   • How closely does the job relate to our mission?

   • How indispensable is the job?

   • How difficult is the job — that is, does it require special skills or training?

   • Does the position generate revenue or support revenue-producing functions?

   • Do political or other factors make this job important?

   Eventually, you produce a ranking or hierarchy of positions. Keep in mind that you're not rating individuals. You're rating the relative importance of each job with respect to your business's mission and strategic goals.

In setting the actual pay scale for specific jobs, you have several options, as the following sections describe.

Job evaluation and pay grading

How this approach works: You look at each job in your business and evaluate it on the basis of several factors, such as relative value to the bottom line, complexity, hazards, required credentials, and so on.

The rationale: In large businesses, you must use a reasonably structured approach to deciding what pay range to apply to each job. Otherwise, you invite chaos. The more systematic you are as you develop that structure, the more effective the system is likely to be.

The downside: Creating and maintaining a structure of this nature takes a lot of time and effort.

The going rate

How this approach works: You look at what other businesses in your industry (and region) pay people for comparable jobs and set up your pay structure accordingly. You can obtain this data from government and industry websites and publications.

Rationale: The laws of supply and demand directly affect salary levels, as do geographic factors such as cost of housing and living, among others.

The downside: Comparing even apples to apples can be difficult in today's job market. Many new jobs that businesses are creating today are actually combinations of jobs in the traditional sense of the word and, as such, can prove difficult to price.

Management fit

How this approach works: The owner decides arbitrarily how much each employee is paid.

Rationale: The owner of a business has the right to pay people whatever that owner deems appropriate.

The downside: Inconsistent wage differentials often breed resentment and discontent. Lack of a reasonable degree of internal equity diminishes the spirit of teamwork and fairness.

Collective bargaining

How this approach works: In unionized workplaces, formal bargaining between management and labour representatives sets wage levels for specific groups of workers, based on market rate and the employer's resources available to pay wages.

The rationale: Workers should have a strong say (and agree as a group) on how much the business pays them. This system, of course, is (arguably) the ultimate form of establishing internal equity.

The downside: Acrimony arises if management and labour fail to see eye to eye. In addition, someone else — the union — plays a key role in your business decisions. Also, in this system, employees who perform exceptionally well can feel less rewarded because their wages are then the same as less proficient colleagues in similar positions.

Accounting for individuals

You pay people, not positions. So, sooner or later, you must program into your salary decisions those factors that relate solely to the individual performing the job. The following list describes the key "people factors" that you may want to consider in defining your pay-scale structure.

- Experience and education
- Job performance
- Seniority
- Potential

The bottom line on overtime

Employees in many industries depend on the extra money they make in overtime wages to support their standard of living. No one disputes that overtime certainly makes sense in many situations. The question you need to ask yourself is whether overtime is the best option for your business in any given situation. The question doesn't lend itself to a from-the-hip answer, but the following list describes basic truths about overtime:

- Responding to increased demand by putting existing workers on overtime is less expensive than hiring new employees.

- Of course, cost savings from using overtime are true only for a short period of time. A steady diet of overtime to increase production can have negative long-term consequences. Numerous studies have demonstrated that excessive, long-term overtime can increase the rate of on-the-job accidents, erode employee morale, and cause family pressures.

- You're best off viewing overtime as a stop-gap strategy, reserving it for short-term situations, such as when people call in sick or take vacations, or when the workload increases in the short term. If the need becomes constant, consider adding a new employee.

Reviewing the Basics of Raises, Bonuses, and Incentives

Offering competitive compensation is key in attracting top talent to your organization, but once employees are on board, salary levels don't stay competitive for long. As staff develop new skills and increase their knowledge of your business, they become more and more valuable to you — and their value in the marketplace increases as well, meaning that they become attractive targets for other businesses. To keep your best and brightest, you need to figure out fair (and affordable) ways to augment what you pay them. Most businesses enhance their compensation through raises, bonuses, and incentives designed to retain their best workers and give them a reason to stay on.

Employers structure effective bonus and incentive programs around the following main principles:

- **Results-oriented:** Employees must accomplish something to receive a bonus.
- **Fair:** The rules for bonuses are clear, and you enforce them equitably.
- **Competitive:** The program rewards extra effort and superior performance.

Pay raises

Traditional pay systems often link raises to *tenure* (that is, time spent in that grade or position). Other systems frequently tie raises to performance. The most common types of raises include the following:

- Seniority
- Merit raise
- Productivity increases
- Cost of living adjustments

Bonuses

Bonuses are one-shot payments that you always key to results: the business's, the employee's, or those of the employee's department. They come in a variety of flavours:

✔ **Annual and bi-annual bonuses:** These bonuses are one-shot payments to all eligible employees, based on the business's results, individual performance, or a combination thereof.

✔ **Spot bonuses:** Spot bonuses are awarded in direct response to a single instance of superior employee performance (an employee suggestion, for example). Employees receive the bonus on the spot — that is, at the time of, or immediately thereafter, the action that has earned the bonus.

✔ **Retention bonuses:** You make such payments to persuade key people — top managers or star performers — to stay with your business. These bonuses are common in industries that employ hard-to-recruit specialists.

✔ **Team bonuses:** These bonuses are awarded to group members for the collective success of their team.

Incentives

Incentives are like bonuses in that they don't increase base pay. The difference is that most incentive programs, unlike bonuses, are often long term in nature to cement employee loyalty or spur productivity. The following sections outline some common incentive programs.

Profit-sharing plans

Profit-sharing plans enable the business to set aside a percentage of its profits for distribution to employees. If profits go up, the employees get more money. You can focus these programs very sharply by allocating the profit sharing on a department or business-unit basis.

Stock

Stock in the business is an incentive that publicly traded firms (or firms planning to go public) may choose to offer their employees. *Stock option* plans give employees at publicly held companies the right to purchase shares in the business at a time of their own choosing, but at a price that is set at the time the option is awarded. Employees are under no obligation to exercise that option, but should the stock go up, employees can buy the stock at the cheaper price and either hold on to it or sell it for the current value, thereby earning a profit.

Stock options have also given small, growing businesses a way to attract top talent without having to pay high salaries.

If your business is thinking about offering stock options as part of your overall benefits package, everyone must be aware of certain aspects of the process. If you're a privately held business, for example, your employees need to recognize that a stock option plan isn't likely to mean anything to them unless your business goes public or is acquired. If you're publicly held, you need to make sure that you have an organized plan and some mechanisms in place that will not dilute the value of the stock to non-employee stockholders. Bear in mind, too, that these programs must comply with tax and security laws.

What's fair versus what works?

The easiest way to start a mutiny among your employees is to institute a raise or bonus process that people don't clearly understand and that neither managers nor employees buy into. The following list offers guidelines to help you avoid this all-too-common pitfall:

- Set clear rules.
- Set specific targets or goals that you can quantify.
- Make the goal worthwhile.
- Don't ask for the impossible.
- Don't make promises you can't keep.

Communicating Your Compensation Policies

Many businesses unfortunately spend a lot of time and effort designing a pay system and then leave it to the paycheck alone to communicate their pay philosophy and administration. You need to thoroughly brief managers and supervisors in particular on your business's pay systems so that they can effectively explain, administer, and support your policies. Managers and supervisors need to possess the following information:

- Your business's pay philosophy
- How to conduct a performance appraisal
- How to handle and refer employee pay complaints
- Legal implications of all compensation policies

You need to advise employees of the business's pay policies and how these policies affect them individually. You also need to communicate and fully explain any changes in these policies promptly. Employees need to possess the following information:

✔ The job's rating system, how it works, and how it affects them

✔ How the performance-appraisal and incentive systems work

✔ How they can raise their own income through performance and promotion

✔ How to voice complaints or concerns

You must keep your compensation system competitive and up-to-date. The key steps in doing so are as follows:

✔ Obtain and review competitive data at regular intervals.

✔ Review — and adjust if necessary — salary ranges at least annually.

✔ Review job descriptions regularly and make adjustments based on disparities between actual work performance and the formal description.

✔ Evaluate the performance-appraisal system. One common problem is that too many employees get superior ratings.

✔ Review salary systems in terms of your business's financial condition to determine whether the system is in line with the business's financial health and is tax-effective and efficient.

✔ Periodically measure and rate productivity and determine whether any links exist between productivity increases (or declines) and pay policies.

Creating an Employee-Friendly Work Environment

A wise man once said that the mark of an outstanding mind is the ability to hold two seemingly opposing ideas at the same time. Consider two aspects of contemporary business: On the one hand, in order to thrive, your organization must be diligent, competitive, and keenly focused on bottom-line results. But at the same time, most businesses that earn respect and profits know that nothing is more critical to attaining their goals than a workforce that feels not just engaged, but valued. Businesses that are appropriately attuned to creating a supportive, nurturing work environment stand the best chance for long-term growth. What appear to be opposite ideas — unwavering attention to business results, coupled with an employee-friendly environment — go together like bees and honey. Your skill in linking the two can go a long way toward building a first-rate organization.

A number of organizations and publications regularly select lists of best employers and best employment practices. While the criteria sometimes differ and the approaches vary, all would agree that the best employers do the following to create a people-friendly workplace:

- Foster employee well-being
- Are reasonably committed to job security
- Provide people-friendly facilities
- Are sensitive to work-life balance issues
- Allow for a high degree of employee autonomy
- Ensure open communication
- Create a sense of belonging among employees

Saying Goodbye to Nine to Five: Alternate Work Arrangements

Broadly speaking, an alternate work arrangement is any scheduling pattern that deviates from the traditional Monday-through-Friday, nine-to-five workweek.

Alternate work arrangements are an approach that employees really care about. Flexibility is the basic idea behind alternate work arrangements. You give employees some measure of control over their work schedules to help them manage non-job-related responsibilities. The business rationale behind the concept is that by supporting employees to deal with pressures on the home front, they'll be more productive when they're on the job — and less likely to jump ship if one of your competitors offers them a little more money.

Looking at options for alternate work arrangements

Alternate work arrangements are generally grouped into the following general categories:

- Flextime
- Compressed workweek
- Job-sharing
- Telecommuting
- Permanent part-time arrangements

Making alternate arrangements work

In theory, alternate work arrangements offer a win-win situation. Many studies have shown that flexible scheduling policies improve morale and job satisfaction, reduce absenteeism, cut down on turnover, and minimize burnout — with no measurable decline in productivity.

But these arrangements don't work for every business at every level, and thus the practices may have to be carefully implemented with some legally sound ground rules. In addition, instituting a policy of alternate work arrangements involves a good deal more than simply giving your employees a broader selection of scheduling options. The process needs to be carefully thought out. It must be implemented with consistency, patience, and discipline because you can easily ruin a good thing. Follow these guidelines if you're thinking of setting up a flexible scheduling policy in your business:

- ✔ Be willing to rethink processes.
- ✔ Establish guidelines.
- ✔ Pay attention to legal implications.
- ✔ Get managerial buy-in.

Telecommuting

Telecommuting is one of the fastest-growing alternate work arrangements. Strictly speaking, *telecommuters* are employees who regularly work out of their homes or other locations all or part of the work week. The key word in the previous definition is *regularly.* The structured aspect of the arrangement is what differentiates telecommuters as a group from employees who routinely take work home from the office.

Telecommuting arrangements vary. In some cases, employees never come into the office except for special events. More typically, though, a business's telecommuters spend part of the week — one or two days, usually — working out of their homes and the rest of the week in the office.

Identifying prime candidates for telecommuting

Candidates for a successful telecommuting arrangement might include those who

> ✔ Perform a function that doesn't require extensive interaction with other employees or the use of equipment found only on business premises.
>
> ✔ Have a compelling personal reason (a long commute, for example, or family responsibilities) for working from home part of the time.
>
> ✔ Have the temperament and the discipline to work alone.
>
> ✔ Can be absent from the office without creating an inconvenience for others in the business.

These factors are just a few to consider when selecting telecommuting candidates. You should also take into account a number of sticky legal and operational aspects:

Home office expenses

The basic question is simple: Who pays for what? The answer isn't simple and can depend on any number of factors, including the safety and health of the employee. The general guideline is that if the expense involves a piece of equipment that an employee must use to perform the job and that the employer would routinely be responsible for if the employee were working on business premises, your business should consider paying for it.

This guideline doesn't mean that you're obliged to replicate the working conditions at your business (the corporate gym, for example) in the telecommuter's home office. But most businesses view basic resources — at least one dedicated phone line, a computer with a high-speed Internet connection, a scanner, photocopier, and fax machine — as business expenses. Common sense needs to prevail.

Viability of service contracts

Some office equipment vendors provide service only at the employer's office locations. If your business intends to furnish a telecommuter's home office with equipment that would normally be covered by a service contract, double-check with the service provider to make sure that your policy covers residential visits.

Security

The mere fact that telecommuters are working out of the office — well outside the sphere of normal business security procedures — creates a hornet's nest of potential security problems. Technology-driven security measures, such as access codes, passwords, and firewalls can reduce but never eliminate the chance that confidential business information will end up in the wrong hands, particularly when the Internet is an integral part of many people's job. At the very least, have a written agreement with all telecommuters that spells out the business's confidentiality policies and sets down specific guidelines.

But does telecommuting work?

Unquestionably, telecommuting provides many opportunities and rewards. It's a highly productive way for certain employees to get their work done. It's also a good way to draw on the skills of talented, high-performing employees who may otherwise be unable to work for your business under a standard scheduling arrangement. This advantage makes it a compelling recruiting strategy.

But you should also take into account other factors before permitting someone to telecommute.

For example, consider the temperament and discipline of the telecommuter. Can the individual continually work effectively in relative isolation? How does the employee's work fit into a broader team environment — not just now, but as you look ahead to future growth? What is the impact of the telecommuting arrangement on others? If the telecommuter is a manager, for example, supervising people even part of the time by telephone and e-mail is not always productive.

Local zoning issues

Many communities have zoning restrictions against conducting certain business activities in residential neighbourhoods. While these rules generally are loosely enforced, the restrictions can create legal problems. Somebody — either the employee or employer — should take the initiative to investigate the situation before a problem arises.

Setting up an agreement for a telecommuter

Consider preparing a formal agreement with any employee who is going to be telecommuting. The agreement, at the very least, should spell out the following:

- ✔ The specific scheduling terms — that is, how much time the employee spends at home or at the office.

- ✔ The specific equipment the business is willing to provide, and how the equipment is to be installed and maintained.

- ✔ Reporting requirements: How often should the telecommuter send e-mail updates? Should the employee be part of a weekly departmental conference call? What kind of voice mail setup will the employee have (on both the business home office line and cellphone)?

- ✔ How proprietary information is to be controlled and handled.

Avoiding Burnout

The Japanese have a word for it: *karoshi.* The term means, literally, "death from overwork." *Karoshi* may not be a major cause of death in Canada, but almost everywhere you look in today's lean and mean environment — even in businesses with employee-friendly policies — you sometimes hear complaints and concerns about employee burnout. Often it relates to the psychological, social, and physical problems that result when workers literally "wear down" from stress and become unable to cope with workday demands.

Most psychologists explain burnout as the convergence of two forces:

- ✔ High job demand
- ✔ Low job control

In a typical burnout situation, employees not only feel tremendous pressure to extend themselves, but they also perceive that they lack the ability or the resources to meet the demands. Whether this latter perception is justified doesn't really matter. As long as employees believe they're both overworked and under-resourced, the potential for employee burnout exists.

Recognizing employee burnout

Employee burnout can manifest itself any number of ways. Among the most obvious signs are the following:

- ✔ Noticeable increase in staff absenteeism or tardiness
- ✔ Any obvious change (for the worse) in the general mood of the workplace
- ✔ Uncharacteristic emotional outbursts from employees who are normally calm
- ✔ Increased customer complaints about the quality of goods and services

Burnout doesn't happen overnight; it's a gradual process. However, if you can become sensitive to the warning signs of burnout, you can frequently avert a crisis.

Your managers and supervisors are your first line of defense against burnout and the workplace problems it causes. Make sure that they're trained to recognize burnout symptoms before the situation gets out of hand.

Being sensitive to extended periods of excessive workload

The prime cause of employee burnout is overwork, or, to be more precise, sustained periods of overwork. Most successful businesses, of course, run into periods of peak workloads from time to time, and expecting good employees to rise to the occasion isn't unreasonable. But even if you're giving your regular employees extra income to meet the increased demand, at some point even the most dedicated employees will reach their physical, emotional, and mental limits. When they reach this point, you have two options:

- ✔ Hire additional full-time employees.
- ✔ Hire supplemental workers to ease the burden.

Giving employees more day-to-day job autonomy

Productive, happy employees generally feel that they're making unique contributions that provide a sense of personal pride. Peter Drucker, the prominent management scholar, repeatedly emphasized the importance of personal ownership. If you've haven't already done so, take a look at the responsibilities your employees have, make sure that they have the necessary resources, and then be certain to provide them with plenty of independence.

You've no doubt heard of or experienced the dreaded micromanager. And perhaps you've found moments when you yourself have taken on some of those characteristics and suffered the consequences. You don't need to abandon demanding accountability (such as weekly update meetings or written reports), but think how you much you like it when your own supervisors display ample trust in your ability to get your work done. Nothing is more important to wedding productivity and an employee-friendly culture than encouraging self-reliance and the accompanying spirit of trust.

Providing help

No matter how good your work environment, some employees will develop personal problems that have nothing to do with your business but that they nonetheless bring to work. The most damaging effects include behaviour and attitudes that hinder their ability to do their jobs. The HR professional has a responsibility to offer resources to assist employees in addressing these issues.

In the HR world, programs that help workers cope with personal difficulties are known as *Employee Assistance Programs* (EAPs). EAPs include such activities as confidential counselling or seminars for employees seeking to better handle job pressures. Employees need to know that help is available and that their careers will not suffer if they seek it.

Keeping Tabs on Morale

In many cases, particularly if your business has fewer than 50 employees, you don't have a hard time getting a good read on the general atmosphere in the workplace. You're able to personally make your way around offices and work areas enough to observe how employees interact with one another, how they feel about the way they're treated by senior management, and whether morale is rising or falling.

Conducting an employee survey

If your business is larger — over 50 employees — periodically conduct a rigorous employee survey. Here are some tips on how to proceed:

✔ Watch your timing. Don't conduct surveys during holidays when many employees may be taking days off. And avoid exceptionally heavy workload periods.

✔ Think carefully about your objectives before crafting your survey questions. What do you want to find out? What do you intend to do with the information?

✔ Share survey objectives with employees, but do so in language that's relevant to them. In other words, instead of using HR terms such as "We want to assess employee attitudes," tell them that "We want to hear your thoughts since we merged with Company X."

✔ Before you unveil your survey to the entire business, test it out on a small group of employees to see whether your questions are appropriate and what you can refine.

✔ A key step: Assure employees that their comments are confidential.

✔ Communicate to employees the results of the survey on a timely basis and take action, as appropriate, when employees make recommendations. Let employees know how their input has affected policies.

Conducting exit interviews

When you're trying to "take the temperature" of the organization, some of the most candid employees are often those who are leaving your business. To gain valuable ideas about improving your working conditions and making the workplace more inviting, consider conducting exit interviews with employees who have resigned or are otherwise voluntarily leaving your business. (People you've had to fire, while potentially the most candid of all, are not good subjects for two reasons: They're unlikely to cooperate and, if they do, their input will probably be overly negative rather than constructive.)

Training and Development

In a perfect world, every employee you hire would already possess the knowledge, skills, and background to perform every facet of the job flawlessly. However, employees can always discover something that can help improve their performance. This simple, universally acknowledged principle underlies the HR function, and is generally known as employee training and development.

Broadly speaking, *employee training and development* refers to a wide range of educational and learning-based tools. These activities aren't inherently built into job functions, but generally produce some positive change in the way employees handle their work. These activities can range from a live seminar, to a CD that employees listen to while commuting, to an online instructional session they participate in at home or at their desks.

Providing training for the good of the business

No matter what the nature of your business, you won't stay on top unless you help your people stay ahead of emerging trends and changing needs. Increasing the knowledge of your workforce not only enhances your business's ability to compete, but also makes for more satisfied employees. Even in lean times, cutting back on training to reduce expenses can be "shooting yourself in the foot," both in terms of business success and employee retention.

Knowing the benefits of training

The biggest change in training is the degree to which it has become intertwined with other HR functions (hiring, promotions, and so on) and the business's long-term goals. Because businesses and employees alike value training, it's become a big business in its own right, with a wide range of products, services, seminars, and materials available for businesses of all sizes.

If you're responsible for training in a growth-oriented business, you're working more closely than ever with senior managers, supervisors, and employees. You're making sure that a logical connection exists between the programs being offered and the skill sets necessary to keep your business competitive. Here are key factors:

- ✔ **The "learning" route to competitive advantage:** Profitable organizations recognize that in today's highly competitive and changeable business environment, what employees currently know does not shape the business's future; what they must *eventually* know is most important. That's why one major objective of training is to increase each employee's intellectual capacity for acquiring the knowledge and skills needed to thrive amid the increasing demands and pressures of a global marketplace.

- ✔ **The need to attract and keep talented employees:** The degree to which your business is genuinely committed to developing the skills of your employees is critical for attracting and keeping high-performing employees. Businesses that provide their employees with opportunities to learn and grow have an edge when recruiting.

- ✔ **The competition for skilled labour:** Simply put, the "shape up or ship out" approach to managing is no longer feasible in most industries, even for entry-level positions. In response to the realities of the workplace, businesses are investing more time and money in training, mentoring, and developing other employee activities.

- ✔ **The disappearance of hierarchies and the emergence of team play:** The ability to communicate effectively and build a spirit of teamwork is important in today's workplace

Assessing your training needs

A growing number of consulting companies and individuals specialize in helping businesses identify their training needs. If your business is large enough and you don't have the time or resources to engage in this process yourself, consider hiring one of these outside sources. If you do decide to manage this process yourself, consider exploring the options in the upcoming sections.

Time, money, mentors: Principles of first-rate training

Fortune 100 companies like General Electric spend in excess of $1 billion a year on training. Though your business does not likely have that kind of budget, you can still show your employees you support their ongoing professional development. Training your employees does, of course, require spending money, but what matters most is the level of your commitment. Here are just a few ways your business can "walk the walk":

✔ A progressive tuition reimbursement policy

✔ A scheduling policy that doesn't oblige employees to attend training sessions during non-working hours

✔ Excellent communication channels between HR professionals involved in training and line managers

✔ Performance appraisal systems that take into account what managers have done to enhance the individual development of the employees they manage

✔ A mentoring program that gives employees the chance to learn from and interact with others in the business who might not necessarily be that employee's immediate supervisor.

✔ If possible, comfortable, well-equipped on-site facilities (a library or training room, for example) where employees have access to books, periodicals, research studies, CDs, DVDs, and self-administered courses. And, of course, to the extent possible, this information should also be available through the company's intranet.

REMEMBER

Keep in mind that some options work better at larger businesses, while others are more effective in smaller businesses.

Employee focus groups

Generally implemented at larger firms, *employee focus groups* often represent the ideal first step to a needs-assessment process. You pull together a group of employees from various departments or levels of your organization. If time permits, you spend a day or two (possibly off-site) discussing as a group what your business needs to do to achieve its strategic goals and what skills are required to meet this challenge. If you don't have much time, even a two- to three-hour session in a conference room at your office can be illuminating.

No matter how much time you're able to take, remember these two keys make sure that this process is productive:

✔ **The make-up of the group:** The group should include representatives from a wide cross section of departments and experience levels.

✔ **The ability of the facilitator:** It can be either you or someone else, but the facilitator needs to promote open discussion and keep the focus group from disintegrating into a "gripe session."

Surveys and questionnaires

Surveys and questionnaires are standard tools in the needs-assessment process. Depending on the size of your business, surveys may represent the most cost-effective approach to needs assessment.

If you intend to survey employees in this way, also gathering feedback from supervisors is a good idea. Each group may offer a unique perspective. You can also use a questionnaire to get some survey feedback from customers.

Employees may well have an accurate sense of what they need to improve in order to perform more effectively, but these areas may not necessarily connect directly to the strategic objectives of the business. The goal is to view the information you gather from employees as simply one tool in a process.

Observation

Simply observing how employees are performing on the job and taking note of the problems they're experiencing can often give you insight into their training needs. Just be careful about the conclusions you draw. When observing employees who are struggling, you may be tempted to attribute the difficulty to a single cause — some problem that you can solve by scheduling a training program or by sending them to a seminar.

One way to avoid the common pitfall of jumping to conclusions is to speak directly with the employees you've observed and give them the opportunity to explain why their performance may be falling short.

Tying training needs to strategic goals

Whatever approach (or approaches) you take to evaluate your training requirements, the needs-assessment process should be strategically driven. After you've gathered the data — regardless of how you've gathered it — you need to process it within the framework of the following questions:

- ✔ What are the strategic goals of this business — both long term and short term?

- ✔ What competencies do employees need to achieve these goals?

- ✔ What are the current strengths and weaknesses of the workforce relative to those competencies?

- ✔ What improvements can training be expected to offer that differ from day-to-day supervision?

- ✔ What kind of a commitment — in money, time, and effort — is your business willing and able to make to provide necessary training?

Deciding whether to train or not to train

The basic question you need to ask is whether a training program represents the best and most cost-effective approach to reducing the gap between job demands and employee capabilities. How do you determine whether or not to train a group of employees, and how do you determine how much time and money to invest? No simple answers exist, but certain factors can help guide you:

- ✔ State of the labour market
- ✔ Current workload in the business
- ✔ Internal resources and budget

Evaluating training options

After conducting the needs-assessment process, the biggest challenge you face is setting up an effective training program. What follows is a brief look at the range of approaches that are possible today, along with the pros and cons.

In-house classroom training

With *in-house classroom training,* the traditional and most familiar form of training, a group of employees gathers in a classroom and is led through the program by an instructor. These sessions occur on-site or off-site and can be facilitated by trainers who are either employees themselves or outside specialists.

Pros: The main advantage to classroom training (apart from its familiarity) is that it provides ample opportunities for group interaction and gives instructors a chance to motivate the group and address the individual needs of students.

Cons: In-house classroom training requires considerable administrative support. This form of training can also entail major expense (travel and lodging, for example), which is not directly connected to the learning experience.

Public seminars

You can encourage employees to attend topic-specific workshops that are organized and run by training companies. These public seminars are usually held at a public site, such as a hotel or conference centre.

Pros: Public seminars require little or no administrative support. The per-person cost is reasonable.

Cons: Most public seminar offerings are, by necessity, generic. Topics covered don't necessarily have direct relevance to your particular business. The quality of seminars may also vary from one to the next.

Executive education seminars

Seminars and workshops offered by universities and business schools are targeted, in most cases, to middle and upper-level managers. Typically they cover a wide range of both theoretical ideas and practical pointers for putting these principles into practice.

Pros: Instructors are usually faculty members with a high level of expertise. These kinds of seminars are a good opportunity for attendees to network and share ideas.

Cons: Courses at the more prestigious schools can take the executive away from the office for more days than desired. They're also expensive, in some cases as much as $5,000 (including room and board) for a five-day course. Make sure that events cover management concepts and techniques that are relevant or applicable to your business's focus and culture.

E-learning

E-learning has gained rapid acceptance throughout corporate North America. The concept of learning from sources based far away is, of course, hardly new. Correspondence courses were popular long before the Internet entered the workplace. But the great payoff of e-learning is its flexibility and speed, delivering the real-time immediacy of classroom instruction without the need to actually be present in a classroom.

Pros: E-learning has a number of important benefits:

- Vastly increases the scope and reach of a corporate training effort
- Eliminates, or greatly reduces, ancillary, non-learning expenses of training, such as travel and lodging costs for participants
- Enables students to work at their own pace and convenience so they avoid production downtime
- Enables participants to not only experience training in real time but also to store and retrieve information transmitted through the course
- Enables students to set up individualized objectives and to establish milestones to mark different levels of achievement
- Liberates you or your training staff from classroom presentations, enabling more one-on-one consultations

Cons: The downside of e-learning is that lack of human interaction and direct instructor involvement might not work well for people who are not self-motivated.

A word of caution

E-learning is a productive training technique, but also one that requires careful attention. You need to determine which mix of approaches best matches your real needs. Create a team consisting of yourself, technology experts, and line managers to figure out the best possible set of solutions. For example, the time and money required to set up an effective system of intranet-based training makes sense only when you have a lot of potential students — and only when your long-term strategy is to make your intranet your primary training delivery system.

Don't forget you've got to monitor and manage e-learning if it's to be success-ful. If you simply upload a slew of training courses and tell employees to "have at it," it won't do much good. But e-learning is easy to monitor. In fact, one of the benefits of e-learning is that you can track its usage to make sure that employees are engaged in the learning and are actively participating and com-pleting the required workshops and courses. Encourage — and maybe even offer incentives (read more about incentives earlier in this chapter) — to employees who complete training. Set aside specific times for training so that employees feel comfortable temporarily stopping their day-to-day tasks to complete an online course.

Mentoring as a training tool

Some skills, such as interpersonal abilities, are not easily taught in the classroom or through online courses. In fact, some skills aren't taught well in groups at all. Enter employee mentors. Just as appointing a more experi-enced employee to serve as a mentor for a new employee can help the new person acclimate to your work environment, well-chosen mentors can like-wise assist staff at any stage of their careers with longer term developmental learning.

In a mentoring role, an employee who excels in a given area — customer service, for example — can help fellow employees discover how to more smoothly interact with customers and colleagues or develop additional skills that require more long-term and individualized attention than a classroom or online course can offer. Regarding interpersonal, or people skills, employees who are paired with an appropriate manager can pick up such abilities as persuasiveness and diplomacy.

Getting feedback on training

E-mail allows you to measure the effectiveness of training in a timely manner. You can quickly send surveys to large groups of employees. If you want, you can distribute them and ask for responses within a few days or even hours of the session's conclusion. You can also record survey responses online, with results organized into databases and available to HR and managers.

Mentors can also serve as valuable training facilitators for high-potential employees you may want to groom to eventually take over key roles. Mentoring programs are among the most effective ways to transfer tacit knowledge from seasoned leaders to aspiring ones. As businesses prepare to lose their most experienced employees due to the retirement of many baby boomers, such arrangements may become important for passing on valuable know-how to less experienced workers and preparing them take on greater responsibility.

Deciding on a training program

Learning is a highly individual process, and because of that you must remain leery of taking the "one-size-fits-all" approach. In general, here are some of the factors that most often influence the effectiveness of a program, regardless of which form it takes:

- ✔ Receptivity level of students
- ✔ Applicability of subject matter
- ✔ The overall learning experience and the variety of learning tools
- ✔ Quality of instructor
- ✔ Reinforcement of class concepts at work

Measuring results of training efforts

HR professionals have long wrestled with the problem of quantifying the results of training — a process that doesn't readily lend itself to quantifiable measures. For example, one of the primary benefits of employee training is that it enhances morale. But how do you measure the bottom-line benefits of morale? Not easily, to be sure. Yet another problem with measuring the results of training is that the skills and knowledge that people bring to a task represent only one factor in job performance. In many situations, factors that are independent of an employee's knowledge and skills will either impede or enhance job performance.

These issues aside, following are four generally accepted practices for measuring the results of training:

- ✔ **Initial employee reaction:** The most common way to gather feedback from participants immediately following a training session is to distribute a questionnaire to each one at the end of the session. The answers give you a general idea of whether your employees thought the training was worthwhile. Post-training surveys measure initial reactions, but offer little insight into how effective the training was in the long run.

- ✔ **Effectiveness of learning:** You can measure the learning that takes place during programs that focus on well-defined technical skills (using software programs, for example) by administering tests before and after the training and comparing the results. Remember, though, that the subject matter of many training programs (leadership skills, for example) doesn't lend itself to specific metrics. One way around this limitation is to observe the accomplishments or behaviour of employees in the weeks and months after soft skills training.

- ✔ **Impact on job performance:** Determining whether training has had a positive impact on actual job performance depends on the nature of the training and the specific tasks. The problem? Performance in most jobs is influenced by variables that may have little bearing on what was taught in a workshop. Participants might bring new skills back to their jobs, but run into resistance from supervisors when they try to put their new skills into practice. That's why educating business managers about the advantages training sessions bring to their employees is important.

- ✔ **Cost/benefit analysis:** Training simply doesn't easily lend itself to familiar cost/benefit analysis. The costs are easy enough to quantify. The problem lies with attaching a dollar value to the many indirect benefits that training brings, which may include reduced absenteeism and turnover, reduced employee grievances, a less stressful workplace (with fewer medical problems), and the need for less supervision.

Key questions to ask in a post-training questionnaire

Employees' answers to the following survey questions can help you gauge the effectiveness of your training sessions:

- ✔ Did the course meet your expectations, based on the course description?

- ✔ Were the topics covered in the course directly relevant to your job?

- ✔ Was the instructor sensitive to the needs of the group?

- ✔ Were the instructional materials easy to follow and logical?

- ✔ Would you recommend this program to other employees?

- ✔ Were the facilities adequate?

Chapter 4

Monitoring Ongoing Performance

· ·

In This Chapter

▶ Evaluating the performance of your workforce

▶ Knowing why employee appraisals are good for your business

▶ Choosing the system

▶ Launching the appraisal program

▶ Ensuring appraisal meetings are effective

▶ Avoiding wrongful dismissal claims

▶ Setting up a progressive discipline procedure

▶ Firing or laying off employees

· ·

*Y*ou've moved mountains to hire the best staff in the world, and you are offering them the most comprehensive and cost-effective benefits package known to man. But you have to keep the machines well oiled, turbo-charge them occasionally, and fix them when they break down. That's what this part of the book is all about. From assessing the way your team is handling their jobs and inspiring them to achieve even more, to handling the not-so-fun aspects of HR, this chapter shows you how to keep it all together.

Assessing Employee Performance

Few management practices are more basic or prevalent than *performance appraisals* — the mechanism through which managers or supervisors evaluate the job performance of their employees. Yet, as common as the practice may be, many businesses, both large and small, experience difficulty in structuring and managing the process.

Effective managers have to monitor the performance of direct reports, note the areas of job performance need to be improved, and then communicate assessments to them in a positive and constructive way. How else would you determine how people get promoted, if they deserve salary increases, and how much they should be making?

The problem seems to be not with the concept, but with the format and mechanics. In many businesses today, managers as well as employees aren't convinced of the value of appraisal systems. To many supervisors, they simply represent additional work, and some employees remain skeptical and apprehensive regarding the process. In addition, traditional approaches to performance appraisals aren't necessarily well suited to today's flatter management structures, which de-emphasize direct supervision, promote employee autonomy, and often involve collaboration with many different employees from a wide range of disciplines. In fact, many younger businesses were created with the goal of intentionally *not* resembling older command-and-control corporations and, as a result, are reluctant to create formal employee performance evaluation procedures. Yet another problem with performance appraisals in today's workplace is that the difficulty in finding highly skilled employees, coupled with the fear of litigation, has made some managers gun-shy about being too critical of staff.

 These problems notwithstanding, performance appraisals are a vital management function, and your business must implement a structured and systematic program that takes into account the realities of today's workplace — and the nuances of your business's unique culture.

Reaping the Benefits of Performance Appraisals

Creating and implementing a structured performance appraisal process is a challenge. For one thing, performance appraisals invariably create additional work for supervisors. The process also puts pressure on employees by forcing everyone to establish specific goals and identify the behaviours necessary to achieve those goals, which some may view in the short term as simply "busy work." What's more, the very nature of appraisal systems puts both employees and supervisors into situations that most people find uncomfortable. Being, in effect, "graded" makes many employees feel as though they're back in school. And most managers, even those who've been involved with an evaluation process for many years, find being candid and constructive difficult when they're conducting an appraisal session that involves negative feedback.

Why, then, should you put in the time and effort to create and implement this process? The answer is that the long-term benefits of an effectively structured and administered performance appraisal process far outweigh the time and effort the process requires. Here's what a well-designed, well-implemented performance appraisal system does for your business:

✔ Creates criteria for determining how well employees are truly performing — and, to that end, clarifies how their job descriptions and responsibilities fit in with business and departmental priorities

✔ Provides an objective — and legally defensible — basis for key human resources decisions, including merit pay increases, promotions, and job responsibilities

✔ Verifies that reward mechanisms are logically tied to outstanding performance

✔ Motivates employees to improve their job performance

✔ Enhances the impact of the coaching that is already taking place between employees and their managers

✔ Establishes a reasonably uniform set of performance standards that are in sync with the business's values

✔ Confirms that employees possess the skills or attributes needed to successfully fulfill a particular job

✔ Irons out difficulties in the supervisor-employee relationship

✔ Gives underperforming employees the guidance that can lead to better performance

✔ Keeps employees focused on business goals and objectives

✔ Helps employees clarify career goals

✔ Validates hiring strategies and practices

✔ Reinforces corporate values

✔ Assesses training and staff development needs

✔ Motivates employees to upgrade their skills and job knowledge so that they can make a more meaningful contribution to your business's success

Deciding on a Performance Appraisal System

All performance appraisal systems are driven by the same objective: to establish a systematic way of evaluating performance, providing constructive feedback, and enabling employees to continually improve their performance.

The basic ingredients in all systems are pretty much the same: setting performance criteria, developing tracking and documenting procedures, determining which areas should be measured quantitatively, and deciding how the information is to be communicated to employees. Methods vary in the following areas:

- The degree to which employees are involved in establishing performance evaluation criteria

- How employee performance is tracked and documented

- How performance is rated and how it's aligned with corporate priorities, objectives, and goals

- The specific types of appraisal tools used — in some cases, for example, certain approaches are more appropriate for evaluating managers and professionals than other employees

- The amount of time and effort required to implement the process

- How the results of the appraisal are integrated into other management or HR functions

- How the actual appraisal session is conducted

The following sections offer a brief description of performance appraisal methods most commonly used today.

Goal-setting, or management by objectives (MBO)

In a typical MBO scenario, an employee and manager sit down together at the start of an appraisal period and formulate a set of statements that represent specific job goals, targets, or *deliverables*.

What makes MBO so powerful is its direct link to organizational objectives and priorities. In the case of MBO, goals, targets, and deliverables should be as specific and measurable as possible. For example, instead of "improve customer service" (too vague), try something like "reduce the number of customer complaints by 5 percent." And instead of "increase number of sales calls" (too vague), go with "increase the number of sales calls by 5 percent without changing current criteria for prospects."

This list of targets becomes the basis for an action plan that spells out what steps need to be taken to achieve each goal. At a later date — six months or a year later — the employee and the manager sit down again and measure employee performance on the basis of how many of those goals were met.

Essay appraisals

The *essay approach* can be useful for a supervisor to periodically compose statements that describe an employee's performance. The statements are usually written on standard forms, and they can be as general or as specific as you want. A supervisor may describe an employee's performance in terms of "the employee's ability to relate to other team members." These written statements can either be forwarded to the HR department or used as one element in an appraisal session. Any written evaluation also needs to include more measurable evaluation tools, such as rating scales applied to specific objectives, tasks, and goals.

Critical incidents reporting

The *critical incidents method* of performance appraisal is built around a list of specific behaviours, generally known as *critical behaviours,* that are deemed necessary to perform a particular job competently. Performance evaluators use a critical incident report to record actual incidents of behaviour that illustrate when employees either carried out or didn't carry out these behaviours. You can use these logs to document a wide variety of job behaviours, such as interpersonal skills, initiative, and leadership ability.

Job rating checklist

The *job rating checklist* method of performance appraisal is the simplest method to use and lends itself to a variety of approaches. To implement this approach, you supply each evaluator with a prepared list of statements or questions that relate to specific aspects of job performance. The questions typically require the evaluator to write a simple "yes" or "no" answer or to record a number (or some other notation) that indicates which statement applies to a particular employee's performance.

Behaviourally anchored rating scale (BARS)

Behaviourally anchored rating scale (BARS) systems are designed to emphasize the behaviour, traits, and skills needed to successfully perform a job. A typical BARS form has two columns. The left column has a rating scale, usually in stages from very poor to excellent. The right column contains behavioural anchors that are the reflections of those ratings.

If the scale were being used, for example, to evaluate a telephone order taker, the statement in one column may read "1-very poor," and the statement in the right column may read, "Occasionally rude or abrupt to customer" or "Makes frequent mistakes on order form."

Forced choice

Forced-choice methods generally come in two forms: paired statements and forced ranking. In the *paired statements method,* evaluators are presented with two statements and must check the one that best describes the employee; it's either one or the other. In the *forced ranking method,* a number of options are listed, allowing the evaluator to select a description that may fall somewhere in between the two extremes.

The following example illustrates how each version may be used to cover the same aspect of job performance for a field service representative.

Paired statements:

____ Provides sufficient detail when filling out trip reports

____ Doesn't provide sufficient detail when filling out trip reports

Forced ranking:

____ Provides sufficient detail when filling out trip reports

____ Exceptional

____ Above average

____ Average

____ Needs improvement

____ Unsatisfactory

Ranking methods

Ranking methods compare employees in a group to one another. All involve an evaluator who asks managers to rank employees from the "best" to the "worst" with respect to specific job performance criteria. The three most common variations of this method are as follows:

- ✓ **Straight ranking:** Employees are simply listed in order of ranking.

- ✓ **Forced comparison:** Every employee is paired with every other employee in the group, and in each case, the manager identifies the better of the two employees in any pairing. The employees are ranked by the number of times they're identified as the best.

- ✓ **Forced distribution:** The employees are ranked along a standard statistical distribution, the so-called *bell curve.*

Overcoming obstacles

Regardless of how much time you take to gather feedback and incorporate it into a new performance appraisal system, you may still face objections. Some employees approach appraisals with skepticism and even trepidation. Some supervisors may not appreciate the reasons for the additional work. And the senior management of some younger businesses, eager not to mimic what they perceive as the harsh, judgmental cultures of older corporations, resists the idea of conducting performance appraisals at all. Show your team that, for businesses to grow, they must evaluate what's working, what isn't, and what can be improved.

When making the case for performance appraisal systems, here's what you can expect — and what to do about it:

Employee resistance: Employees often feel threatened by appraisal systems, and some employees actively dislike being appraised. Respond by communicating as clearly and as openly as possible the purpose and mechanics of the new appraisal system and that it was built with their input. Make sure that employees understand what role the appraisal will play in influencing the things they care about: raises, promotions, and so on. Spell out the role they're expected to play in the process.

Supervisor resistance: Appraisal systems require extra work by supervisors and managers, as well as create additional paperwork and administrative overhead. Try to keep forms and paperwork to a minimum, but provide forms for continuing tasks such as critical incidents reporting. Train evaluators and audit their performance to see whether follow-up training is needed.

Multi-rater assessments

Multi-rater assessments are also called *360-degree assessment.* The employee's supervisors, co-workers, subordinates, and, in some cases, customers are asked to complete detailed questionnaires on the employee. The employee completes the same questionnaire. The results are tabulated, and the employee then compares the self-assessment with the other results.

Launching an Appraisal Program

When you set up a new performance appraisal system, you need to gather input from both senior management and employees and also make sure that the program is workable and well communicated throughout the organization. Use the following general guidelines in setting up and launching your performance appraisal system:

- ✔ Enlist the support of senior management.
- ✔ Give employees a say in establishing performance criteria.

✔ Choose performance measures with care.

✔ Develop a fair and practical tracking mechanism.

✔ Devise a workable evaluation method.

✔ Keep it simple.

✔ Develop a communication game plan.

Getting the Most Out of the Performance Appraisal Meeting

When you're creating a performance appraisal process, you have to address the "people" component — what happens when managers and employees sit down together to set goals or to discuss work performance during the appraisal period.

Preparing for the meeting

Managers should be thoroughly briefed on what they need to do prior to holding a performance appraisal session. The key point is that they must be ready: that is, not wait until the last minute before thinking about how the session is going to be handled. Managers should have a clear idea before the meeting begins of what specific behaviours are going to be the focal point of the session. Other points to stress include the following:

✔ Give employees sufficient time to prepare for the session.

✔ Allot sufficient time to conduct a productive session.

✔ Have all documentation ready prior to the meeting.

✔ Choose a suitable place (private, quiet, relaxing, with no interruptions) for the meeting.

Conducting the session

If more than a handful of managers are involved in the performance appraisal process, training sessions on how to conduct an effective appraisal session may be beneficial. Whether you conduct this training yourself or bring in an outside company, here are the points to stress:

✔ The appraisal meeting should always be a two-way conversation, not a one-way lecture.

✔ Positives should always be emphasized before negatives are discussed.

✔ The emphasis should be always on what needs to be done to improve and not what was done wrong.

✔ Employees should be encouraged to comment on any observations managers share with them.

✔ Managers should know how to explain to employees the difference between *effort* (how hard employees are working) and *quality results* (whether the results of those efforts are contributing significantly to business objectives).

Giving constructive feedback

If your business is like most, the toughest thing about the appraisal meeting will be to talk about performance areas in which the employee is lacking. Working in advance with your managers (or on your own, if you're conducting the appraisals) is a good idea, so that they're sufficiently prepared to handle this undeniably tricky aspect of the process. Here are the points to emphasize:

✔ **Focus on why candor is important.** Failing to focus on the negative aspects of employee performance when necessary not only does the employee a disservice, but can also harm your business. The employee can't very well improve if no one communicates the need. Additionally, if firing an employee becomes necessary, failing to mention the employee's weakness in a performance appraisal can jeopardize the business's ability to defend the firing decision.

✔ **Stress the importance of documentation.** Always be prepared to back up critical comments with specific, job-related examples. Gather documentation for these examples prior to the meeting.

✔ **Highlight the importance of careful wording.** How a criticism is worded is every bit as important as what behaviour is being described. Focus on the behaviour itself and not on the personality quality that may have led to the behaviour. For example, instead of saying, "You've been irresponsible," be sure to describe the specific event that reflects the irresponsibility, as in "For the past few weeks, you've missed these deadlines."

✔ **Encourage employee feedback.** Employees should be given the opportunity to comment on points of criticism. Given a chance, employees will often admit to their shortcomings and may even ask for help.

✔ **End on a positive note.** No matter how negative the feedback may be, performance appraisal meetings should end on a positive note and with a plan for improvement.

Preparing for a negative reaction

In a well-managed business, most employees are probably performing adequately or better, but some people don't take criticism well, no matter how minimal or appropriately delivered. In any performance appraisal meeting, an employee whose work is being criticized has the potential to become agitated, confrontational, verbally abusive, and, in very rare instances, violent. Anyone conducting appraisals must be aware of this possibility and have a strategy for response. Here's some advice on handling these difficult situations:

- ✔ **Within reason, let the employee blow off steam.** Don't respond, comment on, or challenge the employee while the employee is agitated or angry. In certain situations, a calm, nonthreatening demeanour can defuse a situation.

- ✔ **Don't fake agreement.** The worst thing to say in this sort of situation is "I can see why you're upset." It can very well set the employee off again.

- ✔ **When the storm passes, continue the meeting.** A lack of response usually ends most outbursts, and the employee quickly realizes the gravity of the mistake. Accept the apology and move on.

- ✔ **If any hint arises that the employee may become violent, leave the room immediately and seek help.** Call an in-house security guard, 911 for the police, or, if necessary, other nearby employees.

Choosing areas for further development

What's most important after giving any constructive criticism is a mutual effort between employees and managers to initiate changes that will help staff perform at a higher level. As part of the appraisal meeting, supervisors should recommend areas for improvement and, together with employees, build a set of workable performance-development activities.

Prior to the meeting, the one doing the appraisal should create a concise, one-page list of potential developmental activities for the employee. The list can include

- ✔ Recommended readings, both current and ongoing, that the employee can learn from and that are devoted to the topics where development is suggested.

- ✔ Possible classroom or online courses that may help the employee.

- ✔ People within the business who may offer useful input. ("John became a supervisor last year, so you can talk with him about the challenges of managing people.")

Employee development isn't just for underperformers, of course. (Refer to Chapter 3 of this book for more about training and development for employees.) Even the very best employees have room to improve and further develop themselves. For any professional, appraisal time is the ideal opportunity to tie a look backward with a look forward.

Performance-development activities are a means to help employees better achieve their job objectives set at the start of the appraisal period. (See "Goal-setting, or management by objectives (MBO)" in this chapter) As a result, the employee and manager should revisit these objectives during this phase of the appraisal meeting to ensure that they're still on target. Many businesses require an annual goal-setting meeting, and the appraisal meeting may be a good time to tackle that task. You certainly don't want to establish developmental activities around goals that will soon be changing.

Making appraisal followup ongoing

The performance appraisal meeting is not the conclusion of the appraisal process. The truth is, the days following this session are extremely important. Providing adequate followup is key, including regular monitoring of employee progress toward performance-development goals. Without sustained followup — both formal and informal — any input an employee receives is unlikely to be effective in the long run.

The employee and supervisor should have both short- and long-term methods to review progress on the improvement areas discussed and schedule specific dates to do so. Many businesses advise managers to conduct interim meetings after six months, but the interval can be shorter or longer depending on the situation. Between these sessions, supervisors should be encouraged to remain easily accessible so that employees can share thoughts, concerns, or suggestions on any of the topics covered during the appraisal. Real benefits exist to providing input to staff throughout the year: If feedback is ongoing, nothing in the performance appraisal should come as a surprise to employees.

At the end of any appraisal process, evaluate your own performance as the one who created and implemented the process. Were you able to thoroughly explain the evaluation approach to line managers? Did employees feel the session was conducted appropriately, with their supervisors providing enough time for discussion? Did you recommend specific actions to take following the appraisal — courses, reading, or contacts within the organization who may offer a different perspective? Being a "business strategist" requires extensive attention to these very human, delicate matters. Doing so can be quite rewarding — for the business, for employees, and for your own personal growth.

Evaluating your appraisal system

Here's a list of questions to ask yourself about your business's current program. If you can answer "yes" to all the questions, you can probably relax. A "no" answer may indicate an aspect of your program that needs to be re-examined.

✔ Are all performance criteria job-related?

✔ Is the focus on results, as opposed to personal traits?

✔ Do your employees understand how the process works and how appraisals tie into other aspects of their jobs?

✔ Have managers been adequately trained to implement the system?

✔ Do employees thoroughly understand the program?

✔ Have all relevant employee behaviours been documented?

✔ Have promises of confidentiality been kept?

✔ Are all subsequent HR decisions consistent with employee evaluations?

✔ Are follow-up plans built into appraisals?

✔ Have you reviewed all elements of your program with legal counsel?

Handling Difficult Situations

Regardless of how good a job you've done in organizing the human resources function in your business, and regardless of how diligently you handle your day-to-day challenges, you're engaging in wishful thinking if you expect your organization to be entirely free of personnel-related concerns. Even your best employees are going to make mistakes. So are your best supervisors. Even the most closely knit and harmonious group of employees is going to get into occasional squabbles. And unpleasant though the prospect may seem, inevitably, you or the managers in your business will be obliged to take some sort of corrective action — including termination — against an employee whose job performance or conduct falls short of business expectations.

You must ensure that job performance and workplace conduct issues are handled promptly, intelligently, and fairly — and in a way that doesn't diminish productivity, accelerate turnover, or deplete employee morale. And most important perhaps, you have to make sure that your business's disciplinary and termination policies minimize exposure to wrongful dismissal lawsuits.

This area is not one where you can afford to be your own lawyer. Employee disciplinary action, termination, and layoffs are matters that require advice tailored to your particular business and situation. Hire a lawyer.

Establishing an ethical culture

The best overall way to reduce the number of difficult situations you have to deal with is to prevent them from happening in the first place. You can never hope to avert all employee improprieties, poor judgments, and disputes, but establishing a culture based on ethical behaviour can go a long way in diminishing these situations.

From the "tone at the top" on down, become a business that emphasizes the critical importance of employees' ethical behaviour in all interactions, whether externally with customers and vendors or internally among each other. People will always find ways and excuses for wrongdoing just as they will always be capable of making honest mistakes. But including integrity and consideration of others as one of your core values not only prevents many unpleasant situations from occurring, but also helps you develop a reputation as a business people want to work for. (Book 3 talks more about your business's values.)

Managers must be every bit as accountable as employees. Your business should have a formal code of conduct that is not buried on a shelf, but actively reinforced by all managers. When employees hear one set of values but see another enforced — or, for that matter, neglected — by managers, the inconsistent messages confuse them or, cause them to question your commitment to your basic principles. As a result, they will likely become less committed to the overall organization.

Staying out of court

The last thing you want is to have to defend a wrongful dismissal case in court. It will cost you a substantial amount of money. It will take time and take you away from managing your business. How do you protect yourself? In short, protection comes from preventive action. Here are seven key principles to bear in mind:

✔ Have your lawyer review all business recruiting and orientation literature to ensure that no statements could be misconstrued or used against you.

✔ Establish and document specific, easy-to-understand performance standards for every position in your business and make sure that every employee is aware of those standards.

✔ Train managers to maintain careful, detailed records of all performance problems and the disciplinary actions that have been taken in response to those problems.

✔ Make sure that all disciplinary and dismissal procedures are handled "by the book."

✔ Make sure that all the managers and supervisors in your business are well-versed in your business's disciplinary and termination procedures.

✔ Seek legal advice whenever you are uncertain about any aspects of your business's disciplinary or legal policy.

✔ Be sensitive to the possibility that an employee who leaves your business voluntarily as a result of a change in assignment or work practices may be able to convince a jury that the change represented a deliberate attempt on your business's part to force the employee to quit.

Developing Disciplinary Procedures

Some businesses like a formalized disciplinary process, one that reasonably and systematically warns employees when performance falls short of expectations.

A formal disciplinary procedure works best in businesses that are highly centralized, where personnel decisions for the entire business are made within one department (most likely HR), which makes sure that each step of the disciplinary process is implemented properly. The advantage is that the rules and regulations of job performance are consistently communicated to everyone. The disadvantage, however, is that if your business doesn't abide by these self-imposed rules, not even a lawyer can help you.

On the other hand, some businesses don't like such a process. Using a formalized disciplinary process doesn't work as well for organizations that are decentralized, where personnel decisions are made within each office or department on a case-by-case basis in accordance with a business's general expectations. In these situations, ensuring that each office or department follows the same disciplinary procedure is difficult.

Formal disciplinary processes can vary, but most practices are structured along similar lines. To some degree, they all mirror the following phases:

1. **Initial notification:** The employee's manager typically delivers this initial communication verbally in a one-on-one meeting. Details from this and all later conversations should also be documented. The report needn't be lengthy; a few bullet points highlighting the main topics are perfectly acceptable.

2. **Second warning:** This phase applies if the performance or conduct problems raised in the initial phase worsen or fail to improve. The recommended practice is for the manager to hold yet another one-on-one meeting with the employee and accompany this oral warning with a memo that spells out job performance areas that need improvement.

At this stage in the process, the manager needs to make the employee aware of how the employee's behaviour is affecting the business and what the consequences are for failing to improve or correct the problem. The manager needs to work with the employee to come up with a written plan of action that gives the employee concrete, quantifiable goals and a timeline for achieving them.

3. **Last-chance warning:** The "last-chance" phase of discipline usually takes the form of a written notice from a senior manager or, in smaller business, from the owner or president. The notice informs the employee that if the job performance or workplace conduct problems continue, the employee will be subject to termination. What you're doing here is applying the heat.

4. **Corrective action:** Corrective action is some form of discipline administered prior to termination. In union contracts, for example, this action may take the form of a suspension, mandatory leave, or possibly a demotion. In small businesses, disciplinary actions become a little trickier to implement — so much so, that corrective action can become termination itself.

5. **Termination:** Termination is the last step in the process — the step taken when all other corrective or disciplinary actions have failed to solve the problem.

These progressive disciplinary steps serve as general guidelines and aren't intended as a substitute for legal counsel.

However you decide to structure your disciplinary plan, the process itself — apart from being fair — should meet the following criteria:

- ✔ Clearly defined expectations and consequences
- ✔ Early intervention
- ✔ Consistency
- ✔ Rigorous documentation

Firing Employees Is Never Easy

Even when you have ample cause for doing so, firing employees is always a cause for heartache — not only for the employees losing their jobs and the supervisors making the decision, but the co-workers as well.

You can do only so much to ease the pain and disruption that firings create. You can do a great deal, however, to help ensure that your business's approach to firing meets two criteria:

✔ It protects the dignity and the rights of the employee being terminated.

✔ It protects your business from retaliatory action by a disgruntled former employee.

The standard (and recommended) practice in most businesses is for the immediate supervisor to deliver the termination notice. The message should be delivered in person and in a private location. Depending on the circumstances, include a third person, such as another supervisor or member of the human resources department, at the meeting. Do not involve co-workers.

Regardless of why an employee is leaving your business, keep the termination meeting as conclusive as possible, which means you need to prepare prior to the meeting. The following list covers some issues to consider:

✔ **Final payment:** Ideally, any employee being dismissed should walk out of the termination meeting with a cheque that covers everything the employee is entitled to, including severance, money due from accumulated vacation, sick days, expense reimbursements, etc.

✔ **Security issues:** Think about the security of the business, including keys, access cards, and company credit cards. If the employee has been using a password to access the business's files, ask your IT department or consultant (or whoever sets up your computers) to change it on the system. Do the same with credit-card privileges.

✔ **Business-owned equipment:** The employee should return any business-owned equipment immediately. If the equipment is off-site (a computer in the employee's home, for example), arrange for its pickup.

✔ **Notification of outplacement or other support mechanisms:** If your business has set up outplacement arrangements (or any other services designed to help terminated employees find another job), provide all the relevant information. In some businesses, the outplacement counsellor is already on the premises and is the first person the terminated employee talks to following the meeting.

Following post-termination protocol

If your business hasn't developed one, work with your management to develop a disciplined, clearly defined procedure for what happens after you discharge an employee. Make the break as clean as possible — albeit with respect to the feelings and the dignity of the person being fired. Harsh and humiliating though the practice may seem, accompany the dismissed employee back to the employee's office or workstation to collect personal belongings and escort the employee out the door. If the business has confidentiality agreements, remind employees — in writing — of their legal obligations. Also advise employees that they're no longer authorized to access the business's computer systems and any online accounts.

Just cause

Certain employee infractions and misdeeds are so blatant that you can generally terminate the employee without going through the normal disciplinary channels. Your orientation literature should spell out the offenses that lead to immediate dismissal. Here's a list to get you started:

✔ Stealing from the business or from other employees

✔ Possession or use of illegal drugs

✔ Distribution or selling of illegal drugs

✔ Blatant negligence that results in the damage to or loss of business machinery or equipment

✔ Falsifying business records

✔ Violation of confidentiality agreements

✔ Misappropriation of business assets

✔ Making threatening remarks to other employees or managers

✔ Engaging in activities that represent a clear case of conflict of interest

✔ Lying about credentials

Generally speaking, holding the meeting early in the week (not the weekend) and at the end of the workday works best. If you conduct the termination meeting on Monday or Tuesday, you make it easier for the dismissed employee to get started immediately on a job search and for you to begin searching for another employee. By delivering the news as late in the day as possible, you spare the employee the embarrassment of clearing out his or her office in front of co-workers.

Using a waiver of rights

Some businesses ask a discharged employee to sign a statement that addresses confidential agreements and also releases the business from legal liabilities. Often called a *severance agreement,* businesses require employees to sign this document and return it by a specified date before they receive a severance payout. Note that this payout is separate from any compensation regulated by federal or provincial law. The value of this practice is obvious. Although some people believe that employers who present waivers of rights while terminating employees can communicate that they're worried about the legality of their actions, it's common practice and a useful business tool. Have your legal counsel review such a document; encourage the employee to consult legal counsel as well. In fact, a good practice is to discourage employees from signing the document during the exit interview. This is because an argument may be made later that the employee signed the document under duress. Telling the employee to take time to consider the document and to consult legal counsel helps further dispel the notion that the business is trying to hide something.

Easing the trauma of layoffs

Layoffs differ from firings in a variety of ways, but one critical aspect comes to mind: The people being let go haven't done anything to warrant losing their jobs. Layoffs occur for a number of reasons, such as the following:

✔ Seasonal shifts in the demand for a business's products or services

✔ An unexpected business downturn that requires the business to make drastic cost reductions

✔ A plant/company closure

✔ An initiative that restructures work practices, leaving fewer jobs

✔ A merger or acquisition that makes certain positions redundant

Generally, when someone is *laid off,* no expectation exists that the person will be returning to work. Some businesses use the term in a different sense, however. When business is slow and they don't need the entire current workforce, some organizations (particularly those operating in a unionized environment) notify workers that they will be placed on *furlough* for a period of time and will be offered the opportunity to return to work on a certain date or in stages. Some businesses (especially seasonal businesses and those for which losing a major project creates a significant worker surplus) call this arrangement a "layoff" even though they plan to bring people back to work if and when conditions allow.

Whatever the reason for a layoff, the pressure on the HR function is the same. You need to help your business navigate this difficult turn of events with as few long-term repercussions as possible. Remember the following points to guide you through the process:

✔ View layoffs as a last resort.

✔ Know the law around layoffs.

✔ Think through the layoff criteria.

✔ Ease the burden of layoffs with severance packages.

✔ Hire outplacement specialists.

✔ Help former employees take advantage of staffing and placement services.

✔ Address the concerns of those who remain.

Alternatives to layoffs

If the purpose of the layoff is to cut down on costs (as opposed to reduce redundancy), you may want to explore options that, at the very least, can reduce the number of people who need to be let go:

✔ **Temporary pay cuts:** Reducing salary costs is probably the simplest and most direct way to cut staffing costs without cutting staff. The key to this strategy is to ensure that everyone — including senior managers — shares the pain. Many businesses, in their efforts to ensure equality, vary the percentage of reduction according to the amount of salary an employee is earning, with higher-salaried workers surrendering a higher percentage of their regular paycheques than their lower-salaried counterparts.

Downside: No matter how justified the cuts and how many jobs you save, some workers will resent losing pay — and the decision to cut back on pay may induce your best and most mobile workers to quit. Keep in mind, too, that employees who agree to pay cuts will expect the salary to be restored — and then some, when the business turns around. If your business doesn't meet that expectation, you'll likely soon encounter decreased employee commitment and, down the road, a higher turnover rate than desired. Though no legal limit applies to the duration of a temporary pay cut, the sooner you can communicate when wages will be restored, the more positive the impact on morale.

✔ **Workweek reductions:** This option is worth exploring for businesses that have large numbers of hourly workers. You maintain the same hourly rates, but employees work fewer hours. As an inducement to accept the lower take-home pay, most businesses pledge to maintain benefits at full-time levels.

Downside: Reducing hours has no effect on salaried employees and managers who are not paid by the hour.

✔ **Early retirement:** An often-used method of reducing payroll costs is to encourage early retirement, generally through financial incentives. Because senior employees are usually the most highly paid, trimming their ranks can result in significant savings.

Downsides: Senior employees are often your most valued, and losing too many of them at one time can significantly weaken the leadership of your business. Remember, too, that you cannot discriminate against a person because of age and it is therefore not usually possible to force anyone to retire.

In addition, in order to avoid charges of age discrimination, early retirement offers usually have to be extended to wide classes of employees rather than selected individuals. This option can sometimes backfire when large numbers of employees you may want to keep accept the offer.

Book VI
Marketing

In this book . . .

Chapter 1: Getting Started in Marketing 485

Chapter 2: Sharpening Your Marketing Focus 509

Chapter 3: Creating and Placing Ads 519

Chapter 4: Reaching Your Market in More Ways..................533

Chapter 1

Getting Started in Marketing

- -

In This Chapter

▶ Understanding the meaning and role of marketing

▶ Getting started on the marketing process

▶ Knowing who buys from you

▶ Taking a solid look at what you sell

▶ Seeing the unexpected reasons why people buy products

▶ Making more sales

▶ Recognizing all your competitors

▶ Looking at your market share

▶ Coming up with a plan and budget

- -

*O*ne thing is clear. Generally speaking, businesses with a relatively higher expenditure in marketing do better than businesses that spend comparatively less. This assumes, of course, that the marketing money is spent smartly.

This chapter looks at the marketing truths that will fuel your business's success if you spend the time and the money to implement your marketing program successfully.

We begin with some definitions and the work you need to do to define who you are as a business and what you stand for. Then we look at the market environment, essentially your customers and your competitors, to help you create the foundation of your marketing efforts.

Describing the Marketing Process

REMEMBER

To settle the matter right up front, here is a plain-language description of what marketing is all about.

Marketing is the process through which you create — and keep — customers.

- ✔ Marketing is the matchmaker between what your business is selling and what your customers are buying.

- ✔ Marketing covers all the steps of tailoring your products, messages, distribution, customer service, and all other business actions to meet the desires of your most important business asset: your customer.

- ✔ Marketing is a win-win partnership between your business and its market.

Making marketing your key to success

How many times have you heard small-business people say that they just don't have time for marketing?

Think of it this way: Without customers, a business is out of business. Because marketing is the process by which your business gets and keeps customers, marketing is the key to keeping your business in business.

So marketing is the single most important activity in any business — including yours. The fact that you're holding this book means you've made a commitment, and that gives you an edge over many of your competitors.

Going around the marketing wheel of fortune

If you could get an aerial view of the marketing process, it would look like Figure 1-1. Marketing is a nonstop cycle. It begins with customer knowledge and goes around to customer service before it begins all over again. Along the way, marketing involves product development, pricing, packaging, distribution, advertising and promotion, and all the steps involved in making the sale and serving the customer well.

Every successful marketing program — whether for a billion-dollar business or a hardworking individual — follows the marketing cycle illustrated in Figure 1-1. The process is exactly the same whether yours is a start-up or an existing business, whether your budget is large or small, whether your market is local or global, and whether you sell through the Internet, via direct mail, or through a bricks and mortar location.

Just start at the top of the wheel and circle around clockwise in a never-ending process to win and keep customers, and to build a strong business in the process.

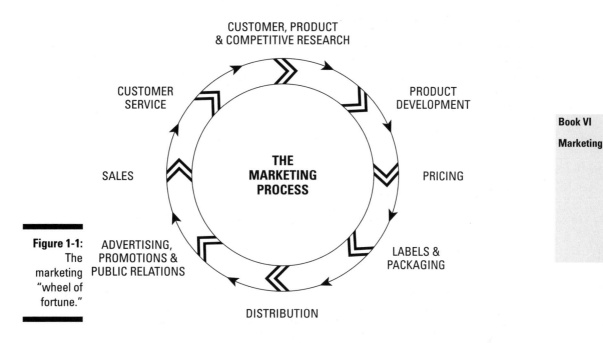

Figure 1-1:
The marketing "wheel of fortune."

As you loop around the marketing wheel, here are the actions you take:

1. **Get to know your target customer and your marketing environment.**
2. **Tailor your product, pricing, packaging, and distribution strategies.**
3. **Create and project marketing messages.**
4. **Go for and close the sale — but don't stop there.**
5. **When you make the sale, begin the customer-service phase.**
6. **Talk with customers to gain input about their wants and needs and your products and services.**

And so the marketing process goes around and around.

Marketing has no shortcuts. You can't just jump to the sale, or even to the advertising stage. To build a successful business, you need to follow every step in the marketing cycle.

Distinguishing marketing from sales

People confuse the terms *marketing* and *sales*. They think that *marketing* is a high-powered or dressed-up way to say *sales*. Or they mesh the two words together into a single solution that they call *marketing and sales*.

Selling is one of the ways you communicate your marketing message. *Sales* is the point at which the product is offered, the case is made, the purchasing decision occurs, and the business-to-customer exchange takes place.

Selling is an important part of the marketing process, but it is not and never can be a replacement for it.

Starting Your Marketing Program

Business owners clear their calendars for marketing activities typically at three predictable moments:

- ✔ At the time of business start-up
- ✔ When it's time to accelerate business growth
- ✔ When there's a bump on the road to success, perhaps due to a loss of business because of economic or competitive threats

Marketing a start-up business

If your business is just starting up, you face a set of decisions that existing businesses have already made. Existing businesses already have images to build upon, whereas your start-up business has a clean slate upon which to write exactly the right story.

Before sending messages into the marketplace, know your answers to these questions:

- ✔ What kind of customer do you want to serve?
- ✔ How will your product compete with existing options available to your prospective customer?
- ✔ What kind of business image will you need to build to gain your prospect's attention, interest, and trust?

Marketing to grow your business

Established businesses grow their revenues by following one of two main routes:

- ✔ Grow market share by pulling business away from competitors.

- ✔ Grow customer share by increasing purchases made by existing customers, either by generating repeat business or by achieving larger sales volume at the time of each purchase.

Almost always, the smartest route is to look inside your business first, work to shore up your product and service offerings, and strengthen your existing customer satisfaction and spending levels *before* trying to win new prospects into your clientele.

Book VI

Marketing

Marketing to compensate for lost business

It happens to every business. Things are running smoothly and a key client merges with an organization and you lose them. Or there's an economic downturn generally or in a specific sector and your client cuts back. Successful clients don't just sit back, they act proactively and market to:

- ✔ Replace a client by looking at businesses in the same sector and taking them away from their existing suppliers

- ✔ Look for businesses in new sectors who may need products or services you can provide

The best strategy is to be very targeted and look at the specific clients you might go after and then go after them in a systematic and planning way.

Scaling your program to meet your goal

Whether you're launching a new business or accelerating growth of an existing enterprise, start by defining what you're trying to achieve.

Ask yourself two questions:

- ✔ How much business are we trying to gain?
- ✔ How many clients do we want to add?

Considering Your Customers

Every marketer mulls over the same questions: Who are my customers? How did they hear about me? Why do they buy from me? How can I reach more people like them?

Successful businesses use the answers to these questions to influence every product design, pricing, distribution, and communication decision they make.

Business owners don't work for themselves; they work for their customers.

The upcoming sections get you thinking about the only boss that really matters in business (and you thought going into business for yourself meant you had no boss!): that person over there with an open billfold — your customer.

Looking at customer segments

An important part of knowing your customer is differentiating who's who among your clientele. It's called *market segmentation* — the process of breaking your customers down into segments that share distinct similarities.

Here are some common market segmentation terms and what they mean:

- ✓ **Geographics:** Segmenting customers by regions, counties or municipalities, provinces, countries, postal codes, and census tracts.

- ✓ **Demographics:** Segmenting customers into groups based on aspects such as age, sex, race, religion, education, marital status, income, and household size.

- ✓ **Psychographics:** Segmenting customers by lifestyle characteristics; behavioural patterns; beliefs; values; and attitudes about themselves, their families, and society.

- ✓ **Geodemographics:** A combination of geographics, demographics, *and* psychographics. Geodemographics, also called *cluster marketing* or *lifestyle marketing,* is based on the age-old idea that birds of a feather flock together — that people who live in the same area tend to have similar backgrounds and consuming patterns. Geodemographics helps you to target your marketing efforts by pinpointing neighbourhoods or geographic areas where residents share the age, income, lifestyle characteristics, and buying patterns of your prospective customers.

Collecting information about your customer

People with the profile of your current customers are apt to become customers as well. That's why target marketing starts with customer knowledge.

Finding the facts

You can get a good start on conducting customer research without ever walking out the front door of your business. Use these strategies:

- ✓ Collect addresses from shipping labels and invoices and group them into areas of geographic concentration.

- ✓ Follow the data trail from credit card transactions to see where customers live.

- ✓ Request postal code information at the beginning of cash register transactions.

- ✓ Survey customers.

- ✓ Observe your customers.

- ✓ Use contests to collect information.

- ✓ Monitor the origin of incoming phone calls.

- ✓ Track responses to ads and direct mailers.

- ✓ Study Web reports to learn about prospects who visit you online.

Book VI

Marketing

Doing your research

Consider the information in Table 1-1 as you make research decisions.

Table 1-1	Research Approaches		
Method	*Purpose*	*Advantages*	*Challenges*
Questionnaires and surveys	Obtain general information	Anonymous. Inexpensive. Easy to analyze. Easy to format and conduct.	Impersonal. Feedback may not be accurate. Wording can skew results.
Interviews	Obtain information and probe answers	Develop customer relationships. Adaptable to each situation. Access fuller range of information.	Time-consuming. Reliant on good interviewers. Difficult to analyze.

(continued)

Table 1-1 *(continued)*

Method	Purpose	Advantages	Challenges
Observation	Document actual buyer behaviour	Anonymous. Immediate findings. Relatively easy to implement.	Can be difficult to interpret findings. Can be difficult to target which behaviours to monitor. Can be expensive.
Documentation review	Study factual history of clients and transactions	Readily available. Not disruptive to operations. Not subject to interpretation.	Time-consuming. May be incomplete. Research is limited to previously collected data.
Focus groups	Learn about and compare customer experiences and reactions	Convey information to customers. Collect customer impressions.	Require expert facilitation. Require advance scheduling. Difficult to analyze findings.

Seeing your business from the customer's perspective

The best products aren't *sold* — they're *bought*. If you're a good marketer, when the time of purchase comes, you aren't *selling* anyone anything. Instead, you're helping customers to select the right products to solve their problems, address their needs, or fulfill their desires. You're helping them *buy*.

As a result, you devote the bulk of your marketing efforts to the steps that take place long before money changes hands. These efforts involve targeting customers, designing the right product line, and communicating your offerings in terms that address the customer's wants and needs. Then when the customer is ready to make the purchase, you facilitate a pleasant exchange and make sure the customer feels good about trading money for the right product.

Giving the Facts about What You Sell

Freeze-frame your business to study the products you offer your customers, and answer these questions:

- ✔ What do you sell? How much? How many? What times of year or week or day do your products sell best?

- ✔ What does your product or service do for your customers? How do they use it? How does it make them feel?

- ✔ How is your offering different and better than your competitors'?

- ✔ How is it better than it was even a year ago?

- ✔ What does it cost?

- ✔ What do customers do if they're displeased or if something goes wrong?

Tallying your sales by product line

Make a list of every kind of product you offer to your customers, along with the revenue each offering generates. Concentrate only on the end products you deliver. For example, a law office provides clerical services, but those services are part of other products and are not the reason why a person does business with the attorneys in the first place — so they shouldn't show up on the attorney's product list.

To get you started, Table 1-2 shows products for a bookstore.

Table 1-2	Independent Bookstore Product Analysis	
Product	*Product Revenue*	*Percentage of Revenue*
Books	$250,000	44%
Magazines	$95,000	16%
Coffee and pastries	$95,000	16%
Greeting cards and gift items	$55,000	9%
Audio books	$45,000	8%
Audio book rentals	$18,500	3%
Pens and writing supplies	$18,000	3%

Using the cash register to steer your business

Your product analysis will detail exactly which products your customers are buying. You can put this information to work by prioritizing and managing your product line:

- ✔ Sell what people want to buy.
- ✔ Promote the products that you've hidden from your customers.
- ✔ Back your winners.
- ✔ Bet on product lines that have adequate growth potential.

Realizing Why People Buy What You Sell

When you can buy bread for under a dollar at the grocery store, why would anyone pay nearly $5 to pick up a loaf at the out-of-the-way Italian bakery?

Why pay nearly double for a Lexus instead of a Toyota, when some models of both are built on the same chassis with many of the same components?

For that matter, why would people seek cost estimates from three different service providers and then choose the most expensive bid when all three offer nearly the same proposed solution?

Why? Because people rarely buy what you think you are selling.

People don't buy your *product.* They buy the promises, the hopes, or the satisfaction that they believe your product will deliver. People may choose to buy from your business over another simply because you make them feel better when they walk through your door.

Don't fool yourself into thinking that you can win your competitor's customers simply by matching features or price. People decide to buy for all kinds of illogical reasons, and then they justify and rationalize their purchases by pointing out product features, services, or even the price tag. They buy because they see some intangible value that makes them believe the product is a fair trade for the asking price. Often that value has to do with the simple fact that they like the people they're dealing with.

Understanding the importance of value

Whatever you charge for your product, that price must accurately reflect the way your customer values your offering.

If a customer thinks your price is too high, expect one of the following:

- ✔ The customer won't buy.
- ✔ The customer *will* buy but won't feel satisfied about the value.
- ✔ The customer will tell others that your products are overpriced.

Book VI

Marketing

Before you panic about a customer calling your business overpriced, remember that it is only bad news if others respect this particular person's opinions regarding price and value. Letting a cherry-picking bargain hunter go is often better than sacrificing your profit margins trying to price to that person's demanding standards. If your prices are on the high end, though, just be certain that the quality, prestige, and service — the *value* — that you offer is commensurate with your pricing.

Looking at the value formula

During the split second that customers rate the value of your product, they weigh a range of attributes (see Figure 1-2).

Figure 1-2:
Many
attributes
besides
price
contribute
to a
customer's
perception
of value.

The Value Formula

How Customers Compute Value

Price
Quality
Features
Convenience
Reliability
Expertise
+   Support
V A L U E

Have you heard the old chestnut, "Price, quality, and speed — choose any two"? Well, for successful twenty-first century small businesses, those days are gone. Your customer expects you to be the best at one and competitive in all *three* areas. Not the *best* in all three areas — but at least competitive.

Here are some well-known examples:

- Costco = Best price
- Holt Renfrew = Best service
- Starbucks = Best product
- Federal Express = Best reliability
- BMW = Best performance
- Rolex = Best quality

Riding the price/value teeter-totter

Before you reduce your prices to increase sales or satisfaction levels, think first about other ways to increase the value you deliver. Consider the following points:

- Your customer must perceive the value of your product to be greater than the asking price. If you charge 99 cents, deliver at least a dollar in value.
- The less value customers equate with your product, the more emphasis they'll put on low price.
- The lower the price, the lower the perceived value.
- Customers like price reductions way better than they like price increases. Upping your prices later may not settle well.
- Products that are desperately needed, rarely available, or one-of-a-kind are almost never price-sensitive.

Tell a person his child needs special eye glasses to see properly and he'll pay whatever the ophthalmologist prescribes — no questions asked, if he can find a way to afford it. But tell him he's out of dishwasher detergent, and he'll comparison shop. Why? Because one product is more essential, harder to substitute, harder to evaluate, and needed far less often than the other. One is a matter of great importance; the other, mundane.

Pricing considerations

Give your prices an annual checkup. Here are the factors to consider and the corresponding questions to ask:

✔ **Your price level:** What is the perceived value of this product compared with its price? What are the prices of competitive products? How easily can the customer find a substitute — or choose not to buy at all?

✔ **Your pricing structure:** How do you price for extra features/benefits? What features/benefits do you include at no extra charge? What promotions, discounts, rebates, or incentives do you offer? Do you offer quantity discounts?

✔ **Pricing timetable:** How often do you change your pricing? How often do your competitors change their pricing? Do you anticipate competitive actions or market shifts that will affect your pricing? Do you expect your costs to affect your prices in the near future? Are market changes or buyer taste changes looming that you need to consider?

Book VI

Marketing

Presenting your prices

The way you present your prices can either inspire your prospects — or confuse or underwhelm them. Use the following list to show your prices in the most favourable light:

✔ Don't let your offer get too complex.

✔ Don't be misleading.

✔ Do present prices so they look visually attractive and straightforward.

✔ Do make the price compelling. In today's world of outlet malls, online bargains, and warehouse stores, "10 percent off" isn't considered an offer at all.

✔ Do support your pricing announcements with positive reasons and added benefits. Price alone is never reason enough to buy.

Increasing Your Sales

Most businesses want to increase sales. There are really only two ways to do this, and most successful businesses have marketing strategies to do both simultaneously:

1. **Sell more to existing customers.**

2. **Attract new customers.**

Figure 1-3 presents questions to ask as you seek to build business from new and existing customers through new and existing products.

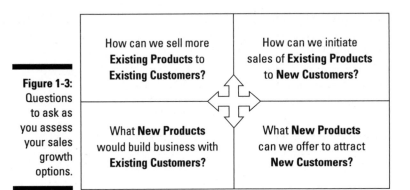

Figure 1-3: Questions to ask as you assess your sales growth options.

How can we sell more **Existing Products** to **Existing Customers?**

How can we initiate sales of **Existing Products** to **New Customers?**

What **New Products** would build business with **Existing Customers?**

What **New Products** can we offer to attract **New Customers?**

Enhancing the appeal of existing products

At least annually, small businesses need to assess whether their products still appeal to customers or whether it's time to adjust features, services, pricing, and product packaging — or make other changes to sustain or reignite buyer interest. Here are some of your options:

- ✔ **Same product, new use:** Start by looking for ways you can re-present your offerings.

- ✔ **Same product, new promotional offer:** Examine ways to update how you offer your product to customers.

- ✔ **Same product, new customer:** Invite new customers into your business with a fairly risk-free introductory or trial offer or some other way to sample your product and service.

Following the product life cycles

Products get old. They follow a life cycle (shown in Figure 1-4) that begins with product development and proceeds until the product becomes old hat, at which time its growth rate halts and profits decrease.

Figure 1-4:
Sales
follow a
predictable
curve
throughout
the product
life cycle.

Sizing Up Competitors and Staking Out Market Share

Every business has competition. Competition may not be obvious or even direct, but it is always there. The sooner you face competition and plan for it, the better. Your business faces three kinds of competition, and the upcoming sections tell you how to recognize them.

Direct competitors

These businesses offer the same kinds of products or services you do and appeal to customers in the same geographic markets where you do business. To increase your market share, think about how you can woo business away from your direct competitors and over to your business.

Indirect competitors

You're either losing sales to or splitting sales with these businesses. For instance, if you're selling paint, and your customer is buying the paintbrush somewhere else, that brush seller is an indirect competitor of your paint store, because it is capturing the secondary sale. To increase your share of customers, figure out what kind of business your indirect competitors are winning.

Phantom competitors

No one *has* to buy what you're selling. In fact, one of the biggest obstacles to the purchase — and therefore the biggest phantom competition — is your customer's inclination to do nothing at all or to find some alternative or do-it-yourself solution instead of buying what you're selling. Taking the paint store example a step further, if you're offering the choice between enamel and latex paint, and your customers are opting for never-need-paint vinyl siding, that siding outlet is a phantom competitor capable of roadblocking your business. For that matter, if your customers decide that their houses can go another year without a paint job, the option to do nothing is your phantom competitor. To increase your share of opportunity, think about where your phantom competitors are hiding. Then find ways to make your product an easier, more gratifying, more satisfying, and more valuable alternative.

How businesses compete

When everything else is equal, most customers opt for the product with the lowest price. If you want to charge more, make sure that everything else *isn't* equal between you and your lower-priced competitor. Most competitors fall into one of the following two categories:

- **Price competitors:** These businesses emphasize price as their competitive advantage. They must be prepared to offset lower profit margins with higher sales volume. They also have to be prepared for some other business to beat their price and take away their one-and-only competitive edge.

- **Nonprice competitors:** These businesses charge a higher price than their competitors. They must be prepared to compete and win based on superior quality, prestige, service, location, reputation, uniqueness of offering, and customer convenience. In other words, they must offer an overall value that customers perceive to be worth a higher price tag. (Refer to "The value formula" earlier in this chapter.)

Winning Your Share of the Market

You win market share by taking business from your direct competitors, therefore reducing their slice of the market pie while increasing your own. To advance in the market share game, here's what you must do:

1. **Know your direct competition.**

2. **Learn why your customers are choosing those competing businesses over yours.**

3. **Analyze how you can beef up the value that the market equates with your business and products.**

Defining your direct competition

On an annual or regular basis, ask yourself these questions:

- Whom does your business really compete with?
- How does your business rate against the businesses that your prospects also consider when they consider your offerings?
- Where does your business rank among your competitors?

Book VI

Marketing

Climbing the competitive ladder

Most businesses misdirect their time and energy by tackling the wrong competitors. They shoot too high — taking on the biggest names in their market area rather than the biggest threats to their business. Who would your clients go to, if you weren't there? Answer that question and you'll have a good sense of what competitors and what competitive level you should be going after. As you develop your competitive plan of attack, follow these steps:

1. **Start by winning market share from the businesses you're actually losing customers to *today*.**

2. **Make a list of the businesses you *wish* you were running with and determine why you're not in that group.**

3. **Consider whether changing competitive levels would be advantageous.**

4. **Change competitive levels if necessary.**

Calculating your market share

Having a sense of your market share gives you a good indication of your competitive rank. It also provides a way to monitor the growth of your business within your target market.

Market share: Sample calculation

Suppose that Green Gardens, a residential landscaping business, serves a market area that includes 20,000 houses, of which approximately 10 percent use landscape services. This creates a total potential residential landscape service market of 2,000 homes. If Green Gardens has a client roster that includes 200 homes, then it has a 10-percent market share based on the total number of potential customers in the area (200 divided by 2,000).

Another way to look at market share is by dollar volume. Green Gardens could estimate the revenues of each of its competitors and then add those figures to the Green Gardens revenue figure. That would produce an estimate of the total amount being spent on residential landscape services. If Green Gardens analyzed its market share based on *unit sales* (number of houses served) *and* based on dollar volume, its owners could conclude that although they have only a 10-percent share of the houses served, they have 15 percent of the total dollar volume. This finding could lead them to conclude that they are serving larger-sized accounts than some of their competitors.

To calculate your share of the market, first define the size of the market in which you compete.

The *total* market includes the entire nation or world — a market area that matters enormously to such major marketers as Nike, Levi's, General Motors, Citibank, or other internationally known brand names.

But to a small business like yours, what matters is your *target* market — the one within the sphere of your business's influence. You can assess the size of your target market by using the following criteria:

- ✔ **Geographic targeting:** Where are your customers?
- ✔ **Customer targeting:** Determine which people fit your customer profile.
- ✔ **Product-oriented targeting:** Analyze how many sales of products like yours are taking place.

Increasing your market share

Be reasonable as you set your market share goals and growth expectations. Also, as you seek to increase market share, steer clear of these landmines:

- ✔ Avoid "buying" market share through price reductions.
- ✔ Be ready to meet increased demand before issuing an invitation to new customers.

Making Your Marketing Plan and Budget

Too many small business leaders feel paralyzed by the marketing process because they don't know where to start. But when they get around to setting their goals, most small businesses find that they face a pretty reasonable marketing task. An accounting firm might determine that it wants to add three new corporate clients. A retail establishment might want to gain $20,000 in new sales. A commercial cleaning business might want to take on five more business contracts.

Knowing the goal simplifies everything.

What's more, when small business owners are clear about where they want to go, they nearly always get there. As a small business marketer, if you start with a goal, a plan, and a reasonable budget for achieving your desired outcome, you'll get where you want to go.

Knowing where you're going

Mission. Vision. Goals. Objectives. What's all this?

Small businesses rarely have time to stop and think about what they're trying to accomplish beyond the survival objective of bringing in enough revenue to cover the expenses. That's why your business will have an edge — and a greater chance for success — if you devote some time up front to setting your sights and aiming yourself and your business.

When market share means market saturation

The common rule is that 25-percent market share is considered a dominant market position. As you calculate your share within your target market area, watch closely as it reaches a dominant position. When it gets there, take time to celebrate, for sure, but then be aware that as your share edges still upward, it will near a level called market saturation.

Market saturation occurs when a business captures the sales of close to a majority of the potential customers within the target market. Usually that figure is pegged at about 40 percent. Market dominance is the dream of every business. But keep your eye on the road in front of you so that should you near saturation, you have a plan for where you'll go next to grow your business. Don't turn from a growing market too soon, and don't cling exclusively to a saturated market too long. Use market share knowledge as your navigating device.

Having a vision

The terms *mission* and *vision* are often used interchangeably, but a fine-line difference exists. Your *vision* is a statement of what your business *strives to be*. Your *mission* is a statement of how to create your vision. (Refer to Book III for more about a business's vision and mission statements.)

Your business's vision is the big picture of where you're going, whereas your mission is the path you plan to follow to achieve success.

A more modern example of vision and mission comes from the Habitat for Humanity program, which now reaches around the globe to provide housing for people in lower-income groups.

> **Habitat for Humanity Vision:** To eliminate poverty housing and home-lessness from the world, and to make decent shelter a matter of con-science and action.

> **Habitat for Humanity Mission:** To build and rehabilitate simple, decent, affordable homes in partnership with those who lack adequate shelter.

Developing your statement of purpose

Some businesses combine mission and vision into a single *statement of purpose* that defines their purpose, long-range goals, and core values.

You must decide whether to create statements of mission and vision or whether to write an overall statement of purpose. Either way, your business will be stronger if you put into writing the ultimate reason that you come to work every day. Consider these questions as you work on your reason for being:

- ✔ Why did you get into this business in the first place?
- ✔ What need did you see that you felt you could fulfill better than anyone else could?
- ✔ What makes your business different from others?
- ✔ What commitment do you make to those you deal with — from employees to suppliers to customers?
- ✔ What is the ultimate reason for your work?

Use the formula in Figure 1-5 to create a sentence that serves as the beacon for your business. As you develop your statement, think in terms of your *vision* (what positive change you are working to achieve) and your *mission* (what you will do to make your vision real).

Formula for a Purpose Statement

BEGIN WITH

A Verb that describes the change you want to make

THEN ADD

A clause summarizing the need your business addresses

AND YOU HAVE

The Purpose Statement for your company

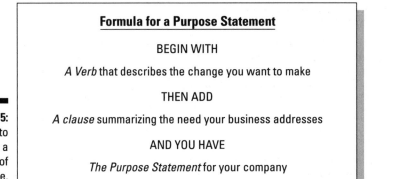

Figure 1-5: How to develop a statement of purpose.

Defining goals

Following are definitions for the terms *goal, objective, strategy,* and *tactic.* To see how they fit together, see the planning pyramid in Figure 1-6.

- **Goal:** The overall sales or professional target that your marketing program seeks to achieve. Your goal is an expression of a realistic and clearly defined target, usually accompanied by a time frame.
- **Objective:** The measurable result that will be necessary to achieve the goal. A plan usually has several objectives that define the major means by which the goal will be met.
- **Strategy:** The plan for achieving each measurable objective.
- **Tactic:** An action you will take to enact your strategy.

THE ACTIONS WE WILL TAKE
HOW WE WILL ACHIEVE IT
WHAT WE WANT
WHY WE DO THIS
Strategy
Objectives
Goals
Vision, Mission and Core Values/Purpose

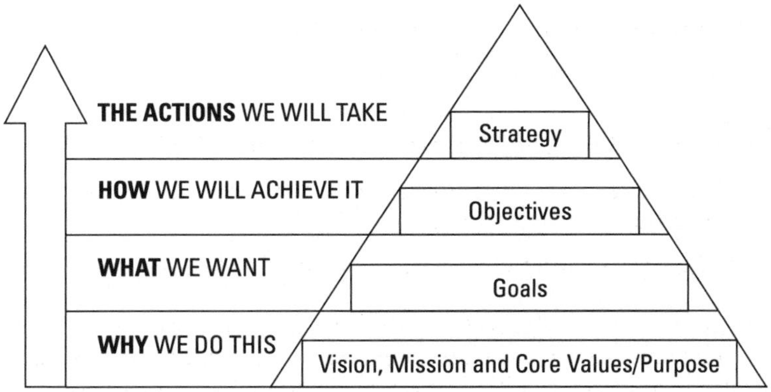

Figure 1-6: The planning pyramid.

Setting strategies

Strategies are the plans for achieving business objectives. They are practical, achievable, and action-oriented. Strategies generally detail changes that a business intends to make to the four marketing functions called the *marketing mix:* product, pricing, promotion, and place (also known as *distribution*). These four marketing mix elements are known as *The Four Ps:*

- ✔ Product
- ✔ Pricing
- ✔ Promotion
- ✔ Place

Taking action

When you're clear about your annual goal, every action becomes a building block toward achieving that ultimate desired end.

Small businesses sometimes falter when asked to state their goals. They say that they're going to open a new office, begin selling a new product, or increase prices in June. But those aren't goals — those are strategies. Knowing your strategies without being clear about the goal you're trying to reach is like wandering the woods blindfolded.

Planning

Successful business marketers follow the same lock-step marketing scenario:

1. **Conduct market research.**

2. **Establish marketing goals and objectives.**

3. **Set the marketing strategies and determine the marketing mix that you will employ to achieve your objectives.**

4. **Choose your marketing tools and tactics.**

Never, ever start with Step 4. Never decide on your tactic — whether to run an ad or hire a new distributor or take on a new partner — until you know your strategies. Tactics *follow* strategies — not vice versa.

Budgeting to reach your goals

Leaders of successful businesses never say, "We'll see how much money is available and then spend it on advertising." They dedicate funds in advance because they know that without good marketing, they won't have any funds to spend, let alone left over funds!

To reach your goals and achieve your objectives, fuel your strategies with a marketing investment that is appropriate to the size of the task.

The most important commitment you can make to your marketing program is to establish and stick to a budget. What is commitment? It has four parts:

Book VI

Marketing

- ✔ Establishing a marketing budget
- ✔ Spending the funds on a planned marketing program
- ✔ Viewing the allocation as an important business investment
- ✔ Managing the program well

Think long and hard before trimming your marketing budget, because it's the one expense item designated specifically to attract and keep customers.

Deciding on how much to spend

Everyone wants a magic formula to know what to spend on marketing, but none exists. Mature businesses in established markets with low growth goals can get away with low marketing expenditures. Businesses targeting high growth must spend far more. A business getting sales primarily as a subcontractor can spend practically zero on marketing, but a business trying to win a broad cross-section of retail customers must budget enough for media ads and promotions.

One industry survey finds that businesses that market primarily to other businesses spend an average of 3.49 percent of revenues on marketing. Other studies show that businesses that market to the public spend closer to 8 to 10 percent. So the answer is always different.

Budgeting considerations

As you determine how much to allocate for marketing, consider the following elements:

- ✔ The nature of your business and your market
- ✔ The maturity of your business
- ✔ The size of your market area
- ✔ Your competition
- ✔ Your objective and task

You can cut your marketing budget and reap an extra $100, $1,000, $10,000, or even $100,000 in the bottom line. But you'll realize that savings only once. Marketing investments keep delivering even after the ad is finished or the sales call has long since ended.

You *must* dedicate time or money, or both, if you want to market your business from where it is to where you want it to be.

Chapter 2

Sharpening Your Marketing Focus

In This Chapter

▶ Conveying the desired image

▶ Looking at your brand

▶ Positioning your business in the market

▶ Writing your tag line

▶ Building a creative strategy

Marketing is both a science and an art. Businesses that are new to marketing often jump to the art first: the creative marketing idea. But a good concept and a good creative idea are only good if they are based on a strategic foundation. How do we want our customers to see us and what would we like their image of us to be?

In this chapter, we look at how to create a brand that attracts the clients you want to attract to your business. We help you understand that everything you do, including your advertising of course, contributes to the overall appeal of doing business with you.

Projecting the Right Image

Right now, your business is making an impression. Somewhere, some prospect is encountering your ad, seeing your logo, placing a call to your business, visiting your website, or walking through your door. Based on what the person is seeing or hearing, the prospect is making quick mental calculations about where you fit in the business pecking order, deciding whether your business looks like a top-tier player, an economical alternative, or a struggling start-up — all based on impressions that you may not even know you're making.

The upcoming sections tell you where and when your business makes impressions and how you can align your communications to get people to form the opinion of your business that you want them to have.

Making first impressions

You've heard the saying a thousand times: "You never get a second chance to make a first impression." But your business most often makes its first impressions when you're nowhere to be found. In your stead is your ad, your voice mail message, your direct mailing, your business sign, your employee, or maybe your logo on the back of some midget hockey player's uniform.

Most of the time, your marketing communications make your business impressions *for* you. Ask yourself the following questions as you assess whether your materials are representing you well:

- ✔ When people receive multiple impressions of your business, do they see evidence of a consistent, reliable, well-managed, successful enterprise?
- ✔ Do your communications look like they all represent the same business?
- ✔ Does your logo always look the same? What about the typefaces and colours you use?
- ✔ If you use a tag line or slogan, is it always the same, or does it change from one presentation to the next?

To evaluate what kinds of messages you're sending — and what kinds of impressions you're making — begin by tracking the ways that customers approach your business. Then work backward to determine what marketing efforts brought those customer to your business. And work forward to determine what kinds of impressions customers form when they actually "meet" your business, whether that first contact is made in person, over the phone, by an ad, or online.

Take some time to role-play, following the path that customers take through your business:

- ✔ Stop where they stop.
- ✔ Shop like they shop.
- ✔ Wait where they wait and for as long.

Taking an impression inventory

The only way you can be sure that you're making a consistent impression in your marketplace is to take inventory and study every communication you have with prospects, customers, and others who deal with your business.

You can take an *impression inventory* using a simple form. Across the top of a sheet of paper label five columns with the words listed in bold and described here:

- ✔ **Impression points:** In this column, list every item that carries your name or logo into the marketplace. Use the "Impression Points" list following this section to trigger your thoughts. No item is too small to include. If your ad is a work of art, but your proposal cover is ratty, the negative impact of one will cancel out the positive impact of the other. Every impression counts.

- ✔ **Target market:** Define the purpose of each communication. Is it to develop a new prospect or to communicate with an existing customer — or maybe a little bit of both? If your business has a number of customer types or product lines, you may want to get even more specific.

- ✔ **Who's in charge** of each impression point? Many impressions that affect a business's image are made by those who don't think of themselves as marketers. Nine times out of ten, no one is thinking about marketing when a cost estimate is presented, a bill is sent, or a purchase order is issued. The key is to think about the marketing impact way in advance so that you create materials and usage systems that advance a positive image for your business.

- ✔ **Costs involved:** What does each communication cost in terms of development, media, printing, or other expenses? When you know the answer, you can add up what you're spending on business development, customer retention, and marketing of each product line.

- ✔ **Evaluation:** Go to the next section, "Rating your marketing communications," for tips on how to evaluate your communications.

With the headers in place, your next step is to list down the left side all the "impression points" that apply to your business. To speed the process, you can add to or subtract from the following list:

Impression Points

Advertising and Sales Materials

Newspaper ads

Magazine ads

Television ads

Radio ads

Phone book ads

Other directory ads

Community publication ads

Website or search engine ads

Transit ads and outdoor boards

Other ads

Direct mailers

Sales literature

Brochures

Newsletters

Printed materials (menus, rate cards, instruction sheets, and so on)

Videos, DVDs, or CDs

Speaker support materials (overheads, PowerPoint slides, and so on)

Presentation materials (proposal covers and so on)

Signage

Building signage

Entry door sign

Department signs

Trade show signs

Event signs

Posters

Office displays

Correspondence

Letters

Memos

E-mail

Faxes

Estimates

Purchase orders

Invoices/statements

Business cards

Envelopes

Package labels

Publicity

News release stationery

Press kit folders

Logo items

T-shirts

Baseball caps

Shopping bags

Specialty items (pens, coffee cups, paperweights, gift items, and so on)

When your inventory is complete, answer the following questions:

✔ Are you allocating your efforts well?

✔ Do your communications fit your image and objectives?

✔ Is your image consistent, professional, and well suited to the audiences that matter most to your business?

Rating your marketing communications

Pull samples of stationery, ads, signs, brochures, coffee cups, T-shirts, and any other items that carry your business name or logo. Line them all up and put them through this test:

✔ Does your business name and logo look the same every time you make an impression?

✔ Do you consistently use the same colours?

✔ Do you consistently use the same type style?

✔ Do your marketing materials present a consistent image in terms of look, quality, and message?

Cull the inappropriate items and then look at what's left:

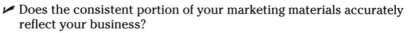

✔ Does the consistent portion of your marketing materials accurately reflect your business?

✔ Do your marketing materials adequately appeal to your target market?

- If you know that your customers value top quality, do your marketing materials convey a top-quality business? Do your ads convey quality? Do you apply your logo only to prestigious advertising items?

- If your customers value economy above all else, do your materials look too upscale?

- If your customers choose you primarily for convenience, do your materials put forth that assurance?

Establishing Your Brand and Position

When people hear your name, they conjure up a set of impressions that influence how they think and buy. Those thoughts define your *brand*.

Branding simply involves developing and consistently communicating a set of positive characteristics that consumers can identify with and relate to your name.

Your brand resides in your customer's mind as a result of all the impressions made by encounters with your name, your logo, your marketing messages, and everything else that people see and hear about your business.

Having a powerful brand

The power of your brand comes from the degree to which it is known. Your small business probably will never have a globally recognized brand simply because you don't have (and for that matter don't need) the marketing horsepower that would fuel that level of awareness. But you *can* be the most powerful brand in your target market by doing the following:

✔ Knowing the brand image that you want to project

✔ Having commitment and discipline to project your brand well

✔ Spending what's necessary to get your message to your target market

✔ Managing your marketing to make a consistent impression that etches your desired brand image into the mind of your target prospect

Staying consistent to build your brand

When your marketing communications create a single impression for your business, they build a strong brand. Stay consistent in your marketing by projecting the following:

✔ A consistent look

✔ A consistent tone in your communications

✔ A consistent level of quality, demonstrated by consistent communications, consistent products, and consistent services

Consistency builds brands, and brands build business.

Following six steps to brand management

Good brand management follows certain steps:

1. **Define why you're in business.**

2. **Consider what you want people to think when they hear your name.**

3. **Think about the words you want people to use when defining your business.**

4. **Pinpoint the advantages you want people to associate with your business.**

5. **Define your brand.**

6. **Build your brand through every impression that you make.**

A well-managed brand creates a strong emotional connection, and a strong emotional connection fosters loyal customer behaviour. Protect and project your brand through every representation of your business in the marketplace.

Filling a Meaningful Market Position

Positioning involves figuring out what meaningful and available niche in the market your business is designed to fill, filling it, and performing so well that your customers have no reason to allow anyone else into your market position. Customers position your business in their own minds. Your job is to lead them to their positioning conclusions through your branding and marketing communications efforts.

How positioning happens

When people learn about your business, subconsciously they slot you into a business hierarchy composed of the following:

- Me-too businesses
- Similar-but-different businesses
- Brand-new offerings

First-in-a-market businesses and first-of-a-kind products have to market fast and fastidiously because, in the end, being first isn't as important as being first into the consumer's mind.

Creating a positioning statement

The easiest way to figure out what position you hold is to determine what hole would be left in the market if your business closed tomorrow. In other words, what does your business offer that your customers would have a hard or impossible time finding elsewhere? Figure 2-1 helps you arrive at your positioning statement. Other questions that will lead to your *positioning statement* include the following:

✔ How is your offering unique or at least difficult to copy?

✔ Is your unique offering something that consumers really want?

✔ Is your offering compatible with economic and market trends?

✔ With which businesses do you compete and how are you different — and better?

✔ Is your claim believable?

Don't aim for a position that requires the market to make a leap of faith on your behalf. If a restaurant is known for the best burgers in town, it can't suddenly decide to try to jump into the position of "the finest steakhouse in the state." Leapfrog doesn't work well when the game is positioning.

Figure 2-1:
This formula helps you build a positioning statement.

Your Name	+	Your Business Description	+	Your Point of Distinction	+	Your Market Description	=	Your Positioning Statement

Your desired position must be

✔ Available

✔ Consistent with the character and offerings of your business

✔ Believable and desirable to the target market

As you write your statement, avoid these traps:

✔ Don't try to duplicate a position in an already crowded category.

✔ Don't base your distinction on a pricing or quality difference that a competitor can take from you.

✔ Don't hang your hat on a factor you can't control.

Conveying Your Position and Brand through Tag Lines

Your *tag line* is the phrase that helps consumers link your name to your business brand and position. A tag line (also called a *slogan*) provides consumers with a quick, memorable phrase that gives an indication of your business brand and position in just a few words.

Positioning statement: For Dummies business and general reference books are lighthearted but not lightweight survival guides that demystify confusing or intimidating topics and give readers everything they need to know without making it seem like a big deal.

Tag line: A Reference for the Rest of Us!

Advancing Your Brand through a Creative Strategy

Your *creative strategy* is the plan that directs the development of all your marketing materials. It defines these elements:

- ✔ Your target market
- ✔ The believable and meaningful benefit you offer to your market
- ✔ The way you present your personality in your communications

Writing your creative strategy

You can write your creative strategy in three sentences that define the purpose, approach, and personality that will guide the creation of your marketing communications, following this formula:

1. **"The purpose of our marketing communications is to convince [insert a brief description of your target market] that our product is the most [describe the primary benefit you provide to customers]."**

2. **"We will prove our claim by [insert a description of why your distinct benefit is believable and how you will prove it in your marketing]."**

3. **"The mood and tone of our communications will be [insert a description of the personality that all your communications will convey]."**

Using your creative strategy

Every time you create an ad, a direct mailer, a voice-mail recording, or even a business letter or an employee uniform or dress code, be 100-percent certain that your communication is consistent with the creative strategy that you've established to guide your business personality. Here are some ways to do so:

✔ Use your creative strategy to guide every representation of your business — and your brand.

✔ Create each new marketing communication with your creative strategy in mind.

✔ Fine-tune your creative strategy annually.

Chapter 3

Creating and Placing Ads

· ·

In This Chapter

▶ Looking at types of ads

▶ Using advertising to move the market to action

▶ Having a media plan

▶ Identifying a well-written ad

▶ Running ads in the best locations and at the right times

▶ Considering broadcast ads

· ·

Contrary to popular belief, great advertising rarely makes the sale for your business. Advertising paves the way, but the sale happens later, after your prospect is motivated by your ad to call or visit your business, request more information, or buy your product.

This chapter offers the information you need to set reasonable expectations for your advertising and to make wise media selections and placements. It also tells you what elements go into effective advertising. (See Book VII for more information about online marketing and advertising.)

Advertising Basics

Basically, ads fall into two categories: ads that promote a business's image and ads that aim to prompt a consumer action. Check out the following two definitions:

- ✔ **Images ads:** If an ad's sole purpose is to build awareness and interest, it is considered an *image ad*. Image ads are also called *brand ads* or *institutional ads*.

- ✔ **Product ads:** If an ad's sole purpose is to present an offer and prompt a corresponding action, it is considered a *product ad*. Product ads are also called *promotional ads, response ads,* or *call-to-action ads*.

Using the image-plus-product advertising approach

Brand advertising is an indulgence that many small businesses, who need every ad to deliver a measurable prospect action, can't afford. Yet call-to-action advertising works best if the prospect already has a favourable impression of the company — achieved through brand advertising. It's a classic catch-22, but one with a good solution.

Instead of choosing between brand ads and product ads, choose *total-approach ads* that build brand awareness, present your offer, *and* prompt consumer action. To create ads that do double and triple duty, follow these steps:

1. **Establish a creative strategy to reign over the creation of all ads, brochures, and communications in your marketing program.**

2. **Establish a creative brief to guide the development of each new ad or other communication effort.**

3. **Hand both your creative strategy and your creative brief to those who will produce your ad.**

Identifying your prospective customer

Before committing dollars to advertising, know your prospect and do everything you can to talk to only that kind of person.

Your *prospective customer* fits the following criteria:

- ✔ Someone who matches the profile of your best existing customers.

- ✔ Someone who wants or needs the kinds of products or services you offer.

- ✔ Someone who can easily access your business, whether by a personal visit or by phone, mail, or Internet.

- ✔ Someone able to purchase from you, by reason of financial ability or ability to meet any qualifications required to buy or own your product.

Creating Ads That Work

Good ads grab attention and lead consumers exactly where they want to go. A good ad accomplishes these three things:

- ✔ Presents *what* the prospect wants to buy.
- ✔ Presents offers that are sensitive to *how* and *when* the prospect wants to buy.
- ✔ Affirms *why* the prospect wants to buy.

Good ads persuade, convince, and nudge prospects into action, all without any apparent effort. They meld the verbiage with the visual and the message with the messenger so the consumer receives a single, inspiring idea.

Creative teams will tell you that making an ad look so simple takes a lot of time and talent — and they're right. If you're spending more than $10,000 to place an ad or more than $100,000 on annual media buys, consider bringing in pros to help you out.

Sampling the Mass Media Menu

Mass media reach many people simultaneously. Mass media reach the population at large rather than specific segments of the population. Advertisers divide mass media into five categories:

- ✔ **Print media:** Includes newspapers, magazines, and directories
- ✔ **Broadcast media:** Includes television and radio
- ✔ **Outdoor media:** Includes billboards, transit signs, murals, and signage
- ✔ **Specialty media:** Includes items imprinted with an advertiser's name and message
- ✔ **New media:** Includes Internet advertising, Web casts, Web pages, and interactive media

For a comparison of different types of mass media, as well as how and why your business might use them, see Table 3-1. The opposite of mass media is *one-to-one communications,* such as personal presentations, telemarketing contacts, direct mailings, and other means of contacting your prospects individually.

Table 3-1	Mass Media Comparisons		
Media Vehicle	**Cost Realities**	**Advertising Considerations**	**What This Medium Does Best**
Newspapers reach a broad market within a specific geographic area.	Inexpensive cost per thousand readers. Inexpensive ad production.	Deadlines allow for quick ad placement decisions.	Good for announcing sales and offers to adults within a geographic area on a frequent basis.
Magazines reach target markets that share specific characteristics and interests.	Advertisers pay for access to highly targeted audience. Advertisers must invest in quality ad design and production.	Ad commitments are due months before publication date. Magazines remain in circulation for long periods of time.	Good for developing awareness, credibility, and interest in complex or high-investment products.
Directories reach prospects at the time of their purchasing decision.	Costs are based on number of categories and ad size chosen by advertiser. Production costs are minimal.	Ad commitments are due months before publication date. Ads are in the market for a year with no chance for revision.	Good at establishing credibility, providing reason to choose one business over others, and reaching prospects when they're ready to take action.
Outdoor Advertising reaches an audience within a geographic area on a repeated basis.	Placement costs are based on traffic counts. Requires investment in sign design/production.	Prime locations are reserved well in advance. Ad commitments usually span a multi-month period.	Good at building name awareness and product interest through a single-sentence message.
Radio reaches a defined local audience — if they're tuned in — with a verbal message.	Airtime is inexpensive and negotiable, but costs more during peak listening times.	Repetition of ad is important. Last-minute decisions and short-term schedules are possible.	Good for building immediate interest and prompt responses to newsy or urgent messages.

Media Vehicle	Cost Realities	Advertising Considerations	What This Medium Does Best
Television reaches a defined audience — if they're tuned in — with visuals and sound.	Reaching large audiences is expensive. Good TV ads often involve significant production budgets.	Repetition of ads is important. Local ads compete for attention with top-quality national ads.	Good at engaging viewer emotions and empathy while explaining or demonstrating products and building credibility.
Web advertising reaches a defined audience — banner ads on commercial Websites can be effective. Search engines like Google can determine who should see what ad and deliver it to their home pages.	Rates are generally moderate but all ad rates are based on the value created.	The opportunity to target very precisely has real advantages but ads are not always seen and consumers can be wary of marketers they haven't heard of.	Good at targeting potential customers by demographic profile based on their Web choices.

Book VI

Marketing

Capturing prospects with a media plan and schedule

The harsh reality is that many prospects disappear en route between your advertising and your cash register. Your media plan determines what specific media you use to best invest your advertising dollar. Your schedule determines when your advertising runs, where, and for how long. With a strong *media plan*, you can increase the number of prospects you bring into your sphere of influence — and almost automatically get more new customers, as well.

Make media decisions based on answers to these four questions:

✔ What do you want your ad to accomplish?

✔ Who and where are the people you want to reach?

✔ What are you trying to say, and when do you need to say it?

✔ How much money is in your media budget?

You can divide your business's advertising budget in a number of different ways, depending on how you decide to balance three scheduling considerations:

✔ **Reach:** This is the number of individuals or homes exposed to your ad. Your media schedule needs to achieve enough reach (that is, your message needs to get into the heads of enough readers or viewers) to generate a sufficient number of prospects to meet your sales objective.

✔ **Frequency:** This means the number of times that an average person is exposed to your message. Your media schedule needs to achieve enough frequency to adequately impress your message into the minds of prospective customers — and that rarely happens with a single ad exposure.

If you have to choose between reach and frequency — and nearly every small business works with a budget that forces that choice — opt to limit your reach to carefully selected target markets and then spend as much as you can on achieving frequency within that area.

✔ **Timing:** This means when your advertising runs. There may be seasonal considerations: you're not going to sell a lot of pumpkins after Halloween. There may be time of day considerations: you're not going to reach a lot of teens with daytime television during the week.

Evaluating Your Advertising Efforts

Your advertising will be more effective if you set objectives and plan your evaluation methods early on. The upcoming sections give you some ideas for evaluating the results of your advertising efforts.

Generating ad responses

The easiest way to monitor ad effectiveness is to produce ads that generate responses and then track how well they do, following these suggestions:

✔ Give the prospect a reason to respond. Offer a brochure, a free estimate, or some other reason to contact your business.

✔ For ads that will be evaluated based on phone activity, visit to a website or response to an e-mail address, create an ad that presents a reason to call, along with an easy-to-read indications of a toll-free number, Web address, or e-mail address.

✔ If you plan to evaluate based on increased foot traffic or cash register activity, present a compelling and time-sensitive offer and be prepared to track which media worked to originate customer activity.

Keying responses

A *key* is a code used to facilitate an advertiser's ability to track the ads that produce an inquiry or order. Here's how to key your ads:

- ✔ Add a unique extension to your phone number.
- ✔ Add a key to coupons that indicate where the coupon was placed.
- ✔ Feature different post office box numbers on ads running in various publications or on various stations.

Writing and Designing Your Ads

Great print ads capture attention, inspire the target market, promote the benefits of a product, prompt the desired consumer action, *and* advance a business's brand. If you're considering creating a print-based ad to attract customers to your business, remember that three important elements of the ad must work together:

- ✔ **Headline:** The print ad's major introductory statement.
- ✔ **Copy:** The words that fill the body of an ad. Good copy talks directly to the prospect. Its point is to connect with and persuade the reader.
- ✔ **Graphics:** The overall look and feel of the ad's design and the placement of elements such as the headline, copy, photos or illustrations, logo and signature line, etc.

Packing power into headlines

Four out of every five people who see your ad will read only the headline. Here's where the rest of the readers go:

- ✔ One reader will see your headline and move on because that reader doesn't have time to study the details at the moment.
- ✔ A second reader will see the headline, but doesn't want or need what you're offering, or can't buy what you're offering at this time.
- ✔ The third reader may find your headline all that's needed to reinforce an existing (hopefully positive) opinion.
- ✔ The fourth (should you be so lucky!) reader will find the headline powerful enough to trigger the desired consumer action.
- ✔ The fifth reader is stopped by your headline and inspired to dive into the ad copy in a genuine desire to learn more. Oh, lucky day!

Attributes of a good headline

Your headline has to pack marketing power. It is your only chance to communicate with 80 percent of your prospects and it's your hook for baiting the other 20 percent into your marketing message. If your headline doesn't grab and inspire readers, your ad copy doesn't stand a chance. Here's what your headline needs to do:

- ✔ Flag the attention of your prospect by saying, in essence, "Stop! This message concerns you."
- ✔ Appeal to your target prospect individually and immediately.
- ✔ Promote an answer or solution to a problem.
- ✔ Convey a meaningful benefit.
- ✔ Advance your brand image.

How to write a headline

Whether you do it yourself or call on the talents of a professional copywriter or advertising agency, follow these headline tips:

- ✔ **Lead with your most powerful point.** Traditionally words like "save" and "new" have stopping power. Try to present the benefit to the reader as clearly as possible

- ✔ **Turn features into benefits.** Windows are a feature. Lots of natural light and views of a mountain are benefits. Think of the reader and present the benefit to him

- ✔ **Use both uppercase and lowercase letters. It's hard for readers to read words and especially sentences in capital letters.**

- ✔ **Don't end your headline with a period. You want the reader to move on, not stop there.**

- ✔ **Use the word *you*.** It's the most magnetic word in advertising. Every time you get ready to write *we,* turn the spotlight to the consumer by using *you.*

- ✔ **Tell *how*.** People are attracted to the feeling of interaction that the word *how* conveys. Write a headline that includes *how to . . .* or *how you . . .* to up your chances that the prospect will continue on to the first line of the ad copy.

- ✔ **Use power words.** Whenever you can, grab your readers' attention with the long-proven power of words such as *free, new, save, better, now,* and other words that communicate that your offer is special and worth reading about.

Writing convincing copy

The first sentence of your ad copy only has to do one thing: Make the reader want to continue to the second sentence. The second sentence needs to lure the prospect on to the third sentence. And so good ad copy goes, carrying consumers through your ad, building credibility and trust, and convincing readers of the merit of your message, until, finally, it makes an irresistible offer and tells readers exactly how to respond.

Making design decisions

When readers are asked which ads they remember positively, the following design traits emerge:

- ✔ **Use visual elements:** Whenever you can, include an attention-getting visual element in your ads. Use a photo or illustration, and let your visual *show* what your ad's headline and copy are *telling* readers.

- ✔ **Keep it simple:** Streamline your design to help readers focus on the important points of your ad. Keep your ad design uncluttered by framing the ad with wide-open space and ensuring the ad is easy to follow.

Looking at Ad Placement

Where and when you place print advertisements is as important as the ads themselves. The following sections give you some advice on putting ads in newspapers, magazines, and other places for readers to see them. Most print publications also have websites and online versions. You can make a media buy that combines print and Web or you can buy each of these separately. With increasing numbers of Web readers, online publications can be part of a strategy for reaching your market segment. For more about online marketing, see Book VII.

Newspaper ads

Myths are rampant about which day gets the most readership, but the fact is this: From Monday through Friday, the number of people who open their papers varies only 3 percent, with Tuesday's paper outpulling the others because in most markets it carries the food ads. If you want your ad to generate results, heed these tips:

✔ Place your ad on the day that makes sense for your market and message.

✔ Advertising in the large weekend edition of the paper usually costs more — and delivers more.

Even though more readers note full-page newspaper ads than half-page ads, and more note half-page ads than quarter-page ads, small-budget, small-size advertisers can still benefit from this type of advertising.

Partial-page ads pull fewer readers — but the reader numbers don't drop as fast as the cost of the space does. For example, while a full-page ad pulls about 40 percent more readers than a quarter-page ad, the quarter-page ad costs roughly a quarter of the price. As you work out a small-budget ad plan with your advertising salesperson, follow some general advice:

✔ If you have to choose, opt for frequency over size.

✔ Match your ad size to the size of your message.

✔ Aim to dominate the page.

✔ If you're not the biggest, be the most consistent.

Placing magazine ads

When a full-page, colour ad in *Macleans* magazine costs tens of thousands of dollars, you may wonder why small businesses should even bother considering magazine advertising. The reason is that thousands of small circulation (and vastly more affordable) magazines exist — plus, many of the best-known magazines print regional or even city editions in which you can place an ad for a fraction of the full-edition price.

Most small businesses limit their magazine ads to publications that serve particular business or interest groups, or — especially in the case of those in the travel industry — to city or regional travel magazines.

Review the magazines that serve your industry or your target market. A good reference is the *Canadian Advertising Rates and Data (CARD)* advertising sourcebook, which is available on the shelves of many public libraries and online at `www.srds.com/frontMatter/ips/canadian`; however, access to the website is relatively expensive.

Out-of-home advertising

Out-of-home ads include billboards, transit displays, waiting bench signs, wall murals, building or facility signs, vehicle signs, movie theatre billboard-style ads, and even flyover signs. In placing and creating out-of-home ads, two truths prevail:

✔ Location is everything. The amount of traffic the location gets, the demographics of the drivers who will see it, and the visibility of the billboard itself are among the important location features.

✔ Ads must pass the at-a-glance test. You've got five seconds to make an impression and probably a maximum of about five words to convey both your name and the reason to buy your product. The kind of type and the size of the type have to make the billboard impression count or it's money wasted.

Broadcasting Ads on Radio and TV

If you plan to venture into the world of broadcast ad production for either radio or TV scheduling and placement, count on the following pages to help guide your decisions.

Whether you're producing a television ad or a radio ad, some general broadcast advertising guidelines apply.

Buying airtime

If you're placing ads on just a few stations in your own hometown market, you can probably handle the task on your own. But if your marketing needs involve multiple market areas, or if you're spending more than $10,000 on a media buy, use a *media buyer* to wheel, deal, apply clout, and bring the kind of muscle that comes from experience in the field. You'll pay an hourly fee or a percentage of your overall buy, but you'll save time and confusion and almost certainly you'll obtain a better schedule and price. If you're using an advertising agency to create your ad, media planning and buying usually come as part of the service.

If you're going to do it yourself, begin by requesting a *rate card* for each station you believe will reach your target market. The rate card will explain the various costs for placing advertising at various times, based on the length of the ad (usually 30 seconds). Use the rate card as a cost guideline. In broadcast, prices vary depending on availability, time of day, time of year, and the commitment you're willing to make to the station.

Achieving broadcast reach and frequency

In the case of the reach and frequency (which we discuss earlier in this chapter) of broadcast advertising, the accepted rule is that a broadcast ad needs to reach a prospect three to five times before it triggers action, which usually requires a schedule of 27 to 30 ad broadcasts.

Increase advertising impact by opting for frequency over reach. Instead of airing ads on ten stations (wide reach), choose two of the stations and talk to the same people repeatedly (high frequency).

It takes *reach* to achieve awareness, but it takes *frequency* to change minds.

Establishing your own broadcast identity

Over time, you want listeners or viewers to recognize your business before they even hear your name. Consider the following identity-building techniques:

- **Sound:** Have the same announcer serve as the voice in all your ads.

- **Style:** Establish a broadcast ad style — for example, an ongoing dialogue between the same two people, or ads that always advance a certain kind of message.

- **Music:** If you use music or sound effects, use the same notable background in all your ads.

- **Jingles:** A jingle is a short catchy piece of music with words written specifically for your business or product. A great jingle creates an ear worm, a song you can't get out of your head. "I'd like to buy the world a Coke" is one example. "I'm stuck on Band-Aid 'cuz Band-Aid's stuck on me" is another. Before investing in a jingle, make sure you will air enough broadcast ads to achieve an association between the jingle and your name, and make sure the jingle is appropriate to your brand image.

Overseeing the writing of your broadcast ad

Don't write your own broadcast ad. Instead, write your ad strategy and objective and then bring in professional help to develop your concept and write your script. As you work with your advertising professional, keep these tips in mind:

- Be strategic.
- Know your objective.
- Develop your ad concept.
- Grab audience attention.
- Tell a story.

Book VI

Marketing

Wanna be a star?

Think long and hard about serving as your own ad talent. Even if you're your firm's best advocate, you aren't necessarily its best spokesperson. Do you have the best voice and appearance to serve as your own on-air talent? Can you commit the time? Can your advertising build a story around you, thereby making your appearance part of your message and not just a substitute for paid talent? Do you *want* to be the spokesperson? If you're considering selling your business in the future, will your presence in your advertising help or hinder that effort?

In a 30-second broadcast ad, you have about 20 seconds to inform, educate, entice, and entertain — and even less if you cede time to a jingle or other sound effects. The other seconds get divided between an attention-getting opening and your ad identification and *call to action*, what you want the listener or watcher to do right after the ad runs (Call 1-800-555-1212 now; Visit us on Main Street next to the Post Office today). Be sure to do the following in your ad:

✔ Feature your name (or product name) at least three times.

✔ Feature your call to action at least once, preferably twice.

✔ If you include an address, provide an easy locator (for example, "Just across from the train station").

Producing good radio ads

If you're opting to advertise your business with a radio ad, the ad needs to accomplish a lot in only 30 or 60 seconds. A good radio ad grabs attention, involves a listener, sounds believable, creates a mental picture, spins a story, calls for action, and manages to keep the product on centre stage and the customer in the spotlight — all without sounding pushy, screamy, obnoxious, or boring.

Great writers tell you to *write out loud* when you create radio ads. Here's how:

✔ Use straightforward language.

✔ Write to the pace people talk.

✔ Include pauses.

✔ Cut extra verbiage.

✔ Write simple sentences.

Along with a well-written script, radio ads should always tell listeners what to do next. Prepare them to take down your business's phone number ("Have a pencil handy?"), or at least repeat your phone number for them. Most important, help them remember your name so they can find you in the phone book or online.

Producing good TV ads

People spend more time with the television than with any other advertising medium. "I saw it on TV" has become a mark of having made it into the advertising major leagues. To get there, though, be prepared to make a financial commitment.

Successful television advertisers have two things in common: They earmark adequate ad production budgets and they fund media schedules that span at least a multi-month period. If you can do both those things — produce a quality ad and fund an adequate schedule — TV advertising will deliver awareness and credibility for your business.

Notice that this section isn't titled "Creating your TV ad." *Do not* create your own television ad.

As you select a creative partner, rely on the following potential resources:

- ✔ Advertising agencies
- ✔ Video production services
- ✔ TV station production facilities

You may not need to produce a TV ad from scratch. High-quality, ready-to-air ads may be available to you through your manufacturers or dealers. *Manufacturer ads* feature the manufacturer's products, but they include time to add a tag line directing viewers to your business. If you go this route, consider the following:

- ✔ Manufacturer ads work best only for products with major sales potential for your business and for which your business is the exclusive regional representative.
- ✔ The ads are likely to be of higher quality than you could afford to produce on your own. By adding your own tag line, you'll gain advertising visibility while benefiting your business through association with a major national advertiser.
- ✔ The manufacturer may be willing to work with you. When airing manufacturer ads, contact the manufacturer to discuss the possibility of obtaining cooperative advertising support in the form of shared costs for the media placements.

Chapter 4

Reaching Your Market in More Ways

In This Chapter

▶ Building relationships using one-to-one marketing

▶ Producing marketing literature

▶ Attending trade shows and offering promotions

▶ Peering at the world of public relations

Developing what is known as integrated marketing communications allows various communications media, including advertising, to build on each other and create an environment that promotes brand recognition and drives sales. In this chapter we look at some of the tools of integrated marketing communications, which you can use alone or combined with advertising to give your business a competitive advantage in the marketplace.

Reaching Your Market Directly

Direct mail is one-to-one communication that delivers your marketing message to carefully selected prospects and customers, one at a time. Some call it junk mail, but it is far from junk in the hands of an able marketer. It is an effective marketing tool when used properly and for the right purposes. That's why most of the mail you receive today is likely to be bills (with direct marketing enclosed) or stand-alone direct mailers in the form of addressed mail, catalogues, and postcards as well unaddressed flyers and other promotional pieces. (Book VII gives you more information about e-mail and online direct marketing.)

One-to-one communication is the exact opposite of mass media advertising. (Refer to Chapter 3 of this book for more on the subject.) *Mass media advertising* uses the shotgun approach — that is, you create an ad and use newspapers, magazines, and broadcast media to spread the message far and wide. *One-to-one communications* aim your message only at specific and well-defined individuals.

Most marketers believe that the two approaches work best as a tag team effort: You use mass media advertising to build awareness, desire, and perceived value for your products and then use one-to-one marketing to call for the order and to form the basis of a lasting customer relationship.

If you can only afford to do one or the other, however, consider placing your bets on one-to-one marketing so that each dollar you spend is aimed straight at a qualified prospect, and not scattered through mass media to reach prospects and non-prospects alike.

When you employ one-to-one marketing, you bypass mass media vehicles and take your ad straight to the mailboxes, telephones, and computer screens of individuals who are prime prospects for your product or service. You may hear the terms *direct marketing, database marketing, direct-response advertising,* and *direct mail* used interchangeably.

Exploring direct sales strategies

Just as you'd guess, marketers who employ *direct sales* strategies sell to consumers directly, without involving middlemen, retailers, agents, or other representatives. Following are three examples of how direct marketing tools can generate direct sales:

- ✔ **Direct response advertising:** A jewellery maker advertises his wares by placing small black-and-white magazine advertisements. But instead of aiming to build general awareness, the ads invite readers to call toll-free to purchase the featured item or, alternatively, to visit the jeweller's website to view and order from his complete line. Either way, the instructions in the ad lead straight back to the jewellery maker and not to any retailer or other intermediary.

- ✔ **Direct mail:** The self-publisher of a book featuring lists and ratings for summer youth camps promotes the book by sending a postcard promoting the book through unaddressed mail to neighbourhoods with a high concentration of families with school-aged children.

- ✔ **Catalog distribution:** A kitchen accessories company generates direct sales by mailing its catalog to the households of current and past customers, ad respondents, and subscribers of gourmet magazines.

Direct mail success factors

Direct mailers are among the easiest of all marketing communications to monitor for success. With each mailing, you know exactly how many pieces you're sending and, therefore, how many prospects you're reaching. And because direct mailers almost always request an easy-to-track direct response (in the form of a sale, an inquiry, a visit to your business, or some other prospect action), within weeks you can count the responses to learn the effectiveness of your direct mail effort.

To increase your chances for success, consider that the most successful direct mailers all rely on these three important factors:

✔ A targeted list

✔ A compelling offer

✔ An attention-getting format

Building your direct mail list

Book VI

Marketing

With direct mail, your marketing investment is aimed precisely at those prospects who possess the exact characteristics that make them likely to buy from your business:

✔ Demographic lists

✔ Geographic lists

✔ Geodemographic lists (a combination of the above)

You can create your own list or you can obtain lists from outside organizations.

Creating your own list

If you market in a local or very clearly defined market area, you'll probably want to create your own list rather than buy one from outside your company. As you go about assembling the names for your list, follow these steps:

1. **Start with your established customer and prospect base.**

2. **Segment names according to past purchasing patterns or interests.**

3. **Turn to local business and community directories to add to the list.**

4. **Enter all the names into a database.**

Getting lists outside your business

If you haven't got much of a direct mail list based on your existing customers, other businesses can help you:

✔ **Mailing services and list brokerage businesses:** These organizations can assist your business with developing a direct mail list or provide list rental services.

Working with an outside organization, be sure you can define your prospect profile by stating where your most likely customers reside geographically and who they are in terms of age, income, family size, education, and other lifestyle facts.

✔ **Magazine subscriber lists:** You may also be able to get a list of magazine subscribers, as many magazines will rent their subscriber lists to businesses with approved product offers.

✔ **RDS Direct Marketing List Source:** This guide, published by the Standard Rate and Data Service, is available from public libraries or you can access it online for a charge at www.srds.com/frontMatter/ips/directmarketing. It features data on thousands of mailing lists in hundreds of categories for sources of mailing in Canada and globally.

An hour or so browsing the catalog will help you focus on the kinds of lists available — useful information to know before you enter discussions about list rentals with magazine publishers or mailing service professionals.

Mailing services go by many names: direct response specialists, bulk mailers, database managers, mail processors, and list managers. They provide professional assistance in taking care of every aspect of your mail or e-mail campaign.

Deciding on a direct mail offer

A successful direct mail offer must relate to — and build credibility in — your product or service. It should also be unique, valuable, and interesting to your prospect.

A good offer contains the following elements:

✔ A great deal (Buy 1, get 1 free)

✔ A guarantee (If it isn't the best book you've ever read, send it back for a full refund)

✔ A time limit (Offer expires January 30, so order today)

The best mailers also state your offer clearly and provide a toll-free number or postage paid card, Web address, or e-mail address for customers to take action.

Although every direct mailer wants a strong response rate, remember that your goal is to receive *quality* responses. If your offer is *too* great, it will generate responses from people who simply want your gift. So don't go overboard.

Writing direct mail messages

First things first: If your mailing is any larger than a postcard or self-mailer, *enclose a letter.*

In your letter, follow each and every piece of advice for writing advertising copy (refer to Chapter 3 of this book), and ensure you do the following:

- ✔ Start with a short, clear, strong first sentence.

- ✔ Tell your prospects what's in it for them.

- ✔ Get to the point quickly.

- ✔ Talk in terms that matter to your market.

- ✔ With direct mail, you can take the time and space you need to make your message clear as long as you can keep your reader interested. Good direct mail letters allow for different levels of reading. Headings and messages in boxes, underlining, and colour draw attention to the central messages, with more detail provided in the regular type.

- ✔ Finish with a P.S. (Some studies show that as many as three-quarters of readers actually read the P.S. first. Use it to summarize your sales message, reiterate key benefits, make a pitch for and reinforce the value of your offer, remind the reader of the time-sensitivity of your offer, and tell how to contact you.)

Following up

Half of all responses arrive within two weeks of the date that people receive a direct mailing.

How many replies should you expect? Brace yourself: 1 to 3 percent is considered a home run with a purchased or outside list. If you use internal lists that are full of highly qualified names, you can hope for a 5 to 10 percent return, or sometimes higher.

But no matter how many responses you get, don't wait even one week to get back to your direct mail respondents. Follow up on responses in the following way:

- ✔ Enclose a letter thanking the respondent for the inquiry.

- ✔ Enclose the item that you promised (the brochure, coupon, or the actual product you promised) in your initial mailing, along with a description.

- ✔ Introduce your business in terms of benefits that matter to the consumer.

- ✔ Offer the next step in the buying process or promote a repeat sale.

If you don't think you can handle the volume of responses in a timely manner, send your mailers out in groups of several hundred every three or four days. This ensures that the responses will be staggered as well.

Creating a database of respondents

After following up on a response you receive, enter the respondent's name into a database. Within eight weeks, contact prospects a second time via a mailing, phone call, or — if they've invited you to do so — an e-mail newsletter or update.

Sending a second mailing to non-respondents

Within 30 days of your first mailing, contact all recipients who have not yet responded. (If you are using an outside list, rent the list for two-time usage and obtain a duplicate set of labels for this purpose.)

Research proves that follow-up with non-respondents increases your overall response rate dramatically. It also gives you much more value for the cost of the list rental, because the second-time usage is usually at a fraction of the cost of the initial usage.

Written Materials, Trade Shows, and Promotions

Mass media advertising and direct mailings are the most obvious ways to promote your business, but the communications toolbox also includes a long list of other effective (and often far less expensive) communication vehicles to consider.

Brochures and fliers, free giveaway items known as *advertising specialties,* product promotions, trade show appearances, and sales presentations are all means of carrying your message into the marketplace.

Most of these alternatives come with low price tags, and for that reason many small businesses use them with a nothing-ventured-nothing-gained-or-lost attitude. The following sections offer advice so that every marketing investment — however large or small — works to your advantage while contributing to a favourable image of your business.

Producing and using marketing literature

Marketing literature is various written pieces such as brochures, catalogues, and flyers that a business produces to provide information and selling features of products and services to customers. If the following scenarios are true of your business, you need some marketing literature:

✔ Your prospects aren't easy to contact in person or by phone but would likely respond to literature about your business.

✔ Your business would benefit from a printed piece that could be sent ahead of sales presentations to pave the way for your visit, or left afterwards to reiterate key points.

✔ You're trying to communicate with individuals who aren't easily or affordably reached by mass media, but who are likely to pick up literature at information kiosks or other distribution points.

✔ Your service or product is complicated and involves details that your prospects need to study in order to make informed decisions.

✔ The price of your product is high enough or the emotional involvement is such that prospects will consult with others before making the decision, in which case they will benefit (as you will, too) from a brochure that conveys your message in your absence when your prospects consult with advisers, associates, or spouses.

Types of marketing literature

Marketing literature runs the gamut from elaborate folders filled with sets of matching fact sheets to laser-printed cards that sit on countertops or in *Take one* racks. The following points help you sort through the opportunities:

✔ **Capabilities brochure:** A *capabilities brochure* is an "about our business" piece that tells your story, conveys your business personality, and differentiates your offerings from those of your competitors.

✔ **Product brochure:** A *product brochure* is a piece that describes a specific offering of your business.

✔ **Modular literature:** Modular literature involves a number of sheets or brochures that all use the same or a complementary design.

✔ **Rack cards:** Rack cards get their name from the fact that they fit into 4-x-9-inch brochure racks.

✔ **Fliers:** The least expensive promotional piece you can print is a flier, which usually takes the form of an 8½-x-11-inch sheet of paper printed on one side or both.

Writing and designing brochures

The best brochures talk directly to the prospect, anticipating questions and providing answers before the person even thinks to ask. As you develop brochure content, refer to these copywriting tips:

- ✔ Include a headline.
- ✔ Use subheads.
- ✔ Write directly to your prospect.
- ✔ Avoid technical jargon, long feature descriptions, and clichés.
- ✔ Tell what to do next (call, go to a website, etc.).
- ✔ Make the next step in the buying process an easy one.
- ✔ Revise and proofread.

You want to ensure that all your marketing materials look the same and offer a positive impression of your business and your brand. (Chapter 2 of this book tells you more about the power of branding.) As you proceed, keep the following tips in mind:

- ✔ Keep your brochure quality in line with the nature of your offering.
- ✔ Know your business's type and colour guidelines.
- ✔ Make your business name and logo visible.

Launching and maintaining newsletters

Newsletters are informal, friend-to-friend communications that deliver newsworthy information, useful updates, reminders of what your business does, and ideas of interest and use to newsletter recipients. They can be printed and distributed, but more often than not are sent electronically today. Regardless of the delivery method you use, keep the following advice in mind.

Planning your newsletter

Newsletters work only when they're produced and distributed on a consistent basis, which means you have to commit to the long haul before you undertake the first issue. As you consider developing a newsletter for your business, do the following:

- ✔ Define the purpose of your newsletter.
- ✔ Establish how often you will produce and send your newsletter.
- ✔ Decide who will receive your newsletter.
- ✔ Set your newsletter budget.

Writing and designing your newsletter

Here is good news for small-budget marketers: The most effective newsletters look newsy and current rather than expensive and laboured, which puts newsletters among the most economical of marketing materials.

In creating your newsletter, consider the following points:

- ✔ Include many short items rather than a few long ones.
- ✔ Establish a simple format and stick with it issue after issue.
- ✔ Invite reader responses to help you gauge the effectiveness of your newsletter.

Converting business material to marketing opportunity

For all the money that small businesses spend on marketing, they often look right past the free opportunities that exist to coattail marketing messages onto their own business materials.

Following are three tactics that deliver excellent return on their almost non-existent investments:

- ✔ Using your packages as advertising vehicles.
- ✔ Building business with gift certificates.
- ✔ Papering the market with business cards.

Choosing and using trade shows

Most industry associations hold trade shows where attendees can hear presentations on industry trends and promote their products and services. Attending trade shows is a great way to maintain customer contacts, introduce products to your business, develop and maintain media relations, and stay on top of industry and competitive developments. The only drawback — and it's a big one — is that even in the most targeted industry, you have a lineup of trade shows from which to choose.

Because attendance at even one show costs a significant amount of time, money, and energy, invest cautiously, using this checklist:

- ✔ Choose shows carefully.

- ✔ Decide whether you need to invest in a booth or whether you can achieve visibility by buying an ad in the show guide, making a presentation, hosting a reception, or simply working the floor.

- ✔ Know whom you want to attract to your booth, what you want to communicate, and what action you want to inspire.

- ✔ Know how you will capture trade show visitor information and how you will follow up with your trade show contacts.

Building sales through promotions

A promotion aims to increase sales over a short time period by offering an incentive that prompts consumers to take immediate action.

Why use promotions

Businesses stage promotions for a number of reasons, such as the following:

- ✔ To increase activity by existing customers.

- ✔ To entice the attention of new customer prospects.

- ✔ To urge customers to adopt new buying patterns, such as greater dollar volume per transaction, more frequent purchases, or purchases via a certain payment method.

- ✔ To stimulate sales during slow seasons by offering limited-time special pricing or added-value offers.

Choosing your promotion incentive

The whole purpose of a promotion is to create a desired consumer action over a short period of time. The objective is accomplished by offering one of the following types of action incentives:

- ✔ **Price savings:** Incentives include percentage discounts, two-for-one offers, buy-one-get-one-free deals, and other appealing reductions. The bigger the incentive, the more attractive to the consumer.

- ✔ **Samples:** Businesses introducing new products or trying to win over competitors' customers offer samples or free trials to prove their advantage and get their products into circulation.

- ✔ **Events and experiences:** Events draw crowds, spurring increased sales and sometimes even attracting media coverage.

Looking at Public Relations

The Canadian Public Relations Society (CPRS) defines *public relations* as "the strategic management of relationships between an organization and its diverse publics, through the use of communication, to achieve mutual understanding, realize organizational goals and serve the public interest" (Flynn, Gregory & Valin, 2008). Other professionals say that public relations involves activities that aim to establish, maintain, and improve a favourable relationship with the public upon whom an organization's success depends.

The field of public relations consists of the following:

✔ Media relations

✔ Employee or member relations

✔ Community relations

✔ Industry relations

✔ Government relations

✔ Issues and crisis management

Focusing on publicity

When you get mentioned in the media, that's *publicity*. Each time you succeed in generating positive publicity, you score a triple victory. First, you win valuable editorial mentions in mass media vehicles. Second, you win consumer confidence, as people tend to find information they receive through the editorial content of mass media more believable than they find paid advertising messages. And third, you can use reprints of the coverage you obtain through your publicity efforts to add credibility to your other marketing communications by enclosing copies in direct mailings, sales presentations, and press kits.

Orchestrating media coverage

If your story conveys timely and useful information — if it tells something new, or a different or easier way to do something — then package it up and get it to the media. Be prepared to proceed with both tenacity and patience, however, because the art of getting your name into the news requires both.

Getting real with your expectations

To generate publicity for your business, commit to a long-haul program and keep the following in mind:

- ✔ Don't expect instant or even consistent results.
- ✔ Tailor your story to individual editorial contacts.
- ✔ Don't try to get news coverage as a perk for your advertising investments.
- ✔ Don't peddle hype as news.
- ✔ Don't hound the media.
- ✔ Aim for quality — not quantity.

Circulating your news with a new release

News releases summarize stories appropriate for coverage in the editorial portion of news media. They are the main tool used in the effort to generate publicity. News releases are also called *press releases,* but with the ever-growing impact of broadcast and Internet news, the term *news release* provides a more appropriate and all-encompassing label.

Increasingly news is submitted electronically using e-mail. You can circulate your business's news in three main ways:

- ✔ Distribute it yourself.
- ✔ Hire a public relations firm.
- ✔ Use a news distribution service such as CNW (Canada Newswire). (See www.newswire.ca.)

In addition to media distribution, leverage your news release by using it in the following ways:

- ✔ Post your release on your website.
- ✔ Distribute your release to those of influence to your business, including clients and those in a position to refer business your way.
- ✔ Post it within your company.

Writing news releases

Develop your release by first deciding on an *angle* from which to present your news. This involves deciding what makes the facts you are sharing timely, interesting, and worthy of media interest.

When you know your angle, begin writing your release in this order:

- ✔ When the news can be released
- ✔ A headline
- ✔ A dateline
- ✔ Clear presentation of the facts
- ✔ Quotes
- ✔ Boilerplate information about your company
- ✔ Whom to contact for more information

Establishing media contacts

Create a list of trade and regular journalists, editors, and reporters that serve your geographic and industry arena, including the following outlets:

- ✔ Your local daily newspaper
- ✔ Regional weekly and business publications
- ✔ The radio and television stations that broadcast in your area
- ✔ Your industry publications

Managing media interviews

When you hit the publicity jackpot and a reporter calls for an interview, be ready!

Before the interview

Get the details. In advance of the interview, confirm the publication or station name and deadline, along with the interview topic, the angle of the story, and the type of questions you will be asked. Ask whether others will be interviewed for the same story.

Then take time to prepare yourself. When you know the scope of the interview, get ready by doing the following:

- ✔ Jot down the two or three most important messages (also called *key messages*) that you want to convey about the topic.

- ✔ Grab any appropriate reference materials that will help you make your points clearly.

- ✔ Consider negative issues that might arise and develop short responses.

- ✔ Think about what photos, charts, industry statistics, or other materials you'd like to offer to the reporter to enhance the coverage.

During the interview

Proceed with confidence — and caution — during media interviews. Answer questions clearly and then stop talking. Bring responses to questions back to your important messages.

Don't say anything you don't want to read or hear later. You can ask not to be quoted by stating that your comments are *not for attribution,* and you can say that a comment is *off the record.* But there are no guarantees.

After the interview

Following the interview, thank the reporter and ask when the article will run or air. Don't demand prior review of the story, but do offer to be available to assist in confirming any facts or quotes.

Guidelines for broadcast interviews

In preparing for and conducting radio or television interviews, follow all the earlier interview advice and then add these items to your checklist:

- ✔ Ask whether the program will be live or taped. The good *and* bad news about live shows is that they can't be edited.

- ✔ Ask the name of the program and host and then watch the show to acquaint yourself with the style.

- ✔ Confirm the interview site and length. If the location is out of town, ask whether the studio pays transportation and lodging costs.

- ✔ Ask whether other guests will be part of the same show. If so, ask the producer who they are and what point of view they represent. The interviewer may be setting up a battleground — in which case, you'll want to arrive at the interview with a bulletproof strategy.

- ✔ Ask whether submitting a biography and list of possible discussion topics in advance would be helpful.

Book VII
Online Marketing

In this book . . .

Chapter 1: Creating an Online Presence for
  Your Business 551

Chapter 2: Getting Started with Mobile Marketing 563

Chapter 3: Getting Ready to Use SEO and Web Analytics ... 571

Chapter 1

Creating an Online Presence for Your Business

In This Chapter

▶ Creating a website that works

▶ Discovering ways to make money online

▶ Blogging for business

▶ Understanding social media

*T*oday — with the world sending 35 billion e-mails a day, the Internet hosting 10 million websites, and e-commerce ringing up retail and travel sales in the billions and growing steadily — it's hard to remember that the Internet didn't even enter business conversation until the mid-1990s, and back then most discussions ended with more questions than answers.

The idea of NOT having a website, of NOT harnessing the power of the Internet to get, maintain, serve, and sell to customers is nearly unthinkable today. Many businesses depend on the Internet for some aspect of their business. Others would not be in business at all if it weren't for the Internet, and that number is growing every day.

This chapter takes you through the basics of creating a website and choosing the functionality you need to support your business. We look at ways to make money online including selling your own products and profiting from helping other businesses sell theirs. And we look at blogging and social media as ways to establish presence, create profile, and drive sales.

Putting a Website to Work for You

Whether you want your business's website to create corporate credibility or act as an area for customers to place and track orders and pay, most businesses today need a website.

As you embark on creating and launching your website, you must ensure you do the following:

- ✔ Define how prospects and customers will use your site.
- ✔ Define your goal for the site.
- ✔ Commit to the cost, including site construction, hosting, and support.
- ✔ Be ready to market your site.

Types of websites

Defining the purpose of a website is just like defining the purpose of any other business communication. You need to know whom you're trying to talk to, what people currently know or think about your business, what you *want* them to know or think, and, most of all, what action you want them to take after encountering this communication with your business.

Most business websites fall into one of three categories:

- ✔ **Contact and brochure sites:** These are promotional sites that tell who you are and what you do. These websites are the easiest and most economical to create and maintain. They allow prospects to find your business online, find out how to contact you, and find out information about your products or services.

- ✔ **Support sites:** These websites provide online customer service and communication. They offer information about product installation, usage, and troubleshooting; share industry trends and product update news; and help customers put products to use. Support sites also often include e-commerce components as well.

- ✔ **E-commerce sites:** The primary purpose of an e-commerce site is to sell goods online. Site visitors can view products, make choices, place orders, and submit payments.

Building your website

Unless you're a Web designer, turn to the pros for assistance in building a custom site for your business. This approach will cost you time and money — that's the downside. The upside is that you'll end up with a website that conveys your unique brand image, with a viewing and navigation system precisely tailored to your business, all built on a platform that can grow with your business.

If you do decide to create your own website, you can use templates provided by Internet hosting and site-development resources. An online search will result in hundreds of potential service providers who can provide templates at little or no cost.

Creating website content

As you prepare content that you want to appear on your website, use the following guidelines:

✔ Organize content into well-defined categories. A modular approach to presenting information works best. (See the section "website navigation" for examples of how to organize the content.)

✔ Limit the number of words you use and use short paragraphs and sentences. Online readers demand clarity and ease of use. Go for visibility over volume.

✔ Make the information easy to skim so readers can scan over the material and stop where and when they find what's pertinent to them.

✔ Communicate directly to your customer, anticipating what the customer is looking for and putting it where the customer will most likely look for it.

✔ Make the visit to your website worthwhile by delivering on the promise. For example, if the goal is to tell prospects about your company, provide names of satisfied clients, areas of expertise, and profiles of the team that will provide an experience equal to the prospect's expectation.

Book VII

Online Marketing

Setting up website navigation

To help visitors get around your site, present them with clearly labelled selections. For example, labels such as Technical Support, Our Products, Our Customers, News, Contact Us, and Frequently Asked Questions tell people way more about what to expect — and are easier to read — than labels like Features, Information, What People Are Saying, or other more ambiguous descriptions. Keep these tips in mind as you develop your site navigation:

✔ Start with a home page that tells visitors exactly what you want them to know about your business — clearly and immediately.

✔ Let visitors jump from section to section and page to page with ease.

✔ Provide a link back to your home page from every page.

✔ Keep choices clear and to a minimum by creating a logical flow in the navigation. websites should rarely be exhaustive in their content. They should generally leave people wanting more — which they can get from you.

✔ Provide a site map so users can see how your site is organized.

Knowing the attributes of a good site

You know a good website when you get to it. You stay there and you get what you expect. You also know what happens when you get to a poorly designed or written website. You get off and go somewhere else fast.

Good websites have some common strengths:

✔ The purpose of the site is clear.

✔ The site immediately tells the visitor what the company is and what it does.

✔ The site is organized so visitors can easily find and access information.

✔ Visitors can quickly learn how to contact people at the business.

✔ The site comes up on all computers with different operating systems quickly and reliably.

✔ The site is easy to read and use.

✔ The look of the site creates a good impression of the business.

✔ The site doesn't crash or give error messages.

✔ The website's content is well written, clear, and directed at visitors' wants and needs.

Generating traffic to your website

Here are five ways to increase the amount of *traffic* (the number of visitors) a website sees, which virtually all businesses can benefit from:

✔ **Free search optimization:** Many search engines and directories don't require you to pay a fee to get listed. Google, MSN, and Yahoo! are good examples. Optimizing your site content can help you appear higher in search engine results and attract more visitors to your website, as Chapter 3 of this book explains.

✔ **Paid search:** With the growth of measurement tools (such as Google Analytics, for example), paid search has become an accepted and essential form of promotion for any product or service. You can put your banner ad or other content on someone else's website and pay them for the privilege as a monthly fee or by the number of visitors that come to you referred by that site.

✔ **Supplying content:** Just when you think every topic of content has been covered, new angles and opinions emerge. Supplying content to the Web through blogs (see the heading "Blogging" a bit later on in this chapter), really simple syndication (RSS), press releases, articles, and forums, and the growing surge of content pushing to cellphones are traffic-generating processes.

✔ **Offline efforts:** Don't overlook your opportunities to use offline resources to promote your website: radio interviews, networking, and public speaking are all good ways to build traffic.

✔ **Referrals:** Whether referrals come from offline or online, always strive to increase visitors who are referred by someone else. This means getting onto other business sites, perhaps by doing the same for them, or by paying for a presence on theirs.

Book VII

Online Marketing

Making Money Online

You can make money online in a variety of ways, and many tools and tactics are out there to help you mine the Internet for traffic and revenue.

The many ways to make money by using the Internet all fall into three main categories:

✔ Promoting affiliate products

✔ Monetizing traffic

✔ Developing and selling your own product or service

The following sections take a look at each category more closely.

Promoting affiliate products

An *affiliate product* is an item that another business produces, delivers, and supports. All you have to do is recommend that others visit that business's website. When someone makes a purchase through that website as a result of your recommendation, you get paid a sales commission.

A first source of affiliates could be products you have used yourself and were impressed with, such as software, a book, or other item. You may also find potential affiliates by doing an Internet search or using an affiliate aggregator such as ClickBank (www.clickbank.com)

Monetizing traffic

You can put ads for other products and services on your website and make money by essentially selling ad space on your site. If you can attract a significant number of website visitors (see "Generating traffic to your website" earlier in this chapter), you can turn that traffic into money — *monetize* — without promoting affiliate products or attempting to sell your own. Google AdSense ads and traditional banner ads cost per-click and are examples of monetizing traffic.

Developing your own online products and services

At first, the idea of developing your own online products and services seems to be the most profitable path, because you get to keep all the money. But this isn't always the case, especially in the short term. With affiliate programs (refer to the heading "Promoting affiliate products"), proven content is normally already provided for you, so ramp-up time is fast, and your investment is low. With monetizing traffic (see the previous section), the ads on your pages are commonly already tested and proven to work.

Creating and selling your own online products and services can prove to be the most challenging, because you have so much work to do before you can begin selling. However, creating your own product does give you creative control and long-term growth potential. Here are some points to remember when considering what types of online products or services you might create for sale on your website:

✔ **Information products are king.** An *information product* — which is essentially a product that provides information and that can be as simple as a how-to book — is still the easiest and least expensive product to produce and deliver. For example, your business may have developed a process or a software application that helps service your customers. You can create a document that outlines how to create and implement a similar product and then sell it on your website.

✔ **Audio is queen.** After you get started with audio, you will quickly realize the unlimited opportunity potential available by producing recorded products and promotional content. If you're a musician, selling downloads of your latest "album" is an obvious one. But you can also sell a series of downloadable material including interviews with experts, panel discussions, etc.

✔ **Video is hot, hot, hot!** Every website can enhance the buyer's experience by offering video, especially when a product is for sale. You can demonstrate how your software works and provide guidance in installing it. You can show people having fun at your club and dancing the night away. The video can be the product or the video can help sell your product.

✔ **Webinars are the ultimate education tool.** Webinars are online sessions that allow you to take people through your presentation or training session. This can happen in real time, with you at your computer and your clients/students at theirs, or the Webinar can be prerecorded for others to download and follow the program when and where they want.

✔ **One product can become a line of products.** For every information product you produce, you can create an entire product line by offering the nearly identical product in e-book form, MP3 audio recording, video, Webinars, and in-person seminar training.

Blogging

The word blog is a shortened form of Web log and has quickly become part of everyone's vocabulary. Essentially bloggers "post" their diaries, recipes, thoughts at large, editorials, photos, anything they want, and anything they believe people may want to read on line. As a small-business person you can use a blog, which may be part of your website or may be on a separate site (see "Introducing blogging tools" later in this chapter), to reinforce your knowledge and expertise with clients and potential clients, or to provide news that your readers may need for their business. If you have a website company you may want to blog about the latest developments or how to decide whether implementing a new technology is right for your customers, for example. Blogs can help you establish your credibility and draw people to using your services or buying your products.

Choosing a topic to blog about

If you're going to write a blog, you need a topic that you can write about regularly, and you have to have something to say about that topic that is meaningful to the readers you want to attract: customers and potential customers foremost. You might rate new products in your field, give tips on how to use a tool, or answer frequently asked questions.

Your goal is to reach the point where your audience seeks you out because you consistently offer information that they find helpful in light of their interests.

If you read nothing else in this section, read these key tips:

✔ Write about something that excites you.

✔ Write about something you know.

Stay focused and stay within your area of expertise. Here's why:

✔ Blogging requires a long-term commitment.

✔ Your audience won't hesitate to point out subject matter mistakes.

✔ Your audience knows if you don't know what you're talking about.

Consider what you do and then ask yourself these questions:

✔ How can I make my blog posts useful?

✔ How can I make this topic funny?

✔ How can I make this topic fascinating?

✔ What can I say about this topic that will prompt discussion?

✔ Which questions are asked repeatedly?

Here are a few ideas on choosing the right blogging topic that will attract the right followers and achieve your business objectives:

✔ **If you're a management consultant,** write a blog about applying your favorite time-management technique to midsize companies.

✔ **If you're a roofer,** create a question-and-answer blog for homeowners.

✔ **If you're a real estate agent,** blog about your favorite staging techniques.

✔ **If you're a freelance personal chef,** write about the best frozen foods with taste testing.

✔ **If you're a tutor,** come up with a daily list of homework tips.

Introducing blogging tools

Behind most blogs is a blogging tool: Blogger (www.blogspot.com), WordPress (http://wordpress.com), TypePad (www.typepad.com), and Movable Type (www.movabletype.com) are popular examples. Each requires an account, and some require you to download software. Others only require you to log in from the Web.

WordPress — the most popular self-hosted blog software, by far — can be downloaded at www.wordpress.org for free. Plus, it offers the easiest way to add affiliate links (see earlier in this chapter) to every post as well as include audio and video in posts.

Using Social Media

The term *social media* umbrellas any website or Web application that allows your audience to interact with your site and each other, directly or indirectly.

Social media sites and tools enable you to build your business's reputation and audience over time. Every friend you add on Facebook, every bookmark you add to StumbleUpon, and every tweet you post to Twitter increases your business's profile.

If you spend this capital wisely, you can use it to

✔ Announce a new product.

✔ Ask everyone for feedback about a new idea or blog post.

✔ Build some buzz and get others talking about your product or service — and your online presence.

Table 1-1 shows the seven basic categories of social media sites.

Book VII

Online Marketing

Table 1-1	Social Media Sites by Category	
Social Media Type	*Description*	*Examples*
Blogs	Allow you to write, journal-style, and then invite comments from your readers	Blogger WordPress
Social networks	Where people can interact and connect online	Facebook Google+ LinkedIn Yammer MySpace

(continued)

Table 1-1 *(continued)*

Social Media Type	Description	Examples
Bookmarking sites	Allow you to save bookmarks, just like you would in your browser, but on a site you can access from any computer	Delicious StumbleUpon
Microblogging sites	Allow you to blog one or two sentences at a time	Twitter Tumblr Plurk
Media sharing sites	Where you can upload and share video, audio, and photographs	YouTube Flickr
Popularity sites	Where you can collect bookmarks and then let visitors vote on them	Digg Reddit
Aggregators	Help the truly social and connected keep up with all this stuff	FriendFeed

Social media, more than any other vehicle, has the potential to spread a message far and fast.

You also need to know what sites are social media hot spots and what each site's specialty is so you can successfully use social media to spread the word about your products or services online.

The following sections explain the top three categories of social media and explore the benefits so you can begin to formulate a social media strategy for your business.

Connecting via social networks

All social networking sites offer a rare opportunity to spread the word about yourself or your business to thousands or even millions of people. Facebook, MySpace, and hundreds (if not thousands) of other sites all qualify as social networks.

At their simplest, social networks offer you — and your online presence — a great opportunity to

- Get a feel for your potential customers
- Get advice from colleagues
- Demonstrate your expertise

Here is a list of social networks that you should be familiar with. They've been around for a while, have thousands or millions of users, and offer access to the widest audience:

- ✔ **Facebook:** This is the dominant site today. Facebook (www.facebook.com) allows you to create your own profile pages, send messages to other members, and make "friends" with them by adding fellow members to your friends list. You can join for free by creating an account in just a few minutes.

- ✔ **LinkedIn:** A members-only network for businesspeople. Businesspeople worldwide can connect with you based on common interests, previous work together, or networking groups. Members can create networks of literally hundreds of people.

- ✔ **Yahoo! Answers:** Have a question? Visit http://answers.yahoo.com. Thousands of helpful members offer answers to questions on topics ranging from Internet marketing to wedding planning to pet care.

- ✔ **Discussion forums:** Forums are still out there. Sites like WebmasterWorld.com (www.webmasterworld.com) and Google Groups (http://groups.google.com) are basically enormous collections of discussion threads where you create your membership and then join the fray. Most discussion forums are free to join.

Microblogging

Microblog sites allow members to make lots of short — often less than 140 characters — blog posts. Microblogs are fast, easy, and can be updated from a cellphone, computer, or even via voice mail.

Microblogs look and feel more like old-fashioned chat rooms than blogs. Participants post statements, which are visible in a common *public timeline,* which everyone can see and read.

You might think that microblogging is just like a social network, but microblogs tend to be more "real time," with some participants posting every few minutes. So they allow for more of an ongoing conversation. But yes, the lines do get blurry at times.

More importantly, participants can follow fellow microbloggers whom they find interesting. After you make friends on a microblog, you follow them, and they follow you. Then their friends see you and follow you, and so on. On most microblogs, you mark people as friends by clicking Friend, or Follow. Then they confirm, and you're friends. It's that easy.

Book VII

Online Marketing

Therefore, microblogging is a great way to build a focused audience to which you can pose questions, make suggestions, or announce a new blog post.

Twitter (http://twitter.com) is by far the prominent microblogging tool with which you can enter 140-character messages. By following other people you find interesting, you'll receive their messages. Think of it as a huge chat room that remembers what you said. It's free to join. Like most social networks, you create a simple identity and can start posting right away.

Media sharing sites

Media sharing sites allow you to upload videos, photographs, and audio to a single directory. Then visitors can browse through and see your masterpiece. If you've been online in the last few years, you know a few of these sites. Here are two examples:

- ✔ **YouTube:** This is the biggest video-sharing site out there. Upload your video (ten minutes or less), and visitors can view and comment on it. Garnering more views and favourites ratings moves you up in the directory. Whole careers have been launched on YouTube (www.youtube.com). YouTube is free and lets you upload video in a wide array of formats.

- ✔ **Flickr:** Use Flickr (www.flickr.com) to upload and manage photographs. You can divide them into groups, organize them by tags, and restrict access as desired. Flickr also lets you publish your photos individually or as a "stream" on other websites. Flickr supports video, as well.

As a small business with an online presence, you can post your videos, photos, and illustrations on these sites. They're not magical marketing tools, but the right content at the right time can get you hundreds, thousands, or even hundreds of thousands of new visitors. That's why you want to put your photos and videos on third-party sites: They get a lot of traffic and put you in front of an enormous audience.

Chapter 2

Getting Started with Mobile Marketing

....

In This Chapter

▶ Seeing how mobile marketing fits into your marketing plans

▶ Running mobile communications campaigns

....

This chapter explains why mobile marketing, done properly, doesn't need to be expensive, complicated, or difficult; it can benefit small businesses just as well as Fortune 500 companies. In fact, mobile marketing can be an effective channel for increasing customer brand awareness, responses, interactions, and satisfaction.

Understanding and Weaving Mobile into Marketing

Mobile marketing is a way of marketing your product or service by engaging people through their mobile devices — cellphones, smartphones, laptops, or tablets — or encouraging people to engage with your business via their mobile devices. It is simply one of the many practices of marketing, such as retail, direct mail, Internet, e-mail, TV, radio, and advertising.

The days of mass-market marketing are waning. We've entered an age of connectedness, in which communication/media channels and markets are segmented down to individual members of the audience. With mobile marketing, you're not broadcasting messages to the masses. Rather, you use mass media and the mobile channel to engage individuals in a one-to-one interactive exchange.

Two main types of mobile marketing exist: direct and indirect.

Direct mobile marketing

Direct mobile marketing refers to the practice of proactively reaching out and engaging individual members of your audience via the mobile channel on their mobile phones. Direct mobile marketing may take place only if customers have given you explicit permission for you to proactively engage them — that is, send them a text message and/or call them.

Indirect mobile marketing

Because mobile marketing requires that individual customers give you permission to interact with them on their mobile devices directly and proactively, you can use indirect mobile marketing to expose people to your offerings and invite them to give you permission to contact them directly. Therefore, *indirect mobile marketing* refers to the practice of mobile-enhancing your traditional and new-media programs, and inviting people to use their mobile devices and respond to your mobile call to action.

On television, for example, your call to action may ask viewers to text a keyword to a short code to cast a vote. Or, you may ask them to fill out a form on the Web or mobile Internet, including their mobile phone number, to participate in the program. A print ad or poster may have a QR Code (that stands for Quick Response Code and is that bar code of black pixels on a white square you see more and more often). It can be scanned by a smartphone, which then takes the person to a website.

Adding mobile to your marketing strategy

You should not consider mobile marketing to be separate from your other marketing activities; rather, you can and should integrate it with those activities. You can use mobile marketing both directly and indirectly to enhance all your marketing activities.

Understanding the Many Paths within the Mobile Channel

It's easy to look at a mobile device and think, "It's just a phone." But it really isn't a phone anymore. Sure, you can make voice calls with it, but that function is just the tip of the iceberg. Today's mobile devices are also newspapers, maps, cameras, radios, stores, game consoles, video music players, calculators, calendars, address books, stereos, TVs, movie theatres, and concert halls. These devices can be much more than most people expect.

You can make them what you want them to be by creating rich, interactive experiences with the many interactive paths to mobile phones, shown in Figure 2-1.

The upcoming sections explain the various mobile paths and applications you can employ to reach your customers via the mobile channel and mobile-enhanced traditional media.

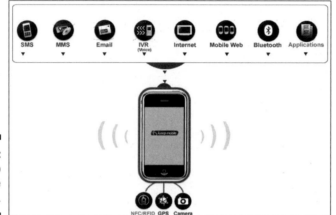

Figure 2-1:
Paths to
a mobile
device.

Book VII

Online Marketing

Understanding SMS capabilities

Short message service (SMS), commonly referred to as *text messaging* or just *texting,* is an incredibly versatile path to nearly all mobile phones on the planet. An SMS is a 160-character alphanumeric digital message that can be sent to and from a mobile device.

More than just a person-to-person channel, text messaging is the cornerstone of mobile marketing. In addition to offering voting services, you can launch trivia programs, provide search capability, send information and text alerts, trigger interactive calls, deliver content, operate coupon programs, and even charge people for content and services consumed on the phone (such as ringtones and television subscriptions).

E-mailing your messages

Mobile e-mail is enabled by smartphones, including Research In Motion's BlackBerry, Apple's iPhone, and devices running Google's Android software or Symbian and/or Microsoft mobile operating systems. E-mail is rarely used for mobile marketing; controlling the user experience is difficult, and many technical hurdles and legal landmines still need to be overcome.

Focus on your target market

Even if a particular mobile path isn't applicable for mass marketing use, you shouldn't ignore it. Services such as video delivery through texting technology or applications (apps), simple software programs that can be downloaded onto a smart phone or tablet, are perfect for niche markets — markets in which you can be fairly sure that your audience members have mobile devices capable of accessing the mobile Internet, that they have *data plans* (they're paying their wireless carriers for data services such as mobile Internet), and that they know how to use the feature.

Business market segments, iPhone users, and high-end niche consumer markets are perfect candidates for a rich mobile experience — for example, iPhone-specific apps and downloads. You can be widely successfully with this path, and many players are seeing their applications downloaded hundreds of thousands of times a month via iPhones, whereas they're not seeing these numbers on a mass market level because the application doesn't meet the mass market criteria. In short, you'll want to rely on voice and text messaging, and then start introducing the mobile Internet, and then other services until you better understand the members of your target market and the phones and services they use. Then, after you know what device they use, you can focus on the services that these people have. For example, 85 percent of iPhone users regularly use the mobile Internet and download apps.

Humanizing your messages with IVR

The *voice path* refers to your phone's standard telephone capability — the means by which you make and receive calls. In addition to talking with a live person, a very popular use of the voice channel is *interactive voice response* (IVR). You're probably familiar with IVR, which is a common prompting system used in automated customer support. When you call many businesses today, you reach an automated prompt that tells you to say or press 1 to get this, or to say or press 2 to get that. That's IVR.

Making connections through Bluetooth

The *Bluetooth path* refers to the use of the Bluetooth communication channel on the phone In addition to working with peripheral devices such as a handsfree earphone and speaker for your cellphone, Bluetooth can be used for mobile marketing — a practice called *Bluecasting*. A marketer places Bluetooth access points and a Bluetooth transmitter in a public area (such as a mall, airport lounge, bus stop, or movie theatre) or at a live event. When a consumer walks by the access point, if the person's phone is set to receive Bluetooth requests automatically, the phone beeps, and the person is asked to accept a pairing request from the Bluetooth access point. If the person accepts the request, the Bluetooth access point sends an image, ringtone, game, or other communication to the phone.

Running Mobile Communication Campaigns

You can use mobile marketing to generate consumer responses to your queries, disseminate information, collect information, entertain your audience, and conduct commerce. The following sections discuss how you can plan a mobile marketing campaign for your business, and the ways you can engage mobile users.

Planning your communication flow

One of the most important aspects of planning your mobile communications campaign is creating *user flows* — documents that show as thoroughly as possible how your users engage in your campaign.

The best way to plan your communication campaign flow is to use *a user-flow diagram* — an image that outlines all the interactions that may occur between a mobile subscriber and your mobile marketing program (see Figure 2-2).

Book VII

Online Marketing

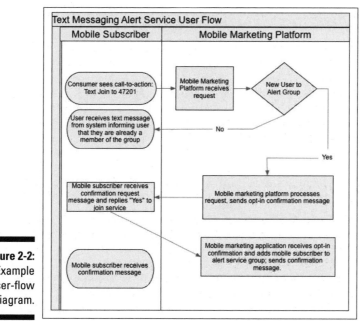

Figure 2-2: Example user-flow diagram.

User-flow diagrams typically are created with software applications such as Microsoft Word, Excel, PowerPoint, or Visio. Some people use standard flow-charting techniques; others use images of mobile devices to map the user flow.

Your application provider or connection aggregator, the businesses that furnish the software and support services you need to manage your mobile campaigns, typically have the most common user flows already designed — as well as the not-so-common ones. Rather than start with a blank piece of paper, ask the provider to give you a few examples. Then you can tailor an existing user-flow diagram to your individual needs.

Providing text promotions

One of the most basic mobile marketing communication programs you may want to run is a text promotion. In a *text promotion,* a mobile subscriber sends a text message to a mobile marketing application, and the application sends a message back. The content of the message depends on the nature of your program, but it may include details about a new movie or a recipe and coupon.

Using quizzes to gather information and entertain

Mobile subscribers interact with quizzes by responding to questions sent to their mobile devices. You can use text messaging in quiz programs to gather feedback, consumer opinions, or votes, as well as to inform and entertain. Your customers can have a great time with trivia programs, for example.

You can also use the application for quizzes to direct mobile subscribers to a particular next step in an application's user flow, such as a product offering (a content storefront, for example) or another text-messaging campaign or service. You can use the response to a question to initiate a mobile subscriber into a horoscope program, for example. When the subscriber answers the question, the subscriber's response is used to configure the next question to be sent to his phone.

Gathering input with open-ended survey questions

You can use open-ended, text-messaging survey programs to gather information such as consumer, candidate, or employee feedback. After a job interview, for example, you could send the candidate a text message like this: "Please give us your feedback on the interview process. Reply to this message with your feedback."

Offering incentives

You probably know that people respond to *incentives*, which are offering that motivate and encourage people to take a certain action. Offer people something of value, and they'll be more inclined to participate in your program and initiate communication with you. Continue offering them value, and they may become customers. Keep offering them value, and they'll become loyal customers. Keep offering them value after that, and you'll turn them into evangelists who'll start doing your marketing for you. This process starts with the first engagement, and an incentive is a great way to kick-start the interaction.

Not surprisingly, offering incentives to mobile device users is also your best shot at getting their participation; many mobile users value unique and/or personalized content.

The most common forms of incentives are

- ✔ **Money:** Coupons, discounts on services, or even hard cash
- ✔ **Content:** Free ringtones, wallpaper, or images
- ✔ **Free stuff and experiences:** Ticket for trial and sample products, free movie admission, or a chance to go backstage and meet the star

Applying user-generated content

The mobile device is an extremely personal device for communicating, gathering information, and conducting commerce and exchange, as well as for personal expression. Over the past few years, we've seen a groundswell of *user-generated content* (UGC, for short). *UGC* is any type of content — videos, pictures, text, news, stories, and so on — that people create and share with their own communities and society at large.

Book VII

Online Marketing

Mobile is a perfect tool for UGC. In fact, some people refer to mobile as the "second mouse" (the first mouse being the device used with a computer). People use mobile devices to send text messages, take videos, place calls, snap pictures, send e-mail, and so on. Mobile subscribers also use every one of these capabilities to create content.

You can encourage clients, suppliers and other people interested in your business offer to send comments, thoughts, photos, text messages to your blog, for example, in order to enhance the content of your own blog and thereby increase its interest and the number users who visit your blog as a result.

Conventional advertising and P.R. agencies, new media marketing agencies, and many internet service providers can provide advice on the mobile campaign that's right for you and can also help in generating content and building traffic.

Chapter 3

Getting Ready to Use SEO and Web Analytics

In This Chapter

▶ Discovering what matters to a search engine

▶ Filling your SEO toolbox

▶ Making an SEO worksheet

▶ Picking keywords your visitors want

▶ Staying visible to search engines

▶ Ensuring a solid website structure

▶ Discovering how analytics software works

▶ Tracking website traffic

▶ Measuring for quality visits

*Y*ou can't sell anything if no one knows you exist. That's why retailers look to locations that provide the highest possible number of target shoppers so they can convert a high proportion of shoppers into buyers. The same is true on the Internet. Visitors have to be able to find you. If they don't find you because they know who you are already, they will probably look for you or people like you using search engines like Google.

In this chapter, we look at how you can help search engines find you and deliver the right visitors to your virtual door. We look at choosing the key words your potential visitors may use and optimizing your website using these key words. We then look at collecting data on your website and visitors to it that will help you understand who is visiting, where they are coming from, and what they looked for.

Understanding Why Search Engines Exist

Search engines are online services you can use to find almost anything and everything online, and they drive the Internet. Type in a few key words, and a search engine comes up with a list of web pages to match your query. If you're going to grow your business online, you're probably going to depend on such search engines as Google, Yahoo!, and Bing to deliver a huge chunk of your customers and clients. A high placement in the search engine ranking can drive tremendous growth.

You can leave those rankings to chance and hope for the best. Or you can use *search engine optimization (SEO),* the practice of providing the best possible target for search engines.

Search engines aim to deliver relevance. *Relevance* means visitors click on search results and are happy with what the search engine found for them. When that happens, visitors come back, traffic to the search engine rises, and the search engine company's stock goes up.

 SEO is a huge field, with thousands of little details that come together to make a successful campaign. If you're looking to dig deeply into this topic, get *Search Engine Optimization For Dummies,* 2nd Edition, by Peter Kent (Wiley). If you want to improve your search rankings and steer clear of trouble, this book is for you.

Search engine terms to remember

Crawl refers to what a search engine does when it reads and indexes a website.

Organic or natural search results are unpaid listings on a search result page.

Search engine ranking pages (SERP) are the result pages you see when you complete a search on a major search engine.

Spiders or robots (bots) are software that the search engine uses to crawl your site.

Black hat SEO uses tactics specifically designed to improve search rankings and fool the search engines into providing a higher ranking than a website should actually receive according to that search engine's algorithms.

White hat SEO uses tactics to make a website as acceptable as possible to both visitors and search engines, without attempting to manipulate the search engines.

Knowing What Makes a Website Relevant

Search engines want to know which website is the most important for a particular concept. These concepts are represented by *key phrases. New York hotels, chocolate candy, bicycles,* and *wedding dresses* are all examples of key phrases.

Search engines are hierarchical thinkers. After reading billions of pages of content by using little software programs called *spiders,* search engines determine the relevance of each of those pages for a key phrase based on a complex series of rules (called *algorithms*).

When you go to a search engine and type in a key phrase (*wedding dresses,* for example), the search engine picks the best matches by looking at the following in hierarchical order:

1. A website's authority on the subject of wedding dresses, as demonstrated by links from other sites about wedding dresses

   Every link from other, relevant sites is a vote for the target site's authority.

2. Whether wedding dresses are the main focus of each website, as demonstrated by site structure

3. Which pages on those websites are most dedicated to wedding dresses

4. Whether those web pages are more relevant than all the other pages in the search engine's index

Table 3-1 describes the factors that make a website relevant as well as the factors that have little or no impact on a site's rankings.

Table 3-1	What Matters in SEO		
Factors	*Matters*	*Doesn't Matter*	*Why*
Title tags	X		Title tags are at the very top of the hierarchy for each page. They're the first thing search engines look at. If the key phrase shows up in the title tag, search engines flag the page as relevant to that phrase.

(continued)

Table 3-1 *(continued)*

Factors	Matters	Doesn't Matter	Why
Keywords meta tag		X	The keywords meta tag was so horribly abused by SEOs that search engines largely ignore it.
Description meta tag	X		The description meta tag actually affects your rankings, but is usually shown as the page "snippet" in the search engine results.
Headings (H1, H2, and so on)	X		Headings provide a content outline to the search engines when they read your pages. If the target key phrase shows up in a heading, that demonstrates relevance.
Paragraph copy	X		The more copy you have on your site the easier it is to rank well. Don't just stuff copy with keywords, though.
Bolded key phrases		X	Bolding keywords in your paragraph text doesn't help.
Hidden text		X	Hiding text on your page and stuffing it with key phrases may seem like a neat trick. But search engines root this stuff out, and if you're caught, they'll penalize your site.
Site age	X		Older sites have higher rankings. You can safely assume that a two-year-old site will have more leverage than a two-week-old one.
Trust factors	X		Having a physical address on every page can definitely help make you look more trustworthy.
Image captions	X		Text captions near images help with image search results.
Bullets and lists			Bullets are more easily scanned, which makes for better linking opportunities. But they don't directly impact rankings.
Links	X		Links equal authority. Authority equals greater relevance. Don't just buy junk links, though. You need relevant links from relevant sites.

Factors	Matters	Doesn't Matter	Why
Link text	X		If the link to your site reads `Click Here`, that tells the search engines that your site is relevant to click here. If the link reads `Wedding Dresses`, it tells the search engine your site is relevant to wedding dresses. See how that works?
File names	X		Keyword-rich file names on images and individual pages insert keywords into the site hierarchy.
URL or Web address	X		Keyword-rich Web addresses can be a huge help, because every link to your site that uses the URL as the link text creates a keyword-rich link. This only works within reason, though.
Submitting a website		X	You can certainly submit your website to Google, Yahoo!, and Bing, but it's better for these search engines to find you through links on other sites.
Number of clicks on my search listing		X	Click your listing as much as you want. The search engines still won't move you up.

Setting Up Your SEO Toolbox

Some fantastic tools are available to help you see how a search engine will evaluate your business's website. Use the tools mentioned in the following sections to set up your SEO toolbox.

Downloading and installing Firefox

Firefox is a Web browser by the Mozilla foundation. It's speedy, allows for tabbed browsing, and most importantly, has hundreds of add-on tools that can help you with SEO. To download and install Firefox, follow these steps:

1. **Go to** `www.mozilla.org/firefox.`

2. **Click the Free Download button.**

3. **After the download is complete, install Firefox.**

Firefox runs on Mac OS X, Microsoft Windows, and Linux.

Installing add-ons

Firefox's number one feature is that it allows developers to create their own add-ons. You can find a huge collection of add-ons at `http://addons.mozilla.org`. The ones you want for SEO include the following:

- ✔ **SeoQuake,** which collects and displays a few dozen relevant search engine statistics, including pages in the Google index, pages in the Yahoo! index, keyword density on the page, site age, and page rank.

- ✔ **Live HTTP Headers** shows what your website is telling a search engine about each page.

- ✔ The **Google Toolbar** gets you a few details about your site as seen by Google.

- ✔ The **Web Developer Toolbar** lets you change how Firefox displays a web page. It's great for testing how your site looks without images or styles (how a search engine sees it).

- ✔ **Yellowpipe Lynx Viewer Tool** enables you to see the web page in a text-only Web browser — another good way to preview how a search engine will see your site.

Setting up and using Webmaster tools

The major search engines provide insight into your site's SEO, too. Yahoo!, Bing, and Google all have Webmaster tools that can do the following:

- ✔ Notify you if they find problems, such as duplicate content

- ✔ Show you who is linking to your site

- ✔ Report the most common queries used to find your site

- ✔ Tell you the last time the search engine crawled your site

- ✔ Allow you to modify (in a few cases) how your listings appear

Using Google Webmaster tools

The Google Webmaster toolset includes more than 20 gadgets. You want to explore them all, but you can't do without these three:

- ✔ **Diagnostics⇨Content Analysis** tells you, at a glance, whether any pages on your site duplicate title or description meta tags, or whether they're missing those tags.

✔ **Links⇨Pages with external links** tells you which pages on your site have links from other sites. And you can drill down to find out where those links come from.

✔ **Statistics⇨Top search queries** allows you to peek at the key phrases (and your rankings for those phrases) that drive traffic.

Google Webmaster tools are a *must have*. Don't leave them out of your toolbox!

Creating Your SEO Worksheet

SEO can take a long time. Plus, changes you make today might impact your rankings months from now, so it's important that you keep a record of relevant data and changes you make over time. That way, you can refer back to those changes and better understand what worked and what didn't.

If you're serious about SEO, you're going to need to track a number of different statistics over time, including:

✔ **Traffic from organic search:** Your Web analytics package (see Book III for in-depth Web analytics information) should show you clicks from unpaid search rankings.

✔ **Keyword diversity:** The number of key phrases driving traffic to your website. Again, your Web analytics package will give you this.

✔ **Incoming links, by search engine:** The number of links reported by Live, Yahoo!, and Google.

✔ **Indexed pages, by search engine.**

✔ **Sales/leads/other results from organic search:** If your site has a goal, and your analytics package allows it, record the results you get. Traffic is great. Sales are better.

✔ **Keyword rankings:** Notice how this is last? That's because *keyword rankings don't matter.*

Keyword rankings don't matter. Traffic and results do. Although ranking number one for a phrase or two is one way to get those extra visitors, getting 500 Top 10 listings for less prominent phrases may get you far more visitors and sales, leads, or whatever else you need. Don't obsess about keyword rankings. Obsess about traffic, keyword diversity, and success.

Record these numbers by month. You can record them by week if you're really obsessive. Whatever you do, don't check them every day — you may lose your mind!

Choosing the Right Keywords

Keywords (or, more accurately, key phrases) are the focus of successful search engine optimization. SEO is a long-term undertaking. You may wait months before you see any results. Choose the right keywords and you can see a nice lift in traffic after all that effort. Choose the wrong keywords and your months of effort won't help your business. The upcoming sections go over how to pick the right keywords to bring traffic to your business website.

Thinking like your visitors

You must understand that you are not optimizing for the keywords *you* like or think *should* be associated with your product or service. You are optimizing for the keywords *potential customers* associate with your product or service.

For example, say you sell salad through the Internet. You've found a miraculous way to keep vegetables crisp and prevent lettuce from wilting, and you ship salad to suburban dwellers everywhere.

You research keywords and find that no one searches for *salad*. They search for *mixed greens* instead. You have a choice to make. You can insist on optimizing for *salad,* because that is what you sell. Or, you can optimize for *mixed greens,* get visitors, and then educate them as to why *salad* is better.

Understanding the long tail

You never optimize for a single word; you optimize for a keyword and the hundreds or thousands of permutations on that word. So, if you're targeting *broccoli,* you're probably also targeting *cream of broccoli soup, broccoli recipes,* and *broccoli coleslaw.* These *long-tail* phrases — longer niche phrases that don't get as many searches — are the real beauty of search engine optimization. By optimizing for one word or phrase, you get the benefit of improved rankings for many more.

Go back to the *salad* example in the preceding section. You decide to optimize for *mixed greens*. After six months of hard work, you're still stuck on the fourth rankings page for that phrase. But your traffic from organic searches has gone up 300 percent. For these reasons, you're not sure whether you should fire yourself or give yourself a raise.

Taking a look at your traffic report, though, you notice something interesting. Traffic from longer phrases that include the words *mixed greens* has gone up. Phrases such as the following are now major traffic generators:

> *mixed spring greens*
> *mixed greens online*
> *buy mixed greens*
> *mixed greens salads*
> *really great mixed greens*
> *where can I buy mixed greens*

All these phrases are driving traffic to your site. Together, the six phrases drive more traffic than *mixed greens* would have.

Behold, the long tail! By optimizing for one phrase, you really optimized for six longer ones. Even though you didn't move up in the rankings for the target phrase, you did move up for these others, and they brought you traffic.

Using the right tools to develop keywords

Luckily, you don't have to guess to find keywords. You can use some of the great tools available to help you with your initial brainstorming.

Using keyword services

Several companies have launched keyword services designed just for search engine optimization pros looking for the right targets. These services include

- ✔ **Wordze:** www.wordze.com
- ✔ **Keyword Discovery:** http://keyworddiscovery.com
- ✔ **Wordtracker:** www.wordtracker.com

All services cost a small monthly fee, but they are a good investment. They provide at-a-glance reports showing keyword demand, competition, and quality.

Working with the Google AdWords keyword research tool

Google's keyword research tool shows search volumes. That makes the Google keyword tool the only source for Google keyword search data.

To show search volumes, follow these steps:

1. **Go to** `http://adwords.google.com/select/ KeywordToolExternal.`

2. **Type in a phrase in the Word or phrase box then Search, and you get a report.**

   The report shows searches performed in the previous month, average monthly search volume over the past 12 months, and advertiser competition in Google AdWords.

3. **Click the Keyword box to display the top 100 Keyword ideas.**

Using Google Trends

All major search engines favour content that focuses on hot key phrases. For example, say that a famous movie star loses 45 pounds on a diet solely composed of mixed greens. The story hits newsstands, and suddenly everyone is searching for *mixed greens diet*.

If you knew that, you could add a few articles to your site about the mixed greens diet. The search engines would see that and quickly move you up in the rankings. You'd get a nice burst of traffic.

To check on trending phrases go to `www.google.com/trends`. Type in any phrase, and you can see whether search volumes are rising or falling. The report even shows specific news stories and whether they affected search volumes.

Watching the news

We are media driven. It pays to keep current on TV, radio, and print news. If a relevant story seems to be gaining a lot of ground, see if you can work it into your website.

Going back to the (now somewhat silly) mixed greens example earlier: If you see on the news that Mark Starguy is the movie star who lost 45 pounds on the mixed greens diet, you might want to mention his name here and there. Chances are other folks watching the news will remember the star's name and *diet,* but not *mixed greens.* If you show up for *Mark Starguy diet,* you're set.

Using your brain

All the computers in the world can't match your brain for its ability to manipulate language. Don't rely on keyword tools alone. They will eventually lie to you (or at least tell a small fib): Keyword tools lack your insight into your customers. They can use only the data they have, and that means sometimes they'll miss important subtleties, such as the difference between *auto* (as in *automobile*) and *auto* (as in *automatic*).

Your brain is the last line of defense against keyword paralysis. If the tools are showing you keywords that simply make no sense, go with your gut and try a different approach.

Comparing competition and search volume

If you're facing 200 million other websites that are all vying for the number one spot, you might want to choose a different keyword.

Go to Google, Yahoo!, and Bing and search for the phrase you've chosen. Look at three competitive factors:

- ✔ **The number of competing sites:** If you find more than 10 million competing pages in the search results, you might be facing an uphill battle.
- ✔ **Where you rank:** If you're already on the second page of the results, you might not care how many sites are competing with you.
- ✔ **Your ability to compete:** If you have a daily newsletter on your site about mixed greens, you might be super-competitive, even if a mob of other sites are trying to beat you. You're adding new, highly relevant content every day, and search engines love that. That steady content growth gives you an advantage.

Always balance competition against search volume. Some terms might be so relevant and offer so many potential visitors that any level of competition is worth it. For example, the phrase *wedding dresses* gets over one million searches per month. It's also one of the most competitive phrases on the entire Internet. But one million searches makes *wedding dresses* so potentially valuable that, if you have any chance of gaining a front-page ranking for it, you have to try. Other keywords might offer only a tiny trickle of traffic — and thus, very little competition.

Your best strategy is to mix your keyword list and optimize for both of the following:

- ✔ **High-volume, high-competition keywords** that require a long effort on your part before you gain any rankings
- ✔ **Low-volume, low-competition keywords** that can produce results sooner

This strategy lets you build traffic sooner while still aiming for the home run phrases later.

Eliminating Search Engine Roadblocks

One way or another, business owners often block search engines from reading their content. And by doing so, they're cutting off a huge segment of their audience. If a search engine can't find your content, it can't index it, which means that it can't determine relevance. When this happens, you don't get ranked.

The following sections explain how to make sure that you're not actively blocking search engines from crawling pages on your website.

Ensuring search engine visibility

websites can completely disappear from the Google rankings because a developer put a tagline on every page of the site that read:

```
meta name="robots" content="noindex,nofollow"
```

Chances are that the developer put that tag there to prevent search engines from reading the site while the developer was building it — like covering a painting until it's unveiled. Leave that tag in place, though, and search engines ignore not only that page but also every single link on that page — which is like forgetting to remove the cover from the painting before the big show.

Checking your robots.txt file

Go to www.*yoursiteaddress*.com/robots.txt. You might get a Page Not Found error. That's okay for our purposes. You might also see a file that looks like this:

```
User-agent: *
Disallow: /blog.htm
```

It might have other lines in it, too. This file is called the robots.txt file. It tells search engine crawlers, also known as *robots,* what to do when they visit your website.

What you *don't* want to see in your robots.txt file is this:

```
Disallow: /
```

This line tells a visiting search engine crawler to ignore *every page* on your website. A developer may add this line while building the site to prevent search engines from crawling it while the site under construction. But if the line is left by accident, your site is invisible to search engines.

If your `robots.txt` file has any `Disallow` commands in it, check with your Webmaster or developer to find out why. `Disallow` can be used to hide pages that change a lot, hide duplicate content, or keep search engines out of stuff you don't want them crawling. Just make sure that you're not accidentally hiding content they *should* see.

Checking for meta robots tags

Using the meta `robots` tag is another way to hide pages from search engines. Go to any page on your website and view the source code. You don't want to see

```
<meta name="robots" content="noindex,nofollow">
```

If the meta `robots` tag is there, and it contains either `noindex` or `nofollow`, or both, remove it. Valid reasons to use this tag exist: You might want a search engine to ignore this page because it's a duplicate of another; you might feel the information on the page is inappropriate for search results; or the developer might have hidden the page during development. But you should know those reasons. If you don't, delete the tag.

Do not trust your developer to remove the meta `robots` tag. When developers build your site, they're working hard, writing code so fast their fingers smoke. Forgetting to remove that one little line of code is easy when you're facing a tough deadline and still have 4,000 lines of code to write. Remind your developer!

Eliminating registration forms

Don't put registration forms in front of great content! Visitors often have to complete these forms before they can download some kind of premium content, such as a white paper, or before they can read some articles on a site. Businesses put these forms in place because they want leads — they want contact information for interested potential customers.

If you have any registration forms hiding white papers, newsletters, or other information, remove the forms.

Your salespeople might howl. Your head of marketing might yell. Your CEO might stamp her feet. Remain calm and ask them for a one-month test — and here's why:

You spent two months writing a white paper. You put it up on your website, and you want to get something in return. So you add a little form that forces visitors to give you their e-mail address and name before they can read the paper.

That form hurts you in two ways:

- It greatly reduces the number of people who will read the content. You wrote that content to spread the word about your business, so you want people to read it.

- Search engines can't fill out forms, so they'll never see that great information. Which means, if you wrote a white paper on making a perfect carrot cake, folks searching for *perfect carrot cake* will never see your information. Never mind whether they'll call. They won't even know you're there.

Eliminating login forms

You've probably already guessed that login forms are bad, too. If you haven't, well, they're bad.

website owners might include login forms for the following reasons:

- They feel that they need to add value for registered members.
- They want to force registration.
- They don't want business secrets getting out.

Remove the forms anyway. If you remove your registration forms, you'll remove the need to add value for registered members. Also, hiding a few white papers behind a login doesn't give perceived value to members.

If you really have top-quality training content, tools, or products for sale for which you're offering a preview, then keep the login. Otherwise, you don't need that form.

Regarding business secrets, you need to think carefully. Is this information really a secret? Or is it just information you'd rather people didn't know? In both cases, a login form won't help you.

If you don't want people to find it, don't put it on the Internet. Someone will find the information, somehow, someday, and republish it to their heart's content.

Dump the login forms.

Avoiding all-Flash pages

Adobe Flash is a great way to create beautiful, interactive animations for your website. Unfortunately, search engines can't read Flash animations. Remember, search engines visit your website as a super-simple Web browser. Flash is a plug-in that you have to add to your Web browser — without it, you can't see any Flash content. Search engines don't have that plug-in built into their software, so they typically can't read any of the content.

Also, Flash compiles links, fonts, and structural information differently than a typical HTML page. So even if a search engine *does* manage to read the content, it may read it as gibberish.

Finally, Flash is often used to load multiple pages of text, videos, and other motion graphics onto a single HTML web page. That creates the problem of hiding all but the very first snippet of information from visiting search engines.

And don't forget, anyone using a mobile device (such as an iPad or iPhone, won't be able to see Flash-based websites.

Structuring Your Site for Search Engines and People

Think of your website as a pyramid. At the top, you have the homepage. One click away from the homepage, you have the second layer of content. Two clicks away, you have the third layer. Each additional click moves you another layer down in the hierarchy until you can't click any further away from the homepage. That's the bottom layer. Search engines award more relevance more readily to content that is closer to the top of the site pyramid.

Creating content clusters

You can bring content to the top of the pyramid by creating *content clusters*, which are groupings of related content, so that you create individual, high-relevance *hub pages* within the site structure. You can then link to these high-relevance pages from your homepage and move the entire cluster up the hierarchy.

You can use content clusters to help build relevance. When you link two or more related pages to each other and to a central *hub* or index page from which a visitor can find all of those related pages, you create a cluster of relevant content.

These links lend authority, just as links from other sites lend authority. If you can link ten pages to and from a single hub page, that creates more relevance than if you had a single relevant page all alone. So, there's strength in numbers — the more related pages you can link in clusters, the greater authority you can generate for your site.

Always link like with like. Keeping your content clumped together has two benefits:

✔ Customers are happier.

✔ Hub pages and clusters make search engines consider your site more relevant.

Creating deep links

Deep linking involves creating a hyperlink that points visitors to a specific page or image on your website instead of to the website's main or home page. These are called deep links. The fact that visitors to your website may bypass your home page and other messages can provide both liabilities and benefits. For example, it might take visitors directly to a page where they may purchase your product. But it may also bypass all the information needed to allow the purchaser to understand you provide the best product or service choice.

Keeping the structure clean and clear

After you do the work to create and improve a search engine optimized site structure, you want to maintain it.

That means never moving content around and reinforcing that structure with great link text. The upcoming sections provide tips for accomplishing these two goals.

Keeping content in one place

Many large websites (particularly online publications) create an archive section. After a few months, old content is moved to this section. So a page that used to be

www.mynewspapersite.com/june/2007/sports

becomes

```
www.mynewspapersite.com/archive/sports
```

Search engines lose track of the content. And when they find it again, it's likely buried in the site hierarchy, five to ten links from the homepage.

The fix is simple: *Don't move your content. Ever.*

Make sure your website is set up to accommodate a lot of content without an archive. Pages that stay where they were originally placed get you far more SEO leverage. If you archive content, you're effectively playing now-you-see-it, now-you-don't with the search engines.

Writing great link text

The text contained in a link provides a hint to both search engines and visitors. A link tells them what they're going to see when they follow the link.

Search engines look at link text to gain insight into the target page's content. If you have a page that talks about bike wheels and a link that reads Click Here, for example, search engines have no idea. Although Click Here is accurate, using something like Click Here for More About Custom Wheels — or even just Custom Wheels — is far better.

Take a link's text and write it on a blank sheet of paper. Read it. Does it identify the page at which it points?

If your website has any of the classic links shown in the left column in Table 3-2, consider your options. Use the examples as a guide to come up with something more relevant.

Table 3-2	Link Text Ideas
Original Link	*Better Link Examples*
Products	Business Gifts Computer Software Bicycles
About Us	Best Bicycle Shop Our Software Geeks 5 Years of Dentistry
Services	Internet Marketing Services Dental Services

Bicycle Repair

Your website designer might say that your site design doesn't have room for long links. However, tweaking the design to allow for a few extra characters is better than having your online store sit, unused, because no one can find it. If you can't change the design, create enhanced links elsewhere on the homepage.

Use great link text and you reinforce your site structure, and the meaning of the content within that structure, to both search engines and people. So, you boost your chances of a high ranking.

Getting Started with Analytics

You build your website, launch it, and wait. And wait. And wait some more. Is it working? Are you getting visitors? Are they doing what you want them to do? How will you know?

Discovering the traffic report

Enter the traffic report. A *traffic report* is a list of numbers and information about how folks are using your site, as Figure 3-1 shows. It is also the foundation for Web analytics.

Figure 3-1:
A traffic report.

Web analytics comprises using a traffic report to draw conclusions and adjust your marketing strategy. So, if a traffic report is the pencil and paper, Web analytics is the process of putting pencil to paper and creating a blueprint for your next steps.

Ultimately, the purpose of analytics is to establish a narrative so that you can tell which changes have a positive or negative effect on your site and on your business over time. That helps you figure out what works and what doesn't, which leads to improved results.

If you want to get a more in-depth look at Web analytics, check out *Web Analytics For Dummies,* by Pedro Sostre and Jennifer LeClaire (Wiley).

Collecting data and what it can tell you

Traffic reports, at a minimum, show you the following information:

- ✔ How many times people visit your website
- ✔ Which pages are most popular
- ✔ What sites send you visitors
- ✔ How much time visitors spend on your site

Those are the basics. Additionally, most traffic-reporting tools provide more powerful features:

- ✔ E-commerce sales tracking
- ✔ Search-keywords reports that show which keywords folks use to find you
- ✔ Campaign performance measurements so that you know which e-mail marketing pieces, banners, and other ads generate traffic

With most traffic-reporting tools, you can

- ✔ Find out your best sources of traffic and business
- ✔ See which pages on your site get the most or least attention
- ✔ Figure out which parts of your *shopping cart,* your actual selecting and paying for products process, drives away visitors
- ✔ Discover which pay per click (PPC) advertising campaign generates the best return on investment (ROI)

Choosing your reporting tool

As of this writing, at least a dozen very good Web traffic–reporting tools are available. Some are free; some aren't. Table 3-3 outlines examples of what you can find on the market as this book goes to press.

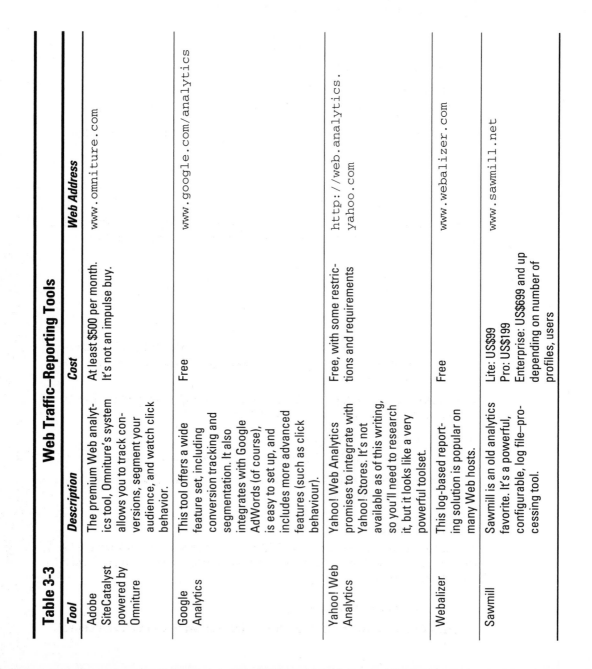

Table 3-3	**Web Traffic–Reporting Tools**		
Tool	**Description**	**Cost**	**Web Address**
Adobe SiteCatalyst powered by Omniture	The premium Web analytics tool, Omniture's system allows you to track conversions, segment your audience, and watch click behavior.	At least $500 per month. It's not an impulse buy.	www.omniture.com
Google Analytics	This tool offers a wide feature set, including conversion tracking and segmentation. It also integrates with Google AdWords (of course), is easy to set up, and includes more advanced features (such as click behaviour).	Free	www.google.com/analytics
Yahoo! Web Analytics	Yahoo! Web Analytics promises to integrate with Yahoo! Stores. It's not available as of this writing, so you'll need to research it, but it looks like a very powerful toolset.	Free, with some restrictions and requirements	http://web.analytics.yahoo.com
Webalizer	This log-based reporting solution is popular on many Web hosts.	Free	www.webalizer.com
Sawmill	Sawmill is an old analytics favorite. It's a powerful, configurable, log file–processing tool.	Lite: US$99 Pro: US$199 Enterprise: US$699 and up depending on number of profiles, users	www.sawmill.net

Setting up Google Analytics

Google Analytics has emerged as the premier analytics tool for small business. It's easy to use, easy to understand, and easy to interpret. Plus it's free! It is certainly the place to start for the small business embarking on a Web presence and/or on Internet commerce.

To create your account, follow these steps:

1. **Go to** www.google.com/analytics.

2. **Click Sign Up Now.**

3. **Enter the Web address you want to track and then click Finish.**

4. **Copy the code and paste it into a text editor so that you have it for later.**

5. **Click Finish again.**

Installing the tracking code

Remember that tracking code you copied in the last step? You need to install it on your website so that it can start sending data to Google Analytics.

This procedure varies depending on whether you have a blog site, a traditional site, or a CMS-driven site. (*CMS* stands for content management system.)

1. **Access your site with whatever editing tool you're using.**

2. **Copy the Google Analytics tracking code to your Clipboard by first selecting all the code and then choosing Edit↪Copy in the text editor where you pasted it.**

3. **In your editing tool, paste the tracking code right before the closing `</body>` tag on each page of your site.**

4. **Save the edited code to your website.**

5. **If necessary, republish the site to update your code.**

6. **Wait a half hour or so. Log back into Google Analytics and look for the profile you added.**

Tracking site search

If you have a search box on your website, it makes sense to track what folks type into it. You can learn a lot about your audience. To set up a site search, follow these steps:

1. **Log into Google Analytics.**

2. **Click Edit next to the website for which you want to track site search.**

3. **Click Edit at the top of the page, next to Main website Profile Information.**

4. **Select the Do Track Site Search radio button.**

5. **Leave this page open in your browser. Open a separate browser window for the next few steps.**

6. **In the new browser window, go to your website.**

7. **Search for** *"buggy bumpers,"* **using your site's search tool.**

8. **Look at the address of the search result page.**

9. **Enter the query attribute into the Query Parameter field in Google Analytics.**

10. **Click Save Changes.**

Excluding your office

Your analytics package won't distinguish between customers and folks at your business unless you tell it to. Because you want the most accurate numbers, set up a filter to exclude everyone who works at your organization.

That kind of filter depends on the IP addresses your office uses. If you don't know what that means, don't fiddle with it. Instead, contact your Webmaster or your Internet service provider for help finding the IP address.

Then you set up the filter, as follows:

1. **Log into Google Analytics.**

2. **Click Edit next to the website profile that needs the filter.**

3. **Under Filters Applied to Profile, click Add Filter.**

4. **Select Add New Filter for Profile.**

5. **Give the filter a name you'll remember, such as** *Exclude IPs.*

6. **Under Filter Type, choose Exclude All Traffic from an IP Address.**

7. **Type in your IP address.**

Tracking Traffic Volumes

The more information you have on your customers and potential customers the better. Understanding where visitors to your website are coming from, how many of them there are, where they are looking, and how long they are staying provides you with crucial information for understanding what is working and what you need to change. You need to understand the five measurement criteria or metrics that the upcoming sections discuss. Google

Analytics is used for most of the examples, but the reports and such are much the same from one reporting package to another.

Seeing why hits are a lousy metric

First off, though, you need to avoid one metric when tracking traffic and user behaviour: hits.

You probably hear a lot of folks talk about hits. "I got a million hits last month!!!" is a claim people hear a lot.

That's great, but hits are almost meaningless for measuring audience or marketing performance. Simply defined, a *hit* is any one *file* downloaded from your website, any one time. Every image, script, and style sheet linked to a page counts as one file — and, thus, one hit. Seeing as how one page can contain 1 file or 1,000 files, hits don't tell you much from a marketing viewpoint.

Understanding the five basic traffic metrics

Traffic, in terms of Web visitors, actually comprises five different ingredients:

- ✔ **Sessions (also called *visits*):** A *session* is any one person visiting your website any one time. If a person visits your site ten times in a week, that person's visits count as ten sessions, whether the person stayed on the site for 5 minutes or 50.

- ✔ **Unique visitors:** A *unique visitor* is any one person visiting your website any number of times during a defined period. If a person visits your site ten times in a week, that person still count as only one unique visitor.

- ✔ **Pageviews:** A *pageview* is any one visitor viewing one page of your site, one time.

- ✔ **Time on site:** This is the total amount of time one visitor spends on your site in the course of a single session. Average time on site is an invaluable measure of visit quality and visitor interest.

- ✔ **Referrers:** If a person clicks a link at Google.ca and lands on your website, then Google is the *referrer.*

Any traffic-reporting toolset — even the most basic — must provide these five metrics.

Tracking sessions (visits)

Because a *session* is defined as any one visit to your site, sessions are a good general measure of site use and load (more on this in a moment). Think of sessions as foot traffic in a traditional retail store: The same people might go in and out of the store, but that doesn't matter. If the store's full, it's full.

In your traffic-reporting tool, you'll find sessions either under a section called Sessions (surprise!) or Visits.

Use sessions to see the following information:

- ✔ How busy your site is in the broadest possible terms
- ✔ Conversion rate based on foot traffic to your site
- ✔ General interest in your site
- ✔ Peak times of day, month, or year

Among analytics experts, sessions can sometimes get a bad reputation. Folks will skip them and move on to unique visitors, which appear to provide better data. However, sessions do provide valuable information.

Tracking unique visitors

Unique visitors reports are a good measure of audience size, ad performance, and the effect of blog mentions or other *noise* — news reports about you or a competitor, for example — on your business's website.

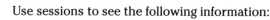

Use unique visitors to measure

- ✔ Audience size
- ✔ Overall ad performance
- ✔ Changes over time
- ✔ Comparison with sessions

See how these metrics build on each other? Sessions alone are useful, as are unique visitors, but sessions compared with unique visitors is even better.

Check your traffic reports to make sure you're measuring unique visitors. They're a must-have metric.

Tracking pageviews

If unique visitors are the people, then pageviews are their footprints. Pageviews are the measure of interest in specific areas of your site. Most traffic-reporting tools will give you a few different ways to look at pageviews:

- ✔ Overall pageview count for your entire site
- ✔ A page-by-page look at which pages get the most attention

Use pageviews to measure

- ✔ Visitor interest
- ✔ Content performance
- ✔ Ad performance

Again, see how the different metrics can be combined? Pageviews are a great measure of raw site usage. Pageviews per visit (per session) give you an added dimension: visitor interest.

Tracking time on site

Time on site is a useful metric when combined with pageviews, visits, sessions, and average time. Together, they give a more complete view of site performance and user interest. Consider the following examples:

- ✔ A visitor came to your site, visited 10 pages for five seconds each and then left. You might think you had a quality visitor, but that visitor was only on the site for 50 seconds, which makes it unlikely it was a meaningful visit.
- ✔ Your results show that a given page is the second most popular page on the site. The data also shows that visitors are spending more time on that page than any other. That can tell you the page is a strong performer.

Tracking referrers

Referrers complete the basic traffic-reporting toolset. A *referrer* is a web page that points to your website. When someone clicks a link, that web page becomes a referrer. Referrers come in many flavours:

- ✔ A traditional web page that might have a link to your site
- ✔ A link in an e-mail that someone reads in a Web-based e-mail reader, like Hotmail or Gmail
- ✔ A search result on a search engine

So, a referrer tells you where visitors came from when they reached your site.

Think about it: If you ran a vegetable stand and every single person who walked up had a sign on their forehead that read, "I saw your ad in the newspaper" or "John at the corner store told me about you," you'd immediately know which advertising worked and which marketing didn't.

Referrers are like that kind of sign telling you which referrers generate quality traffic. That makes referrers a must have in your analytics toolset. If your reporting tool doesn't show referrers, get a new tool.

Measuring Visit Quality

Measuring visit quality is not a science. The following sections discuss setting some benchmarks that you can try to improve upon. Your mission, should you choose to accept it, is to accomplish the following:

- ✔ Build traffic, but not at the expense of these benchmarks.
- ✔ Increase time on site and pageviews per visit.
- ✔ Keep these benchmarks in mind as you look at other statistics.

Setting quality targets

You need to set target numbers for the kinds of visitors you want. Even if you have a goal on the site — such as a sale, lead, or white paper download — you still need these separate measures of visit quality. The key is to figure out what your benchmarks are so you can focus on improvement rather than producing a perfect set of numbers.

So why not just focus on sales or whatever your ultimate goal is? Well, because even if visitors don't make a purchase, they might still show enough interest to return later, or tell a friend, or do something else you want them to do. You can't just rule out visitors who don't buy anything. Rather, think of their potential: They might still have a lot to offer your business.

Setting benchmarks for pageviews per visit and time on site

To set benchmarks for these numbers, you need to have been running your traffic-reporting tool for at least two to three months. That gives you enough data to set your benchmark, which you do by following these steps (which use Google Analytics as an example):

1. **In Google Analytics, from the main dashboard, click Visitors in the sidebar on the left.**

2. **Click the Visitor Trending option and then click Average Pageviews.**

3. **Look at the average for the past two to three months.**

4. **Navigate to your Time on Site report and, again, find the average for the last two to three months, which will be your target to improve upon.**

Calculating your loyalty benchmark

This section explains how to find out how many returning visitors you have and how to use this as a benchmark for increasing the percentage of returning visitors, which reflects visitor loyalty. The following steps help you set the target, again using Google Analytics as the example reporting tool:

1. **Open the report that calculates your percentage of repeat visitors.**

2. **Take a look at the percentage of returning versus new visitors: that's your target to improve upon.**

Learning more with bounce rate

You can further measure visit quality with *bounce rate*. A bounce occurs if someone visits one page of your website and then leaves without clicking to any other pages.

Bounce rate is the ultimate arbiter of visit quality. It shows you a few things:

- Pages that just drive people away.
- Pages that draw visitors further into your site.
- Most important, problems that exist with landing pages.

Bounce rate is a great statistic to analyze for your homepage. Unless you have a one-page website, chances are you want as low of a bounce rate as possible.

Sometimes, a high bounce rate is okay. If you have a blog, for instance, a lot of readers will drop in from an RSS feed or a link on another site, read something, and then leave. The more article-focused your site is, the less bounce rate might matter.

Index

• *Numerics* •

"80/20" rule, 120
360-degree assessment (multi-rater assessments), 469

• *A* •

absolute discharge, bankruptcy, 93
absolute novelty requirement, 142
Abstract section, patent specification (application), 148
acceleration clause, commercial term loans, 89
accidents, preventing, 58–59
Account column, chart of accounts, 346
account format, balance sheet, 354
accountants, seeking professional help from, 26–27
accounting, defined, 326
accounting cycle, 329–331
accounting equation, 333
accounting firms, 241
accounting period, 328, 359
accounts payable, 328
Accounts Payable account, 339
accounts receivable
  defined, 328, 349
  non-payment of, 61
Accounts Receivable account, 337
accrual accounting, 332
Accrued Payroll Taxes account
  Canada Pension Plan, 340
  Current Liabilities accounts, 340
  Employment Insurance, 340
Accumulated Depreciation — Buildings account, 337
Accumulated Depreciation — Equipment account, 338

Accumulated Depreciation — Furniture and Fixtures account, 338
Accumulated Depreciation — Leasehold Improvements account, 338
Accumulated Depreciation — Vehicles account, 338
acid test (quick) ratio, 357–358
acquiescence
  infringement dispute, 187
  IP rights, 187
act of bankruptcy, 109
action incentives, 542
action plan, 211
ad placement
  magazines, 528
  newspaper, 527–528
  out-of-home advertising, 528–529
  overview, 527
add-ons, SEO and, 576
adjusted cost base, 100
adjusted sale price, 100
adjusting journal entries, accounting cycle, 330
Adobe SiteCatalyst, 590
adopted trademarks, 162
adopting trademarks, 160
ADR (alternative dispute resolution)
  arbitration, 97–98
  mediation, 97
  overview, 97
Advanced Personnel Systems, 393
Advertisement stage, trademark registration process, 163
advertising
  ad placement, 527–529
  broadcasting ads on radio and TV, 529–532
  designing ads, 527
  determining need for advertising firm, 27
  effective, 521

advertising *(continued)*
evaluating, 524–525
identifying prospective customer, 520
image-plus-product advertising
approach, 520
mass media, 521–524
overview, 519
product packaging, 250
specialties, 538
writing ads, 408, 525–527
Advertising account, 344
Advil, 126
advisors, professional, 84–85
affiliate aggregator, 556
affiliate products, promoting, 556
agent, insurance, 27, 64
aggregators, 560
algorithms, search engine, 573
Allen, Paul, 296
all-Flash pages, avoiding, 585
Allowance stage, trademark registration
process, 163
allowances, 342
alternate work arrangements, 446–447
alternative dispute resolution (ADR)
arbitration, 97–98
mediation, 97
overview, 97
Amortization — Patents account, 339
Amortization account, 344
angel capital, 116
angle, news releases, 545
annual bonuses, 443
annual reports, 328
annuities (maintenance fees), patents,
134, 150
application
industrial design, 179
patent, 145–150
arbitrary marks, 158
arbitration, 97–98
arbitrators, 97
archives, copyrighted works, 176
arrears of rent (rent owing), 91
artistic reputation, protecting, 174–175
artistic works, copyright, 169

aspirin, 126
Asset accounts
Accounts Receivable account, 337
Accumulated Depreciation — Buildings
account, 337
Accumulated Depreciation — Equipment
account, 338
Accumulated Depreciation — Furniture
and Fixtures account, 338
Accumulated Depreciation — Leasehold
Improvements account, 338
Accumulated Depreciation — Vehicles
account, 338
Amortization — Patents account, 339
Buildings account, 337
Cash in Chequing account, 336
Cash in Savings account, 336
Cash on Hand account, 337
Copyrights account, 339
Equipment account, 338
Furniture and Fixtures account, 338
Goodwill account, 339
Inventory account, 337
Land account, 337
Leasehold Improvements account, 338
Patents account, 339
Prepaid Insurance account, 337
Vehicles account, 338
assets
bought on credit, inability to pay for, 90
current, 336–337
defined, 39, 327
dividing and listing on balance sheet,
348–351
finding buyers for, 106
long-term, 337–339
overview, 336
protecting without incorporating, 54–55
sale of, 103–104
valuing, existing business, 40–41
assigning
copyrighted work, 171
versus licensing, 194
patent, 139
assignment in bankruptcy, 93
assumptions, competitors', 270

athletic shoe market, 244
authorship, copyrights and, 169
averaging cost formula, 359

• *B* •

background checks, 430
Background of invention section, patent
    specification (application), 148
backward integration, 266
balance sheet
  account format, 354
  debt, 351–352, 358–359
  defined, 327
  dividing and listing assets, 348–351
  existing business, 39
  financial position format, 355–356
  generating electronically, 359
  investments, 352–353
  overview, 353
  report format, 354–355
  testing liquidity, 357–358
balance sheet accounts, 336
balancing out, 336
Ballard Power Systems, vision
    statement, 220
Bank Service Charges account, 344
bank websites, 21
bankruptcy, 93–94
Bankruptcy and Insolvency Act, 92–93
base salary, 436
behaviourally anchored rating scale
    (BARS), 467
Beliefs and Principles Questionnaire,
    215–217
bell curve, 468
benchmarking, 368
benefits
  defined, 437
  versus features, 252–253
bi-annual bonuses, 443
BioWare Corp, 276
BizPaL online business permits and
    licences service, 19
Black hat SEO, 572
BlackBerry e-mail software, 155

blind spots, industry, 270
Blogger, 559
blogging
  choosing topic, 558
  overview, 557
  tools, 559
Bluecasting, 566
Bluetooth, 566
bolded key phrases, SEO, 574
bonuses, 436, 442–443
book value, 40
bookkeepers, 326
bookkeeping
  accounting cycle, 329–331
  accrual accounting, 332
  balance sheet, 327
  bookkeepers, 326
  cash-basis accounting, 331–332
  chart of accounts, 335–345
  converting from manual to computerized
    bookkeeping, 379–380
  credits, 335
  customizing software to match
    operations, 378–379
  debits, 335
  double-entry bookkeeping, 333–334
  income statement, 327–328
  overview, 325, 373
  software, 373–376
  terminology, 328–329
bookmarking sites, 560
boss-employee relationship, 120
bots (robots), 572
bounce rate, 597–598
brand, 513–515
  advancing through creative strategy,
    517–518
  consistency and, 514
  conveying through tag lines, 517
  critical success factors, 241
  management, 514–515
  overview, 513–514
  powerful, 514
  trademarks and, 157
brand ads, 519
breach of contract, suppliers, 83

break-even cost, 33

broadcast media, 521

broadcasting ads on radio and TV, 529–532
  buying airtime, 529
  establishing broadcast identity, 530
  overview, 529
  reach and frequency, 529–530
  writing broadcast ad, 530–532

brochure websites, 552

brochures, 539–540

broker, insurance, 27, 64

budget, marketing, 507–508

Buildings account, 337

Bulk Sales Act, 105, 107

bullets, SEO, 574

burden of proof, 185

burnout, avoiding
  giving employees more job autonomy, 451
  minimizing extended periods of excessive
    workload, 451
  overview, 450
  providing help, 451–452
  recognizing employee burnout, 450

business coach, 27

business description section, business
  plan, 210

Business Development Bank of Canada
  website, 205

business environment section, business
  plan, 209

business evaluator, 27

business incubators, 22

business management techniques
  boss-employee relationship, 120
  delegating, 119
  embracing change, 120
  focusing on strengths, 120
  overview, 119
  setting goals, 119–120

business model
  competitive advantage, 295–297
  core competence, 297–298
  earmarking resources, 299–300
  finances, 293–294
  overview, 293

sustaining competitive advantage, 298–299
  timing revenue flow, 294

business networking organizations, 207

business plan. *See also* NCI sample
    business plan
  action plan, 211
  business description section, 210
  business environment section, 209
  business strategy section, 210
  executive summary section, 208
  financial review section, 210–211
  general business overview section, 209
  goals and objectives, 227–230
  mission statement, 221–224
  overview, 203
  resources, 204–207
  setting ground rules, 207
  values and principles, 211–219
  vision statement, 219–221

business strategy section, business plan, 210

Business Strengths and Weaknesses
    Questionnaire, 275

business-owned equipment, employee
    termination meeting, 478

buying existing business, 35

by-laws, corporation, 54

• *C* •

call-to-action ads (product ads), 519

Canada Awards of Excellence (CAE), 277

Canada Business organization
  accessing services, 19–20
  network services, 18–19
  overview, 18

Canada Business website, 19, 205

Canada Pension Plan (CPP), 340

Canada Revenue Agency (CRA)
  business-planning info, 205
  cash-basis accounting, 332
  statutory liens, 92

Canadian Advertising Rates and Data
    (CARD), 528

Canadian Association of Women
    Executives & Entrepreneurs, 28

Canadian Council for Aboriginal Business, 28
Canadian Council of Human Resources Associations (CCHRA), 393
Canadian Federation of Independent Business (CFIB), 205
Canadian Gay & Lesbian Chamber of Commerce, 28
Canadian Humanitarian, mission statement, 224
Canadian Innovation Centre (CIC), 30
Canadian Institute of Chartered Business Valuators, 42
Canadian Intellectual Property Office (CIPO)
  accrediting patent and trademark agents, 129
  assigning IP rights, 194
  copyright application, 171–172
  first-to-file priority system, 148
  patents, 138
  registering transfer of IP rights, 187
  Trademark Register, 162
  Trademarks Journal, 163
Canadian Public Relations Society (CPRS), 543
Canadian Security Administrators, values statement, 213
Canadian Youth Business Foundation, 28
capabilities and resources
  competitors', 266–267
  customer base, 278
  distribution and delivery, 281–282
  financial condition, 282–283
  management, 276
  operations, 279–280
  organization, 277
  overview, 275
  research and development, 279
  sales and marketing, 280–281
capabilities brochure, 539
capacity levels, 238
Capital account, 341, 352
capital cost allowance (CCA), 100–101, 104
capital gains
  calculating, 100–101
  taxation of, 100
capital loss, 100

capital property, 100
car manufacturing, 259
CARD (*Canadian Advertising Rates and Data*), 528
Carnegie, Andrew, 290
CAs (Chartered Accountants), 241
Cash in Chequing account, 336
Cash in Savings account, 336
Cash line item, balance sheet, 349
cash on delivery (COD), 79
Cash on Hand account, 337
cash-basis accounting, 331–332
catalog distribution, 534
CCA (capital cost allowance), 100–101, 104
CCHRA (Canadian Council of Human Resources Associations), 393
cease and desist letter, 184–185
CEED (Centre for Entrepreneurship Education and Development Incorporated), 21
Centennial College Centre of Entrepreneurship, 21
Centre for Entrepreneurship Education and Development Incorporated (CEED), 21
certification marks, 157–158
Certified General Accountants (CGAs), 241
CFIB (Canadian Federation of Independent Business), 205
CGI Group Inc., vision statement, 220
chart of accounts
  assets, 336–339
  balance sheet accounts, 336
  equity, 341
  income statement, 341–345
  liabilities, 339–340
  overview, 335
  setting up, 346
Chartered Accountants (CAs), 241
chattel mortgage, 90
checking references
  background checks, 430
  overview, 429
choosing your business
  avoiding difficult business start-up, 13–14
  looking for business start-up, 13
  overview, 12–13

chronological resume, 414
CIC (Canadian Innovation Centre), 30
CIPO (Canadian Intellectual Property Office)
  accrediting patent and trademark
    agents, 129
  assigning IP rights, 194
  copyright application, 171–172
  first-to-file priority system, 148
  patents, 138
  registering transfer of IP rights, 187
  Trademark Register, 162
  Trademarks Journal, 163
claim, patent application, 149
Claims section, patent specification
    (application), 148
class market, 251
classification, balance sheet accounts,
    348–349
clearing mark, 161
ClickBank, 556
clicks, search listing, 575
clients. *See* customers
closed-ended interview questions, 419
closing books, accounting cycle, 330–331
closing the sale, 66
cluster marketing (geodemographics), 490
CMS (content management system)-driven
    site, 591
co-branding product, 197
COD (cash on delivery), 79
Cognos Incorporated, mission statement, 224
co-inventors, 144
collecting data, 589
commercial lease, 48–49
commercial source loans, 89
commercialization strategy, 195
commercializing IP, 189
commissions, 437
commodities marketplace, 235
common shares, 53
Common Shares account, 341, 352
common-law tort, trademarks, 167–168
company information, job ad, 408
company profile, 246–247
compatibility, Microsoft's competitive
    advantage, 296

compensation, employee
  accounting for individuals, 441
  basing on scale, 437–438
  bonuses, 442–443
  communicating policies, 444–445
  consistency and flexibility, 437
  defined, 436
  fairness, 444
  incentives, 443–444
  overtime, 441
  pay levels, 439–441
  pay raises, 442
compensation for damages, infringement
    dispute, 188
competency models, employee
    recruitment, 400–401
competition
  avoiding, 13
  car manufacturing, 259
  choosing battles, 272
  data sources about, 271–272
  identifying competitors, 261–266
  overview, 258–259
  predicting competitors' moves, 269–270
  product/service development, 31–32
  role in price strategy, 34
  tracking competitors' actions, 266–269
  understanding value of, 259–260
competitive advantage, 295–299
competitive intelligence, 31
competitive principle, employee
    bonuses, 442
competitive view, business analysis,
    274–275
competitors
  direct, 31, 499
  emerging, 265–266
  first-tier, 261–262
  head-to-head, 261–262
  indirect, 31, 261–262, 499
  IP rights and, 126
  measuring business against, 285–287
  nonprice, 500
  phantom, 500
  price, 500

computer systems consultant, 27
computerized bookkeeping
 converting manual bookkeeping to,
  379–380
 customizing software to match
  operations, 378–379
 overview, 376–378
conditional discharge, bankruptcy, 93
conditional sales agreement, 90
confidential disclosure agreement,
 36, 102–103
confidentiality
 industrial design, 178
 IP professionals, 130
consistency
 brand, 514
 employee compensation, 437
consulting agreements, 105
consumables, 294
contact websites, 552
content, website
 generating traffic with, 555
 as incentive to mobile device users, 569
content clusters, 585–586
content management system (CMS)-driven
 site, 591
contingency search firms, 411
contingent employees, 387
continuing education courses, 25
contracts
 consulting lawyer regarding, 68–69
 contracts for sale of goods or services,
  67–68
 overview, 66–67
 suppliers, 80–81
contractual rights, intellectual property
 and, 125
conventional wisdom, industry, 270
Cooper Virtual Office Services, mission
 statement, 224
co-ownership, 50–51
co-ownership agreement, 171
copies for the blind, literary works, 176
copy, print ad, 525
copying, forbidding, 173
copyright licence, 191

copyrights
 barring public performances, 174
 defined, 168–170
 exceptions, 175–176
 forbidding copying, 173
 infringement, 182–183
 infringing, 172–173
 as intangible asset, 350
 intellectual property and, 125
 making official, 171–172
 overview, 168
 ownership issues, 170–171
 preventing unauthorized distribution, 174
 prohibiting preparation of derivative
  works, 173–174
 protecting artistic reputation, 174–175
 scope of your rights, 186
Copyrights account, 339
core competence, 297–298
corporate culture, 40
corporation
 bankruptcy, 93
 overview, 52
 owning, 53
 running, 53
 setting up, 54
corrective action, employee disciplinary
 process, 477
Corvette, 261
cost
 industry analysis, 238
 IP professionals, 133–134
 patenting, 140–141
 prior art search, 147
cost of goods sold
 defined, 328, 362–363
 gauging, 364–365
Cost of Goods Sold accounts
 Freight-In Charges account, 343
 Purchase Discount account, 343
 Purchase Returns and Allowances
  account, 343
 Purchases account, 343
Cost of goods sold item, income
 statement, 360
cost of sales, tracking, 343

cost/benefit analysis practice, employee training, 461
Costs involved column, impression inventory, 511
counterclaims, 98
court proceedings, infringement, 185
CPP (Canada Pension Plan), 340
CPRS (Canadian Public Relations Society), 543
CRA (Canada Revenue Agency)
  business-planning info, 205
  cash-basis accounting, 332
  statutory liens, 92
crawl, 572
creativity
  employee, 428–429
  entrepreneur, 16
credit
  establishing with suppliers, 79–80
  extending to corporations, 71
  inability to make payments on assets bought on, 90
  not extending, 61
  payment, 71–72
Credit Cards Payable account, 340
credit rating, 80
credit sales, 328
credits
  bookkeeping, 335
  double-entry bookkeeping, 333
crisis communications, 547
crisis management skills, importance of, 16
critical incidents method, performance appraisal, 467
critical success factors (CSF)
  adopting new technologies, 240
  branding, 241
  customer loyalty, 241
  distribution, 241
  government regulation, 241
  handling operations, 240
  human resources, 240
  location, 241
  logistics, 240
  monitoring, 284–285
  overview, 239

current assets, 39, 336–337, 349
current liabilities, 339–340
Current Liabilities accounts
  Accounts Payable account, 339
  Accrued Payroll Taxes account, 340
  Credit Cards Payable account, 340
  Goods and Services Tax or Harmonized Sales Tax, 340
  Goods and Services Tax Payable account, 340
  Provincial Sales Tax, 340
  Retail Taxes Payable account, 340
current ratio, 39, 357
customer loyalty
  critical success factors, 241
  customer buying decisions, 254
customer motivation
  overview, 494
  price, 496–497
  value, 495–496
customer relations, 68
customer research, 31
customer service, 66
customer targeting, 502
customers
  analysing to determine competitor's capabilities, 267
  customer research, 491–492
  dealing with unhappy, 69–70
  existing, 114–115
  geography, 246
  identifying, 255–256
  identifying prospective, 520
  interviews, market research, 257
  keeping happy, 69
  lifestyle, 247–248
  making the sale, 65–66
  market segmentation, 490
  motivation, 252–255
  new, 115
  notifying when going out of business, 107
  overview, 64–65, 490
  personality types, 245–246, 248–249, 258
  privacy, 72–73
  profile, 246–247

seeing business from customer's
  perspective, 492
separating into groups, 244
typical business transaction, 65

● *D* ●

damages
  caused by careless advice, 59–60
  caused by not fulfilling contract, 60
  caused by suppliers, 83–84
  to premises, 60–61
damages (money compensation), 91
data plans, smartphones, 566
death of business owner
  keeping it in family, 111
  overview, 109–110
  selling to outsider, 112
  short-term planning versus long-term
    planning, 110–111
debenture, 109
debits, 333, 335
debt
  balance sheet, 351–352, 358–359
  paying off when going out of business, 107
  personally guaranteeing business debt,
    90–91
  when selling business as going
    concern, 105
debt-to-equity ratio, 39, 358
decision-making process (DMP), 254–255
decision-making unit (DMU), 254
Declaration of Entitlement, filing, 149–150
deep links, 586
delegating
  business management techniques, 119
  personal management techniques, 118
deliverables, 466
delivery. *See also* distribution and delivery
  analysing to determine competitor's
    capabilities, 267
  product, 251
Delta Elevator, mission statement, 223
demand bank loan, 351

demographics
  customer data, 246–247
  market segmentation, 490
depreciation, 328
Depreciation account, 344
derivative works, prohibiting, 173–174
description, industrial design
    application, 179
Description column, chart of accounts, 346
description meta tag, SEO, 574
Description of preferred embodiments
    section, patent specification
    (application), 148
descriptive marks, 158
designing ads, 527
diffusion of innovation, 249, 258
direct competitors, 31, 499
direct distribution channel, 33
direct mail
  lists, 535–536
  messages, 536–537
  offers, 536
  success factors, 534–535
direct mobile marketing, 564
direct response advertising, 534
direct sales strategies, 534
director, corporation, 53
directories, advertising, 522
disciplinary procedures, 476–477
disclosure of invention, 142
Discount Car & Truck Rentals, 296–298
discounts, income statement, 369
discussion forums, 561
disputes
  alternative dispute resolution, 97–98
  litigation, 98–99
  negotiating settlement, 94–97
  overview, 94
distinguishing guise, 157
distrain, 91
distribution and delivery
  analysing to determine competitor's
    capabilities, 267
  critical success factors, 241

distribution and delivery *(continued)*
  importance of, 281–282
  where consumers find products, 251
distribution channel, 237
distribution systems, 237
diversity, workplace environment, 399
dividends, 327
DMP (decision-making process), 254–255
DMU (decision-making unit), 254
documentation review, customer
    research, 492
double-entry bookkeeping, 333–334
dramatic works, copyright, 169
draw, 437
drawings, industrial design application, 179
Drawings account, 341, 352
Drawings or figures section, patent
    specification (application), 148
Drucker, Peter, 451
due diligence, 45
Dues and Subscriptions account, 344
duration, IP licence, 192

• *E* •

EAPs (employee assistance programs),
    387, 452
early adopter customer personality type,
    248, 258
early majority customer personality type,
    248, 258
early retirement, 481
earmarking resources, 299–300
earnings, recording, 342–343
e-commerce websites, 552
educational use of copyrighted works, 176
effectiveness of learning practice,
    employee training, 461
EFTs (electronic funds transfers), 374–375
EI (Employment Insurance), 340
"80/20" rule, 120
e-learning, 458–459

electronic funds transfers (EFTs), 374–375
e-mail
  Canada Business, 20
  mobile marketing, 565–566
embezzlement, 62
emerging competitors, 265–266
employee assistance programs (EAPs),
    387, 452
employee focus groups, 455
employee-friendly, 387
employees. *See also* recruiting employees;
    retention, employee
  contingent, 387
  copyright ownership of work created
    by, 170
  firing, 477–481
  furlough, 480
  industriousness, 428
  intelligence, 428
  layoffs, 480, 481
  making employment offer, 430–433
  motivation, 428
  ownership of industrial design created
    by, 178
  as source of data on competition, 271–272
  temperament, 428
  training and development, 453
employment agencies, 411
employment contracts, 433
Employment Insurance (EI), 340
employment offer, making
  avoiding delays, 431
  checking in, 433
  clarify acceptance details, 433
  hiring details, 431
  knowing when to walk away, 433
  negotiating salary, 432
  overview, 430
  setting deadline, 431
  staying connected, 431
ending inventory, 362
enforcement, IP licence, 192

enforcing trademarks
  infringing on rights, 166–167
  overview, 165–166
  passing off action, 167–168
Enron Corporation, 219
entrepreneurship centres, 21–22
entry barriers, 264
ephemeral recordings, copyrighted
    works, 176
Equipment account, 338
Equipment Rental account, 344
Equipment under Capital Lease asset,
    balance sheet, 350
equity
  defined, 327
  investments, 352
Equity accounts
  Capital account, 341
  Common Shares account, 341
  defined, 336
  Drawings account, 341
  Retained Earnings account, 341
equity investment, 116
essay appraisals, 466–467
ethics
  establishing culture of, 475
  ethical dilemmas, 212–213
  human resources, 388–389
evaluating your business
  capabilities and resources, 275–283
  competitive advantage, 295–297
  considering independent viewpoints,
    274–275
  core competence, 297–298
  critical success factors, 284–285
  earmarking resources, 299–300
  finances, 293–294
  measuring business against competitors,
    285–287
  overview, 273, 293
  sustaining competitive advantage,
    298–299

timing revenue flow, 294
  value chain, 287–293
Evaluation column, impression
    inventory, 511
evaluation process, recruiting
    employees, 413
events, as promotion incentive, 542
Examination stage, trademark registration
    process, 163
Examiner's Report (office action), 150
exclusive IP licence agreement, 192
exclusive licences, IP, 127
exculpatory clause, contract, 68, 74–75
executive education seminars, 458
executive search firms, 411
executive summary section
  business plan, 208
  NCI sample business plan, 301–303
executor of will, 110
exemption clause, contract, 68, 74–75
exemptions, copyright, 176
existing customers
  doing more of same work for, 114–115
  doing new and additional work for, 115
exit barriers, 264
expanding your business
  business management techniques,
    119–120
  defined, 112–113
  existing customers, 114–115
  financing, 115–116
  finding new customers, 115
  marketing, 489
  overview, 112
  personal management techniques,
    117–119
expense accounts
  Advertising account, 344
  Amortization account, 344
  Bank Service Charges account, 344
  Depreciation account, 344
  Dues and Subscriptions account, 344

expense accounts *(continued)*
Equipment Rental account, 344
income statement, 341
Insurance account, 344
Interest account, 344
Legal and Accounting account, 344
Maintenance and Repairs account, 344
Miscellaneous Expenses account, 344
Office Expenses account, 345
overview, 343
Payroll Benefits account, 345
Postage and Delivery account, 345
Rent Expense account, 345
Salaries and Wages account, 345
Supplies account, 345
Telephone and Internet account, 345
Travel and Entertainment account, 345
Utilities account, 345
Vehicles account, 345
expenses
chart of accounts, 343–345
defined, 38, 328
income statement, 366
IP, 134
experience curves, 238
experiences, as promotion incentive, 542
expungement, 164
extraction business, 12

● *F* ●

Facebook, 409–410, 561
face-to-face interviews
closed-ended questions, 419
goals, 416
hypothetical questions, 420
knowing what you can't ask, 420–421
leading questions, 420
meeting candidate, 417–418
open-ended questions, 420
overview, 416
Q&As, 418–419
setting stage, 417

Fact sheets, 19
fair dealing concept, copyrights, 175
fair market value, 40
fair principle, employee bonuses, 442
false assumptions, industry, 270
features
versus benefits, 252
defined, 249
fiduciary duty, IP professional, 130
Field of invention section, patent
specification (application), 148
field of use, IP licence, 192
file names, SEO, 575
filling jobs from within organization
developing employee skills inventory, 407
internal hiring process, 407
overview, 406
final payment, employee termination
meeting, 478
finances
bankruptcy, 93–94
business model, 293–294
competitor, analysing to determine
capabilities, 267
inability to make payments, 88–90
inability to pay mortgage on real
property, 91–92
inability to pay rent, 91
inability to pay taxes, 92
industry analysis, 237–239
insolvency, 92–93
maintaining healthy business, 282–283
overview, 87–88
personally guaranteeing business debt,
90–91
financial position format, balance sheet,
355–356
financial review section, business plan,
210–211
financial statements
accounting cycle, 330–331
balance sheet, 39
income statement, 38
overview, 38

financing
   expanding business, 115–116
   market segments, 251
   product/service development, 32
finding help
   accountant, 26–27
   insurance agent or broker, 27
   lawyer, 26
   overview, 26
   peer support, 28
finding new customers, 115
finding suppliers, 77
finished-goods inventory, 365
Firefox, 575
firing employees
   easing trauma of layoffs, 480–481
   overview, 477–478
   post-termination protocol, 478–479
   waiver of rights, 479
first stage financing, 116
first-tier competitors, 261–262
first-to-file priority system, 146, 148
first-to-invent system, 142
fiscal year, 378
Fisher, Roger, 96
fixed assets, 39
fixed fee, IP professional services, 134
flexibility
   employee compensation, 437
   workplace, 387
Flickr, 562
fliers, 539
focus groups, 492
focus strategy, 268
forced choice methods, performance
      appraisal, 468
forced comparison ranking method, 468
forced distribution ranking method, 468
forced ranking method, 468
Ford Motor Company, mission
      statement, 226
foreclosure, 91
Formalities stage, trademark registration
      process, 163

forward integration, 266
franchise
   advantages of, 43
   disadvantages of, 43–44
   doing due diligence, 45
   evaluating, 44–45
   finding, 44
   overview, 42
franchisee, 42
franchisor, 42
free search optimization, generating
      website traffic with, 555
Freedom-to-operate analysis, 155
Freight-In Charges account, 343
frequency, advertising, 524
functional resume, 414
furlough, employee, 480
Furniture and Fixtures account, 338

• **G** •

GAAP (generally accepted accounting
      principles), 332
Gain or Loss on Sale of Fixed Assets
      account, 343
Gary, Elbert, 290
Gates, Bill, 296
general business overview section,
      business plan, 209
general ledger, 329
general security agreement, 109
generalists, HR, 385
generally accepted accounting principles
      (GAAP), 332
generic strategies, 267–268
genericide, 167
geodemographics, 490
geographic indications, 158
geographic targeting, 502
geographics, market segmentation,
      245–246, 490
goals
   competitors', 269–270
   defined, 505

goals *(continued)*
importance of being goal-orientated, 15
marketing plan, 505
goals and objectives, in business plan
avoiding business-planning pitfalls,
228–229
creating, 227
defined, 225–227
laying out, 228
matching with mission, 228
overview, 209
time frame, 230
going concern, selling business as
allocating purchase price if assets
sold, 104
consulting agreements, 105
dealing with prospective buyers, 102–103
knowing what business is worth, 102
non-competition agreements, 105
overview, 101
paying business debts, 105
sale of assets or sale of shares, 103–104
going out of business
finding buyers for assets, 106
joint venture, 99–100
negotiating with landlord, 108
notifying clients or customers, 107
notifying suppliers, 108
overview, 99, 106
paying off debts, 107
put out of business by secured creditors,
108–109
put out of business by unsecured
creditors, 109
taxes and, 100–101
unloading leased equipment, 107
goods
contract, 67
suppliers of, 83
Goods and Services Tax or Harmonized
Sales Tax (GST/HST), 340
Goods and Services Tax Payable account,
340

goodwill
defined, 102
as intangible asset, 351
valuing, existing business, 41–42
Goodwill account, 339
Google AdWords keyword research
tool, 580
Google Analytics
excluding office, 592
installing tracking code, 591
overview, 590, 591
tracking site search, 591–592
Google Toolbar add-on, 576
Google Trends, 580
Google Webmaster tools, 576–577
government regulation
critical success factors, 241
factor in business venture decision, 14
graphic designer, 28
graphics, print ad, 525
gross profit, income statement, 365–366
Gross profit item, income statement, 360
growing markets, 235
GST/HST (Goods and Services Tax or
Harmonized Sales Tax), 340

• *H* •

Habitat for Humanity program, 504
Harris Hatch Inn, 294
Harvard Negotiating Project, 96
headhunter (human resources specialist),
28, 411
headings, SEO, 574
headline
job ad, 408
print ad, 525
head-to-head competitors, 261–262
help resources
accountant, 26–27
insurance agent or broker, 27
lawyer, 26

overview, 26
peer support, 28
hidden text, SEO, 574
hiring criteria, job ad, 408
hiring decision
  ability to cope with stress, 428
  annual needs assessments, 398
  creativity, 428–429
  decision-making process, 425
  industriousness, 428
  intelligence, 428
  motivation, 428
  overview, 396–397, 424
  resourcefulness, 428–429
  resources for, 425–426
  strategic staffing, 397–398
  teamwork abilities, 429
  temperament, 428
  weighted system, 426–427
hits, 593
home office expenses, telecommuting, 448
hourly fee, IP professional services, 134
How-to guides, 18
HR (human resources)
  adapting to changing workplace, 386–387
  critical success factors, 240
  easing work/life conflict, 387
  ethics, 388–389
  keeping pace with technology and new
    skills, 388
  managing, 384
  overview, 383
  software, 390–393
  strategies, 389–390
  thinking strategically, 385–386
HR (human resources) software
  being an educated buyer, 391–392
  features, 392–393
  overview, 390–391
HRIS (Human Resource Information
    Systems), 390

hrVillage, 393
hub pages, 585–586
Human Resource Information Systems
    (HRIS), 390
human resources (HR)
  adapting to changing workplace, 386–387
  critical success factors, 240
  easing work/life conflict, 387
  ethics, 388–389
  keeping pace with technology and new
    skills, 388
  managing, 384
  overview, 383
  software, 390–393
  strategies, 389–390
  thinking strategically, 385–386
human resources (HR) software
  being an educated buyer, 391–392
  features, 392–393
  overview, 390–391
human resources specialist (headhunter),
    28, 411
human rights laws, 421

• *I* •

IFRS (International Financial Reporting
    Standards), 353, 355
IHRIM (International Association for
    Human Resource Information
    Management) e-Journal, 393
image, projecting
  impression inventory, 511–513
  making first impressions, 510
  overview, 509–510
  rating marketing communications, 513
image captions, SEO, 574
image-plus-product advertising
    approach, 520
images ads, 519

impact on job performance practice,
    employee training, 461
impression inventory, 511–513
Impression points column, impression
    inventory, 511
incentives
  defined, 436
  mobile marketing, 569
  overview, 443
  profit-sharing plans, 443
  stock, 443–444
income accounts
  Gain or Loss on Sale of Fixed Assets
    account, 343
  Interest Income account, 342
  Other Income account, 342
  Rent Revenue account, 342
income statement
  classifying accounts in, 360–361
  defined, 327–328
  drawing remaining amounts from
    worksheet, 363–364
  existing business, 38
  expenses, 343–345, 366
  formatting, 361–362
  gauging cost of goods sold, 364–365
  gross profit, 365–366
  overview, 341–342, 359
  preparing, 362–363
  recording earnings, 342–343
  tracking cost of sales, 343
  using to make business decisions,
    366–369
incoming links, SEO, 577
incorporation
  considering options, 51
  overview, 51
  versus unincorporated business, 51–52
indefinite duration, IP professional
    fiduciary duty, 130
independence, importance of, 15
indirect competitors, 31, 261–262, 499
indirect distribution channel, 33
indirect mobile marketing, 564

industrial design
  application, 179
  basics, 178
  defined, 176–177
  determining proprietorship, 178–179
  infringement, 183
  intellectual property and, 125
  overview, 176
  registering, 177–178
  scope of your rights, 186
Industrial Design Office, 177
industriousness, employee, 428
industry analysis
  distribution systems, 237
  finances, 237–239
  growing markets, 235
  overview, 232–234
  product differentiation, 235–236
  product substitution, 236
  satisfied customers, 237
  shrinking markets, 235
  solidifying structure, 234
  supply and demand, 236–237
Industry Analysis Questionnaire, 233
Industry Canada website
  business-planning info, 205
  government assistance for small
    business, 368
  researching business, 23
inertia, 31
Info guides, 18
information product, 557
infringement
  cease and desist letter, 184–185
  copyright, 182–183
  copyrights, 172–173
  court proceedings, 185
  industrial design, 183
  overview, 181, 184
  patent, 182
  trademark, 182
  on trademark rights, 166–167
infringement IP opinion, 154
in-house classroom training, 457

initial capital, 282
initial employee reaction practice, employee training, 461
initial notification, employee disciplinary process, 476
injunctions, infringement dispute, 188
injuries, preventing, 59
injury to business
  computer and Internet hazards, 62
  damage to premises, 60–61
  loss of paper records, 62
  non-payment of accounts receivable, 61
  overview, 60
  theft and embezzlement, 62
injury to others
  damage caused by careless advice, 59–60
  damage caused by not fulfilling contract, 60
  overview, 58
  physical injuries and damage, 58–59
innovator customer personality type, 248, 258
insolvency
  bankruptcy, 93
  dealing with secured creditors, 92–93
  dealing with unsecured creditors, 92
  defined, 109
  overview, 92
institutional ads, 519
insurance
  agent or broker, 27, 64
  determining need for, 63–64
  Employment Insurance, 340
  overview, 63
  policies, 64
Insurance account, 344
insurance agents (brokers), 27, 64
intangible assets, 339, 350
intangibles
  creativity and resourcefulness, 428–429
  industriousness and motivation, 428
  intelligence, 428
  overview, 428

teamwork abilities, 429
temperament and stress-coping ability, 428
intellectual property (IP)
  benefits of protecting rights, 125–128
  commercialization strategy, 195
  defined, 124
  infringement, 181–185
  licensing, 189–197
  overview, 123–124, 181
  professionals, 128–134
  rights, 185–188
  types of, 124–125
  using filings as research tool, 197–199
intellectual property (IP) opinions, 154–155
intelligence, employee, 428
interactive voice response (IVR), 566
interest, 329
Interest account, 344
Interest Income account, 342
interior designer, 28
interlocutory injunction, 188
internal view, business analysis, 274
International Association for Human Resource Information Management (IHRIM) e-Journal, 393
International Financial Reporting Standards (IFRS), 353, 355
international priority date, 164
Internet. *See also* online presence; websites
  handling application submissions, 409
  preventing injury to business, 62
  using website to attract job candidates, 409–410
interviews
  customer research, 491
  ending, 424
  face-to-face, 416–421
  phone, 415–416
  questions to ask and interpreting answers, 421–424
Intuit QuickBooks Pro program, 374
invented marks, 158

invention
  describing on patent application, 149
  qualifying, 144
  summarizing on patent application, 149
  writing description, 143
invention-assignment clauses, 145
inventorship, determining, 144
inventory
  averaging cost formula, 359
  defined, 77, 329
  employee skills, 407
  ending, 362
  finished-goods inventory, 365
  impression, 511–513
  opening, 362
  parts suppliers and, 78–79
  raw materials, 365
  work-in-process, 365
Inventory account, 337
investments
  balance sheet, 352–353
  from within business, 116
  from outside business, 116
IP (intellectual property)
  benefits of protecting rights, 125–128
  commercialization strategy, 195
  defined, 124
  infringement, 181–185
  licensing, 189–197
  overview, 123–124, 181
  professionals, 128–134
  rights, 185–188
  types of, 124–125
  using filings as research tool, 197–199
IP (intellectual property) opinions, 154–155
IVR (interactive voice response), 566

• J •

Jaguar, 161
Japanese car manufacturing, 259
jingles, broadcast identity, 530
job ad, writing, 408

job descriptions
  flexibility, 404
  job title, 405
  sample, 402–403
  setting salary range, 405
  soft skills, 404
  specificity, 404–405
  tasks and qualifications, 403
job rating checklist method, performance
  appraisal, 467
Johnson & Johnson Credo, 214
joint ownership, copyrights and, 171
joint venture, 99–100
journal entries, accounting cycle, 329–330
journals, 329
judicial sale, 91

• K •

key messages, media interviews, 546
key phrases, website, 573
key success factor (KSF). *See* critical
  success factors
Keyword Discovery website, 579
keyword services, 579
keywords
  comparing competition and search
    volume, 581
  developing, 579–581
  diversity, SEO, 577
  Google AdWords keyword research
    tool, 580
  Google Trends, 580
  keyword services, 579
  long tail phrases, 578–579
  overview, 578, 579
  rankings, SEO, 577
  staying current, 580
  thinking like visitors, 578
  using brain, 581
keywords meta tag, SEO, 574
Kijiji, 48
knockout, 161

knowledge workers, 388
KSF (key success factor). *See* critical success factors

• L •

laggard customer personality type, 248, 258
Land account, 337
landlord, negotiating with when going out of business, 108
last-chance warning, employee disciplinary process, 477
late majority customer personality type, 248, 258
launching business, 32
Law Society of Upper Canada, 172
lawyers
  interviewing, 131
  seeking professional help from, 26
layoffs
  alternatives, 481
  defined, 480
  easing trauma of, 480–481
lease with an option to purchase, 90
leased equipment, unloading, 107
Leasehold improvements account, 338, 350
leasing options, 251
Legal and Accounting account, 344
Legal Line website, 205
lessor, 107
Lexus, 161
liabilities
  current, 339–340
  defined, 39, 327
  long-term, 340
  overview, 339
Liabilities section, balance sheet, 351–352
Liability account, 336
libraries, copyrighted works and, 176
licensee, IP, 190, 196

licensing
  versus assigning, 194
  benefitting from someone else's IP, 196–197
  copyrighted work, 171
  IP rights, 127
  licence agreement, 192–193
  overview, 190
  patent rights, 139
  remuneration, 193–194
  reporting, 194
  selling and, 189–190
  types of licences, 190–191
  using with trademarks, 196–197
licensing body, trademarks, 158
licensor, IP, 190
lifestyle, customer, 245, 247
lifestyle marketing (geodemographics), 490
link text, 575, 587
LinkedIn, 409–410, 561
links
  SEO, 574
  value chain, 288–289
liquidation sale, 106
liquidation value, 41
liquidity
  acid test (quick) ratio, 357–358
  current ratio, 357
  defined, 39
  overview, 357
list brokerage businesses, 535
lists, SEO, 574
literary works
  copies for the blind, 176
  copyrights, 169
litigation
  being sued, 98–99
  overview, 98
  suing, 98
litigation lawyer, 131
Live HTTP Headers add-on, 576

loans
    from commercial source, 89
    demand bank, 351
    from non-commercial source, 88–89
Loans Payable account, 340
location, business
    critical success factors, 241
    existing business, 37–38
    overview, 46
    renting, 47–49
    space-sharing arrangements, 47
    working from home, 46
    working from real business premises, 46–47
login forms, eliminating, 584
logistics, CSF, 240
long tail phrases, 578–579
long-term assets, 337–339
long-term liabilities, 340
long-term liability accounts, 340
loss
    capital, 100
    net, 328
    suffering because of suppliers, 83–84
    terminal, 101
love money, 88–89
low cost strategy, 268

• M •

magazine ads, 522, 528
magazine subscriber lists, 536
Magna Entertainment Corp. (MEC), 269
Magna International, 276
Magnetic Hill Zoo, mission statement, 224
mailing services, 535
Maintenance and Repairs account, 344
maintenance fees (annuities), patents, 134, 150
making the sale
    first impressions and customer service, 66
    overview, 65
    pitch and close, 66

management
    analysing to determine competitor's capabilities, 266
    brand, 514–515
    evaluating, 276
management by objectives (MBO), 466
management consultant, 28
manual bookkeeping, converting to computerized books, 379–380
manufacturer ads, 533
manufacturing business, 12
Marineland, 199
market
    measuring, 235–236
    NCI sample business plan, 306–311
    overview, 533
    promotions, 542
    public relations, 543–547
    reaching directly, 533–538
    trade shows, 541–542
    written materials, 538–541
market expansion, 265
market saturation, 502
market segmentation, 490
market segments
    based on product delivery, 251
    customer geography, 246
    customer lifestyle, 247–248
    customer motivation, 252–255
    customer personality, 248–249
    customer profile, 246–247
    defined, 244
    identifying customers, 255–256
    overview, 243–245
    purchase patterns, 249–251
    reaching, 256
    separating customers into groups, 244
    sizing up, 255
market share
    calculating, 501–502
    competitive plan of attack, 501
    increasing, 502
    indentifying competition, 501
    overview, 500–501

marketing. *See also* mobile marketing
  analysing to determine competitor's
    capabilities, 267
  brand, 513–518
  budget, 507–508
  to compensate for lost business, 489
  competitors, 499–500
  conveying position and brand through
    tag lines, 517
  customer motivation, 494–497
  customer research, 491–492
  customers, 490–492
  defined, 65
  expanding business, 489
  importance of, 280–281
  increasing sales, 497–499
  key to success, 486
  market segmentation, 490
  market share, 500–502
  marketing cycle, 486–487
  NCI sample business plan, 312–314
  overview, 485, 509
  plan for, 503–506
  positioning, 515–516
  product analysis, 493–494
  projecting right image, 509–513
  versus sales, 488
  seeing business from customer's
    perspective, 492
  start-up business, 488
marketing consultant, 28
marketing literature
  brochures, 539–540
  newsletters, 540–541
  producing and using, 538–539
  types of, 539
marketing mix, 506
marketplace. *See also* competition;
  market segments
  critical success factors, 239–241
  defining personality types, 257–258
  industry analysis, 232–239
  opportunities, 242
  overview, 231

  researching, 257
  risks, 243
  understanding your business, 232
Marx, Karl, 219
Mary Kay Cosmetics, 251
mass market, 251
mass media advertising
  media plan and schedule, 523–524
  versus one-to-one communications,
    533–534
  overview, 521–523
MBO (management by objectives), 466
MEC (Magna Entertainment Corp.), 269
media buyer, 529
media interviews, 545–547
media relations firm, 27
media sharing sites, 560, 562
mediation, 97
mentoring, 459–460
merchandising licence, 191
meta robots tags, 583
microblogging, 560–562
microblogging sites, 560, 562
Microsoft
  competitive advantage, 296
  core competence, 297–298
minimizing risk
  injury or death of key person, 62–63
  injury to business, 60–62
  injury to others, 58–60
  overview, 57–58
minimum performance clause, exclusive IP
  licence agreement, 194
minutes, meeting, 117
Miscellaneous Expenses account, 344
mission statement
  business plan, 209, 221–224
  versus vision statement, 504
mitigating damages, 75, 83
mobile marketing
  adding to marketing strategy, 564
  applying user-generated content, 569–570
  Bluetooth, 566
  direct, 564

mobile marketing *(continued)*
  e-mail, 565–566
  indirect, 564
  interactive voice response, 566
  offering incentives, 569
  open-ended survey questions, 569
  overview, 563
  planning communication flow, 567–568
  providing text promotions, 568
  quizzes, 568
  short message service, 565
mobility barriers, 264
Modify Report feature, 380
modular literature, 539
monetizing traffic, website, 556
money, as incentive to mobile device
      users, 569
money compensation (damages), 91
money-back guarantees, 251
monitoring ongoing performance
  disciplinary procedures, 476–477
  firing employees, 477–481
  handling difficult situations, 474–476
  performance appraisal meeting, 470–474
  performance appraisal system, 463–469
monopoly, 234
moral rights, 174–175
morale, workplace
  employee surveys, 452
  exit interviews, 453
  overview, 452
Morgan, J. P., 290
mortgage on real property, inability to
      pay, 91–92
mortgagee, 91
motivation, employee, 428
Movable Type, 559
multiopoly, 234
multiple interviews, job applicant, 418
multiple of earnings method, 41
multi-rater assessments, performance
      appraisal, 469
multi-step format, income statement,
      361–362
music, broadcast identity, 530
musical works, copyright, 169

• N •

name search database, 162
National Inventor Fraud Center (U.S), 30
National Quality Institute (NQI), 277
natural search, 572
NCI sample business plan
  company, 303–304
  current company status, 304
  executive summary, 301–303
  financial data, 317–321
  marketing and sales, 312–314
  markets and competition, 306–312
  objectives, 304–305
  Phase I, 305
  Phase II, 305–306
  Phase III, 306
  products, 314–316
  risk analysis, 317
negotiating settlement
  calling it quits, 96
  opening discussions, 95–96
  overview, 94–95
  preparing for negotiations, 95
  research resources, 96–97
net loss, 328
net profit, 328
net sales, 362
net worth, 39
Network Components, Inc. (NCI) sample
      business plan
  company, 303–304
  current company status, 304
  executive summary, 301–303
  financial data, 317–321
  marketing and sales, 312–314
  markets and competition, 306–312
  objectives, 304–305
  Phase I, 305
  Phase II, 305–306
  Phase III, 306
  products, 314–316
  risk analysis, 317
new customers, finding, 115
new media, 521

news releases, 544–545
newsletters, 540–541
newspaper ads, 522, 527–528
non-commercial source loans, 88–89
non-competition agreements, 105
non-current assets, 349–351
non-current liabilities, balance sheet, 352
non-exclusive IP licence agreement,
    127, 192
non-obviousness test, patents, 143
non-offering (private) corporation, 52
non-payment of accounts receivable, 61
nonregistered IP attorneys, 129
Norco Product Ltd., 229
Nordstrom, 278
North American car manufacturing, 259
Notes Payable account, 340
not-for-attribution comments, media
    interview, 546
notice of intention to make a proposal, 93
notification of outplacement, employee
    termination meeting, 478
novelty test, patent, 142
NQI (National Quality Institute), 277

• *O* •

objectives, 505. *See also* goals and
    objectives, in business plan
objectivity, importance of, 16
observation
    customer, 492
    employee, 456
off the record comments, media
    interview, 546
offering (public) corporation, 52
Office Expenses account, 345
official marks, 158
offline resources, generating website traffic
    with, 555
offshoring, 399
off-the-shelf business
    buying existing business, 35
    corporate culture, 40
    financial statements, 38–39

location, 37–38
overview, 35
reason behind business success, 37
reasons for selling, 36
reputation, 37
researching existing businesses, 36
oligopoly, 234
Omniture Adobe SiteCatalyst, 590
one-to-one communications, 521
ongoing services, 77
online payment, 72
online presence
    attributes of good site, 554
    blogging, 557–559
    building, 553
    creating content, 553
    developing online products and services,
        556–557
    generating traffic to, 554–555
    monetizing traffic, 556
    navigation, 553–554
    overview, 551, 552
    promoting affiliate products, 556
    types of, 552
    using social media, 559–562
Ontario Small Business Enterprise
    Centres, 21
open-ended interview questions, 420
open-ended survey questions, 569
opening inventory, 362
Operating expenses item, income
    statement, 360
operating your business. *See
    also* customers
    contracts, 66–69
    getting repeat business and referrals, 70
    injury or death of key person, 62–63
    injury to business, 60–62
    injury to others, 58–60
    insurance, 63–64
    overview, 57
    payment options, 71–72
    suppliers, 76–85
    terminating business relationship, 73–76

operations
analysing to determine competitor's
capabilities, 267
critical success factors, 240
Discount Car & Truck Rentals core
competence, 298
importance of, 279–280
opportunism, importance of, 16
opportunities, marketplace, 242
Opposition stage, trademark registration
process, 163
optimism, importance of, 16
ordinary marks, 157
organic search
defined, 572
SEO, 577
organization
analysing to determine competitor's
capabilities, 266
evaluating, 277
organizational talents, importance of, 16
original expression, copyrights and,
169–170, 172
Other expenses item, income statement, 360
Other Income account, 342
Other income item, income statement, 360
outdoor advertising, 522
outdoor media, 521
out-of-home advertising, 528–529
outside view, business analysis, 274
outsourcing, 399–400
overtime compensation, 441
ownership
changing to protect personal assets, 54–55
co-ownership, 50–51
copyright, 170–171
establishing, 159
overview, 50
sole-ownership, 50

• P •

packaging, product, 250
pageview, Web traffic
defined, 593
setting benchmarks for, 597
tracking traffic volumes, 595

paid search, generating website traffic
with, 555
paired statements method, 468
panel interviews, job applicant, 418
paper records, loss of, 62
paragraph copy, SEO, 574
Paris Convention of 1883, 152
parties, contract, 67
partnership
bankruptcy, 93
selling business, 103
part-of-the-action fee arrangement, 133
parts suppliers, 78–79
passing off action, 167–168
patent agents, 129, 131
Patent Cooperation Treaty (PCT), 152–154
patent licence, 190
Patent Office Search Report, 150
Patent title search, 155
patents
alternatives, 155–157
assessing rights, 143–144
benefits to country, 138–139
benefits to inventor, 139
defined, 138
determining ownership, 144–145
filing internationally, 151–154
infringement, 182
as intangible asset, 350
intellectual property and, 125
overview, 137
patent application, 145–150
patentability test, 141–143
professionals, 154–155
pros and cons, 140–141
rights and limitations of ownership,
139–140
scope of your rights, 186
Patents account, 339
Patton, Bruce, 96
pay levels
collective bargaining, 440–441
going rate, 440
job evaluation and pay grading, 440
management, 440
overview, 439

pay raises, 442
payments
    credit, 71–72
    inability to make, 88–90
    online, 72
    overview, 71
    planning, 71
pay-over of profits, 188
payroll, 329
Payroll Benefits account, 345
PCT (Patent Cooperation Treaty), 152–154
peer support, 28
people skills, importance of, 15
performance appraisal meeting
    choosing areas for further development,
        472–473
    conducting, 470–471
    followup, 473–474
    giving constructive feedback, 471
    overview, 470
    preparing for, 470
    preparing for negative reaction, 472
performance appraisal system
    behaviourally anchored rating scale, 467
    benefits of, 464–465
    critical incidents reporting, 467
    essay appraisals, 466–467
    forced choice, 468
    goal-setting, or management by
        objectives, 466
    job rating checklist, 467
    launching, 469–470
    multi-rater assessments, 469
    overview, 463
    ranking methods, 468–469
permanent injunction, 188
persistence, importance of, 15
personal guarantees, corporate
    shareholder, 71
personal information, customer, 73
Personal Information Protection and
    Electronic Documents Act (PIPEDA), 72
personal management techniques
    avoiding procrastination, 118
    delegating, 118
    learning when to say no, 118–119

overview, 117
    scheduling time, 117
    screen and bundle, 118
Personal Property Security Act, 72
personal use exemption, copyrighted
    works, 176
personality types, customer, 245–246,
    248–249, 258
pharmaceutical companies, 126
phone interviews, 415–416
physical (tangible) assets, 40, 350
physical injuries, 58–59
PIPEDA (Personal Information Protection
    and Electronic Documents Act), 72
Pirate Bay website, 172
pitching sale, 66
plan, marketing
    goals, 505
    overview, 503
    setting strategies, 506
    statement of purpose, 504–505
    taking action, 506
    vision statement, 504
planning pyramid, 505
pleadings, 185
point-of-sale software, 375–376
Polaroid, 166
popularity sites, 560
positioning, 515–517
positioning statement, 515–516
positive cash flow, 282
Postage and Delivery account, 345
poster ads, QR Code, 564
posting, accounting cycle, 330
post-termination protocol, 478–479
post-training questionnaire, 461
power of sale, 91
power words, advertising, 526
preferred shares, 53
prefiling search, patent, 146–147
Preliminary Examination Report, 153
Prepaid Insurance account, 337
press releases, 544
preventive action, wrongful dismissal case,
    475–476
price savings, 542

pricing
  contract for sale of goods, 67
  customer motivation, 496–497
  information sources for valuing
    business, 42
  overview, 40
  product/service, 33–34
  valuing assets, 40–41
  valuing goodwill, 41–42
primary links, value chain, 288–289
principles. *See* values and principles,
    business plan
print ads, QR Code, 564
print media, 521
prior art
  defined, 142
  searching for, 146–147
priority date, patent, 145
privacy, customer, 72–73
private (non-offering) corporation, 52
privileged communications, 130
privileges, copyright, 176
procrastination, avoiding, 118
product ads, 519
product analysis
  overview, 493
  tallying sales by product line, 493
  using sales to manage product line, 494
product brochure, 539
product differentiation, 235–236
product expansion, 265
product life cycles, 498–499
product substitution, 236
product-oriented targeting, 502
product/service
  development, 30–32
  NCI sample business plan, 314–316
  pricing, 33–34
  product packaging, 250
  usage and competition, 262–263
professional associations, 23–24
professional journals, 23–24
professionals
  accountant, 26–27
  advisors, 84–85

insurance agent or broker, 27
IP, 128–134
lawyer, 26
patent, 154–155
profile, customer, 245–247
profit
  defined, 38
  industry analysis, 238–239
  net, 328
  pay-over of, 188
  testing, 369–371
profit margins, 238
Profit or loss item, income statement, 360
profit-sharing plans, 443
promissory notes, 340
promotional ads (product ads), 519
promotions
  incentives, 542
  product packaging, 250
  promotional ads, 519
  text, 568
property. *See also* intellectual property
  capital, 100
  inability to pay mortgage on, 91–92
  insurance, 64
  tangible, 189–190
  transferring, 54–55, 111
property rights, 124
proposed use, trademark, 160
proprietorship, industrial design, 178–179
prosecuting IP, 129, 149–150
protocol, processing employee
    applications, 406
Provincial Sales Tax (PST), 340
provincial/territorial government
    websites, 20
provisional applications, patent, 146
PST (Provincial Sales Tax), 340
psychographics, 247–248, 490
public (offering) corporation, 52
public performances, barring, 174
public relations
  crisis communications, 547
  establishing media contacts, 545
  focusing on publicity, 543

media interviews, 545–547
news releases, 544–545
orchestrating media coverage, 543
overview, 543
realistic expectations, 544
public seminars, 457–458
public timeline, microblog, 561
publicity, 250
publishing invention, 156–157
Purchase Discount account, 343
purchase money security interest, 90
purchase patterns, customer
  overview, 249
  product distribution and delivery, 251
  product features, 249–250
  product packaging, 250
  product pricing, 250–251
Purchase Returns and Allowances
    account, 343
Purchases account, 343

• **Q** •

QR (Quick Response) Code, 564
qualifications, job ad, 408
qualifying inventions, 144
qualifying IP professionals, 130–131
questionnaires
  Beliefs and Principles, 215–217
  Business Strengths and Weaknesses, 275
  customer research, 491
  employee, 456
  Industry Analysis, 233
  post-training, 461
quick (acid test) ratio, 357–358
Quick Response (QR) Code, 564
QuickBooks, 374, 376–377
QuickBooks Pro, 375–376
quizzes, mobile marketing, 568

• **R** •

R&D (research and development)
  analysing to determine competitor's
    capabilities, 267
  importance of, 279

rack cards, 539
radio, broadcasting ads, 530–532
radio advertising, 522
raises, 436
ranking methods, performance appraisal,
    468–469
rate card, 529
ratio tests, liquidity, 357–358
raw materials, 365
RDS Direct Marketing List Source, 536
reach, advertising, 524
recapture of capital cost allowance, 101
recruiters, 410–412
  on campus, 412
  employees, 412
  finding, 411–412
  knowing when to use, 411
  overview, 410
  types of, 410–411
recruiting employees
  assessing potential employees, 412–413
  checking references, 429–430
  competency models, 400–401
  ending interview, 424
  face to face interviews, 416–421
  filling jobs from outside organization, 399
  filling jobs from within organization,
    398–399, 406–407
  hiring, 396–398
  hiring decision, 424–429
  with Internet, 408–410
  job descriptions, 401–405
  making employment offer, 430–433
  outsourcing, 399–400
  overview, 395
  phone interviews, 415–416
  questions to ask and how to interpret
    answers, 421–424
  reading resumes, 413–415
  recruiters, 410–412
  resourceful recruiting, 405–406
  writing job ad, 408
references, checking, 429–430
referrals
  generating website traffic with, 555
  getting, 70

referrers, Web traffic
  defined, 593
  tracking traffic volumes, 595–596
registered trademarks
  finding, 162
  retaining, 164
registration forms, eliminating, 583–584
Registration stage, trademark registration
    process, 163
regulation, government
  critical success factors, 241
  factor in business venture decision, 14
relationships
  boss-employee, 120
  Discount Car & Truck Rentals core
    competence, 298
  industry analysis, 236–237
  with suppliers, 81–82
  terminating business, 73–76
relevance, search engine and, 572
reliability, importance of, 15
reminder (tickler) system, 117
renewal, trademark, 164
rent, inability to pay, 91
Rent Expense account, 345
Rent Revenue account, 342
renting, business location, 47–49
repeat business, 70
replacement value, 40
report format, balance sheet, 354–355
reporting results. *See also* balance sheet
  income statement, 359–366
  return on assets ratio, 371
  return on equity ratio, 371
  return on sales ratio, 370
reputation, existing business, 37
research and development (R&D)
  analysing to determine competitor's
    capabilities, 267
  importance of, 279
Research In Motion
  BlackBerry e-mail software, 155
  patent infringement case, 184–185

researching your business
  existing businesses, 36–37
  Industry Canada, 23
  marketplace, 257
  overview, 22
  trade and professional associations,
    23–24
  using IP filings for, 197–199
resourcefulness
  employee, 428–429
  entrepreneur, 16
resources. *See also* capabilities and
    resources
  business plan, 204–207
  obtaining business goals, 225, 228
response ads (product ads), 519
response method, job ad, 408
results-oriented principle, employee
    bonuses, 442
resumes, reading
  basics, 414
  overview, 413
  reading between the lines, 414–415
  red flags, 415
retail business, 12
Retail Taxes Payable account, 340
retained earnings, 116
Retained Earnings account, 341, 352
retainers, 61
retention, employee
  alternate work arrangements, 446–447
  avoiding burnout, 450–452
  compensation, 436–441
  employee-friendly work environment,
    445–446
  morale, 452–453
  overview, 435
  telecommuting, 447–449
  training and development, 453–461
retention bonuses, 443
return on assets (ROA) ratio, 371
return on equity (ROE) ratio, 371
return on sales (ROS) ratio, 370

returns, 342, 369
revenue
  defined, 38, 328
  monetizing IP, 126–127
Revenue accounts, 341
rights, IP
  acquiescence, 187
  adding value to business, 127–128
  cashing in on, 188–189
  copyright, 186
  developing new revenue source, 126–127
  exhausting, 187
  industrial designs, 186
  invalidating claim, 187
  keeping competitors at bay, 126
  overview, 125–126, 185, 186
  ownership, 187
  patents, 186
  rulings, 188
  settlements, 188
  trademarks, 186
risk-management instincts, importance
  of, 16
risks, marketplace, 243
risks, minimizing
  injury or death of key person, 62–63
  injury to business, 60–62
  injury to others, 58–60
  overview, 57–58
ROA (return on assets) ratio, 371
robots (bots), 572
robots.txt file, 582–583
ROE (return on equity) ratio, 371
Rogers Communications Inc., 265
RONA Inc., vision statement, 220
ROS (return on sales) ratio, 370
royalties, 193
rulings, IP rights, 188

• *S* •

Sage Simply Accounting Pro program, 374
Sage Simply Entrepreneur, 374

Salaries and Wages account, 345
sales
  analysing to determine competitor's
    capabilities, 267
  importance of, 280–281
  increasing, 497–499
  versus marketing, 488
  NCI sample business plan, 312–314
Sales and Service Revenue account, 342
Sales Discounts account, 342
sales on account, 328
Sales Returns and Allowances account, 342
Sales/Revenues item, income statement, 360
samples, as action incentive, 542
satisfied customers, 237
Sawmill, 590
scheduling time, 117
scope of your rights
  copyright, 186
  industrial designs, 186
  invalidating claim, 187
  overview, 186
  patents, 186
  trademarks, 186
Sea Ray Sundancer, 261
search engine optimization (SEO)
  add-ons, 576
  eliminating search engine roadblocks,
    582–585
  Firefox, 575
  keywords, 578–581
  overview, 575
  search engines, 572
  structuring site for search engines and
    people, 585–588
  Webmaster tools, 576–577
  worksheet, 577–578
search engine ranking pages (SERP), 572
search engine roadblocks, eliminating
  avoiding all-flash pages, 585
  checking for meta robots tags, 583
  checking robots.txt file, 582–583
  eliminating login forms, 584

search engine roadblocks,
eliminating *(continued)*
eliminating registration forms, 583–584
overview, 582
search engines, 572
seasonal work, 13
Second Cup company, 215
second stage financing, 116
second warning, employee disciplinary
process, 476–477
secured creditors
being put out of business by, 108–109
insolvency and, 92–93
security
from lender, 108–109
telecommuting, 448–449
security interest, 72
security issues, employee termination
meeting, 478
self-confidence, importance of, 15
self-determination, importance of, 15
self-discipline, importance of, 15
selling
existing businesses, reasons for, 36
licensing and, 189–190
selling business as going concern
allocating purchase price if assets
sold, 104
consulting agreements, 105
dealing with prospective buyers, 102–103
knowing what business is worth, 102
non-competition agreements, 105
overview, 101
paying business debts, 105
sale of assets or sale of shares, 103–104
selling to outsider, on death of business
owner, 112
seminars, 24
SEO (search engine optimization)
add-ons, 576
eliminating search engine roadblocks,
582–585
Firefox, 575

keywords, 578–581
overview, 575
search engines, 572
structuring site for search engines and
people, 585–588
Webmaster tools, 576–577
worksheet, 577–578
SeoQuake add-on, 576
SERP (search engine ranking pages), 572
service and support, Microsoft's
competitive advantage, 296
service business, 12
service contracts, telecommuting, 448
service suppliers, 79, 82–83
services
contract, 67
trademark use concept and, 160
sessions (visits), website
bounce rate, 597–598
loyalty benchmark, 597
overview, 593–594, 596
setting benchmarks for pageviews per
visit and time on site, 597
setting quality targets, 596
setting precedents, 98
settlements, IP rights, 188
settlements, negotiating
calling it quits, 96
opening discussions, 95–96
overview, 94–95
preparing for negotiations, 95
research resources, 96–97
severance agreement, 479
shares, sale of, 103–104
shopping cart, online, 283
short message service (SMS), 565
shrinking markets, 235
Simple Start QuickBooks, 374
Simply Accounting Pro program, 374
Simply Accounting Pro software, 374–375
Simply Entrepreneur, 374
single-step format, income statement, 361
situational analysis, 242

sizing up, 255
skills
  crisis management, 16
  developing employee skills inventory, 407
  keeping pace with technology, 388
  people, 15
  soft, 404
  survival, 15
slip-and-fall incidents, preventing, 58
slogan (tag line), 517
small business centres, 21–22
small business essentials
  advantages of, 10
  bank and trust company websites, 21
  business incubators, 22
  Canada Business organization, 18–20
  choosing business, 12–14
  deciding whether to quit day job or not, 17
  determining if you have the small
    business personality, 14–17
  disadvantages of, 11
  obtaining essential business skills, 24–25
  overview, 9
  peer support, 28
  professionals, 26–27
  provincial/territorial government
    websites, 20
  researching business, 22–24
  small business or entrepreneurship
    centres, 21–22
Small to Medium Enterprises (SMEs), 368
smartphones
  data plans, 566
  mobile e-mail, 565
  QR Codes, 564
SMEs (Small to Medium Enterprises), 368
SMS (short message service), 565
Snow, Michael, 175
Sobeys Inc., vision statement, 220
social media
  connecting via social networks, 560–561
  defined, 559
  discussion forums, 561

Facebook, 409–410, 561
LinkedIn, 409–410, 561
media sharing sites, 562
microblogging, 561–562
overview, 559–560
Yahoo! Answers, 561
Society for Human Resource
  Management, 393
soft skills, 404
software
  BlackBerry e-mail, 155
  bookkeeping, 373–376
  human resources, 390–393
  point-of-sale, 375–376
  QuickBooks Pro, 375–376
  Simply Accounting Pro, 374–375
sole IP licence agreement, 192
sole proprietorship
  advantages of, 50
  bankruptcy, 93
  selling business, 103
something different strategy, 268
sound, broadcast identity, 530
space-sharing arrangements, 47
special shares, 53
Specialized Research Service, 19
specialty media, 521
spiders, 572
spot bonuses, 443
staffing firms, 411
standard form lease, landlord, 49
start-up costs, 14
statement of earnings (income
  statement), 327
statement of financial position, 327, 355
statement of purpose, marketing plan,
  504–505
State-of-the-art search, 155
Statistics Canada website, 205
statutory lien, 92
stock, 443–444
stock investments, 353
stock option plans, 443

straight commission, 437
straight ranking, 468
strategic business thinkers, 386
strategic goals, 456
strategic groups, 263–265
Strategic Leadership Forum, mission statement, 224
strategic staffing model, 396
strategies
  competitor, 267–269
  defined, 505
  human resources, 389–390
strengths and weaknesses, identifying
  capabilities and resources, 278–283
  critical success factors, 284–285
stress-coping ability, employee, 428
stretch goals, 228
Stronach, Frank, 269, 276
The Stu Clark Centre for Entrepreneurship, 21
style, broadcast identity, 530
success-management instincts, importance of, 16
suggestive marks, 158
suing, 98–99
Summary of drawings/figures section, patent specification (application), 148
Summary of invention section, patent specification (application), 148
suppliers
  avoiding problems, 82
  choosing, 78–79
  contracts, 80–81
  determining what's needed, 77
  establishing credit with, 79–80
  establishing good working relationship, 81–82
  finding, 77
  inventory and parts, 78–79
  notifying when going out of business, 108
  overview, 76
  of professional services, 84–85
  reviewing essential goods and services, 77
  service, 79, 82–83

suffering loss or damage because of, 83–84
suppliers of goods, 83
Supplies account, 345
supply and demand, 236–237
support websites, 552
supporting links, value chain, 289
surveys
  customer research, 491
  employee, 456
survival skills, importance of, 15
sustained competitive advantage, 299
SWOT analysis, 286–287

• T •

tactics
  defined, 505
  when to decide on, 506
tag lines, conveying position and brand through, 517
tangible (physical) assets, 40, 350
tangible image, business, 223
tangible property, 189–190
target market, 32–33, 502
Target market column, impression inventory, 511
tax updates, 376
taxes
  calculating capital gains, 100–101
  inability to pay, 92
  overview, 100
  taxation of capital gains, 100
team bonuses, 443
teamwork abilities, employee, 429
technology
  critical success factors, 240
  human resources, 388
telecommuting
  home office expenses, 448
  local zoning issues, 449
  overview, 447–448
  security, 448–449
  viability of service contracts, 448
  work agreement, 449

Telephone and Internet account, 345
television advertising, 523
temperament, employee, 428
temporary pay cuts, 481
terminal loss, 101
terminating business relationship, 73–76
termination, employee disciplinary
    process, 477
termination, IP licence, 192
test marketing, 257
testing liquidity
  acid test (quick) ratio, 357–358
  current ratio, 357
  overview, 357
testing profits
  overview, 369–370
  return on assets, 371
  return on equity, 371
  return on sales, 370
text messaging, 565
text promotions, 568
theft, 62
third-party claims, 98
Thomson, Beverly, 280
360-degree assessment (multi-rater
    assessments), 469
tickler (reminder) system, 117
time on site, Web traffic
  defined, 593
  setting benchmarks for, 597
  tracking traffic volumes, 595
timeframe, contract, 68
timing
  advertising, 524
  revenue flow, 294
title, industrial design application, 179
Title section, patent specification
    (application), 148
title tags, SEO, 573
TMO (Trademark Office), 163
tools
  blogging, 559
  Google Webmaster, 576–577
  Web traffic-reporting, 589–590

toothpaste market, 254
Toronto Stock Exchange (TSX), 332, 353
total market, 502
total-approach ads, 520
Toyota, Lexus, 161
tracking traffic volumes
  hits, 593
  overview, 592–593
  pageviews, 595
  referrers, 595–596
  time on site, 595
  tracking sessions (visits), 594
  tracking unique visitors, 594
  traffic metrics, 593
trade associations, 23–24
trade journals, 23–24
trade name, 158
trade secrets, 125, 155–156
trade shows, 24
trade-in arrangements, 251
trademark agents, 129, 131
trademark licence, 191
Trademark Office (TMO), 163
Trademark Register, 162
trademarks
  adopted, 162
  applying for registration, 162–163
  categories of, 157–158
  clearing mark, 161
  deciding whether to register, 160–161
  foreign, 164–165
  infringement, 182
  infringing on rights, 166–167
  as intangible asset, 350
  intellectual property and, 125
  overview, 157, 165–166
  passing off action, 167–168
  registered, 162, 164
  scope of your rights, 186
  types of, 158–159
  using licensing with, 196–197
Trade-Marks Act, 164
Trademarks Journal, 163
trade-secret licence, 191

traffic metrics, 593
traffic report, 588–589
training and development
  deciding on training program, 460
  e-learning, 458–459
  employee focus groups, 455
  executive education seminars, 458
  in-house classroom training, 457
  measuring results of training efforts,
    460–461
  mentoring, 459–460
  observation, 456
  public seminars, 457–458
  strategic goals and, 456
  surveys and questionnaires, 456
transactions, accounting cycle, 329–330
transferring ownership, copyright, 171
transferring property, 54–55, 111
Travel and Entertainment account, 345
treaties, patent, 152–154
trending phrases, 580
trial balance, 329
trial balance, accounting cycle, 330
trip-and-fall incidents, preventing, 58
trust company websites, 21
trust factors, SEO, 574
trustee in bankruptcy, 109
TSX (Toronto Stock Exchange), 332, 353
TV, broadcasting ads, 530–532
Twitter, 562
Tylenol, 126, 213
Type column, chart of accounts, 346
TypePad, 559

• U •

UGC (user-generated content), 569
unauthorized distribution, preventing, 174
undepreciated capital cost, 101, 104
undischarged bankrupt, 94
uninterrupted power supply (UPS), 62
unique visitors, website
  defined, 593
  tracking, 594

United States
  first-to-invent system, 142
  National Inventor Fraud Center, 30
  Patent Office website, 147
  Steel industry, 290
United States Patent and Trademark Office
  (USPTO), 151–152, 198
University of Calgary Continuing
  Education, 25
University of Toronto School of Continuing
  Studies, 25
unsecured creditors
  being put out of business by, 109
  insolvency and, 92
UPS (uninterrupted power supply), 62
Ury, William L., 96
usage gap, 235
use concept, trademark, 160, 164
user flows, mobile communication, 567
user-generated content, mobile marketing,
  569–570
user-generated content (UGC), 569
USPTO (United States Patent and
  Trademark Office), 151–152, 198
Utilities account, 345
utility test, patent, 141

• V •

Validity analysis, IP opinion, 154
value
  customer motivation, 495–496
  defined, 34
  IP rights and, 127–128
  trademark, 166
value chain
  building, 289–292
  links, 288–289
  overview, 287
  summarizing business, 288
  value proposition, 292–293
value equation, 260, 287
value proposition, 292–293

values and principles, business plan
Beliefs and Principles Questionnaire, 215–217
clarifying, 214–215
ethical dilemmas, 212–213
importance of, 212
integrating into daily business operations, 218–219
overview, 211
value of having, 213–214
values statement, 213, 217–218
values statement, 209, 213, 217–218
valuing your business
assets, 40–41
goodwill, 41–42
information sources for, 42
Vehicles account
asset accounts, 338
expense accounts, 345
venture capital, 116
versatility, importance of, 16
video, as online product, 557
vision statement
business plan, 209, 219–221
marketing plan, 504
visits (sessions), website
bounce rate, 597–598
loyalty benchmark, 597
overview, 593–594, 596
setting benchmarks for pageviews per visit and time on site, 597
setting quality targets, 596
voice path, 566

• *W* •

waiver of rights, 479
Wal-Mart, 279
wares
defined, 157
trademark use concept and, 160
weaknesses. *See* strengths and weaknesses, identifying

Web advertising, 523
Web analytics
bounce rate, 597–598
choosing reporting tool, 590
collecting data, 589
Google Analytics, 591–592
hits, 593
loyalty benchmark, 597
measuring visit quality, 596–598
metrics, 593
overview, 588, 592–593
pageviews, 595
referrers, 595–596
sessions (visits), 594
setting benchmarks for pageviews per visit and time on site, 597
setting quality targets, 596
time on site, 595
traffic report, 588–589
unique visitors, 594
website relevancy, 573–575
Web Developer Toolbar add-on, 576
Website designer, 28
Websites
attributes of good, 554
building, 553
creating content, 553
generating traffic to, 554–555
navigation, 553–554
overview, 552
relevancy, 573–575
types of, 552
Web traffic-reporting tools, 589–590
Webalizer, 590
Webinars, 557
Webmaster tools, 576–577
weighted system, hiring, 426–427
WestJet Airlines, 250
White hat SEO, 572
wholesale business, 12
Who's in charge column, impression inventory, 511
WordPress, 559

Wordtracker, 579
Wordze, 579
work agreement, telecommuting, 449
Workforce Online website, 393
work-for-hire, copyrights and, 170
working from home, 46
working from real business premises,
    46–47
working relationship, suppliers, 81–82
work-in-process inventory, 365
work/life conflict, easing, 387
workplace
  contingent employees, 387
  employee-friendly, 445–446
  flexibility, 387
worksheets
  accounting cycle, 330
  income statement, drawing remaining
    amounts from, 363–364
  search engine optimization, 577–578
workshops, 24
workweek reductions, 481
WorldatWork website, 393

writing ads
  broadcast ad, 530–532
  convincing copy, 527
  headlines, 525–526
  job ads, 408
  radio ads, 532–533
wrongful dismissal case, avoiding, 475–476

• Y •

Yahoo! Answers, 561
Yahoo! Web Analytics, 590
Yellowpipe Lynx Viewer Tool add-on, 576
Youth Employment Services (YES), 22
YouTube, 562

• Z •

ZENN Motor Business, mission
    statement, 224
zoning issues, telecommuting, 449

Notes

Notes

Notes

Notes

Notes

Notes

BUSINESS & PERSONAL FINANCE

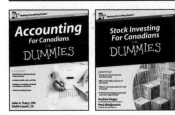

978-1-118-13346-0   978-0-470-73684-5

Also available:

- ✔ 76 Tips For Investing in an Uncertain Economy For Canadians For Dummies 978-0-470-16099-2
- ✔ Bookkeeping For Canadians For Dummies 978-0-470-73762-0
- ✔ Business Plans For Canadians For Dummies 978-0-470-15420-5
- ✔ Canadian Small Business Kit For Dummies 978-0-470-93652-8

- ✔ Investing For Canadians For Dummies 978-0-470-16029-9
- ✔ Personal Finance For Canadians For Dummies 978-0-470-67988-3
- ✔ Trading For Canadians For Dummies 978-0-470-67744-5
- ✔ Wills & Estate Planning For Canadians For Dummies 978-0-470-67657-8

EDUCATION, HISTORY & REFERENCE

978-0-7645-2498-1   978-0-470-46244-7

Also available:

- ✔ Algebra For Dummies 978-0-7645-5325-7
- ✔ Art History For Dummies 978-0-470-09910-0
- ✔ Canadian History For Dummies 978-0-470-83656-9
- ✔ Chemistry For Dummies 978-0-7645-5430-8
- ✔ English Grammar For Dummies 978-0-470-54664-2

- ✔ French For Dummies 978-0-7645-5193-2
- ✔ Statistics For Dummies 978-0-7645-5423-0
- ✔ The Canadian GED For Dummies 978-0-470-68091-9
- ✔ World History For Dummies 978-0-470-44654-6

FOOD, HOME, & MUSIC

978-0-7645-9904-0   978-0-470-67895-4

Also available:

- ✔ 30-Minute Meals For Dummies 978-0-7645-2589-6
- ✔ Bartending For Dummies 978-0-470-05056-9
- ✔ Brain Games For Dummies 978-0-470-37378-1
- ✔ Diabetes Cookbook For Canadians For Dummies 978-0-470-16028-2

- ✔ Gluten-Free Cooking For Dummies 978-0-470-17810-2
- ✔ Home Improvement All-in-One Desk Reference For Dummies 978-0-7645-5680-7
- ✔ Violin For Dummies 978-0-470-83838-9
- ✔ Wine For Dummies 978-0-470-04579-4

GARDENING

978-0-470-58161-2   978-0-470-57705-9

Also available:
- Gardening Basics For Dummies 978-0-470-03749-2
- Organic Gardening For Dummies 978-0-470-43067-5

- Sustainable Landscaping For Dummies 978-0-470-41149-0
- Vegetable Gardening For Dummies 978-0-470-49870-5

GREEN/SUSTAINABLE

978-0-470-84098-6   978-0-470-59678-4

Also available:
- Alternative Energy For Dummies 978-0-470-43062-0
- Energy Efficient Homes For Dummies 978-0-470-37602-7
- Green Building & Remodelling For Dummies 978-0-470-17559-0

- Green Cleaning For Dummies 978-0-470-39106-8
- Green Your Home All-in-One For Dummies 978-0-470-59678-4

HEALTH & SELF-HELP

978-0-471-77383-2   978-0-470-16036-7

Also available:
- Borderline Personality Disorder For Dummies 978-0-470-46653-7
- Breast Cancer For Dummies 978-0-7645-2482-0
- Cognitive Behavioural Therapy For Dummies 978-0-470-01838-5
- Diabetes For Canadians For Dummies 978-0-470-15677-3

- Emotional Intelligence For Dummies 978-0-470-15732-9
- Healthy Aging For Dummies 978-0-470-14975-1
- Neuro-linguistic Programming For Dummies 978-0-7645-7028-5
- Understanding Autism For Dummies 978-0-7645-2547-6

HOBBIES & CRAFTS

978-0-470-28747-7   978-0-470-29112-2

Also available:
- Crochet Patterns For Dummies
  97-0-470-04555-8
- Digital Scrapbooking For Dummies
  978-0-7645-8419-0
- Knitting Patterns For Dummies
  978-0-470-04556-5
- Oil Painting For Dummies
  978-0-470-18230-7

- Quilting For Dummies
  978-0-7645-9799-2
- Sewing For Dummies
  978-0-7645-6847-3
- Word Searches For Dummies
  978-0-470-45366-7

HOME & BUSINESS COMPUTER BASICS

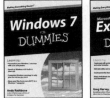

978-0-470-49743-2   978-0-470-48953-6

Also available:
- Office 2010 All-in-One Desk Reference For Dummies
  978-0-470-49748-7
- Pay Per Click Search Engine Marketing For Dummies
  978-0-471-75494-7

- Search Engine Marketing For Dummies 978-0-471-97998-2
- Web Analytics For Dummies
  978-0-470-09824-0
- Word 2010 For Dummies
  978-0-470-48772-3

INTERNET & DIGITAL MEDIA

978-0-470-44417-7   978-0-470-39062-7

Also available:
- Blogging For Dummies
  978-0-471-77084-8
- MySpace For Dummies
  978-0-470-09529-4
- The Internet For Dummies
  978-0-470-12174-0

- Twitter For Dummies
  978-0-470-47991-9
- YouTube For Dummies
  978-0-470-14925-6

MACINTOSH

978-0-470-27817-8   978-0-470-58027-1

Also available:
- iMac For Dummies
  978-0-470-13386-6
- iPod Touch For Dummies
  978-0-470-50530-4
- iPod & iTunes For Dummies
  978-0-470-39062-7

- MacBook For Dummies
  978-0-470-27816-1
- Macs For Seniors For Dummies
  978-0-470-43779-7
- Mac OS X Snow Leopard All-in-One
  Desk Reference For Dummies
  978-0-470-43541-0

PETS

978-0-470-60029-0   978-0-7645-5267-0

Also available:
- Cats For Dummies
  978-0-7645-5275-5
- Ferrets For Dummies
  978-0-470-13943-1

- Horses For Dummies
  978-0-7645-9797-8
- Kittens For Dummies
  978-0-7645-4150-6
- Puppies For Dummies
  978-1-118-11755-2

SPORTS & FITNESS

978-0-471-76871-5   978-0-470-73855-9

Also available:
- Exercise Balls For Dummies
  978-0-7645-5623-4
- Coaching Volleyball For Dummies
  978-0-470-46469-4
- Curling For Dummies
  978-0-470-83828-0
- Fitness For Dummies
  978-0-7645-7851-9

- Mixed Martial Arts For Dummies
  978-0-470-39071-9
- Sports Psychology For Dummies
  978-0-470-67659-2
- Ten Minute Tone-Ups For Dummies
  978-0-7645-7207-4
- Wilderness Survival For Dummies
  978-0-470-45306-3
- Yoga with Weights For Dummies
  978-0-471-74937-0